The Spy Who Saved the World

Also by Jerrold L. Schecter:

The New Face of Buddha
Khrushchev Remembers: The Last Testament
Khrushchev Remembers: The Glasnost Tapes
An American Family in Moscow
Back in the U.S.S.R.
The Palace File

Also by Peter S. Deriabin:

The Penkovsky Papers
The Secret World
Watchdogs of Terror

The Spy Who Saved the World

HOW A SOVIET COLONEL CHANGED THE COURSE OF THE COLD WAR

by Jerrold L. Schecter and Peter S. Deriabin

CHARLES SCRIBNER'S SONS
New York
MAXWELL MACMILLAN CANADA
Toronto
MAXWELL MACMILLAN INTERNATIONAL
New York   Oxford   Singapore   Sydney

Charles Scribner's Sons
Macmillan Publishing Company
866 Third Avenue
New York, NY 10022

Maxwell Macmillan Canada, Inc.
1200 Eglinton Avenue East, Suite 200
Don Mills, Ontario M3C 3N1

Macmillan Publishing Company is part of the
Maxwell Communication Group of Companies.

Library of Congress Cataloging-in-Publication Data

Schecter, Jerrold L.
    The spy who saved the world: how a Soviet colonel changed the
course of the Cold War/by Jerrold L. Schecter and Peter S.
Deriabin.
        p.   cm.
    Includes bibliographical references and index.
    ISBN 0-684-19068-0
    1. Espionage, Soviet. 2. Pen'kovski, Oleg Vladimirovich,
1919–1963. 3. Spies—Soviet Union—Biography. 4 Soviet Union
—Politics and government—1953–1985. I. Deriabin, Peter, date.
II. Title.
DK266.3.S365   1992   91-28072 CIP
327.12′092—dc20

Sch
300-3586

Macmillan books are available at special discounts for bulk purchases
for sales promotions, premiums, fund-raising, or educational use. For
details, contact:
                    Special Sales Director
                    Macmillan Publishing Company
                    866 Third Avenue
                    New York, NY 10022

10 9 8 7 6 5 4 3 2 1

Printed in the United States of America

For Isabel and Leona

Contents

Maps

Acknowledgments

The authors would like to thank the former CIA officers who generously contributed their knowledge of the Penkovsky case and the history of their times: Charles Beling, Joseph J. Bulik, Dr. Cleveland Cram, Walter Elder, Katherine Colvin Hart, Donald Jameson, Quentin Johnson, Edward Proctor, and Richard Malzahn. Eunice Evans and John Carver were professional and cooperative in assisting our research efforts. We are also indebted to intelligence officers in the United States and Great Britain who choose to remain unnamed publicly. Assistance in research was provided by Peter Novick, Vadim Biryukov, Helen Clegg, and Douglas V. Henry. Thanks also to friends in the Soviet Union who asked to remain unnamed.

The authors benefited from critical readings of the manuscript by Zbigniew Brzezinski, Gregory Freidin, Lawrence Linehan, Strobe Talbott, Evelind Schecter, Steven Schecter, Kate Schecter, Doveen Schecter, Barnet Schecter, and Michael Shafer. Leona Schecter, our agent, was responsible for vital suggestions in structuring and editing and played an instrumental role in the creation of the book.

At Charles Scribner's Sons our senior editor, Ned Chase, nurtured and sustained our efforts with constant support and sharp insights. Bill Goldstein provided excellent suggestions for style and structuring. Hamilton Cain and Charles Flowers graciously assisted in keeping the book on schedule.

Susan Forbes of the Kennedy Library, William H. McNitt of the Ford Library, and the National Security Archive facilitated our efforts to obtain relevant materials and information.

Transliteration of Russian Names

In transliterating Russian names, we have followed a simplified version of the system used by the Library of Congress. Simplifications include the substitution of *y* for *iy* in surnames such as Penkovsky (not Penkovskiy). In first names *i* is substituted for *iy* as in Yuri, Georgi, and Valeri, not Georgiy, Valeriy, or Yuriy. The apostrophe used to signify a soft sign is omitted. The *y* between the letters *i* and *e* is omitted, as in Sheremetievo airport, not Sheremetiyevo. Russian names standard in Western publications, such as Khrushchev, Beria, Joseph Stalin, and *Izvestia*, are retained as commonly used.

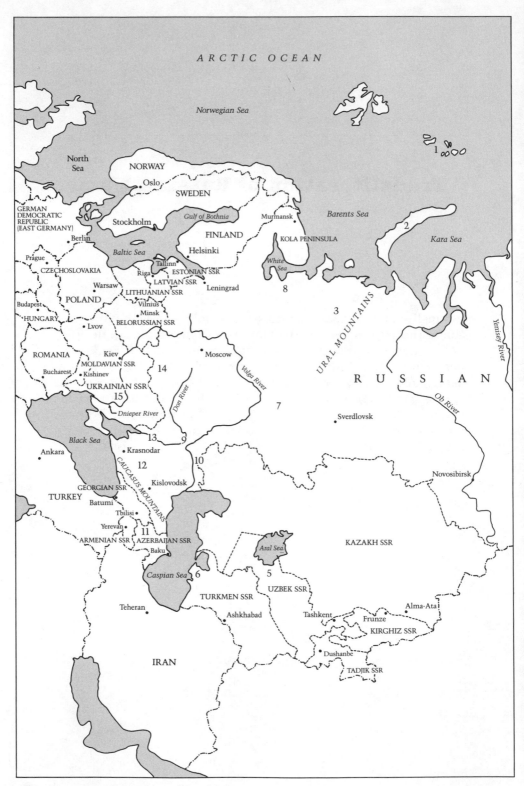

ARCTIC OCEAN

Norwegian Sea

North
Sea

NORWAY
Oslo

SWEDEN

GERMAN
DEMOCRATIC
REPUBLIC
(EAST GERMANY)

Stockholm

Berlin

Prague

CZECHOSLOVAKIA

Warsaw

POLAND

Budapest

HUNGARY

ROMANIA

Bucharest

Lvov

Kishinev

Baltic Sea

Gulf of Bothnia

FINLAND

Helsinki

Tallinn

Riga

Vilnius

Minsk

BELORUSSIAN SSR

Kiev

MOLDAVIAN SSR

UKRAINIAN SSR

15

Dnieper River

Murmansk

Barents Sea

Kara Sea

KOLA PENINSULA

White
Sea

8

3

URAL MOUNTAINS

Leningrad

ESTONIAN SSR

LATVIAN SSR

LITHUANIAN SSR

14

Moscow

Volga River

Don River

2

Yenisey River

RUSSIAN

Sverdlovsk

Ob River

7

13

9

Black Sea

Ankara

Krasnodar

CAUCASUS MOUNTAINS

12

Kislovodsk

GEORGIAN SSR

TURKEY

Batumi

Tbilisi

Yerevan

ARMENIAN SSR

11

AZERBAIJAN SSR

Baku

Caspian Sea

6

10

Aral Sea

5

KAZAKH SSR

Novosibirsk

TURKMEN SSR

UZBEK SSR

Teheran

Ashkhabad

Tashkent

Frunze

Alma-Ata

KIRGHIZ SSR

Dushanbe

IRAN

TADJIK SSR

xii

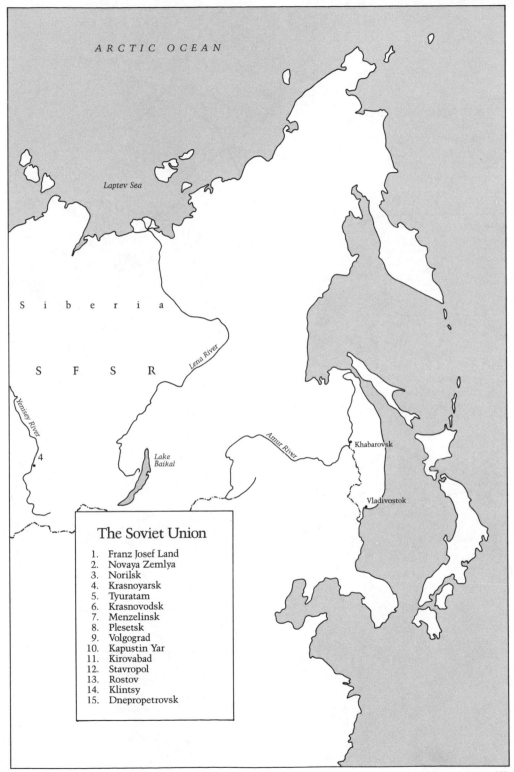

ARCTIC OCEAN

Laptev Sea

Siberia

S F S R

Yenisey River

Lena River

Amur River

Lake Baikal

Khabarovsk

Vladivostok

4

The Soviet Union

1. Franz Josef Land
2. Novaya Zemlya
3. Norilsk
4. Krasnoyarsk
5. Tyuratam
6. Krasnovodsk
7. Menzelinsk
8. Plesetsk
9. Volgograd
10. Kapustin Yar
11. Kirovabad
12. Stavropol
13. Rostov
14. Klintsy
15. Dnepropetrovsk

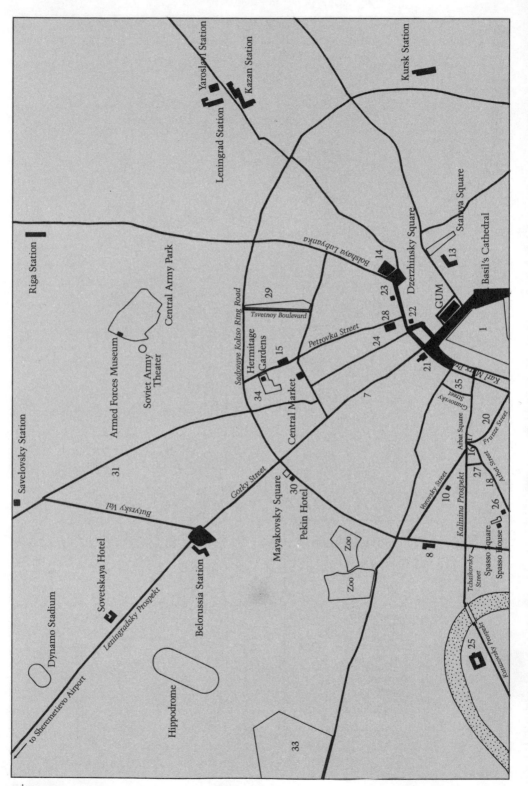

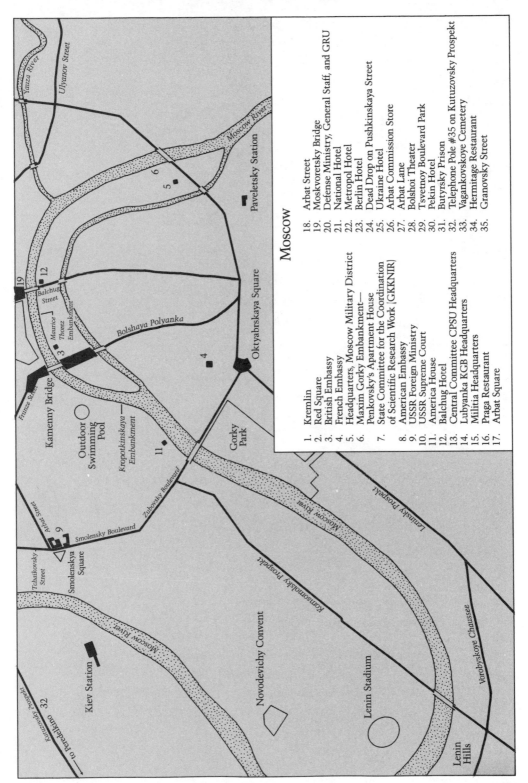

Moscow

18. Arbat Street
19. Moskvoretsky Bridge
20. Defense Ministry, General Staff, and GRU
21. National Hotel
22. Metropol Hotel
23. Berlin Hotel
24. Dead Drop on Pushkinskaya Street
25. Ukraine Hotel
26. Arbat Commission Store
27. Arbat Lane
28. Bolshoi Theater
29. Tsvetnoy Boulevard Park
30. Pekin Hotel
31. Butyrsky Prison
32. Telephone Pole #35 on Kutuzovsky Prospekt
33. Vagankovskoye Cemetery
34. Hermitage Restaurant
35. Granovsky Street

1. Kremlin
2. Red Square
3. British Embassy
4. French Embassy
5. Headquarters, Moscow Military District
6. Maxim Gorky Embankment—
7. Penkovsky's Apartment House
   State Committee for the Coordination
   of Scientific Research Work (GKKNIR)
8. American Embassy
9. USSR Foreign Ministry
10. USSR Supreme Court
11. America House
12. Balchug Hotel
13. Central Committee CPSU Headquarters
14. Lubyanka KGB Headquarters
15. Militia Headquarters
16. Praga Restaurant
17. Arbat Square

Range of Soviet Missiles Based in Cuba

──────── Approximate range of
medium-range missiles (1020 miles)

─ ─ ─ ─ Approximate range of
intermediate-range missiles (2100 miles)

The Spy Who Saved the World

Prologue

My Dear Sir!

I request that you pass the following to the appropriate authorities of the United States of America. It is your good friend who is turning to you, a friend who has already become your soldier-warrior for the cause of Truth, for the ideals of a truly free world and of Democracy for Mankind, to which ideals your (and now my) President, government and people are sacrificing so much effort.

I have consciously embarked upon this path of struggle. Many things have contributed to this. In my life, the last three years have been very critical, both in my way of thinking and in other things, about which I will report later.

I have thought long and hard. Now I have taken a mature and, for me, a correct final decision which has impelled me to approach you.

I ask that you believe the sincerity of my thoughts and desires to be of service to you. I wish to make my contribution, perhaps a modest one but in my view an important one, to our mutual cause, and henceforth as your soldier to carry out everything which is entrusted to me.

You need not doubt that I will give all my strength, knowledge, and my life to this new obligation.

In presenting the above, I want to say that I am not beginning my work for my new cause with empty hands. I understand perfectly well and take into full consideration that to correct words and thoughts must be added concrete proof confirming these words. I have had, and do have now, a definite capability to do this.

At the present time I have at my disposal very important materials on many subjects of exceptionally great interest and importance to your government.

I wish to pass these materials to you immediately for study, analysis and subsequent utilization. This must be done as quickly as possible. You will determine the manner of transmittal of this material yourself. It is desirable that the transfer be effected not through personal contact, but through a dead drop.

Again I request that you "relieve" me as quickly as possible of this material which I have prepared; this should be done for many valid reasons.

Your reply: Please inform me (preferably in the Russian language) through my dead drop No. 1 (see its description and manner of use) concerning the manner, form, time, and place for passing of the indicated material.

If you designate your own dead drop for my passing the material, please take into consideration that your dead drop should be able to contain material equivalent in size to the book, *Van Cliburn* by S. Khentov, published in 1959.*

After you receive the material from me, it would be desirable to arrange a personal meeting with your representative during the second half of August of this year. We must discuss many things in detail. I request four to six hours for this. Saturdays, Sundays, and evenings are convenient for me. You decide the place and manner of setting this up.

I will wait for your orders regarding the questions raised above, through drop No. 1 starting from 15 August 1960.

I ask that in working with me you observe all the rules of professional tradecraft and security and not permit any slipups.† Protect me.

---

* With his victory in the first international Tchaikovsky Competition in Moscow in April of 1958, Van Cliburn, a twenty-three-year-old pianist from Kilgore, Texas, captured the imagination of the international musical world.
† Professional tradecraft in Russian is *po vsem pravilam iskusstva*, literally the rules of art.

May the justice of the ideals and goals to which I am devoting myself from this day forward aid us in our future collaboration.

Always yours. . . . . . .
19 July 1960

P.S. My best, best greetings to my first good friends, Colonel Charles Maclean Peeke and his wife. Mentally I send greetings to my friend Cotter, Koehler, Ditta, Beckett, Daniel, Glassbrook, and others. I remember with great pleasure the time I spent with them. I had planned to meet your representative and pass him this letter before 9 August 1960, but it did not work out. Now this must be postponed to 15 August.[1]

With this letter Colonel Oleg Vladimirovich Penkovsky made his first contact with the United States Central Intelligence Agency in August 1960. For the next two years Penkovsky supplied the CIA and MI6, the British Secret Intelligence Service, with highly classified Soviet war plans, nuclear missile diagrams, and more than 10,000 pages of military information. His contributions changed American and British thinking about Nikita Khrushchev's strategic nuclear capabilities and intentions. Penkovsky's material made it clear that the U.S.S.R. lacked the nuclear missile capability Khrushchev claimed, thus enabling President Kennedy to call Khrushchev's bluff. During the Berlin crisis of 1961 and the Cuban missile crisis in 1962, Penkovsky was the spy who saved the world from nuclear war.

Approaching the Americans

LIGHT RAIN WASHED THE COBBLESTONES OF RED SQUARE AND GLIS-
tened on the marble of the Lenin Mausoleum on the night of August
12, 1960. At about eleven o'clock, two young American tourists
crossed the square past the floodlights illuminating the brightly
painted orange, red, and blue onion domes of Saint Basil's Cathedral.
Eldon Ray Cox and Henry Lee Cobb were returning to their hotel
after enjoying a performance of the Bolshoi Ballet. They headed
toward the Moskvoretsky Bridge over the Moscow River. When they
neared it a Soviet citizen came up behind them, tugged at Cobb's
sleeve, and asked for a light for his cigarette. He started a conversation in English, asking if they were Americans and if it was their first
time in the Soviet Union. The two men said, "Yes." That excited the
Russian and set him to talking rapidly. At the same time he looked
around to see if they were being observed. The man was about forty
years of age, of medium build, five feet nine inches tall, his red hair
showing gray on the sideburns. He wore a suit with a shirt and tie
and appeared to be a reputable person.

While the three men walked across the bridge the Russian pleaded,
"I beg you to help me. I was on the train with you three or four
nights ago from Kiev. You were in a student group in the same car
that I was in. There was an agent assigned to watch you. I did not
approach you at that time because of the presence of the agent."[1]

Cox and Cobb were put off by the man's furtiveness and the tension he exuded while he continued to watch for surveillance. When
it was clear they were alone, he continued: "At one time I worked
in Turkey with the Soviet Embassy. I had a very good friend in
the American Embassy and I have wondered many times what has
become of him." The Soviet citizen claimed to be an infantry officer.

"Are you a Communist?" the Americans asked him.

"I was," the man replied. His English was passable.

Russians sometimes approached foreigners to practice their English, but not at eleven on a rainy night. Although Cox was initially perturbed by the advances, he found himself quickly attracted to the man and his manner. Yet the thought also occurred to Cox that he might be the object of a setup by the KGB, the Soviet secret police. At the back of Cox's mind a warning flashed: beware of a provocation. This could be an attempt to entrap and blackmail him. Yet the more the man talked, the more Cox felt his sincerity. Cox could also sense his frustration. "I cannot go to the American Embassy myself," the Russian said.[2]

When other Soviet citizens on the bridge walked toward them, the man changed the conversation to the weather and questions about how they liked the Soviet Union. When they had crossed the bridge and were again walking alone along the embankment, the man said, "I have tried to get in touch with other Americans, but so few of them speak Russian. I recognize you to be intelligent Americans. I have some information which I wish to give directly to the American Embassy."

The Russian told the two Americans he wanted them to give the information only to Edward Freers, the deputy chief of mission, or the military attaché. He had been carrying a letter for about a month, trying to find a way to get it to the proper person. It contained information that might enable him to go to the West someday. "Do not open it and do not keep it overnight in your hotel. Go immediately to the American Embassy with this letter," the Russian commanded. "Your government will be grateful for this information." The Russian pressed the envelope into Cox's hands and kept repeating how important it was that the two letters in the envelope be taken directly to the embassy.[3] He refused to give his name, but they kept talking.

They walked back and forth along the river embankment and the Russian told them he had secret information on the U-2 spy plane piloted by Francis Gary Powers that was shot down near Sverdlovsk three and a half months earlier on May 1, 1960. Powers was captured and the incident was still on everyone's mind because Powers was to go on trial in Moscow on August 16, 1960, only four days later.

All over the world there was speculation about exactly what had brought down the U-2 and how Powers had emerged alive. No American officials had been permitted to interview Powers. The official Soviet explanation that he had been shot down with a single surface-to-air missile did not seem credible because the U-2 was supposed to fly above the range of Soviet antiaircraft missiles.

The initial official Soviet version, given by Nikita Khrushchev, said only that the U-2 had been shot down by a single rocket at over 20,000 meters (65,000 feet). The U-2 violation of Soviet airspace had angered Khrushchev and he demanded an apology from President Eisenhower. At first the U.S. issued a cover story that the U-2 was on a weather mission and had lost its way. Then, when Khrushchev revealed that the pilot, Gary Powers, was alive in the Soviet Union, Eisenhower became the first president in American history to confess that his government practiced espionage. Eisenhower canceled all U-2 flights. This was not enough to satisfy Khrushchev, and the May 1960 Big Four summit in Paris among Eisenhower, de Gaulle, Khrushchev, and Macmillan broke up in disarray.[4]

The Russian assured the two young Americans that he had the answers on what happened to the U-2. He told them exactly fourteen rockets had been fired at Powers' U-2 from a SAM-2 surface-to-air missile site. There were no direct hits, but one warhead burst near the U-2, forcing it out of control. While the U-2 was spinning to earth, Powers ejected, but he was unconscious when he landed.

The man told the two students that there was a MiG-19 jet fighter trailing the U-2 at a lower altitude. This plane was inadvertently destroyed by one of the fourteen surface-to-air missiles. The MIG pilot was killed. The mysterious stranger now told the Americans he had received his information on the U-2 from a close friend in the military service.

He also told them that an American RB-47 reconnaissance bomber had been shot down by rockets fired from a MiG-19 on July 1, 1960, in the Barents Sea. When it was hit, he said, the RB-47 was definitely over international waters, not over Soviet territory as the Soviet Union had publicly claimed.[5]

Cox was fascinated by the striking intensity in the Russian's eyes. Already Cox felt an unusual emotional kinship that disturbed him. He had met many people in other places in the world where he traveled—Japan, the Philippines, and Mexico—but none had the same effect on him. Cox felt as if he had met an old friend.

Cobb, however, was not comfortable. He still feared the man might be a provocateur, and decided to return to his room in the nearby Balchug Hotel. When they passed an alley two policemen appeared and the man grew apprehensive. Cox and Cobb sensed his fear. In Russian, which the students understood, the man told them to follow him into the entrance of a nearby building to finish their conversation. Unnerved, the two students walked away. The Russian kept watching them as if he were afraid they might throw away the material he had given them.

7

Cox was convinced of the importance of the Russian's U-2 story and decided to go directly to the American Embassy.[6] By the time he found a taxi near his hotel, the Russian was gone. Cox recrossed the Moscow River. While he rode up Gorky Street to Mayakovsky Square in the drizzle, Cox grew apprehensive; he replayed the scene on the bridge and the embankment through his mind. Should he trust his instincts toward the stranger and deliver the envelope? The cab turned left onto the Garden Ring Road in the direction of the American Embassy on Tchaikovsky Street. Cox decided to take a chance.

He paid the driver at the main entrance to the embassy and looked up to see a tall Soviet policeman in a gray uniform standing outside the heavy iron gate. Cox's step faltered. Again he wondered if he was being set up by the Russians to be arrested as a spy, but he reassured himself. "Why in the world would a Russian take this kind of risk?" he asked himself. His heart was pounding when he approached the gate.[7]

The policeman barred the way to the embassy and asked Cox for his identification. The police are there ostensibly to protect the embassy, but in reality they are KGB officers, on duty twenty-four hours a day, whose function is to prevent Soviet citizens from entering the compound and defecting. Cox showed the policeman his driver's license; his passport was being held at the hotel front desk, normal practice in Moscow. The policeman assiduously compared the photograph on the license to the red-bearded face of the young man in front of him. He returned the driver's license and waved Cox inside the gate.

It was now shortly after midnight on August 13, 1960. Cox did not look around. Quickly, he headed straight to the Marine guard on duty. He asked to see the deputy chief of mission, Edward Freers. Cox showed the guard his driver's license; home address, Lubbock, Texas; date of birth, October 1, 1933.

The deputy chief of mission was not available. The embassy security officer, John Abidian, officially listed as Special Advisor to the Ambassador, Llewellyn Thompson, was working late in his office on the ninth floor. He came down to meet Cox.

Abidian went over and over with Cox what had happened on the bridge. Which side of the bridge had they been walking on? Where had the letters actually been turned over? The meeting with the Russian lasted about twenty minutes, certainly not more than half an hour, Cox said.

While Cox told Abidian about the intense Russian, the security officer tried to assess Cox. Cox told Abidian that he and Cobb had served together in the U.S. Air Force as Russian-language specialists.

When they were discharged from the air force, Cobb continued his Russian studies at the University of Indiana. Cox loved to travel and had just come back to his home in Texas from a 1500-mile bicycle trip to Vera Cruz, when Cobb contacted him and urged him to join the university's two-week summer program in the Soviet Union. The idea appealed to Cox, so he signed up for the course and an opportunity to visit the Soviet Union for the first time. Now, at the end of their program, Cox and Cobb were scheduled to depart Moscow on August 15.[8]

Abidian strongly advised Cox to reject all future contacts with Russians of the type he met on the bridge and to disregard all future references to the incident which might be made by Soviet citizens or by his American colleagues. There could be no certainty whether the approach was genuine or a provocation.

Cox asked what the embassy was going to do with the letters, but the security officer was noncommittal and indicated that the embassy "gets a lot of stuff like this from tourists." If Cox were needed he would be contacted, Abidian assured him. He told Cox where to find a cab a few blocks from the embassy. Cox returned to the Balchug and found Cobb sleeping soundly.[9]

Cox was furious because of what he considered a lack of cooperation at the embassy. He thought the embassy officer was not interested in his story.[10] Security Officer Abidian had been listening carefully, but he wanted to keep Cox and Cobb from any further involvement with the Russian while they were in Moscow.

Planting classified information, arranging sexual liaisons for foreigners, and then photographing men and women in heterosexual or homosexual acts, to be used for blackmail, were standard practices to create fear, and a constant threat to foreigners in Moscow. Any offer to exchange money on the black market could be a provocation.

In the summer of 1960 a young American elementary school teacher from the Midwest visited Moscow and Kiev as a tourist. In Kiev, the capital of the Ukrainian Republic, she was greeted by a good-looking "student" who introduced himself as a dissident. He said he disliked the Soviet system of government and showed the naive American around the city. Then he invited her to a park to rest. Late in the afternoon romance rose from the grass. While the two lay in a compromising position, the KGB photographers went to work. The following morning the American teacher was summoned to the police station, where plainclothed KGB officers showed her the indelicate photos. If she did not work for the KGB in the United States, they said, they would publish the pictures and inform her school. Terrified, the teacher left for Moscow immediately, but she was afraid to report the entrapment to the American

Embassy. She flew from Moscow to Vienna and there contacted the embassy, whose officers advised her to forget the incident and report to the FBI if she ever received a call from the Soviet Embassy in the United States. She never did.

Abidian immediately prepared a memo of his conversation with Cox and called Deputy Chief of Mission Freers at 2 A.M. to advise him the letter had arrived. At 10 A.M. Abidian and Freers met with embassy political officer Vladimir I. Toumanoff in the embassy secure room, nicknamed "the bubble" because it is a soundproofed, floating plastic box. The bubble is suspended on wires from the ceiling and the floor to make it invulnerable to listening devices known to be planted by the Soviets in the walls of the embassy. Abidian and Freers opened the envelope, which contained two sealed letters. By opening the letters together they provided witness that security had been maintained and that nobody had tampered with the letters. Freers asked Toumanoff, a native Russian-speaker, to assess the letters. He might be able to detect manipulative language that would tip off a setup.

Toumanoff began freely translating bits of the letters for Freers and Abidian. The Russian who had accosted Cox and Cobb had written, "I have at my disposal very important materials on many subjects of exceptionally great interest and importance to your government." Freers' assessment was to pass the letter to the CIA for further evaluation. Freers told Abidian, "Take it from here."[11]

Abidian sent a back-channel message to the State Department for delivery to the CIA, summarizing Cox's report on the U-2 and RB-47. The back channel is a secure, classified communications link with its own code that is separate from the regular embassy system. Back-channel messages are person-to-person communications that are not saved in official files. The two letters and a report of the meeting with Cox were placed under seal in the diplomatic pouch and sent by courier to the State Department in Washington, which immediately forwarded them to the Central Intelligence Agency. At the Agency, the letters were turned over to John M. (Jack) Maury, the head of the Soviet Division in the Directorate for Plans (Clandestine Operations).

On the basis of the initial report from Abidian, Maury was interested in checking out the Russian's offer. Abidian received a cable praising him for his handling of the letters and telling him the Russian sounded like the kind of man the CIA was looking for.[12] Maury gave the letters to Joseph J. Bulik, head of the branch dealing with CIA operations inside the Soviet Union. It would be Bulik's job to identify the man who had written the intriguing letter and determine whether he was sincere or a provocateur. If the Agency believed the Russian was acting on his own motivation, it would initiate contact.

In 1960 Bulik was forty-four years old and at the peak of his career. His family originally came from the eastern Carpathian region of Slovakia, inhabited by rugged mountain people, the Huzul, noted for the quality sheep they raised. Bulik, fluent in Russian, had a reputation as a strict, meticulous officer. Friends joked that if you passed Bulik in the corridor and asked him what the weather was he would stop to think if you had "a need to know" before answering.

Handsome and vibrant, Bulik's rangy height, rugged jaw, and dimpled chin added to his presence. His brown hair, cut close at the sides, was high and wavy on the top, in the latest style. Bulik was a pragmatic type who had learned to cut hair at a barber college on New York's Bowery to help him pay his way through college. After graduating from the University of Wyoming in 1937, with a specialty in animal husbandry, Bulik received a master's degree in agriculture from the University of Minnesota in 1939. He started his career with the Bureau of the Census in 1940. When the U.S. entered World War II he joined the Foreign Agriculture Service of the Department of Agriculture and served with the Combined Food Board, which organized food shipments to America's allies. From D-Day in 1944 until 1948, Bulik was the agricultural attaché at the American Embassy in Moscow. He worked on the Lend-Lease program, providing sugar, Spam, and C rations to the Russians during the war and in the aftermath.

Bulik sympathized with the wartime suffering of the Russians, but life in the Soviet Union made him painfully aware of the shortcomings and abuses in the Communist system. He returned to the United States in 1949 and joined the CIA, where he became an analyst in the Directorate of Intelligence, the overt research and intelligence side not involved in clandestine operations. The Agency was still in its infancy, and Bulik's firsthand experience in the Soviet Union was highly prized. He had traveled extensively during his tenure as agricultural attaché. In 1952, when the CIA expanded because of the Korean War, Bulik was asked to join the covert side of the Agency by Peer de Silva, one of its renowned clandestine operators, who appreciated Bulik's hands-on knowledge of the Soviet Union. An officer who actually had tramped through the back alleys of Moscow and the collective farms of the Ukraine was a rare find. Bulik knew the sounds and smells of Moscow and he had a feel for how to work there. Inside the clandestine side of the Agency he rapidly rose to head the Internal Soviet branch. Now Bulik was facing what would become the biggest challenge of his career.

Bulik did not circulate the letters in the packet, but after studying the debriefing of the two students he asked for a "blind" assessment of the information—that is, circulating only the facts without saying who had provided them or when and where they had come from. When the reports on the U-2 and RB-47 were read by experts in the Soviet division, the positive responses that came back to Bulik were unanimous. All who read the reports sensed authenticity and important information. "This material has the ring of truth to it. It could be the real thing," said Charles Beling, one of the officers who evaluated the reports on the U-2 and the RB-47. "It looks like we've got a live son of a bitch here."[13] The details were precise and embarrassing to the Soviet Union, yet they offered the first realistic explanations for two incidents of which the CIA knew little.

Bulik looked at the material in the packet before reading the two letters. There was a picture of a Soviet colonel with an American army colonel, but the Soviet's head had been cut from the photo. It was an unusual way of signaling that he was a bona fide officer without prematurely divulging his face and name. If the letter writer was sincerely disillusioned with Communism and wanted to work for the United States, the value of a Soviet colonel with high-ranking connections in Moscow would be fabulous. Bulik's role and that of his branch would be expanded.

Bulik read the letter, typed on a Cyrillic typewriter, and was impressed by the way the writer had coupled his desire to work for the United States with a promise to provide information. The letter promised more high-level intelligence from a source with unparalleled access. Bulik had seen efforts by the KGB to plant agents by providing what appeared to be real information but which on checking turned out to be false, or what the Agency called "chicken feed."* The report on how the U-2 and RB-47 had been destroyed by Soviet missiles and aircraft was too highly classified, the CIA believed, to be provided as chicken feed for establishing a Soviet penetration agent in the CIA.

Then Bulik turned to the second letter in the packet, a diagram and detailed description of dead drop No. 1, through which the writer could be contacted. A dead drop is a hiding place to leave materials and messages for pickup, preferably to be used only once. The dead drop chosen by the letter writer was located in Moscow at the corner

---

* "Chicken feed" is a controlled transmission of information meant to obtain advantage over a rival service. The key to chicken feed is not so much its triviality as its propensity to pollute and confuse. Chicken feed has to be reliable data before it is "planted" or tampered with in some way. It may confirm data known to be already in the hands of a rival. Data released to secure the bona fides of an agent would qualify as chicken feed.

of Proyezd Khudozhestvennogo Teatra (Art Theater Lane) and Pushkinskaya Street. The entrance to the drop was located on Pushkinskaya Street, between the store number 19 "Myaso" (Meat) and the
store "Zhenskaya Obuv" (Women's Shoes). (See map, pages xiv–xv.)
The instructions read:

> The main entrance is open twenty-four hours a day. The entrance
> is not guarded, there is no elevator. In the entrance foyer to the left
> upon entering a dial telephone, no. 28, is located. Opposite the dial
> telephone, to the right as one goes into the entrance hall, is a steam
> heat radiator, painted in oil paint in a dark green color. This radiator
> is supported by a single metal hook, fastened into the wall. If one
> stands facing the radiator, then the metal hook will be on the right,
> at the level of one's hand hanging from the arm.

> Between the wall, to which the hook is attached, and the radiator,
> there is a space of two-three centimeters. For the dead drop it is
> proposed to use the hook and the space (open space) between the
> wall and the radiator.

> METHOD OF USING THE DEAD DROP

> It is necessary to place and camouflage any written material, for
> example, in a matchbox, then, the box should be wrapped with soft
> wire of a green color, and the end of the wire bent hook-shaped,
> which will permit the small box to hang from the hook or bracket
> of the radiator between the wall and the radiator.

> The location of the dead drop is on the unlighted right-hand corner
> of the entrance hall. In the entrance hall it is convenient to make
> a call on the dial telephone and it is very simple and easy to hang
> some type of small object on the indicated hook.

> The site for placing the signal indicating that material has been
> placed in the drop, is located at a five minutes ride from the dead
> drop, or a fifteen minutes walk. Thus the time that the material is
> in the dead drop can be held to a minimum. I will await the signal
> indicating placing of the material in the dead drop after 1200 and
> after 2100 each day beginning with 15.8.60.

Included with the description was a diagram of the dead drop and a
diagram for finding the phone booth at another site, which was to
be marked, indicating that the drop had been filled. The phone to be
marked was in the entranceway of a house on Kozitsky Lane off
Gorky Street in downtown Moscow, only four or five blocks away

from the dead drop. (See Appendix A diagram for dead drop and marking site.)

Bulik immediately recognized that the writer of the letter was a unique person. He was dazzled with the precise description of the dead drop and the signaling system, clearly the mark of a professional intelligence officer who knew his trade. The writer should be identified and contacted as soon as possible. He mused on what an exciting and valuable prospect the writer could be if he fulfilled his promise. There was nobody like him on the Agency's roster of Moscow agents or sources.[14]

The next step for Bulik was to identify the Soviet officer in the picture that came with the letter. He knew the Russian had worked in Turkey. He had told that to Cox. It was easy to match the American army colonel in the photograph with the name in the postscript of the letter. He was Colonel Charles Maclean Peeke, army attaché in Turkey from 1955 to 1956. From CIA files Bulik obtained photos of the Soviet military attachés in Ankara during the same period. It is standard Agency practice to keep a record of all Soviet military attachés around the world because they normally serve as intelligence officers. The senior attaché was Soviet army general Nikolai Petrovich Rubenko, a.k.a. Savchenko. The assistant attaché was a colonel in the Soviet Army, Oleg Vladimirovich Penkovsky. The headless uniformed figure in the photo was a colonel. In addition, Bulik could tell from photos that between the two men, Penkovsky's head fit better than General Rubenko's on the physique in the picture.

From the CIA records Bulik determined that General Rubenko and Colonel Penkovsky were members of the GRU, *Glavnoe Razvedyvatelnoe Upravlenie*, the Chief Intelligence Directorate of the Soviet General Staff. Both were using their attaché positions for cover while gathering intelligence and running spies. General Rubenko's real name was Savchenko. He took the name Rubenko in an effort to conceal his GRU affiliation, since Western Intelligence might have his real name on file from previous postings overseas.*

Then Bulik tracked down the students, Cox and Cobb. Bulik arranged to meet Cobb at a Washington, D.C., safe house, a secure CIA-controlled house used for meetings with agents or sources. Bulik did not tell Cobb the name of the Soviet officer, but Cobb confirmed from a spread of ten pictures of Soviet military officers which one was the man he had met on the bridge in Moscow. Bulik felt he

---

*In his obituary in *Krasnaya Zvezda* (Red Star), the Soviet military newspaper, on July 25, 1970, he was identified as Rubenko-Savchenko.

was on the right track, but he wanted further confirmation of the photograph from Cox.

Bulik left Washington on a Friday night and flew to Anchorage to meet Cox, who by then worked as a transportation expediter for the Federal Electric Corporation, building the DEW (Distant Early Warning) Line, a radar system against nuclear missile attack. Cox was gratified to meet Bulik. He realized the brave choice he had made that August night in Moscow was taken seriously by the American government. When Cox saw the layout of pictures he quickly recognized Penkovsky's face. Cox told Bulik he was definitely the same man who had given him the envelope on the embankment in Moscow. Bulik leaped from his chair when Cox made the identification. He was elated.[15] Then Bulik flew back to Washington to report the good news at the opening of business on Monday morning.

Bulik assumed from the letter that when Penkovsky had been military attaché in Turkey from 1955 to 1956, he and Colonel Peeke had been cautiously friendly. Like all military attachés around the world, when they meet adversaries on social occasions they probe each other for weak points and insights, much as dogs come up and sniff one another for identifying signs. There was a report on file that Penkovsky had sold jewelry and made an abortive attempt to sell a camera on the local Turkish market because he needed money, but there was no indication from the Ankara CIA Station that he wanted to defect or that Peeke had attempted to recruit him.[16]

Peeke returned to the U.S. for emergency home leave when his father-in-law became ill and died in October 1956. In November, by the time Peeke returned to Turkey, Penkovsky had gone to Moscow for home leave.

Bulik did not speak to Peeke because he did not want to widen the circle of those who knew about the letters from Penkovsky. In later years Peeke recalled that he liked Penkovsky. He found him intelligent, alert, and a cut above the hard-drinking, fat, and sloppy General Rubenko, who was the senior Soviet attaché. Penkovsky helped to arrange visas for Peeke and his wife to visit the Soviet Union. He visited the Peeke home in Ankara, and at one point Peeke joked that both he and Penkovsky had the job of trying to recruit one another as spies. Peeke said he had given the name of Penkovsky to the CIA as a possibility for recruitment, but there is no record the lead was ever followed up.[17]

None of the warmth of Peeke's relationship with Penkovsky was known to Bulik. He could only surmise that the greeting to Peeke in the postscript of the letter presumed and exaggerated their friendship in order to make Penkovsky welcome and credible.

With the information Bulik had in hand, he recommended Penkovsky be contacted and asked for a meeting with Jack Maury, head of the CIA's Soviet Clandestine Operations Division. After reviewing the material, Maury arranged a meeting with Bulik, Paul Garbler, the new Moscow Station chief, and Richard Helms, then the chief of operations for the Directorate for Plans (DP), which managed the Agency's covert activities. This high-level group pored over Bulik's report, searching for clues that would tell them whether the new walk-in was leading them to a gold mine or quicksand. (A walk-in is an unsolicited agent who volunteers his services.) Assuming Penkovsky was the writer of the letters, was he setting a conduit for disinformation and trickery or was he really a disillusioned Communist who wanted to counter Khrushchev's warmongering?

The hesitation and doubt about Penkovsky's intentions were directly related to the case of Lieutenant Colonel Pyotr Popov, a GRU officer who had spied for the CIA from 1953 to 1958. First based in Vienna, and then in Germany, Popov had been the most important Soviet intelligence officer in the GRU to be run by the CIA since World War II. He approached an American vice-consul in Vienna on New Year's Day in 1953 and asked for directions to the office of the American Commission for Austria. When the vice-consul replied, Popov handed him a note offering his services and naming a meeting place. At the first debriefing, Popov told his case officer that he needed money to straighten out an affair with a woman.

Popov was short, thin, and uptight, without any flair or imagination. He had risen from a peasant background to the officer corps mostly by managing to survive the battles of World War II. His Soviet colleagues remember him to be a subdued loner, who did not mix well with other officers. His GRU assignment was to recruit agents and work against the Yugoslavs.[18] Popov provided the West with the first inside information on GRU personnel and how they operated. He also gave the CIA important details on Soviet policy in Austria until he was transferred back to Moscow in 1954. He returned to the West in 1955, stationed in East Berlin, where he continued to offer information on GRU activities and Soviet policy in East Germany. In 1958 Popov was suddenly ordered back to Moscow, where he was confronted and forced to cooperate with the KGB to reveal the CIA's operations in Moscow. When he met his CIA contact on a Moscow bus, Popov pointed to a tape recorder on him so that the CIA officer would know he was under hostile control. It was too late. Popov and Russell Langelle, a CIA officer in the Moscow Station, were arrested on the bus. Langelle was declared persona non grata. Popov was sentenced to death and executed. According to a Soviet account, Popov "died like a mad dog." Several unconfirmed Western sources say he was executed by being thrown alive into a roaring furnace before an audience of GRU officers ordered to watch the fate of a traitor who spied for the Americans.[19]

Jack Maury and the men and women in the Agency's Clandestine Soviet Division saw Penkovsky's approach to be a possible provocation in retaliation for the deep embarrassment suffered by Soviet Military Intelligence because of Popov. The case forced a major reorganization of the GRU. As a result, General Ivan Serov was transferred from his position as chairman of the KGB to head the GRU at the end of 1958. Serov was trusted by Khrushchev from their days together in the Ukraine.

As head of the Soviet Division, Jack Maury had to make the recommendation to Dick Helms on how to respond to Penkovsky. Maury's legal training contributed to his persuasive briefing abilities. He had a reputation as an adroit bureaucrat, skillful in advocating positions and covering bases.

Maury was an American aristocrat, a member of the exclusive FFV, First Families of Virginia. He was born on April 24, 1912, at Donlora in Albemarle County, Virginia, Thomas Jefferson's second choice for the site of his home, after Monticello. Maury attended the University of Virginia and received his law degree from the University of Virginia Law School. While at the university he was a tour director in the summer for the Swedish American lines. On one trip to Leningrad he jumped ship for a couple of days and went to Moscow.

When he went into Marine intelligence work during World War II, Maury was asked which foreign country he knew. The Soviet Union, he replied. He was assigned to be a Marine Corps intelligence liaison officer in Murmansk. After the war he joined the CIA at its inception in 1947. His good looks, fine manners, and a sharp eye for women, supported by a pipe and flashy MG sports car, created for Maury the image of a romantic intelligence officer. His impeccable social connections only added to the allure. Maury worked on Soviet affairs in the Directorate of Intelligence, the analytical and estimating side of the Agency. Allen Dulles called on him to improve relations with the Directorate of Plans, the covert side of the Agency. Maury was so successful that in 1955 he was named head of the Soviet Division in the Directorate for Plans.[20]

Weighing the pros and cons on Penkovsky, Maury decided that the initial information on the U-2 and the RB-47 and his letter, with the dead-drop site, were so impressive in their professionalism that Penkovsky should be approached. He made the presentation to Helms, who approved trying to contact Penkovsky. Bulik was directed to commence the operation in Moscow, but the Agency had

17

no man in place to run an agent. Bulik needed a CIA officer to contact Penkovsky, clear his drops, and provide him logistic support. Except for the station chief and a deputy station chief, the CIA had no other personnel in Moscow. The only cover positions for CIA officers were on the embassy staff. The State Department limited them because of obtrusive KGB surveillance on all embassy personnel and the strong belief that CIA activities would disrupt diplomatic relations. State considered a low CIA profile in Moscow the best way to avoid a scandal that would enrage Khrushchev. The American ambassador, Llewellyn (Tommy) Thompson, refused to permit any State Department foreign service officers to clear or fill the dead drop described by Penkovsky, fearing they might be arrested.

State and the CIA had never worked well together. Under the Dulles brothers, with John Foster Dulles as secretary of state and Allen Dulles at CIA, foreign and national security policy had become a family affair. The closeness and informality between the Dulles brothers excluded State Department professionals from policymaking. Instead of being briefed by his own staff, John Foster Dulles often preferred Allen Dulles' experts for guidance.[21]

During the McCarthy hearings on Communism in the early 1950s, the State Department bore the brunt of the Wisconsin senator's unsubstantiated charges, while the CIA escaped virtually unscathed.[22]

State Department career officers resented the Agency's elite status, which gave CIA officers better housing and more independence at overseas posts. "Gentlemen don't go into trade or dirty tricks," was the diplomat's opinion of the Agency. In the Eisenhower years, however, the CIA was the favored policy arm of the government. In Operation Ajax, in 1953, the CIA's foremost covert operations expert, Kermit Roosevelt, was instrumental in mounting a coup against Prime Minister Mohammad Mossadegh in Iran and restored Shah Mohammad Reza Pahlavi to the throne. In 1954 the CIA's Operation Success overthrew the leftist government of Jacobo Arbenz in Guatemala after it had nationalized United Fruit Company holdings.

The Moscow Embassy evaluation of the situation, approved by the ambassador: Penkovsky's offer was a provocation. The U-2 Affair, for which Eisenhower accepted responsibility, and the cancellation of the Paris Summit had cast a pall over U.S.-Soviet diplomacy. Caution was the watchword. Thompson and the State Department still hoped for an improvement in relations with the Soviet Union after the 1960 election battle between Richard Nixon and John F. Kennedy. A new president could make a fresh start.

State's bureaucratic interest was in easing tensions with Moscow.

CIA's mission was to face risks in order to gather intelligence of national security interest. Conflicting goals created an inertia at State that avoided cooperation with the CIA.

As a rule, if agreement cannot be reached between the CIA and the State Department, the president makes a decision on how to resolve the interagency conflict, based on his own personal evaluation of the value of the spy and his importance to national security. At this early stage, the CIA had still to prove Penkovsky's worth, and the State Department was not anxious to cooperate in contacting him.

A young officer in the CIA's Soviet Division at headquarters in Langley, Virginia, was chosen to go to Moscow with the task of contacting Penkovsky. He was a bachelor who had served in Germany and did not know Russian well, but he seemed eager for the job. The officer was given the code name COMPASS. A colleague remembers him to be short, about five feet, six inches, blue-eyed and balding. On the surface he was cocky and self-assured, with a good sense of humor. He spoke rapidly and "credited himself with more intelligence and brain power than he had. He chewed his fingernails."[23] COMPASS was not an ideal officer for the job, but if Penkovsky were to be approached promptly, and considering the time necessary to train another officer and provide him with a cover position to operate from within the embassy, there was no alternative.[24]

There were no additional embassy slots available for a CIA officer because of a lack of housing accommodations. State was inclined to keep all the positions for Foreign Service officers and not allot any to the CIA. "It was a situation perceived as 'what I gain you lose' between State and the CIA," recalled a CIA officer who served in Moscow. "State did not want to give up its slots."

The compromise was to provide a low-profile, junior-administrative position to a CIA officer. Only three people—Ambassador Thompson, the CIA Station chief, and his deputy—knew of his cover. COMPASS's duties included janitor's chores at the American bachelor living quarters called America House, located at 3 Kropotkinskaya Embankment, along the Moscow River (see map, pages xiv–xv). The facilities at America House consisted of rooms for the Marine guards and other servicemen who worked in the embassy. They also provided quarters for bachelor Foreign Service officers. America House had a juke box with the latest hits, and movies flown in from West Germany three times a week. There was a billiards room and an outdoor swimming pool.

COMPASS arrived in Moscow on October 4, 1960. His life was bleak in the gray Moscow winter, which came early in 1960. Rain,

19

snow, and sleet turned the city into a dark and gritty river of slush. COMPASS settled into America House, in a corner room with a large window facing onto the street, across from a cement factory.

COMPASS, an inexperienced field officer, found it rough going. He was lonely and drank heavily. He knew little of the Russian language and the atmosphere was depressing, even frightening. To compound the physical darkness of the Russian winter and his personal isolation there was KGB surveillance whenever he moved from the embassy or America House. COMPASS had no office of his own, and had to write his letters furtively, by hand, then deliver them to his contact at the embassy for packeting by diplomatic pouch to Washington. He had no safekeeping facilities in his room or the embassy, so he could not retain copies of his reports or letters.

In his first letter to Bulik, COMPASS explained that "surveillance coverage so far noted is tight. I've made no checks for it, but even then it is obvious." He insisted that whenever he went for a walk along the Moscow River to the Kremlin he had teams of watchers surveilling him. He was watched at the Kremlin and St. Basil's Cathedral. Then, when he returned along the river to America House, the KGB tails were still there. He wrote:

> Reaching the large heated swimming pool along the river to America House I strolled in, and there were two new ones, undoubtedly for me. Not my imagination, and there were no repeats spotted in any of my coverage.

> Back along the river border and on to America House I spotted four or five possible "friends" and one positive [KGB surveillance officer]. The positive was a girl about 25, strolling ahead of me, who foolishly turned about halfway down the block to gesture twice to whoever was behind me that they should hold off. She then crossed the street to go under the bridge and make sure from there that I returned to America House. Lord, how they communicate I don't know, but the area is simple to cover.[25]

COMPASS suggested a plan to contact Penkovsky, now codenamed CHALK, through the dead drop on Pushkinskaya Street, the one Penkovsky described in his first letter. Since a dead drop normally is only used once and then abandoned, COMPASS would leave instructions for Penkovsky to toss his material over the corner of the twelve-foot-high wall of America House at a specific time when COMPASS would be waiting to receive it:

> I'm sure they have coverage from the building facing down over the yard but it doesn't cover the corner wall we discussed for CHALK.

I have official daytime access and can have official evening access to back yard storerooms, but I can't carry my ambition as building superintendent too far. Inside the wall is a dog kennel with 2-3 months old pup. I'm getting very well acquainted with him as fast as I can.

The wall itself is about 12 feet high and a minimum of 36 feet long and [it is feasible] to have a package come into America House compound. However, Sovs have jumped over that wall and—no details—all four sides of the House seem to have tight coverage.

In his disjointed, self-contradictory letter COMPASS warned that the wall around America House was under heavy surveillance and that CHALK [Penkovsky] would be taking a grave risk if he tried to throw a package into the yard at night. At best it would be a one-time means of contact. CHALK would have to use his own judgment during the day. COMPASS noted that the No. 17 bus passed across from the cement factory and foot traffic was heavy, including military men in uniform, making it "probably as deadly" during the day as at night. In any event CHALK would have to wait until COMPASS could give more specific information on his "cooling off," meaning when surveillance on him decreased.[26]

Please give my intermediary instructions that he has got to get to me regularly and I will hand him a blank envelope, which unless otherwise specified, goes directly to you.

Don't dare go down side streets as desired for CHALK, since as it turned out I'm the "hottest" thing in town.

signed//   COMPASS

No copy retained, got to keep it in my head. OHHH![27]

COMPASS's letters to headquarters continued to describe his miserable personal situation and suggested new possible drop sites. A dead drop he proposed in the back of the Anglo-American School was considered and then abandoned. COMPASS complained that the gentle puppy at America House had grown into a fierce, forty-five-pound watchdog that had not been trained. He had to approach the dog with rolled-up newspaper in hand. The drudgery and boredom of embassy life in Moscow were a constant refrain in COMPASS's letters, which he filled with complaints of how hard he was working as a glorified janitor in his cover job.

COMPASS admitted that he was "personally dissatisfied" with his own progress, but he could find no dead-drop site for Penkovsky other than the yard of America House. He urged that he be authorized to tell Penkovsky in his first message "to be prepared to make a quick heave over a twelve-foot wall as though he were throwing away a package of 'dirty pictures' or a book he'd prefer not to be caught with. He should practice with snowballs over twelve feet (sic) walls before he tries America House.[28]

"The dog situation, the lighting of the backyard, the access to the backyard, can all be handled by COMPASS on the basis of being sick with too much drink, interest in the dog, loneliness and anything else that will take care of getting out in the backyard at the right time and with a good excuse. Plan on the wall. If CHALK buys it we will know soon enough! Anything that comes over the wall, except for a person, which has not happened since COMPASS has been here, COMPASS has all the reasons he needs to get the package to himself."

In his letters COMPASS complained: "There are many personality conflicts, inter-service rivalries, and housing problems here in the city and at the American Embassy which complicate rather than simplify the problems. Realizing the absolute need, despite the local problems, COMPASS hopes that what is sent here will enable you to make a plan for CHALK. COMPASS is as anxious, and perhaps more so than those of you at home, that this will work out." In December of 1960, two months after COMPASS arrived in Moscow, the Americans still had failed to contact Penkovsky.[29]

The British Connection

EARLY IN NOVEMBER 1960, OVER A FINE LUNCH AT THE EXCLUSIVE IVY Restaurant in London, Dickie Franks, an officer in MI6, the British Secret Intelligence Service (SIS), asked Greville Maynard Wynne, a British businessman, to make contact in Moscow with the State Committee for the Coordination of Scientific Research Work (GKKNIR or *Gosudarstvenny Komitet po Koordinatsii Nauchno-Issledovatelskikh Rabot*). Ostensibly the committee develops and monitors the implementation of a unified state policy for science and technology. However, it has also served as a cover organization for KGB and GRU agents spying on Western technology. *

"You might want to see about getting together with some of their people. Among other functions, they have a department that's been put in charge of monitoring contacts between Soviet scientists and technicians and visiting delegations from the West," Wynne's MI6 liaison told him.[1] In the 1960s there was little direct contact between Western businessmen and Soviet organizations. Invitations to discuss trade deals were tightly controlled by the State Committee, which made all the arrangements and supervised the visits. Wynne's business activities would enable him to measure the State Committee's official interest in sending technical trade delegations to Great

---

* The name was changed to the State Committee for Science and Technology in 1965. In 1986 Aleksei Yefimov, a KGB officer who claimed he worked for the State Committee, was involved in the compromise of an American Marine guard. Known only as Uncle Sasha to Sergeant Clayton Lonetree, a Marine guard at the American Embassy in Moscow, Yefimov attempted through Lonetree's Soviet girlfriend to obtain access to American secrets. Lonetree was court-martialed for giving secrets to the Soviet Union and sentenced to thirty years in prison.

Britain. He would see what kinds of machinery and industrial processes the Soviet Union was trying to purchase in the West.

Wynne was forty-one, and trying hard to establish himself as an independent businessman in Eastern Europe and the Soviet Union. He had no previous intelligence experience or training; he was simply a British businessman trying to do business with Eastern Europe. His frequent travels behind the Iron Curtain made him a candidate for MI6's frequent-travelers program, an effort to debrief businessmen and academics visiting the Soviet Union on what they saw and heard. CIA had a similar program. Wynne had the rough charm of an ambitious working-class achiever trying to rise on his own. He was short and well groomed, his black hair and moustache neatly trimmed. Wynne's peppery, emotional personality made him likable but unpredictable. Born in Shropshire in 1919, he grew up in a poor Welsh mining village where his father was an engineer who serviced mining equipment. Wynne was fascinated with electricity and got his first job when he was nineteen as an apprentice repairing machinery in the factory of the Ericsson Telephone Company. He attended college at night in Nottingham, and worked during the day.[2]

In his memoir, The Man From Odessa, Wynne claims he spent most of World War II working for MI5 under cover, conducting surveillance on suspected German agents.[3] His war record, made available to the authors by his family, shows Wynne was posted twenty-three times, including three tours at Officer Cadet Training Units (OCTU), a clear indication he was working for the British Army Intelligence Corps field security as an investigator. Gordon Brook-Shepherd says, "It is not true that Wynne 'served in MI5 during the war.' "[4]

After the war Wynne became an industrial sales consultant representing British electrical, steel, and machine-making companies, first in Western Europe, then in Eastern Europe and the Soviet Union. He developed sales leads for companies that did not have their own traveling representatives or permanent sales offices. By representing several companies in different fields of manufacture, Wynne could present a variety of machinery. He received a commission on the sales. After he began traveling to Eastern Europe and the Soviet Union, he was called on by MI6 to report on what he had observed. Wynne was never a member of MI6, but he agreed to become an MI6 agent because he was a loyal British subject.[5]

On December 1 Wynne visited Moscow and was granted an interview at the State Committee's Gorky Street headquarters, not far from Red Square. "Armed guards stood in the reception hall, and there was a general bustle of messengers and secretaries, at least half of whom were girls. Not pretty girls. The Western business wolf would be disappointed in Moscow. The office girls wear white coats, unironed, and thick low heeled shoes. Buxom healthy girls, but with bad complexions and no makeup. Brassieres and deodorant are unknown to them," recalled Wynne.[6]

Wynne was introduced to the members of the Foreign Relations Department of the committee, then headed by Dzhermen Gvishiani,* and his deputy, Yevgeny Ilich Levin, a KGB colonel assigned to the State Committee as the *rezident*, KGB Station chief inside the committee. When he shook hands with the officials sitting around a table covered with green felt and bottles of mineral water, Wynne noted that most of them were badly dressed and physically unimpressive. One man, however, stood apart from the rest. He had a very straight back and did not wiggle or slouch. He sat quite still, his pale firm hands resting on the cloth. His nails were manicured. He wore a soft silk shirt and a plain black tie. His suit was immaculate. Sunlight filtering through the uncleaned windows showed up his glossy reddish hair and deep-set eyes. His nose was broad and his mouth full-lipped and strong on a powerful, imaginative face. His name was Oleg Penkovsky.[7]

Wynne proposed to the committee that instead of merely taking his brochures and catalogs to the appropriate ministries, he should be allowed to bring to Moscow a delegation of technical specialists from the eight main companies he represented. The company experts would meet with Soviet personnel of a similar caliber. This would allow for direct discussions and avoid the tedious bureaucratic channels that slowed the process of developing trade. Wynne said he could arrange for a delegation to come to Moscow before the end of the year.

Wynne's suggestion was welcome, and his group arrived on December 8, 1960, aboard a British European Airways flight from London. The twelve-member delegation from eight companies came to discuss the latest British technical developments in cement, metallurgy, computers, engine fuels, and welding techniques. Wynne billed the group as the first privately organized trade and technical delegation to visit Russia since the war.[8] Penkovsky was assigned to be the senior Soviet liaison with the delegation and to arrange for their needs.

He was their guide and accompanied them to Leningrad on December 12. That night Penkovsky approached Dr. A. D. Merriman, a

---

* Gvishiani's father, a distant relative of Stalin's, was a KGB major general. He named his son after Felix Dzerzhinsky, the first head of the Secret Police, and Vyacheslav Menzhinsky, his successor, hence Dzhermen. Gvishiani was married to the daughter of Alexsei Kosygin, who was chairman of the Council of Ministers from 1964 to 1980 under Leonid Brezhnev.

specialist in metallurgy, and W. J. McBride, his colleague, when they were about to retire for the night. Penkovsky asked Merriman if he had any spare cigarettes, and they went up to Merriman's room in the Leningradskaya Hotel to get them. McBride said goodnight and left. Then, Penkovsky locked the door, turned the radio on full blast, and drew from his coat pocket a folded packet of papers wrapped in cellophane. Penkovsky said they were secret documents he wanted to put in the hands of the American Embassy.[9] Merriman refused to touch them.

In his eagerness to make contact, Penkovsky had made an approach so blatant that in the context of the times it suggested provocation. Merriman had been warned to avoid any such offer. He had spent a year in the Soviet Union after the war as a steel expert and often made trips as a consultant for British steel companies. He also conferred with MI6 after his trips, a relationship that stemmed from wartime service in British Intelligence. It was a delicate balancing act, and Penkovsky's offer might be a test; he feared jeopardizing his position with the Soviet Union. Pinning an intelligence label on him could be used by the KGB to discredit his business contacts and all British trade delegations. Compromising of foreign diplomats or businessmen followed by blackmail and recruitment to spy for the Soviet Union was common practice in the 1950s and '60s.

In the early 1960s the KGB was busy seducing the French ambassador, Maurice Dejean, with a "swallow," a KGB female prostitute.[10] Early in the summer of 1962, the KGB used the same technique to entrap Colonel Louis Guiband, an air attaché at the French Embassy in Moscow. They confronted Guiband with compromising photographs of himself and his Russian girlfriend and offered him the choice of collaboration or exposure. Guiband returned to the French Embassy and shot himself rather than make the choice. The episode was never openly discussed, and Guiband was said to have committed suicide as a result of "psychotic depression."[11]

In an earlier episode the KGB established that a French diplomat was a homosexual who was attracted to a Soviet Militia captain guarding the French Embassy in Moscow. The captain was in reality a KGB officer who was ordered to submit to the diplomat. Then the KGB photographed the "love affair" of the two men and presented the diplomat with the pictures. When the KGB urged the diplomat to spy on his country he smiled, placed the photos in his pocket, and said, "These will be a good addition to my collection, especially the photos with the Soviet captain." The following day he returned to France.

The KGB also used such incidents to arrest foreigners and hold them as hostages to exchange for Soviet spies arrested in the West. The KGB considered the Westerners they held to be pawns who could be sacrificed in a trade for the KGB's highly prized knights of espionage.* Penkovsky, after pleading in vain with Merriman, put the papers away and departed.

When the delegation returned to Moscow, Merriman did not want to be seen entering the American Embassy, but he told the British ambassador about his encounter with Penkovsky in Leningrad. Merriman did not tell Wynne of Penkovsky's approach, but Wynne sensed that the Russian wanted to become friendly with him and was leading up to talking with him privately. Penkovsky hinted to Wynne that he would like Wynne to take something to England for him, but he did not come right out and ask him to do so.

Five minutes before Merriman was to depart for London, Penkovsky showed up at Sheremetievo Airport to say goodbye. He called Merriman aside and said, "I realize you are reluctant to become involved, but it really is important that I establish contact with someone in the American Embassy." Penkovsky asked Merriman to advise the Americans that he would be waiting for a telephone call at his home phone, 717-184, every Sunday at 10 A.M. "All the American has to do is call and I will give him further instructions," said Penkovsky.

Merriman was noncommittal. He asked Penkovsky where he lived. Penkovsky, sensing he had failed, and trying to cover himself, said he lived at 11 Gorky Street, the offices of the State Committee for the Coordination of Scientific Research Work.

On his return to London, Merriman informed MI6 and they put him in touch with the CIA's London Station to describe the incident with Penkovsky in Leningrad.[12]

---

* Yale University professor Frederick Barghoorn was arrested and accused of spying in November 1963, after a Soviet spy had been arrested in the United States. Only after President Kennedy said he regarded the arrest as "a very serious matter" that had "badly damaged" the "reasonable" atmosphere between the U.S. and the Soviet Union was Barghoorn released on Khrushchev's direction. However, the charges against him were not withdrawn.

In 1978 Francis Jay Crawford, an American working for International Harvester in Moscow, was arrested and charged with currency speculation. He was to be part of a trade for Vadik Enger and Rudolf Chernyayev, two Soviet employees at the United Nations arrested on May 20, 1978, by the FBI while engaging in espionage activities. Crawford was fined and expelled. The two Russian spies were convicted and sentenced to fifty years in prison in October 1978. In April of 1979 they were exchanged for the release of five leading dissidents.

In August 1986 Nicholas Daniloff, the *U.S. News and World Report* correspondent in Moscow, was arrested on charges of spying and held in prison for thirteen days until a trade was arranged for Soviet spy Gennady Zakharov, arrested in New York City.

*   *   *

Had Merriman taken the letter, MI6 would have read Penkovsky's reminder to the Americans that four months had passed since his first approach and still he had received no word. "This is a period of torment for me," he wrote. He urged the Americans to speed up their decision on how he should transmit the materials he was holding and tell him how a meeting could be organized.[13]

With no word from the Americans, and the British members of the trade delegation unwilling to accept his letter, Penkovsky turned to the Canadians. They also made their official contacts for visits of businessmen and scientists through the State Committee for the Coordination of Scientific Research Work. On December 30, 1960, a bitter cold, overcast day, Dr. J. M. Harrison, Director, Geological Survey of Canada, arrived at Sheremetievo. He was in the U.S.S.R. to assess Soviet geological developments and to arrange future exchanges between the two nations' specialists. Penkovsky's mandate for developing espionage through the State Committee included the United States and Canada. He met Harrison at the airport and accompanied him throughout his eleven days in the Soviet Union. Harrison visited geological institutes, universities, and museums. Penkovsky took him to the Kremlin Museum, where the two men were fascinated by the collection of Scythian gold artifacts on display. In his diary Harrison noted the contrast between the openness of Penkovsky and the rigidity of the Intourist guide, who was always spouting official propaganda.

When Penkovsky and Harrison traveled to Leningrad they shared a sleeping compartment with an elderly lady. It is standard Soviet practice to put men and women who are total strangers together in a sleeping car, and the two men stood in the corridor chatting while she changed into her nightclothes. Penkovsky's comments were critical of the Soviet system, and his candor made Harrison "wonder what was going on."

Early in the morning they were blasted awake by the train's public address system. "This is another example of Russian bureaucracy," grumbled Penkovsky, complaining about being arbitrarily awakened. When they left their hotel in Leningrad for an appointment at the Institute of Arctic Geology, Penkovsky told Harrison that he would catch up with him at the institute. "I have to report to Moscow on how you are behaving," Penkovsky said, smiling in a disarming manner. Clearly, he was trying to win Harrison's confidence and intimate that he was not really a heavy-handed official spying on him.

When they returned to their hotel there was no service in the dining room because they arrived during the staff's lunch hour. Penkovsky excused himself and went into the kitchen. When he returned to the table he told Harrison that he was a colonel in the Soviet Army. "I had to pull rank to get our lunch," said Penkovsky. Harrison had seen Penkovsky only in civilian clothes and was not aware of his military rank.

On the Red Arrow express train back to Moscow, Penkovsky and Harrison had a compartment to themselves. Penkovsky continued his criticism of the bureaucracy while they sat together drinking tea from glasses. He voluntarily described the Soviet Union's shortcomings, and was relaxed enough to make derogatory remarks about the people with whom he was working. Harrison listened in fascination, but, to avoid further involvement, pleaded fatigue and went to bed.

The next day Penkovsky asked Harrison to introduce him to William Van Vliet, the commercial counselor, at the Canadian Embassy. Penkovsky escalated his campaign to ingratiate himself with Harrison by inviting him to the Bolshoi Ballet performance that night. Penkovsky's wife, Vera, and their fourteen-year-old daughter, Galina, joined them in a box next to Nikita Khrushchev. Prima ballerina Maya Plisetskaya danced the lead in *Swan Lake*. Her performance was so stunningly beautiful that it left the audience in awed silence when the curtain fell. When the audience recovered, the waves of applause continued for more than ten minutes.

Harrison, in an effort to return Penkovsky's hospitality, invited the Penkovsky family to an Armenian restaurant near the Bolshoi, but because he was a novice in Moscow he had failed to make a reservation. When they arrived, the restaurant was full. Penkovsky disappeared with a few dollar bills from Harrison and soon they were shown to a table directly in front of the floor show. When Harrison asked how Penkovsky accomplished the feat, he replied with flattery, "Oh, I told them that a distinguished Canadian scientist was here and they immediately made things available."

Penkovsky's all-out courtship of Harrison reached its climax the next day in Harrison's room at the National Hotel. Penkovsky indicated he wanted to talk confidentially. Harrison gestured toward the telephone on the table where they were sitting. Penkovsky got up, reached to the end of the table, and yanked some wires out of the wall, making it appear they had broken. "That should take care of that," he said, indicating that if there was a listening device in the phone, he had deactivated it.

Penkovsky asked Harrison about his feelings toward Russians— but not toward the Communist Party—and whether Harrison was prepared to help promote better relations between the U.S.S.R. and Canada. When Harrison replied in the affirmative, Penkovsky came right out and asked the big question. Would it be possible for Harrison to invite Penkovsky and his family to visit geological centers in Canada? Harrison backed off, telling the Russian that although he was a senior civil servant, he did not have influence in the government.

Penkovsky was not deterred. He said he understood Harrison to be a millionaire, with a big house, a car, garage, and washing machine. For Russians, even those like Penkovsky who had traveled to Turkey, Harrison's private home and ordinary household possessions seemed unattainable. In 1960 most Russian families were still living in one-bedroom apartments or shared a *kommunalka*, a communal apartment, which was broken up to accommodate several families, but with only one shared kitchen and toilet. Harrison stalled again and Penkovsky repeated his request to meet Van Vliet, the commercial attaché. By the end of the conversation Harrison's mind was in a whirl while he tried to figure out Penkovsky's motives. He did agree to introduce Penkovsky to Van Vliet.

The following day Harrison told the story of the meeting to the Canadian chargé d'affaires, but never uttered Penkovsky's name. He wrote it on a piece of paper and told the chargé that the discussion referred to the name he had written: Penkovsky.[14] If the KGB had been taping the conversation in the Canadian Embassy, as was always the assumption, it might have been able to track down Penkovsky as the source of the request to be invited to Canada.

That same evening, January 9, 1961, Penkovsky came to Harrison's room to meet Van Vliet. Penkovsky had worked it all out in advance that he would give secret information for the Americans to Van Vliet, who had a diplomatic passport. Harrison, a civil servant, had an ordinary passport. Van Vliet had diplomatic immunity and he also had official dealings with the State Committee for the Coordination of Scientific Research Work. At worst, Van Vliet would be declared persona non grata and expelled. If Harrison were found with the papers he could be arrested as a spy. It would be safer for Van Vliet to handle the information Penkovsky had prepared on the construction and characteristics of Soviet nuclear missiles.

After brief small talk, Penkovsky went into the bathroom and turned on the water to muffle the conversation in case it was being taped. He sat in a chair near the open bathroom door and asked Van Vliet to deliver a letter for him to an American friend through the military attaché at the American Embassy. Before Van Vliet could respond, Penkovsky thrust a package into his hands and in English urged him "to be a patriot." He told Van Vliet, "I know that you can sell me down the river—but what will you get out of that?"

Penkovsky left quickly, and said he would return the next day. Van Vliet and Harrison went downstairs for dinner in the National Hotel.

The two Canadians discussed the incident at length, but reached no conclusion on what to do with the packet from Penkovsky.[15] When Harrison left, Van Vliet again stared at the package he had received from Penkovsky but did not open it. Van Vliet saw that it was a bulky envelope, doubly sealed with tape and without the name of the addressee. It did not look like a personal letter to the American acquaintance whom Penkovsky said he had met in Turkey when he was a military attaché there. Van Vliet decided to return the envelope to Penkovsky at the first opportunity, with the explanation that he was in no position to pass over a packet with unknown contents to the American military attaché.

Two days later Penkovsky visited Van Vliet in the hotel room and asked him if he had delivered the material to the U.S. Embassy. "I am not concerned with such matters," Van Vliet said, and returned the unopened packet to him. If he were being set up by the KGB, Van Vliet would have to explain to the ambassador why he had accepted the letter when it was against embassy policy. He would be expelled and have to leave the Soviet Union. He was a bachelor with a Russian girlfriend and was enjoying his stay. He did not want to take chances. Nothing but trouble could come from cooperating with a member of the State Committee in such an enterprise.

Being expelled from the Soviet Union would be a black mark on a rising diplomat's record, even if the expulsion was the obvious result of a Soviet effort to create a false case. To cover himself, Van Vliet described his meeting with Penkovsky in a memorandum to the Canadian ambassador.

On Wednesday at 7 P.M. Mr. Penkovsky dropped in and I offered him a drink and a chair, he taking the former, but declining the latter as it faced onto the door, and instead asked if he might sit on a divan on the opposite side of the room. I happened to have the record player on, and in view of this start of proceeding kept it on during Mr. Penkovsky's stay.

I started the conversation on topics of our mutual interest vis-à-vis the State Scientific and Technical Committee. Mr. Penkovsky almost immediately asked me if I had delivered the letter, to which I replied that I had not since I was in no position to deliver unknown contents on behalf of Soviet citizens. He took the letter. Mr. Penkovsky appeared somewhat agitated upon first entrance and never seemed to regain full composure. I tried to cut the trend of conversation and discuss only those matters which came strictly within the realm of normal liaison function on behalf of the State Committee.

31

This was to no avail and Penkovsky persistently reverted to the theme of the importance for him to meet with someone from the U.S. Embassy.

Penkovsky said that although he could perhaps understand my action in not undertaking to be a go-between with the Americans, his fate was now in my hands—he hoped I would not inform anyone (presumably the Soviets). He said he had been trying desperately the last six months to find some way of approaching the Americans and thought that his present position for the State Committee would make this possible. He offered to show me the contents of the original letter, which I declined, and said that in addition to a document on ballistic missiles, it contained his personal letters to each of President Eisenhower and President-elect Kennedy. He said he hoped to pass on more documents, thereupon taking out of his pocket a large thickly packed envelope.

His determination remained, he said, to contact the Americans, to whom he wanted to pass valuable information, and that a final objective was to get out of the Soviet Union with his wife and daughter. Almost in passing, he mentioned that he was experiencing financial problems.

Again, he asked that I arrange for him to meet someone from the U.S. Embassy, either through an invitation to the Canadian Embassy, or a luncheon invitation, and if neither of these, that at least I inform the Americans of his interest. Penkovsky explained his inability to go directly to the U.S. Embassy because of the Soviet police guards, and that even at the State Scientific and Technical Committee it was an almost invariable rule that two Soviets must be present when a foreigner calls. He offered me his home phone number, which I expressed myself willing to have, but suggested that I would be able to reach him at his office.

The Canadian official said he "declined everything resulting from this one-sided gushing flow, maintaining only that I would hope to be in touch with him at the State Committee on our continuing commercial interests. I invited him to stay for dinner but he said he just didn't feel up to it and so ended our 40 minute conversation in English."[16]

Van Vliet explained to the ambassador that he was at a loss to assess the motivations behind the visits.

Mr. Penkovsky is about 47, he has a pleasant personality and would appear to have reasonable capacity. The rush of events in our brief meetings certainly instilled me with deepest caution. He apparently is the type that has little hesitancy to ask for personal favors as evidenced by his requests for various items from Canada, such as salve for eczema, which he assumes will be sent to the Embassy to be passed over. He certainly went into uncalled for detail in our conversations in commenting on matters such as having the record player on, the hazards of phoning his office, repeating his fate was in my hands, specifically mentioning documents and letters, expressing his regret that apparently I was not quite convinced of his sincerity of purpose in wishing to contact the U.S. Embassy, etc; a partial explanation might be the melodrama of his previous position as military attaché.

Very obviously his position with the State Scientific and Technical Committee is a minor one, with low salary, and is a great comedown from his military career. It is likely that he is a disgruntled citizen.

If he is honest in his professed desire to pass information of value to the Americans and have he and his family leave the Soviet Union, he is dangerously talkative. If these are not the motivations, association of Canadian personnel with him, except at the strictest official level, is highly undesirable.[17]

Van Vliet had no way of knowing that Penkovsky was a full colonel in the Soviet Army assigned to the Chief Intelligence Directorate of the General Staff, and was using the State Committee, where he appeared in civilian clothes, as a cover. Dr. Harrison had not told Van Vliet of the incident in Leningrad when Penkovsky revealed he was a colonel in the Soviet Army in order to commandeer their lunch. When he returned to Canada, Dr. Harrison, who had no security debriefing from the Canadian government, wrote a letter to the Canadian chargé d'affaires in Moscow thanking him for the embassy's cooperation. He joked in the letter that if Penkovsky ever came to Canada he hoped to be far away in Alaska. Harrison sent the letter to Moscow through the open mail, which is routinely read by the KGB and could have compromised Penkovsky before he started to work for the West. Apparently the KGB did not get the joke or did not read the letter.

Penkovsky's approaches to the Canadians and the British occurred during the same period that COMPASS was in Moscow, unable to make contact with Penkovsky. The CIA was unaware of Penkovsky's approach to the British until Merriman reported to MI6, who put Merriman in touch with the CIA Station in London. On January 12, 1961, the CIA requested MI6 cooperation in further debriefing Merriman. The British had no objection but replied that they be-

lieved Penkovsky was "a routine provocation." Because of the blatant directness of his approach, Penkovsky was seen by British
Intelligence to be part of a scheme designed to compromise an American or British diplomat. The CIA still had not told the British that
Penkovsky had succeeded in sending a letter with the student, Cox,
the previous August.

On January 14 COMPASS, the CIA's man sent to Moscow to
contact Penkovsky, met with American Embassy officials to discuss
the case. With its traditional caution, the State Department refused
to risk endangering U.S.-Soviet diplomatic relations by encouraging
an unproven Soviet officer who said he wanted to spy for the West.
The judgment of the embassy officials, led by Ambassador Thompson, was that Penkovsky was a provocateur; the embassy wanted no
part of him. At this stage the decision was made by the ambassador
on the spot. COMPASS would have to keep Penkovsky away from
the embassy and America House to avoid any unpleasant entangle-
ment. The ambassador again refused to allow American Embassy
personnel to unload the dead drop Penkovsky proposed in his letter.
The ambassador also refused to allow America House to be used as
a drop point for Penkovsky to deliver materials. COMPASS was on
his own to contact Penkovsky and unload the drop Penkovsky had
proposed.

The CIA could turn to the British Secret Intelligence Service for
cooperation, but many in the Agency were deeply concerned with
Soviet penetration of the British intelligence establishment. British
diplomats Guy Burgess and Donald Maclean defected to the U.S.S.R.
in May 1951. Harold (Kim) Philby, the MI6 man in Washington
from 1949 to 1951, was forced to return to London, where he was
suspected of being a Soviet agent. Philby was forced to resign from
MI6, but later official statements spoke only of his resignation from
the Foreign Service. Since the SIS does not officially exist, "the
Foreign Service" is used as a euphemism to avoid mentioning MI6.
Philby was technically attached to SIS for up to five more years,
because it often takes that long to build a case against someone
under suspicion. A mock trial by MI5 and MI6 efforts to force a
confession from him failed. In November 1955, J. Edgar Hoover
pressed for a full-scale British investigation of Philby and he was
named in Parliament as the Third Man in the Burgess and Maclean
team. Philby's supporters produced a brief which leaned heavily in
favor of his innocence and Philby was cleared in a statement by
Foreign Secretary Harold Macmillan. In 1956, Philby's friends at
MI6, Nicholas Elliott and George Young, arranged a job for him as
a "stringer," a part-time, nonstaff correspondent, for *The Observer*
and *The Economist* in Beirut while the investigation of his past

continued. In 1963 MI6 sent Nicholas Elliott to Beirut to force a confession from Philby, but he fled to the Soviet Union.[18]*

The CIA's concerns about the security of the British service clashed with the imperatives of the moment, which demanded action. Neither intelligence service had a high-ranking source inside the Soviet military establishment.

When the Moscow Embassy's decision not to participate in the running of Penkovsky reached Washington, Dick Helms decided to seek British assistance. Given the urgency of determining whether or not Penkovsky could be a bona fide agent for the West, and the lack of CIA personnel in Moscow, Helms judged the British to be the best source of help. The CIA has a special working relationship with the SIS and shares information on the highest level. Helms felt more comfortable working with MI6 than exposing the details of the Penkovsky case to the State Department where he feared a leak might occur. Helms turned to MI6 because they agreed to cooperate in contacting Penkovsky. Besides, MI6 already knew of Penkovsky and there was no way out without straining relations.[19]

Going to the British was an unhappy choice for Bulik and Quentin Johnson, the Soviet Division's chief of operations; but there was no immediate alternative. "The big lesson on the Penkovsky case is never to enter into a joint operation with another service," Bulik insisted in retrospect. "Joint operations, by definition, double the risks of exposure. The differences in any two services' operating styles lead to confusion, misunderstandings and raise the possibility of compromise."[20] Since Penkovsky had also approached the British, cooperation was the order of the day.

MI6 knew that Penkovsky's offer was directed toward the Americans, and they raised the issue in Washington in January 1961 when Harold Taplin Shergold, one of the toughest and most experienced agent handlers in MI6, visited CIA headquarters. On January 27, 1961, Joe Bulik informed Shergold of Penkovsky's initial approach to the two American students five months earlier. It was standard operating procedure to share information in such a situation, but a face-to-face meeting was necessary. Bulik was ready to tell Shergold of Penkovsky's August overtures and show him the U-2 and the RB-47 information. The British still had to be convinced.

The Americans respected Shergold. He was trim, with crisp, pleasing features, a sharp but not prominent nose, well-shaped chin and

---

*Philby lived in Moscow until his death in 1988, never fully trusted by the KGB despite their efforts to laud him as a hero publicly. Privately, his bona fides remained in doubt and he was not given access to highly classified information. For sharp insights into Philby's character, or lack of it, see Nicholas Elliott, *Never Judge a Man by His Umbrella*, London: Michael Russell, pp 182–190.

high forehead. His bright eyes and compressed vitality suggested intelligence, competence, and tight restraint. He was born on December 5, 1915, and educated at St. Edmund Hall, Oxford, and Corpus Christi College, Cambridge. After graduation he taught at Cheltenham Grammar School until the war intervened. In 1940 he joined the Hampshire Regiment and soon switched to the intelligence corps. Shergold's first professional experience came in World War II as an interrogator of German prisoners of war in the Middle East. From there he was seconded to the Eighth Army and was in charge of all interrogations from the battle of El Alamein in Libya to Cassino in Italy. Shergold's British Combined Services Detailed Interrogation Center (CSDIC) was based in Rome under the Allied command at the same time as two young Italian-speaking American officers, James Jesus Angleton and Raymond Rocca, from the fledgling Office of Strategic Services (OSS), were also interviewing German and Italian prisoners of war. Angleton and Rocca knew Shergold professionally and socially during this early period of their careers.*

Angleton rose rapidly after the war to the post of CIA chief of counterintelligence from December 1954 to December 1974. Rocca, his deputy from 1969 to 1974, remembers Shergold as "a strict, hard working operator who did the best job he could for his own country."[21] During World War II the British SIS was wary of losing its control in Europe to the American upstarts and was determined to keep the OSS less than fully informed.[22]

Shergold began his postwar career as a case officer for MI6. As a junior officer he ran agents in Germany from the main British station at Bad Salzufflen, as well as in Berlin and Cologne. He built a formidable reputation as a cool, precise agent handler with a keen instinct for getting the most from his agents. He was ready for Penkovsky.[23]

Shergold was impressed with the possibilities and said MI6 would reconsider whether or not to try to approach Penkovsky and take his measure as part of a joint operation with the CIA. After the Washington meeting the matter moved quickly. On February 3 Quentin Johnson flew to London to meet with Shergold. The Americans and the British agreed to exchange information and arranged for a security "button-up" with the Canadians. It was necessary to prevent Penkovsky from being compromised by Van Vliet and Harrison and to "vet" or closely examine and remove all references to Penkovsky in the Canadian files. This also meant getting those who had read Van Vliet's and Harrison's reports on Penkovsky to sign security pledges not to discuss them.

* The Office of Strategic Services was founded on June 13, 1942, by Franklin D. Roosevelt and headed by William J. Donovan, a Wall Street lawyer.

From February 6 to 8, 1961, a high-ranking CIA counterintelligence officer visited his counterparts in Ottawa and arranged to have Van Vliet's and Harrison's reports on Penkovsky removed from the Canadian security files.

On Sunday morning, February 5, 1961, COMPASS finally tried to phone Penkovsky at home in Moscow. In the intervening four months since he had come to Moscow in early October, COMPASS was unable to service the dead drop or contact Penkovsky. He wrote interminable letters to CIA headquarters explaining how difficult it was to do his cover job in the embassy and carry out his assignment without embassy support. Although he reconnoitered the location of the dead drop on Pushkinskaya Street, he never marked the telephone to indicate that he had actually left a message in the dead drop for Penkovsky.

COMPASS never explained to Bulik's satisfaction why he failed to leave a message for Penkovsky; he always claimed he was never free from KGB surveillance. Bulik believed COMPASS had lost his nerve and kept prolonging the operation without acting.[24] The February 5 phone call was his first attempt at direct contact. COMPASS's instructions were to call at 10 A.M. and speak in Russian, but in a letter to Bulik, speaking of himself in the third person, he wrote:

> ... hope the following amendments to your instructions of Letter No. 8 will be acceptable. They are based on his experience here and use of public telephones. First, if a male answers the phone of Feb. 5, COMPASS will use familiar Russian for Hi, Oleg!
>
> If the answer is Yes! (Da!) COMPASS will reply, "Reply only in Russian. This is your intimate friend!"
>
> Then COMPASS will continue in English. If CHALK [Penkovsky's cryptonym] tries to insist on knowing who is calling, COMPASS will insist "Listen!" in English and go on as instructed. CHALK must have some guide to a cover story in case he is not alone when COMPASS calls and, in the event the number is wrong, or a male answers who is not CHALK, the use of the familiar [pronoun] in Russian should allay suspicion.

Then COMPASS said the other instructions would be followed "to the letter."[25]

Use of the familiar pronoun in Russian when speaking to Penkovsky would appear to anyone tapping the line that the caller was a close friend and not a foreigner who had never met him. If COMPASS's letter sounded confusing, it was. He had problems speaking

Russian and had worked himself into a psychological state of turmoil.

COMPASS called Penkovsky's telephone number, 717-184, at 11 A.M., and Penkovsky, who had stayed out late partying, at first thought it was his friend from the previous evening. COMPASS was supposed to speak only in Russian, but he spoke in English. Penkovsky could not understand him on the phone and could not reply because his wife was listening. He did not want her curiosity aroused by his speaking English on the phone, something he never did at home. He said he could not understand what the caller had said. Listening to an unfamiliar foreign voice was difficult for Penkovsky, whose English was limited. He did not expect the call and was confused about who it might be because it came at the wrong time. Penkovsky hung up in frustration, so that if his phone was monitored there would be no indication that anything more had occurred than that a wrong number was called.

On February 9 Bulik again conferred with Shergold at CIA headquarters in Washington and they agreed to proceed jointly to contact Penkovsky. Shergold gave Bulik more details from the meeting in Leningrad between Penkovsky and the members of the British trade delegation.

At the beginning of March 1961, the Canadian commercial counselor, Van Vliet, received the assignment of an apartment in Moscow and moved from his hotel room. Van Vliet, who hoped to maintain contact with Penkovsky for legitimate Canadian trade and commercial work through the State Committee, invited him and his wife to a reception to celebrate the move. Penkovsky again carefully put together the material that he had collected on the operational characteristics of Soviet missiles and took it with him to the party. He placed the packet in an ordinary letter envelope which he could easily hand over, but double sealed it with tape.

When he entered Van Vliet's apartment, Penkovsky shook hands with the Canadian diplomat and said he hoped Van Vliet had thought the matter over and would accept the material. Van Vliet simply avoided responding to the entreaty. He greeted Penkovsky and his wife, Vera, in a friendly manner, but stayed away from the Penkovskys during the entire time they were at the reception. Penkovsky never had an opportunity to ask Van Vliet to carry out the missile secrets or contact the Americans for him. Frustrated, Penkovsky left with his secrets tucked inside his breast pocket.[26]

Wynne, however, was hard at work to get a Soviet delegation to come to Great Britain. In early April 1961, he flew to Moscow to discuss arrangements for a Soviet delegation to return the visit he had made in December. Penkovsky presented Wynne with the list of Soviet representatives who had been chosen to visit England. Wynne protested that they were inexperienced in industry and unsuitable because they were clearly people who would be interested only in gathering technical industrial intelligence. They were not likely to place any orders. Penkovsky explained to him that the list had been drawn up by the State Committee and could not be changed. The relationship between the two men had ceased being formal and they now called each other by their first names. Penkovsky asked Wynne to call him Alex, because he said "it sounds better in English than Oleg." To Penkovsky, Alex was more elegant and foreign.

Wynne and Penkovsky walked across Red Square in a spring snowstorm arguing over the composition of the delegation. Wynne insisted that he wanted "top technical advisors or no one." If he didn't get them he would complain to the committee.

Penkovsky was in anguish, "No, no, Greville, you mustn't do that. It would mean that the delegation is canceled."

"I'm sorry, Alex, but I have to insist. I would like to show you London, but not if it means wrecking the whole purpose of the visit. My companies want experts."

In *Contact on Gorky Street*, Wynne wrote, "At that point Penkovsky clapped his hands together and cried, 'But it is not the delegation that matters. It is I who must come to London, and it is not for pleasure. I have things to tell you, so many things, I have got to come. I have got to.' "[27]

Then, for the first time, Penkovsky told Wynne that he had materials for the West. In Wynne's hotel room on April 6, 1961, Penkovsky gave Wynne a bulky package with a complete dossier on himself and film of Soviet military documents. When Wynne accepted the handover from Penkovsky he was no longer a naive businessman who by chance had befriended a spy. Wynne's role was to become that of a courier cum comrade-in-arms for Penkovsky, but he was never to be told the details of the documents Penkovsky gave him. Wynne was never given intelligence material orally by Penkovsky. This was standard intelligence tradecraft. By not letting Wynne know the details of anything Penkovsky might give him, Wynne, if arrested, could claim that he did not know he was involved in spying.

In this first instance Wynne immediately went to the British Embassy to get rid of the papers. It was the end of the day and the ambassador was not available. Wynne put the material in a sealed envelope and left it with the British security guard. He returned the following day, retrieved the papers, and gave them to an embassy officer who was assigned to see him.

At the April 6 meeting Penkovsky asked Wynne to meet him during the weekend for dinner. He said he felt he should not invite Wynne to his home. Soviet officials did not invite foreigners to their homes without official permission, and if they did, a full report on the conversation was mandatory. Wynne was reticent. He had not expected to be given documents, and asked for a day or two to think things over. Wynne did not know what was in the envelope Penkovsky had given him and he still was not certain whether Penkovsky's approach was genuine or an attempt to entrap him. They agreed to meet on Monday, April 10, at the final committee meeting at 2:30 P.M., and not before.

Penkovsky came down from committee headquarters to greet Wynne at the front door of No. 11 Gorky Street. They were alone in the elevator and halfway up to the meeting place when Penkovsky asked, "What have you done with the papers? Are they all right?"

"Yes," replied Wynne.

Penkovsky acknowledged the answer with a gesture of relief, but said nothing more when the elevator stopped and they entered the meeting together.

The meeting to work out final details for the visit ended at about 5:30 P.M., and Penkovsky asked Wynne, "Can I see you once more?" Wynne agreed and Penkovsky came to his room at the Berlin Hotel. They talked committee business and then Penkovsky repeated his performance of tiptoeing to the bathroom and turning on the water taps to generate noise. "The papers are all right?" asked Penkovsky.

"Yes," said Wynne.

"Will you take the others? They are very important," implored Penkovsky.

"No. I am not taking any more."

"If you won't take these others, will you take a single sheet saying what I can discuss with your people?" asked Penkovsky, slapping his pocket to indicate where he was holding the papers.

"No, I have done all I can," Wynne insisted.

"Please stay one more day and think it over," argued Penkovsky.

"All right."

That night Penkovsky and his wife took Wynne to the Bolshoi with an official invitation from the committee. Afterward, unofficially, they went to dinner to celebrate Vera's thirty-third birthday. Penkovsky told Wynne he would be forty-two years old on April 23.

The following evening Penkovsky came to the hotel to say goodbye to Wynne and again requested that he take more papers with him to London. Wynne stayed up for hours pacing back and forth in his room trying to decide what to do. The fear of being searched at customs and arrested for spying fought with the desire to bring the material to the West. Although he had carried one batch of material to the British Embassy for Penkovsky, he now was "clean." It was only if he was caught carrying state secrets that he would be liable to arrest and imprisonment. There was no time to return to the embassy.

At 7:20 A.M. on Tuesday morning, April 11, Penkovsky came to the hotel in an official committee car to drive Wynne to Shereme-tievo and see him through customs. While the baggage was being put in the trunk, Penkovsky put his finger to his lips, warning Wynne not to discuss anything sensitive in the car. Their conversation might be monitored on a tape recorder or overheard by the driver, who most likely was a KGB informant. On the way to the airport they talked about committee matters and the forthcoming visit by Penkovsky and the delegation to London later in the month.

At Sheremetievo, Penkovsky pulled out his credentials from the committee and breezed Wynne through the departure formalities. Twenty minutes before Wynne was to board his flight to London, Penkovsky looked in the direction of the men's room and indicated for Wynne to follow him. Penkovsky cased the toilet stalls and when he was certain they were alone he said formally, "Mr. Wynne, you must now decide whether to trust me. There is no more time; take the package of remaining papers, or the smallest thing you can do is to take this sheet. If you won't take the papers then take this single sheet." Wynne accepted the single sheet and put it in his inside breast pocket. Penkovsky embraced Wynne and said, "You have done the right thing."

Penkovsky had handed Wynne a letter addressed to the leaders of the United States and the United Kingdom. The letter, by then outdated, was written on December 25, 1960, and revealed Penkov-sky's state of mind:

My Dear Gentlemen:

On August 12, 1960, I resorted for help to two American citizens, tourists and teachers of the Russian language; they stayed in Mos-cow at the Balchug Hotel and left Moscow for the USA on 8-15-1960. I sent with them, for transmission to you, two envelopes with a personal letter and other materials (three pages and one photo). I am very grateful to those gentlemen for their kindness and the great attention they displayed in carrying out my request. Almost four months have passed (it was a period of torment and waiting for me) and there is no answer to the questions and requests raised by me.

At this time I decided to send to you part of some materials (for this I started to look for the right moment).

I am asking you to speed up the decision about the way to transmit to you the rest of the very important materials and to organize a meeting with your representative, that is absolutely necessary for me for personal reasons.

Please inform me about your decision: by writing to me using dead drop #1 (the description of which I sent to you 8-12-60); or organize a meeting with your representative.

The conditions for meeting you decide yourself. From my side I also propose my variant: 5, 10, 15, 20, 25 January 1961 and 30 January; 5, 10, 15 February 1961, beginning from the moment of transmission of this letter from 9:00 to 9:15 (in the evening) I will wait for your representative at the following address: Moscow, Kadashevskaya Embankment. I will walk along the embankment, across Repin's Memorial (which is located at the opposite side of the canal). This memorial faces Kadashevskaya Embankment and Lavrushensky Lane. I will be dressed in a light overcoat of dark brown color and a cap with ear flaps; I will be smoking cigarettes. (In the spring a raincoat of gray color and hat.) Your representative (male or female) should have an eye glass case in the left hand and at the beginning of our talk should send me a greeting from C. Peek [Colonel Charles Maclean Peeke].

I remain, yours,
12-25-60

P.S. In any case I will inspect dead drop #1: 4, 9, 14, 19 January 1961 at 8.00 in the evening + 24, 29 January; 4, 9, 14 February 1961.

P.P.S. That means each day which can be divided by five from the day of transmittal of this letter [referring to the days he would wait for a meeting on the embankment].

On his return to London, Wynne called the telephone number he had been given by Dickie Franks of MI6. Although SIS knew that Wynne was making the trip to Moscow, when Wynne delivered Penkovsky's letter, the SIS discovered for the first time that Penkovsky had decided to use Wynne as a courier. Shortly afterward SIS received the same news from Moscow as a result of Wynne's approach to the British Embassy there. At this point SIS arranged to debrief Wynne thoroughly. Penkovsky and his delegation were scheduled to arrive on April 20. When Penkovsky applied for a visa to come to Great Britain, the CIA agreed to take no further action to contact him until he arrived in London. CIA and SIS agreed on a joint operation to run Penkovsky from London as an agent. Shergold, in consultation with Bulik, would control Penkovsky through the British Embassy in Moscow. In the week remaining, a flurry of cables went back and forth between the CIA and SIS establishing joint U.K.-

U.S. operational arrangements for Penkovsky's visit to the United Kingdom. The initial CIA objective was to maintain him as an agent-in-place and to offer him terms of "employment."

Because of the difficulties with the American Embassy in Moscow, the Agency decided not to approach the State Department for cooperation in running Penkovsky in Moscow. Since the British had contacted Penkovsky through Wynne, the operational details would be handled initially by the British SIS Station in Moscow.

Two Americans flew to London to meet Penkovsky. Joe Bulik headed the team. Bulik chose George Kisevalter, a member of his staff experienced in handling Soviet agents, to join him. The son of a German father and a French mother, Kisevalter was born in 1910 in the North Caucasus, where his father, an engineer, was building railroads for the tsar. During World War I the elder Kisevalter was sent to the United States to buy arms and equipment for the tsar. When the Russian Revolution intervened in 1917, the Kisevalters settled in America. Young George quickly became Americanized, but he retained his Russian-language skills. Later he attended Dartmouth, where he studied mathematics and engineering. One of Kisevalter's best friends at Dartmouth was Nelson Rockefeller. They graduated in 1930 and remained lifelong friends.

During World War II, the U.S. Army used Kisevalter's Russian-language skills to assist in transferring Lend-Lease equipment from Alaska to Siberia. At the end of the war he joined the OSS in Europe, where he began as an interpreter. In 1952 Kisevalter was recruited by the CIA to be one of the first case officers in the Clandestine Soviet Division. Kisevalter's reputation as an effective case officer rose when he was put in charge of handling GRU Lieutenant Colonel Pyotr Popov. Kisevalter put Popov at ease, and the spy looked upon his case officer as a friend. Kisevalter was comfortable with Popov's peasant directness and lack of pretense. Kisevalter had an easygoing, rumpled manner and a prodigious memory. He liked to drink, and his drinking bouts with Popov after operational sessions were well known in the Clandestine Service.

It was an insider's joke that the CIA even had its own cow on a Soviet collective farm—Popov bought a heifer for his brother, a member of a collective farm, with rubles given him by Kisevalter. While he worked the Popov case, Kisevalter let it be known to his colleagues that he was running an important Soviet agent. Bulik thought he talked too much, but he called him into the Penkovsky case because of his language skills and thorough familiarity with the structure of the GRU from handling Popov.[28]

Bulik and Kisevalter would team up with Harold Shergold, or Shergie, as the Americans called him, and Michael Stokes, a Russian-speaking MI6 officer. Shergold was to be the senior MI6 officer on the case. He had just added renown to his name inside the Secret Intelligence Service by obtaining the confession of George Blake, a traitorous MI6 officer who had served the KGB as a Soviet penetration agent into the British Secret Intelligence Service from 1953 until he was discovered and arrested on April 4, 1961, two weeks before Penkovsky's arrival in London. Blake's arrest was not publicly announced until April 22, but CIA's London Station had been informed at the time of his arrest.

At CIA headquarters in Washington, Blake's arrest added additional concern about the risk of compromising Penkovsky by joining in the operation with the British. Was Blake operating alone or was he part of another group like Philby, Burgess, and Maclean? The specter of Soviet penetration was aroused again. The Americans, however, respected Shergold for his hard-driving approach and his careful efforts to maintain total control over his agents. They had no doubts about his professionalism. He was not a man who warmed to his colleagues, but his analytical abilities were unsurpassed. He had an uncanny facility for coming directly to the point and pressing it, however far away his agent's thoughts might have wandered. "He was not the kind of guy who volunteered information. He didn't speculate or engage in small talk. He would say only what had to be said," recalled Bulik.[29]

Before Penkovsky arrived in London, Shergold invited Bulik and Kisevalter to dinner at his home in Richmond Park, outside of London. There, over drinks and a tasty meatless meal cooked by his wife, Bevis, a vegetarian and former Olympic discus thrower, Shergold told the two Americans about Blake's confession and arrest. Pointing to Bulik, Shergold said, "You are sitting opposite me just the way George Blake did when he confessed."[30]

Blake was very much on the mind of the Americans. When he was a junior MI6 officer in London in 1954, Blake was a note taker at an early planning meeting between the CIA and SIS for Operation Gold, tapping the Soviet's communication lines through a Berlin tunnel that the Americans and British dug from West Berlin to East Berlin to tap Soviet military communication lines.

After he left the planning meeting, Blake made a chalk mark on a lamppost so his Soviet control officer would contact him. He informed his Soviet control officer of the plans for the tunnel that same evening. Although the KGB knew of the plans, they did not inform the GRU, and tapes of the tapped telephone lines in the tunnel provided a source of valuable operational information about Soviet forces in Germany. However, highly classified communications between Soviet and East German leaders were not transmitted through the tapped lines. The Russians seized their end of the tunnel in April 1956, ending Project Gold. When Blake was arrested, intelligence officials began to speculate in private that the tunnel had been kept open to protect Blake. An early closing of the tunnel would have forced an internal CIA and MI6 counterintelligence investigation that might have exposed Blake as the source of the leak.

In 1955 Blake had been sent to West Berlin by MI6 while the tunnel was still in use. For three years, in Berlin, Blake revealed secret information on Western strategy to his KGB controllers. In Berlin, Blake was a member of the SIS Soviet Operations Section, and betrayed the names of British and German agents to the Soviet Union. At dinner Shergold remarked to the two Americans that Blake had been brought back to London for questioning from Lebanon, where he was studying Arabic for a new assignment. Blake had been arrested before the onset of the Penkovsky case and therefore could not compromise him.*

Bulik and Kisevalter kept a low profile in London while waiting for Penkovsky. They spent hours playing cribbage until Greville Wynne called to say that Penkovsky had arrived as scheduled at Heathrow on Aeroflot.

---

* Blake escaped from a British jail, where he was serving his forty-two-year sentence, on October 22, 1966. He fled to the Soviet Union and lives there in obscurity. Blake's autobiography, *No Other Choice*, was published in London in 1990 by Jonathan Cape Ltd.

London at Last

Wynne met Penkovsky at Heathrow on a crisp but cloudy spring morning and drove him into London. The initial meeting at the airport, when the two men shook hands, was friendly but formal. Penkovsky carefully concealed his elation. Once they were together in the front seat of Wynne's Humber sedan, Penkovsky quickly passed a package of documents to Wynne. By this time Wynne knew what to expect in dealing with Penkovsky. He put the documents inside his coat pocket without comment. Penkovsky arrived in London April 20, 1961, the day that Fidel Castro proclaimed victory at the Bay of Pigs. The last Cuban invasion forces sponsored by the CIA were captured at Playa Giron near the original landing point. A week earlier, on April 12, Major Yuri Gagarin, the Soviet cosmonaut, had become the first man to successfully orbit the earth.

Wynne booked the six-man Soviet delegation into the Mount Royal hotel, near Marble Arch. It was a tourist-class hotel with 1400 rooms, inexpensive but serviceable, which suited the Soviet delegation's small hard-currency allowance for room and board. The Mount Royal takes up the entire block on Oxford Street and is bordered by Portman and Old Quebec streets.

Penkovsky was entitled to a single room and he had asked Wynne to reserve a large one for him. He was determined to fully enjoy every moment in London and to use his position as head of the delegation to obtain every special treatment due him. His visa had arrived only at the last moment, after approval at the Central Committee of the Communist Party; foreign travel was a rare privilege and requests were screened for security clearances at the highest level.

Penkovsky planned to create an impression of leadership and prestige in order to distance himself from the others in the delegation, but he was also careful to look after them well. Then the delegation would speak well of him when they returned to Moscow, smoothing the way for further travel abroad. He was booked into room number 566, on the corner overlooking Portman and Oxford streets. The others in the delegation had to share double rooms or were assigned small single rooms.

Penkovsky was not only the head of the delegation, but he was known by the others in his group to be a GRU officer. The delegation's purpose was to acquire Western technology such as high-temperature steel, radar specifications, new communications developments, and advanced systems for concrete processing.

After checking in the delegation, Wynne went to Penkovsky's room. A broad smile brightened Penkovsky's face when Wynne entered. Penkovsky gripped Wynne by the shoulders, held him at arm's length, and said, "I can't believe it, Greville. I just can't believe it."[1]

Wynne told Penkovsky that the first meeting in London with American and British Intelligence would be held that evening right there in the Mount Royal. After the welcoming reception and dinner, Penkovsky was to proceed to a secure room on the third floor.[2]

In the meantime MI6 looked at the packet Penkovsky handed Wynne in the car. The British quickly notified the interviewing team that the material contained descriptions and diagrams of the latest Soviet missiles and launchers. The team waited for nightfall with excitement and anticipation. After dinner with the delegation at the Mount Royal, Penkovsky left his group on the pretext of going to bed.

Penkovsky arrived back in his room at 9:40 P.M. His real evening of work was about to begin. He walked through the corridor to a stairway on the opposite side of the hotel and then down to the third floor, where the British had arranged rooms 360 and 361. Penkovsky was ready. He squared his shoulders and knocked on the door. He was greeted formally in the anteroom to the hotel suite by a man who introduced himself as Joseph Welk. The American had a wireless tape recorder on him in order not to miss any of the conversation, but when he checked it just after Penkovsky knocked on the door, it was not working, so he decided not to waste time on small talk. Penkovsky called him *Gospodin Iosif*, Mr. Joseph. Welk's real name was Joseph Bulik and he was as tense as Penkovsky. Bulik had never had a bigger case.[3]

Bulik guided Penkovsky into room 360 and introduced him to Shergold, the head of the British team, who used the name Harold Hazelwood. Michael Stokes, the junior member of the SIS team, was introduced as Michael Fairfield. The other American, George

Kisevalter, told Penkovsky his name was George McAdam. Kisevalter would do almost all of the direct questioning of Penkovsky and translating for the team.

The adjoining rooms 360 and 361 faced onto an interior court and were free of street noise. The actual meetings were in room 360, a modest-sized room, 12 feet by 18 feet, furnished with a couch, five straight-backed chairs, and a small cocktail table, around which Penkovsky and the joint Anglo-American team gathered. Room 361 was to be used for training sessions.

Kisevalter, who had such an open manner that his friends said he was like a teddy bear, asked Penkovsky if he would prefer to speak Russian or English. "I can express myself much better in Russian," said Penkovsky.

"I graduated from the Military-Diplomatic Academy in 1953. In 1955 I went to Turkey. My working language there was English. I had many difficulties there and during the past four years, I simply forgot much of my English by disuse. Well, gentlemen, let's get to work. We have a good deal of important work to do."

Penkovsky wore a business suit, white shirt, and tie. His red hair was thinning and gray at the temples. He lit a cigarette, the first of many. His weight of 180 pounds was well proportioned on his five-foot-nine-inch frame, and there was no sign of flab. Penkovsky had the self-possessed good posture and military bearing of a general officer. His face was intelligent and alert, radiating intensity and openness.

Kisevalter, portly and dressed in a wrinkled suit, sought to reassure Penkovsky. "You know now that you are in good hands."

"Yes," replied Penkovsky, "I have thought about this for a long time. I have attempted to make this contact, taking a very devious path about which I feel I must report to you in full."

Kisevalter explained that the British and Americans had received his original letter with the plan for a dead drop.

"You mean the one I gave to the two teachers," said Penkovsky. "If you knew how many gray hairs I have acquired since that time; if you had only marked the signal just so I would have known that the message got into the proper hands. I worried so much about this."

To reassure Penkovsky, Bulik pulled out the original copy of his first letter and the photograph he had enclosed.

Kisevalter told him, "This was shown you to reassure you, and in two words I can tell you why a response was not made immediately after receiving the letter. We deliberately delayed signaling you until a secure manner for receipt of the materials you wanted to pass could be devised. This was done exclusively in consideration of your security."

Penkovsky was not assuaged. "Between friends, admit that you did not trust me. That is most unpleasant and painful to me."

"No, it is quite the opposite," insisted Kisevalter.

Penkovsky was not impressed, and he poured out his anxieties:

I was exposing myself constantly to considerable danger. I had expected to be met by an American representative—why do I say American? Because a good friend of mine was the military attaché in Turkey, Colonel Charles Peeke, and I also have many other American acquaintances, among whom were the naval and air attachés. Due to this friendship I wanted to arrange with Colonel Peeke some sort of a future plan that I already had in my mind, but unfortunately just prior to my departure the father of Colonel Peeke's wife died and he and his wife flew back to America for the funeral. I did not want to speak to any of the other attachés, with whom I was not as well acquainted. Besides, when I left Turkey I expected to return. I thought I was going on leave, but they deceived me in Moscow and did not send me back.

Kisevalter took charge and laid down a set of operational requirements for Penkovsky to follow. He insisted that the first and most important consideration for Penkovsky's own security was that he have absolutely no clandestine relations in any way with Greville Wynne or the British businessman whom he had asked to carry out his documents in Leningrad. All contact was to be restricted to public meetings related to their official functions.

Penkovsky listened carefully. Then he said, "In addition to them I also was in contact with a Canadian person and he must be buttoned up. He turned out to be a very unserious person."

"We know about him," replied Kisevalter. "He was an employee in the Canadian Embassy's commercial attaché's office."

"I gave him an envelope and requested that he deliver it to the American Embassy," explained Penkovsky. "I told him that I saw in him an honest face. He is a Canadian citizen, a patriot, and friendly to the American people. He took it and promised to deliver it. A day went by. The Canadian met me and returned the package, saying, 'I cannot deliver this; I do not know you, and my purpose here is only commerce.' I really believed that he would deliver my envelope. You can imagine how dejected I was when I left him."*

Kisevalter asked Penkovsky if he had received a phone call in

---

* Van Vliet was not told of developments in the Penkovsky case, but he was transferred from Moscow to Washington in June of 1961 in an effort to prevent him from being in a position where he could compromise Penkovsky. He died on April 11, 1968.

Moscow from an American who was sent to contact him. "Yes, I did, but this gave me absolutely nothing at all. The only word I understood in the whole message was the word 'March.' In a telephone conversation I do not understand English at all. Therefore, I requested that when a telephone call was to be made, that it be made in Russian. In addition the call should be made from a public booth."

"It was," said George.

"The night before I was at a friend's house at a party and the following morning when the telephone rang I thought it was him. My control time for the call was at 10:00 hours and the call came at 11:00 hours."

"That is correct," said Kisevalter.

"I understood nothing and I couldn't ask questions very well since my wife was walking around. My mother and daughter were also in the room. Although they realize that I can speak English, to engage in a serious type conversation would raise the question to whom I was speaking."

"Is your wife absolutely unwitting of your intentions?" asked Kisevalter.

"She doesn't know a thing."

The team decided to let Penkovsky take the lead during the first meeting and discuss whatever he wanted, in whatever order he chose. Penkovsky, an experienced intelligence officer, did what he would have wanted his own agent to do: relate his biography. He knew the Americans would want to check him out and establish to their satisfaction whether he was a bona fide agent or a plant sent to infiltrate the American and British Services. He began by telling the team about himself.

"I was born April 23, 1919, in Ordzhonikidze in the Caucasus.* My father was a first lieutenant [*poruchik*] in the tsar's army. My father's name was Vladimir Florianovich Penkovsky. My grandfather came from Stavropol." Penkovsky asked the team if they would like to "jot down some of this data since it would be hard to remember." If Penkovsky was aware that the meeting was being recorded, he gave no indication of concern, and the team took notes for form's sake. Speaking in rapid-fire manner, Penkovsky often left thoughts incomplete while he unburdened himself. He was intense and excited, shifting from one subject to another when ideas triggered points he wanted to be sure to make.

My grandfather's name was Florian Antonovich Penkovsky and he was a well-known judge in Stavropol. Only recently have I been

*Formerly and presently known as Vladikavkaz.

accused and confronted with having come from a background of the gentry [*dvoryanstvo*]. Allegedly this information came from one of the countries of the People's Democracies.*

I was the only son. My father graduated from a polytechnic institute. He was a mining engineer. Either he died of illness or was shot during the Revolutionary days since there were very violent conflicts in that district of the Caucasus.

Well, both my grandfathers died; my mother brought me up all by herself. I finished high school and immediately enrolled in the Second Kiev Artillery School. My father had vanished without a trace. It is not possible to simply state in one's official records in the Soviet Union that you have no record of your father's death. One would be blocked for life from progressing in any specialty. They would not accept you in the Party and one would just about have to be a common laborer. Therefore, I worked out a legend that he had been killed in 1919. Actually we did find out from records later, and my mother knows this—she is living with me now—that he was killed during the siege of Rostov and that he had been promoted to first lieutenant in May 1919, in the White Army. Everything was accepted and I had no difficulty.

Penkovsky was obsessed by the legacy of his father's service as a White Russian officer in the civil war. Had the records of this appeared earlier, he would never have been permitted to rise as high as he did. The KGB's criteria for loyalty included a thorough background check of an individual's class background. Those whose families fought against the Bolsheviks were considered suspect and

* Shortly before the end of World War II, Stalin and his senior military and security officials issued an order establishing special detachments to seize the archives of government organizations including intelligence, foreign affairs, armed forces, secret and regular police, as well as emigré organizations in countries liberated by the Red Army from German occupation. The special detachments were composed of operational officers from the Commissariats of Internal Affairs, State Security, and Counterintelligence and Defense. The records they confiscated were brought to the Soviet Union during the years 1946–1950. Several railroad cars from Germany, Czechoslovakia, Yugoslavia, and Bulgaria contained the records of military organizations of the White Army that had been collected and maintained by emigré groups in those countries. They contained the details on officers and men who had escaped after the defeat of the White Army and a rundown on the members of the emigré communities in those countries. The archives were put at the disposal of the KGB and gradually the material in the railroad cars at the station of Veshnyaki, about eighteen miles southeast of Moscow, in the vicinity of the KGB Higher Intelligence School, was processed and integrated into the KGB files. Small groups of KGB officers worked on the archives from 1947 to 1953. In 1952 the First Chief Directorate of the KGB assembled a team to integrate the archives into the KGB records. It is possible that from these files came the records of Penkovsky's father in the White Army.

eliminated from consideration for top security clearance positions, even if, as in Penkovsky's case, they had never seen their father.

"In my early years," Penkovsky continued, "I decided I had better conduct myself with enthusiasm in the Communist cause, and to be perfectly honest, I did serve quite faithfully. I am almost forty-two now—in fact the twenty-third of April will be my forty-second birthday—this coming Sunday."

Kisevalter interrupted. "We'll celebrate it."

Penkovsky continued:

I joined the Komsomols [Young Communist League] and I considered myself a progressive man of our country fighting for the ideas of Lenin. My ambition then was to join the Party and in 1939 I was already a candidate for Party membership. Also, in 1939, I graduated from the Kiev Artillery School. Immediately upon graduation I was taken for a twenty-day assignment to liberate the Western Ukraine, and our action was in the direction of Tarnopol-Lvov, at that time a part of Poland. [He was referring to the Soviet takeover of the Polish-Russian borderlands in 1939 after the signing of the Hitler-Stalin Pact, which ceded the Baltic states and the borderlands to the Soviet Union.]*

At that time the *Yezhovshchina* [the bitter expression for the purges of 1939 named after Nikolai Ivanovich Yezhov, head of the NKVD] was in full force and there were many executions, even of army people. Since I was a Party candidate I was assigned, together with a lot of other candidates, to serve as a political commissar [*politruk*] with various army units. I worked in that capacity for four years. My rank was Senior Politruk [senior political officer responsible for the political education and reliability of the troops at company level]. There was little loss of life in this campaign in Poland. This was in September and October 1939, when we were engaged in liberating Byelorussia and the Western Ukraine.

When Kisevalter interrupted him to ask, "This was Polish territory?" Penkovsky replied: "Yes, it was, but we were liberating it, just as the Red Army liberated the Baltic States. At that time I was on what was known as the Western Front."

* From November 1939 to August 1940, the Soviet Union conducted so-called Liberation Operations and annexed the Western Ukraine and Western Byelorussia from Poland. Bessarabia and Northern Bukovina were also annexed from Romania. They remain part of the U.S.S.R. The Baltic States of Latvia, Estonia, and Lithuania were annexed on August 3, 1940. They were overrun by the Germans in 1941, but returned to the U.S.S.R. in 1944–1945. They declared their independence from the central government in Moscow after the August 1991 coup failed, and quickly received international recognition.

In November 1939 the war with the Finns began, and in January 1940 our division was sent to fight on the Karelian Isthmus against the Finns. The division was in reserve almost all of the time, but two days prior to the arrival of Kalinin [Mikhail Ivanovich Kalinin, president of the U.S.S.R. from 1919 to 1946]—who was to participate in signing a peace treaty with the Finns—our division was thrown into action and only ten percent survived. All regimental commanders were killed and I was fortunate to escape without a scratch. This was due to the fact that I was an artilleryman and our positions are somewhat behind the front line. Despite the hardships of this conflict, I was still full of enthusiasm and when this war ended, I was accepted into the Party in March 1940.

The team was concerned about Penkovsky's security, and Kisevalter asked him how much time he could spend at the meeting.

"I am very glad that you have my original letter. My spirits have been buoyed up considerably and I am no longer tired," he replied.

"Can you get into trouble for being away?" asked Kisevalter.

Penkovsky said that he had no problems.

I have received a special intelligence mission during this trip. I can leave at any time to do my own work and I will tell you after what my mission is. The other members of the party realize that I am not an engineer or a specialist and that I am a member of this delegation because I work in the foreign relations section of the GKKNIR [the State Committee for the Coordination of Scientific Research Work]. They know that many intelligence personnel work in this committee and in fact in all ministries. All I need to say is that I want to go off. I would say that today I have about two hours' time. If anyone calls me on the phone I will say I was tired and had disconnected the phone and did not hear it. I simply said, "Good night" to the other fellows and went to sleep. That's all there is to it.

Kisevalter warned Penkovsky, "At any rate you must be on your guard constantly, and it is difficult for us to determine what is dangerous for you and what is not."

"Yes, I have asked you to protect me and I will protect myself," Penkovsky agreed.

"Enough dangerous risks have been taken by you already and by the grace of God everything turned out all right. Therefore, that is all the more reason for being extra careful now," added Kisevalter.

"Yes, after all the chances I took, thank God everything turned out all right and thank you for your consideration," said Penkovsky.

The mood of the meeting was changing. The room was stuffy from cigarette smoke, yet all the windows remained closed for security. The men removed their jackets and loosened their ties. The intensity level rose. The team realized that they were about to acquire a serious senior officer with access to Soviet military secrets and top military personalities. Neither the Americans nor the British had such a spy.

Penkovsky continued his life story.

After I became a Party member and the war with Finland was over, I transferred to the Moscow Military District. My assignment there was Deputy to the Chief of the Political Section dealing with Komsomols in the Krasin Artillery School. I worked there until the beginning of World War II. When the war began I was transferred to the headquarters of the Moscow Military District. There I worked as a senior instructor in the Political Directorate of the Moscow Military District and again this involved work with the Komsomol. I was still full of enthusiasm and was already a senior political officer. I was twenty-three years old then. After a year I was transferred to the Military Council of the Moscow Military District in the section of Extraordinary Missions [Penkovsky worked on highly classified security matters].

A member of the Military Council was Dmitri Afanasyevich Gapanovich, a lieutenant general whose daughter I married and to whom I am married today. I have been married now for fifteen years. He was a prominent political worker and a very fine man; he helped me a great deal and he liked me. He saw that I was very enthusiastic, which was quite true at that time, and I do not deny this to you. I only make this remark now to explain why later I changed all my views and how I became more mature in my thinking.

I worked for the Military Council until November of 1943. At that time the recapture of Kiev was being celebrated and I thought that the war would end very soon. Here I was with no distinctions or decorations. I received nothing for the Finnish campaign, only a commendation and a cigarette case. There were already a thousand Heroes of the Soviet Union, so I submitted a request for front-line duty and was sent to the First Ukrainian Front. I was assigned to a subdivision of the huge headquarters by General Sergei Sergeyevich Varentsov, who is now a marshal. Note his name; I will tell you much about him later. He was at that time a colonel general of artillery and the chief of the artillery of the First Ukrainian Front. He liked me because I was full of enthusiasm, and assigned me to be the commander of a training reception center for antitank artillery regiments. At that time we had twenty-seven antitank artillery regiments in action on the First Ukrainian Front combating German tanks. Therefore the general gave me this assignment, emphasizing how important it was to have a constant flow of replacement units to the front.

I had three training units and worked there for three months, but I wanted to go on line duty and submitted a request. I was assigned to be a deputy for personnel matters to a regiment. I was again a line officer and I worked for two months under my commander, a Hero of the Soviet Union named Tikhvich. He was a good fellow, but he was a drunkard. He raped a pregnant woman and was removed, so I became the commander of the 323rd Artillery Antitank Regiment of the Eighth Artillery Antitank Brigade.

Penkovsky also told the team that

during one battle we faced massed attacks by German forces trying to relieve their threatened formations. We endured fierce tank and infantry assaults which caused us tremendous losses—some of our gun crews were reduced to one or two men instead of seven. It was here that I was compelled to shoot dead one of our own Soviet officers, an infantry lieutenant charged with protecting our regiment, who cracked under the strain of battle and fled. I felt no compunction at all at the time, and apparently my action won approval from both my superior officer and the political staff. There was a certain feeling, however, in my regiment that I was overzealous and even cruel, but times of crisis call for decisive actions like this, and I'm sure I did right.

Then I was wounded and was sent to Moscow in June 1944. I was hospitalized for two months. I was released in July and prepared to return to the front. I was a major at that time, the youngest regimental commander on the front. I had two decorations then; now I have, altogether, five orders and eight medals. Just when I was about to go to the front I heard that General Varentsov, who was en route to visit General Konev, was injured in a tank accident and was flown to Moscow. He was in a so-called Marshals' Hospital on Serebryany Lane. His hip was damaged and as a result one leg was shorter than the other. He was suspended by a pulley in the hospital for four months. Since he was my commanding officer, I brought gifts to him. He already knew me well and assigned me to be his liaison officer at the front. He wanted me to do this during his recuperation. Varentsov told me that when we returned to the front together he would give me back my old regiment. I told him that would be fine and since the war would end soon and the Germans would be crushed, I would like to go to a military academy. He said he would arrange this. I went back and forth to the front a number of times and reported to him.

Varentsov had a very beautiful first wife, Anya, who died of tuberculosis. Later he married his present wife, Yekaterina Karpovna. He snatched her away from a Leningrad doctor to whom she was married. At this time Yekaterina, his mother, and his two daughters were in Lvov [in the Western Ukraine]. They lived on Pushkin Street during the time the marshal was hospitalized, and they had a hard time getting food and fuel. Therefore, I took care of the family; not only was the marshal a very nice person, but I knew that he would reward me tenfold for anything I did for him. From his first marriage the marshal had a daughter, Nina. When Varentsov was recuperating and Marshal Konev was demanding his earliest return to the First Ukrainian Front as chief of artillery, Nina's husband was shot together with two others who were engaged in black marketing in Lvov. Her husband, Major Loshak, who happened to be a Jew, and with whom she was deeply in love, was convicted of participating in a black market ring. They were charged with committing sabotage and undermining the power of the Red Army. It was proven that Varentsov had no personal interest in the black market deal whatsoever, but he was accused of political shortsightedness in allowing this to go on under his nose. He was called before the minister of defense, who reprimanded him. However, the minister said, "Let us forget the whole matter; go back to the front."

His daughter, Nina, worked as a nurse's aide in a military hospital. When her husband was executed she was distraught, but she returned to work at the hospital. In the hallway she saw a wounded pilot awaiting treatment. She approached him, leaned down and pulled his pistol from its holster and killed herself.

I sold my last watch and went down to Lvov to bury the girl. I bought her a black dress and her coffin. When he was returning to the front by rail I accompanied him, and it was then I told him about the unfortunate situation with his daughter. He was emotionally upset. That was in March 1944. After we returned to the front and he knew what I had done, the marshal said, "You are like a son to me."

Later he gave me 5000 marks and said to order the best possible monument in Vienna to place on her grave in Lvov. Three months later Varentsov received the order of Hero of the Soviet Union.[4] Anyway, that is the story of a good friend of yours, indirectly, through me. I am going to buy him an expensive watch and inscribe it from my wife and myself. I can photograph this watch and send you a picture.[5]

Up to this moment Varentsov supports me, and it is partially due to him that I am sitting with you now. Even yesterday they were still hesitating to send me here. Although I had my visa from you on the 8th of April, they were still undecided in the Central Committee yesterday about whether I should be sent or not. This is because my father was a White officer. On the other hand, I have had a distinguished military record in three campaigns. I have been decorated and have no black marks whatsoever on my Party records. If it were not for my father, I should not be isolated. In fact, I once was slated to go to India to be the military attaché and was not permitted to go even though I was completely prepared to go. I studied all the required codes and ciphers.* I was to have gone as the *rezident* [station chief].[6]

They did not let me go and transferred me instead to another section, this committee. Of course the work is along the lines of intelligence, but of a more passive variety, namely to work with foreign delegations, the purpose being to obtain information—possibly to steal some documents of value, and, of course, the ever present mission of recruiting someone in a foreign delegation. At any rate this latter mission thus far has been unsuccessful so far as I am concerned.[7]

It was the problem of my father again. They christened me—I was born in Ordzhonikidze, and my name is in the church register in Stavropol. They searched for the entry in the archives which were taken away by the Germans when they destroyed the city. They are still studying them. The KGB is studying every name in the archives. That's the way they work. Well, they turned up the fact that my father was a White Army officer, a second lieutenant, that in May 1919 he received the rank of first lieutenant in the White Guards, and that he was killed when his unit was surrounded near Rostov. That's what my mother heard—you know these rumors— and what she told me. But Major General A. A. Shumsky, the GRU deputy chief of personnel, confronted me and said, "Your mother reported that he died of typhus during an epidemic." My mother did not want to wreck my life. She gave me this cover story and that's what I wrote at the beginning. I suspected, of course, that this was not true. My father was wellborn. He finished at the Lyceum. He was a mining engineer. Then he joined the Whites and fought against the Soviet régime in the civil war. Well, I felt this. My mother told me all this because I never saw him and never called him father. I was four months old when he last held me in his arms and he never saw me again. That is what my mother told me.

Shumsky said, "Well, there you are. Write me an explanatory note." I took a small piece of paper and wrote. My wife does not know about this. She loves me and I love her. She has a sister, a brother, and a mother. They are of proletarian descent. Her father [Lieutenant General Gapanovich] was a political commissar [*Politrabotnik*]

---

* Penkovsky is referring to the system of encyphering words for sending secret messages and the ciphers or keys to decoding the messages.

who died in 1952; he had two stars. He was a good man. He swore at Stalin; his family didn't agree with him but he criticized everything. He was a straightforward sort of person.[*8]

I called my mother to my aunt's house. My mother's sister lives on the Fourth Meshchanskaya Street. I called my mother there and told her what happened. She said, "Oleg, I knew nothing about this." I asked her to write me an explanation. She let me have a letter explaining that in such and such a year she had gotten to know so and so; he said he was an engineer and showed her his papers; they got married and the civil war began; she bore a son shortly after this and her husband disappeared without a trace. This two-page letter is now in Shumsky's safe. Now, when I was filling out the form for the trip here I went to Shumsky and said, "What can I write after what you have told me about my father?" He said, "Write just as you have always written."

The KGB supplement reporting all this was in the file, with a note on top stating, "We trust Colonel Penkovsky." That saved me from being dismissed from Intelligence. They must believe me because they gave me my passport even though it was held up. As you know, they gave everyone their passports except me. I got mine at the last moment. The Foreign Travel Commission of the Central Committee examined it at the last moment. *Svolochi* [scum] of the KGB sit there. If they hadn't given it to me, I would have gone straight to the British or American Embassy and said, "To hell with you. Goodbye!"

Kisevalter asked Penkovsky if he worked for the KGB. "No," replied Penkovsky, who explained that he was a member of "the GRU, the Chief Intelligence Directorate of the General Staff. I am an officer of Strategic Intelligence of the General Staff."

For the first time the team had confirmation from Penkovsky that he was a military officer who had gone to work in Military Intelligence. He was not, he insisted, working for the KGB, the Committee for State Security. The distinction is important because it gave Penkovsky access to a broad range of strategic and tactical military information that does not fall in the KGB's domain.

"Even up to now are you GRU?" asked Kisevalter.

"Yes," replied Penkovsky. "They had no cause to shoot me or to arrest me. About a year ago I was called up by the chief of the Personnel Directorate, who questioned me about my father. He said, 'This is what you have declared your background to be and this is

---

[*]Deriabin worked under General Gapanovich from 1939 to 1941 as a Komsomol secretary in the Trans-Baikal Military District. Gapanovich, short and stocky, was totally bald. He was chief of the political administration for the district and was known to be well liked by Stalin.

what we have found out about your father. You said your father simply died.' I replied, 'I have never seen my father and never received a piece of bread from him.' The general said, 'But evidently you have concealed the fact.' To which I replied, 'If I had something to conceal I had a tenfold opportunity to run off during the war or on my assignment abroad in Turkey and I did not do this. I was even in all of the countries of the People's Democracies."

"Who was this personnel chief?" asked Kisevalter.

"The chief of the Personnel Directorate is Lieutenant General Smolikov. The chief of the GRU is General [Ivan Alexandrovich] Serov, previously the chief of the KGB.* They asked me how long my length of service was, and I said twenty-four years, and in 1962 I will complete my twenty-five years of service. If I had already completed my twenty-five years, they would have discharged me on pension because for them I am politically unreliable. That is what I feel. Up to a certain degree they trust me, but they watch me closely. I believe they actually trust me because about a year and a half ago, before they unearthed anything about my father, they sent me to higher academic courses on new technology. It is from there that I wrote up all this material on rockets for you. In my opinion, had they already known about father, they would not have sent me there."

The team realized they had just heard the crucial fact behind Penkovsky's decision to work for the West. The explosive factor that forced him to act was the discovery of his father's past and how it was shackling his career. In the transcript of the first meeting in London with the American and British teams there is a note on the KGB's doubt about Penkovsky's father that reads: "This is a most salient theme in Subject's recent life and has contributed significantly to his decision to approach the West. Specifically it involves his lifelong legend that his father had died of typhus in 1919. Actually, he was killed while fighting with the White Army against the Reds as a first lieutenant in the city of Rostov. The significance of the fact lies in a KGB accusation that Subject had deliberately concealed the true circumstances and this accusation was a matter of record in his GRU file."

Penkovsky returned to his life story. "Well, anyway, when Varen-

---

* General Serov was a favorite of Khrushchev's since they had served together in the Ukraine during World War II. Serov headed the KGB from 1954 to 1958. He was known as "the Butcher of Budapest" for his role in crushing the Hungarian revolution of 1956. During World War II Stalin put Serov in charge of forcing the Crimean Tartars from their homelands. He also relocated the Chechen Ingush people from the Crimea and was responsible for forcing thousands of people from the Baltic republics into exile and forced labor in Siberia.

tsov returned to the front at the request of Konev, I also went along and was given the command of another regiment, the Fifty-first Artillery Antitank Regiment, a GHQ unit, part of the reserve of the commander in chief. This regiment was independent and not part of the brigade. I requested Varentsov to release me, saying that my bride, Vera, is in Moscow and has just graduated from high school."[9]

Vera Dmitrievna Gapanovich was a radiant fourteen-year-old when she met Penkovsky for the first time. They met in 1942, during the dark days of World War II, when Penkovsky worked for her father, Lieutenant General Gapanovich, as a junior political officer in the Moscow Military District Political Directorate, before he was sent to the Ukraine. The general invited Penkovsky to his apartment for dinner and introduced him to Vera, a dark-haired, diminutive beauty with shining eyes. Penkovsky saw Vera again when he was recovering from his wounds in Moscow in 1944 and "fell in love with her there and then." When he returned from the war they were married; she was seventeen. It was a marriage made of good chemistry and convenience. General Gapanovich's position assured Penkovsky of having a patron and shrewd adviser.

Varentsov approved Penkovsky's move to Moscow to enter the Frunze Military Academy. "I arrived two months after the course began, but I passed the examination successfully and was admitted. Since I had commanded a regiment, I had no trouble passing a battalion commander's examination. So I entered, and in 1948 I graduated from the Frunze Military Academy. Immediately upon graduation I was offered the opportunity of entering the Military-Diplomatic Academy to study strategic intelligence."

"How long were you in Frunze?" asked Kisevalter, checking carefully to establish the chronology of Penkovsky's career to make sure that no time was unaccounted for. This would help to establish Penkovsky's credibility.

It was a three-year course. I consulted my father-in-law, General Gapanovich, who advised me to work for a year instead of transferring from one classroom to another at once. So I worked for one year in two places. My first assignment was as a senior officer in the Mobilization and Organization Directorate of the Headquarters of the Moscow Military District, where I had previously worked in a lower capacity. I worked there for six months and then I was transferred to the headquarters of the ground forces. I was also there as a senior officer and was perfectly satisfied with the job, since it paid 200 rubles a month more. But I did have in mind to enter the Military-Diplomatic Academy in 1949, and fortunately we have a regulation which says that the pay of an officer received just prior to entering the MDA is retained by that officer during the period that he is a student. Therefore in 1949 I was accepted at the MDA, which is near the subway station Sokol.

"Is it not 13 Peschannaya Street?" asked Kisevalter, displaying his own expertise of the GRU to impress Penkovsky.

"That's exactly right. I studied there for four years, from 1949 to 1953. It was then a four-year course, but now it has been reduced to a three-year course."

By offering the exact address of the academy, Kisevalter was building a credibility which the team hoped would enhance Penkovsky's confidence. The relationship between a control officer, or handler, and a spy is difficult and delicate. If there is no rapport the spy may balk or lose motivation. If the handler is too aggressive the spy may worry he is not doing satisfactory work or is incapable of fulfilling the requirements demanded of him. Penkovsky had come forward with information about himself, intent on establishing his own credentials. He was not about to be intimidated by Kisevalter.

Penkovsky answered questions about the staff of the academy and said he would tell the team how he obtained his information later. He insisted on continuing the story of his own career.

"After graduation I was placed in the Fourth Directorate of the GRU. This Directorate is the Eastern Directorate [Strategic Intelligence]. There are other Directorates, for example the Anglo-American Directorate, the European Directorate, and the First Directorate, which is the directorate for illegals. We will come to these directorates later. Anyway I worked there for about a year on the Egyptian desk. I became familiar with the agent nets there and remember something about it still."

Penkovsky said he was called in and told he would be sent to Pakistan to be the senior assistant to the military attaché, who was the GRU *rezident* in Pakistan. Then the Pakistani government refused permission to expand the size of the military attaché's office and his visa was denied. Penkovsky spent several more months on the Egyptian desk until he was called up again and told, "We are thinking of sending you to Turkey."

"This was already at the end of 1954. Again I prepared myself to go and studied codes, the operational program, the economics of the country, and the armed forces. I arrived in July of 1955 and became the *rezident*, the chief of the station. My official position was Acting Military Attaché, and I took over the whole agent operation net."

61

"What rank did you hold—lieutenant colonel or colonel?" asked Kisevalter.

"I was already a colonel—let me clarify this. At the end of the war, just prior to my entry to the Frunze Academy, I was promoted to lieutenant colonel, and I was promoted to full colonel in February 1950. I was already working about eleven years as a full colonel in February 1960, and they will never make me a general because of my father. They have already said so and they have said I was unreliable. Maybe I will become a general in another army," he added jokingly.

This bitter joke struck Joe Bulik as a key reason for Penkovsky's defection. It summed up with humor his frustration and anger at having his brilliant career cut off because of his father's past.

So I arrived in Turkey with my wife and took over the *Rezidentura*, the GRU's Ankara Station. During the course of one month my predecessor, Colonel Kondrashov, turned over all the responsibilities to me, and I had for my assistant the naval attaché. At that time there was no air attaché. Seven months later, Major General Savchenko arrived to be the *rezident*, but he arrived under the false name of Rubenko. Many of our people use false names.

This Rubenko was previously military attaché in Afghanistan. When this old man arrived—he was over sixty years of age—I turned over everything to him and he became the *rezident*. I became his assistant. I worked until November 1956 and then we had a compromise of one of our assistant attachés. This took place three months after Savchenko's arrival, and the attaché involved was Lieutenant Colonel Nikolai Ionchenko. He was simply approaching Turks in restaurants and offering them money to work for him. Ionchenko was attempting to purchase military manuals from Turks in this crude manner. Naturally, the Turkish Counterintelligence was efficient and they noticed this. Now I will confess to you: my relations with Ionchenko were extremely bad; he and Rubenko were trying to undermine me, to have me expelled from the Party. I will tell you the details of this later.

I made an anonymous telephone call from a public phone booth to the Turkish Counterintelligence informing them of Ionchenko's activities and specifying where his agent contacts were made.

"What was his rank?" asked Kisevalter.

"He was a lieutenant colonel; his first name was Nikolai. Ionchenko was very bitter against me. Since he had studied the Turkish language at the academy, he was indignant that I, with the English language, was sent out to be the senior deputy to the *rezident* instead of himself. He was very friendly with the general, and the two of them made my life so miserable that I wrote a letter to headquarters requesting a transfer—anywhere. They replied that I should wait. By nature I am a vengeful person, but I am fair. Even then, when I saw how unjustly I was being treated I had already decided to come over to you. I want to take an oath and to sign my willingness to serve you and spend the rest of my days, whatever they may be, in a new life.

Three months later Ionchenko was compromised again and was declared persona non grata. I accompanied him through Istanbul and he went home via Bulgaria. The general wrote a cable to headquarters stating that the Turks and the Americans ran a provocation against Ionchenko. He was seized while he was purchasing fruit. Incidentally, at this time the shah of Iran and his wife were on an official visit, and Turkish security and counterintelligence services were intensively alert in protecting the visitors. We even had instructions from the GRU chief not to run any operations during that period. However, the general permitted Ionchenko to go out for an agent meeting scheduled for the 10th of May. I remember the date because it is my mother's birthday. The incident actually occurred at the time that a Turkish lieutenant was handing Ionchenko a military manual.

I was sitting in his office when the embassy duty officer reported to the general and said, "Comrade General, your assistant has been detained by the Turkish Counterintelligence due to his attempt to obtain a military manual from a Turkish officer." The general was very upset and told me to go and get him out. I said: "Why did you let him go to this meeting?" The operational funds in Turkish lire were in my hands, but the general gave Ionchenko money out of his own pocket, some 200 lire [$40 dollars in 1956] to pay the Turkish officer for the manual we were given. This was done so that I would not know about it. This is a considerable sum and it was not taken from the operational fund so that I wouldn't know. Now, when this compromise occurred, the general admitted it to me. We had an argument. I told him that he had always accused me of being a bad operator, inexperienced, and not recruiting agents. He was preparing a cable to Moscow and I asked him, "Are you a Communist?" When he answered yes, I asked him why he had to lie and not admit that he had disobeyed orders not to conduct operations during the shah's visit. He asked me to leave the office, saying the affair was none of my business, and I said that I would report on the matter through another channel.

Then I actually reported the incident through the KGB channel, our neighbor's channel. Colonel Pavel Dmitrievich Yerzin was then the KGB *rezident* and it is about him I am reporting to you. Yerzin now is the recruiter at the university of these Negroes who are sent here from Africa to study, the Patrice Lumumba Friendship University. These students are going to form powerful *rezidenturas* for us when they return to their own countries. I believe Yerzin has already been promoted to general. He also had been the KGB *rezident* in India and his cover position was that of counselor.

My cable was received by Serov, the KGB head, the same Serov who is now chief of the GRU. Serov immediately reported this cable to Khrushchev since all compromises of officers must be reported to the Presidium, but Lieutenant General Mikhail A. Shalin [head of the GRU] brought in a cable from Rubenko, which covered up his failure to obey orders. Marshal Zhukov was then the defense minister and the cable went to the chief of staff. When Khrushchev saw my cable and Rubenko's cable he yelled, "Which fool is the liar, Penkovsky or the general? Figure this out and report." I had told the truth and all I could be accused of was having spoken coarsely to the general. But that was because he was always criticizing me unjustly. I did not receive any reprimand, not even along Party lines, but General Rubenko received a severe reprimand from Zhukov, "incompetence in duty."

Shortly after my departure from Turkey he was removed and recently he was discharged. He is now working in the Institute for Area Studies as a department chief. Serov remembered my name because of the cable. We call the KGB "neighbors" and they refer to us as the "nearest neighbors."

While in Ankara, Penkovsky's wife, Vera, was propositioned by the KGB *rezident*, Vavilov, who succeeded Yerzin, a matter which Penkovsky did not take lightly.[10] Intramural adultery is well known in the Soviet diplomatic and intelligence community. It is considered safer to sleep within the official family rather than outside it with foreigners who are security risks and potential spies. (Penkovsky was having an affair with Vavilov's wife.) In one conversation Penkovsky told Mrs. Vavilov to "take a bath, I'm coming over."[11]

Well then, gentlemen, up to November I was still working there. I called the Turkish Counterintelligence anonymously once more to tell them that an assistant case officer together with some Bulgarian agents stole a military manual at a Turkish military exhibit. The officer I spoke to on the phone said to me in clear English that I should drop in to speak with him, but I refused because at that time I was still undecided. If at that time they had made this accusation with respect to my father and had expressed political distrust, I probably would never have gone back to the U.S.S.R. I called up the last time on the 4th of November 1956, the eve of the Suez crisis.

You can check this because the call must have been officially recorded.*

Penkovsky had called the Turks to expose his fellow officer Ionchenko and take revenge on his superior, General Rubenko. If Rubenko was exposed for mishandling his position, he might be recalled to Moscow and Penkovsky promoted in his place. At the time, Penkovsky was considering an approach to Colonel Peeke to ask him how to open a channel to the CIA, but he had still not made up his mind.

On the 6th of November 1956, Penkovsky and his wife left Turkey by train and entered the Soviet Union through Armenia. Upon his arrival in Moscow he found himself under pressure from his superiors. "Evidently this Rubenko is their close friend. He had sent them all kinds of gifts and they had drunk vodka and wine together. The senior officers in Moscow were indignant that such a 'snot-nosed' young colonel could have behaved that way with respect to a general. They assumed that I wanted to trip up the general in order to be the military attaché in Turkey. To tell the truth, when I was acting military attaché, there was more organization than under the general and I could have run the agent net effectively. But I swear to you that was not my motive even though I would have liked to have been the military attaché."[12]

At that point, sandwiches were served with a dry white German wine, Liebfraumilch, the only alcoholic beverage the men consumed throughout the meetings. Penkovsky was ready to relax after his initial performance. He sensed that the questioning had gone well. For the Anglo-American team, Penkovsky's detail was impressive. Kisevalter, the expert on the GRU, found all Penkovsky's dates and personalities checked well on first hearing. The team knew they had a professional intelligence officer in their midst and they primed Penkovsky for another round of questions and revelations.

---

* The call was never checked with the Turks despite a request from James Angleton, the CIA's head of Counterintelligence, because at the time it was feared such an approach would create more problems than it could solve, and might expose Penkovsky.

Life and Times

DURING THE BREAK PENKOVSKY TOLD THE MEMBERS OF THE INTERRO-
gating group about his life in Moscow. Although he was a privileged
member of the officer class and had been given a choice apartment
at the end of World War II, he said his living accommodations were
cramped. There was little if any privacy, especially since his mother
was living with him. Bulik asked Penkovsky about his normal movements, where he lived and worked, how he spent his day.

"I live on Naberezhnaya Maksima Gorkogo [Maxim Gorky Em-
bankment] 36, Flat 59. The entry is from the courtyard, third floor,
third entrance—if there were no surveillance I could have you all as
guests in my home for tea. There is an elevator. The attendant is an
old woman." Any foreigners visiting a Soviet home in 1961 would
be grounds for suspicion. Surveillance would begin with the old
woman running the elevator, who would report on Penkovsky's
guests to her local district KGB officer.

Bulik interjected to ask the height of the building. The team
wanted a complete picture of his physical living conditions and daily
movements because they would become important operationally in
planning how to contact him. Knowing his routine in detail also
gave them a realistic sense of his lifestyle and role in Soviet society.
This would enable the team to devise ways of making contact with
him through American, British, or third-country agents.

Penkovsky told them it was a nine-story gray concrete building
with a balcony on the top floor, built in 1944. "That's where all the
big people live," Penkovsky said, explaining it was located near the
headquarters of the Moscow Military District, which was responsible for the military security of the capital and the surrounding re-

gions. Kisevalter brought out a map in order to fix the location of Penkovsky's house, which was across the river from the Kremlin.

Bulik wanted to know how many families lived on each floor of Penkovsky's building. Of the four apartments per floor, two had two rooms and two had three. There was one family per apartment, an improvement over *kommunalkas*, or communal apartments, still prevalent in the 1960s, where several families shared the kitchen and a bathroom. Penkovsky lived with his wife, daughter, and mother in a two-room apartment of approximately 400 square feet. "A two-room apartment would be adequate for a couple," Penkovsky explained, but his daughter and his mother slept in the living room, where Penkovsky kept his private desk with a custom-made lock. The family's television set was in the living room, too. The second room was the bedroom for Penkovsky and his wife. They rarely invited friends to the apartment and did their entertaining at restaurants and the Bolshoi Theater; Penkovsky received funds from the State Committee to entertain foreign guests.

Penkovsky said he usually retired early and awoke at 6 A.M. He left for work at 8 A.M. and normally had lunch from 2 to 3 P.M. Sunday was his day off and he often drove the family to his wife's uncle's dacha. His family did not know that he intended to spy for the West, he said.

The team went through Penkovsky's daily routine, plotting out on the map his routes to work by foot and bus. In good weather he walked across the Moskvoretsky Bridge, leading into Red Square, and from there to 11 Gorky Street, the headquarters of the State Committee for the Coordination of Scientific Research Work. In bad weather he went by bus along the Gorky Embankment past the British Embassy, over the Kamenny Bridge, and got off at the Arbat.

Penkovsky explained that in the morning he had to sign in at the State Committee, but he also had to spend time at the GRU offices in the General Staff headquarters in the Ministry of Defense nearby on Frunze Street, to which he walked. He made a point of telling the team that he used entrance number 5, the same entrance as the minister and his deputies. "As a rule, though, the minister goes through the gates from Gritsevets Street in his car, a Chaika," explained Penkovsky, showing he understood this information might be of operational interest to the team.[1]

When he left work, Penkovsky passed the Church of the Resurrection, where he occasionally entered to pray. Across from the church there was a public bath (*banya*) with a counter where he sometimes stopped to drink beer. Occasionally he would go to a restaurant or theater in the evening and would not return home until well after midnight. He told the team that he had casual affairs with secretaries in the Defense Ministry and a salesgirl. To his wife, he made excuses about working late.[2] Such behavior was considered standard practice for military officers and other members of the Communist Party elite. Usually Penkovsky saw male friends or his girlfriends before returning home. He followed this pattern except when foreign delegations arrived and he was required to accompany and entertain their leaders. His mission was to report on the prospects for exploiting or recruiting the foreigners for the GRU.

After sandwiches and wine the meeting turned to a discussion of the structure of the GRU; Penkovsky answered Kisevalter's questions on how its directorates were organized and who headed them. Then Penkovsky moved on to the subject of nuclear weapons. Within moments he was revealing to the team the most fundamentally significant information about the Soviet military capacity to destroy the West.

In 1961, Penkovsky said, "All of the People's Democracies [East European satellites] must be furnished with nuclear missiles. Varentsov and his people are also working on the development of bases, storage areas, launching sites, and the training of cadres for the countries of People's Democracies. The missiles being delivered to these countries are now being mass produced." They included, he said, the R-11, a powerful medium-range ballistic missile designated as the SS-1 by NATO. Penkovsky had already passed a report on the SS-1 to the team. He said that the SS-1 "and all those which are on the production lines, are being given to all the People's Democracies except Albania." The Albanians were critical of Khrushchev's denunciation of Stalin's crimes at the Twentieth Party Congress in 1956, and by 1961 were openly supporting Chairman Mao's criticism of Khrushchev's policies.

Penkovsky was in command of his audience. "In the GDR [East Germany] we now have four rocket brigades, and of these, two brigades are equipped with nuclear warheads. All of the rockets stationed abroad remain under the control of Soviet forces. In the GDR they also have special storage facilities, and the engineers of the Dzerzhinsky Artillery Academy are working on this."

The team took notes but did not follow up on his revelations with questions. They let him set the pace and the subject matter. Penkovsky returned to his own career. He told them how, with Marshal Varentsov's help in September 1958, he was sent to the Dzerzhinsky Military Academy to the courses given for the General Staff on the study of new technology. "Previously this was purely an artillery academy, but now it is an academy for missile and rocket artillery, under the control of Marshal Moskalenko. There are now

2,500 students there who are trained as specialists and engineers in the employment of all types of missiles. The emphasis is on training specialists to service the missiles on their testing pads prior to launching. This training is under the direction of very experienced engineers, of whom there are not too many—about thirty or forty. I graduated from these courses with distinction on May 1, 1959." Penkovsky revealed that the Soviet nuclear program was indeed in its infancy and that the number of skilled engineers qualified to teach officers was very small.

With his new rocket and missile skills Penkovsky had a better chance of finding a slot in the GRU. "Immediately after graduation, Ivan Serov, who took over as GRU head in 1959, was informed of my progress. He suggested that I go to India, since India is considered to be our territory and we might want to conduct operations in that territory in the future. Therefore it would be desirable that an officer with my background in rockets should be sent there, since it is possible that in the not too distant future rockets may be given to India," Penkovsky related. His disclosure that Khrushchev was considering supplying missiles to India was new and important, for it exposed Soviet intentions and strategic thinking—

I was almost completely processed to go. Just as I was all set I was called in by Major General Shumsky, who is the deputy to Lieutenant General Smolikov [GRU head of personnel]. Well, then, they did not send me to India. I was very disappointed about this and was very worried.

To be quite honest with you, my disaffection with the whole political system began quite a long time ago. I disagreed with many facets of life there. I will not bother you by listing categories, but the whole setup was one of demagoguery, idle talk, and deceit. The people were waiting patiently for a long time and now they are tired of waiting and they are restless. Actually, Khrushchev to some degree has decreased KGB controls. Many persons have been rehabilitated or received amnesties, and now one can say certain things—not everything of course—without being immediately arrested like in the past. Of course, if this is done to excess a man can be ejected from the Party. He can be arrested and his working future will be limited.[3]

The team listened carefully but did not comment so as not to distract Penkovsky and set him off on a tangent. Good professional tradecraft in handling an agent required that the team listen, record his information, and then compare it against what was already known or predicted to see what Penkovsky had added. The depth of

Penkovsky's knowledge and his authority was impressive to the team, and they had no reason to stop him. He was a control officer's dream, demanding only great endurance for the roller-coaster ride of emotions and state secrets that swooped up and down from the recesses of his mind.

Penkovsky explained, "There is a difficult situation in the country right now. Everything is subordinated to the armaments race. Also, billions have been spent to sustain the countries of the People's Democracies. China has been given a great deal and now everything is directed to equipping our forces with missiles. Everything is going for missiles. In this respect they have already attained a measure of success." Some missiles "are already proven," Penkovsky said, "and some are not yet properly developed." He explained that "the greatest deficiency is in the field of electronics." He pinpointed the U.S.S.R.'s main missile test site in Kapustin Yar, sixty miles southeast of Volgograd—formerly Stalingrad—and the impact area in Kazakhstan in Central Asia. "There were very many cases where rockets struck railroads or a settlement because they had deviated from their assigned course," Penkovsky revealed, pleased to be able to provide information that the Soviet missile program was far from as perfect as Nikita Khrushchev was describing it in his speeches.

"But a great effort is now being made; they have mobilized scientists, the most outstanding ones. Some of them have received four decorations each as Heroes of Socialist Labor, but they never appear in the newspapers. They may be seen on occasion at Party congresses. They constitute a small circle and are given no publicity. There are little settlements near Moscow and there is one settlement [gorodok] at Krasnogorsk, on the northwest outskirts of Moscow, in which German scientists live. These are the ones who were involved in the development of the V-2 [the German rocket used to terrorize London during World War II]. These Germans are used to a great extent, and they are very well subsidized with the comforts of life, including automobiles. Their families are with them and they have special schools for their children. Similarly, all other scientists are kept isolated and in secrecy."[4] This confirmation of the role of German scientists in the development of Soviet missiles filled out the material which Peter Deriabin had revealed to the CIA when he defected from Vienna in 1954. Keeping track of the German scientists taken as prisoners of war by the Soviets was one of the many arcane ways the U.S. intelligence community and air force tried to gauge the state of Soviet missile development.

This train of thought stimulated Penkovsky to tell the team the real story of the death of Marshal Nedelin on October 24, 1960. The Soviet press initially reported only that he had died in the line of duty in an aircraft accident. "It was not an aircraft accident. The report was a big lie deliberately told to the world. Nedelin was killed when they were testing a new rocket. It was a two-stage rocket. Let's see what else my notes have. On Marshal Nedelin's death: A very large rocket using atomic energy for motive power was being tested when Nedelin was killed. He was in a bombproof shelter, a deep reinforced concrete structure where people sit during test observations. After ten or fifteen minutes Nedelin received a report that the rocket engine malfunctioned and he came out of the bunker to see for himself. But at that time the fuel system of the second stage ignited and an explosion occurred, killing him and a large number of service personnel as well as scientists." Penkovsky urged that Khrushchev should be confronted with the true story of Marshal Nedelin's death. "A great number of people know the truth," said Penkovsky.*

These scientists were the ones who were engaged in developing a new type of fuel that requires a strong storage space and operates on the principle of atomic fission in the rocket engine. This is what our scientists are working on now, and they have achieved a small degree of progress. Although nothing has been perfected, this is the basic idea on which they are working. The purpose is to eliminate the large space required for the fuel tanks and oxidizer tanks by substituting a lighter and smaller fuel component. This will possibly afford a larger warhead for conventional explosives and for atomic types.[5]

Please keep in mind that this is a two-stage rocket and that basically all our rockets are two-stage. When you report this to your scientific experts, emphasize this so they won't have to guess. Even when Nixon was there [in Moscow in July 1959 as vice president, during which he had his famous "Kitchen Debate" with Khrushchev at an American exhibition], a question was asked whether solid or liquid fuel was used. Only liquid fuel is used. Thus far no type of solid fuel has been developed which can propel a large rocket at a great range. A high-caloried fuel has been developed using boron as a component. However, I do not know what proportion of boron is used.[6]

---

* The public announcement attributed Nedelin's death to an airplane crash. The Soviet Military Encyclopedic Dictionary, published in 1983, did not describe how he died, stating only that he died in 1960. Another account said he died in "an aviation catastrophe." In April 1989 Ogonek no. 16 gave full details of the missile disaster and acknowledged publicly for the first time that a fully fueled intercontinental ballistic missile exploded on the launch pad, killing a number of people including the head of the Soviet Rocket Forces, Marshal of Artillery Mitrofan Nedelin. The magazine blamed the accident on the U.S.S.R.'s rush to catch up with the United States in the missile race and on the resulting flouting of safety rules.

Penkovsky's report on the state of development of fuel for Soviet missiles and attempts to use nuclear reactors to fuel them was a significant revelation to the CIA's scientific experts. In 1961 solid fuels for missiles were still in their development stage. There was a race on to replace bulky liquid rocket fuels, which required hours of fueling time on the launching pad, with solid fuels, which were stable and remained in the missiles, enabling rapid launching. The United States also experimented with a nuclear-powered rocket, but discarded it as unfeasible and too dangerous until research was resumed in the 1980s as part of the Pentagon's Star Wars plan to send armaments into space for the destruction of enemy missiles.[7]

By the way, when the Sputnik was launched, it was with a two-stage rocket. The fuel was liquid; I wrote up the composition of the fuel. The very first Sputnik was launched with the help of a cluster of rockets. Later, I will draw what this cluster looked like. The overall weight of the rocket was about one hundred tons, of which the weight of the fuel was sixty-eight tons. An outstanding engineer told me this when I was studying at the Rocket Academy. Boron was one of the basic fuel components, and this was being tested for the action of a new type of fuel, namely the fission of atoms in one stage. The accident occurred because the upper portion of the rocket was ignited. This upper portion, upon being set off, fell toward the earth, and an explosion took place. Many scientists were killed, and among them was Marshal Nedelin.

Just now Gagarin was launched with the help of a large two-stage rocket. They say that the overall length of such a rocket is twenty-four to twenty-eight meters. They are erected by a special hoist and tower and have their own launching pads. These launching pads are special ones, not the type that I have described for the ordinary free rockets and guided missiles. This is the field of endeavor now.

This rambling report on Soviet missile development would be handled by the CIA and MI6 much as a miner pans for gold in a stream, washing the extraneous material away until the new, shining facts emerged to be processed into a report of high-quality intelligence information that carried American and British knowledge of the Soviet state of missile art to a new level of understanding and confirmation. The miners were the CIA's and MI6's scientific experts on Soviet missiles, the men and women who coordinated the information from overhead photography, agent reports, and the information gathered from the National Security Agency and the Defense Intelligence Agency.

Penkovsky asked to return to his biography.

Let me finish my thought now or I will be out of sequence. I was thinking of becoming a soldier in a new army, to adopt a new people, to struggle for a new ideal, and in some measure to avenge my father and millions of other people who have perished in a terrible way. I thought that words are, after all, just words, but I should bring something tangible from the place where I sat. I was the head of my class of eighty students. At any rate I had a certain amount of authority. My own studies were outstanding; I had the opportunity of taking books and classified lectures from the special *fond*, a classified library. By means of a pass I had the opportunity of working independently. I had a notebook—I even blocked the door by placing a chair under the knob—and I studied by myself. If anyone knocked I would slide everything into my briefcase, which was sealed, and I would simply say that I was studying.[8]

"And this is the manner in which you wrote up all of your material?" asked Kisevalter.

"I copied everything down and, not having any camera, this writing took a very long time.

"This was done during my courses. Everything was done consecutively, and I did most of this writing in the evening. We were first taught free rockets, then guided missiles, and then all types of launching equipment and technical checking at various stages. Then we were given an examination. I graduated with distinction and received a certificate which I now have at home and which I can show you if you like."

Penkovsky was trying to convince the team of his bona fides by offering to show them the certificate. He was an experienced intelligence officer and understood the importance of establishing an agent's credibility.

"Did you study ICBMs [intercontinental ballistic missiles]?" Kisevalter asked, hoping to spur Penkovsky to further disclosures.

"No, we did not study them. But I can tell you this. There is nothing at all that is unusual about them. All these ICBMs and the rockets for launching humans into orbit are constructed in exactly the same way as the others except that they are much larger and have a very large fuel capacity to give them a greater thrust. The working principles, however, are identical."

"Are the guidance systems for those large ICBMs not yet perfected?" asked Kisevalter, pursuing a question high on the requirements list developed from the needs of intelligence community analysts in Washington.

"The electronics development is far behind. They are struggling with this. We always get technical briefings for conducting technical intelligence. When our scientists and technicians are sent abroad, they don't tell them to spy. They simply urge them to 'study' the problem. So they give them a free ticket, money, and send them off to study processes that can be usefully installed in our own industries."

Penkovsky explained that he had read twenty-two reports on synthetic rubber, reports "which are of great interest to us now since we have trouble in its production. I can only judge by the twenty-two reports in my hands what shortsightedness and blindness there is to permit access of Soviet scientists to such important centers, especially when the scientists have been specially trained in such matters."[9]

Penkovsky talked at length about the State Committee for which he worked and how it operated by showing foreign specialists "worthless installations." He warned the team that the Soviet Union was taking advantage of the United States and Canada through the guise of scientific exchange and that there should be a serious effort made to create realistic reciprocity.[10]

Kisevalter moved back to his requirements list, and asked Penkovsky, "Would you know of the location of any missile bases which may be planned or under construction even though they are not yet in use?"

"You must realize such locations are kept in utmost secrecy. In our organization the only ones who would know about these would be Serov and the directorate chiefs. I doubt if any subordinates would know these sites. However, our country is full of rumors. I have heard, for example, that bases and troops, that is, rocket troops for use against England, are located north of Leningrad, toward Murmansk, and to the north. The exact coordinates of their location are known to a very small group of people, and the data lies in underground safes in the Arbat district.

"The General Staff of the Ministry of Defense is located in the Arbat area, that is, in the blocks bounded by Frunze Street, Gogolevsky Boulevard, and the Antipyevsky Lane. [See map on pages xiv–xv.] This headquarters should all be blown up with small, two-kiloton bombs."

A two-kiloton nuclear weapon, the equivalent of two thousand tons of TNT, would be devastating in the heart of Moscow. The bomb dropped on Hiroshima had a yield equivalent to 12,500 tons of TNT. The total tonnage of bombs dropped on London from September 1940 to May 1941 during the Blitz was 18,800 tons—18.8 kilotons. Nuclear weapons small enough to be carried by one man had been developed in the U.S. by the 1960s. Known as SADMs, small atomic demolition munitions, portable nuclear weapons have a yield equivalent of two—one hundredths of a kiloton, 200 tons of TNT, one-tenth of the destructive power Penkovsky was recommending for use in Moscow. There are also MADMs, medium atomic demolition munitions, with a one-kiloton yield, in the American arsenal.[11]

Kisevalter did not reply directly to Penkovsky's suggestion that small nuclear weapons be placed in Moscow; he continued to question him. The rest of the team was staggered by the suggestion but said nothing. It was important to listen and extract from Penkovsky the most complete information possible. By keeping him going they hoped the keys to his motivation would emerge.

Penkovsky pointed out that the Ministry of Defense was connected to the Kremlin by means of a subway tunnel. He noted the location of the various directorates of the ministry and said,

> As a strategic officer, a graduate of two academies, and having worked for some time in the General Staff, I know what the sensitive spots are. I am convinced that my viewpoint is absolutely correct, namely that in case of a future war, at H-hour plus two minutes, all of these critical targets such as the General Staff, the KGB Headquarters on Dzerzhinsky Square, the Central Committee of the Party, which organizes everything, and similar targets must all be blown up by pre-positioned atomic bombs rather than by means of bombs dropped from aircraft or rockets, which may or may not hit the vital targets.

> In our Soviet Army we have a five-kiloton, a ten-kiloton, and bigger weapons, but they have not yet been able to produce a one-kiloton weapon. Our scientists are still working on it. I know this exactly. Such weapons would not need to be set within the buildings themselves, but there are many adjacent buildings where they can be concealed. Dwellings and stores are adjacent. For example, there is a large *Gastronom* [food store] next to the KGB Headquarters.

> A small group of saboteurs equipped with such weapons, governed by a time mechanism, should plant them in the locations from which all these headquarters can be destroyed. Irrespective of what other attacks will be made at H-hour, these essential headquarters must be destroyed. These headquarters can be easily spotted in every major city. They are easy to find in Leningrad, Sverdlovsk, Voronezh, and Novosibirsk, for example. All one would need would be one man to do this for each military district. This would destroy the mobilization and organizational directorates that are the backbone of the army. If these headquarters of the General Staff and the Military Districts are destroyed, this will reduce the combat strength of the Soviet Army to a very great degree. A number of months would be required to assemble more or less experienced

men from the reserves. Furthermore, not all of these can be trusted like the ones now sitting in headquarters. The complete disorganization that would be created would permit the execution of a military decision [in favor of the West].

It would be well to destroy also all of the Military Commissariats [*voyenkomaty*] in the regions. [These commissariats, under the Ministry of Defense, control draft records and mobilize manpower.] These are all easy to locate. In these Military Commissariats are also located the records and personnel of the city, district, and even settlement. All are responsible for mobilizing draftees down to the village level. Of course it is difficult to destroy a headquarters down to that level, but to destroy the headquarters of the regions [*oblasti*], of which there are many, is mandatory.

During World War II the Germans did very little damage. A few minor fires and broken roofs and glass, but the staffs remained in operation. This was due to inaccurate bombing. But now, with the possession of atomic weapons, small-size weapons of one or two kilotons as required, these vital targets can be completely destroyed. The exact timing for this destruction is up to the big people who have to make the decisions."[12]

Penkovsky's proposal still drew no response. The team was determined not to engage him in a debate over how unrealistic his proposal appeared. Was he serious? they wondered. Perhaps this was a fantasy of his role as a spy. Or was he simply trying to prove that he was willing to go to any lengths to establish his loyalty to his newly adopted countries?

Michael Stokes, the junior member of the British team, a Russian-speaking SIS officer, was appalled by what Penkovsky was saying and told a colleague, "I thought he was crazy. But as I listened to Penkovsky pour forth details and provide information, I became convinced of his veracity and importance as an agent."[13]

Not immediately obvious to the team was that Penkovsky was reflecting the then current Soviet view of nuclear weapons: that they could be used to win battles in a limited nuclear war. In the 1950s the Soviet Union hailed nuclear power as the harbinger of progress. Soviet scientists wrote how peaceful nuclear explosions could create new rivers to irrigate deserts and open new paths to economic development. There was no discussion of nuclear fallout and the threat to food and water supplies. Nuclear power was portrayed to be manageable; so was nuclear war. The meaning of the American strategy of massive retaliation and the concept of total destruction of Soviet society was seen largely by the Soviets as Cold War propaganda. The Soviet view of the superiority of Communist man over nature was reflected in their naive view of the dangers of nuclear power. Soviet efforts to establish a civil defense program and minimize the dangers of nuclear radiation were part of the countereffort. The Ministry of Health published a major monograph on the effect of nuclear weapons assuring a fairly high survival rate if fallout shelters were utilized and radioactivity were washed from the body.[14] Without an antinuclear movement, and cut off from outside information on the destructive power of nuclear weapons, the Soviet Union in the early 1960s viewed nuclear weapons as a powerful but controllable phase of warfare. They were still in the dark night before the dawn of nuclear reality, which did not come until the Cuban missile crisis and again at Chernobyl. Penkovsky's bold unreality reflected the internal debate that was raging within the Soviet military on whether a limited nuclear war was possible and how it should be fought.

Then Penkovsky harked back to the subject of his father. "Incidentally, neither Serov nor Varentsov know anything about my father or that his archival material has been unearthed. They do not know why I was held back in Moscow. I said simply that the climate in India is bad, pretending that I didn't want to go there myself, although I had already given my consent to go." Some of his superiors, he said, "waver and consider that it is not right that a son of a White Army officer should have extensive privileges. There is no such thing as the 'democracy' they speak about. It is all a lie and a bluff. Thus far I can maintain myself because they know they cannot simply dismiss me." If that were to occur, Penkovsky said, "Then I would have every reason to go over to the other side. They would have to isolate me and keep me under constant surveillance. Right now I am receiving commendations and even monetary rewards."[15]

Penkovsky turned to his notes and told the team that the town of Perkhushkovo, about fifty miles from Moscow, "is now the headquarters of Moskalenko, and the strategic rocket forces." [Marshal Kirill Semenovich Moskalenko was commander in chief of strategic rocket forces from 1960 to 1962 and deputy minister of defense.] This spurred Penkovsky to turn to the shooting down of the U.S. Air Force RB-47 reconnaissance aircraft on July 1, 1960. "I made a note here to tell you the RB-47 was brought down by rockets fired from a MiG-19 [over the Barents Sea]. This MiG is equipped with four rockets—two upper rockets and two lower rockets. The rockets have a homing device; their range is between 2.5 and 3 miles. The point I wish to make is this: when the plane rises to its top altitude of between 59,000 and 65,000 feet, it still has the capability of firing an additional 2.5 to 3 miles, even though we have no planes which can do this yet—they are still experimenting. Thus, the effective ceiling is actually above 65,000 feet when one considers the additional range of the rocket. Anyway, the MiG-19 fired a rocket at the RB-47, and I can say with full assurance, since I have checked this with many sources, that the RB-47 did not violate our [Soviet] borders, although it was close. It was actually over neutral waters. Our pilot had itchy trigger fingers and fired the rocket that knocked it down. The length of the rocket is three meters. Only the two upper or the two lower rockets may be fired simultaneously; otherwise the plane would break up."[16] This was the first authoritative account of how and where the plane had been shot down. It confirmed American radar plots of the aircraft's course, which indicated that it had not penetrated Soviet air space.

Penkovsky thumbed through his notes and told the team, "There is a town called Klintsy [200 miles southwest of Moscow] where atomic warheads are assembled. I told you earlier that there are rockets based north of Leningrad directed against England. There is a city called Severomorsk. A PVO [antiaircraft] regiment is stationed there. This regiment is equipped with V-75 rockets [SA-2 surface-to-air missiles]." He listed the centers for training officers in the rocket command and the production and storage centers for nuclear warheads.[17]

He then announced: "Here is another new item. There is a new rocket. It is called the R-14 [SS-5]. It is a long-range rocket, over 1000 kilometers [over 600 miles]. I have no data on it." Then Penkovsky repeated "how easy it would be to blow up the General Staff." He returned to the subject of the new rocket. "This rocket is fired from Kapustin Yar, and the impact area is in Kazakhstan. The impact area consists of high wooden towers which are erected in a triangulation pattern. Soldiers man these towers, and there has not yet been a case where a tower has been struck by a direct hit from a rocket. The rockets fall at different points, which are then resected from optical instruments to determine the errors in lateral deviation and errors in range. There are radio communications for relaying the moment rockets are launched. I already mentioned that there were many cases where rockets struck buildings, railroads, and other sites."

Kisevalter looked at his watch. "According to your time schedule you have about twenty minutes left. We can't cover everything in this session. I hope you don't mind if I interrupt you from time to time and ask questions."

"Not at all," said Penkovsky, "that is a very good idea because it helps me to remember. Please prepare a set of photographs for me for identification. Now, as to the tenth point I have on my agenda which I have already mentioned, that is, about what should be destroyed." Then he smiled and said, "If necessary I will take the mission upon myself to blow up the General Staff."[18]

Penkovsky produced a torrent of information, skipping from point to point for fear that he might leave out something important in this first meeting. Often one thought triggered another when he spoke of a GRU or KGB officer. He had his own set of notes for what he wanted to accomplish in the first meeting.

At this point Joe Bulik interjected to ask Kisevalter, "Since he has been speaking of boron, maybe his memory is refreshed concerning what he said about the first Sputnik."

"I will repeat it again," replied Penkovsky amiably. "Only the first Sputnik was fired by using a cluster of rockets. There were three rockets below and one above, all clustered together." He repeated the specific measurements.[19] This information confirmed to the United States and Great Britain that the Soviet Union had a basic design for missiles that was modified to meet mission requirements but was essentially the same design for military missiles and space exploration.

"My next item: the Sixth Assault Artillery Division is located in the GDR now. Remember that in the Soviet Union there are also artillery corps. This division is four brigades. In addition there are four other brigades that are rocket artillery brigades. Two of these are equipped with atomic warhead rockets. The atomic warheads are not assembled on the rockets but are stored in special atomic storage depots. I don't know where these depots are, but it should be very simple for you to find out."[20]

In a detailed exchange with Kisevalter, Penkovsky explained the independent nature of the strategic rocket forces. Kisevalter asked to whose command the brigades report, and Penkovsky explained that "they are under Moskalenko because these are considered to be strategic weapons." They were not under Varentsov, who was in charge of the tactical artillery, the ground forces artillery. This consisted of rifled artillery, free rockets, and guided missiles of a short range—tactical missiles—but strategic missiles were under Moskalenko. He controlled the ICBMs, the launching of Sputniks, and the strategic rocket brigade.

Penkovsky listed the military districts and groups of forces in the Soviet command structure with their headquarters. "All of these headquarters must definitely be blown up. Please destroy these slips and notes of mine later as you wish."

Joe Bulik asked Penkovsky to elaborate on the point he had made earlier, that Marshal Varentsov and other high-ranking officers were dissatisfied with the régime.

79

I mentioned this before and wrote in my letter that Marshal Konev and Marshal Sokolovsky were absolutely healthy people and are Varentsov's friends. They did not agree with Khrushchev about his policy on reducing the size of the army. I didn't finish about the other marshals. When Khrushchev found out that they did not back him, he simply ordered them retired. They are living on pension now, just like Zhukov. Timoshenko was also retired but he had started to drink heavily some time ago. Many officers are displeased because many healthy generals and officers are being retired and because of the reduction in pay they have no other means of earning a livelihood. For example, a reduction from 500 rubles income to an income of 200 rubles per month in retirement is very difficult when one has a family.

Thus Penkovsky provided the first hard evidence to the West that the Soviet military high command was at odds with Khrushchev.[21]

I am your soldier. I must report to you that the Soviet Union is definitely not prepared at this time for war. All of this agitation for peace on one hand, and intimidation on the other hand, which unfortunately many Western leaders succumb to, proves nothing. Back in 1956, when the Egyptian affair [the Suez crisis] was going on, the Soviet Union should have been sharply confronted, and even today this should be done. With Cuba for example, I simply can't understand why Khrushchev should not be sharply rebuked. I do not know what answer Mr. Kennedy will give him, but he certainly should be accused of arming Cuba with Soviet tanks and guns, right under the gates of America. Czechoslovakia also sent considerable quantities of arms. Kennedy should be firm. Khrushchev is not going to fire any rockets. He is not ready for any war.

I respect and love the United States, and I, certainly, in Kennedy's place, would be firm. When we helped the régime in Hungary maintain its power, everyone knew then what we were doing. Why shouldn't Kennedy have the right to help the patriotic elements in Cuba, when you know what arms have been sent to Cuba from the U.S.S.R.? This is my opinion and the opinion of many of our officers.[22]

I would say that of the total Communist Party strength of seven to eight million members, there are no more than two to two and a half million strong, fanatical Communists. If a war began today on the scale of Hitler's war, even with conventional armament, countless numbers of officers and soldiers would simply desert to the other side. This is because all of these ideals for which many of our fathers, brothers, and relatives died have turned out to be nothing but a bluff and a deceit. There is always the promise that things will be better, but actually nothing is getting better and things are only getting worse. I swear to you that only in Moscow and Leningrad can one even purchase decent food. In Voronezh and Orel—a friend of mine recently came from there and said that they are eating horse meat, nine rubles per kilo [$8.10 at the exchange rate in 1961]. Even sausages are made of horse meat and it is difficult to get bread. There are no roads, which results in unbelievable transportation delays and breakdowns; grain is rotting since it cannot be delivered. The country is large and can produce much wheat, but such a large percentage is lost because they cannot make equitable deliveries. Much cattle was lost due to lack of fodder.

Last December a delegation of Englishmen, thirteen of them, came to me and I was arranging to show them the refrigeration equipment of the Refrigeration Plant Mikoyan Number 1. They were from the John Thompson firm, which manufactures refrigeration equipment in England. Suddenly I received an order to cancel this because the cattle which were brought there were just skin and bones, and they did not want the Englishmen to see this. They told the Englishmen that repairs were going on. You can check what I say with this delegation. They did not see the plant. I could tell you much more, my friends, and I'm sure you know a great deal more yourselves.

But I would like to emphasize one fact and that is that Khrushchev has not renounced war and is patiently awaiting the time when we can begin a war. He has given himself the mission of being the instigator of war. He wants to make a "rain of rockets" under which, as he says, "to bury imperialism." I am confident that my government now—the U.S.A. and England—with the other free countries of the world such as France and West Germany, are sufficiently flexible to withstand the onslaught of Soviet rockets and arms. All will not be destroyed and recovery may be possible. But still it seems to me that Khrushchev should not be permitted to initiate the war. Today he will not begin a war. He will rant and rave and even send arms here and there just as he did in Cuba and possibly even send small-caliber rockets there. In fact, there was talk about this with Castro and possibly a few rockets are already there.[23]

Thus, toward the end of his first meeting in the West, Penkovsky raised the specter of Soviet missiles being placed in Cuba more than eighteen months before the Cuban missile crisis. At that time, surface-to-air missiles, SA-2s, were being sent to Cuba, but the decision had not been made to send strategic missiles.

Penkovsky spoke with pain about the dissatisfaction of the younger generation and their poor incomes.

They have few decent clothes, and when they see your tourists and your visiting delegations, and see how well dressed foreigners are, this has an effect on them. Our youths have no money and theft is common. All kinds of crimes occur about which nothing is written. After all, the press is entirely controlled. The people cannot organize. There is no opposition to the régime, and when a small opposition does arise, such as Molotov and Malenkov, they are immediately eliminated.* The people are afraid to do anything because if they open their mouths they will lose even the little bit they have. There is no money in the banks; there is no property, nothing from which to draw sustenance. There is internal dissension. Hitler was right when in his time he attempted to create minority conflicts. All of these weak spots must be exploited before the external blow is dealt during a war. Even the Soviet help to the countries of People's Democracies may serve a good purpose in that it is draining the national treasury.

Penkovsky was aware of the deep-rooted tension among the Great Russians and the minority peoples of the Soviet Union. He had seen some of them—the Baltic Republics, Ukrainians, and Tatars—fight against the Russians during World War II in support of the Germans, who they thought would give them their independence. He sensed that worsening economic conditions in the Soviet Union would again bring this resentment to the surface.

Valuable production results from our labor even though the individual worker gets only pennies. But all of these billions are going out of the country and it's become a serious drain. Relations are not always the best with the Satellites. For example, with China we are having difficulties. Mao said that his own specialists have now been sufficiently trained. It can even happen that if we stop supplying the Satellites, more of them, like Poland, will be asking you for aid. There simply is no monolithic Warsaw Pact.

Another item I am reporting is that military pensions are being reduced still further. Now full colonels will receive only 150 rubles per month pensions, and generals up to 200 rubles. Now all of us are being squeezed more and more. Even of my present 5400 rubles [annual salary], I pay 500 rubles tax. They took away allowances for household help for high-ranking officers. They took away privileges from those who were decorated in Stalin's time, who had been declared exempt from income taxes. All of this is done because they need more and more funds to build factories and other equipment for the manufacture of rockets. The discipline and morale of the army has fallen greatly. There are countless cases of drunkenness, pilferage, and immorality. By itself it may not be a decisive factor,

* Penkovsky was referring to Molotov and Malenkov's efforts to oust Khrushchev. Their so-called Anti-Party Group was defeated in June 1957 and they were removed from power.

but it all adds to the general situation and can be exploited. Of course, I am sorry for the people, but they have suffered so much already that if they suffer just once more for the sake of a really better future, it would be worthwhile having this war. But in that case, let me know when I should be in Moscow.

Having fought in World War II, Penkovsky believed that wars could be won. He saw a better Soviet Union emerging from a war won by the West. He did not conceive of a nuclear war destroying life on earth, nor, despite his training, did he really appreciate the dangers of nuclear fallout and radiation.

Kisevalter asked, "Are you the representative of any group of disaffected persons?"

"No, I am all alone," replied Penkovsky. "All I have is my mother, my daughter, Galya, and my wife. I am entirely in your hands. You can do with me as you will, and I wish only to work with you honestly. All the materials I pass to you are mine and all of my experiences and intelligence training are at your disposal. I received a great deal of training earlier from the Soviet government. I am associated with no one whatsoever. I would be afraid of this and I do not wish it."

Penkovsky repeated, "I would like to have agent communication with you via a dead drop. Please give me a small Minox camera. I know it and I have worked with it before. Even though I have my own apartment, I will not develop the film, so that neither my wife nor anyone else will notice. I will deliver only undeveloped film to you and I will place it wherever you tell me to. I have many Secret and Top Secret journals such as *Voyennaya Mysl* [Military Thought], manuals, and classified lectures by prominent people.* I have a chance to get these items in my hands for possibly an hour, and I can photograph them. I will not have time to write. I wrote up this rocket material because I knew it was important. I did it carefully because I knew you would check every word and if it were perfect maybe I would get a decoration."

"That's fine," said Kisevalter. "Now the time is drawing to a close, let us plan for the future."

"In the summer of 1960," Penkovsky continued, "they assigned me to the commission for accepting students to the MDA [Military

* *Voyennaya Mysl* was published in Secret and Top Secret versions. It is the internal magazine for the Soviet armed forces to discuss strategic and tactical problems at the highest level. The CIA had not seen this publication in its Top Secret edition before Penkovsky offered to provide it. The Top Secret editions were restricted to a circulation limited to general officers in command of any army or positions of higher responsibility.

Diplomatic Academy]. At first I was to be the chief of the incoming class, but later I was told that this is not compatible with my background, that is, my father's having been a White Russian officer. Then I was transferred to the State Committee for the Coordination of Scientific Research Work. But in the meantime I was writing up all the data on these students from their personnel files. There were many who came to Moscow from foreign assignments, and there was one illegal. I will think of his name in a minute."

Kisevalter offered: "He is Shcherbakov."

Penkovsky said, "That is exactly right."

Kisevalter was again displaying his knowledge of the GRU acquired from Popov before Penkovsky. Kisevalter was trying to impress him, but instead it made Penkovsky uneasy. How had Kisevalter acquired this information? He had never told Penkovsky about Popov, and at one point Penkovsky said, "Only someone on the inside would know this information."

Kisevalter told Penkovsky, "It would be very helpful if you could write out the names, ranks, and what you know briefly about other GRU officers, particularly your own classmates, because you probably remember them better than others."

"If you would only show me a set of photographs, we would do a lot of good work since I can identify a pretty large number, well over a hundred," Penkovsky offered.

"Are you personally acquainted with any illegals at all?" Kisevalter asked. Illegals are agents who operate independently under deep cover and are not responsible to the local KGB or GRU residency. They have a "legend" which establishes an identity and record of birth and education based on false documentation.

"I can tell you about those who have returned from illegal work who are members of the present incoming Military Diplomatic Academy. I can also tell you which of my classmates are being trained as illegals. But whether they were dispatched out or not I do not know. The GRU has many cover installations such as those used for training illegals. All this is handled by the First Directorate," Penkovsky replied. The mission of the First Directorate of the GRU is to position and control illegal military intelligence spies abroad. The most famous GRU illegals were Richard Sorge, who spied for the Soviet Union in Japan before World War II, and Colonel Rudolf Abel, who operated in New York City for ten years before he was arrested in 1957. Abel was traded for Gary Powers in February 1962.

Penkovsky thought about Kisevalter's request to name illegals and came up with Colonel Fedorov, who ran illegal operations. "Fedorov is a particularly effective and dangerous intelligence officer. He was previously in England in the *apparat* of the military attaché and he graduated with me. He is an artillery engineer. Right now he is military attaché somewhere in the Scandinavian area. He has many agents." Penkovsky named GRU officers with extensive agent contacts and said he was prepared to give the team a list of fifteen of them presently located in Ceylon [renamed Sri Lanka in 1972], Pakistan, and India. "Those in India are being held in reserve. I have all this material," Penkovsky said.

As if to underscore how well he was doing in the State Committee and how extensive his contacts were, Penkovsky, out of the blue, announced: "I found out from one person that a prominent American industrialist, Cyrus Eaton, has offered himself to Khrushchev to serve as an informant."

Cyrus Eaton (1883–1979) was the founder of the Republic Steel Corporation, one of the largest manufacturers of flat steel, with a long history of ill-treatment of its workers. In 1954 millionaire Eaton secretly approached the Russians to do business and traded Republic's steel for Soviet chrome ore. Eaton sponsored the first Pugwash Conference of American and Soviet nuclear scientists in 1957, an informal forum that contributed to Soviet-American understanding of nuclear strategy and the dangers of nuclear war. Pugwash provided an opportunity for contact at a time when the Cold War made such meetings difficult. Eaton was widely viewed as a self-serving eccentric in his efforts to become an intermediary for improved relations between the Soviet Union and the United States.

Penkovsky insisted, "A prominent person told me this [about Eaton]. This is something you should look into. The industrialist also has a friend, an old man whom I believe has also been in the Soviet Union twice, and who also was involved quite willingly in similar conversations with some of our leaders. But allegedly the industrialist told Khrushchev that he was in full accord with Khrushchev's peace policy and that he would inform Khrushchev of important matters. I do not have a document to support this, but I know this is a fact."

"Where did you find this out?" Kisevalter asked.

"The man who told me this is a civilian who works in the Central Committee of the Communist Party; his name is Viktor M. Churayev [deputy chairman of the Communist Party Bureau for the Russian Federation]. At a dinner party given by Varentsov, Churayev said that the industrialist, having drunk a bit, simply offered his services. Whether his services were accepted or not, I do not know," explained Penkovsky.[24] In 1991 Richard Helms recalled that the CIA did not follow up on Penkovsky's tip. Eaton had no access to classified documents and his pro-Soviet views were well known.[25]

From his grand design to destroy Moscow's military command

85

and control network, Penkovsky veered back to the personal, seeking a reaction from the team to his ideas and the information he had provided. "Please give me your opinion of me as a strategic intelligence officer, now your soldier, your worker ready to fulfill any mission you may assign to me now and in the future. All I ask is for you to protect my life, and I only have three persons close to me, my wife, my mother, and my daughter. I would be happy now to go to England or America myself, but I cannot leave them behind. Thinking about them would drive me insane in time, should I leave them behind. I have to prepare a basis for my future existence, and I believe that I can serve you most usefully in place for at least a year or two, particularly if I work under specific directions set by you to fulfill missions within my capability. All I have said about destroying our headquarters is my opinion."[26]

Penkovsky had stated his conditions. He was ready to spy for the West for another year or two, but he wanted to be assured a future in the West for himself and his family. The team was not prepared to negotiate details of the arrangement, but Kisevalter moved to assure him and sign him up. "With respect to what you have asked us, we are completely prepared to grant you your minimum requests. It is most gratifying to us to realize that you can still continue to work inside for a year or two. We can give you in hand whatever you need and the balance we can deposit for you in the bank. Not only will this be an accumulation of monthly payments, but after you have joined us, we will review your entire scope of activities."[27]

Penkovsky immediately agreed.

That's right. Just so I have a nest egg. I see in your faces that you are official, responsible, high-status workers, my comrades. Also, being an intelligence officer, I know how to run and control agents. There is no need to keep things in the dark. I wish your governments, and I consider them both my governments, to trust me as their own soldier. It doesn't matter whether you confer the title of colonel on me or not. I am still full of energy, although Wynne may have reported to you I have been nervous recently; and I have this eye disturbance which I picked up in Turkey, although my vision is perfect.

My request to you is to establish a material basis for my work. In general, I am a man of some achievements. I have been a colonel now for eleven years. Previously I received 500 rubles [$450] per month; now [at the State Committee] I receive 450 rubles [$405].*
I have an apartment with quite a few personal items. I have been a

* Monthly salaries for workers and doctors ranged from 75 to 200 rubles—$67.50 to $180.

regimental commander and I have also been abroad. It is normal for me to have something. I married the daughter of a lieutenant general who had given her a lot of money, and in general my standard of living is good. But I would like to live even better, and to provide luxuries for my family. This is all easily explained at home because anyone who has been abroad would normally acquire all sorts of things to bring back. These things are acquired from one's own savings. As you well know, there are many things completely unavailable in the U.S.S.R. and others that are extremely expensive.[28]

I would like to have a certain amount in hand, which we can discuss. I was thinking of acquiring a dacha just outside Moscow. A modest dacha is entirely normal for someone of my age and status. This would cost about 10,000 rubles [$9,000]. After returning from the front I had a Mercedes-Benz, but after riding around in it I sold it since I couldn't get parts and I was thinking about buying a Volga. All my comrades have cars. From my small savings and the money I have, I usually spend quite a bit on my family and to go out to restaurants. I am not an ascetic.[29]

I would like to swear an oath of allegiance to you, to give you a signed statement in order to formalize our relationship. Secondly, we need to work out a communications system with me without personal meetings—providing me with dead drops where I can pass materials. I would prefer not to meet with anyone. I did have the desire before of meeting with an American or British representative and to ask them to take me off somewhere overnight. Our counterintelligence is not operating as intensively as it would seem. People are caught primarily because of crude errors. Now that we have met, thank God—and I have begun to believe in God—we can consult on all these things together, and frankly I would like to avoid personal meetings.[30]

I request that you evaluate my submitted material with respect to its financial worth. I am certainly not going to bargain about it, and I am a soldier. Whatever you determine I should get, I will accept. Please place whatever you decide in the bank and I will request small sums when I need them. During this trip I will ask you for some money, not this minute, but during my stay. I have to buy quite a few things. Some of the things I buy I can take with me. I can even take two suitcases with me if it is necessary since it is entirely normal, or I can leave one suitcase behind with Wynne and get them from Wynne next time he comes to Moscow. I have many purchase orders to fill for my friends, my wife, and others. I have complete trust and know that you will decide this properly. Basically these are all my requests.

"I am sure everything will be arranged accordingly," said Kisevalter.

"Fine," agreed Penkovsky. "Now consider how to establish a system of dead drops. I think that we can arrange all this prior to the 30th of April, and it seems that there may not be any reason to make it necessary for me to meet with someone until five or six months after this."

"Are you planning to return here again in the fall?" asked Kisevalter.

You see, that all depends. Tomorrow I will tell you all about my mission here and what data I have to get in terms of certain catalogs, so that they will see that I have obtained something and brought it back. I have the assignment of obtaining a steel called Nimonic 105, a heat-resisting steel which is available here in England. The firm that makes it is Henry Wiggin.

Then there is another mission, that of turning over some of my acquaintances to local contacts. I will tell you about that tomorrow. I will ask your advice and possibly your help in some of these matters. Then it all depends on how all this will be accepted at home. If they trust me, they may even send me with my wife and family overseas. This could be to the United States, to England, or to Canada. By my experience and maturity I am eligible, but it's a matter of whether they trust me.

"How about your mother?" asked Kisevalter.

"No, they would not let her go. You will have to help me arrange to get my mother out some other way."

"Could your mother get to East Germany?"

"Yes, it is possible that she could go there as a tourist."

"In that case it will not be a difficult matter to get her out through East Berlin."

"That is a possibility. I have another possibility in mind. After I have completed all my assignments for you in Moscow, I could go with my family to live in Riga or elsewhere in the Baltic States. Then I could get out either by submarine or surface craft. This may sound naive at this point, but it is still a possibility."

"It would be much better if she could go as a tourist to East Berlin and then simply get to West Berlin."

"Anyway, think about this. The only other thing I want to mention is that you will be satisfied with me."

"We are sure of this," said Kisevalter emphatically. "Now let's arrange about tomorrow."

"I believe that I can meet with you again tomorrow in the evening, late, between 2100 and 2200 hours. That would be the best time for me, because the others will already be tired and be falling asleep."

"Can there be any difficulty for you from anyone in your delegation?" asked Kisevalter.

"No, none at all. I am perfectly sure of this. Tell me, what danger do you think there can be?"

"We don't know the exact circumstances, but we are afraid that if a pattern of your disappearance is noticed, someone will report this to your people," Kisevalter said.

"Nothing can happen. My room is locked. Here is my key. If the phone rings there will be no answer, and I will simply say that I was asleep," explained Penkovsky.

"Suppose they keep knocking loudly on your door?"

"First of all, there are double doors, and secondly why should anyone knock on my door? I said goodnight to them quite properly and said I would retire. I am positive none of them are surveilling me," Penkovsky insisted.

"We are raising these points entirely for the sake of your security," Kisevalter assured him.

"That is fine, and you can say anything with respect to matters that I am aware of. But these things I know, so far as my delegation is concerned."

"We certainly are most happy to meet with you as much as possible. Don't misunderstand," Kisevalter said.

"I believe that we can work during the night. Tomorrow I will come here about 2200 hours," Penkovsky said.

"Yes, come straight to this room."

"This is about all I had in mind to tell you tonight. Now I would like to be completely honest in my relations with you and I would like to formalize our relationship by an official *akt** so that you can properly report this to your top people. I will sign all necessary obligations, oaths, etc. I want to have a clear soul that I am doing this irrevocably for my whole life. These are not impressions as the result of one day. After all, I felt these urges far back in the days when I was in Turkey. Maybe the Turks even suspected, although I was never identified to them by name. Now that I've patiently waited almost one year, God has granted our getting together," Penkovsky explained.

"That is why no further unnecessary chances should be taken from now on. God has protected you so far, but there is a limit to taking chances," Kisevalter said.

"Yes, God does not bless fools," agreed Penkovsky.

"No matter how much we want to meet with you for long sessions and often, we must be careful," reiterated Kisevalter.

* An *akt* is an official agreement, the Soviet version of a contract.

"Well, then, let us say goodnight until tomorrow. Tomorrow I will come as soon as I can, but it may be as late as 2200 hours," concluded Penkovsky.

"Come when you can. We will be waiting for you. Let us take you out and show you a rear stairway of the hotel, right across from this room. You can go right up to the fifth floor without being seen by anyone. This will avoid taking the elevator," Kisevalter said. He handed Penkovsky his key to room number 566 and escorted him to the stairway. Penkovsky left the first meeting shortly after midnight on April 21, 1961. He had been with the American and British team for three hours and thirty-five minutes.

Hitting the Jackpot

AFTER THE FIRST MEETING THE BRITISH AND AMERICAN TEAMS WERE elated. They had struck gold. Penkovsky, although high-strung and a heroic romantic, clearly had access to secret materials that could reveal Soviet nuclear missile strength and Nikita Khrushchev's plan of action in case of a nuclear war. For the two teams, the scope of Penkovsky's revelations and the candor and detail with which he presented them branded him genuine. No planted agent sent to penetrate Western Intelligence would offer such secrets.

At stake were the answers to such critical issues as Khrushchev's intentions toward West Berlin and whether a missile gap existed between the United States and the Soviet Union. Nikita Khrushchev claimed publicly that the Soviet Union's missiles were rolling off the assembly lines like sausages and implied that his country had more and better nuclear weapons than the United States. Penkovsky's information belied those claims. His descriptions of food riots within the Soviet Union were a revelation. In those days Moscow was the best city in the Soviet Union in which to live because food and goods were commanded to the capital by the central planners who controlled the economy. Communist Party control emanated from Moscow, the Center. Tight security made travel for Western correspondents difficult, and even then, on their few forays outside the capital, everything was arranged in advance to present a rosy picture of reality. The tradition of "Potemkin villages" was maintained in the style of the favorite statesman of Empress Catherine II. Prince Grigory Aleksandrovich Potemkin erected fake villages in the steppe area north of the Black Sea and the Sea of Azov to make them appear more populated than they actually were when the empress visited the area in 1787. In 1961 Soviet officials were still painting the fronts of buildings and offering banquets to visitors on collective and state farms to make them appear prosperous, but life was harsh away from the Center.

Bulik and Kisevalter, who stayed at a hotel near the Mount Royal, were mindful to carry out the empty wine bottles and drop them in trash cans on the street in order not to arouse suspicions among the hotel staff that there had been a meeting in room 360. The following morning Bulik went to the American Embassy on Grosvenor Square and prepared a cable summarizing the first meeting for headquarters in Washington. An additional message was sent outlining Penkovsky's information on nuclear missile developments in East Germany. The cables were transmitted by Carleton B. Swift, Jr., the deputy chief of the London Station.

Then Bulik and Kisevalter spent the day going over their notes, listening to the tapes of the meeting, and preparing for the next encounter with Penkovsky. They were joined by Leonard McCoy, who worked diligently with them, going over the questions for the next meeting. McCoy, a reports and requirements officer who specialized in the Soviet Union, was brought to London at Bulik's request to provide the specific American requirements for interrogating Penkovsky. After meeting together, Bulik and Shergold decided it would be helpful to have McCoy serve both the Americans and the British since his grasp of the subject areas was so extensive.

A reports and requirements officer is the link between the Agency's clandestine operations officers and the users of their information in the rest of the intelligence community. The Reports and Requirements staff of the Soviet Clandestine Division is responsible for a general awareness of the needs of all the government's agencies, including the analytical side of the CIA, the State Department, the Defense Intelligence Agency (DIA), and the National Security Council (NSC), which advises the president. By knowing the operational capabilities of the clandestine service of the CIA, Reports and Requirements makes certain that the right questions are asked of the Agency's agents and assets in the field. The resulting information is then disseminated to the intelligence community on a "need-to-know" basis. An agent, or spy under control and on the Agency's payroll, or an informant, a person who only occasionally provides information to CIA officers, is never directly named in an intelligence report, but only described in general terms and given a grade for reliability.

Reports and Requirements separated Penkovsky's material into two categories of highly classified reports created especially for the operation. One series of reports dealt with the documents Penkovsky photographed and sent to the West. This was known as the IRON-

BARK series. The other category dealt with Penkovsky's subjective reporting on personalities and their comments on vital issues. This was named the CHICKADEE series. Included in this second category were Penkovsky's own impressions of political and military developments based on his sources' information.

Penkovsky's dynamism and enthusiasm, his wide-ranging and passionate denunciations of the Soviet system and its leaders, illustrated with anecdotes, fascinated and captivated the American and British teams. Never before had there been a Soviet spy like him.

It was only after the first meeting that the team first laid eyes on the list of materials that Penkovsky handed Wynne at Heathrow. The list added to the team's excitement. The documents appeared to be authentic and broke new ground. Neither the British nor the Americans possessed such Soviet materials. With Penkovsky's clarification and perspective, the information would be passed on to the appropriate military officials and policymakers. In this first handover Penkovsky provided seventy-eight pages of Secret and Top Secret material, most of which he had copied by hand. He also provided four photocopies of plans for construction sites of missile-launching installations which would later play a critical role during the Cuban missile crisis. The material was primarily about missiles, including the deadly V-75, designated the SA-2, GUIDELINE, by NATO, an antiaircraft missile of which little was known at the time. Penkovsky also supplied information and manuals on the R-5, R-11, R-12, and R-14 medium- and intermediate-range missiles and their ground equipment. In the West the missiles were given the NATO designations: SS-6, SS-1, SS-4, and SS-5. He also gave them an operating code of intelligence terminology and five pages of material on Khrushchev's "improper activities, reducing the size of the armed forces and cutting military pay and pensions."

Penkovsky's desire for recognition, acceptance, and honor from the West were a constant theme that emerged in the debriefing sessions with him. His enormous ego and his desire to be the best spy in history left the team limp with fatigue at the end of each of their sessions. Then they had to process the "take."

Bulik requested a Minox camera for Penkovsky from headquarters so he could readily copy classified documents. Penkovsky also told the team about stolen American weapons manuals he had seen in the classified library of the rocket and missile forces, and offered to copy them. By examining the manuals, a CIA counterintelligence unit could find out from where in the American military establishment they had come and begin to track down the spies who provided them to the Soviets. Penkovsky gushed like a swollen stream; the team struggled to assimilate and sort out the information he provided at the meeting. Kisevalter worked on the translation of the taped transcripts of the meetings, and an MI6 team in London translated the documents Penkovsky had provided.

The second evening, at 9:25, April 21, Penkovsky returned to the meeting room at the Mount Royal. The team's initial wariness had ebbed, replaced by a professional acceptance of his bona fides and a desire to maximize the time available. Penkovsky came to the meeting from a dinner at the Soviet Embassy with a GRU officer who had carefully described the GRU setup at the Soviet Embassy in Kensington. Penkovsky passed on the names, assignments, and office locations of the GRU staff in London. The fact that he and his GRU colleague had consumed half a bottle of cognac became quite evident while the meeting with the Anglo-American team progressed. Penkovsky digressed even more than at the first meeting when answering direct questions or when striking out on his own, but he never appeared drunk, only excited and stimulated by the revenge he was exacting by betraying the secrets of Soviet military strength and intelligence organization.

During a break in the questioning Penkovsky signed an *Akt na verbovku*, literally a recruitment contract, an agreement to work for the American and British governments. Such a contract is standard for recruitment of agents on both sides, but Penkovsky, rather than his handlers, had taken the initiative at the first meeting and requested that he be allowed to sign one. He wanted to win the confidence of the British and American Services. The *akt* was drafted by members of the debriefing team. It read:

1. I, Oleg Vladimirovich PENKOVSKY, Colonel in the Soviet Army, do hereby on this 21st day of April in the year 1961, offer my services totally and unreservedly to the Governments of the United States of America and Great Britain. I undertake to serve these Governments loyally and faithfully and to carry out to the best of my ability the orders transmitted to me by the representatives of these Governments.

2. I undertake to serve the Governments of the United States of America and of Great Britain by working on their behalf in the U.S.S.R. until such time as my services there lose their value. At that time I request the Governments of the United States of America and of Great Britain to grant me and members of my family political asylum and citizenship of one of these countries and a status in the country of my choice in accordance with my rank and the services I have rendered.

3. Henceforth I consider myself to be a soldier of the free world

fighting for the cause of humanity as a whole and for the freeing from tyrannical rule of the people of my homeland Russia.

4. I hereby declare that I sign this *Akt* in all solemnity and of my own free will.

The wording of the *akt* was more detailed than a normal contract between a spy and his handler. Most contracts are insisted upon by the control officer to reinforce the spy's determination to serve. They represent a point of no return so that the spy cannot change his or her mind. In Penkovsky's case the *akt* underscored his sense of mission and importance. It was a tangible symbol of his new role of self-fulfillment and revenge.

After signing the contract, Penkovsky's excitement quieted and he was at ease while he listed for the team the GRU assignments he had been given to fulfill in England. He was expected to study his British contacts and estimate their potential value as agents, and to report this to the GRU *rezident* in London. In addition he was to determine and report on the methods used by British Counterintelligence against his delegation. Finally, Penkovsky was to gather technical information on a range of subjects, including turning seawater into fresh water, the manufacture of artificial fur, British progress on synthetic rubber, and new technology in metallurgy and machine building.

Penkovsky was anxious to discuss how the secret military material he had provided the team could be used by the U.S. and Great Britain without compromising him. At stake was his own protection. If the material he had stolen was circulated too widely, word might get back to Moscow that the British and Americans had a good new Soviet source, and a full-scale search for the leak would be started, much as the Americans were now eager to track down the source of the American military publications in the Soviets' hands. It was the classic intelligence dilemma: how to maintain a spy in place, take advantage of his revelations, and yet protect him from exposure.

The second meeting focused on technical aspects of how the GRU works. Penkovsky had copied by hand the latest GRU operational code names, and he told the team how to use them. He gave an elaborate description of the GRU's operational automobiles, particularly foreign-model cars which were kept at the GRU Auto Base (*Avtobaza*) on Gritsevets Street, two blocks from the Ministry of Defense, close to the Arbat. (See map, pages xiv–xv.)

Penkovsky proudly reported that he had spent thirty hours studying how to avoid foreign counterintelligence there. "I know where there are hiding places in the Pontiac, the Ford, and the Mercedes-Benz; for example, the floor and the armrests. In front where the driver and the passenger sit, the floor opens up and there is a hole underneath. If I was followed, the material could be jettisoned. I throw the stuff out, I am picked up; I have nothing in my hands. Therefore the cars are adjusted so that when the car stops or brakes, there is no red brakelight at the back. The car is dark when picking people up or dropping them off and there are many hiding places. All operational cars are equipped like this. But such ingenuity! They take off the metal upholstery holders and make a hiding place. You would never guess that there is a hiding place there."

Penkovsky stressed the importance for the GRU of radio monitoring as a source of intelligence, and he identified listening posts in each Soviet military district bordering a nonsocialist country. Then, like players from opposing teams who have suddenly joined forces, Kisevalter and Penkovsky one by one reviewed the careers of top GRU personnel. When Kisevalter described each officer, Penkovsky added personal details: one general's gold teeth, another's approach to Penkovsky asking for help in obtaining a telephone; how the attractive wife of another was prone to affairs.

They went down the list and Penkovsky digressed to describe the political conditions inside the Soviet Union. He recounted a hunger strike in Voronezh, 200 miles south of Moscow, which was put down with force. He told the team of the miserable conditions in rural areas, the refusal by the state to allow collective farm members to own their own cows, and the failure of the collective farm system. While such information was of interest, it was not on the team's immediate requirements list. Kisevalter tried to steer the talk back to operational matters, the question of Penkovsky's personal security, and how to continue communications.

Penkovsky was not ready to talk about that. Still smarting from the pain of his long wait, he asked why he had not been contacted sooner. "Why couldn't two words have been posted, stating, for example, that I should wait for eight months?" he asked.

"That could have been done," replied Kisevalter, "but we deliberately refrained until we could give you instructions for a secure way of passing material. This was to provide maximum security for yourself as well as for our man."

Penkovsky, evidently haunted by the danger of his high-risk approach to the two American students, once more relived his own concerns about their meeting. "I made a mistake. I wanted to say farewell to them properly at the embankment, but I went to the alley, and ran into two militiamen. The students saw that I was apprehensive. When I told them in Russian to follow me into an entryway to finish our conversation, they became afraid and went on. They walked along Osipenko Street toward the Balchug Hotel and I surveilled them for a distance because I was afraid that they might throw away the material. Later, after there was such a long interval of silence, I began to think that although they did not throw away the material, they may have disposed of it later in the toilet of the hotel.[1]

"Now let me mention this: in the future, if a telephone call is to be made to me, do not speak in English. By the way, what was the substance of what this man who tried to call me at 1100 hours on Sunday tried to tell me? All I could get was one word, 'March.' "

"March of course is the month," explained Kisevalter. "He tried to say that during the month of March or April there would be a signal for you. Furthermore, he said that you should wait for this patiently and should not contact anyone until you see the signal. A signal will be placed and you will be called again."

"This all could have been said in two words," grumbled Penkovsky. "Why couldn't you have placed this information behind the radiator?"[2]

"Because such a signal would say only one thing—keep waiting. Then, to go back again to the same dead drop with a complete set of instructions would create an additional risk of compromise."

"People go there all the time," argued Penkovsky, who had chosen the drop because it was near a busy corner usually jammed with people.

"Why should the dead drop be used for this purpose twice when one time would serve more securely?" asked Kisevalter.

"Still," Penkovsky insisted, "all that needed to be done was for a signal and a note to be placed telling me to wait and that the material got into the right hands. I am sure that there is no surveillance on me at all at this time."

"Most probably not," agreed Kisevalter, "but there is certainly surveillance on our man whom we planned for you to contact. Consequently this surveillance is also a source of danger to you."

"But you did believe me, that I had this other material that I wanted to pass?"

"Of course—we believed you because the material that you first sent made it very clear what the situation was."

"You checked all that?"

"Of course we did," said Kisevalter.[3]

Kisevalter used the moment to revive a plan for future contact: the possibility of Penkovsky throwing material over the wall of America House at the point where the wall joins the building itself. Although initially ruled out by the ambassador, it could be reconsid-

97

THE SPY WHO SAVED THE WORLD

ered once Penkovsky's bona fides were approved. Penkovsky assured the team he knew where America House was and could avoid the Soviet policeman on duty near its entrance.

"Now listen carefully," Kisevalter said. "The concept is that at a point of time, that is, giving yourself a five-minute interval to be sure that you are not observed, you would throw the package of your material over the wall where it joins the building. Our man would be waiting to pick it up exactly during that time interval."

Penkovsky nodded and explained, "There is no policeman there. He is in front of the house."

"That is right," said Kisevalter, "but no one should see you throw a package at all. The concept is that if during this short interval you do not find a secure opportunity to throw the package, you could come back for a second or a third alternate time after a week, and then two weeks, but at a specific hour on a specific day."

Penkovsky agreed with the idea. "Absolutely. At night it is dark. There are no policemen there. They are on the other side. People just walk their dogs around there. This can work well."[4]

Bulik interjected in English to suggest they move to the operational side and discuss communications. How were they going to contact Penkovsky in Moscow when there was such heavy KGB surveillance of American and British diplomats? Bulik suggested they work out methods that would protect Penkovsky and permit secure and efficient contact. The answer: use diplomats whom Penkovsky would normally see in the course of his work for the State Committee.

It was agreed. Penkovsky would avoid dead drops, except in an emergency. He was, instead, to make contact "only with those with whom you have normal contact in an official capacity."

"You mean one who has a diplomatic passport?" he asked.

"Of course," replied Kisevalter. "Someone who will be at those receptions whether he has anything to do with this business or not. You, of course, will know him."

"That is good. That's quite right."

"You could go to the toilet, say, and he could follow you five minutes later and pick up your message. There is no need for personal conversation or anything. In that way it is safe because you know within two or three minutes that the material is in safe hands and that the business is completed. There is also no need to travel around," said Kisevalter. "You understand, this is the method which gives us the greatest security."

Penkovsky listened, then replied, "The question is, what will my position be? Suddenly things will get bad for me. Some member of the Central Committee—you know the sort of scum [*svoloch*]—will say, 'Such a man [Penkovsky] cannot be tolerated in the GRU. Let's finish with him.' Besides, they know that Major General Shumsky told me officially, 'This report has come from the KGB archives saying that Colonel Penkovsky made a false declaration. When he reported on his father it did not tally with the actual facts. His father, Vladimir Florianovich, was of noble descent.' "

Penkovsky again noted that his grandfather was "a great jurist, a high-placed official. He had a rich home and everything was elegant." Penkovsky's concern about his status was a theme he returned to over and over again. If he was dropped from the State Committee and forced to retire, he would have to live on a pension which had been reduced by Khrushchev. No longer would he have access to secret materials, and his spying would be limited to repeating information he gathered at social meetings with senior officers. His access would be severely curtailed and so would his lifestyle.

Penkovsky urged the team to think about the development of one or two dead drops, but Kisevalter tried to dissuade him. "For you to fill and clear a dead drop when there is no surveillance is no problem; but although you live in Moscow and although you are forty-two years old, I am sure that you can have no idea how heavy the surveillance is on all our people in Moscow."

"I do understand," said Penkovsky.

"Then double this understanding and you will be closer to the actual facts. There is a great danger. Understand me, we are not worried about our man. What can happen to him as a diplomat? A small scandal and he is thrown out. He will be alive and well, but—"

"I am gone," said Penkovsky.

"Thank you, that is right. Secondly, even with an ideal dead drop there is uncertainty if hot material is in it for any length of time."[5]

Kisevalter cautioned Penkovsky on Wynne. "We know Wynne is a good chap and that he has helped us a lot, but after all, he is not an intelligence officer and he may talk. We are engaged in a big affair and if we start using him as an intermediary—"

Penkovsky interrupted. "If he sees that I have some money of my own he's going to think that I have got it from you. You had better warn him."

"There is no need to tell him," insisted Kisevalter.

"There is nothing to fear from Wynne," agreed Penkovsky, trying to ease Kisevalter's concern.

"Nevertheless there is no reason for him to know or for you to stir up his curiosity," warned Kisevalter, who was following standard tradecraft procedure by trying to keep the courier and contact free of any knowledge of the substance of the materials being handled.

In that way if Wynne was compromised or arrested he could not reveal the full extent of the operation.

"Incidentally, he asked me if I was with you yesterday. I said yes," recalled Penkovsky.

"All right, but do not tell him anything unnecessary again—it is not his business."

Penkovsky was growing restless and squirmed in his chair. "I have not yet finished my sheet of paper with my agenda," he said.

"Finish it, by all means," urged Kisevalter.[6]

"What concerns me," Penkovsky said, "is the West's failure to understand the true motives of the Soviet Union as a dangerous foe who wants to be the first to attack and smash us, and she will do this. When all is prepared she will do this some dark night. She will do it.

Our General Staff is not sleeping. It is planning hundreds of variations of attack, but they do not know the exact targets since many of the locations are secret and cannot be discovered. That is why Khrushchev and his General Staff have set a goal: to eliminate large areas with atomic and hydrogen bombs. Do you understand? To create "a rain of missiles"—this is Khrushchev's own expression. This was told to me by Varentsov. I believe Varentsov as I believe Churayev—who said that Cyrus Eaton had offered his services. Such dangerous people we are dealing with. How you deal with Eaton is your business. As far as my own safety is concerned, I am aggressive and have iron willpower. I am just a cog, especially now, in fulfilling new assignments.[7]

It seems to me that in spite of the tremendous tasks which are being accomplished by the American leaders and the British and American military commands, the evaluations are wrong. There is too much giving in, compliance, and indifference. For instance, whatever amount of dollars and pounds you expect to allot in your planning, you must triple this amount in order to be really strong. Then when you hear by your "grapevine" that Khrushchev is ready, that he has many missiles—and I also will hear things through some of my channels either in my present line of work or through other channels with which I have indirect contact—then the first blow must be struck. A knockout blow. Then we will be in a winning position. You must be as sure that two times two equals four—that such targets [the Defense Ministry, the KGB, and the Central Committee headquarters] will no longer exist.[8]

Penkovsky referred to himself and the Western allies as "we" throughout the meeting. His sense of his own mission to alarm and arm the West had to be taken seriously. It was not the mission of a disinformation agent. It was a timely warning that had to be factored into the Western hesitation about how to conduct the Cold War.

In 1960 and 1961 the U.S. was involved in an internal debate over Soviet missile strength. Air force estimates of the number of Soviet missiles relied on U-2 photos and deductive estimates of Soviet production capabilities based on secondary sources. Estimates of the number of Soviet missiles, made on the basis of the size of factories and calculations of uranium production, erroneously gave the Soviet Union a decided advantage in missile strength. Among CIA analysts there was a joke that whenever cloud cover blocked a view of the ground below, the air force added a new Soviet missile site to its estimate.

The "missile gap" became a major issue in the 1960 presidential campaign between John F. Kennedy and Richard Nixon. The Democrats charged that the Republicans had allowed the United States to fall behind the Soviet Union in the development of ICBMs. Kennedy referred to the Soviet missile "advantage" and branded the Republicans as "the party which gave us the Missile Gap."[9]

When Francis Gary Powers had been shot down near Sverdlovsk on May 1, 1960, the U-2 program over the Soviet Union ended. There was a blackout period over the summer of 1960 when the U.S. satellite program to photograph Soviet missile launching sites suffered from a series of failures. The first satellite photos of these bases became available in August 1960, and by the end of the year and spring of 1961 there was regular coverage. The new photographs showed that the estimates of Soviet missile strength apparently were too high.

Penkovsky provided the first reliable human intelligence on Soviet missile strength. His information came while the satellite information was being assembled and evaluated. He provided a rational explanation to accompany the satellite evidence, which led to a revision of the National Intelligence Estimate (NIE) on Soviet missile strength in the fall of 1961. His reporting was later corroborated by the satellite photographs.[10] A National Intelligence Estimate is the collective agreed view of the intelligence community on a foreign situation, trend, or development. It identifies major elements, interprets their significance, and appraises future possibilities. The director of the CIA is responsible for presenting the NIEs to the president. The organizations in the community include the CIA, the Defense Intelligence Agency, the National Security Agency, and the State Department's Bureau of Intelligence and Research. NIEs are the basis for policymaking decisions by the president and are the highest form of intelligence since they represent a consensus of the intelligence community. They are revised annually or as events demand.[11]

Penkovsky was unaware of the missile gap debate. For him the existence of such an argument would have been unbelievable. He knew the sorry state of Soviet offensive missile development. He was also aware of the resources that were being committed to remedy that condition so that the Soviet Union would have a first-strike capability against the United States. Penkovsky's plan was how to cripple the Soviet Union from within with small nuclear weapons in order to head off a Soviet first strike against the West. He knew that any Soviet attack would be followed by massive American retaliation. Such a full-scale nuclear attack against a first strike, the U.S.'s announced strategic doctrine, would destroy his country and probably the world as we know it.

Penkovsky told the team:

> If Hitler had destroyed our military command centers, he would have won the war. After all, what did Hitler do? He wasted millions of tons of metal, but did not completely destroy even one military headquarters. This I know exactly. I read it in the reports of the General Staff and heard it in lectures given us on military strategy by the deputy chief of the General Staff in 1947. He said not one of the Military District headquarters—which provided the front with the batallions, regiments, brigades, and divisions—was destroyed by Hitler. All the millions of trained people in the Moscow Military District, from Kalinin to Kazan, remained intact. The Moscow District General Staff, located on Osipenko Street, and the Moscow Defense Zone were intact. If Hitler could have blown them up with commando groups, if he would have done away with the core that does all the planning, that had the experience and the know-how, then the Soviet government and military leadership would have been powerless.[12]

> That is why I insist that you consider these targets such as the General Staff—the Chief Artillery Directorate, Antiaircraft Defense, the Central Committee of the Communist Party of the Soviet Union [CCCPSU], where all the scum [svolochi] who rule everything are presiding—all the inspectors who have the privileges of an Oblast Party Secretary [obkom]. They have a salary, cars for their own use, and an allowance. I am not mentioning the bases and ammo dumps that are underground, but the military districts. There are nineteen. In a few months I shall be able to report to you that there are even one or two less. They are being consolidated. It would be desirable to destroy the headquarters. It would be good strategy to get rid of the experienced commands because they are the heart of the army.[13]

The team was absorbed and did not respond. They were determined to hear out Penkovsky and not intrude with their own ideas on his train of thought. Penkovsky expanded on how to target and destroy the General Staff with small weapons of two kilotons.

This is just my own idea. The weapons should be small enough to be put into a little suitcase or a little satchel and left next to a house. Not inside. You don't even have to go inside. There are guards all around and you need a pass to go inside, and if you don't have one you might get killed. But the things can be placed all around the building—right next to the guards—with a clock mechanism, and let the whole establishment go up in smoke. Then, when the leaders, the framework of the working body, the framework of the General Staff and the central directorates, which are the brains of each type of troops—tanks, artillery, aviation—when these are all destroyed, then let's see them pick themselves up and recover quickly. Then they will have to use some old, sclerotic goats, not fit for military duty. They will not be able to do anything. Then you destroy all the operational documents. Not from the air. Not by rockets. You know how many errors can be made by missiles and aircraft—pray God the accurate missiles will be on your side, not mine.[14]

Here was Penkovsky at his most audacious. His plan sounded reckless, even mad. Yet the logic of destroying command and control centers in the case of all-out war has now become accepted doctrine. Since 1961 the U.S. has changed from its massive retaliation strategy of destroying the Soviet Union by a first strike that would try to devastate all of that nation's military and industrial power in a single massive attack. While nuclear targets in the Soviet Union remain highly classified, the concept of decapitation—withering an adversary's military power by removing its leadership in a nuclear attack—is now part of American strategic doctrine.

Penkovsky's proposal to place portable nuclear weapons at key command centers was never seriously considered, but his information was valuable for targeting, and contributed to the evolution of American nuclear strategy.

Penkovsky sounded as if he wanted to start a nuclear war, but he also told the team that he hoped the Russian people would not have to be destroyed. His proposal was for an extreme situation. He was trying to prove to the team that no task was too great for him. The Soviet Division's chief of operations, Quentin Johnson, recalled:

Penkovsky was completely bitter about the Soviet system, going back to his White Guards father, having to hide his father's record and being passed over for promotion. He was resentful of and hostile to the system. What he wanted to do was to get a nuclear device from us and put it, as he said, "where it should be placed." He did not realize how powerful nuclear weapons are. Our problem was to convince him that placing tactical nuclear weapons in the middle of Moscow was not a smart thing to do, but that he could achieve the same kind of satisfaction and get back at the Soviet system— which is what he really wanted to do—by alerting us and giving the West information which would erode the power of the people who were in authority. We had to help him rationalize the problem and bring him around from blowing up Moscow to a long-term commitment to provide intelligence which would enable him to achieve the same kind of personal satisfactions that he was out for. Remember, he was willing to give up his life.[15]

Penkovsky was filled with gossip and reports of the leadership's private meetings. He told the team about the Sino-Soviet split and a conversation between Khrushchev and Liu Shaoqi, a deputy to Mao Zedong. "You know this leader. He, like all the Chinese, is defending Stalin and berates Khrushchev, and says that by his unwise, loud, worldwide disclosure and denigration of the personality cult, he has undermined the authority not only of Stalin but of the entire Communist Party. Stalin was the symbol of the Party and of the people, even of the people of other countries. Khrushchev became quite agitated when Liu praised Stalin and told him: 'Take your Stalin out of here together with his box.' In other words—'Take Stalin's body if you love him so much.' And you know, there was a time when they wanted to put Stalin into the ground, there was such a time."[16]

Penkovsky was referring to the discussion over removing Stalin's embalmed body from Lenin's Mausoleum after Khrushchev's revelations of Stalin's crimes at the Twentieth Party Congress in February 1956. Stalin's body was removed from Lenin's tomb after the Congress and placed in a grave on the left side of the mausoleum, with a granite tombstone and a small statue of Stalin. Later Penkovsky gave the team a sample of new jokes going the rounds in Moscow. A favorite question for Armenian Radio was: Why did Khrushchev remove the body of Stalin from the mausoleum? Answer: The mausoleum is only big enough for two people. (Khrushchev wanted Stalin's place next to Lenin.)[17]

Kisevalter asked Penkovsky about the Soviet view of American nuclear weapons. Penkovsky replied:

I know that in some aspects your "missile business" is going very well. We know that it's better than ours in many respects from the information we got from our agents. We know it's better than we are doing in the Soviet Army. But we also know that you are not entirely ready. We know that all the guidance assemblies are not perfected and that your scientists are still working out problems. God willing, I hope any so-called copied labors of mine will help your scientists, who in the space of the next few months must study all this, assimilate it, and see how to resolve the problems. Perhaps the information may not be there in detail. After all, it is condensed from courses, at the academy. I did not study five years as one does at the Dzerzhinsky Academy—but the push in the right direction is all there for the specialist who will study this.[18]

At the time of Penkovsky's meeting in London, the U.S. was deploying Jupiter and Thor medium-range missiles in Turkey and England that could reach targets in the Soviet Union, but their accuracy was still being perfected.

There are many differences of opinion between the Satellites and the U.S.S.R., but Khrushchev knows how to localize these things and put them aside. Take a look—rocket weapons are delivered to all the People's Democracies with nuclear warheads, with the exception of East Germany, which already has them. You know this. There are two brigades there and two dumps of atomic warheads. The weapons are controlled and in the hands of the Soviet Army, not the Germans. The Eastern Sector welcomes Soviet power like a fifth wheel on a loaded wagon. Well, Khrushchev knows how to handle such things. Right now many specialists, such as engineers, have been sent to these countries. You know. You have your own channels to watch such moves. There are all kinds of things going on—construction of launching platforms, building up cadres.[19]

Penkovsky was asked how many nuclear submarines the Soviet Union had. "We were told up to ten," he replied.[20] "All of this began from the original V-2 of the Germans, whose scientists are still working for us. Speaking of Germans, you have seen how often Khrushchev threatened to make a separate peace with the GDR. He will not do this because it would involve a war. He is not ready to fire missiles now and he will avoid a war at this time. He is giving rockets and training personnel to the GDR, but they are still far from being ready to use them."[21]

The Four Power allied occupation of Germany was still in effect in 1961, and no peace treaty ending World War II had been signed. Khrushchev, pressing for East German domination over West Berlin, threatened to sign a separate peace treaty in 1958. He backed off but raised the issue again at the end of 1960.

105

While the evening wore on, Kisevalter asked Penkovsky about arrangements for the next day's meeting. "Are you tired already?" asked Penkovsky with a smile.

"Not at all," replied Kisevalter, "but how about yourself?"

"Last night when I left you, I spent two hours thinking, analyzing everything and preparing notes. This morning, when I met the members of my delegation, there was not a word mentioned about last night. No one wanted to contact me. This may be none of my business, but how is Colonel Peeke getting along? Is he a general yet? He was very nice to me."

"He is doing very well and as a matter of fact, he is not very far from being a general," said Kisevalter.[22]

"I spent many years among generals and marshals. Even my wife's father was a general, and my grand-uncle also was one; but I am only a colonel. I'll never be made a general because my father was a White Army officer. They don't trust me. My problem now is to do our work and be ready to fulfill your orders."

The team was impressed by Penkovsky's anguish. Kisevalter told him, "I want you to realize that the most basic consideration we have toward you is humanitarian, irrespective of how important you may be as a source of information. We regard you as an individual first of all."

"I understand you and am very grateful for this. It is quite different with us, and many good people have perished."

"The difference in the systems is very simple to understand. All government leaders in the countries of the Free World are servants of the people. We even use the expression that a man is in the service when he is military or in government work. In the U.S.S.R. the government is everything and the individual is nothing," said Kisevalter.[23]

Penkovsky was winding down. He told the team he had been up since 7 A.M. and had worked all day. What he really wanted was to see London. "There are many fine things to see in the stores, and my wife has given me a whole list of things to get." He recalled that at the end of World War II he had helped liberate a porcelain manufacturing town in Czechoslovakia and brought home "all kinds of porcelain vases. I have many expensive things at home, including rugs from Turkey, and I live on a high scale for Communists."[24]

Living well under Khrushchev was not easy, said Penkovsky, who told the team about a general he befriended.

This aide-de-camp to Marshal Varentsov, Buzinov, is always broke. He has three children and he often asked me to take him somewhere. So, having money that my wife doesn't know anything

106

about, I buy him cognac. He knows that when one is abroad there are always extra allotments in foreign currency, so he is not surprised that I have all kinds of things—that is normal. I like to live freely and now and then take a lady out.

I know how to approach them and I never drink to excess like Buzinov. I say all this to you because I feel you should know all about me, and if you ordered me to stop doing all these things, I'd have to stop. You know what the moral views of our government are, and so far I've never been in any trouble, but all these activities require money for gifts and entertainment.[25]

Anyway, I got myself into debt and I wish you would consider how to reinforce my financial basis a bit. I've already thought of buying odds and ends here that I can sell at a profit there. I know some wealthy Jews in Moscow who can even handle diamonds. Whatever is not too bulky. I may need to buy five or six heavy sweaters and other stuff. Wynne can bring that to me later, but if that is impossible, I would like to have more money to buy these things while I am here. I need as many rubles as you can spare to take back with me. Frankly, I have one debt of 1020 rubles. A good friend of mine gave me the money to get him a suite of furniture through my connections in Moscow. I ordered it and have the receipts to show, but I spent the money gradually. How many rubles did you plan to give me?

"About 1000," replied Kisevalter, deliberately mentioning a lower figure than the 3000 rubles the team planned to give Penkovsky.

"You see, that would just about cover my debt less twenty rubles and would leave me nothing at all. Well, I'll be able to buy the furniture since I have it ordered. I have just bought a new television set. I thought of buying a small transistor radio here. [Later Penkovsky was given a Sony transistor radio for operational use.] I swear by my daughter and my future work with you that I must do the following. I must bring each and every friend of mine some small item, since they know that I am going abroad. It does not have to be an expensive item in every case, but it would be extremely bad to neglect anyone."

Penkovsky listed a variety of items such as fountain pens, neckties, nail polish, lipstick, and a range of medicines for casual friends. He had a list of more expensive items for influential friends such as generals, marshals, and colonels.[26]

Suddenly, Penkovsky shifted to a new subject. "By the way, I just remembered something important. We are conducting scientific intelligence against the U.S. The assigned intelligence missions for the year [1961] cover all conceivable types of industries; there were 150 specific intelligence targets listed. On each target there are supplemental questions—two, three, or more. The targets, broadly speaking, were nonferrous metals industries, the steel industry, and all phases of the oil industry. The interesting thing is that all U.S. targets were also given to the delegations going to Canada. I know this because I gave it to them with my own hand."

"I suggest we discuss his financial situation again tomorrow," said Bulik, who felt that Penkovsky was being kept on too tight a financial leash in London by the British team leader, Harold Shergold.

"I just thought of something," Penkovsky interjected. "If I could have a one-carat diamond, exactly one carat, not more or less, I am sure that I could cash it in for 1200 rubles. Consider this, and possibly we can work it out so that you will not be concerned about passing any monies to me through contacts in Moscow for some time."

"We will consider all this and we'll talk about it some more tomorrow and will try to comply with all your requests, which are reasonable," said Bulik.

"Very well, I will go now, and tomorrow let us plan on meeting between nine and ten P.M. if I can."

Penkovsky left for his room at 1:40 A.M. on April 22, 1961.[27] Ten minutes later he returned with only his trousers and jacket on over his underwear. He had come to look for a lost notebook. Fortunately it had fallen between the cushions of the armchair in which he had been sitting. In the notebook was a neatly itemized shopping list in red ink which his wife had prepared for him. It was accompanied by clippings from fashion magazines for a full array of ladies' fine underwear. There were also tracings of the feet of his wife and daughter so he would be sure to buy the right size shoes.

In their comments on the transcripts of the meetings Bulik and Kisevalter noted: "It should be stressed here that many of these items would unquestionably have important operational significance, since they will be given to important Soviet personages who will automatically be valuable, unwitting informants."[28] By providing gifts to senior generals and marshals, Penkovsky was developing intimate personal relationships that would allow him to be present at their social occasions. Through this kind of private contact with his superiors he could glean highly classified information.

With his shopping book and lists safe in hand, Penkovsky retired for the night. He and the team met later that day in London. Then Penkovsky prepared for a fact-finding mission to Leeds.

Penkovsky's Travels in England

ON APRIL 23 THE MORNING SKY WAS GRAY AND OVERCAST WHEN PEN-kovsky and Wynne drove 175 miles, from London to Leeds, with the Soviet delegation. They visited British machinery factories en route and stopped for lunch at a small restaurant outside Leeds where Penkovsky, enjoying the atmosphere, quaffed a full liter of cold beer with abandon. No sooner did he sit back to relax than he suffered intense stomach pains and cramps. At first he thought he had appendicitis. The cramps persisted and Wynne called a British doctor who examined the Russian in a room above the restaurant. The doctor said Penkovsky had not had an attack of appendicitis, but he recommended that he be hospitalized in Leeds if the pains continued. The doctor told Penkovsky that his problem was guzzling too much beer too quickly, and that it had caused an extreme kidney irritation. After a rest of two hours the pains subsided.

When Penkovsky entered the lobby of the Hotel Metropole in Leeds at 8:30 that night, he was escorted by Kisevalter to room 31. The first thing he talked about was his close call with being hospitalized. "I'm feeling better except that I'm a little weak from the anxiety of this ordeal. I was terrified about going to a hospital since the people back home, who were not too willing to have me [come to England] in the first place, would probably criticize me for doing this deliberately. They would say, 'Why did he have to go to a hospital in England when we have adequate facilities at the embassy in London or in Moscow?' Now I feel all right and I think we can work a little here."[1]

Penkovsky's fear of being placed in a British hospital arose from the Soviet intelligence system's inbred fear of being compromised by foreigners. A stay in a foreign hospital would raise doubts about Penkovsky's reliability and make it unlikely he could go abroad again. According to the KGB and GRU way of thinking, Penkovsky could have been drugged, sexually blackmailed, and recruited while in the hospital. Being under the control of an adversary or enemy was enough to discredit a Soviet intelligence officer, no matter under what circumstances. During World War II, Soviet soldiers who had been captured at the front by the Germans were considered traitors at war's end and were ordered by Stalin to be shot or sent to labor camps when they were forced to return to the Soviet Union.

Penkovsky told the team that he could not stay very long because he had told his delegation that he was going out for a walk. He promised to work all night at the next meeting.

The first part of the meeting was taken up by Penkovsky's agenda. He began by reviewing his plan to destroy the major military and KGB headquarters in Moscow with one- or two-kiloton tactical nuclear weapons in case of an all-out war between the United States and the Soviet Union. In discussing the means to destroy the General Staff headquarters, Penkovsky noted:

A five-kiloton bomb is the smallest we have developed. I know this for sure because Marshal Varentsov told me so. They have computed a one-kiloton charge, but they have not developed the practical adoption of it yet. [The size of the nuclear weapon intended to destroy the General Staff] should be designed for extensive subterranean damage which could effect a shock wave. The timing for this destruction is very important and I suggest that it should be several minutes before H-hour, the signal for an all-out attack by bombers and rockets. The KGB structures are mostly old buildings, although there are some new ones. In between the four main buildings are many private dwellings with dark entryways. It would be simple for anyone to place a suitcase or trash can or a spittoon there. No one would pay any attention to a spittoon; they would simply spit in it. The best time to set the explosion is between 1000 and 1100 hours because all of the command personnel will be in the buildings.

Penkovsky described the buildings and the sites where the nuclear charges should be placed, including the toilets or the pass bureau of the GRU [the public reception area], where parcels and a suitcase might be checked.[2]

While relating details about the Moscow Military District headquarters near his apartment house, Penkovsky digressed to recall that Lavrenti Beria, the dreaded chief of the MVD, the precursor of the KGB, established in 1954, was brought to the basement of the headquarters "and was shot there by a general in the presence of other generals.* This building complex was surrounded by armored cars and tanks, all in firing positions, during the night of December 21, 1953, when Beria was executed. There was some apprehension that Beria's MVD cohorts would make an attempt to seize this headquarters at the time. After he was shot, Beria's body was burned with gasoline." The full account of Beria's removal from power and execution were not known in the West and remained a subject of fascination—how the Soviet leadership dealt with a potential revival of Stalinism.[3]

Penkovsky continued to run down the list of targets, including the Antiaircraft headquarters and Marshal Moskalenko's headquarters for the strategic rocket forces at Perkhushkovo, outside Moscow. He plotted a total of twenty-four suggested target sites on an enlarged section of the Moscow map covering the center of the city.

When Penkovsky finished his strategic agenda he began to express his material concerns. A good deal of the meeting was taken up with discussion of Wynne's expenses and Penkovsky's need to provide gifts for friends in Moscow. Kisevalter reassured Penkovsky, "We will treat Wynne very well. Everything will be taken care of, but do not get yourself involved in any personal dealing with Wynne."

"Of course, he asked me to help him, and he has turned out to be a wonderful person," said Penkovsky.

"Our clandestine relationship is one thing, but our dealings with Wynne are something different, and under no circumstances should you be involved in this," reiterated Kisevalter.[4]

"I felt it my duty to report this to you," Penkovsky persisted.

"Remember, he may inadvertently talk too much either here or in Moscow," Kisevalter argued.

"He is afraid and will not talk," insisted Penkovsky.

"He is inexperienced in clandestine matters," warned Kisevalter.

"That's right, he is inexperienced. However, he did take my one letter and a document when I saw him off at the airplane," Penkovsky reminded Kisevalter and the rest of the team.

"I assure you Wynne will be adequately taken care of and everything you request will be included, but don't talk to him about this again."

"Very well. I won't speak about Wynne anymore," agreed Penkovsky, although the subject was still on his mind and would recur frequently in later meetings.

*Beria was head of the NKVD from 1938 to 1945 and of its successor, the MVD, which combined state security and internal security, from March to June of 1953, when he was arrested, tried, and executed.

111

With Penkovsky ready to turn his attention to Kisevalter's questions, Kisevalter went to work to get through all the items on the team's agenda for debriefing the Russian. The discussion centered around Soviet strategic and tactical nuclear missile development and who controlled the missiles. The question of defining the type, numbers, quality, and range of Soviet intercontinental ballistic missiles and their stage of development was a vital American and British concern. For the Soviets, everything with a range over 1000 kilometers (about 600 miles) was a strategic missile. (In 1962 the United States divided these missiles into two categories: medium-range missiles [600 to 1500 nautical miles; 1080 to 2700 kilometers] and intermediate-range missiles [1500 to 3000 nautical miles; 2700 to 5400 kilometers]. Missiles with a range greater than 3000 nautical miles qualified as intercontinental ballistic missiles, ICBMs.)

"To what extent were you told about ICBMs?" asked Kisevalter.

"We were told that they exist and, as I have written, the basic characteristic is that they are two-stage rockets. Emphasize this to your scientists to spare them an analysis for more than two-stage rockets, which do not exist. Next, the fuel capacity is much larger, and of course so is the overall space in the rocket."

"Are there any operational ICBMs at all or are they only experimental?" asked Kisevalter.

"They are all experimental for strategic purposes except for the one I mentioned, which is as you said of an intermediate range. I give you my word, and I swear by my child, that Marshal Varentsov has often told me, 'You know, Oleg, with respect to ICBMs, we still don't have a damn thing. Everything is only on paper, and there is nothing in actual existence.' He was specifically referring to ICBMs. Varentsov said, 'For short ranges we can fulfill the missions, but beyond that what? There is nothing.' "[5]

Kisevalter pressed hard, focusing on the state of Soviet nuclear weapons development. "I understand what you want to know about rockets," replied Penkovsky. "All I can say is that the experimental effort now to make ICBMs is all based on those shorter-range rockets that have already been proven except that all dimensions will be proportionately increased."[6]

The team was interested in Penkovsky's knowledge of nuclear submarines and he replied at length that he knew atomic components were manufactured in the town of Menzelinsk, on the eastern border of the former Moscow Military District, 540 miles from Moscow. Penkovsky smiled and recalled that he had almost married Masha, the daughter of the rear admiral who commanded the base there. He had met her before he was married.[7] Kisevalter and Penkovsky discussed the Soviet nuclear submarines' rocket-launching capability above and below the surface and then went on to the question of storage facilities for nuclear weapons.

Penkovsky told the team that nuclear submarines were based in the Leningrad area. He had found this out, he explained, when he met a captain in the submarine force while on vacation at the House of Rest, the former naval sanitarium in Sukhumi on the Black Sea. During their walks at the sanitarium, the captain talked about his work and told Penkovsky that there was a dock north of Leningrad where nuclear submarines were assembled. "I'll give you his address," Penkovsky volunteered, so that the captain could be contacted for possible recruitment. "He was with his wife and so was I. We got to know each other."

Penkovsky said he had heard that "there are two hidden storage areas in the German Democratic Republic where atomic warheads arc stored."[8] He was asked the size of Soviet nuclear weapons and how many had been produced. In reply he repeated that the Soviet Union had nuclear bombs as small as five kilotons but nothing lower. Soviet nuclear strategy at that point was not concerned with smaller nuclear weapons for tactical use. There were twenty-five-kiloton bombs and those of greater TNT equivalent. The Soviet Union had also successfully tested hydrogen bombs of greater than twenty-five-kiloton equivalents, he said.

"Do you know where they are stored?" Kisevalter asked.

"I have no idea."

"Don't be disturbed. These questions must be asked," explained Kisevalter so that Penkovsky would not feel frustrated at not having the answer. In some ways the requirements list was a wish list and questions were asked on the off-chance Penkovsky might have some knowledge of a vital piece of information that had come through his high-ranking personal contacts.[9]

In response to further questioning, Penkovsky confirmed the Soviet shift in emphasis from bombers to missiles for offensive weapons. "To sum up," he said, "aviation as a whole has been radically reduced in favor of rockets." However, Penkovsky agreed that Kisevalter was correct in saying that a number of select modern models of long-range bombers were still being produced and improved.[10]

Asked if any Soviet attempts had been made to develop an atomic-powered aircraft engine, Penkovsky replied: "No. All they are testing now is how to have a rocket engine work on the fission of nuclear energy."[11]

The Americans and British finished their list of questions and ended the meeting at 11:35 P.M., agreeing to meet again the following evening at 8. Kisevalter escorted Penkovsky to the street corner and both men returned to their hotels.

The following evening, April 24, at 8:45, after a day of visiting factories, Penkovsky returned to the Metropole in Leeds to meet the American and British team for the fifth time. He had been tied up with his delegation and arrived forty-five minutes late. Penkovsky, with a smile, said Wynne was in his room washing and getting himself ready to go dancing. "Let me begin by telling you what's on my mind before I forget. First of all, in the Ministry of Defense there are 28,000 employees." He proceeded to explain how the staff was distributed and in which complex of buildings they could be found.[12] He also noted that the *apparat*, the working officials of the Central Committee, "has expanded considerably and it includes all kinds of sections." There was even, he said, a commission that handles all personnel being sent abroad. They brief people on behavior abroad and question them on what they expect to do. Then they fill out a Top Secret form.[13]

> The first page of this form is a declaration that I must sign. It reads something like this: "I, Oleg Penkovsky, about to go abroad, promise to maintain the dignity of the Soviet Union as the representative thereof, promise not to enter into any contacts or discussions that are not authorized and to maintain state secrecy." On the opposite page are vital statistics of the individual. This includes his Party record. The whole document is Top Secret. The reason is that, according to our advertised democratic principles, to ask these questions would be improper, so they made the form Top Secret. The pretense is that a specific ministry simply sends someone abroad, and the Central Committee has nothing to do with it. But this is absurd. Of course, a ministry may nominate a person to go abroad, but then everything is checked minutely by the KGB. When their acquiescence is obtained, the Central Committee commission takes this Top Secret obligation from the individual and then permission is given for the issuance of a diplomatic passport by the Ministry of Foreign Affairs.[14]

Returning to his main theme, Penkovsky said there were 50,000 key people in Moscow who would need to be eliminated if war occurred. He gave his estimates of personnel strength: the General Staff of the Ministry of Defense, 28,000; the Central Committee of the Communist Party of the U.S.S.R., 5000; the KGB, 5000 to 6000. In addition, he said, there are naval and air forces. He also included the other regional headquarters in about twenty military districts with another 100,000 people. "Therefore this total of 150,000 experienced generals, officers, and men of the headquarters in the U.S.S.R. must be destroyed according to the plan that I have proposed."

Penkovsky entreated his questioners,

Please consider my plan and report it to your headquarters. No doubt destruction has been considered by them as an inevitable action in case of war. Perhaps my grasp of the whole problem may be inexact and requires much adjustment and reorientation. I am ready to accept any assignment to blow up what I can in Moscow, any assignment that may be given to me. Wiser and more experienced heads will probably come up with a better solution than I have offered.[15]

I would like to suggest another possibility. Your scientists may consider this. The nuclear mines, with TNT atomic equivalent, should be concealed in a device, for example standard Moscow refuse cans, which can be found in every house entrance. A false bottom should be prepared in the trash can. I should be able to set a time mechanism for the desired detonation time. The materials should be obtained in a Soviet store so that these cans resemble Soviet ones. Then the prepared materials can be sent by means of heavy diplomatic packages and passed to me through dead drops. Then assume that I can concentrate all this in the basement of my dacha. These cans or spittoons I can haul either in suitcases or better yet, in the trunk of my car.[16]

If I were assigned the mission of blowing up seven targets, this may require some fifteen mines. I could run around and set all these in the proper places. It may require several trips to get them all placed. But I could run back and forth as if I am shopping. I could even have some items placed in the suitcase. These I could leave at the baggage storage area I described to you or in the proper driveways—with everything set by a time mechanism. This is what occurs to me. Maybe the whole scheme is very primitive in your eyes, but to me this seems to be one of the first essentials of our common mission.[17]

Kisevalter, who had been listening carefully, replied, "Your intentions are good and when the time comes to consider this, your proposition will not be ignored."

"The destruction of such a group of military and Party leaders included in the 150,000 I mentioned would cause immediate capitulation. Of course, this may not get Khrushchev, who could be at his dacha." Khrushchev had three dachas: one near Moscow University, another on the Rublevskoye Highway beyond Kuntsevo, seven miles from Moscow, and the third near Dmitriyevo.

"We have a lot of questions here we would like to ask you," said Kisevalter. "Even though you may not answer all of them, just reply to whatever you can."[18]

In response to Kisevalter's list of questions, Penkovsky explained the construction details of Soviet rocket nozzles and how they controlled the mixture of fuel and air. All Soviet rockets, he said, began

115

from the German V-2 and followed them in principle. "The ICBM is exactly the same type of a two-stage rocket as the tactical rockets except that everything is on a massive scale and the fuel component has a mixture of boron in order to develop a higher-caloried fuel mixture for increasing the specific thrust."[19]

Penkovsky explained how the rocket course was taught at the Dzerzhinsky Academy and who the teachers were. He told the team that the East Germans would be supplied with their own tactical rocket units by the end of 1961.[20] "I know that in the Group of Soviet Forces in Germany (GSFG) there are exactly four brigades of rocket artillery. Two of these are designated as atomic-weapon rocket brigades and the other two are normal rocket brigades, that is, high explosive. This is in Soviet hands and will not be given to the Germans. But the countries of the People's Democracies will have their rocket units trained by us and they will be armed with rockets, that is, with the exception of Albania. Possibly, Castro has received some rockets, but I am not sure."[21]

In April 1961 the Soviet conventional arms buildup of Cuba was under way, but the decision to place medium-range and intermediate-range nuclear missiles did not come until Khrushchev's visit to Bulgaria from May 14 to 20, 1962, when he had the idea of installing missiles with nuclear warheads in Cuba without letting the United States find out about them until it was too late to do anything.[22]

Penkovsky leavened his technical comments with high-level gossip about Varentsov and his family. Penkovsky knew about the poor morale of Soviet troops stationed in East Germany from General Ivan Vladimirovich Kupin, whose nephew married Varentsov's daughter, Yelena. Kupin was commander of artillery of the First Army in Germany and often stayed with Varentsov when he came to Moscow. He sometimes called Penkovsky and they would have a meal together and talk about difficulties in the field.[23]

Penkovsky was still deeply troubled by the fate of his father and raised the question with the team. "On the 5th of January 1960, General Shumsky, deputy chief of GRU personnel, called for me and said, 'Here is the information submitted to us by the KGB on your father.' I would appreciate it if you would check to see if my father is still alive, since he disappeared without a trace. We know that there was an encirclement at Rostov and it would have been difficult to escape from there to Taganrog." Penkovsky was referring to the possibility that his father escaped from the battlefield at Rostov and joined the White Army forces, which fled from Taganrog on the Sea of Azov to Bulgaria and Yugoslavia in 1920.[24]

"We will run a check," Kisevalter assured him.

Penkovsky persisted. "Secondly, possibly through your information channels, you may find out if anybody reported on me about my father. Thirdly, you may know that there were some records in the German archives that fell into the hands of the KGB and which they have been analyzing for years. Our people don't know what to do with me about this matter. They can openly discuss my case without arresting me, but if they did not give me a passport to come here now, I would have made a run for it somewhere, possibly to your embassy."

Penkovsky was referring to the possibility of seeking asylum in the American or British Embassy in Moscow. For the KGB to find out that his father was a White Russian officer created the suspicion that Penkovsky himself was tainted and might be a traitor, especially if his father were still alive and could contact his son. While such a theory seems farfetched today, it was an essential part of Soviet security doctrine for the top intelligence services of the KGB, GRU, and Kremlin Guards.

Anyway, Shumsky called me and said, "Your father was a White Army officer and had a higher education and your grandfather was a nobleman, a judge in Stavropol." My uncle once-removed was also mentioned. He was once a commander of an antiaircraft defense regiment in the Far East before the war, and at one time he was also in prison [from 1937 to 1939] because of his background. His name is Valentine Antonovich Penkovsky. After he was released from prison he was then the chief of staff of the 21st Army during the war. Then he was commander of the 6th Guards Army. Then at the end of the war he was sent to the Far East and he participated in the campaign against the Japanese Kwantung army. He remained there after that and became the chief of staff under Malinovsky. When Malinovsky was finally brought in to replace Zhukov as the minister of defense, he left my uncle out in the Far East since he knew the area well. He avoids contacting me and I do the same, since we do not wish to contaminate each other with our backgrounds.[25]

When Shumsky confronted me with all this he ordered me to write up my version of it. I told him what I had already written about my background, but possibly my mother could add some supplemental information. My mother wrote a statement and I submitted it, but they immediately stopped processing me to go to India as the GRU *rezident*. I should have gone as the military attaché but instead they sent some general who has no diplomatic or other background. When this was done I had no assignment for a month, then two, and I was worried. I was in the GRU reserves. This all happened after I had finished the advanced rocket course. I was very lucky that I had been to these courses, otherwise I could never have gotten this information for you. You would have had information only about the GRU.[26]

I was sitting worrying during these two months and I felt that the big break in my life was going to take place. I had already stolen or copied the material from the academy. The reason I had done this was because I was already distrusted. They would not return me to my post in Turkey after I had this run-in with General Rubenko, who had also made charges against me. I felt insulted by this and wanted to go to Turkey very badly since I had a wide circle of acquaintances, including Colonel Peeke, within the diplomatic colony. I had already made up my mind to approach you, but was biding my time because I was taught to be careful. So I collected this material because I thought it would be useful in the future when I had the opportunity of approaching you.[27]

I became the head of the class since I was the senior colonel. There were six or eight other colonels in the class. The rest of them were lieutenant colonels, majors, and there were a few captains. So I copied everything word for word but had to use abbreviations. Later, at home I wrote out all the abbreviations so that you would understand them. The only place where I did any shortcutting was in describing certain launching-site equipment, because after describing one in detail the other types were similar.[28]

Anyway I was doing this for almost a year and then one day when I was the duty officer, the Powers incident took place. I told the two American students about this. When I was duty officer I had all the room keys but not the safe keys because the safe keys are submitted and placed in a sealed box. At that time I wasn't thinking of opening safes, but now if you can prepare me a similar seal I can open safes. That night I made my rounds and took turns with my assistant, each sleeping for a while. During this time I had some black carbon paper and I copied down the code names from the Red Book [a compendium of code names and real names]. Later, at home I typed them in the form in which I gave them to you. Of course they could trace me by my typewriter, but if it went to that extent I would be shot anyway. I was nervous while copying, even though I was alone at the time. At any moment a special high-ranking duty officer, such as a general from the First Directorate of the General Staff, could come in. There were all kinds of special cables that could come in at night, particularly dealing with information about overflights. I knew when your planes were flying over Kiev.[29]

I was the duty officer during the night of the 1st of May to the 2nd of May. The tour begins at 1500 hours. No sooner did I take over the duty when in came the communication saying that an American pilot had been taken into custody when a U-2 was shot down, and they described the circumstances, which I know exactly. When

Powers was flying near Sverdlovsk, the poor fellow had the misfortune of running into a battalion of V-75s [SA-2 surface-to-air antiaircraft missiles]. He did not fly directly over the position, but slightly to one side of it, and was already being followed by a MIG-19. The pilot was a lieutenant. The battalion on the ground was on alert because of the holiday [May 1 is International Workers Day] and they opened fire. They were firing a defensive barrage since they were alerted that a hostile aircraft was flying overhead.[30]

There were no direct hits, only damage to the tail and wing assembly. The damaged parts were not shown at the Moscow exhibition [of the plane] and your intelligence personnel should have spotted that. He was within the radius of explosion, and as the result of the shock wave from the explosion, the plane was damaged and poor Powers sustained a concussion. I don't know what he reported to his parents or others, but while falling he blacked out several times. He was not conscious when he parachuted to earth or when everything on him was seized. The claims of a direct hit, were, of course, absurd. I reported this to you already on the 12th of August last year, and I reported on the RB-47.[31]

The further details were of great interest to the team because nothing more had been learned on how Powers had been downed. A special report for the intelligence community was prepared on the U-2 incident based on Penkovsky's information.[32]

Penkovsky said Powers was brought to Moscow by plane, and when he arrived, the KGB at that moment didn't have an English interpreter. "I was supposed to talk to him since I was the only one around who had some sort of understanding of English, and I had already reported the incident to some generals. If they had not found a KGB interpreter at the last minute, I would have been the first one to interview Powers."

In fact, the KGB chairman, Alexander N. Shelepin, who had been the Komsomol chief before he replaced General Serov, wanted to make the report to Khrushchev personally.* "Shelepin got an interpreter and picked Powers up. The military people knocked Powers down and Powers was considered to be a military man. Therefore he should have been turned over to us, the General Staff. But the KGB seized him, took him to Dzerzhinsky Square, and made their own report. He was being treated medically because he was still in shock. You could have traded Powers for this Melekh whom you

---

* Alexander N. Shelepin, born 1918, was chairman of the KGB from December 1958 to November 1961. Until Khrushchev's ouster in October 1964, he served in high party and government posts, and as a Politburo member. Brezhnev, fearing him to be a threat, gradually demoted him out of office and power.

were in such a hurry to release." Penkovsky was referring to Ivan Y. Melekh, a GRU officer under cover as a United Nations official from 1955 to 1960, who was arrested on espionage charges in October 1960, and who Penkovsky evidently believed was released too soon. He was expelled in April 1961 on the condition he never return to the United States.[33]

"How is it that Serov had no influence?" asked Kisevalter.

"Serov has none," replied Penkovsky. "If it weren't for the fact that he is remotely related to Khrushchev, he would have been shot for his past association with Beria. He was in the position of a minister, but he had a chance to save his skin and he was made chief of the GRU. Serov is not the most brilliant man. He knows how to interrogate people, shoot them, and imprison them. Although he has studied intelligence, Rogov, his deputy, does most of the executive work. The other deputy, Khadghi Mamsurov, is simply in charge of the household and administrative functions. So I am glad to have the opportunity of telling you the true story about Powers. If he had arrived in Moscow a half hour earlier, I would have been the one to interrogate him."[34]

Penkovsky assumed that the United States operated the same way as the Soviet Union does, fabricating cases or imposing harsh sentences to create human pawns to trade in spy cases:

If we had only made contact sooner, I would have told you all about Melekh, that he was a Soviet spy and an intelligence officer, and you certainly should not have let him go. You could have sentenced him to be shot, and you could have traded him for Powers. When the original bail money was put up, Khrushchev made the decision, not Serov. The bail was $50,000, even though it was later returned. For operations, Serov can make a decision on his own to spend only up to about $2000.[35]

On the 5th of May, after Powers was knocked down, Khrushchev ordered a suspension of agent operations to avoid a possible flap. At that time I was running an agent about whom I will tell you everything. He was obtaining data on electronic computing machines through a third party, and we were getting the material via dead drops. I had to stop this. There were many protests against dropping scheduled meetings and other contacts, but it had to be done. The *rezident* in Pakistan decided on his own to pick up material from a dead drop that was already loaded in order to avoid possible compromise to the agent. He did this but was severely reprimanded by his superiors at GRU, even though it was the right thing. Thus Khrushchev ordered cessation of agent contacts during the period when he was going to capitalize on the Powers incident, despite the damage it did to the agents' net. That's all I have to say. I am ready to answer your questions.[36]

Kisevalter asked, "Are the 3R-1, 3R-2, 3R-3, and 3R-7 now in serial production?" He was referring to a series of Soviet tactical ground-to-ground missiles for battlefield use.

"Absolutely, and in addition, they already have atomic warheads developed for them."

"Were all these shown in the Moscow parade of 1960?"

"No, not all of them. I'll tell you which ones. They were the 3R-1, the V-75, the R-2, the R-11, and the 3R-7. I am checking these from the pictures," said Penkovsky, looking at pictures of Soviet medium- and intermediate-range missiles.[37]

"What is the principle of allocation of these rockets? Is it to the front or the army, or what unit?" asked Kisevalter.

Penkovsky explained that in case of war "the strategic long-range missiles will be commanded by the chief of the rocket forces of the General Staff, the way it is now established. Tactical weapons will be in the hands of the ground forces commander, and through him Varentsov and their direct subunit commanders, such as a front commander. In case of war, the army artillery will have these weapons under its command. However, they will only be conventional-type weapons because the employment of atomic weapons will be the exclusive decision of the Presidium of the Central Committee of the Communist Party through the Ministry of Defense. The atomic weapons will be deployed in such locations that when their use has been authorized, the warheads will not be far from the units which could employ them."[38]

The team looked on while Kisevalter again asked Penkovsky if he knew of any actual locations where nuclear warheads are stored. "Of course I do not know, and one can find out only by chance conversations. There are, I have heard, assembly points for atomic warheads in the Klintsy area [300 miles southwest of Moscow, near Bryansk]. Generally, the hollow rockets are stored separately in entirely different areas. Only when they are to be used with atomic warheads are both the rockets and the warheads brought to some forward assembly point."[39]

Penkovsky discussed details of the Soviet medium- and intermediate-range ballistic missiles being developed, including the R-11, which NATO had designated the SS-1. The center for launching such missiles, he said, was at Kapustin Yar, in the Urals, south of Volgograd, and the impact zone for the tests was in Kazakhstan.[40]

Penkovsky told the team how he had developed "an excellent

121

source of information in this area, a captain who is a friend of mine."
The captain's wife came to Varentsov's aide-de-camp, General Buzinov, and said that her husband was being assigned to Kapustin Yar after graduation from the Dzerzhinsky Artillery Academy. She was a student at a medical school and wanted to remain in Moscow to finish her studies. In addition, she would have to give up her room, a nice one, which was allotted to the family while the husband was at the academy. Her request was for help in getting her husband transferred so he could remain in Moscow. "His name is Vladimir Kashin. He is an engineer captain."[41]

"Well, this General Buzinov, it seems to me, took a liking to the lady. He already had trouble in this direction once before. He flirted with some officer's wife in Leningrad and the husband made a scandal, the result of which was that Buzinov received a Party reprimand. If it weren't for Varentsov he probably would have been thrown out. Well, anyway, I don't know how far his interest in this lady went, but it is common practice that all generals have girlfriends, even Lieutenant General Smolikov of the GRU.[42]

"He came to me and said that this captain should be helped. At that time I was working as chief of the acceptance commission for the incoming class of the Military-Diplomatic Academy [MDA]. I saw his personnel file and it was outstanding. While a student at the academy he had even invented some device which was of value.[43]

"In my discussions with him about what was going on at Kapustin Yar, he told me how often the guided missiles tested were way off their planned course. In the future I will know how to ask him about the vital details which you are interested in. I will surely get him into one academy or the other."[44]

Kisevalter asked if the R-2 and R-11 [SS-1] rockets were already issued to troops outside of the U.S.S.R.

"This I don't know. But I know that it is planned to give all kinds of missiles to satellite countries by the end of 1961," replied Penkovsky. "They were first issued to troops about two years ago, about the time when Khrushchev first bragged about them to Nixon."[45]

The pace of questioning on missiles eased and Penkovsky switched subjects. Turning to Harold Shergold, the British team leader, he asked, "Mr. Harold, what is the status of my request to formally meet a government representative? I want to present myself officially. It doesn't have to be a specific lord, and I don't expect to see the queen."

"Rest assured this is being taken care of," interjected Kisevalter after translating Penkovsky's request for Shergold.[46]

"Also, I will need some more money," Penkovsky told Shergold.

"The fifty pounds you gave me is not sufficient. I haven't spent them yet, but I know I will need more since I have many things that I must purchase. I want you to realize that all of these items I plan to purchase are perfectly logical for me to have. In fact, they can be obtained through our commission stores in Moscow, but at a very high price. In my status it is entirely proper and normal for me to have certain things. On a representational basis, given my position, it is mandatory. Even when I returned from Turkey I had a large suitcase full of things. Nothing was said at all, and there was no customs check. Now I am returning officially with the committee and there will be no trouble at all." Penkovsky again itemized a long list of purchases and opened his notebook filled with shopping requests and the cutouts of foot sizes for his wife and daughter.[47]

"Are you considering my dacha?" Penkovsky asked.

"We are considering all your requests, but whether or not it's purposeful for you to have a dacha now is not so evident," replied Kisevalter.

"I would like to know what value is being placed on the material that I have submitted. Each one should have what he earns. You told me that you have established a monthly salary for me and I am very grateful. If you had set it at half that figure I would not have complained. I am not a tradesman and do not want to bargain. Everyone must try to attain something. I am sure that you are in the same situation.[48]

"I am thinking that anyone may have a black day. For example, I was thinking of this when I was ill yesterday. I could even have died, and in the future I may perish in some way. If that happens I request that my wife and mother be approached, but in only one way since they have no inkling of what I am doing. I have not established any plans for their defection across any border. Simply tell them that I have withheld one fact from them. Say that prior to the death of my father, he had set up either a trust fund or left valuables in a foreign bank, and since I am no longer among the living this sum of money is available for my wife. At least this way my daughter may have some financial help until she is grown up."

"We will do this," Shergold promised.

"My wife is totally unaware of what I am doing and she has been brought up under comfortable circumstances as the daughter of a general," said Penkovsky. "However, she knows what deceit and lies exist in our way of life, and she was very much impressed by Western life when she was in Turkey. She filled this whole notebook with purchase requests."[49]

Penkovsky was baring his deepest concerns. Cut loose, with no certainty of his future, the practical side of his nature emerged. If he was satisfying his American and British questioners, then there had to be a reward, something for his wife, mother, and children to survive on when he was gone. The ambivalence of his position was not lost on him, yet he was careful to try to maintain the high ground of a devoted agent to whom money was secondary to the success of his mission.

For the team, dependence of an agent on money was a key element of control and security. Given too much money, Penkovsky's spending habits might come under investigation and he would be exposed. If he was not given enough money, so that he felt appreciated, he could become disgruntled and unproductive. Shergold insisted that Penkovsky had to ask for every advance of British pounds for his shopping, while Bulik was inclined to give him money to bolster his self-esteem. When it appeared to Bulik that Shergold was being too tightfisted, he and Kisevalter gave Penkovsky additional funds for shopping and entertainment in London. There was clearly a difference in operating style between the British and American teams. An effort was made not to let Penkovsky sense this difference, but it was a private annoyance to Bulik.[50]

Talking about his days in Turkey, when he was a GRU officer, reminded Penkovsky of the illegal GRU *rezidentura* (military intelligence station) in New York City, and he told the team how it was organized. Kisevalter asked him to find out the number of GRU officers assigned to the United Nations.[51]

You should know how pleased the GRU was that I was given a visa. Then I can fulfill GRU missions while heading this delegation. I request that you do all you can to help me fulfill my missions. I will write up an effective report. I need help from you in introducing an English acquaintance to the local GRU case officer here in London. All that has to be done is to maintain some contact, and possibly your man would pass some sort of material once in a while. The material can be worthless, but it would be good if your man would accept money occasionally. There is no need for the man to accept recruitment. All he has to do is to string the case officer along until the time I defect. This is how I visualize it. If necessary the man could be recruited, but he has to work properly. Otherwise he would be traced back to me as my man, and if they smelled provocation, they would put me away so you would never see me again.[52]

"All of the problems you have raised in our operational plans are now being worked on, and as soon as we return to London, we will accomplish everything," promised Kisevalter.

"I understand this perfectly," said Penkovsky. "I realize that you have more experience, scientific approaches, and better heads than I have, even though I have been in Intelligence since 1953, except for a short interlude thanks to being contaminated by Rubenko in Turkey."

Penkovsky rose to leave. Then he stopped and said, "It would be well if you could get Wynne in contact with me in a couple of months. He doesn't need to be trained or told anything. He can be unwitting, but of course he knows who you are and that I am in contact with you."

"We will take care of all that," said Shergold.

"Wynne may not be the sharpest man or the wealthiest, but he treats me very well and with respect. I would say that he is a good patriot and an honest man," explained Penkovsky.

Penkovsky was thinking ahead to his return to Moscow and how he would transmit the information he acquired. Wynne's personal security and his position as the contact man and courier held his legitimate business ventures in the Soviet Union hostage to the continued success of Penkovsky. An experienced intelligence officer, Penkovsky knew better than to rely on dead drops in Moscow except in extreme circumstances. Wynne was his best bet. By telling the GRU that he was exploiting Wynne and turning in high-quality intelligence from his trip to London to prove it, he just might pull off his duplicity.

Kisevalter reminded Penkovsky, "Take your key."

"I wish I could have all of you in Moscow for a month," said Penkovsky.

"I will take you down out of the hotel and walk you to the corner," offered Kisevalter.[53]

Penkovsky left at 12:20 A.M. on April 25.

The following afternoon at 4:15, Penkovsky met again with the team at the Metropole. He had spent the day with officials from the Board of Trade and he complained that the British had asked him what the Russians were going to buy. "They told me that we must buy more. It was all about buying, what could I tell them?" Then, in English, Penkovsky added: "It's terrible!"

It had now become his routine to go through his agenda first. He asked to have a single room on the fifth floor of the Mount Royal, not together with anybody in the delegation, when they returned to London. His room was to be next to the staircase leading down to the room used for meetings. "Doing it this way," he explained, "will remove any grounds for members of the delegation to report later about unusual room assignments."

"Very well, we shall see what we can do," said Shergold.

125

Then Penkovsky insisted that Wynne not be permitted to take his wife to Moscow with him in May. "She is absolutely unnecessary. It would be an unnecessary waste of money and she will just interfere. I request that she be left in London."[54]

Penkovsky had been thinking about his earlier proposal to single out targets for destruction in Moscow. "With respect to the main objectives in Moscow that should be destroyed, you can logically ask me why I did not include the Rocket Academy, since rocket warfare is so vital. I do mean to include it and will describe how this can be done," he said.[55]

Bulik and Kisevalter laid an enlarged map of the center of Moscow on the cocktail table and asked Penkovsky to mark every main military objective on it. While he indicated the targets, Penkovsky provided a running commentary on the personalities in charge of the units. He offered details on how Khrushchev had taken away the biggest official cars, ZISs, from senior officers and replaced them with smaller Chaikas. Penkovsky digressed to explain how he was issued two civilian suits and an overcoat every five years.[56]

Then he pinpointed new targets on the map and described the rivalry between Marshal Varentsov and Marshal Moskalenko, the commander of the rocket forces. In the process he explained to the team that "Moskalenko is commander of the rocket forces of the land—everything—all the strategic rockets with atomic and hydrogen weapons. He commands all this destructive power. Nuclear weapons for aviation and the fleets are also included.[57]

"There is a struggle. Each commander realizes that he needs as much technical equipment as possible and that there is no money forthcoming. So they swear at each other and the matter goes to the highest Military Council, headed by the commander-in-chief, Nikita Sergeyevich [Khrushchev]. Varentsov was there and told me how the meeting went. He said: 'Oleg, not a word about this.'

"Varentsov told me that at the last [Military Council] meeting they talked about everyone's troubles with agriculture. After that, Khrushchev traveled all over the country. He arrived in Tbilisi, you remember, and then went to the East, to the virgin lands, talking about the great new territories and towns." Penkovsky related that during the time that Khrushchev was in the East dreaming of new fields of corn, the Military Council met with Presidium members Anastas Mikoyan and Mikhail Suslov to air their complaints. The military wanted more money to test missiles and solve problems, because there had been numerous failures.

"Varentsov told me, 'Do you know that there was no one there who would support this! Stalin would just have banged on the table and that would have been that.' You ought to give me a small recorder so that I can tape what Sergei Sergeyevich [Varentsov] tells me. I can talk to him at the dacha or anywhere. He tells me about sessions with the marshals," Penkovsky said.[58]

"Now about Latvia, the military headquarters in Riga, and about the Baltic region in general. The Baltic peoples live and wait for liberation. The mood there is bad, but good for us. I would, of course, be sorry if it were necessary to bomb or annihilate the three Baltic republics. This is a question for great strategists, but now you know my point of view. Perhaps sometime you will send me on a mission to Riga and from Riga perhaps I can come to you— or perhaps from some other port. Anyhow, all I want to say is that it is not necessary to annihilate the Baltic peoples," Penkovsky said in English.[59]

As the evening came to a close, Penkovsky talked about himself. "How did I get into the State Committee and how did I come to England? Well, on February 29, 1960, I received my orders to be a senior officer on the Pakistan-India-Ceylon desk of the Fourth Directorate of the GRU. I accepted the assignment, began to work, and conducted the officer training program. My work was praised at the Party meetings. I wrote telegrams and worked with agents. Then a reduction in staff personnel began. For the most part they removed the old men, the invalids, those who were unsuitable or politically unreliable. What supported me? I had been apprehensive for a long time because of my father. Many people knew about him. I saw they were purging people all the time. They left me for about three months after that.[60]

"Then, in June 1960, I was assigned to the Military Diplomatic Academy, as a member of the Mandate Commission, which processes the incoming students. I was designated to be the chief of the class of 1960, which would graduate in 1963. As head of the course I would have received a general's pay since in the past the duty status was that of a *general mayor* [the Soviet equivalent of a U.S. one-star brigadier general]. If I were head, my earnings would have been high, you well know."

"How much?" asked Kisevalter.

"Now it is 500 rubles a month [$450]. And it is a general's position. I have the experience for such work. I commanded a course at one time and a regiment; it's within my character and ability to run such a class."[61]

"So that's where you got your information on the GRU personnel?" asked Kisevalter.

Of course. When I returned from my leave in July and early August, I was told that I had been removed as class chief, but I could serve

127

as an instructor or in the Information Directorate of the GRU. I refused both offers and was placed in the GRU reserves again.

I was sent to GRU Personnel to see Shumsky. He said, "What's this all about?" and he sent me to Smolikov. Smolikov likes to drink and he always has women about.

Smolikov said to me, "How long have you served?" My knees were knocking. I said, "In 1962 it will be twenty-five years." Then came the question about my father. He said my father was the reason I was not sent abroad, but still he kept me. The Central Committee of the Communist Party of the Soviet Union had a personality profile of me included with the proposal for the trip to England sent by the committee, as if I were a demobilized colonel. In addition the GRU military section recommended me favorably to the committee. There is nothing against me except my father. But of course this hinders the GRU from letting me get ahead. "It is awkward," Shumsky told me. "How could a man with such a past be an instructor of sixty future intelligence officers? It may mean nothing to me, but the Central Committee is interested and checks on it. It is impossible to confirm you."

When I was in Odessa and Kiev on leave, they changed my assignment to an instructor. That was not acceptable. I would give lectures and instructions in methods of work. That is for a man who is inactive. Perhaps they considered that they were showing me trust to make me an instructor, but I refused categorically to work with them. It is no life, you understand. I decided to defect. Three times to risk one's life; to be in the Party for twenty-one years—I don't know what I have not done for the country. "Give me some operational work in India or Pakistan," I told them. I showed them I could manage this. "We can't do it." In other words they did not want to have anyone on the operational staff with the slightest mark against him.

On the 15th of November—I have the order at home—I was appointed to be an expert in the Department of Foreign Affairs on the State Committee for the Coordination of Scientific Research Work.

One day I was told, "Wynne's delegation is coming. You will work with this delegation." I arranged the entire visit for Wynne's seven-member delegation. I had to prepare all the lectures and to get together a panel of experts for each lecture—engineers of this and that—and send telephone messages, summon specialists and others to attend the lectures of the English experts.[62]

I met Wynne at Sheremetievo. I worked well with the English delegation. All the lectures and the receptions were well organized. The specialists gave nothing but good written reports, and the delegation was also pleased, as you know.[63]

I worked from beginning to end with Wynne's delegation and then took them out to the airport. When we were there, on the 16th of December, I had the idea of suddenly handing over my materials to Merriman in the aircraft and saying, "Here you are." It could have been done somewhere—in the toilet for instance—but he would just have repeated again, "My business is cement."[64]

One thing which I want to say quite simply—as one who considers himself your worker, your intelligence officer—I would like to express a few political thoughts connected with our work.

I am one of those who believe that from time to time there should be local wars that do not involve our own powerful leading countries [America and Great Britain]. It is necessary to bleed them, to suck the Soviet Union dry of materials, and play on the morale factor, which as you know is unfavorable for them. I am speaking of local wars in which atomic weapons are not used, only classical artillery and close-combat weapons. Then you will see for yourselves the morale level of the Soviet soldiers and officers. The war should last three or four months somewhere, like the one there was in the Far East in the last decade.* Blood must be spilled. Somehow the U.S.S.R. must be weakened materially. It is good that Khrushchev sticks his neck out. Let him help Castro more. Right now Castro has almost used up his supplies. Let Khrushchev give more—a lot more. Of course, I would not have permitted him to deliver those arms. I am not the president, but I am an intelligence officer and I have a little experience.[65]

You must excuse me for passing judgment on such large questions, but I feel myself to be free. I am in the Free World. It is necessary somehow to drain their energy, to divert the great material and living strength of the Soviet Union but not to bring about a world conflict. I wrote all this down once and I am repeating it. I think it is necessary to have meetings, secretly conducted—not summit meetings, which Khrushchev welcomes. He will try to use the decisions reached at summit meetings to his own advantage and increase his own prestige vis-à-vis the U.S. and England. This you understand very well. It is necessary to call together all the leaders of the Free World and to coordinate their unity and the material sacrifices they must make in the name of common victory.[66]

If this is not done, there will be a great disaster. Khrushchev and the General Staff can leave you behind. He is throwing together these missiles and he can do terrible damage with them. In my estimation, and according to powerful people in the leadership, he will need two or three more years. But not longer, gentlemen, not longer, believe me.[67]

* Penkovsky was referring to the Korean War, June 1950 to July 1953.

Kisevalter and Bulik looked at each other with satisfaction. Shergold and Stokes were wide-eyed but tried to mask their excitement. Penkovsky had presented them with a staggering thesis, and they would have to sort out the facts from his own opinions and conclusions. Then the team would present its own assessment for their superiors at CIA and MI6. This was the kind of information that would be passed to the president and the prime minister when it had been prepared in a formal report, sourced to a senior Soviet military officer. It would go through the new system arranged to keep Penkovsky's information in a tight, high-level circle of officials who needed to know about Soviet strategic thinking and intentions.

In the meantime, however, there was a long list of requirements to go through. Shergold presented Penkovsky with a pile of photographs of KGB and GRU officers to identify. MI6 officers and CIA personnel assigned to keeping tabs on Soviet diplomatic personnel at Soviet embassies and consulates around the world had taken the pictures or acquired them from friendly intelligence agencies. When he started to peruse the photographs, Penkovsky looked up; suddenly he had a thought and announced that "the first secretary of the Afghan Embassy is an active agent, paid and everything."[68]

While he thumbed through the pictures he told the team, "It is very necessary to sharpen the weapons of the experienced, esteemed, long-established British Intelligence Service and of the militant young American Service—young when compared with the English—and, in general, the intelligence services of the whole world. Everything that can be done must be done to neutralize the illegals [undercover agents] the Soviet Union is planting; to reveal them and destroy them. This is a primary goal for the future."

"We agree completely," said Kisevalter.

"We are stealing from you. We buy up clean documents and all forms; for instance, materials for passports for illegals to settle into organized work."[69] Penkovsky suggested that a metal wire be inserted in passport paper so it could be detected as genuine or false, and thus prevent illegals from being given forged passports.

The meeting ended after midnight. Penkovsky had to be up early to travel to Birmingham to visit British steel factories. Now he would begin his work for the GRU, spying on the latest British technology—with the help of the CIA and MI6.

Trading Secrets

BY APRIL 27, 1961, PENKOVSKY AND HIS DELEGATION WERE HARD AT work in Birmingham studying British steel manufacturing. Penkovsky had been directed by the GRU to find out all he could about high-temperature-resistant steels that could be used in missiles. Although the British stopped short of providing exact formulas and processing details, enough information was released so that the GRU and the State Committee would be convinced of Penkovsky's value and he would be permitted to travel abroad again. After a full day of meetings and observation of production lines, Penkovsky had an early dinner with his group and excused himself to retire early. Instead of going to bed, at 9 P.M. he went to the lobby of the Midland Hotel in Birmingham, where Kisevalter was waiting for him. They acknowledged each other with eye contact and Penkovsky followed Kisevalter to the hotel room where the four-man Anglo-American intelligence team was waiting.

The group greeted Penkovsky warmly and Kisevalter told him that the team had been considering his request to be introduced to a senior official—before leaving London Penkovsky had told the team he wanted to meet "an important man." Only the previous week, Soviet cosmonaut Yuri Gagarin had been introduced to Queen Elizabeth. "Has he done more for you?" asked Penkovsky, pressing to meet the queen. He wanted praise and reassurance that his information was reaching senior decision-makers. His ambition and a burning desire to be the center of attention were never far beneath the surface.

"Tell us what you yourself have in mind; obtaining such a person is no problem for us," said Kisevalter. "However, you know yourself that prominent people who give commands do not all understand secrecy as we do. The fewer people who know about you, the more secure things are. But we can do it, nevertheless."

"I will try to explain to you," said Penkovsky. "We are meeting today for the seventh time. I calculated we have now worked together for a total of twenty-five hours. That is a long day, during which we have sat without sleeping, eating, or going anywhere. I feel that we are on the same wavelength, meeting for the solution of great and important matters. I am glad that you so deeply examine and understand me, and that I find myself in such trustworthy hands. This inspires me.[1]

"I consider that I am not just some sort of agent. No, I am your citizen. I am your soldier. I did not come to you to do little things. In spite of my hatred and contempt for corrupted Leninism, if I did not have sufficient clandestine capabilities I would not have come with definite demands. Believe me. I consider that I have such unusual and special capabilities and accessibilities for agent work that I shall be able to prove this by helping my queen and president as a front-line soldier." Penkovsky spoke in a highly emotional tone. He was flushed with self-praise and passionate with desire to prove his worth to the team, who sat quietly listening to him.[2]

"Now I enter with you on the second half of my stay in Great Britain. I have realistically assessed everything that I have done in the past year. I consider that I am not contributing just one little grain but maybe a larger grain for our common cause. However, your frequent prompting is invaluable to me.

"After every meeting with you now, my brain works to contrive new things. I am now an inventor developing the possibilities open to me. I want you to test me again; to try me out on important matters, on any task which is within my capabilities to accomplish, using my education and my training." Penkovsky's voice rose to the point where Kisevalter had to interrupt and warn him to speak quietly so he would not be overheard.

"I reject that you do not believe me. You are already my dear friends, my comrades-in-arms. But perhaps somebody who cannot look into my eyes like you, will say, 'He copies all this about rockets out of *Pravda.*' "

Penkovsky was struggling to strengthen his relationship with the team and to reassure himself that they understood and trusted him. The risks he was taking and would undertake when he returned to Moscow were daunting. Was he seeking a new surrogate father in Bulik and the team? CIA psychiatrists have noted that it is a characteristic of defectors who have either lost their fathers early in their lives or have grown up estranged from them to be in search of a new father or authority figure. Although Marshal Varentsov appeared to be that figure in his life, Penkovsky was prepared to betray him because he saw his career at a dead end—due ironically to who his father had been. Varentsov, his surrogate father, had also failed him because Penkovsky had not been promoted to general. Had he been recognized and promoted to general after twenty years as a colonel, it is difficult to imagine Penkovsky turning to the West to fulfill his sense of destiny.

"You must understand me correctly," implored Penkovsky. "I am a mature human being approaching fifty, as are you. Maybe Mikhail [Stokes] and Joseph [Bulik] are younger in age, but perhaps in experience they are older than me. I cannot say."

"Thank you," said Joe Bulik with a smile.[3]

"If the governments which I now serve value my effort, carried out under conditions of exceptional danger, and of definite self-sacrifice, believe me . . ." Penkovsky paused in the middle of his thought without completing it, then continued:[4]

If there is real value in what I have done already, if you believe in my great possibilities and want me to be useful to the end—if I am not just an ordinary run-of-the-mill person for you, your superiors, and for your government—then attention from above to me would demonstrate an appreciation of my work. May God grant it.[5]

If you consider that I am just mediocre, then I too will reach this conclusion. I asked you to reward Wynne, to give him money. Already a week has passed and you have said nothing. I shall soon be going away. Will you give him money or not? Wynne needs the money; Wynne has done everything to bring us together so that I can fulfill my life's mission with you. If you consider my opportunities, tasks, ideas, abilities are small, you should say to me; 'Keep silent. Be more modest. Be quiet. You know you think a lot of yourself.'[6]

But I want to do such great things—so that I will be your Number One—for your governments, for your high commands, and for the human goal, the battle against Communism. You already love me in your way as a friend and as a comrade. You believe me. But all the others, those who direct things, are not here. May God grant that you can convey to them all my wishes and abilities. You understand my rebellious nature. You know that I am an unusual, energetic person. I feel that you are still taking my measure, still studying me. Perhaps there is some contradiction about me in your eyes; if so, tell me. Perhaps I can clear it up, because I believe in my power and abilities and in the truth with a capital T.

In the light of this I ask you to evaluate me before my departure on either the 2nd or the 6th of May. When I decided to come to you,

I did not think all this out lightly. I ask you to understand me, evaluate me correctly, and believe in me. Give me as quickly as possible an extremely difficult mission so that I can fulfill it. Perhaps then you will evaluate me differently. I want you to use me only for big things.[7]

Kisevalter tried to break in and speak, but Penkovsky would not let him. "Just a minute," Penkovsky said.

I will finish shortly. If the American students [Cox and Cobb] who helped me did something worthwhile, reward them. This is an indication that you value me. If you do nothing for them—or just a little—well, then I am also only a little item for you, now and in the future.

For me, the measure of your attitude will be the way in which the government assesses those two young Americans, Wynne, and yourselves. You can ask what business is it of mine how the government regards them and us? But it is not a matter of indifference to me how the work that you have put into our collaboration, for the good of the common cause, will be assessed. May God grant material fortune and well-being. I only want to work on large principles, serious principles, and let them be dangerous ones. I am sure that if I were to perish, if anything should happen to me, you would not forget my daughter, my mother, and my wife. You know my suggestions about this and you would contrive something and not leave them in need.[8]

Penkovsky had now spoken for more than ten minutes. The team allowed him to continue because mixed with the obsessive self-aggrandizing were important revelations about reduced military pay scales and the deteriorating quality of life in the Soviet Union, which contrasted sharply to Khrushchev's claims.

You know that in the Soviet Union the material side of life presses hard on everyone. Even a minister who receives 1200 to 1800 rubles a month [$1080 to $1620]—if he has not saved something, and if they get something on him and he is driven out of work and he uses it up or drinks it away and has debts to pay or something else—after that he just drags his life out.

The minimum living wage of socialism is not established and what sort of wage is it? It is really a gray and hungry life—believe me. I live under Communism myself. One must think of the people—the foolish Russian people. The Russian people are fools—they are good and fine—but foolish. They easily allow themselves to be enslaved. They endure continuously—perhaps there will be something better tomorrow, perhaps the next day. Thank God that there is bread and salt, because that is all there is.[9]

The people are fools who cannot organize themselves. But if we can establish conditions under which the KGB cannot shoot them in the head from behind, then people will say that they have suffered enough and have been deceived too long. That is how Lenin came forward with such a jump in 1917. The tsar took completely wrong attitudes to many of the people's questions. If there had been a more clever tsar there would have been no revolution.

Listen, I can tell you all kinds of things. With us in the seventh basement where the KGB sits, there are chambers where Russians—prominent people, patriots, wise people—were exposed to rats. I was told this by a man who knows, the former assistant commander of the Moscow Military District. I have all his details. There is one special room which is completely glazed. Anyone who cannot be broken or who will not say what they want him to say, or who will not sign something, is put in the middle of this room. There are pipes leading into it made up of clear plastic. Through these—there is no exit above or below—they release dozens of rats which run around the man. Through a microphone they say, "Well, now, will you say with whom you are working?" If the man does not confess or says, "I will not tell you who I was working with," they open a valve, which releases a single rat. The rat, which has not eaten for several days, begins to run around and to bite the man. They let in two or three more. It is terrible. People have gone out of their minds. When they have got what they want, they turn on water under high pressure and the rats are chased away, back to their cages. The Russian people have been tortured and shot. Everybody knows this.[10]

Khrushchev can see that if in addition to this gray, half-starving existence is added the further horror of imprisonment or execution as it was in Stalin's time—but of course, Stalin had support all around—then the people might really say, "The hell with it!" This is why he is giving little inducements. For instance, he gave a general amnesty for those who were chewed up by rats; to those shot, for their families, he gave pensions—not very large—but they get something. Or he rehabilitated their names so that their sons or daughters would not have to put down that their father was imprisoned as an enemy of the people. This would immediately incriminate them from the start.[11] [Penkovsky's own situation was not too different.]

I wanted to make a declaration. You have worked with me exactly a week. I beg you—and I will be only grateful to you if you will tell me—"You know, Penkovsky, everything is not as you judge it. Your material is mediocre and we really don't want to use you; not in the various ways you have suggested. So take it easy. The whole thing does not appear in the same grandiose light as you think." I have offered my ideas to you [to plant small atomic bombs at key military staff locations in Moscow]. If you consider them suitable, then I ask you to develop the plan and give me support and security so that I can execute it. Tell me, "You will arrive on the 6th, and on the 15th you have to blow up the KGB." At eleven o'clock in the morning on the 15th the KGB will cease to exist. Just give me the means to do this and there will be no KGB. Now I am finished with what I have to say.

Penkovsky's intensity was awesome. The team of professional case officers, while deeply impressed, were careful to reassure him but still leave him on edge. Their job was not to get involved with his schemes, but to use him to provide the intelligence information American and British decision-makers needed to understand Soviet military capabilities and intentions. Control of an agent is the key to effective use.

Kisevalter responded in Russian to Penkovsky on behalf of the team. "On certain points we can give you answers right away. In the first place, we trust you; in the second place, we wanted to find out why you desire this meeting with a high-level official. This will be done. In the third place, we want you to be perfectly at ease about Wynne. We are going back to London and everything will be done properly."

Penkovsky, who was smoking a cigarette, interrupted Kisevalter to say of Wynne, "He's really a wonderful guy. I am very much taken with him." He praised the arrangements and hospitality that Wynne provided for his group and noted how well he handled everything.

Kisevalter agreed. "We are aware of all this, but while he is running back and forth between you and the representatives of the companies you are visiting, it's impossible to tear him away, in any sense of the word, even for two or three hours. When he comes to London everything will be taken care of properly."[12]

"Well," said Penkovsky, "I'm closing my testament with this. I want you to trust me completely, one hundred percent. In order to gain this, I want and demand that you give me an assignment that will guarantee me full recognition. If at present you trust me ninety-five percent, this is not enough for me. Ninety-nine percent is not enough; I want one hundred percent or nothing—or kill me."

Kisevalter asked, "How about a hundred and five percent?" His forced attempt to break Penkovsky's mood with gentle humor did not work and the intense Russian bored in again—

Please understand me correctly, because we don't have much time. We have to make concrete decisions.[13] My next point. I want you to advise me on the priority sequence of all my assignments. What you direct will be my orders. Here is my idea of what I'm supposed to do when I get to Moscow. First: the working out of what we discussed in connection with strategic targets. I'll make an outline with dimensions. On each separate sheet of paper I'll repeat again data about the General Staff because the other data is abbreviated and possibly there may be a few inaccuracies. At that time I was working at high speed. This time I'll be doing it thoroughly. I will give the logical and most suitable places for placing a small atomic weapon, for the purpose of blowing up the targets when it is necessary. This is the first thing to work out. I will take it upon myself to designate the targets in Moscow and put the entire thing into action. If you say that this is too much for me to do, please give me another order.[14]

Secondly, I'll be working—and since working with you I understand it even better—to collect all available materials on illegal intelligence operations. Cases that are SOV-SEKRETNO [Top Secret] will go under a special category. Perhaps in this theoretical part we will find some principles of operations against which we can apply preventive measures. This is how I see it. Of course I do not promise you that I will get you the entire *agentura* [control center, in this case of a network of agents].[15]

Kisevalter agreed. "This will be a slow process and will take a lot of scrutiny."
Penkovsky continued:

I feel that this is a very important and big part of the work, because the basic threat to us comes from the direction of the *nelegaly*, the illegals. I want to repeat that there is one task that confronts the illegals, including myself. The entire Strategic Intelligence Staff has the basic mission to warn the Supreme Command, the Central Committee, and the Presidium about H-hour—the start of an attack by the Free World. Our primary mission is to warn the command of the beginning of a war, even a few minutes beforehand. For this purpose tremendous resources are being developed.

I stressed the importance of this point when I told you the meaning of Signals Intelligence [interception of radio, telephone, and telegraph communications]. It is carried on here in England, in the U.S., everywhere. This is their bread, because the number of agents is sparse and there are not many valuable agents. Whatever is picked up can be recorded just as it is. With the help of these interception points, the rest of the radio stations, which are normal transmitting stations, can send signals to intelligence centers at military command posts. An attack alarm signal is already worked out. If an attack is imminent, a signal is sent and sealed envelope number 1

137

is opened at the intelligence center by the duty officer. It contains instructions on how to respond to an attack. The warning signal, of course, goes to Moscow, relayed by all possible duplicate means of communication.

In summing up his mission, Penkovsky stressed that he felt his primary task was to alert the United States and Great Britain in case of a Soviet attack. Early warning of a Western attack was the primary mission of the GRU, and Penkovsky was determined to provide the same early warning to the West. His other assignments were to break down the organizational structure of the GRU and to provide information on the channels through which the GRU accomplished its espionage activities, such as Signals Intelligence and illegal or legal *Rezidentura* (intelligence stations). A legal *Rezidentura* is so designated because its officers operate under the cover of an embassy section or trade representative's office but not under the office of the military attaché. Illegals have no such diplomatic or official government organization cover, but function totally on their own with false documentation.[16]

It is very important for you to know all the methods used to train an intelligence officer in his work. I will collect all their lectures on intelligence and operational-tactical matters. The doctrines also contain important operational information. They have the troop density calculated for each kilometer of the front. They explain how many of each type of weapon are needed and the number of troops to man them. All these lectures I will get for you.

As for Technical Intelligence—with which I am directly connected—that is all in my hands. I can get you a suitcase of this material. We were given 150 intelligence requirements. For 1961 these were sent as requirement missions to the United States in all fields of industry, manufacturing, and agriculture and then duplicated to all countries. I have thirty intelligence requirements specifically for Canada. Scientists assign them and then they are all gathered together in the State Committee. In the field of agriculture there is even a requirement—it does not seem to work for us—on how to grow vegetables without soil in water and chemicals. It's some sort of discovery. The requirement is to determine what the components are.* You see, even these assignments are performed by Intelligence—and we think that we can divorce politics from Intelligence! We can't![17]

---

* Penkovsky was referring to hydroponics, a science the Soviets hoped to develop. After his forced retirement in 1964, Nikita Khrushchev experimented with growing vegetables using only water and mineral solutions.

"Why are copies of the 150 requirements sent to all the other capitalist countries?" he explained in response to a question. "Because there is much of the British and American technology in the other countries of the world. If you can't get into the U.S. and you can't get into England—then clear up the question in Germany.[18]

"I must warn you through all channels available to me if, God forbid, they decide on some adventure. As for the countermeasures to prevent an attack, that will be for the command and the government to decide. We won't have enough brains for that!"[19]

Kisevalter asked Penkovsky to provide special manuals and lectures from the *Sekretny Fond*, the Secret Collection of Marshal Varentsov's artillery library, which contained highly classified materials with restricted access. "They will show us not only the philosophy, but any change in the doctrine regarding the use of atomic weapons," he said.[20] Then Kisevalter lifted a glass of white wine and proposed a toast to Penkovsky's health. The team raised their glasses and drank to the Russian.

"Thank you. I am quite well. It will be sad for us to part. Let there be no day in which you will not think of me, or I will not think of you, even for a moment. Not only when you receive the material from me, but anytime," Penkovsky said.

"Of course, certainly," replied Kisevalter.

"It's after one A.M.," Bulik interjected. The team had spent more than four hours with Penkovsky.

"All right, tomorrow we meet at nine o'clock, right?" Penkovsky said. Then he reviewed the list of purchases he had to make for his wife. "I need to buy a light coat, red with white buttons. They take advantage of me. She likes to dress well and of course I spoil her. I'm going to such a 'wealthy' country—what am I going to do, bring her a little blouse? I'm going to have to scurry around and look. My program is here, I've given you all the papers. Right? So, tomorrow at nine P.M. or earlier."

"It can be earlier," suggested Bulik.

"Let's say eight-thirty," added Kisevalter.

"Fine, tomorrow we'll work some more. Good night. Until tomorrow." The meeting ended at 1:05 A.M. on April 28.

When he returned to London the following day, Penkovsky called the Soviet Embassy and learned that he and his delegation could extend their stay until May 6. He would have to report to the embassy to discuss the details. That evening at 9 he came to room 360 of the Mount Royal and told the team the good news. They settled down to explain how to use the Minox, small enough to fit in the palm of Penkovsky's hand. Kisevalter told Penkovsky not to be concerned about inadvertently getting himself in any picture when practicing with it: "The man who develops the film works for us and we have the negative."

Then came a full debriefing on the requirements list drawn up for the team by Leonard McCoy. McCoy, an expert on Soviet missilery, never met Penkovsky, but he played a vital role in defining the questions that were put to him by Kisevalter and the team. The British were so favorably impressed that they dropped their own requirements officer from the group and relied on McCoy to prime the pump for Penkovsky.

The meeting again lasted until after 1 A.M. and included full discussions of GRU tradecraft and the use of aliases. Penkovsky dropped tantalizing tidbits from his conversations with Marshal Varentsov, the Soviet Army ground forces rocket commander, who he said had told him that the solid fuel used in Soviet missiles was not reliable and that Khrushchev had lied and overstated the range of Soviet missiles.[21]

Penkovsky's days in London were spent with his Soviet delegation in meetings with British Trade Board officials and business executives. There was time for sightseeing and shopping with Wynne. Penkovsky's energy never flagged, and he even found time to take dancing lessons; he wanted to learn the Twist. Wynne took him to see a revival of *Roman Holiday*, the 1953 movie starring Audrey Hepburn and Gregory Peck. Penkovsky fell in love with Audrey and told the team he wanted to meet her someday.

Wynne was a man with a bluff, open personality and a zest for good living. His thin, carefully trimmed moustache gave him a slightly officious air, but it was only a front. He was easily offended and bristled when he thought he was not being taken seriously. Wynne was in his element drinking beer with the boys. He was a fine organizer and delighted in getting things arranged—in that sense he had fulfilled his destiny in bringing Penkovsky to the West. He responded to Penkovsky's enthusiasm and together they explored the pleasures of London.

Surprising sides of Penkovsky's character emerged, including his desire to stop and pray at the Brompton Oratory, the domed Italian renaissance–style church with marble and gilded altar ornaments, on the Brompton Road in Kensington. He returned to the Mount Royal Hotel in the evening for his ninth meeting with the team.

On Sunday, April 30, Penkovsky spent the day sightseeing with his delegation. The itinerary included Windsor Castle, which he was particularly excited to see, given his fantasy of one day meeting the queen. Penkovsky arrived at room 360 in the Mount Royal at five minutes after eight that evening for the tenth meeting. He quickly turned to business and told the team that when he returned to Moscow on May 6, he would ring a phone number that they should give him so that he could report his safe arrival. "I will ring at a designated hour. Just let the phone ring—say three times—and do not pick up the receiver. This will signify that all is in order. If I ring more than three times, that will signify that something is not in order and I will attempt to advise you in some other way if I can. For example, if things are not in order it means there is surveillance of some sort on me."

Kisevalter assured Penkovsky that he would be provided with a telephone number and a time to call it before his departure. Penkovsky added, "Things can be worked out simply; if I do not get everything from you prior to my departure, or if Wynne can't bring it, anyone speaking Russian, man or woman, could call me from a phone booth and say something irrelevant." Penkovsky meant that there would be a prearranged code so that the "irrelevant" phrase would signal a meeting or loading of the dead drop.

"Yes," replied Kisevalter, "but the point is that we do not wish to cut in unnecessary people to know about you."

"I understand this and am grateful to you for this."[22]

They spent much of the meeting discussing coded radio transmissions and how to use one-time cipher pads.

On Monday, Penkovsky said he would not go with the delegation but instead would visit the Soviet Embassy to arrange for money for their extended stay. "I will go shopping with Wynne first. My delegation members are all very happy. They will be able to buy all sorts of junk with the money they saved on their per diem, since they were fed everywhere. I'll meet them at three or four o'clock. They are happy with me since they feel I have organized everything well for them personally. There hasn't been one word of criticism to date. I even told them that if they write good reports on their work here and do good work they will come with me again in October. I told them I would also write a favorable report and they are all happy."[23]

Penkovsky was surprised at the access the British gave to his delegation. "Your people are not shown our [Soviet] factories of any significance," he continued. "Only certain carefully selected ones are offered for inspection," he said, pointing out that transportation to the few open factory sites was restricted to train travel "since too many antiaircraft installations can be seen from the highway. They show very little or things of little interest. Why do you not restrict our delegations? Of course, not the ones which I lead." Everybody laughed, and Penkovsky added, "Seriously, you should restrict them. The Americans are already doing this on a reciprocal basis only."[24]

Penkovsky speculated that one member of his delegation was co-opted to work for the KGB. "His mission is primarily political intelligence, although they do have a secondary mission of general intelligence. Of course they report on all others of the Soviet delegation. For example, last December when I invited Wynne to a reception, I also invited some of our specialists. Since the food and drink were free, they got drunk. The KGB report said that those specialists should not be invited again since they don't know how to behave before foreigners."[25] Penkovsky had been told about this from Evgeny Levine, a KGB colonel posted to the State Committee.

"I will send you an organizational chart of the State Committee and a classified telephone directory, which I can get with ease. There you will find the full names and telephone numbers of all the members. In addition, I have locked up in the right-hand drawer of my desk at home reports of all my agent material [the reports, manuals, and notes he had copied by hand]. I would have brought it this time but I was afraid to. I knew it would not fit into my pocket. I wouldn't like to entrust it to a suitcase. I thought that even though customs would never search me unless I was under suspicion, it is possible that they may request to see the contents of my suitcase. To date, that has not been done, since they know that I am a colonel. If they ever did, I'd have to run to one embassy or the other. I don't know which one," said Penkovsky with a smile.

"I suggest you run to the nearest one," said Kisevalter, attempting a bit of black humor.

Penkovsky remarked that before the West "accepted" him, it had irritated him to realize that he lived on the same street as the British Embassy and his office was quite near the American Embassy. "I sat across from the U.S. Embassy but nobody would walk out to whom I could give my material."[26]

Penkovsky wrote out in his own handwriting which medicines he needed to take back to Moscow for his high-ranking friends. Kisevalter assured him that in translating his requests, security would be maintained. Penkovsky handed over the list of the medicines and prescriptions, including a request for Sustanon, a drug to increase male potency, for Marshal Varentsov.[27]

The team's eleventh meeting with Penkovsky was held on Monday, May 1, in room 360 of the Mount Royal Hotel at 3:02 P.M. On the cocktail table were the medicines Penkovsky had ordered. "These are your medicines, but we will change the labels so that no person's name appears on them," Kisevalter said.

"Why can't I simply say that I bought them at the pharmacy? Can't I say that?" asked Penkovsky.

"No, because it's a prescription," explained Kisevalter.

"And if I rip the whole label off?"

"No. We will take care of it by seeing that they are not mixed up and then give them to you," said Kisevalter, explaining that the labels would be "sanitized," with no reference to Penkovsky.

"Very well," said Penkovsky.

"But you must know which ones are the tranquilizers," said Kisevalter. The team and Penkovsky laughed.[28]

Penkovsky had come from the Soviet Embassy and told the team, "The new hard line America is taking toward Cuba has everyone talking at the embassy. They are alarmed by it. They say if America undertakes anything on her own, not using the Cuban exiles in the U.S., then we [the Soviet Union] will be in a difficult position. Why? Because we can only send food, weapons, and gold. There are no men. If we give them rockets there will be a war. I spoke to the counselor and people from the office of the military attaché. Their thinking is that the Americans will adopt a very severe course of action and we will be in a very difficult position because we will have to do something. Tomorrow I promise to find out something more about their report. I won't force [my contact]; it wouldn't be normal. But I will at least get a summary of the report."[29]

Changing the subject, Penkovsky said, "I want to report to you what I did yesterday. Mrs. Wynne and I went to Harrods, where we spent three hours."

Kisevalter and Mike Stokes broke into a grin and said, "Aha!" They were delighted that Penkovsky had seen the paragon of British department stores, near Hyde Park, with its lavish food halls, flowers, and wide range of high-quality items of clothing, furnishings, and accessories. To a Soviet starved for consumer goods, the choices offered in Harrods were overwhelming and exhausting.

"It was the best. I consider it right that Khrushchev was not taken there when he was in London. He didn't deserve it. He should look at gardens, singing birds, and fountains. I was sorry I couldn't take Varentsov with me; he would have bought all the roses."

Penkovsky's remarks on his mentor, Marshal Varentsov, drew laughter from the group, and he continued in the same vein. "I should have loaded up a car and sent it. We looked at everything.

Things are expensive there. Mrs. Wynne helped me greatly and I made a decision and bought her a suit for twenty-four pounds as a gift. She was delighted. Wynne has all the bills and receipts."

"We don't need the receipts," said Kisevalter.

"No? So that you can check?"

"Who cares if it's more or less?"

"It is just that one of your people might think that I took more pounds than necessary. I have three pounds left," sighed Penkovsky.

"You have three pounds left? That's good," said Shergold.

"I didn't buy much. I bought my wife a regular spring-autumn coat, a coat for my daughter, a suit for my wife—like the one I bought for Mrs. Wynne, the same price, quality, and light-green color. I bought one white blouse, bathing suit, and bathrobe for my daughter. I also bought two kerchiefs, two bottles of perfume, four lipsticks. I bought some after-shave lotion for myself. But things are expensive. Coats cost twenty-five to twenty-six pounds [$70–$72.80], suits twenty-four pounds [$67.20], a few other minor things and three pounds remain. Please take some money from my account and give it to me. I have not yet bought the watch or the ring, not a single pair of shoes or the purse for my mother."

"But you did get a sizable percentage of the things?" asked Kisevalter.

"Yes."

"At least in quantity," said Kisevalter.

"Wynne has everything. I did not bring anything here," Penkovsky said.[30]

Mrs. Wynne later recalled the shopping trip differently and insisted that Penkovsky never bought her a suit. "I would certainly recall trying one or more on and the embarrassment of having it paid for by him." She did recall clearly the coat for his daughter having to be modeled, amid laughter, by the assistant who was the right size. Mrs. Wynne said, "While I fully understand that Pen wanted to be liked and thought generous, I assure you that the only gifts I received from him were a small Russian lacquer box and a picture of a cat."[31]

The CIA expenses for the Penkovsky operation came to $40,000 in 1961, the equivalent of $174,800 in 1990.*[32]

Penkovsky proposed that Wynne carry the presents to Moscow,

---

* In 1961–1962 the Penkovsky operation cost $82,000, today's equivalent of $358,000. This included travel and per diem for the CIA officers, hotel cost, supplies and equipments including gifts, cameras, and custom signaling devices, write-offs of foreign currency and rental of vehicles.

adding that he would escort Wynne through customs with his official pass. He would get a car for Wynne driven by one of his friends. "I will drive him to the hotel. He will enter with his suitcase and mine will be left in the car."

"That's not too bad," agreed Shergold.

"It's all right, but we must check this out," said Kisevalter.[33]

"Thank you for worrying so much, but I will work well for another two to three years. Then I will run," said Penkovsky.

"So it would be better if you took less and Wynne took more?" asked Kisevalter.

"One suitcase will be taken by Wynne and one by me," said Penkovsky.[34]

Kisevalter handed Penkovsky 100 pounds [$280]. "You gave me 150 and now I get 100 more," said Penkovsky.

"That's 250 [$700]," said Kisevalter.

"Should I sign a receipt for this?" Penkovsky asked.

"You are our co-worker, not an agent. With agents you have receipts," said Kisevalter.

"We take receipts from agents," replied Penkovsky, referring to the Soviet procedure of getting signed receipts from agents both for accounting and blackmail purposes.

"For agents, yes, but you are in a different category," said Kisevalter.

"As long as you have reminded me of money, I would like to state my opinion and then we won't return to this subject. If you have a plan, I can flee unexpectedly with the family and leave everything, things worth many thousands of rubles. The hell with them. Let them choke on them. You consider my date of entry April 1, 1961, but I have been working for you much longer. My thoughts and opinions split away long ago, just to work with you. Many Soviets have the idea they would like to work for you. But ideas are nothing; it is only a bluff. Action is important. I started working a long time ago. Today it is two years since I finished those courses. Almost two years have passed and I have had that material in my pocket. I wanted to start working for you actively eight months ago. You know this very well.[35]

"Since there is this system of document evaluation, and it is important for me, I want to live well during the period that fate will have me live in the Free World."

"Of course," said Kisevalter. "We understand."

"I don't have diamonds—my father did not leave me anything in the English or American banks. I can defect to you in six to eight months, in a year. Two to three years would be better in order to do more with my position in the General Staff and my being stationed and working in Moscow. But it might happen that I will come to you earlier."

"Of course."

"I would like to request that all my materials be evaluated separately. How will you evaluate them? In any way you choose."

"Okay," agreed Kisevalter.

"Considering, of course, that I have already been given sums by you already."

"Of course, of course," said Kisevalter, putting him off and not wanting to get into the specifics of how Penkovsky's work and information would be valued in monetary terms.

"It has to be done very honestly. What one has earned is what one should have. A person's ability determines what he has in the Free World. The stupid one is the street cleaner; the smarter one has his little shop. That is the way it seems to me objectively. A person should get what he earns."

"Yes," said Kisevalter.[36]

"The work that I did in advance during this period I considered important. I strived for it. I attained it. I did everything I could regarding these matters. Now I will work on my new assignments and you will get reports from there. I will work actively in all ways and at a deeper level of comprehension. That is why I request—if you consider the material to be of no value or if it is only average, that is a different matter. However, if some of them have a certain value . . ." Penkovsky's voice dropped, leaving the suggestion that a dollar value be assigned to the documents he produced; he didn't want simply to be paid a retainer. "I recently read in the papers that an American paid one million dollars for a file of some sort in Brazil. That's what we heard. A million! Now you will receive from me the names of fifteen recruited agents who are working against you. This also has some value."

"Yes," said Kisevalter.

Knowledge of the agents would enable surveillance to be conducted against them to expose their sources and how they operated, thus revealing other spies. With the names of fifteen agents, the CIA and MI6 could mount a counterintelligence effort to compromise the Soviet agents and try to turn them to work in place for the West. While no specific monetary value was ever put on the names of the illegal agents, experts believe Penkovsky's information was worth a million dollars a name. Certainly, a good agent could cause at least that much damage from stolen communications secrets, military plans, or new technology.

146

"If I must come to you in eight months, then I will have $8000 in my account."

"No! No! This is not the way it works," insisted Kisevalter, trying to put off explaining to Penkovsky how much more he would get than the total of his $1000-per-month salary when he defected to the West. The team's psychological strategy was to keep Penkovsky hungry and dependent on them, but he was balking.

"This will not satisfy me. That is not enough. I'm telling you this," asserted Penkovsky.

"You don't understand," said Kisevalter.

"I am telling you honestly," said Penkovsky.

"Of course. We are talking about a general principle," explained Kisevalter, again stalling Penkovsky over how much he was to be paid. For the CIA and MI6 the $1000 a month was an initial commitment to be reviewed periodically as the relationship developed and the worth of the materials Penkovsky provided was evaluated. The team was not ready to revise its evaluation at this point.[37]

"I thought this through deeply today when I prepared this. You are working with me now, but in a year or two you [people] may get a promotion. New people, whom I don't know, will contact me. They won't know me or will only know about me from what you tell them. This is just an example—suppose you get a promotion at work," said Penkovsky by way of explanation.

Shergold interjected to say, "I think you better tell him that while this goes on we shall stay."

"We will be working with you permanently," said Kisevalter.

"And if you get a high position?"

"No, that won't happen," insisted Kisevalter.

"Then I will have to start proving everything again."

"No, no," argued Kisevalter.

"We have become acquainted. I confessed everything to you as one should," Penkovsky said with frustration in his voice.

"We understand your predicament, and we both vouch that we will work with you permanently," Kisevalter reassured him.

"Thank you," said Penkovsky.[38] "Now the last thing—despite the greed of Khrushchev, we are very limited in our payments to persons who help us. If I ever got something of value for you about rockets, please pay the persons who have helped me. That is all that I will say about the subject. I came to you because of political conviction. I started working for you in Turkey. Check all the files for my anonymous phone calls against [the assistant Soviet military attaché] Ionchenko, against the military attaché, General Rubenko, and against the régime. Was I not ready morally? Yes, I was."

"All this will be considered," said Kisevalter.[39]

"Later, when I knew everything that was happening in the Kremlin, I went out toward the Balchug Hotel. For some reason I was drawn there. I had the inclination to approach the West. I knew foreign tourists who were staying there. I thought I would stop them and tell them what was happening in the Kremlin. What a struggle was going on."

"You can be sure," said Kisevalter, "that everything that happened will be taken into account."[40]

"When I come over to you, I would like to live decently. Will I have the right to live my last years in such a manner?"

"What is even more important, you will have a financial base with which to provide yourself with a house, car, and other things. You will have good, honest, and worthwhile work with us," said Kisevalter.

"I will give all my strength to this, all my faith. If you have this system of payment, then consider that I have worked actively for two years. Then allocate my earnings for two years at the monthly rate. If I had savings in the bank, I would say that I don't need anything," replied Penkovsky. "This is secondary to me, believe me, but I also have to provide for my family and myself. All I'm concerned with is whether I shall be able to do that for them."

"I understand and sympathize with your views," said Kisevalter.

"I want to earn this. I don't want a gift. Don't say that Penkovsky is a good person, let's give him whatever he needs. I want to earn what I get."

Shergold agreed. "Very well."

"I did not say to you—'Here is one rocket, two. This is a code. This is something else.' I gave everything. I am willing to work with my heart, soul, head, health, and strength."

Eager to reassure Penkovsky, but even more anxious not to make a commitment to him, together, the team responded, "We understand your views."

"I am thinking of my future. You are very nice while talking to me, but maybe you won't be here. That is what I am afraid of; maybe you will be transferred."

"No. This will not happen. Never!" insisted Shergold.

"This will not be," repeated Kisevalter.

"Then I will not detain you. I will go to dinner. Do you regard me well now?" asked Penkovsky.

"Yes," said Kisevalter.

"I swear by my mother, child, and conscience, by my brain and my heart, that you will have an even higher opinion of me, about ten times higher."

"Then you will be here at 2100 hours."

"Yes, and we shall work. I am not saying goodbye." Penkovsky left at 3:45 P.M.[41]

That same evening, at 9:12, Penkovsky returned to room 360 at the Mount Royal for his twelfth meeting with the Anglo-American team. "Well, shall I work some more to celebrate the first of May?" Penkovsky quipped, and the group laughed at his reference to the International Workers' Holiday, celebrated in Moscow with a parade and display of military equipment in Red Square. "In the Kremlin on May 1, they invite the cream of the crop. The same ones are invited all the time, the ministers and their wives, the Party hierarchy, the marshals and one or two workers from the plants."[42]

Penkovsky quickly shifted back to business. "I have all this information on our equipment. Of course there are many new secret ones there. It is in my workbook, where I have military notes written down."

"Where is your notebook? In the GRU?" Kisevalter asked.

"In my desk at home. That is my workbook on military matters, strategic directions. If it should be found it would be bad for me."

"Of course," said Kisevalter.

"My desk is locked and I have the key with me in London."

"Don't lose it," said Kisevalter.[43]

They moved down the requirements list and Kisevalter focused on Soviet missiles in East Germany.

"There are two separate underground atomic stockpiles on GDR territory. I know this exactly, like two plus two equals four, two stockpiles, two locations. I don't know how many warheads there are in each, but of course it's not one or two. They are held in reserve. The command will be given from the Presidium, from the commander in chief. There is a roundheaded commander in chief, without a single hair on his head, or anything in his head," said Penkovsky, referring to the bald Nikita Khrushchev and drawing a laugh from the team while they took notes and savored the revelation on the atomic stockpiles. Penkovsky's report would be added to the Agency's estimate of Soviet nuclear capacity in East Germany and passed to the Pentagon for use in current intelligence estimates of the Soviet order of battle in Germany.

"From him [Khrushchev] to the GDR [East Germany], that's it. Similar stockpiling exists on Soviet territory," said Penkovsky.[44]

"Who is in charge of this stockpiling?" asked Kisevalter.

"I'm telling you, Zhdanov [Colonel General N. N. Zhdanov, chief of the Main Directorate of Artillery]."

"The materials and the bombs?" asked Kisevalter.

149

"He is in charge of the warheads and the bombs. But they are not armed."

"So he controls the bombs also?"

"Of course, that is part of the equipment."

"What exactly does he control?"

He controls the safekeeping, the technical supervision, the maintenance, the technical engineering control. He is in charge of how stockpiling is conducted. Is there any radiation? Is there deterioration of material from the engineering standpoint? That is Zhdanov's responsibility. To issue [nuclear weapons] to someone in a brigade, because he wants them, is prohibited. Only the defense minister can do this. The minister is told by the Central Committee. The minister will act through Moskalenko, who heads the rocket and missile forces. What concerns the ground rocket troops will be through Varentsov. Zhdanov's dumps are controlled by the KGB. Zhdanov has "neighbors" [GRU slang for the KGB] sitting all around him. The security of these atomic installations is maintained by divisions of KGB Special Purpose troops.[45] That is the structure. No one can do anything independently. Varentsov can't demand even a single bomb for use in maneuvers. No. It has to originate in the Central Committee.[46]

The meeting ended at 1 A.M., and Penkovsky said he would be busy the following evening. "After talking with you earlier, I saw Wynne and he invited me to a nightclub tomorrow night—with your permission." They laughed. "Wynne said, 'Very expensive,' but that is okay. One should go to a big nightclub once," rationalized Penkovsky.

"Of course," said Kisevalter, ever the patient, unobtrusive case officer. With his pleasant manner, Kisevalter masked his acute memory and his persistent goal, to enlarge the CIA's portrait of GRU operations, his specialty. His engineering background gave Kisevalter a special feel for Soviet missile developments. He was careful not to display emotion and set off Penkovsky's volatile, tripwire personality.

"And you are not going to take us with you?" asked Bulik, drawing a laugh from the team.

"If you like, of course," replied Penkovsky, at first not sure if Bulik was serious or joking.[47] Then, realizing that to be seen in public with anybody on the team would be compromising, he said goodnight and walked up the stairs to the special room that he had requested on the fifth floor.

Meeting a Cabaret Girl and "C"

ON THE EVENING OF MAY 2, PENKOVSKY WENT TO A NIGHTCLUB WITH Wynne instead of meeting with the team. The next day he showed up at the Mount Royal Hotel shortly after 1 P.M. for a brief meeting, their thirteenth. Penkovsky told the team about his evening at the cabaret and his encounter with a woman hired for him by Wynne. "I can give you her telephone number. First we went to one club, then to the cabaret. The show started at one o'clock in the morning with very nice, classical music in the Turkish style, as if to order. They picked up a twenty-three-year-old girl for me at the club—a good girl. She has a pretty name—Zeph. Here is her telephone number. Now everybody knows it." The team laughed and Penkovsky said, "I spent two hours with her. I had to get some sleep. At eight o'clock this morning I had already eaten my breakfast."

"Were you at her place?" asked Kisevalter.

"Yes, I was at her home. She has her own apartment. Everything was modest, but good. Her place is bigger than mine in Moscow. I don't have such a nice one! The rooms are small but all the conveniences are there. She was a nice girl, somewhat experienced in her line of work, but that was okay. I spent two hours with her. It was getting light when I left."

"The phone number was what? Once more," said Shergold.

Everybody laughed again.

"Did she charge you much?" asked Kisevalter.

"Wynne said she wanted fifteen pounds [$42]. I gave the money to him. He gave it to her and asked her not to ask me for more. She didn't ask me for a penny more. She was told that I was Alex from Belgrade, Yugoslavia. We had a good table. Everything was fine."

"One more question," interjected Kisevalter. "Could there be any consequences because of the girl?"

"I don't think so. It is true that Wynne gave me a condom, but I—"

"This is important."

"Of course it is. I considered it. I came home and washed and everything. She was clean. I think she takes care of herself. Wynne guaranteed her, but at the same time he gave me a box of condoms."

When the team members laughed at him, Penkovsky said, "No. No. Everything is okay. I have a little experience. I am responsible."

"There is a proverb," said Kisevalter. "If one is unlucky—"

Penkovsky completed the line, "one can get gonorrhea from one's sister."

"That's it. You know the proverb," said Kisevalter.

"If anything happens I can get cured, there is nothing to fear, but I do not think there will be a problem.[1]

"I was up at seven, ate at eight, and at nine we went to the embassy. We received our [additional per diem] money. Then I went to the *rezident*'s office. I spoke alone with him for thirty minutes and told him all about my trip. I showed him my daily itinerary. I showed him the brochures you had given me. He had everything packaged up, called the code clerk in my presence, and sent it out."

Penkovsky was upset that he could not give the team the name of the GRU London Station chief. He did not know his name, and the professional code of behavior did not permit him to ask the *rezident* his name. "See what it means not to have shown me all the photographs," he complained. If he had seen the captioned photographs of Soviet intelligence officers the team had compiled, he might have been able match a picture to the man he was meeting and thus identify the GRU Station chief by name.[2] With that, Penkovsky dashed off and promised to return in the evening.

At 9:15 P.M. Penkovsky arrived in room 360 for his fourteenth meeting with Bulik, Kisevalter, Shergold, and Stokes. The Russian had taken some pictures with the Minox for practice, and the team critiqued his work. He had spent the early evening arranging a meeting between a British businessman and a GRU contact at the Soviet Embassy. This was part of his campaign, with the team's help, to win approval back home for his GRU intelligence work while in England.

Shergold asked, "Can we break off now and talk about what will occur shortly?"[3] Penkovsky settled down and concentrated on Shergold.

"Now listen attentively. In ten or fifteen minutes a high-ranking representative of the Ministry of Defence of Great Britain will come here. He is personally speaking for Lord Mountbatten, the minister of defence," Shergold said in his most official manner.*

"I know who he is," said Penkovsky.

"I don't know what he will have to say to you, but I want to go over with you what you will say," continued Shergold.

"I will say just a few words of thanks and appreciation and you will translate."

"It seems to me that it would be logical to go through in sequence, starting from the substance of the declaration which you yourself made in writing to us earlier, not word for word of course, but that would be a good start," suggested Shergold.

"I agree," said Penkovsky. "That is perfectly clear and logical."

"Then you can express your sincerity and your desires. I cannot predict what he will say, but he is fully knowledgeable of you. The most important thing for you is to realize that he is in a position to give you complete assurance for your future, for the promises given to you, and to confirm what we have told you," said Shergold.

"I thank you very much for all of this, but you will translate, will you not?" asked Penkovsky.

"Of course I will," said Kisevalter. "Just one thing—the slower you speak, the clearer everything will be for you."

"I understand."

"The man who is coming is called Sir Dick White," said Kisevalter, who did not explain that Sir Dick was head of MI6.†

"I will simply call him *Gospodin* [Mister]. I will be speaking Russian, after all," said Penkovsky, aware of the word's formal meaning of gentleman or master.[4]

Penkovsky returned to the role of Soviet intelligence officers in Great Britain. "Since you have already identified KGB persons here [in the Soviet Embassy], it would be a good idea to push this further. But don't bother the GRU. You will know all about them in the future, but don't touch them. You must take protective measures so that no repercussions will fall back on me through any action. But press against the KGB. Make it so tough that the *rezident* will be

* Shergold referred to Mountbatten as defence minister in order to stress Mountbatten's importance. Actually, Vice Admiral Lord Louis Mountbatten was appointed Chairman of the Chiefs of Staff Committee, the British equivalent of the American Chairman of the Joint Chiefs of Staff, in 1959 and held that post in 1961. A first cousin of Queen Elizabeth, Earl Mountbatten of Burma had had a distinguished career that included serving as Supreme Allied Commander South East Asia Command in World War II and as the last Viceroy of India. He was killed on his sailboat by an IRA bomb while vacationing in 1979.
† Sir Dick White, known by the ideogram "C," was the head of MI6, the British Secret Intelligence Service, from 1956 to 1968. Previously he was the head of MI5, the British internal security organization the American counterpart of which is the FBI.

153

removed. This will upset their activities considerably and before new people can arrive here and become oriented they will lose a great deal."[5]

The team noted the rivalry between the GRU and the KGB and how Penkovsky wanted to discredit the "neighbors."

There was a knock on the door and Sir Dick White entered the room escorted by a member of the debriefing team. His stocky build conveyed a quiet strength; his neatly combed, graying brown hair added a grace note of tradition and ease. He was self-assured but not overbearing. Sir Dick wore the mantle of command easily and Penkovsky, despite his nervousness, relaxed when he saw him. Shergold introduced Sir Dick to Penkovsky and to the team. Sir Dick spoke directly to Penkovsky. "Well, Colonel, the message I have to deliver to you is from Lord Mountbatten, the chief of the Defence Department of England." Then he stopped and asked Kisevalter to translate into Russian.

"First," Sir Dick continued, "Lord Mountbatten regrets very much that he cannot see you personally. He asked me to relay this message to you. 'I have been shown the oath of allegiance which you have made for the governments of Great Britain and the United States. I am filled with admiration for the great stand that you have taken, and we are mindful of the risks that you are running. I have also had reported to me the information which you have passed on to us. I can only tell you that it would be of the highest value and importance to the Free World.' "[6]

Penkovsky replied:

My dear sir, I am most grateful to Lord Mountbatten and to you for this attention that you are extending to me now. This attention on the part of the Lord and yourself is to me an indication of your recognition of me. I place myself under your banners in full consciousness. I have hoped for this for a long time. I did the best I could to prove my faithfulness, my devotion, and my readiness to fight under your banners until the end of my life. During the course of the past two weeks I have had the good fortune and the opportunity to consider many important matters together with the gentlemen present in this room. These matters were of a military, strategic, and political nature. I wish to state to you boldly and honestly that I will have sufficient strength and health and sufficient training of both a theoretical and practical nature in order to give meaning to my new missions and to execute them in the best manner possible for our Free World.

I wish to assure the Lord and yourself that very little time will pass before you will recognize me still further and even have an affection for me. Just recently I had the opportunity to discuss all of the

154

missions which are placed before me now and in the immediate future. I am sure that I will fulfill these missions well as a soldier should do. I swear to you as representative of your governments that I will accomplish this. I would also like to add and to express the great desire which I have carried in my soul and which I carry now—I even thought about this in Moscow—and that is to swear my fealty to my queen, Elizabeth II, and to the president of the United States, Mr. Kennedy, whom I am serving as their soldier. Although unfortunately due to circumstances, this is not possible now, I hope that in the future I will be blessed by this fortune personally by the queen.[7]

"Yes. Well, I would like to reply to that," said Sir Dick. "First, now that Colonel Penkovsky is going back to Russia, I beg that he proceed with caution in view of the great risk. But I want him to know that should the time come when he must leave Russia and make his home in the Western world, the obligations that we undoubtedly have toward him will be firmly and clearly fulfilled."

"It is clear to me and I thank you," said Penkovsky. "I would like to add two more words, if you will permit me. I request that you convey my gratitude to Lord Mountbatten, my gratitude for his attention, and I would like to thank you again for your attention. Please fulfill my request that the Lord at some convenient moment state to her Majesty, the queen, that her forces have been increased by one member—this colonel who is located in Moscow on the Soviet General Staff and who is fulfilling special assignments, but actually is a colonel in her Majesty's service. Furthermore, please say that I will serve exactly as instructed and that I am in very competent hands."

"Of that I feel sure," replied Sir Dick. "To meet you has been delightful."

White wine was poured and Sir Dick proposed a toast. "You have had many hours together to make this possible. Well now, we shall all drink to the colonel's health."

"Thank you for your attention and thank you for having brought me this very good fortune," replied Penkovsky.

"You understand English a little, do you?" asked Sir Dick.

"I know English, as one says, 'fifty-fifty' or less. You know I was in Turkey and I was assistant attaché. How do you say? 'Acting intelligence chief.' After this I had no opportunity to improve my English. I did not have practice. But I promise in the future I will improve."

Sir Dick smiled and added, "Now that you're a colonel in the United States Army, I think that this will be necessary."

"You will also have to learn American," joked Shergold.

155

"I can see that you have plenty of stamina to work so intensively and still be on your feet," said Sir Dick, complimenting Penkovsky.

"Yes, we have worked a great deal and I also had this delegation to take care of, with trips to make. We often worked until two o'clock in the morning. We had important matters to consider, and these matters were more important than worrying about one's health."[8]

"I would like Lord Mountbatten, Sir Dick White, and my controlling case officers, who are concerned about me and who will be receiving materials from me in the future—I wish all of you to know that I will serve to the very end in an honest, faithful manner and will be resolute to the end. That is my character and I am confident of my power to do so."

"That is the impression we have and we are strongly convinced of this," said Sir Dick.

"Thank you. I will attempt to justify your faith."

"I think that you have conveyed your desire very clearly to us and I think that we understand this clearly and entirely."

"It is very pleasant for me to hear these words and as a soldier I receive them willingly," replied Penkovsky, relieved and elated.

"Now then, if you will excuse me, I think I will leave you to your work. The very best of luck to you in the accomplishment of your missions. My very best regards to you gentlemen."

Shergold escorted Sir Dick from the room.[9]

"Did I say everything properly?" asked Penkovsky.

"Yes, you did very well," said Kisevalter. "You didn't overdo it."

When Shergold returned to the room, Kisevalter told him, "Our friend is anxious to know what impression Sir Dick has of him."

"Oh, very good indeed," said Shergold.

"I tried to say everything honestly and briefly," explained Penkovsky.

"That was good, and I feel sure that Lord Mountbatten will tell her Majesty about you," said Kisevalter.

"This obligates me even more to work hard. By the way, Lord Mountbatten is the uncle of Prince Philip and was not his mother Russian?" asked Penkovsky.

Shergold explained, "Prince Philip comes from the Greek royal house, but they were intermarried with the Russian royal family and the queen's grandmother was a cousin of the [last] tsar."[10]

Penkovsky appeared to be satisfied. He had asked to meet Queen Elizabeth, but was told it was not possible. Penkovsky complained to Bulik and Kisevalter and asked if he would have difficulty meeting American royalty, referring to President Kennedy. Through Dick

Helms, Bulik arranged for Penkovsky to meet Attorney General Robert Kennedy if he came to the United States, but there were no plans for Penkovsky to meet President Kennedy. Sir Dick was the British sop to Penkovsky's desire to be recognized for his work by high-ranking members of British royalty.

They returned to work and Kisevalter asked Penkovsky to explain the numbering system for Soviet military vehicles. This prompted Penkovsky to add that Varentsov and Moskalenko have their own airplanes assigned to them, Il-14s, and Varentsov "also has his own railroad car. Two conductors service it and sometimes he takes the wife and family along in order to save on paying their fare."[11]

Kisevalter had a long requirements list that had been prepared by the CIA in Washington and Leonard McCoy in London. The subjects ranged from counterintelligence information to efforts to understand Khrushchev's thinking and intentions.

"What did Khrushchev imply when he said in early 1960 that fantastic new weapons had been developed which are more dangerous than the ICBM?" Kisevalter asked.

Penkovsky clarified for the Americans that when Khrushchev spoke of achievements he was referring only to research projects under way for a nuclear reactor to power rockets. "He had given instructions to develop a new rocket fueled on the fission of atomic energy for its propulsion system. They are working on this intensively with huge monetary allocations to develop an atomic energy fuel," explained Penkovsky.[12] In addition to nuclear energy fuel for rockets, Penkovsky said efforts were under way to develop an extremely high-calorific fuel using boron for one of the ingredients.

"Have you ever heard that in your agent net or the KGB agent net there are highly valuable American, British, or Canadian agents?" asked Kisevalter.

"I know definitely that in the hands of the Soviet strategic intelligence agent net they have American, English, French, and German agents. It is another matter to estimate their value. In Turkey some agent candidates had very little operational capabilities, but still the order was to recruit them. No one had any expectations of being able to recruit a top-ranking general."

"This is all from the GRU?"

"Yes."

"How about the KGB?"

"Of course they have them. The KGB borrowed money from my operational funds to pay their agents. The illegals also have their own network. They don't use the people native to that country necessarily; they also use people brought in from third countries.

157

Very soon I will give you a complete list of operating agents, particularly in Ceylon."[13] Penkovsky had learned of the agents in Ceylon when preparing to go to India as military attaché.

"We are not going to touch them," said Kisevalter.

"Suppose I don't come over to you for two years?"

"If taking action against them would in any way endanger your security during this period of two years, then I would say we would not take action until you came out."

"I understand."[14]

Bulik asked Penkovsky whether he had ever heard of any technical devices being used against foreign embassies in Moscow.

Not only have I heard of them, but I have seen them. Many of the types have been copied from your equipment. They have thin membranes about a half centimeter thick which act as a microphone and which can be plastered into a wall. Wires lead out to some transmitter that is monitored. In general, these are copies of instruments which you Americans have installed that have been discovered.[15]

This brings me to a point which I want to emphasize. All the numerous Soviet employees at the American, British, and Canadian embassies, all of them, report to the KGB. For example, my own aunt, Yelena Yakovlevna Shivtsova, worked for a long time in the Afghan Embassy and she was an informant for the KGB. She is the sister of my mother and has recently been pensioned. She was working there as a housekeeper and a nurse. She hated to do this [spying] but she was ordered to under threat, and one of her assignments was to make wax imprints of the locks. Her son, Igor, was ill and they gave him medical attention, thereby exerting more control over her. She is a gentle woman. She had worked at this embassy prior to the war and later she was transferred to the Italian Embassy. She was always terrified and confided in my mother. We were very concerned because any mishap she might have with the KGB would reflect on us. We were very pleased when she retired two years ago.[16]

In Turkey, we never used local technicians or cleaning personnel, only Russians. But here in Moscow you have large numbers of servant personnel. Everyone has a KGB mission to fulfill and must constantly report. Why can't you cut out these people and have your own cleaning people do the work? It is no disgrace to clean up floors for your own people to protect security. But no, you always have to bring in so many personnel and every one is seeking a crumb of information for which they can get paid. There are absolutely no exceptions. Often your kindnesses to certain individuals serve a very bad purpose. You can be sure I know about this when I tell you my own aunt was forced to work for the KGB in a foreign embassy.*[17]

Ever since the Soviet launching of Sputnik in 1957, Khrushchev had publicly boasted of Soviet nuclear superiority. In November 1959 he said that the Soviet Union had "such a stock of rockets, such an amount of atomic and hydrogen warheads, that if they attack us we could wipe our potential enemies off the face of the earth."[18] Khrushchev claimed that a single Soviet plant produced 250 rockets in a year. He told a team of Hearst journalists, "We will not be bullied, we will not be scared. Our economy is flowering. Our production of rockets is like sausages coming from an automatic machine, rocket after rocket comes off the assembly line."[19]

Kisevalter now asked Penkovsky to tell the team about the factory of which Khrushchev publicly boasted. He replied that the Soviet Union could produce rockets for space exploration on a large scale, but it was not true that there was mass assembly-line production of ballistic missiles.

Penkovsky looked at copies of photos from the previous year's May Day parade to identify any new missiles that were shown, and pointed out tactical surface-to-surface missiles for troops in the field, the SA-2 antiaircraft missile, whose blast had disabled Powers' U-2, and the SS-1, a medium-range ballistic missile.[20]

Kisevalter pressed on with the requirements list and asked about the size of atomic bombs carried by aircraft. Penkovsky said he had heard of a fifty-kiloton bomb.[21]

"Do you have any idea of what methods they use to fasten the atomic warheads on the rockets?" Kisevalter asked.

Penkovsky recalled details of the techniques used from his course in rockets and missiles at the Dzerzhinsky Academy. They also discussed the temperature limitations on missiles, especially how cold weather might affect their performance, and how the missiles were inspected and transported.[22]

This spurred Penkovsky to tell the team,

> You did not detect all the nuclear tests. The smaller explosions are done in deep trenches. You may have picked them up as an indica-

---

* Only in 1986, after the United States insisted that the Soviet Union reduce the size of its official representation in the United States, did the system change. The Soviets withdrew all their nationals from the American Embassy in Moscow as retaliation for the American reduction of Soviet personnel in America. No longer does the American Embassy in Moscow rely on Soviet employees to do secretarial and maintenance service work inside the embassy. An American contractor now supplies the personnel.

tion of a slight earthquake, but they were not seismic manifestations. You must be made aware that there were many tests, but with very small equivalent charges. After these tests, we would watch what would appear in the press—TASS for instance—and with very few exceptions, there was no mention of them. The scientific experimental work here is shooting forth like a geyser. All this is done in the central part of the Soviet Union, nearer to the Southern Republics. All this about stopping the nuclear tests is just empty talk—just bluff. Khrushchev will get rid of all the scientists if they stop testing. And why is this still going on? Because there are still many problems which are not solved. It is done very carefully, on a small scale."[23]

Penkovsky's reports on Soviet testing violations were of great interest to the U.S. and British governments, and the information he provided helped the Western alliance to establish new criteria for monitoring nuclear testing. His information, gathered from conversations with friends in the military, proved accurate in almost all cases. In only one case—when he reported the failure of a Soviet space mission, based on rumors he had overheard, could his information not be confirmed. Only that one time was his material not distributed to the American intelligence community.

Penkovsky spoke about his trade delegation as "My little bunnies. I got them five cartons of cigarettes at the embassy yesterday. They were so happy they almost kissed me. They are afraid of me." Kisevalter reassured Penkovsky, "You did very well in the meeting with Sir Dick White." Penkovsky left at 12:05 A.M.

The following afternoon, May 4, at 2:20, Penkovsky knocked on the door of room 360 in the Mount Royal. His visit was not scheduled, and only Shergold and Bulik were present. Penkovsky had found a telephone message in his mailbox and he did not understand from whom it came. But that was not his only reason for coming unannounced. "I ran here for a few minutes to mention two things. First of all I have a very important announcement."

A GRU officer in the Soviet Embassy in London had told Penkovsky he was going to the Pakistani Embassy to meet one of his agents. "Today Shapovalov is going to meet his recruited agent as well as other people at the Pakistani Embassy. He must be watched. He told me today that he was in contact with and wants to recruit an English Communist. Simply conduct surveillance on them. They can be easily spotted."

Shapovalov would arrive at the Pakistani Embassy at 7 P.M. in car number 462, Penkovsky said.

Shergold repeated the number, 462, to make sure it was correct.

"Yes, that's right. The sum of the numbers is twelve—that makes it easier to remember," said Penkovsky.

The team agreed that no action would be taken against the GRU officer in London. If a GRU officer were expelled for illegal activities, an after-action report or review of the case might lead to Penkovsky.

Penkovsky also asked the team to investigate the number on the phone message and find out who had called him. He could not imagine who would be contacting him and it perturbed him. An unspoken contest quickly developed between the Americans and British to locate the source of the message. Shergold phoned back to his office to have the number traced. Bulik called the other members of the American team and after consulting among themselves they looked up the number of the TASS news agency in the London directory, which matched the number of the mysterious caller. Wynne had been in touch with TASS to publicize Penkovsky's delegation. The TASS man only wanted a story on the delegation's activities. Penkovsky relaxed and left for the Soviet Embassy.[24]

Penkovsky spent the remainder of the day with Wynne, who found time to take him for a dancing lesson. Penkovsky said he needed a rest after his evening at the cabaret. By 8:10 P.M. he was ready to join the team in room 360 for their fifteenth meeting. The first part was again devoted to a critique of the practice photos Penkovsky had taken. An MI6 photo instructor was present to offer pointers on how to improve picture quality when lighting conditions were poor. The instructor showed Penkovsky how to avoid jamming the film and how to prevent double exposures.

After the camera work, Penkovsky told the team of the gossip he had picked up that day in the Soviet Embassy. The trial in London of Soviet spy George Blake, an MI6 officer, had created a sensation around the world. Blake was a great embarrassment to the British government, and efforts were made to play down his role as a traitor, but his stiff sentence of forty-two-years in jail indicated that he had done great damage betraying British secrets and intelligence personnel to the KGB. "I heard that the embassy was very impressed, and has already notified Moscow, about his sentence of forty-two years. This is a very grave sentence. I heard the wretch who received it is thirty-eight years old. With a forty-two-year sentence he will be eighty years old when he gets his freedom. A very strong impression! The order has come down from the center to work seriously and be very security conscious."

"This is today's order?" asked Shergold.

"Yes, the embassy informed Moscow yesterday. Their mood right now is very bad. They say this will discourage people from working with us."[25]

Penkovsky again brought up his relationship with Wynne; difficulties arose because Wynne was only a contact man and courier, and was not an MI6 officer privy to operational secrets or cleared to know what Penkovsky was sending to the West.

"I am sly; I seem to look at things simply but I understand everything," said Penkovsky. "Wynne feels right now that I have a good deal of money, that I have been rewarded. He give me glances and hints that say that I should 'fix him' also. I ask you to have a talk with him—a good, friendly talk. Explain to him that he will be paid well and that if he continues to work well with me he will always have enough of everything, even in the future."

Shergold and Kisevalter agreed with Penkovsky.

"You should tell it to him like this: 'Penkovsky is a generous fellow, but you should not take money from him.' This is so he won't think that I am greedy."[26]

Although Penkovsky said he was no longer a Communist, his thinking was still affected by the moral values of Communism: those who make more money than their neighbors must be doing something illegal. Rather than try to emulate a rich neighbor, the morality is to cut a neighbor down to the common denominator. Being considered greedy in Soviet society carried the connotation of moral corruption and antisocial behavior.

Penkovsky repeated his reasons for initially approaching Wynne in Moscow, concluding succinctly, "Wynne did not want to do it at first. He was afraid. Oh, how he was afraid! How I begged him and persuaded him. Of course he understood that if I met with success, I would get him gold medals! After all, he is a merchant—you must realize this."[27]

"We will take first-rate care of him. You said yourself that he was pleased when you saw him," said Kisevalter, trying to soothe Penkovsky. But for five more minutes, Penkovsky kept repeating his point.

"He is satisfied. He is very well reimbursed and feels quite happy," insisted Kisevalter.

"I swear I am not wrong," replied Penkovsky, who knew what Wynne really felt. "I think that I told him in Moscow, 'If I have it good you'll have it good.' And now he is wondering why I changed my line. This is a very important matter, especially since I'm going to meet him at the end of May. Reassure him tomorrow, tell him that Penkovsky is a kind man."

"We will tell him that we have forbidden you to give him money," said Kisevalter.

"That's it. Tell him you have forbidden me!"

"That is right," added Shergold for reassurance.[28]

Kisevalter had become impatient with the time taken up by Penkovsky's concern with Wynne. "Listen, you have about a half hour now. We have a very important program. You can finish up the photographs another time. We are going over the operational instructions, what and how things will be done. Then I will explain, first briefly and then in detail, the main missions you will be given," said Kisevalter.[29]

"This is an historic room. Someday there will be a memorial plaque here," replied Penkovsky.[30]

Kisevalter showed Penkovsky how to listen to the radio code and how to transcribe the numbers into plain language text. At 9 P.M. Penkovsky left for dinner with his delegation in the Mount Royal. He returned an hour later after telling his "bunnies" he was disconnecting his phone and going to sleep.

The first order of business that night was for Penkovsky to choose from five color samples the materials the team would supply him to replace six defective false teeth. He had lost the teeth when he was hit by a German artillery shell during World War II. The materials for false teeth in Moscow were inferior and did not last, said Penkovsky, pleased with the variety of colors to pick from. After consulting with the team, he ordered a color that blended well with his real teeth.[31]

Since Moscow dental standards are so low, it was common practice for Soviet officials traveling abroad to see dentists approved by the KGB. Penkovsky's new false teeth would not attract attention when he returned to Moscow.

Kisevalter went over detailed instructions for the Russian's next meeting with Wynne in Moscow. Setting a specific time would allow Wynne to go to the British Embassy just before and pick up the material for Penkovsky without having to keep it in his hotel room.

They discussed a range of possibilities for meeting agents and delivering materials. The team had developed an identification signal. If Penkovsky met an American or British diplomat at a reception wearing a tie clip with red stones, and was offered greetings from Charles Peeke and his wife, he would know he had found his man. Bulik, who had purchased a few sets of similar tie clips, showed one to Penkovsky so he would be sure of what to look for.

Another option was for Penkovsky to throw a package over the wall of America House at 10 P.M. on the first Saturday of the month, beginning in July 1961. The alternate time was to be on Sunday, the day after the first Saturday, at the same time. "The spot is where the wall joins the building on Turchaninov Lane," explained Kisevalter, referring to the spot that the hapless American CIA officer, COMPASS, had suggested earlier. By this time the importance of Penkovsky's work was recognized in Washington and the CIA had contacted the State Department, at the level of Under Secretary of State U. Alexis Johnson, who cabled the Moscow Embassy urging cooperation. Ambassador Thompson had only been told of a high-level Soviet source; he knew it was Penkovsky from Penkovsky's jeopardous early approaches. No longer was Penkovsky considered a potential provocateur, but his identity was carefully shielded from others in the embassy.[32]

The British developed another scenario for contacting Penkovsky in Moscow. Shergold told Penkovsky he would meet the wife of a British diplomat while she was walking her children in the park. Kisevalter translated for Shergold: "You may tell him I will decide which is the best place for her. Then we will photograph her and the children in the park so that he will recognize the wife, the children, the baby carriage, and the place in the park where they will be playing."

"Very good," said Penkovsky.

"Can you tell us what will be the best day for you?" asked Kisevalter.

"For this operation, Sunday. It is my day off," replied Penkovsky.[33]

Then Penkovsky went back to identifying pictures of GRU and KGB officers, providing biographical details on them until it was time to leave at 1:15 A.M. on May 5. The team had a farewell toast of white wine to celebrate the conclusion of a session that had lasted three hours and fifty-five minutes. The record of the meetings notes: "As a matter of principle all participants decided to serve only a mild wine at meetings. This served to quench thirst which was stimulated by being forced to sit in a hot, stuffy, smoke-filled room for hours. The windows had to be shut to keep conversation from being overheard."[34]

They agreed to meet again at 9 P.M. Penkovsky again praised Wynne's efforts on the delegation's behalf. They had been invited to several lunches and dinners, which meant they did not have to use their food allowances and could save the money for gifts and personal items. "This helped me to 'buy' the group. They are very pleased," said Penkovsky.

"Have you bought everything you need?" asked Kisevalter.

"Not yet. I have to buy a few more presents and some odds and ends. I'll have time to do this tomorrow."

"Did you get Varentsov's present yet?" asked Kisevalter.

"Yes. It is very fine."

"It will be from Mr. and Mrs. Penkovsky and from us," said Kisevalter with a laugh. "You'll have time to finish shopping tomorrow. It won't hurt to buy a few extra things for presents."[35]

Penkovsky and Kisevalter clinked their wineglasses. "Now we've finished," Penkovsky said. "We'll say goodbye the day after tomorrow. Everything is right; the money I received was both for operational and personal purposes. After all, the presents, are they not operational expenses?"

"Yes, of course," said Shergold.

"I don't think I'll telephone her tonight. I'm tired. Today I rode past her house. You know, she really fell for me," said Penkovsky, referring to Zeph, the woman he had met at the cabaret with Wynne. "She was quite sincere, exceptionally so. Two hours was very short. She was really a bit surprised that I left so soon. She is an experienced girl. I asked her, 'Why don't you get married?' She comes from a good family and lives pretty well." Penkovsky reiterated that the team should reconvene at 9 P.M. and was off.[36]

Penkovsky spent the day at the Soviet Embassy, checking the accounts for his delegation and shopping with Wynne. He arrived at room 360 of the Mount Royal at 9:05 P.M. for his last working meeting with the team.

"Then you have done everything?" Kisevalter asked.

"Not everything. I will ask you to help me in some things. I've done everything for myself and I've got the presents—everything has gone well," said Penkovsky. "At six-thirty P.M. I went to Wynne's home. He said, 'Well, let's have a last drink.' Then he said, 'My wife and I will come and say goodbye to the delegation.' We had a drink or two. I rang from Wynne's, telling the delegation we were coming in ten minutes—everyone arrived. Mrs. Wynne came; we went to the bar and had a drink, sat for a couple of minutes, and then they went off. I went to my room, collected some photographs and catalogs of where we had been; the others went to do their packing, and then I came to you.

"I had a conversation with Wynne. He told me that he had spoken with you and had received instructions. Regarding money, I said that in general I am not working for money—that it is not necessary to give me money. . . . You see, when it is necessary to speak English, I understand Wynne very well. Well, he said, 'I'll do everything that they ask me to do and I only need money.' So Wynne's mood is not a bad one."

"Excellent," Kisevalter replied.[37]

Penkovsky asked the team to arrange that his delegation's bags not be opened at Heathrow and Shergold promised that Wynne would pay for any excess baggage.

As soon as Wynne's name was mentioned again Kisevalter turned to Penkovsky and said, "I beseech you, do not promise Wynne all sorts of things. It is not necessary to make him promises which will be difficult to fulfill. As you can see, this influences him."

165

Penkovsky was still concerned about his relationship with Wynne and how Wynne would respond in Moscow. He started to explain himself again but Kisevalter interrupted and said, "Now you can set your mind at rest. You know yourself that you have taken steps."

"Well, so much for Wynne," said Penkovsky with a nod of his head.[38]

Penkovsky was also concerned with the performance of a British expert, arranged by Shergold, whom Penkovsky introduced to a GRU contact at the Soviet Embassy. At the meeting Penkovsky asked the British expert to write an article on high-temperature-resistant steel that could be printed in the Soviet Union. "I told him we often publish articles by foreign authors on technical questions. He said, 'I will think about it. I know one of your main specialists is interested in heat-resistant steels for rockets . . .' Why did he say rockets?"

Penkovsky was annoyed because the reference to rockets put the GRU officer on guard. He was concerned that his GRU colleague might sense something amiss with the British expert.

"He is a rocket man, that's the way he thinks," said Shergold, explaining the British expert's response. "Because he is a simple mortal, he does not assess things as you and I do. He is not an intelligence officer," added Kisevalter.[39]

Penkovsky moved on. "Something else. Are you getting ready a second Minox?"

"Wynne will give it to you in Moscow," said Shergold.

"I do not want to keep two Minoxes at home. I will think about it," said Penkovsky.

"We could put the Minox in his dead letter box," said Shergold to Kisevalter, referring to the dead drop Penkovsky had designated.

"You have given me enough film for a thousand frames," said Penkovsky. "My number one project is the Field Service Regulations because it is very important and interesting. There is one booklet by Chief Marshal of Artillery Varentsov, a modern evaluation of rocket forces. This is theoretical—there are no descriptions of rockets—with views on their massed employment in military operations. It is a good booklet. It is Top Secret. One can see it only by presenting a pass. If I can work on it, it will be very interesting. Then I will have the basic manual and there will be lectures on special training [for intelligence].

"To take the Regulations, which are 250 to 270 pages, with two frames to a page, will need 500 frames. Then I will already have used more than half. I am worried about film. Additional film should also be provided because I already have another book to copy."

Kisevalter said, "The pages of the Regulations are small enough for one frame each."

Speaking in English to Kisevalter, Shergold spoke of Penkovsky in the third person. Shergold said, "I propose that he should receive more cassettes from Wynne. How many does he think he will be able to take from Wynne so that he has got a supply for two or three months?[40] We are giving him twenty films through Wynne. When would he want to pass over further material? Does he think that he will want to do it at the end of June or July—that is, after Wynne's visit? Does he want to do it every month or every two months?"[41]

"Let's not wait for many months," Penkovsky replied. "I have thought about this. Here is my plan: I will prepare as much as possible before the arrival of Wynne—some of this I have already done—you will have enough work for a month.

"I have thought about the following suggestion, although I did not mention it before. There is a British diplomat who knows me, he invited me when I was looking after Wynne's delegation. I met him and his wife and got to know him well when I was at that fool's—Van Vliet's. Let your diplomat organize something and invite about ten people from the committee. Some celebration should be arranged—the birthday of the queen's son—and with this as a pretext he could organize a party. I liked him—if he would take films and additional material when I offer it to him I would give it to him—with your permission and on your orders."

"No," said Shergold firmly, not wanting to mix a member of the embassy staff with the MI6 man in the embassy.

"No? Then another man in his place?" asked Penkovsky.

"Another man—our man," replied Shergold.[42]

"I could be invited to Van Vliet's. But I do not want to work with Van Vliet," said Penkovsky.

"We don't want you to, either!" said Shergold, agreeing emphatically.

"He kept my packet for two days. After that they rang him up from the committee. Van Vliet has an interpreter-secretary—I gave you his name—a Russian who works in the First Chief Directorate [of the KGB]. Half these people should be chased off. They are informers. Without doubt Van Vliet already knows that I have been in England for sixteen days. He knows of the wishes which I admitted to him," complained Penkovsky.

"He did not understand your wishes. He did nothing. He is a complete fool!" argued Kisevalter.

"He understood everything. He even asked me whether I wanted to live in the Soviet Union or to leave," insisted Penkovsky.

"Oh really?" asked Bulik with concern.

"That's a new one," said Michael Stokes, who was also disquieted.

"I told the man everything about why I was making the requests—and he understood everything, but you are right—he is a complete fool," said Penkovsky.[43] Even though Van Vliet did not see the rocketry information Penkovsky asked him to transmit, the Canadian diplomat could easily drop a careless remark in Moscow that would label Penkovsky politically unreliable and compromise him.

Shergold turned to Kisevalter and asked him to tell Penkovsky, "Under no circumstances must he attempt to say anything or pass anything to the diplomat [in the British Embassy]. If he arranges an invitation for members of the committee, then he must only act when a man makes himself known to him."

"And what will you say to this man?" Penkovsky asked.

"He will have the signal," said Kisevalter, showing the tie clasp that had been given to Penkovsky. An identical one would be worn by anyone who was to contact him.

"Tell this man I will walk around and look at everything—all the rooms—I will go into the kitchen, to the toilet. Your man should watch me. I will contrive a situation in which I am alone and I will give him a package of exposed film," said Penkovsky.

"He will be our own trusted man and no one else will know," replied Kisevalter.

"Once he has the films, then it is your business. Has the diplomat already been warned that he should keep silent? He knows everything regarding the two British businessmen I approached," explained Penkovsky.

"I know. I have done this," said Shergold.

"Will Van Vliet interfere?" asked Penkovsky.

"No," said Kisevalter firmly.

"Harrison [the Canadian geologist] will keep quiet too?"

"Absolutely," Kisevalter said.

Penkovsky was relieved.[44]

Shergold asked Kisevalter if Penkovsky "only wants to hand over material at an embassy meeting? Does he rule out any question of the lady with the pram and all that?"

"Oh no, no," said Kisevalter, explaining that Penkovsky had also agreed to meet with the woman and her children.

"Fine," Shergold replied. "I should like to get back to this time factor."

"There will be new material from me each month—sometimes a large quantity, sometimes less. But you cannot invite me to an English function every month. I can be invited by the Australians, the English, and the Canadians and the Americans—once by each in every three months, without repetition by anyone in that time," said Penkovsky. This was the rule established at the State Committee for visits to foreign embassies.[45]

"It is possible that you will be invited once in two months on an average," said Kisevalter.

"No. I don't want to keep material for two months," complained Penkovsky.

"Once a month. That's all I wanted to know," said Shergold, "because if we are going to use the lady with the pram in the park during the summer, I have to give her instructions how often she has to be there."

After Kisevalter translated Shergold's remarks, Penkovsky said, "This is my suggestion: on the first Sunday of each month—at different places, the first place would be where I suggested—opposite the statue of Repin [on Repina Square opposite the Kremlin]. Can she go out walking with the child in the evening?"

"No, it would not be normal," said Kisevalter.

"And she will only push the children out in the pram in the immediate neighborhood where she lives. She can't push it all over town without taking a car," Shergold added.

"Doesn't she take the child out for air before it goes to sleep?" Penkovsky asked.

"She lives perhaps two or three blocks from the park; she can sit or walk in the park. It will always be in a park. But in which park? The one not far from her flat," Shergold said firmly.[46]

Penkovsky stated, "I have a question. What if suddenly I have an urgent message—like the occasion when Marshal Rokossovsky was sent to the Transcaucasus and Varentsov was there—all the rockets were prepared and ready to fire at Turkey—this actually happened. If something like this should happen again, how could I keep silent? Through what channel could I inform you?"

Penkovsky was referring to Khrushchev's response to the American landing in Lebanon in July 1958, when Rokossovsky was appointed the commander of the Transcaucasian Military District as a sign of Soviet mobilization in response to Eisenhower's move to defend Lebanon.[47]

Shergold said to Kisevalter, "This is a thing on which I propose to give him instructions through Wynne. We can tell him that we have left a message in his *tainik* [dead drop], but we have not yet given him any instructions on the return method. I am hoping to lay on a drill involving a telephone call at a given time on a given day once a week, so he can tell us to go and clear the dead drop, but only once a week. He should be able to deliver more bulky material such as Minox cassettes once a month. He also should be able to inform us

169

of something brief in his small dead drop once a week. I am hoping to have all this arranged so that I can send in the instructions through Wynne."

Penkovsky said, "That is very good. But one must foresee this—for what could happen? The marshals and everyone go somewhere—this is the very basis of our work. Such a situation might arise. Rokossovsky and Varentsov and another general sat ready. They were ready to strike Adana [an American air base in Turkey]."

"Wynne will carry a message from us," said Shergold.

"Then all is agreed: I will be told, when you work it out, how to contact you in an emergency, but only when I have something of real importance to report—such as the removal of Khrushchev or the imminence of military action."

Shergold added to Kisevalter for translation, "Or if he knows, for instance, that he is going to Canada; then he should use it, because the sooner we know, the better we can arrange things."

The size, composition, and location of the Warsaw Pact headquarters was the next item on Kisevalter's list of requirements, and Penkovsky poured forth what he knew from the General Staff, interspersing locations of bases with anecdotes on the personality of the marshals and generals. Kisevalter was fascinated and asked about Marshal Georgi K. Zhukov, considered to be the Soviet Union's greatest World War II commander. Zhukov was defense minister from 1955 to 1957. In June 1957 an old guard group of Politburo members led by Georgi M. Malenkov, Lazar Kaganovich, and Foreign Minister Vyacheslav M. Molotov attempted to overthrow Khrushchev. Zhukov aided Khrushchev by flying Central Committee members to Moscow in military planes so they could vote for Khrushchev and counter the power play. Four months later Zhukov was rewarded with a trip to Yugoslavia. When he returned he found that he had been dismissed as defense minister, removed from the Central Committee and Presidium, and disgraced for "adventurism" and "Bonapartism." Khrushchev was taking no chances that Zhukov's popularity would make him a successor.

Penkovsky said that Zhukov had an apartment in town but spent most of his time at a dacha out along the Rublevskoye Highway. By order of the Council of Ministers he was given a pension of 550 rubles ($495) a month.

"Is that all?" Kisevalter asked.

"It's a disgrace," said Penkovsky. "According to the regulations, a marshal has no right to retire. He is listed as continuing to work actively—like Marshal Budenny [the famed cavalry hero], who does nothing, but who has an office in the gray building on Antipievsky Alley and a colonel as his aide. Sometimes he comes to large lectures.

I have seen him. He has a phone to the Kremlin but he does nothing. He receives his full salary as a marshal. Since the last reform he receives 1200 rubles [$1080] a month."

"Is he higher than Zhukov?" asked Kisevalter.

"Yes," answered Penkovsky. "The Council of Ministers decided to retire Zhukov. I saw the order. If I had a Minox you could have had a photograph of it! It was signed by Khrushchev and witnessed by the ministers. It read, 'The Ministers of the U.S.S.R. agree to the request of G. K. Zhukov, Marshal of the Soviet Union, that he should be allowed to retire.' A special resolution can remove a marshal or create a generalissimo—and this was a special resolution. Then later there were similar resolutions on Konev, on Sokolovsky, and on Timoshenko, and like Zhukov, their pensions were set at 550 rubles. Zhukov had money from savings. As minister he received 2500 rubles [$2250] a month and he had a representation allowance." Penkovsky then enumerated the pay of several levels of officers.

"Marshal Varentsov receives 1000 rubles [$900] per month. Varentsov used to get 1200 rubles [$1080], now it is less—everyone gets less. They have cut them down.

"The head of the General Staff receives 2000 rubles. The commander of a branch of service—a marshal of the Soviet Union like Biryuzov, head of the antiaircraft forces, receives up to 1800 rubles. Khrushchev said, 'They have grown very fat. We cannot create intellectuals and capitalists like this . . .' and so on. A marshal of tanks—a commander—received 1800 rubles. Such commanders, chief marshals and marshals of the U.S.S.R., or a chief marshal in charge of a service branch.

"When my father-in-law died—this is how I know this in such detail—his wife received 750 rubles. A major general's widow got 500; a colonel general's widow got 1000. Now if anyone important dies, the widow receives rubles. That is not a pension but a single payment to cover funeral expenses. My mother-in-law lives on her savings. She has 5000 rubles left. This is how they save billions for rockets. Any complaints and the little bit will be taken away. All are restless—one says to a trusted friend—Khrushchev should drop dead, the scum."

Penkovsky went on to tell the team how suspicion of foreigners had become a fact of military life. "When I was studying at the Rocket Academy there was an important case against one of our officers, a student in the rocket faculty. One day the officer walked by the Udarnik cinema. He saw a foreign car stop and was asked in broken Russian and English, 'Where is America House?' He said, 'I know. I will show you.' He got in the car, saying, 'Go that way.' A

171

policeman saw that the car had a diplomatic D on it and then he saw a Soviet military uniform in the car. They stopped the car at the first crossroads with a red signal and the police pulled the Soviet officer out. The officer was thrown out of the Academy and was reprimanded along Party lines. This was done as an example to everyone else. All he wanted to do was to show them the way. The foreigners in the car were not detained. The foreigners were going to America House. Perhaps they were tourists."

Kisevalter asked, "Can anyone go there?"

"Yes," said Penkovsky. "If I stop a diplomatic car, I should do so in a suitable place, like the Ukraine Hotel where one goes under the bridge. I know many places where one could stop a car without being seen by the police. Then I could get to the American or British Embassy at great speed. I know, however, that they would not let me out of the country. They would invoke an alarm that a General Staff officer disappeared and all frontiers would be closed! Anyway, I do not think that this danger exists."

"But it is better to know beforehand what to do," Kisevalter said.

"Of course."

"The fact remains that we do not have planes that fly in regularly. Even if we did, only the embassy itself is considered extraterritorial. It isn't that we don't want to help!" said Joe Bulik.

Kisevalter said, "My advice would be that if you suspect anything, you should try—together with your family—to get to East Berlin under some pretext."

"They would not allow it," said Penkovsky. "If a thousand tourists are going, they check ten thousand and reject nine thousand."

Shergold joined in to say, "If they know what he is doing, they wouldn't give him the opportunity to get to an airport. But if he feels that there might be some suspicion that they cannot prove, then he stops work immediately in order to allay their suspicions."

Penkovsky replied, "There can be no question of going to an embassy under any circumstances. They would catch me immediately. But if in the case of danger I could stop a diplomatic car at some favorable spot—"

"Then where would you go?" asked Kisevalter. "To the embassy— and then what? There would be discussions and so forth and they would demand that you be handed back as a Soviet citizen. It is better to devise beforehand a plan for getting somewhere to safety by secret means—to a frontier, the Finnish frontier, whichever is nearest."

Bulik turned to Kisevalter. "George, we have been stressing from the very beginning that security is the most important factor. We would rather not see him or hear from him for one year than risk his neck in any way."

Penkovsky asked, "How can I endanger myself? I shall photograph so carefully that no one will know. I will not have contact with anyone, so that I cannot be followed to an operational meeting."

"But," said Bulik, "you can become so interested in what you are doing that you forget and don't even hear with your own ears the noise that little Minox is making."

"If he is doing it in a locked room, closed, he should be all right. He can't use it under any other circumstances," said Shergold, trying to lay down an operational rule for Penkovsky.

To reassure his handlers that he was security conscious at all times, Penkovsky said, "I locked the door when I was writing about rockets and put a chair under the doorknob, not a stick or a board, but a chair. I did this on purpose—locked the door—so that the few evening classes there were would not disturb me. I said that I was going to be busy."

"Well, let's hope nothing happens," said Kisevalter.

Penkovsky spent the rest of the session identifying pictures and providing biographical data on KGB and GRU officers. When they were finished going through the pictures, the team was very pleased. They had covered an estimated 7000 available photographs from the files of the CIA, MI5, and MI6. They were categorized by country and when the person was last seen. Penkovsky identified 7 to 10 percent of the people, mostly GRU officers. He recognized and commented on two to three hundred KGB officers.[48]

"That was a fine set of photographs," he said.

With his identifications the CIA and MI6 would be able to follow KGB and GRU officers to discover their contacts. Counterintelligence could now target these people for recruitment or defection. The heart of the Soviet intelligence operations overseas had been revealed.

Mike Stokes poured white wine for a toast to Penkovsky. Individual and group photographs were taken with a Polaroid camera. Penkovsky was pleased with the way the visit had turned out and he told the team, "We have worked intensively and achieved productive and valuable results." He took a sip of the white wine and it reminded him that Khrushchev had changed the names of Georgian wines to numbers because the wines had been named after Georgian princes. "You know," he said, "there is a very nice girl here at the hotel but I had no time to get acquainted with her. She is a receptionist. I asked her if she had a photograph of herself and she said no. So I gave her five pounds and asked her to have her picture taken. She took the money and this morning she gave me this photograph and wrote this nice letter. She explained that it is forbidden for employees to go out with guests and she sent her best wishes. You see how I spent the last of my pounds!"

The team raised their glasses to Penkovsky and offered best wishes for his success and security. Bulik said goodbye to Penkovsky and they embraced. Carefully, Penkovsky put all compromising notes into his pocket. Bulik told Penkovsky that these meetings were only the beginning of a long and fruitful association. "I am completely at ease," replied Penkovsky. "Please protect me. I promise to fulfill all my missions. I will continue until the end of my days. Let's hope we all meet again." At 12:45 A.M. May 6 Penkovsky left for his own room.

Later that morning, at 10:15, Penkovsky met for the seventeenth time with his American and British handlers to bid a hasty farewell before leaving for Moscow. "I almost feel like weeping," Penkovsky sighed. "In this room we have resolved many important matters of historic significance. It is difficult now to judge how important. Time will confirm and show us. We worked hard and now it is time to rest."

Again Penkovsky asked the Americans and British not to "touch" any of the GRU officers in the Soviet Embassy in London. Shergold and Kisevalter assured him they would not. "Even if there is a flap here involving the GRU, do me a favor and play it as if you didn't see it," said Penkovsky. "As far as the KGBniks are concerned, knock them dead."

Penkovsky still had not finished shopping for everything on the list and asked the team to buy him an inexpensive crystal chandelier and two small matching wall candelabra for his apartment. He tried on Mike Stokes' jacket for size and asked for a good black suit he could wear to receptions. He left the request list of what he had not gotten with the team: a cheap raincoat for himself and fox trot records for his wife and daughter. Wynne would bring everything when he next came to Moscow. "Well, I have told you everything. Now, what have you to say to me?"

"Just goodbye and good luck," said Shergold.

"And everything we agreed on. Let's embrace like brothers," said Penkovsky in Russian, hugging the team members and kissing them on the cheeks.

"And Sir Dick White asked me to give his special regards to you," added Shergold amid the embraces.

"I know you will take care of the money to be put into my account so I will have something," said Penkovsky.

"You may even get a small package through the embassy. Well, my dear one, regards to your family; stay in the best of health. We'll meet again soon!" Kisevalter said emotionally.

"Thank you," replied Penkovsky. He stayed for only fifteen minutes before departing for Moscow armed with his new assignments.

Colonel Oleg Vladimirovich Penkovsky in dress uniform with the medals he received for his bravery during World War II. *(CIA)*

Penkovsky's pass to the Second Directorate of the General Staff of the Soviet Army, the GRU or military intelligence. *(CIA)*

Penkovsky's passport, issued in 1960 for his trip to London, identifying him as a reserve officer. *(CIA)*

Penkovsky shaking hands with Canadian geologist Dr. J. M. Harrison in the National Hotel, Moscow, 1961. *(Courtesy of Dr. J. M. Harrison)*

Left to right: Colonel Charles MacLean Peeke, Penkovsky, and the Yugoslav assistant military attaché, Major Grueisic, at a reception on May 9, 1956, in Ankara, Turkey, where Penkovsky was serving as an assistant attaché. *(Courtesy of Lt. Col. Milford A. Koehler)*

The picture with his head notched out that Penkovsky sent in his recruitment letter, delivered by American student Eldon Ray Cox. *(CIA)*

Left to right: American military attaché Colonel Charles Maclean Peeke, Soviet military attaché Major General Nikolai Petrovich Rubenko, a.k.a. Savchenko, Penkovsky, and the Yugoslav assistant military attaché, Major Grueisic, in Ankara. *(Courtesy of Lt. Col. Milford A. Koehler)*

Мои Родител

Penkovsky's mother and father. *(CIA)*

Marshal Sergei Sergeyevich Varentsov, Penkovsky's friend and protector. *(CIA)*

At the First Ukrainian Front in 1944. *Left to right:* driver; Colonel Andrei Romanovich Pozovny, Varentsov's aide; Lieutenant General Varentsov (with cane); and Penkovsky. *(CIA)*

Greville Wynne (with hands in pockets on extreme right) with a British trade delegation in front of the Bolshoi Theater, December 1960. *(Courtesy of Greville Wynne)*

Greville Wynne at his trial in Moscow in 1963. *(Courtesy of Greville Wynne)*

The British and American team that ran Penkovsky. *Left to right:* Michael Stokes, Harold (Shergie) Shergold, Joseph Bulik, and George Kisevalter in the Mount Royal Hotel, London, 1961. *(CIA)*

Penkovsky (with back to camera) making a point to the MI6 team leader, Harold Shergold. *(CIA)*

Penkovsky and Bulik toast each other in the Mount Royal Hotel, London, 1961. *(CIA)*

Roderick (Rauri) Chisholm, second secretary, British Embassy, Moscow, and MI6 Station chief. *(KGB)*

Janet Anne Chisholm, wife of Roderick Chisholm and Penkovsky's contact in Moscow. *(KGB)*

Rodney Carlson, attaché, American Embassy, Moscow, and CIA officer. *(KGB)*

Captain Alexis Davison, assistant military attaché, American Embassy, Moscow. *(KGB)*

Greville Wynne, British businessman and courier for Penkovsky. *(KGB)*

Hugh Montgomery, attaché, American Embassy, Moscow, and deputy chief of CIA Station. *(KGB)*

Gervase Cowell, second secretary, British Embassy, Moscow, replacement for Roderick Chisholm. *(KGB)*

Richard Jacob, secretary-archivist, American Embassy, Moscow, and CIA officer. *(KGB)*

Penkovsky in an American Army colonel's uniform in London, 1961. *(CIA)*

Penkovsky in a British Army colonel's uniform in London, 1961. *(CIA)*

Return to Moscow

PENKOVSKY RETURNED TO MOSCOW ON SATURDAY, MAY 6, AND TO the delight of his family spent a quiet weekend lavishing gifts from London on them. On Monday, May 8, he returned to the committee offices on Gorky Street. At 2100 hours he stopped at a pay phone booth a block from his apartment house, lifted the receiver, inserted a two-kopeck coin, and dialed the number 948-973, which he had been given in London. He let it ring three times, then hung up. He counted to sixty, a full minute, then dialed again and waited for the phone to ring three more times, the agreed-upon signal that all was well. If something had gone wrong, he would have rung five times in the same sequence. The trip to England had been a success on all counts.

The Anglo-American intelligence team provided Penkovsky with enough booklets and brochures on British steel technology to make it appear that he had done some first-rate industrial spying. The materials he had gathered on British manufacturing processes were highly regarded by the State Committee for the Coordination of Scientific Research Work and the GRU. Penkovsky, thanks to the team's efforts, introduced a British steel expert to a GRU officer in the London Embassy to use as a source. His delegation completed its intelligence-gathering assignments successfully and he received a recommendation of high performance from the GRU *rezident* in London. Penkovsky's bountiful shopping, aided by the CIA and MI6, made him appear to be a reliable, understanding friend. He dispensed medicine, cigarette lighters, and small gifts to his associates and big gifts to Marshal Varentsov. To the wife of his boss, Gvishiani, he presented perfume, powder, lipstick, a deck of cards, and several

175

packets of cigarettes. He estimated the cost of presents at 100 pounds ($280).[1]

Penkovsky went about his normal routine at the State Committee, then headed for the library of the artillery command in the Ministry of Defense complex on Frunze Street, where Marshal Varentsov had arranged a special pass for him to have access to Top Secret files in the Special Collection. Ostensibly, Penkovsky was researching an article on nuclear strategy to be published in a military journal. In the library he placed a chair under the doorknob to avoid being surprised and photographed Top Secret documents on the requirements list generated during the London meetings.

Within three weeks, on May 27, Greville Wynne returned to Moscow. His stated purpose was to attend the French trade show and to arrange a return visit of British businessmen to the Soviet Union. Wynne's Aeroflot flight flew over the green forests on the outskirts of Moscow and landed at Sheremetievo Airport on a sunny, cool Saturday afternoon. He had three suitcases and a parcel of umbrellas with him. One of the suitcases contained the purchases on Penkovsky's shopping list. Everything Alex—as Wynne called him—had asked for was there with the exception of the crystal chandelier and the matching candelabra, which were too large to fit in the suitcase.

When he emerged from the plane and walked down the gangway, Wynne was dismayed because he saw no sign of Penkovsky. However, walking from the plane toward the bus that would take him to the terminal, Wynne spotted his contact hurrying across the tarmac toward him. When the bus stopped at the terminal, Penkovsky flourished a pass that ensured Wynne's passage through customs and immigration formalities in record time, without having to sign a single form. None of the suitcases was opened and there were no questions about what he was carrying.

Once they were outside the terminal Penkovsky directed Wynne to a shabby old black car with an elderly driver. The car was heavily loaded with parcels that Wynne thought might have been purchased on the black market. Penkovsky motioned to Wynne to get into the backseat with his own suitcase, and the driver put the suitcase containing Penkovsky's purchases into the trunk. Penkovsky introduced Wynne to the driver as his friend, and they drove farther away from the city, past white birches lining the road, toward the countryside. When they passed the large white dacha between straight, tall pines that had been Security Chief Lavrenti Beria's country hideaway, the driver explained that the size of the house reflected the differences between the Party hierarchy and ordinary people.* They arrived at the driver's home, a wooden shack, where the driver's wife appeared and helped to unload all the parcels in the car before the return trip to take Wynne into Moscow.

While the driver was busy unloading the car and could not overhear them, Penkovsky used the opportunity to set a meeting with Wynne at 10:30 that evening next to the statue of Karl Marx near the Metropol Hotel, where Wynne would stay. On the way back into town Penkovsky handed a briefcase to Wynne and, while continuing to point out the sights, he handed over three packages which Wynne put in his own briefcase. All this was done in silence out of the driver's line of sight in the rearview mirror. Thus Penkovsky delivered his first load of film taken with the Minox, three undeveloped rolls.

During the drive to the Metropol, Wynne gave Penkovsky six bottles of whiskey, several cartons of cigarettes, and hair tonic purchased in Copenhagen. Wynne gently reminded Penkovsky that while in London Penkovsky had poured a bottle of Old Spice aftershave lotion over his hair and this had turned it from its normal red to a slightly purple shade. Wynne told Penkovsky he could use the new bottle of hair tonic on his hair, but warned him to stay away from after shave-lotion on his scalp.

To reach the Metropol they had to pass Red Square and the massive walls of the Kremlin. The line for Lenin's tomb stretched from the mausoleum through the square and into the Alexander Gardens, beneath the Kremlin wall. It was a reminder to Wynne of the hold of Soviet power over its people and their veneration for Lenin. Penkovsky pointed to young married couples who had come to lay flowers at the gravestone of the Unknown Soldier of World War II, one of the 20 million victims of the war.[†] Soviet radio, newspapers, and television repeatedly reminded the younger generations that the country had sacrificed its blood and wealth to protect them. World War II was the rationale for the failure of the Soviet state to prosper.

When they arrived at the Metropol, Penkovsky again pulled out his identity card. He presented a letter from the State Committee requesting that Wynne be given special consideration at the hotel and that a car should be available to him during his stay. Wynne made a point of using this car when he visited the trade fair each day.

---

*The dacha was infamous among guards and state security officers as the site of Beria's debauches. Beria's rapes of women he accosted on the street, including eleven- and thirteen-year-old girls, were included in a secret Communist Party indictment.
†An eternal flame was established for the World War II Unknown Soldier on May 8, 1967, and the tradition of paying homage on one's wedding day continues.

After Penkovsky left the Metropol, Wynne unpacked and quickly settled into the room. Then, without opening the briefcase or inspecting what Penkovsky had given him, Wynne headed for a prearranged meeting with the MI6 representative at the British Embassy. From the Metropol it was only a short walk through Red Square and across the Moskvoretsky Bridge over the Moscow River to the stately British Embassy at 14 Maurice Thorez Embankment, directly opposite the Great Kremlin Palace. Wynne entered the dark-wood-paneled reception room and then was escorted to the office of the MI6 representative in Moscow, where he handed over the material he had received from Penkovsky. In return Wynne received a package of material London had prepared for Penkovsky. Wynne would deliver it at his 10:30 meeting that night.

Wynne and the MI6 officer, Roderick (Rauri) Chisholm, did not speak during their meeting to avoid being recorded on listening devices planted in the embassy by the KGB. At all times they communicated with each other either by signs or by written notes that were subsequently burned.

Wynne then headed back to the Metropol and met Penkovsky near the bust of Karl Marx. They joined the strollers along Karl Marx Prospekt before moving off onto a side street to discuss their plans. They ended up having dinner in a small café near the Bolshoi Theater. Penkovsky assured Wynne that if they were seen together talking English this way it was all right because the State Committee had authorized him to look after Wynne during his visit. "It will be fine for us to meet at least once a day. I have seen your official dossier and there is no Intelligence interest in you. You are described as a 'purely commercial representative.' " Of course Penkovsky had been assigned by the GRU to exploit Wynne as a source; he was to ask him to arrange meetings for Soviet experts working for the GRU so they could gain access to British industrial and defense technology.

While they walked back to the Metropol, Wynne turned over a letter to Penkovsky and a packet with 3000 rubles [$2700]. Wynne in turn received a letter from Penkovsky, but he did not read it before passing it to his contact at the British Embassy the following day. Shergold had devised the operating plans in coordination with Bulik and CIA headquarters. Wynne and Penkovsky carried out their tasks according to strict instructions. In a memorandum from the British team, the CIA was informed: "Before subject [Penkovsky] leaves Wynne at the hotel and before Wynne leaves for the British Embassy, subject will arrange with Wynne the time and circumstances under which they will be able to meet alone again. Depending on these circumstances, Wynne will arrange a time when he can collect from the person in the embassy material for subject. This material should be in Wynne's possession for the shortest possible period of time. The material will include among other things, a re-supply of Minox cassettes, special shortwave radio receiver, and instructions for delivery of further consignments of material."[2]

Wynne also showed Penkovsky a black-and-white picture of Janet Anne Chisholm, the wife of Roderick Chisholm, which he had received at the British Embassy. Mrs. Chisholm was the contact who would be in the park with her three small children, two boys and a girl (also in the photograph), to whom he could deliver material and from whom he would receive messages and resupplies of film. Wynne did not tell Penkovsky her full name, but called her Anne, her code name, and, to help identify her, said she had dark hair and brown eyes. Wynne showed Penkovsky a diagram of the park along Tsvetnoy Boulevard near the Central Market and gave him instructions on the time to meet Anne. Penkovsky was to sit on a bench near the entrance to the park and wait for Anne, or if she was there with a baby carriage, he should approach the children and give them a box of Drazhes, chocolate-covered candies with sweet, liquid fillings. Penkovsky would hand the box to Anne, who would put it under the blanket in the baby carriage and withdraw another box of candy, which she would give to the children. Penkovsky, whose American code name was HERO, was told to be sure that the mother of the children was nearby when he offered them the candies. The meeting time was set for as close to 1530 hours as possible.

Wynne kept the pictures of Anne and her children with him throughout the visit so that it would appear to anyone watching that Wynne was showing Penkovsky pictures of his own wife and children. Penkovsky studied the photographs at every suitable opportunity in order to make sure that he would recognize Anne and her children, but he did not retain any of the photographs. Wynne handed the photos back to Rauri Chisholm in the British Embassy before he left Moscow; Wynne assured him that they had never left his possession and could be regarded as completely uncompromised.

Janet Chisholm was thirty-two years old in 1961. She had been a secretary for MI6 before marrying Rauri and was familiar with security procedures. The danger that Janet Chisholm, the mother of three charming blond children, would be identified as an MI6 officer by the KGB was judged by Shergold to be a risk worth taking. She was poised and calm, an attractive, no-nonsense person with keen intelligence. She would meet with Penkovsky after Wynne left.

Not a single day passed without some form of meeting between Wynne and Penkovsky. Wynne's presence encouraged Penkovsky, who told Wynne he looked upon him as a "representative of the queen." On Wednesday, May 31, Wynne met Penkovsky and received a sealed envelope from him which Wynne passed to Chisholm. In accordance with British SIS instructions, Chisholm did not open the envelope. He sent it in a sealed diplomatic pouch to headquarters in London. Wynne told Chisholm that Penkovsky was worried about whether the films he had handed over on May 27 would be legible because they had been exposed under various light conditions. On June 5, 1961, Penkovsky handed Wynne one more letter and received one from Wynne.

On June 6 Penkovsky took Wynne to Sheremetievo Airport and again ensured that he was not embarrassed by any customs or immigration formalities. The visit had gone well and Penkovsky was gratified.[3]

The handwritten note from Penkovsky, which Wynne did not read, said, "In July I will hand over the sweets to the children. I was very pleased with the conditions of contacting the lady, worked out by you." He anticipated one meeting with Anne to transmit information while Wynne was out of reach over the summer.

Thereafter he planned to collect material and hand it over to Wynne when he returned to Moscow at the end of August. Penkovsky expected that by the end of the summer he would accumulate a considerable quantity. In a note to the Americans in Washington, the British, who had received Penkovsky's letter from Moscow, reported, "In addition to documents and films, he intends to hand over to Wynne at that time a small optical instrument connected with the sighting or guiding of missiles."[4]

Penkovsky emphasized that as a result of what he would give Wynne at the end of August there would be a great deal of work for his friends. He would therefore need at least three weeks in Great Britain, during a planned October visit with a Soviet delegation, in which to answer all the questions his friends would want to put and to assimilate future requirements. In this connection Wynne was doubtful about whether he could find reasonable excuses to make the visit of the proposed thirty-man delegation last for three weeks. He was, however, confident he could make it last for at least two weeks.[5]

On June 3, 1961, President Kennedy, triumphant after being feted in Paris by Charles de Gaulle, arrived in Vienna on a gray, rainy Saturday morning for two days of talks with Chairman Khrushchev. Kennedy and Khrushchev had met briefly in 1959, when Khrushchev visited the Senate Foreign Relations Committee during his trip to the United States. Khrushchev remembered that Kennedy had come late and they had not had an opportunity to say more than hello and goodbye.

Their first meeting, held in the American Embassy at 12:45 P.M., started with pleasantries and careful verbal fencing. Kennedy said later that he found Khrushchev to be a combination of external jocosity and internal rage.[6] Both men believed that the fighting in Laos between forces supported by the United States and the Soviet Union should be halted without further escalation, and they agreed to make a cease-fire in Laos a priority. It was the only piece of business they resolved in Vienna. On the question of a nuclear test ban, Khrushchev was adamant that inspections be monitored by representatives of three world groups—Communists, neutrals, and the Western states—who would be empowered to adopt only those decisions agreed upon by all. Khrushchev insisted that the test ban itself had little importance and must be linked to general and complete disarmament. They went around and around. Kennedy warned that unless there was a test ban, nuclear weapons would spread and there would be ten or fifteen nuclear powers in a few years. Khrushchev insisted that the Soviet Union would not accept controls it considered equivalent to spying. Later, in his memoirs, Khrushchev admitted the reason he would not accept a test ban was because he did not want the West to see the true, inferior state of the Soviet nuclear weapons program in 1961.[7]

After an unsatisfactory discussion on controlling nuclear weapons, they turned to Berlin and the German situation, which Khrushchev said was "intolerable" and would have to be changed. Kennedy replied that the Western allies were in Berlin as a result of the victory gained in World War II. Berlin, he told Khrushchev, was of primary and vital concern to the United States, and if the U.S. allowed itself to be expelled, American pledges and commitments elsewhere in the world would be regarded as mere scraps of paper. The abandonment of West Berlin would mean the abandonment of Western Europe.

Khrushchev insisted that sixteen years after World War II the time had come for a peace treaty with Germany. If the West refused to sign one, the Soviet Union would go ahead on its own. This act would end the state of war, he explained, and cancel all existing commitments, including occupation rights, administrative institutions, and rights of access to East Berlin. East Germany would be totally responsible for its own territory. The treaty would establish the Free City of West Berlin. There would be no interference with its internal affairs or its communications, though agreement on access would have to be reached with the German Democratic Republic.

Western troops would be acceptable in West Berlin under certain conditions—and of course, with Soviet troops too. "And if there is any attempt to interfere with these plans," Khrushchev added, "there will be war."

Kennedy did not flinch. He looked straight at Khrushchev and said, "Then, Mr. Chairman, there will be war. It will be a cold winter."[8]

In 1948 Stalin had tried to force the Western allies from Berlin by halting road access through the corridor connecting Berlin to the Western zones. For fifteen months, from June 1948 to September 1949, the Allies, led by the United States, airlifted in hundreds of thousands of tons of supplies to keep West Berlin and its 2.5 million people alive. Now Khrushchev was threatening to turn control of the access routes over to East Germany and disrupt the balance of power in Europe. Here was a critical test of Kennedy's resolve.

At the Bay of Pigs, in March 1961, Kennedy had refused to commit American military power. Now Khrushchev thought he could test the president again and find him wanting in resolve. When they parted, Khrushchev told Kennedy he would not resume nuclear tests in the atmosphere unless the U.S. did so first.[9] Then Khrushchev handed Kennedy an aide-mémoire on Berlin, the formal and precise Soviet position, reflecting Khrushchev's remarks. Khrushchev had once told Secretary of State Dean Rusk that Berlin exposed "the 'testicles of the West,' which he could grab and squeeze whenever it suited him."[10]

Khrushchev was beginning to squeeze them. Dean Rusk's biographer, Thomas Schoenbaum, noted, "to those involved, Berlin was the most serious crisis since the end of World War II, because it involved a direct face-off between the United States and the Soviet Union in a situation where both sides (and especially the West) were committed to the possible use of nuclear weapons."[11]

It was NATO doctrine to resort to the use of nuclear weapons in response to a Soviet attack on Western Europe. During the Eisenhower administration, American nuclear strategy was dominated by the concept of massive retaliation to a Soviet attack on the United States or abroad. The U.S. nuclear response would be to attack a combination of military, urban-industrial, and government command-and-control targets in one great spasm. This strategy was incorporated as NATO's doctrine in May 1957, and it called for a massive nuclear response to any sustained Soviet attack, whether or not the Soviets used nuclear weapons.[12]

The Vienna meeting had a powerful impact on Kennedy. James Reston, columnist, *New York Times* bureau chief, and the most powerful and influential journalist in Washington at the time, asked for a private meeting with the president after his final encounter with Khrushchev.

Reston flew to Vienna and avoided fellow journalists. He waited in a darkened room in the embassy. The president arrived wearing a hat. He sank into the couch. Reston recalled later that Kennedy "pushed the hat over his eyes like a beaten man, and breathed a great sigh."

"Pretty rough?" Reston asked.

"Roughest thing in my life," the president answered. He was, Reston thought, genuinely shaken.

Kennedy told Reston, "I've got two problems. First, to figure out why he did it, and in such a hostile way. And second, to figure out what we can do about it. I think the first part is pretty easy to explain. I think he did it because of the Bay of Pigs. I think he thought that anyone who was so young and inexperienced as to get into that mess could be taken, and anyone who got into it and didn't see it through had no guts. So he just beat hell out of me. So I've got a terrible problem. If he thinks I'm inexperienced and have no guts, until we remove those ideas we won't get anywhere with him. So we have to act."[13]

Khrushchev was creating a crisis that threatened nuclear war over Berlin. Kennedy's Soviet advisers saw in the blunt, crude Soviet leader his usual pattern of exaggeration and threat, not to be taken at face value. For Kennedy, however, with his finely tuned sense of image and political advantage, Khrushchev had issued a challenge that could not be ignored. It was to be a sustained crisis that many of those involved believed came closer to nuclear war than the Cuban missile crisis a year later. Penkovsky's information was to prove crucial in accurately forecasting Khrushchev's intentions, his plan of action, and how he would react to Western responses.

As soon as he returned to Washington from Vienna on June 6, 1961, President Kennedy moved to set up a Berlin task force to respond to Khrushchev's new challenge. Ever since 1958 Khrushchev had been threatening to move unilaterally on Berlin, but he had failed to act. Kennedy knew Berlin was a potential flash point and in March of 1961 he had asked former Secretary of State Dean Acheson to do a study of the Berlin situation. The final version was submitted to the president three weeks after Kennedy's return from Vienna.

Acheson warned the president that a Communist takeover of the city in any form would profoundly reshape the alignment of power in Europe. An American willingness to fight for Berlin was essential if the Soviet Union was not to dominate Europe, and by so doing, dominate Asia and Africa too.

Acheson recommended that the president publicly request from Congress a large increase in the military budget as soon as the Soviet Union stepped up tensions on Berlin. Acheson urged the president to declare a national emergency, which would allow him to mobilize the reserves, extend terms of service, bring back dependents from Europe, and impress all concerned—particularly Khrushchev—with the gravity with which the United States regarded the situation.

President Kennedy accepted many of Acheson's recommendations, but took the advice of his Soviet experts, Charles Bohlen and Tommy Thompson, not to escalate the tension with strong pronouncements that would force the Soviet Union to escalate beyond the rhetoric. On June 8 Ambassador Thompson was shown the recent intelligence produced by the CIA clandestine services regarding the Soviet ICBM and other missiles. He expressed only casual interest in this material, but did remark that he personally agreed with one report, that the Soviets did not have a capable ICBM at present and that their security measures might be designed to conceal weakness rather than strength in this regard. The ambassador asked particularly whether the U.S. had any intelligence indicating how seriously the Soviets took the announced Western determination to hold firm in Berlin. He was particularly interested in what kind of intelligence the RIS [Russian Intelligence Service] might be collecting on the Western contingency planning on the Berlin issue.[14]

On Sunday, July 2, 1961, Penkovsky met in the park off Tsvetnoy Boulevard with Janet Chisholm. The sky was overcast when he walked under an archway of plane trees that lined the hard dirt midway of the park. The park was active with children and pensioners. Some sat on long wooden benches along the sides of the park. At the entrance, stands selling ice cream and sweets served the spillover from the Moscow Circus and the Central Market across the street. Penkovsky watched for a foreign woman with a baby carriage and three blond children. He spotted her but waited; there were too many people around. When rain threatened, the crowd thinned and Penkovsky walked toward the bench where Mrs. Chisholm was sitting. He stopped, smiled, and chatted with her and the children, then offered them a box of candy, a seemingly spontaneous gesture inspired by the charm of the youngsters. She thanked him on behalf of the children, placed the box of sweets under the carriage blanket, and took out another box of chocolates which she opened and offered to the children. In the candy box Penkovsky handed to the children in Janet Chisholm's presence were two typewritten sheets of paper and seven containers of undeveloped film. The type-written sheets contained an important statement on Berlin by Marshal Varentsov and details of the Soviet missile brigades in Germany. The Berlin matter required urgent treatment because the president would have to respond to Khrushchev. Penkovsky wanted to help shape that response.

On July 4 Penkovsky was called into the office of his chief, Dzhermen Gvishiani, and told that he had been promoted to deputy chief of the Foreign Department because of the excellent work he had done on his trip to Great Britain. While Penkovsky savored the good news, Gvishiani handed him a secret directive from the Central Committee for organizing the Soviet Industrial Exhibition in London later in July. One of the instructions was for the State Committee to arrange for a delegation of forty to fifty individuals from Soviet economic organizations to acquaint themselves with British companies and establish business contacts in Great Britain.

"You are the deputy head of the section," Gvishiani told Penkovsky. "You have all the cards in your hand, you are energetic and sensible, you can again organize all this and do it. We need to have it done urgently. The decree was signed on the first of July but we only received it today on the direct phone from the Kremlin." There was no time to waste; the delegation was due to leave within the month.

Penkovsky hurriedly put the delegation together, but just before it was scheduled to leave, it was canceled on Central Committee orders. Infighting in the Presidium and a defection from a Soviet ballet company in France made the control organs, the KGB, and the Central Committee more careful. In the end only Penkovsky, who worked for both the State Committee and the GRU, was authorized to go to Great Britain for three weeks and make arrangements for future delegations. He was also given a list of intelligence requirements to fulfill while in London. He could not have been happier.[15]

On July 7 a note from Maurice Oldfield, the British Secret Intelligence Service liaison in Washington, to Jack Maury, informed the Agency that Penkovsky's July 2 meeting with Mrs. Chisholm had resulted in the delivery of seven rolls of undeveloped film and two typewritten sheets containing "an important statement on Berlin by the Chief Marshal [Varentsov] and further details of the rocket brigades in East Germany." Penkovsky's report was dated June 26, 1961, and marked *Especially Important and Urgent*. Penkovsky wrote that

On June 25, 1961, I was at Varentsov's dacha on the occasion of the celebration of his promotion to chief marshal. A party of friends gathered to confer upon him the new rank. Only close friends were at the dacha.

In a private conversation he said to me, "Soon after the completion of the Party Congress a peace treaty will be signed. This is the final decision of Khrushchev and his leadership. The signature will no longer be put off. Firmness in politics is necessary, in particular on the German question, and the West will retreat before this firmness. The Soviet government knows that signing this treaty means a certain risk and danger, but they are not worried, because they know that the FRG [West Germany] still is not ready for war and needs two or three years more. The U.S., Britain, and France, because of this, will not start a big war and will retreat. We also do not want a big war, but we want to force the West to begin to negotiate with the GDR [East Germany] on the procedure for movement along access routes, the procedure for entrance and exit from Berlin, etc. These first negotiations with the GDR will amount to the first recognition of the GDR, and this is important for history. It is necessary to force by firmness at least partial recognition of the GDR and restrict the West in Berlin.

"Immediately after the signing of the treaty a state of battle alert will be ordered and the troops of the GDR will cut off and block the main road at Helmstadt and other dangerous highways with tanks. Air patrolling will be strengthened.

"Battle readiness will also be declared for Soviet troops located in the GDR as well as Czechoslovakia. We are ready to support the GDR with a multitude of tanks, and if necessary with other means if the West moves its tanks and other weapons to hold and reinforce its access to Berlin. However, we want this clash to be short and limited in scale. After the signing of the treaty the GDR will establish new travel regulations for the use by the West of railways leading to Berlin and for other communications procedures with Berlin. We do not intend to forbid the West to communicate with Berlin, but there will be particular restrictions and it will be necessary for the U.S. to negotiate with Berlin, which is very important. While recognizing the risk, we believe that there will not be a major war, but there may be a local clash restricted only to the territory of Germany, and to a small area."

The CIA titled the translated report from Penkovsky "Statement by a Soviet Senior General Staff Officer on the Soviet Plans to Sign a Peace Treaty with the German Democratic Republic." The source was described to be a reliable and well placed Soviet official who received the information from a confidential discussion with a senior

Soviet general officer who was directly concerned with Soviet military preparations for Berlin. The report said the statement was made while the two were alone at a private party.

Penkovsky also added his own interpretation of Varentsov's comments and his recommendations, which were not circulated within the intelligence community. Under the heading "Remarks," he wrote:

1. A treaty will be signed.

2. The firmness of Khrushchev must be met with firmness.

3. It seems to me that Khrushchev might also retreat on the period of signing the treaty, if he feels that we [referring to the West, which Penkovsky considered himself part of in his work] are not confused and if we prepare significant strength for the defense and reinforcement of communications with Berlin. He is not prepared for a big war, and is waging a war of nerves. It would be advantageous to announce widely and broadcast the large redeployment of NATO troops, of the bringing of the troops to battle readiness, of the great strength and power of the FRG, of the placement in Europe of several thousand tanks and airplanes, of the simulated movement of troops, etc. It is necessary that all this be exaggerated, but it is necessary also to actually increase our strength in this theater for a short punch in the teeth.

What we should do is to announce that we shall not be the first to fire a shot in Germany. But, if they use force to block our roads to Berlin, we shall sweep everything from the roads, secure them, and cease fire. We shall maintain the previous procedure for the use by all countries of the means of communications, i.e., all may stay in Berlin.

On the same sheet of paper Penkovsky confirmed that there were four Soviet missile brigades in the German Democratic Republic.

Col. V. I. Fedorov commands the brigade deployed in Weissenfels. He is the garrison commander in the town. A motorized infantry regiment is also deployed there. Fedorov's son is studying in Naumburg, which is about fifteen kilometers [nine miles] from Weissenfels. Fedorov was in Moscow and told me that the average German is not friendly toward the Soviets; that in the event of some danger, if the Soviet troops do not quickly pull out of the towns into the countryside, the populace can blockade the roads leading to the city limits. They will kill all the Soviet troops and destroy the equipment. That is, the Soviets are afraid of getting stuck in populated areas with their equipment, for this will be the end for

187

all. According to Fedorov, if the Soviets manage to pull out into the countryside and take up defense positions, they will destroy everybody and everything around them.

"We," said Penkovsky referring now to the Americans, British, and Western allies, "must take this into consideration and at the appropriate moment destroy the roads of the towns where Soviet troops are located, keep them covered, and not give the troops the opportunity to leave the towns to take up fire positions."

Some of Fedorov's missiles are stored in parks in Weissenfels. Not long ago it was noticed that some of the missile compartments had holes and began to leak when placed in a test fueling position. The electrical systems also were not in order. In September Fedorov wants to send his wife and two children to Moscow. They generally send a large proportion of the families home whenever a critical situation arises. Fedorov himself would like to return to Moscow and work for Varentsov again. He finds commanding the brigade a strain. He told me that if even a small fire occurred in the garrison or if one of his soldiers ran off, he would be reprimanded and removed from the command of the brigade, but that Sergei Sergeyevich [Varentsov] would still take him back. I think that we ought to help him out in this regard by creating some kind of unpleasantness in the brigade. In the uproar Sergei Sergeyevich would have him transferred to his command. To me and to us in our work, he is more valuable in Moscow. I ask you to help me in this. I am one hundred percent certain that Sergey Sergeyevich will take him back, but there is no reason at present. We must cooperate in this matter.

One of the missile brigades in the GDR is commanded by Major General Vinogradov. Not long ago three soldiers in Vinogradov's brigade raped and then robbed a German woman.

On the afternoon of July 11, Dick Helms, chief of operations in the Directorate of Plans, and Jack Maury, chief of the clandestine service's Soviet Division, met with Allen Dulles, director of the CIA, to discuss the handling of Penkovsky's report on Berlin. Of course Penkovsky was never referred to by his real name, but only by a cryptonym that changed every few months. To protect Penkovsky's security his name was known only to a small number with a direct, must-need-to-know, Jack Maury among them. Other senior officials not involved in running Penkovsky knew only that their source was a colonel on the Soviet General Staff.[16]

Allen Dulles noted that the National Security Council was meeting on July 12, and that he would be seeing the president on Friday morning at 11:00. "I would like to hand the report to the president at that time," said Dulles, who was also shown Penkovsky's recommendations on Berlin in case he chose to raise them with the president.

Dulles asked Maury and Helms what they thought of Penkovsky's bona fides. Maury had discussed the question at length with James Jesus Angleton, the head of Counterintelligence at the Agency and a key person to pass on Penkovsky's credibility as an agent. In a memorandum for the record, Maury said he "believed that Mr. Angleton shared my view that the scope, variety, and complexity of material reported on by the Source, ranging all the way from technical data on missiles to identities of illegals being trained for assignment to the West, was too big a mouthful for the Soviets to handle in a single controlled operation. Mr. Helms fully supported this view, which the Director seemed to accept. The Director asked about the Subsources and Mr. Helms said that on the identity of the Subsource all concerned had sworn themselves to secrecy but, in fact, he was a Marshal for Soviet artillery."

Because of the quantity and quality of his information, Maury argued that Penkovsky could not conceivably be a plant penetration agent for the KGB or the GRU but was a bona fide agent serving the CIA and MI6.

Dulles clearly did not want to be upstaged before he saw the president alone with the Berlin report from Penkovsky. He said he wanted the "disseminations to reach the other consumers" at approximately the same time he took it up with the president on Friday morning, July 14, 1961. The report on Berlin was not to be circulated to those cleared at the State Department, the Defense Department, and other U.S. intelligence agencies until then.

At this meeting Dulles instructed that the material on Berlin not be handled through one code-word channel, since he felt this would unnecessarily spotlight the source as having access to both high-level political information and written missile information.[17] By keeping the documentary material that Penkovsky passed on in one channel, to be called IRONBARK, and the political material gathered at personal meetings and through word of mouth in another code-word channel, which was code named CHICKADEE, it was possible to make it appear within the intelligence community that the material was coming from different sources within the Soviet military establishment. The IRONBARK documentary material on details of equipment, operating techniques of the GRU, and Soviet military doctrine went to top-level analysts specifically cleared for the code-named project. This system kept the list of those cleared, the so-called BIGOT list, small and under tight control. The other category of code-word material, CHICKADEE—political and military information Penkovsky overheard or acquired in social meetings, some of it simply high-level gossip—was passed on to the president, the National Security Council, and senior intelligence analysts in the State Department and within the CIA itself. This material helped to provide a background for the hard statistics and photointelligence material that was being received from other channels.

Robert Gates, director of the CIA, explained, "Until Penkovsky we had the words and the music but not the rhythm of Soviet military and strategic doctrine. With him the focus clarified because we learned of Khrushchev's intentions."[18] Penkovsky's inside access to the top leadership and what was being said by the defense minister and the top military about Khrushchev and his policies was invaluable, especially at a time of unprecedented tensions that threatened nuclear war.

The so-called compartmentalization of Penkovsky's information helped to protect him by not making it so readily apparent that the sudden and valuable flood of intelligence data from the Soviet Union was all coming from a single person. However, many of the key players in the State Department and the CIA soon realized that the two different categories of Top Secret code-word material all did come from the same source.[19]

The Agency was now working full time to translate the documents Penkovsky had provided in the form of Minox photographs. None of them had previously been available to the West. In Washington the Agency set up a translation team in the former Women's Army Corps barracks south of Fort Myer in Arlington, Virginia, and had twenty people devoted to the project, while the British had a team of ten people translating the documents in London. A sampling of the list of documents Penkovsky supplied included the Soviet Armed Forces Field Service Regulations (Division-Corps) dated 1958.

This secret 320-page document, the Agency told its consumers in the Defense Department, "is the tactical operational Bible for the Soviet Armed Forces. It was previously issued in 1948 and is revised infrequently. Possession of this manual will permit us to reorganize our own forces and train them to meet the Soviet tactics spelled out in great detail in these regulations." The Field Service Regulations provide full instructions on organization for combat and the deployment of combat arms. It includes diagrams for deployment of forces for defense and attack and the formations to be used for marching to war. It defined the distances forces could travel to keep up with their logistics.

Penkovsky also provided artillery training manuals and copies of *Military Thought (Voyennaya Mysl)*, volumes 5, 6, and 7, all published in 1959. These Top Secret journals, whose circulation was restricted to general officers in command positions, contained articles debating military and nuclear strategy. They provided rare insights into Soviet thinking on the use of chemical warfare, whether to build aircraft carriers, and how to deploy battlefield nuclear weapons.

At his meeting in the White House on July 13, Allen Dulles told President Kennedy that the CIA and MI6, in a joint operation, had a colonel on the Soviet General Staff spying for the West. Dulles showed Kennedy Penkovsky's account of his meeting with Varentsov on June 25, and told the president about Penkovsky's recommendations for dealing with Khrushchev. Kennedy was clearly in agreement with the Soviet colonel's suggestions that he be firm and not give way to Khrushchev's threats, and he later incorporated some of these ideas in a speech on Berlin.[20] Kennedy told Dulles to keep him informed of the spy's progress and directed him to advise General Maxwell Taylor, his military adviser, about the new Russian source.*

An internal CIA memo on the subject of what material to show Taylor suggested "articles from the Top Secret and previously unavailable supplement to Soviet military publications Military Thought." The memo said the articles were "described by a recent Soviet defector—a Navy Captain—as the most authoritative and highly classified Soviet military publication in existence. Among the headings are Missiles, Anti Missile Defense, Support of Missile Forces, Naval Problems, Tank Troops, Naval Role in Closed Seas and Tactical Reconnaissance. Also included is a map of GSFG [Group of Soviet Forces Germany] paper exercises showing the order of battle, assembly areas, break-out routes, etc."[21]

Penkovsky's gossip on impending military organizational and personnel changes, including the transfers of high-ranking officers, would also be of interest to General Taylor.

In addition to his Berlin message, Penkovsky's film contained:

- A thirty-six-page Top Secret document of the Military-Diplomatic Academy titled "Personal Communications in Agent Intelligence," by Vice Admiral L. K. Bekrenev, which provided a key to GRU operating techniques.

- Another Top Secret document, sixty-eight pages long, titled

*General Maxwell Taylor (1901–1987) was appointed military adviser to President Kennedy in April 1961, after the Bay of Pigs, and chairman of the Joint Chiefs of Staff in 1962. He held that position until 1964, when President Johnson named him ambassador to South Vietnam. Taylor was chief of staff of the Army from 1955 to 1959.

191

"Matters Concerning Agent Communications and the Control of Agents."

- A thirteen-page letter of the Central Committee of the Communist Party of the Soviet Union, dated May 19, 1961, on the tasks of the Party organizations in respect to some aspects of cheating the government in the economic sphere.

- Forty-three pages of instructions from the Council of Ministers of the U.S.S.R., dated May 30, 1961, outlining tasks to be carried out by the State Committee for the Coordination of Scientific Research Work in the third quarter of 1961, and documents reviewing the achievements of the State Committee, dated March 15, 1961.

The first two documents were the most important. Penkovsky had supplied the list of sixty students enrolled at the Military-Diplomatic Academy in Moscow, all of them future GRU officers. By June 10 the CIA had assembled biographical data and pictures of fifty-two of the sixty men. American Intelligence would now know most of the military intelligence operatives the Soviets were sending abroad.

The other document, which provided detailed material on GRU communications methods and operational procedures, exposed the inner workings of Soviet Military Intelligence.

With the president directly involved and the Berlin crisis demanding an American response, Penkovsky's material took on an unparalleled urgency and relevance. As his value became more apparent, the Agency tried to devise safe ways to contact him in Moscow. One scheme was to use a foreign diplomat from a friendly Western European country to load a dead drop in Moscow. The Western diplomat was briefed in a safe house in Helsinki and asked if he were willing to load the drop, but was not told who the Soviet agent was. He was to receive the material for the dead drop from a magazine rack in the second-floor toilet in America House, but the plan was never put into operation.[22]

This was part of elaborate backup plans devised in case Wynne was unable to visit Moscow. Shergold, who initiated the British operational plan, subject to American concurrence, told the Americans that the alternative would be to leave a message for Penkovsky in his dead letter box (DLB) with instructions for delivery of his material. "We will indicate to him that material is ready for his collection in his DLB by ringing his home telephone number punctually at 1000 hours on a Sunday morning from a call box. The person making the call will allow the phone to ring three times. Subject should aim to clear the DLB as soon as possible after receipt of the above signal.

"If subject should be approached at a social gathering, where Western diplomats are present, by somebody who introduces the name Charles Peeke into the conversation, subject will know that this person is an emissary of ours and will be ready to receive a message from subject. As a further identification the diplomat will wear the agreed tie clasp.

"Only if there is breakdown in all of the above systems of communication, subject should pass a message and material to us by throwing it over the wall of America House at the agreed point at 2200 hours on the first Saturday of any month, with alternative of 2200 hours on the Sunday following the first Saturday of any month, beginning with July.

"If subject should be in any country outside of the Sino-Soviet Bloc,* and have been unable to notify us of his departure in advance, he should inform us of his presence and give an indication of where he can be contacted by sending a telegram to the telegraphic address LABORICI London. Such a telegram should be signed ALEX."[23]

How to present the new Russian source to the intelligence community and how much to tell the consumers inside the community was an overriding issue. The British sent a message to Washington stating that as far as they were concerned Penkovsky's bona fides were clearly established "beyond any reasonable doubt." On July 13, before Allen Dulles went to tell President Kennedy about Penkovsky, Dick Helms, Jack Maury, and James Angleton had discussed the bona fides of their new Soviet source with Dulles.

One concern of Maury's was that Penkovsky might become compromised. Would he be discovered and turned to work against the Americans and British? That question would linger and gnaw. The case of Pyotr Popov, the GRU officer who spied for the United States and was then discovered by the Russians and turned, was a wound that still rankled. Maury was concerned that Penkovsky might be discovered "and played back like Popov." Helms did not want to go as far as the British in "going bail," as he put it, for Penkovsky, but he added that "deception up to now was virtually ruled out." Helms was convinced for the moment but was continually reassessing. Jim

---

*At that time the split between China and the Soviet Union was just becoming public, and it was still commonplace to refer to the Sino-Soviet Bloc, despite Mao's growing impatience with Khrushchev.

Angleton found the material of great importance but he character-ized the new source as "an anarchist and a crank who for some obscure reason is trying to get us into a war with Russia."[24]

The complexity of Penkovsky's character was hard to fathom. His zeal and intensity were disconcerting, but there was no evidence that he was controlled by the KGB or GRU and was disseminating false information. He told too much and what he provided was too damaging to Soviet interests. Yet the CIA would proceed with cau-tion, protecting the new source carefully, while continuing to check his bona fides.

Officials reading Penkovsky's reports had no idea who he was. How much weight should be given to his reports? Was this really the inside explanation of policy decisions or was it speculation from the officers' mess?

To explain his background, an operational history of Penkovsky, dated July 18, 1961, was drawn up by the CIA's Soviet Division. It described him only as "a senior-grade Soviet Army staff officer presently in intelligence, whose career up to a certain point was successful and indeed brilliant. Many details of his career have been checked from independent sources and others have been substanti-ated by documentary evidence. There is no doubt that he occupies the position of responsibility and authority that he claims."

In examining Penkovsky's motivation the CIA report said:

> At a certain point Subject's further advancement in his career was hampered through disagreement on matters of principle with his superiors. At this time the first seeds of discontent were probably sown and he began to consider the possibility of entering into an arrangement with the Western powers. His tour of duty in a West-ern country was abruptly terminated; while there he was definitely attracted by the good things in life the West has to offer. Both from the career and materialistic points of view, dissatisfaction grew and he began to prepare actively for the day when he could make contact with the USA. As early as 1958, Subject, according to his own statement, began to collect some of the material which he has since handed over. Though these statements cannot be checked fully, there is supporting evidence to show that they are probably true.

The evaluation, based on more than fifty hours of personal meet-ings with Penkovsky, stated:

> It is the considered and unanimous judgment of the four case offi-cers, and of the experts in Washington and London who have evalu-ated the material received, that the Source genuinely desires to serve the West, and that he does indeed have extraordinary access

to extremely sensitive information as well as to senior Soviet policy makers. These conclusions are in large measure supported by collateral evidence.

Since the London contacts Subject has provided, in response to our requirements, highly valuable information including details on the official Soviet policy on the Berlin question and details on the training, operation methods and communications procedures of Soviet clandestine agent contact. His recent information was acquired through clandestine contact arranged by the British. The British have informed us that this capability cannot be provided beyond October. Unless we can arrange adequate and suitable facilities we are faced with the prospect of losing contact with this valuable source of information at precisely the time when the Berlin crisis may be approaching a climax.

The British were uncertain that Wynne would be able to return to Moscow and the decision to use Janet Chisholm to meet Penkovsky on a regular basis had not been made when this report was written. A preliminary "Evaluation of the Counterintelligence Product" supplied by Penkovsky was also made by the CIA and it summarized that he had provided:

A. Unique information concerning the current Soviet intelligence structure, including identification of a staff component concerned with sabotage, subversion, and assassination in support of military operations.

Similarly unprecedented information on the role of the CPSU Central Committee apparatus as the principal consumer of the Soviet Intelligence product and as the policy coordinator-supervisor of Soviet Intelligence;

B. A reaffirmation that the prime Soviet Intelligence objective is to furnish early warning of foreign attack;

C. Identification of more than 300 Soviet Intelligence officers and of more than a dozen Soviet Intelligence agents active in the West;

D. Documentary evidence regarding the Soviet intelligence training including procedures for agent clandestine contact and communications;

E. Reports indicating CPSU Central Committee and Soviet Intelligence intent to increase the already great emphasis on the so-called Illegal operations.

The Agency was convinced of Penkovsky's worth and credibility; the president had been informed and agreed the Soviet colonel's material was fascinating and vital. Now Penkovsky was ready to be marketed to the intelligence community and senior policymakers.

On July 22, 1961, Dick Helms met for thirty minutes with General Maxwell Taylor to discuss the material Penkovsky had delivered. Taylor was deeply impressed and told Helms, "This is the kind of thing a lot of us don't hear anything about." At one point in the briefing, Taylor expressed surprise at Penkovsky's statement that early warning was the prime Soviet intelligence objective. Taylor asked to be put on the list for future distribution of all of Penkovsky's material and that which had already been disseminated. "I think Allen [Dulles] ought to brief the president on this and let him know what we have here," Taylor told Helms, not knowing to what extent the president had already been briefed by Dulles.

When he returned to CIA headquarters on the Mall, near the Potomac, Helms directed Maury to provide Taylor with the processed material on the Soviet ICBM program, the shooting down of the RB-47, the shooting down of the U-2, and Soviet plans for Berlin. The Agency had also prepared a report on Penkovsky's account of the circumstances surrounding the death of the head of the Soviet missile forces, Marshal Nedelin, during a missile misfiring accident in 1960. Maury provided this to General Taylor along with translations of the Field Service Regulations and all of the *Military Thought* articles. Most important, on July 24, Maury brought General Taylor Penkovsky's account of Khrushchev's plans for Berlin that Allen Dulles had shown President Kennedy ten days earlier.[25] Penkovsky's information, carefully placed with influential advisers and decision-makers, quickly had an impact during the critical period.

The essential issue that remained unresolved was Penkovsky's bona fides. There was no way to protect against his being doubled, therefore they had to remain vigilant. Was he really the man he said he was or were the GRU and KGB feeding him material as part of a massive disinformation plot? What was his real motivation? One way to tell to the Agency's satisfaction would be to subject Penkovsky to a polygraph—lie detector—test when he next came to the West. Would he submit? No one had raised the question with him.

On July 18, 1961, Penkovsky returned to London for work at the Soviet Exhibition at Earls Court and another round of meetings with the CIA-MI6 team.

Return to London

WHEN PENKOVSKY ARRIVED AT HEATHROW AT 9:45 A.M. ON JULY 18, he had four GRU assignments and a long list of requirements to fulfill for the State Committee in the next three weeks. His immediate task at hand was to take care of the wife and daughter of GRU chief, Ivan Serov, who were on the special Aeroflot flight with him from Moscow. Penkovsky and the Serovs were assigned to a plane that flew to London to pick up the Kirov ballet company.

At Sheremetievo, before leaving, Penkovsky approached Serov and discussed his mission in London. The GRU chief, dressed in civilian clothes, told Penkovsky he was pleased Penkovsky had been chosen to go to England when the visas of other officials had been canceled by the Central Committee. "Travel three or four times to the Capitalist countries. If you are not recognized [as an intelligence officer] after having worked as a military attaché and chief assistant in Turkey, we shall propose you for a prolonged mission. We shall test the attitudes of the Americans, British, and French towards you since you were a military type, but now you are a civilian," Serov said, referring to Penkovsky's civilian cover as a member of the State Committee.[1]

Serov introduced Penkovsky to his wife and daughter and told him to be sure and look after them in London. Penkovsky said he would be pleased to assist forty-eight-year-old Vera Ivanovna Serov and her attractive twenty-one-year-old daughter, Svetlana, a student. The day before they left, Serov had summoned Penkovsky to his office and informed his subordinate that his wife and daughter were traveling to London as tourists. Penkovsky was to ensure they had a car at their disposal, accompany them shopping, and generally make certain they had a good time in London. Serov had visited London

197

to arrange Khrushchev's visit to England in 1956, but the public protests against him because of his heinous career as Stalin's executioner were so great that he was forced to leave. For Serov's wife and daughter to go sightseeing in 1961 was unprecedented at a time when foreign travel was highly restricted for Soviet citizens.

When they collected their bags and cleared customs at Heathrow, Penkovsky quickly realized that nobody from the Soviet Embassy had come to greet the Serovs, despite a message from the GRU chief himself. Penkovsky took command, and waited an hour with the Serovs until an embassy car arrived to take them to their hotel. Since he had been to London once before, Penkovsky posed as an old hand, and extolled the pleasures of the city. He promised the grateful Serovs that he would personally show them the sites and help them shop. Penkovsky could hardly believe his good fortune at being able to ingratiate himself with his chief's wife and daughter. He would have three weeks in Great Britain, part of it with Mrs. Serov and Svetlana.

Penkovsky called Greville Wynne at his home on Upper Cheyne Row in Chelsea and told him that the Soviet Embassy had booked a room for him at the Kensington Close Hotel, off Kensington High Street, not far from the Soviet Embassy. Wynne set up a rendezvous point near the hotel for Penkovsky to meet Mike Stokes, the junior member of the British team. Stokes booked a room at the same hotel where Penkovsky was staying and escorted Penkovsky to the apartment of another MI6 officer, at the Little Boltons in Kensington, which was used as a safe house for the meetings.

Penkovsky had no idea that prior to his arrival CIA headquarters in Washington had suggested to the team in London that he be subjected to a polygraph test, standard treatment for all agents once they are recruited. The use of lie detector tests, nicknamed "fluttering," is a standard part of the Agency's security routine. The tests are administered at regular intervals to all CIA personnel including the director. The polygraph measures changes in heartbeat and pulse rates based on the subject's response to an agreed-upon list of questions. Standard questions ask whether an individual has taken drugs, been involved in criminal activities, or had meetings with foreign agents. The British eschew the use of fluttering, and a high-level, sensitive transatlantic debate was conducted over how to deal with Penkovsky.

Dick Helms, Jack Maury, and Eric W. Timm, chief of the West European Division, told the case officers in London that in view of the importance, past and prospective, of Penkovsky's reporting on critical issues such as Berlin, serious consideration must be given to submitting him to LCFLUTTER, the cryptonym for a lie detector test, during the upcoming meetings. At the same time, Helms and his Washington team acknowledged that preserving Penkovsky's motivations, confidence in, and rapport with his case officers remained, of course, overriding considerations. They concluded that whether LCFLUTTER could be administered without any risk must be left to the best judgment of the case officers involved.

CIA headquarters also informed the team that Penkovsky's Berlin report on Khrushchev's plan to sign a separate peace treaty with East Germany had been called to the personal attention of the highest State Department officials.

The day that Penkovsky arrived in London, July 18, CIA's London Station reported to Washington that the reaction to the LCFLUTTER proposal was "strongly and unanimously negative" on the part of the British and the two American case officers. Shergold, who strongly opposed the idea, asked Sir Dick White, the head of MI6, for his opinion. After balancing the risks involved, White concluded that the possibility of a seriously adverse effect upon the relationship with Penkovsky outweighed the gains that could conceivably be anticipated by submitting him to the test.

Sir Dick readily acknowledged that his own and MI6's lack of experience with the polygraph technique was a cause for his concern. He found it difficult to visualize, even under the most favorable circumstance, that a fully reassuring result could be obtained through such a test. He stressed the unique character and quality of Penkovsky and said he would be extremely reluctant to run the risk of prejudicing and conceivably losing a source of such very great value, both demonstrated and potential. Finally, Sir Dick made the point that the various possibilities of unwitting deception on the part of the source could not in any case be resolved by LCFLUTTER, and emphasized that only the passage of time, results, and the accumulation of opportunities to observe and check Penkovsky would provide the answer.

Shergold agreed fully with Sir Dick and warned that even if Penkovsky were to submit to LCFLUTTER it was a certainty that the experience and his subsequent reflection upon it would leave him in a very different state of mind, with the strong probability that the change would be for the worse. Shergold raised the prospect that if Penkovsky were shaken in his faith by the team's acquiescence to the test, which he would be likely to interpret as a lack of trust and confidence, it was quite conceivable that he might collapse. Failing that, Penkovsky might decide to limit himself in future reporting to strictly documentary material, thus avoiding all risks of prejudice to his reputation and ultimate prospects in the West. The London Station reply warned that the lie detector test should not be undertaken unless headquarters was prepared to face a showdown of such magnitude that it would surely disrupt the operation.

The London reply caused deep concern in Washington and there was another round of consultations and memo writing. The acting deputy chief of the Soviet Division wrote to Maury on July 19, addressing the question: "Is the Subject reliable and loyal to us?"

> Subject has tried every reasonable way possible to convince us of his reliability, loyalty and worth at the risk of his life. By any standards his performance has been outstanding. We have not yet caught him in any serious or deliberate error of fact. He is not merely responsive to our requests; he has demonstrated from the beginning of the operation tremendous initiative in volunteering information of great interest and value to us. There is a very great difference in dealing with an agent who volunteers information and one who merely responds to specific requests. We should not do anything to dampen his enthusiasm.

> Subject has been led to believe that we accept him as bona fide and he believes he has achieved acceptance by us. In my opinion this is the *key* to understanding the motivation of almost every one of our highest level agents as well as our highest level Soviet defectors. They turn elsewhere for acceptance when they do not find it at home. This is what subject has done. I believe there is considerable risk that the disillusionment involved in being asked at this stage to submit to LCFLUTTER will never be fully overcome and I do not consider that any possible benefit derived from LCFLUTTER is great enough to warrant this risk.

> LCFLUTTER is not infallible. It is claimed that it has never convicted an innocent person. But we all know of instances where the guilty were not caught by it. It could indicate that Subject is clean. It would not necessarily prove that the operation is controlled by the RIS [Russian Intelligence Service]. I think we have enough information to make the determination that Subject is clean. If he isn't, we should not complain too much—he is in any event a fertile and prolific source of valuable, accurate and detailed intelligence information.

It was left to Jack Maury to sum up the situation for Dick Helms, with whom the final decision rested. In a memorandum to Helms on July 19, 1961, Maury reviewed the pros and cons of LCFLUTTER for Penkovsky. First, Maury listed the arguments in favor of administering a lie detector test:

> a. It is a generally well-proved and accepted tool of the trade, and in a case of this significance, we should certainly avail ourselves of all the useful tools.

b. In view of the critical significance of at least two subjects reported on by HERO [Penkovsky's code name]—the Berlin crisis and the Soviet missile program—the value to the Soviets of an effective channel for deception on these subjects is obvious.

c. Although as far as we know the Soviets have not recently engaged in deception of this kind and scope, they may feel that they have learned enough of our interest and methods from [former GRU agent Pyotr Popov] to make such an effort worthwhile; there are, indeed, certain common characteristics in the two cases.

d. Although deception may be the most dangerous possibility in the HERO case, there is also grave danger in our failure to give full weight to a unique and reliable source; any case of this kind creates uncertainties, and the value of the present case depends on our ability to dispel as many of these uncertainties as possible. Therefore, if LCFLUTTER would reinforce our confidence in the case, its value would be enhanced accordingly.

e. HERO has apparently burned his bridges behind him. Even if the administration of LCFLUTTER creates adverse psychological effects, they will probably not be fatal to his relationship with us. Moreover, it may be argued that we would be wise to keep HERO "a little bit hungry" for our confidence, rather than to let him think we accept him blindly.

f. In view of HERO's past protestations of a desire to prove himself, he could not logically object to a procedure to which all members of the club to which he wishes to belong are subjected.

After making the case for LCFLUTTER, Maury proceeded to demolish it. He wrote:

a. LCFLUTTER is only a tool, and the interpretation of the results is not an exact science. It may be decisive in matters regarding the sex life of a JOT [junior officer trainee] and the bona fides of a low-level border crosser, but here we are dealing with a far more complex individual. Moreover, in the present case we have a number of other yardsticks upon which some reliance can be placed.

b. While we must be always mindful of Soviet deception in a case of this kind, the nature, scope, variety and complexity of the material reported on to date by HERO seems to me to be too big a bundle to be manageable. The agent has been personally exposed to us for 52 hours of meetings, during which he was under close scrutiny of four seasoned case officers. He has provided some 2,200 pages of documentary material on the most sensitive subjects. I cannot believe that the Soviets would have enough confidence in the acting ability of the agent or in their own knowledge of what we know and don't know about the matters he has reported on, to be willing

201

to expose themselves to the problems that such an operation would pose. Surely they could find an easier and safer way of accomplishing substantially the same purpose.

c. If the case does involve deception, presumably the purposes concern Berlin, yet it is hard to see how what the Source gives us as his own opinion would serve Soviet purposes in this regard.

d. Although a successful LCFLUTTER might give us reassurance regarding HERO's bona fides, the real problem here is consumer evaluation, and I doubt that an LCFLUTTER (or anything else) will be likely to eliminate the inevitable confusion in the minds of consumers when confronted with any significant report of clandestine service (CS) origin.

e. Believing, as I firmly do, in the bona fides of the case to date, I am particularly concerned about two hazards: (a) the unconscious bias of the Source and Subsources in reporting on matters of opinion and judgment, and (b) the possibility that, like [Popov], Source might be apprehended and brought under hostile control against his will at some unidentifiable moment. However, LCFLUTTER provides little reassurance on these points. We can only say that Subject's arrival in London on 18 July eliminates the latter possibility at least for the moment.

f. Assuming, as we must, that each meeting with HERO may be the last personal contact, and thereafter we may be able to communicate with him only through drops or brush meets [where material is exchanged without verbal or eye contact], we can ill afford to send him back to the lonely task of working for us in place in the USSR with a sour taste. If we could be certain of continued personal contact, we could perhaps heal any psychological wounds which LCFLUTTER might create, but of this we can never be certain.

g. On the basis of eighteen years of dealing with the Russians, both covertly and overtly, I am convinced that the human element— "personal rapport"—is a dominant factor in their motivation and behavior. In the present case it is difficult to imagine more advantageous circumstances in this regard, and any action we might take which could damage this relationship will involve grave risks.

In conclusion, I believe that:

a. It would be dangerous and irresponsible for us in Headquarters to overrule the best judgment of the four case officers involved.

b. Any attempt to overcome the apparently strong views of our British colleagues might endanger the harmonious relationships which have existed to date, and which are an important element in the successful joint handling of the case.

Later that day, July 19, Maury met with Helms and Timm to resolve the issue. The three senior officers in Washington upheld the judgment of the team in London. After the meeting Maury wrote a memorandum for the record summing up the result of their discussion: "It was agreed that no further action in this respect was feasible at this time as the operational risk to the agent's motivation outweighs the value of the polygraph."

The contributing factors, Maury believed, were British sensitivity, the case officer evaluation, and the scope of intelligence information, since it was doubtful that the Soviets would deliberately release such a wide range of materials. "They could not prepare all of it for our consumption as one knowledgeable defector or separate source would destroy their operation," wrote Maury.

Underlying the arguments over the polygraph test was the essential question of Penkovsky's loyalty and reliability. When he entered the second round of London meetings—ten sessions lasting more than forty hours—Penkovsky was the subject of heavy scrutiny in Washington. The wealth of material he supplied created a major translation and distribution problem in Washington and London. The recipients had to reach prompt conclusions on how to evaluate his material; they had to protect him from exposure, yet at the same time distribute his spectacular information to achieve maximum effectiveness in the intelligence community and at the highest levels of the government.

Allen Dulles, the director of the CIA since February 1953, was in critical disfavor with President Kennedy because of the Bay of Pigs debacle in April 1961. Although Kennedy had publicly taken the blame, Dulles knew he was on his way out. Kennedy held Dulles and his deputy director for plans, Richard Bissell, responsible for the failure and asked them to resign.[2] Then the Penkovsky case heated up. Dulles was a skilled, highly respected professional, determined to show the Agency's best side to the president and end his career on a high note.

Dulles followed his usual careful evaluation of the source and his material. Much to the chagrin of the Soviet Division, he called a Soviet expert from the Agency's Directorate of Information, the so-called overt branch of the Agency. The Directorate does not have covert agents in the field, but relies on analysts to sort through and synthesize the field reports and assess them.

Raymond L. Garthoff, a young Soviet analyst in the Office of National Estimates, was asked to review and comment on information from a new Soviet source. Dulles wanted to know if Garthoff thought the information was valid and should be distributed in the intelligence community. Garthoff said the information on Soviet missiles and missile forces appeared to be accurate and some of it could be confirmed. Other information was too new to confirm yet but "seemed to be on track." He told Dulles some information "seems to be out of line with our estimates and raises a question. If the source was genuine the information he was providing was extremely important and should be distributed."

Garthoff recalled in 1990 that Dulles was initially wary of the information and also "to the reception that might be accorded to the source and to CIA's acceptance of it if he disseminated information that seemed out of whack. But of course his principal purpose was in having an additional feel of the source that I, as an intelligence analyst, could offer as opposed to an espionage operator.

"What I recommended to the director, and what he decided, was to disseminate the material with attention to the fact that the source had different knowledge of different matters. Assertions had to be judged with that caveat, but he appeared to be a reliable source."[3]

A more important player in determining the credibility of Penkovsky was James J. Angleton, the Agency's head of Counterintelligence, responsible for preventing penetrations by the KGB and other hostile services at home and abroad. In the spring of 1961 Angleton was valued highly by Allen Dulles, who counted heavily on his judgment to evaluate the bona fides of Penkovsky. Maury, in an effort to win acceptance for Penkovsky, met with Angleton on June 30, 1961.

Maury wrote a memorandum for the record on his conversation with Angleton. He quoted Angleton as saying, "This was undoubtedly the most important case that we had for years." Angleton told Maury that he had read parts of the transcript of the first set of meetings in London and was completely convinced of the bona fides of the agent and the validity of the information he reported. As a result, Angleton said, he had concluded that it would be impossible to protect the source if they disseminated to general consumers reports that would fully reveal the significance and validity of the material. Maury wrote that Angleton felt "the general consumers could not be made aware of the full value of the case, but it was terribly important that the President, who was now faced with crucial problems regarding Berlin, should have the benefit of the full story."

Angleton strongly recommended that the president read the transcripts of the agent's meetings with the team in London. He said, "the full impact of the case could only be gained from reading a firsthand account of the agent's remarks. The transcript revealed so much about the agent's access and the validity of his information that this should be made available to the man who had to make crucial decisions regarding the Berlin crisis."

Maury raised the possibility of deception, remarking that in his judgment the total scope of the source's reporting was so broad that it was virtually unmanageable from the standpoint of a controlled deception operation. Recording his own comments for the record, Maury said: "I added that if the RIS [Russian Intelligence Service] attempted to mount a deception operation against us encompassing all of the military, technical counter espionage (CE), political and related fields upon which HERO had been reporting, they would be taking a terrific chance of tripping themselves up, since they could hardly know with certainty the extent of our solid knowledge in all of these fields. The complexity and variety of the subjects upon which HERO was reporting, and apparently reporting accurately, was, to me, the best reassurance we could have against deception."

Angleton said he completely agreed with this view, and told Maury that in reading the transcripts he had become convinced that a controlled agent simply wouldn't talk the way HERO talked. It would be totally out of character, for example, for a controlled source to express himself the way HERO had about Khrushchev, about the Soviet system, and about his own personal attitudes.[4]

Later, Angleton became obsessed with the idea that the Soviet Union was mounting a massive disinformation plot against the West and he cast doubt on all of the Agency's Soviet agents who appeared in the West after 1961. He mounted a furious search for a Soviet penetration agent, a mole in the CIA, which undercut the effectiveness of the Soviet Division.

In the summer of 1961, the dangers of nuclear war inherent in the Berlin crisis made Penkovsky's contribution paramount; his material checked out and gave senior American officials a unique insight into Khrushchev's plans and capabilities.

At 8:20 P.M. on July 18, Penkovsky was ready for his first meeting of the trip with the team at the safe apartment in Kensington. It was the eighteenth time he had been debriefed. Penkovsky and the team were genuinely glad to see each other again. He was in good form. He started with his agenda and rolled off a long list of complaints and suggestions, then went over the schedule for his mission at the Soviet Trade Fair in London. Clearly, he was bursting to finish the operational details and present the prize material on Soviet thinking and preparations for Berlin he had brought with him.

Penkovsky raced on to the events in Berlin:

Our command [American and British] must pay special attention to antitank defenses. Why? Because two full tank armies—consisting of regiments, brigades, and two corps with all auxiliaries—are on the territory of the East German Republic. Check it through your other channels—two tank armies are already there. This does not take into account the tank armies which are on the second echelon and also in Czechoslovakia and Poland. At present Khrushchev is carrying on a very cunning masked policy with his General Staff; he is putting much emphasis on tank forces. The tanks will have cannons and rockets on them. Our task will be to bring our antitank forces to the highest state of perfection now and to have antitank forces in each infantry section. I have in mind bazookas and other advanced equipment. These things must be available. The troops must be trained daily, like violinists being trained to play the violin. They must practice direct fire daily.

Penkovsky was concerned that the West not be fooled by an air show Khrushchev had ordered; must not think that the emphasis was shifting to aircraft. He insisted that missiles and tanks were the top priority and that a battle was going on between the commanders of the armies for more equipment. The emphasis, he insisted, was on tanks, submarines, and rockets. Aviation, he said, is

a spectacle. These new airplanes exist, they are not yet in mass production, some are in serial production, but very few. The immediate question is Berlin. After the signing of the peace treaty they want to blockade the approaches with tanks. The whole problem is to respond by hitting them hard in the teeth. Khrushchev wishes the nature of these battles to be localized, but we ·[he again was referring to the Americans and British] must hit them so hard that they are all destroyed. For this reason the antitank forces must be raised to an as yet unheard of level now. We must increase antitank forces, rockets, conventional artillery, bazookas, and mines. It is so good that Mr. Kennedy and Mr. Macmillan have declared such a firm stand. This has created quite a panic in Moscow.[5]

Kennedy had visited Prime Minister Macmillan on his way home from Vienna after meeting with Khrushchev. Privately Macmillan told Kennedy, "The East-West conflict cannot be solved by weakness or moral or physical exhaustion of one side or the other. It cannot, in this nuclear age, be resolved by the triumph of one side over the other without the extinction of both. I say, therefore, we can only reach our goal by the gradual acceptance of the view that we can all gain more by agreement than by aggression."[6] On July 4, 1961, Macmillan backed Kennedy's Vienna statements and told the House of Commons that Great Britain would reject any proposals for Germany and Berlin that did not provide for German reunification. The prime minister was rejecting Khrushchev's threat to react unilaterally and sign a peace treaty with East Germany.

Berlin was the burning issue. On the requirements list was a series of questions for Penkovsky about his initial report of Soviet strategy, which had been sent to the president by Allen Dulles. Kisevalter asked Penkovsky to expand upon and clarify the report, and pressed him to tell who else was present when Varentsov made his remarks.

> I will tell you exactly how it happened. First of all, everyone had a few drinks and my wife quite innocently said, "Sergei Sergeyevich, looking at things from the viewpoint of a woman and a mother, do you think we will sign the peace treaty with East Germany?" He said, "Yes, this will be done." We drank well throughout the meal, vodka, wine, and cognac. After the meal the children left the table. Varentsov drank a toast to me, and so we drank more. It was all a matter of feminine psychology, you understand, the women do not want war. My wife asked Sergei Sergeyevich, "But will the agreement be signed now?"
>
> "Yes, it will be signed," Varentsov replied.
>
> The subject was dropped and we drank again. Then we returned to the German problem, this time on my initiative, taking advantage of the lead my wife had achieved on her own. I hadn't asked her to do so. This is only a detail, but an important one. Then Varentsov cursed and said, "We are definitely embarking on a risky action." He mentioned that Khrushchev is prepared to support the original clash with considerable reinforcements by tank forces. But he does not want the war to spread further. He realizes that the NATO powers have strong nuclear capabilities, but he is relying on the assumption that they would not use nuclear weapons in the first phases of such a conflict. If Khrushchev had such capabilities, his concept would be to launch an all-out initial smashing blow, but he does not have this and I have heard this view expressed many times by many officers on the General Staff. The people do not want to fight for anything in East Germany.[7]

Was the Soviet Union ready for nuclear war? Kisevalter asked.

"They are not ready. Khrushchev's statements about this are all bluff, but he is preparing as fast as possible. Our officers do not want an atomic war. Local atomic strikes are possible since they have enough nuclear weapons to spit with, but insofar as blanketing important military centers or concentration points, they do not have the capability."

Penkovsky was describing Khrushchev's dilemma. By threatening the West with his alleged nuclear strength, Khrushchev was risking a strong Western counterreaction and arms buildup. Although the Soviet Union had enough nuclear weapons to cause major casualties in the United States, the Soviet missile program could not carry out a first strike that would wipe out the more extensive American nuclear retaliatory power, which consisted of a triad of ICBMs, bombers, and submarine-based nuclear weapons. The theories of how a nuclear war could be fought, and the concept of limited nuclear war were still being debated: in the Soviet Union the discussion was limited to classified debates within the military; the official American strategy was still massive nuclear response. The concept of limited nuclear war was still in its nascent stage.

"Where does Varentsov himself get this information?" queried Kisevalter.

"He got that from the Supreme Military Council, where Khrushchev sits as chairman and the active voices are usually Kozlov and Mikoyan. The other members of the Presidium are silent. These three are pressing and demanding that the German question be resolved by signing the German peace treaty and that this position cannot be put off any longer because the U.S.S.R. would then be in a laughable position before the whole world.[8]

"Other high-ranking officials including Varentsov, who is a big man, realize that we have certain strengths but that in many respects we are not ready for a prolonged conflict, but they simply give orders to produce [more weapons]. They must support and execute their orders; they have no choice but to do it. If they refuse they will be removed. To keep their positions and not get thrown out they would sell their souls to the devil.

"Everyone knows how Khrushchev is lying when he says that we have caught up with America in milk and meat production when they are slaughtering rabbits and horses for meat.

"Look at Varentsov. Since he became a chief marshal he raised his glass and offered a toast to Nikita Sergeyevich. I was aghast. I raised my glass, but what the hell would I drink to Khrushchev for? I thought of you and drank to your health. Of course all people are human and when one receives these great distinctions and power one will use this power. Now Varentsov is favorably disposed toward Khrushchev."[9]

Kisevalter asked Penkovsky to describe any new developments in the Soviet position since his last report in June.

"The Soviet situation is as follows: first of all if it were possible [for the NATO allies] to deploy a huge army on a wide front, using only conventional weapons and no rockets with atomic warheads, there would probably be mass Soviet troop defections to our side [the West]. I mention this as a preamble."

"Is this your view or do Varentsov and others share this view?" asked Kisevalter.

This is the general view, because our situation at home is rotten. The people don't trust Khrushchev, they don't trust the Soviet government, and the people remain half fed. The people are very displeased with Khrushchev's militant speeches and they say this audibly since it is easier to express oneself now that Beria is gone. The current belief is that, thanks to Khrushchev's militant speeches, Kennedy, Macmillan, and de Gaulle have been forced to increase their armament programs by two or three times. If Stalin were alive he would do everything quietly, but this fool is blurting out his threats and intentions and is forcing our potential enemies to increase their military strength. They dislike him and say that he is hurting his own cause and that he talks too much about Soviet military accomplishments in his effort to frighten the Western leaders.[10]

We [the West] should not repeat the Suez fiasco [1956]. We should react with firmness if he blocks the access roads to Berlin. Those [Soviet] blocking forces should be smashed. This should be done without striking with atomic bombs at industrial centers or rear areas. Should Khrushchev attempt to do this [blockade Berlin], he should be repaid in kind and the whole world told that the West is protecting its vital interests, which Khrushchev trampled upon in violation of the Potsdam Agreement.[11] If he expands the conflict to some degree, then he should be answered with corresponding counterblows. Actually Khrushchev and the Soviet Army at this time are unprepared.

Penkovsky went on to describe how Khrushchev was personally pressing the Central Committee of the Communist Party to establish a mass production program for all types of armaments, with emphasis on missiles. To implement this, committee officials and the responsible ministers "are actually physically present at the production centers for which they are responsible."[12]

Of particular importance militarily, explained Penkovsky, was the integration of East German forces into the Soviet Army. In all maneuvers, an East German infantry division trains with Soviet troops.

"What type of division is it?" asked Kisevalter.

"It is a standard German Democratic Republic infantry division, which operates exactly as Soviet doctrine prescribes, training with the Soviet Army in all maneuvers. It may take place within any country of the Warsaw Pact and also within the U.S.S.R. itself. This is a new measure which is designed to train the GDR army in tactics and strategy for joint operations."[13]

Kisevalter said to Penkovsky, "This is an important question. What is the degree of confidence of Varentsov and other high-ranking Soviet military officers regarding the readiness of Soviet forces to meet the consequences of Khrushchev's Berlin policy? That is, if physical resistance develops?"

Penkovsky framed his answer carefully. "If we consider today's situation, the Soviet Army is not ready for any widespread war. Varentsov said there is no confidence that our forces are prepared. I even wrote you this and Varentsov said specifically that in going forward this way we are proceeding toward a definite risk. We are preparing our troops and training them to be ready for any eventuality, but at this time there is no confidence that they are prepared."

"Did Varentsov say that?"

"Yes, he said that. They are trying to establish this confidence. The Central Committee members, the various Party members, and the ministers are all at the production centers to develop the needed equipment preparedness. The marshals and generals are constantly with troops to develop their combat efficiency. As an example, during the recent maneuvers in Odessa Military District, look at how many generals perished there." Penkovsky was referring to the death of at least four generals in a helicopter accident near Odessa. The helicopter crashed when one of its blades broke loose.[14]

"How do they regard the military feasibility of containing the military conflict within the GDR?" Kisevalter asked.

This is a purely adventuristic concept. They plan to block all access roads through the GDR to Berlin with tank forces. Of course the first echelon of forces will be East German troops, and back of them, in a second-echelon support role, will be Soviet troops. As soon as this barrier is smashed, then additional reinforcing troops will be brought up. The entire plan involves coordinated action on the part of East German and Soviet troops. The thinking is that if these reinforced troops can strongly repulse the Anglo-American, French, and West German forces, then they will abandon further conflict and negotiate with the East German government in order to obtain transit to Berlin. Further conflict will then be avoided, and the Soviet thinking is that the Western powers will be afraid of further conflict. The Soviet estimates are that the West German army is not prepared for conflict. Specifically they are considered to be at eighty percent of strength in equipment and manpower.[15]

The next night Penkovsky called the Serovs at the Bayswater Hotel and arranged to meet them. Although they were already in their dressing gowns and preparing to go to bed when he arrived, Penkovsky prevailed on them to come out with him. He took them to his hotel restaurant, where he could sign the bill, and ordered an excellent meal with wine. He saved the bill to present to Shergold for reimbursement.

Svetlana flirted with him, Penkovsky told the team. During the taxi ride back to her hotel, she squeezed up against him. Unmistakably, but very skillfully, Penkovsky said, she rubbed knees with him while he pointed out the sights of London and promised again to help the Serovs with their shopping. He loaned Mrs. Serov twenty pounds to buy a swing for the garden of their dacha.[16]

On July 25 President Kennedy addressed the nation in what his chief speechwriter, Theodore C. Sorenson, said was "a speech more somber than the American people were accustomed to accept, more somber than any previous presidential speech in the age of mutual nuclear capabilities."

"West Berlin," said Kennedy, "has now become the great testing place of Western courage and will, a focal point where our solemn commitments . . . and Soviet ambitions now meet in basic confrontation."[17]

The president asked Congress to increase the military budget by 3.2 billion dollars. Kennedy did not declare a national emergency, but he tripled the draft calls and he did request standby authority from Congress to call up the reserves. In his memoirs, Paul Nitze, who was the Defense Department representative on the Berlin task force, noted, "Our NATO contingency plans called for sending a small military force down the Autobahn to Berlin and, if resisted, moving to the nuclear response envisioned in MC 14\2. . . . In spite of our inferiority in military conventional forces in the European theater, we had, in my opinion, superior strategic capability behind us. Even though we very much wished to avoid a nuclear exchange, it was my opinion that the Soviet Union would wish to avoid one even more fervently. Even so, the risks were great and miscalculation on either side was our greatest potential enemy. To my mind, the Berlin crisis of 1961 was a time of greater danger of nuclear confrontation with the Soviet Union than the Cuban missile crisis of 1962."[18]

On July 28 Penkovsky met with the Anglo-American team in the Kensington safe apartment at 3:10 P.M. A Zenith shortwave radio was presented to him, and Kisevalter explained in Russian, "This gift shows that money is not a problem but security is." Penkovsky beamed with pleasure when he received the radio and thanked the team profusely. He said he would prefer that Wynne carry it to Moscow on his next trip. He assured the team that similar models were available for dollars in special shops for foreign tourists in Moscow and he would have no problem explaining how he came to own it. Kisevalter agreed, but he refused Penkovsky a small tape recorder to record his conversations with Varentsov and other senior military officers. "You would be suspect having it and risk a disaster trying to record Varentsov. You should abide by our advice and decisions regarding future requests of a security risk nature and minimize your acquisitive desires."[19]

Limiting the risks Penkovsky was willing to take in his efforts to be the best spy in history was a constant problem for the team. The Russian needed constant reassurance and praise. Kisevalter took out a report from headquarters in Washington concerning Kennedy's July 25 speech on Berlin and handed it to Penkovsky. "This is so you will know that your information is definitely reaching our leaders. I won't read it to you, but I can point out that in a number of the president's statements, exactly those thoughts which you suggested were mentioned by the president."[20] Penkovsky smiled broadly and savored the quotes from President Kennedy's speech:

"West Berlin has now become the great testing place of Western courage and will, a focal point where our solemn commitments . . . and Soviet ambitions now meet in basic confrontation.

"We cannot and will not permit the Communists to drive us out of Berlin, either gradually or by force. For the fullfillment of our pledge to that city is essential to the morale and security of Western Germany, to the unity of Western Europe, and to the faith of the entire Free World."[21]

Then Penkovsky lifted his head and said:

You should know what is going on in the leadership and how Khrushchev is promoting generals to win their loyalty. Among the leadership there exists a secret opposition, which remains secret because the majority are still Khrushchev's protégés and the others don't want to lose their jobs.* But there could be a realignment of forces and a split as a result of the Berlin question. All of those aware of the economic and military points will say, "It is too early to go to war. We've got to wait. What's the point of heating up the

---

*In Khrushchev on Khrushchev, his son Sergei tells how the plot to overthrow his father in October 1964 was carried out in secret by KGB chairman Vladimir Y. Semichastny, supported by Shelepin, Podgorny, and Leonid Brezhnev.

situation because of a Berlin which has existed for the last sixteen years?" Should this occur, it is possible that Khrushchev will carry the day and win once again; on the other hand the reverse might happen. We have to take this into consideration. They could either remove Khrushchev saying he was ill, or else he might resign—as Malenkov did. Or they could say, "You go on being the boss, but let's retreat on the Berlin question, let's think something up. Let's say outright that we are defenders of the peace, the Anglo-Americans have taken the extreme view of our declaration and are preparing for war, we don't want war, there's no hurry, we'll settle the Berlin question one day." There are lots of diplomatic words that can be found in order to meet the situation and to fool the people and lie again.[22]

The decision on what action to take will be made at the Twenty-second Party Congress in October. It doesn't appear on the agenda, but as I have told you before, whenever there is one of these big gatherings they have secret sessions, and I am positive that this matter will be discussed. It might even be discussed before the official opening of the Congress. So we must keep in mind three possibilities.

First, Khrushchev may crush all opposition and proceed to sign an East German peace treaty, inviting local hostilities and risking general war.

Second, Khrushchev may be forced to compromise and delay signing a peace treaty in view of Western opposition and propagandize this more as his desire for peace—still postponing possible action on East Germany and Berlin to a further date.

Third, Khrushchev may be deposed.[23]

Penkovsky added, "Judging by the telegrams received by the ambassador in London and the *Rezidentura*, the Soviet government is already in a difficult position. Therefore my desire and that of all progressive Russians is to increase your military preparedness in order to make the Soviet position still more acute."[24]

Kennedy had already asked Congress to increase defense spending by $3.2 billion dollars in response to Khrushchev's threats. A new and expensive lap of the great nuclear arms race was under way.

Much of Penkovsky's time with the team was taken up with operational matters. He provided a diagram of the Soviet Embassy in London and identified still more pictures of GRU and KGB agents. There was intricate planning for future meetings in Moscow so he could deliver his film and communicate with the team. The first item was to evaluate his meeting in the park with Mrs. Chisholm.

Penkovsky asked, "Well, did I work correctly with this lady or not?"

"You stayed a little too long with her," said Shergold.

Excuse me, I also am a clever man. It's impossible to sit, hand over the material, and vanish. It is impossible. The baby carriage is empty and she is holding all three children. She is dressed in the same brown suede jacket I was told she would be wearing so that I should always recognize her. I appraised the whole setup. The rain is approaching. I purposely waited for the rain to begin so that as many people as possible should leave. The place is bad. It would be better to go farther toward the edge of the park; there would be fewer people walking by. She was sitting beside the path opposite the circus and the cinema. Everyone goes and sits there. When it is sunny there isn't space for a sardine there. People are all around, but farther in the park it is empty. The rain was coming. I thought, "Let the first drops fall, then I'll approach her."[25]

Penkovsky said he came to the park again on the following Sunday, the 9th of July, but she was not there, although he had a message for her. His boss, Gvishiani, had informed him on July 4 that he was ordered to London, and he could have passed this message on via "the girl," as he called Mrs. Chisholm. "She understood me despite my bad English," said Penkovsky, "but I will improve my English. There was nothing to fear, especially the intervention of the policeman, as I had my military identification with me [identifying him as a colonel of the General Staff] and would have told the policeman to 'shove off, scum.' I would have let the girl go and discussed the matter with the policeman. The British are the leaders and mentors here [in London], but over there I know what to do.

"All went well. She was a heroine. She was most natural, she didn't get nervous. It was quite correct and natural that I should have chatted with the children—otherwise why should I have approached them at all?"

Shergold told Penkovsky that he did not like the idea of using Mrs. Chisholm again. Shergold expressed his views, and Kisevalter translated them into Russian, saying, "It was all right once, but it would not be a good thing often. If we have to use her again, the briefer the meeting the better."[26]

It was agreed that if they had to meet in the park again it would be better to meet farther inside the park to the left of the entrance because there were likely to be fewer people there. They would not meet near the kiosks.

Penkovsky complained to the team that they were sending him duplicate radio messages and he was wasting time decoding them.

Why was it necessary to repeat the messages? "What do I need it for? On Saturday I again received forty-one groups of numbers. [The groups of numbers are decoded into words]. What do I need it for? I don't understand."

"Of course you understand," replied Kisevalter, patiently explaining the importance of a backup in communications. "Just think. Every Saturday and Sunday during the course of a month this is being sent to give you the chance to listen whenever it's best for you."

To reassure Penkovsky that he had done well, Kisevalter said, "Now that you know Mrs. Chisholm, the matter is quite different."

"Now that she is in England you can meet her in a short while," said Shergold.

Penkovsky replied: "I have an idea—I would ask you to analyze this matter and solve it scientifically. Why shouldn't this lady be invited to the Canadian Embassy, say to a reception, so that I could become acquainted with her at the reception? Then I could meet her quite openly in the street, the same way I would come up to the Canadian ambassador [Arnold Smith] if I saw him in the street, for a chat, even if there are a hundred policemen present." The team nodded to each other and it was agreed that such a meeting would be arranged.[27]

Penkovsky expanded on the idea and suggested that arrangements be made to meet him at other diplomatic receptions by inviting him through the State Committee. "Regarding the American and British embassies, I'm quite clear about it now. Perhaps that will also develop gradually," said Penkovsky. Bulik explained that the American Embassy had called the State Committee and asked for a guest list of people to invite to a reception, but his name was not on it.[28]

This would change soon, explained Penkovsky, because he had been made the deputy head of his section and thus he would be included on the list of those to be invited to diplomatic receptions.

Penkovsky was always thinking of ways to improve his access to secret materials and to raise his own status within the Soviet hierarchy. He still nurtured the hope he would become a general officer and left nothing to chance in his rigorous campaign, even while he increased the intensity of his spying.

He came up with the idea of having the Americans write an article on military theory for him in Russian. "Now please write an article for me because I am very busy, and then when I finish work I'm too tired to write anything for the Soviet régime. In the past, when I received permission to look at classified material, it was for background for writing some articles. That will be my cover story, then I shall open up vast treasures in the secret section."

"How can you account for the sources of data in such an article?" asked Kisevalter.

"Quite simply," explained Penkovsky. "We receive masses of unclassified military journals from you, from the British, from the French. I finished courses at two military academies. For the third time I am today on a mission to a foreign country. If I want to be clever, if I am a military strategic intelligence officer, if I absorb like a sponge everything that goes on here, I should be able to do this, but now I have enough other work for the present for the committee, for the GRU, and our basic work." Then he stopped and corrected himself. "I didn't start in the right order—our basic work, the GRU, and the committee. I get tired. I come home and fall into bed. I fall asleep. In the morning I do my gymnastics, eat, and go out. In the past I came up with small inventions. I proposed an artillery angle-measuring device. Before, when I burned with the courage of an eagle, I wrote in the papers a little. Why should I not write now, if I sit down in front of all the material which we get through our Intelligence from you?[29]

"By the way, how was the list, good or not, of the agent network?"

Shergold replied, "All good, yes."[30]

Penkovsky stopped for a moment and said, "If you like I will send you a bibliography and you can write the article based on the bibliography. Your expert can write it so that it would appear logical that a forty-two-year-old colonel who finished two academies, traveled abroad, has for eleven years had experience in intelligence, could have done it."

"That would be much better," Kisevalter said.[31]

Penkovsky was enthused by his idea and assured the team that if he produced a list of materials from which to write the article there would be no trouble coming up with the source material to show his superiors once the article was written. The rewards would be tremendous because not only would he then have greater access to secret documents, but his career would be enhanced by publishing. Then, as always, when he discussed his career, a black cloud descended. "I am on this trip right now. They consider me to be useful. Why do they still keep me in spite of my father? You don't know anything about my father, do you?" asked Penkovsky.

"No. But I will inform you if I find out," said Kisevalter, who had promised Penkovsky at an earlier meeting that an effort would be made to check on whether there was any record of how his father had died, or if by a quirk of fate he were alive in the West.[32]

They know that I can work, they taught me, a fool, for many, many years. They say I have initiative, am gifted, quick on the uptake—

they expect a return from me. If there is no return, they will say, "That means he is slipping. He no longer has a future." I don't care what they say, in any case I shall be with you in two years' time. If I have something printed, even several pages, I can go to them and say, "I have had this printed. I want to produce something else now. I have more thoughts, ideas are coming to me. I must read what the views are on such and such a subject." When I read I take photographs of it all! All those journals which I brought just now on film are an example. When I told Varentsov that I wanted to write military articles, he told me to use his office. Tomorrow there will be more and you will say of me, "Excellent chap!"[33]

Penkovsky arrived at the last meeting of his second London trip in a good mood. He reminded the team how he had given them the name of a GRU officer in London who was going to meet a recruited agent at a diplomatic reception. "You can arrest the agent tonight if you like. Then you can give me a decoration." He laughed. Of course, Penkovsky knew that the British would not arrest the officer or his agent for fear his betrayal would lead back to himself, but it pleased him to play this game and hint that he should be given a decoration for his work.

For the last time Penkovsky urged the team to inspire Wynne by paying him. He warned that if they disciplined Wynne it would be dangerous and would put Wynne in a doubtful mood when he came to Moscow on August 22.

At this point Joe Bulik and Harold Shergold brought out British and American colonel's uniforms and Penkovsky tried them on. First he slipped into the British uniform, and before he was dressed Bulik photographed him in his undershorts with the jacket and cap on, while everybody laughed. Once fully dressed, Penkovsky's military bearing and strength were apparent. He was elated with the two uniforms, and a full set of pictures was taken with a Polaroid. The American uniform had ribbons denoting medals and campaigns, and afterward Shergold complained to Bulik that the British had not been informed that the American uniform would be decorated. The British colonel's uniform was plain except for the shoulder pips.[34]

The uniforms were an effort to boost Penkovsky's morale and compensate for his not having met the queen or other recognizable high-ranking British officials during the London visit. While Sir Dick White, the head of MI6, was a key figure, Penkovsky did not really understand his role and importance since Sir Dick was not in the limelight. For Penkovsky, the queen of England, Lord Mountbatten, President Kennedy, or one of the Kennedy family would have been more his idea of recognition.

In his farewell statement to the team Penkovsky spoke of the importance of the meetings as "an opportunity to get to know each other better, as well as to give a more concrete form to future plans, all of which can contribute to the improvement of our collaboration." He predicted the tempo of his work would increase and asked for weekly meetings in Moscow. Then he thanked the case officers and requested that they all be given bonuses of 1000 pounds each from his salary of $1000 per month. Janet Chisholm, the photographer, and the radio operator who trained him in London were each to receive 250 pounds. All the technical secretaries and translators should each receive 100 pounds. "This is from me, my modest present, and I ask my government to fulfill this request."[35]

The team hedged an answer and never paid the bonuses from his funds as he requested. Later the American members of the team were given cash awards, medals, and promotions by the CIA. Mrs. Chisholm received 5000 pounds paid jointly by the Americans and British.

Penkovsky was concerned with his future in the GRU and discussed it frankly with his colleagues. For him the two American and two British agents were his lifeline. While he worked hard to be accepted as a professional intelligence officer, he also craved their personal acceptance and respect. He wanted them to accept him as a friend, to share and support his emotional needs. Despite his bravado and single-minded sense of purpose, Penkovsky had no place or person to turn to except his case officers. He poured out his anxieties, telling the team how there was a division of opinion in Moscow about "what to do with me. Some wish to make me a general and bring me on because I have become ripe. I have sufficient education, experience, and age. Others keep a brake on me like [GRU personnel chief] Shumsky and those at the Central Committee, because of my father. It is still a riddle to me how this matter of my father became known. I ask you to help me in this—to clear things up. Why wasn't it known before that my father was a White Guards officer? Why? If it had been known earlier, they would have told me about it earlier. They would not have let me go to Turkey on a long mission. They of course take into account my record; they have to. Thanks to the fact that I served extremely well in the Soviet Army, was a political commissar, was in three campaigns, was decorated at the front, twice commanded a regiment, and fulfilled my tasks with a fine efficiency report. But what do you think? You are intelligent people. Why did the matter of my father become known? Why wasn't it known before?"

"They dug and dug and got to the bottom," said Kisevalter. "Possibly Rubenko [the military attaché in Turkey] gave a hint to the 'neighbors' to investigate."

Penkovsky interrupted Kisevalter. "But Rubenko knew nothing, just as no one knew anything."

"That was just the thing! That's why the KGB said, 'Search, find out something,' " said Kisevalter.

"They got to the bottom," said Penkovsky. "There were some archives coming from the People's Republics and Germany, I think. I ask you once more, my dear friends, find an acquaintance of my father's. I am sure there are acquaintances of his alive who served with him. My father was active in Rostov, Vodosalsky Stepi, and toward the Black Sea, in the Novorossisk direction.[36]

"The information my mother had was that my father had fallen near Rostov. They say that a large party of White Guards officers had been taken onto the river on rafts and shot. It may have been there. Of course I exclude the possibility that my father managed to get abroad. There were years when he might have managed to get into contact. He loved my mother very much. If you like I shall send you a photograph of my mother; she was an exceptionally attractive woman in her youth. She was simply beautiful!"

"Could he have been afraid of harming her by attempting contact from abroad," asked Kisevalter.

"No."

"Or perhaps he wrote but the letters were intercepted?" suggested Kisevalter.

"I'll tell you, there were, after all, masses of cases where both letters and money reached their recipients, under all sorts of cover. But of course there are former friends of his at work still living, and there is detailed information buried in the hands of Soviet organs regarding his rank in 1919. I've already told you about it. I'll send you a photograph of my father without fail. My mother and I have about five photographs, when he was a student at the Lycée, when he finished school, and with my grandfather."

"Where did he graduate? Where did he study engineering?" asked Kisevalter, ever the diligent case officer. Not only was he trying to find a way to help Penkovsky, but the information would also be important to double-check Penkovsky's own legend.

Kisevalter, who had been the case officer for Popov, did not take readily to Penkovsky and his aristocratic manner. Kisevalter's strength with Popov was his ability to win Popov's confidence by long hours of drinking and talking together. With Penkovsky and a team of three others, his style was cramped. He was forced to show his knowledge in the questions he asked. His knowledge of the GRU was so extensive, as a result of the Popov interrogations, that Penkovsky often wondered how Kisevalter had acquired it. At one point he even joked that "only somebody on the inside could know this." For Kisevalter, not having Penkovsky totally dependent on him, the way Popov was, distanced the two men. Kisevalter often complained privately to Bulik that he found Penkovsky overblown, romantic, and difficult to control. Bulik felt that Kisevalter chaffed at being subordinate to him. "Kisevalter felt he should have handled Penkovsky himself after his success with Popov," recalled Bulik.[37]

Penkovsky explained that his father graduated from the Warsaw Polytechnical Institute but his family had no direct connection with Poland, despite their Polish name that came from distant Polish forebears. "My father spent all his life in Stavropol and was a big lawyer there, a member of the gentry. For those who are in the intelligence services it is written in my file that my grandfather was a *dvoryanin* [nobleman]," said Penkovsky, laughing bitterly. "They are swine in general. Had they been intelligent they should have kept quiet about it. So what!"

"And who was Lenin's father?" interjected Kisevalter, alluding to the fact that Lenin's father, Ilya Ulyanov, was not a worker or peasant, but also a member of the gentry.

Incidently, so that you should know, my wife doesn't know a thing about my father. I haven't told her, only my mother and my aunt—my mother's sister—know. My mother wrote an explanation to Shumsky. She was eighteen years old when she met my father, Vladimir Florianovich Penkovsky. She married him soon afterward; a child was born. He frequently went on journeys. "He told me he was an engineer; it was easy for anyone to see and understand, but I knew nothing about the details of his service." That is the way she wrote, and they have this explanation. "He may have been occupied in some activities—as any man had to—he was called into the army and had to serve in it. I did not know anything about his political views and service. He used to disappear, go off on business, make journeys lasting several days because the times were troubled and all men were occupied." That is the spirit in which she wrote. She wrote the explanatory letter very intelligently. Shumsky read it and said, "No, no, that's not it. That's not the way she ought to write."

"Why, Comrade General?" I asked him.

"Well, what she has written here is how she brought you up and what she told you. She didn't want to tell you of the fact that she really knew that her husband was a White officer. She brought you up in the tradition that you are the son of an engineer and an employee," Shumsky replied.

"All right, what's it got to do with me?" I asked.

"Comrade Penkovsky, it's got nothing to do with you! Nothing to do with you."

Shumsky told me so at once. When they put off my mission to India [as military attaché] I said, "What's the matter?"

They said, "Nothing to do with you. We just wanted to tell you so that you would know who your father was."

Joe Bulik tried to lighten the mood by telling Penkovsky that there would be a submarine coming for him from Tokyo with the four members of the team on board to pick him up in the Soviet Far East if he were assigned there.[38]

Ever optimistic when with the team, Penkovsky looked at the brighter side. "After all, the Central Committee may say, 'The devil take him. Let him go!' It may happen because there is at present a certain softening in this respect. It's not like it was in Stalin's time and Beria's." Penkovsky explained that since the Twentieth Party Congress speech exposing Stalin's crimes, Khrushchev had released those held illegally in prisons or labor camps and had posthumously rehabilitated some of those who had been shot as "enemies of the people." In such an atmosphere Penkovsky was hopeful his father's past might not affect his future.

He embraced the team and kissed each officer on the cheek in Russian style, then left with Michael Stokes, who escorted him to meet a prearranged "date" with a lady of the evening cleared by MI6. Penkovsky had called Zeph, the woman he saw on his first visit, but she was out of town, performing as a dancer. Rather than risk security the British arranged an evening of pleasure for Penkovsky with a reliable date before departing.[39]

Penkovsky returned safely to Moscow on August 7, 1961, and continued his work for the State Committee, the GRU, the CIA, and the British SIS.

While Penkovsky was in London the CIA once again made an effort to obtain State Department cooperation in handling him. Ambassador Thompson was still cautious and agreed to cooperate only if the State Department considered the information to be obtained justified the risks. Thompson wanted the "subject" to be instructed to pass only information considered to be vital and not attempt to set up a scheme for collection of material that was "only interesting." Thompson warned that, in view of the close Soviet surveillance of the embassy staff, an eventual blowup was highly probable, and he wanted the operation to be carried out by a trained CIA officer.

The only trained officer in Moscow was COMPASS, and he was considered inadequate. At noon on July 25, 1961, Dick Helms met with Jack Maury and Quentin Johnson, the chief of operations for the Soviet Division, to discuss COMPASS's unreliable performance in Moscow and "the fact that his judgment and actions appear to be seriously affected by a fear complex." They decided to recommend that John Abidian, the security officer in the embassy, be utilized "because of his past training, motivation, awareness of surveillance and sound judgment."

In a memorandum for the record Maury noted that in discussing COMPASS, Dick Helms voiced his considerable displeasure over the fact that COMPASS "had been oversold to him and that henceforth no Agency personnel could be assigned to the post until a very thorough psychological assessment of them had been made and personally reviewed by Mr. Helms." Helms directed that COMPASS be recalled from Moscow at the earliest practicable time and separated from the Agency.[40]

At the beginning of August the question of how to distribute the Penkovsky materials and at the same time protect his identity persisted and demanded attention. The flood of material from Penkovsky could be expected to continue when he returned to Moscow, but the Agency had nobody in Moscow to service him. In a discussion with his key officers in the Soviet Division on August 3, Maury considered the pros and cons of cutting in the government's leading Soviet expert, Charles E. (Chip) Bohlen, former ambassador to Moscow and President Kennedy's special advisor for Soviet affairs, "in view of the obvious advantage of getting his cooperation in the matter of internal support after HERO returns to Moscow." They agreed that if Penkovsky came out again, there might be some advantage in having Bohlen actually meet him, since he "would be flattered by such attention." However, they noted that "if HERO is ever picked up, his having met Bohlen would certainly be an embarrassment to the Department." Maury mentioned this possibility to Helms, who told him to "defer consideration of it for the present."[41]

Ambassador Bohlen was shown material on the Vienna meeting that Penkovsky had acquired on August 2. Bohlen reacted enthusiastically, saying it was "terribly exciting" and "the real thing beyond any shadow of a doubt." Bohlen noted that "the significance of the material lay in the extent to which Khrushchev had disseminated it abroad, especially among underdeveloped nations, and the extent to which this dissemination constituted a commitment by Khrushchev from which it would be hard for him to back down."

Immediately after reading the material, Bohlen said Secretary of State Dean Rusk should be informed and went to the secretary's office to do so. CIA director Allen Dulles was also on his way to see Rusk. Maury wrote:

> At Helms' instructions, I hurried to intercept the Director before the Secretary was informed. However, I missed connections since the Director was at that moment in the White House. As a result, the Director went to a meeting with the Secretary at four o'clock still unbriefed on the Vienna material, and at the meeting the Secretary mentioned the material to him.
>
> Later, when the Director met and talked to me, he was incensed and threatened to fire Bissell [deputy director for plans (DDP)], Helms and me. I explained how the situation had come about, assuring him that the Secretary had not gotten a piece of paper, but had only been told briefly of the existence of the material by Bohlen. I also explained to him our fervent efforts to get to him before Bohlen got to the Secretary. The Director was entirely pacified and asked for a write-up of the material which he could show the President this morning.
>
> When we talked to Bohlen, we obtained from him the very closely held American version of the Vienna talks to aid our translation. I assured him it would be used by only one officer and would be returned promptly.
>
> This morning the Director briefed the President and showed him the Vienna material. The Director later told me that the President was most enthusiastic and would like to be informed, after the transcript is complete, of the extent to which it varies from the American version.[42]

President Kennedy was intrigued with Dulles' presentation and impressed with his Soviet colonel's work. He directed that the Soviet transcript be compared with the American to see what changes, if any, had been made and how the Soviets had shifted the emphasis in the exchange of views. On August 9 the CIA transmitted a copy of the Soviet account of Khrushchev's and Kennedy's conversations in Vienna to President Kennedy. Included was a comparison to the American transcript.

Penkovsky's copy of the English translation came from a Central Committee resolution approving Khrushchev's performance in Vienna. The resolution and the English translation were sent to socialist bloc leaders, Fidel Castro, and the Soviet ambassadors in Paris and Rome. The ambassadors were directed to brief the French Communist leader Maurice Thorez and the Italian Communist leader Palmiro Togliatti. It was also sent to the Soviet ambassadors in eighteen nonaligned countries for them to brief heads of state. Penkovsky had copied the resolution and the transcript of the Vienna meeting with his Minox.

In reading the two accounts of the Vienna meeting it was clear that Khrushchev was trying to capitalize on his tough talk to President Kennedy and gain support for the Soviet demand for a separate German peace treaty before the end of the year. Kennedy saw that Khrushchev emphasized the correctness of his case, stressed Soviet determination to press ahead, and downplayed American determination. The reading of the transcripts was a lesson to Kennedy in how Khrushchev operated and how the United States could not allow itself and its allies to be bullied.

Paris

WHEN PENKOVSKY'S AEROFLOT JET LANDED AT LE BOURGET ON Wednesday morning, September 20, 1961, the air had turned cool and comfortable after a record heat wave. Penkovsky was in high spirits. His trip to the Soviet Trade Fair in Paris had been personally approved by the head of Soviet Military Intelligence, General Ivan Aleksandrovich Serov. Neither the "neighbors" [the KGB] nor the Central Committee had asked any questions about Penkovsky's leaving the Soviet Union to go to France. Penkovsky had become a *vyezdnoi*, a person who could travel abroad because of his good record. He had the right sponsors, had performed well on previous trips, and had returned.

The Soviet exhibit, now a week old, had not impressed Paris. Attendance was well below that of the same fair in London in July. Parisians complained about the slow service and high prices at the Soviet specialty food shops. The front pages of French newspapers carried reports of the unilateral renewal by Nikita Khrushchev of Soviet nuclear tests in the atmosphere. The news stories said radioactivity in the air had increased at "an alarming rate" in the forty-eight hours before Penkovsky's arrival. No matter. Penkovsky would not allow a little radioactivity to spoil his first visit to Paris. Leading the news was a terrorist, ultrarightist OAS (Secret Army Organization) plot to kill de Gaulle. Yves Saint-Laurent's decision to leave Christian Dior and open his own fashion house also made the front pages. Bulik, Kisevalter, Shergold, and Stokes had come to learn the latest developments in the Soviet missile and nuclear warhead programs while Penkovsky would sample the pleasures of the grandest city in Europe.

One thing was bothering him. He would tell the team that they

225

must devise a system that would enable him to pass critical information to them quickly.[1] Penkovsky had been in Moscow on Sunday, August 13, cut off from contact with his case officers, when the East Germans, backed by Soviet troops, rolled out barbed wire and began construction of the Berlin Wall. "Border control," Khrushchev had called it. In an effort to stop the East-West flow of refugees, which rose to more than 150,000 in the first six months of 1961, Khrushchev and his top military advisers came up with a plan to close off free access for East Germans to West Berlin. East German leader Walter Ulbricht beamed with pleasure, but the rest of the world was outraged.[2]

Penkovsky had found out details of the plan to build the Wall four days before it was executed, but he was unable to send word to the Americans or British. Had President Kennedy known of Khrushchev's intentions, he could have undermined the Soviet action, possibly forcing them to abort it by exposing the plan to build the Wall and, at the least, alerting the West Germans.*

Penkovsky finally passed his information on the Wall, including the actual specifications for its construction, to Greville Wynne in Moscow ten days later, on August 23. Wynne's trip was officially billed at the State Committee as an opportunity for him to see the French Exhibit in Moscow and to organize the visit of a British delegation in the fall. This permitted Penkovsky to meet alone with Wynne and to pass six rolls of film, the material on the Berlin Wall, books he had copied, and the missile guidance device he had promised the team.

On August 25 Wynne and Penkovsky had dinner in the restaurant of the Budapest Hotel in downtown Moscow. At the beginning of the meal Wynne handed Penkovsky a letter. Penkovsky took it into a stall in the men's toilet, read it, flushed the toilet, washed his hands, and returned to the table. He gave the letter, which laid out the contact arrangements for Paris, back to Wynne. "It is all very satisfactory, but you must be in Paris, too," Penkovsky said.

Outside the customs hall at Le Bourget on September 20 was cheerful Greville Wynne, ready to take Penkovsky to the Hôtel Cayre on the Boulevard Saint-Germain, on the Left Bank. During the ride into Paris Penkovsky passed Wynne a package of eleven rolls of undeveloped Minox film. MI6 officer Roger King picked up

---

* Allied intelligence on Berlin indicated that the East Germans might make a move on the city itself, but there was no hint of a wall being built. When the East Germans moved with Soviet backing the Allies were caught by surprise. Paul Nitze, the head of President Kennedy's Berlin task force, noted in an interview with the authors in 1991 that "the situation was strategically intolerable."

the film from Wynne and sent it by courier to London for processing. King was Wynne's contact, and the team's driver and general utility man for the Paris operation. King, the liaison between the team and Wynne, was introduced to Penkovsky, but like Wynne, did not attend the meetings. King was another means of preserving security. This way Wynne did not need to know the names of the four members of the team. King instructed Wynne to accompany Penkovsky from his hotel to the Solférino footbridge on the Left Bank at 7:30 that evening. It was only a short walk from the hotel down the Boulevard Saint-Germain to Rue de Bellechasse, where they were to turn right and follow the street to its end at the river. Penkovsky was to walk alone across the bridge, toward the Tuileries on the Right Bank, and look for a member of the team.

As soon as he crossed the river, Penkovsky spotted Kisevalter and followed him along the riverbank to a parked car. They arrived at the safe house in a quiet, expensive residential area on the right bank, just north of the Pont de Grenelle, in the 16th arrondissement. The British had rented an apartment at 6 Hameau Beranger, on the third floor opposite the elevator. The newly built five-story apartment house stood in the corner of a closed, tree-lined street that ended in a crescent of stylish private homes. With no outlet, traffic was restricted. The garage to the apartment house was accessible from the street, enabling the team to go directly to the elevator from inside the garage and not expose Penkovsky in the lobby.

Kisevalter and Stokes had been living in the apartment since the beginning of September. While they waited, uncertain of Penkovsky's exact arrival date, tensions arose between them. Normal everyday chores became the cause for open bickering. Who would return the Perrier bottles to collect the deposit? Who would remove the garbage? Because of the need to maintain security, they could not be seen frequently in Paris; keeping each other company in such close quarters had become a strain.[3] Penkovsky's arrival cleared the air; now work could begin and their shared sense of purpose was strengthened. There were hearty greetings all around. Penkovsky presented Joe, Mike, George, and Harold with jars of black caviar and highly polished Georgian hollowed cow horns set in sterling silver for drinking on festive occasions. He also brought caviar for Janet Chisholm.

It was five months since they had first met. They drank a toast with white wine to their first meeting. Penkovsky announced that his wife, Vera, was expecting their second child in five months. The others proposed another toast of congratulations.

Asked about his future prospects in Moscow, Penkovsky said, "It all depends on the attitude of the Central Committee. Just prior to this trip they requested a new character evaluation on me.* There has even been a proposal approved by two generals in the GRU that I be sent on a tour of duty to Washington as a counselor in the Soviet Embassy there. Of course I would be working for the GRU. All of this depends on the Central Committee."

Penkovsky explained that the proposal had been submitted by the GRU and agreed to by Gvishiani at the State Committee. What happened next would depend, he said, on how they regarded the story of his father. "I have only come on this trip because no negative statements were submitted by the 'neighbors' against me personally.

"Even though the [Berlin] situation looks very bad, I am very glad that our governments [the United States and Great Britain] have displayed such firmness and decisiveness." The Soviets, Penkovsky explained, had not expected such a firm stand. "This has placed them in a difficult position," he said. "Mikoyan [first deputy chairman of the Council of Ministers] does not get along at all with Khrushchev. They are still not sure of themselves and they know they do not have everything that they need. They could launch a massive nuclear attack, destroying several cities and ten million people, but that will not solve all of their problems."[4] Penkovsky was speaking in technical shorthand, but the team knew he meant that the Soviet Union, although it had enough nuclear weapons to inflict limited casualties on the United States, did not have enough for a first strike that would wipe out the American ability to retaliate and inflict even greater damage. He knew that the prevailing American nuclear strategy was massive retaliation, which would mean a full-scale, all-out nuclear war against the Soviet Union if the U.S. were attacked.

Then Penkovsky gave the team his report on Marshal Varentsov's sixtieth birthday party, also celebrating his promotion to chief marshal of artillery, which had taken place the previous Saturday, September 16. Penkovsky had met the marshal at the train station on his return to Moscow from Leningrad on Friday. To begin the birthday celebrations he gave Varentsov presents supplied by the CIA and MI6: a rocket-shaped cigarette lighter, a silver cigarette box, and a sixty-year-old bottle of cognac. Actually it was several years younger, and the cognac bottle label had been prepared by MI6's Technical Service Division to make the year match Varentsov's age. Varentsov was flattered. He told Penkovsky to come to his dacha at Babushkin,

---

* A *kharakteristika*, or efficiency report, was required of all persons who travel overseas. It is a complete personal history as well as a character evaluation by superiors. Those who attest to a person's character are held responsible by the Communist Party for the person's behavior.

on the northern edge of Moscow, the following day and to be sure to "bring them all," meaning Penkovsky's wife, daughter, and mother.

Outside the sunlit dacha were poised highly polished Chaika and ZIS limousines,* their military drivers at the ready. Inside, tables heaped with food and drink awaited the high-ranking officials invited by Varentsov. Leading the guest list were Defense Minister Marshal Rodion Malinovsky and Viktor Mikhailovich Churayev, one of Khrushchev's close aides and a member of the Central Committee. Churayev, Khrushchev's deputy in charge of the Communist Party organization for the Russian Federation, had vast influence through political patronage.

The generals and their wives and children were in a festive mood when they offered presents to Varentsov on that mild September afternoon. Only Marshal Malinovsky was in uniform. The first toast, proposed by Malinovsky, came from the bottle of cognac that Penkovsky had given to Varentsov the day before. Everyone except the children drank, and all toasted to Varentsov's health before draining their glasses in the traditional manner. The effect of the rare cognac was exhilarating. Warmth and good feeling spread quickly. Malinovsky wanted to drink only the cognac so Penkovsky poured three rounds, giving full glasses only to the defense minister, Varentsov, Churayev, and himself. When it was Penkovsky's turn to toast Varentsov he proposed congratulations to Sergei Sergeyevich for having been awarded the Order of Lenin, the highest government award, on his sixtieth birthday.

Penkovsky explained his scheme to the team members. "When they began to applaud I thought I would pull a fast one on the minister [Malinovsky] by praising him too, so I continued by saying that this award represents high esteem for Sergei Sergeyevich by the Party, the government, and personally by the minister of defense. After that he beamed and I could talk to him as a Comrade." His flattery of Malinovsky had worked.

When the cognac was finished, Malinovsky requested that the magnum of champagne he had brought for a gift be opened, and all drank from it. Before the men adjourned for a smoke to a nearby room, Penkovsky's mother asked Marshal Malinovsky if there was going to be war over Berlin. "It is hard to say. I do not want to talk about it because I have to think about it all the time. However, I can say that the situation is difficult. Our enemies are not giving in to us although it is true that they have swallowed a pill. We handled this one well [the Berlin Wall], but how will it be in the future? All

---

*ZIS is the Russian abbreviation for *Zavod Imeni Stalina*, a factory named after Stalin.

I can say is that we are keeping everything in readiness."[5] Malinovsky was referring to the fact that the United States and its allies had not known that the Berlin Wall was going to be built and had not made any move to stop it.

Penkovsky revealed that many generals, including two of Varentsov's deputies, were not present at Varentsov's party because they were involved in training and testing exercises. From his talks with Varentsov and other generals, and the discussions at the birthday party, Penkovsky knew what was about to happen.

In the beginning of October this year extensive general maneuvers will begin. They will start between the 3rd and 5th of October and continue until the end of the month. All headquarters of all military districts and all headquarters of groups of forces will participate. Even all rear services in the military districts will participate in these maneuvers. In other words, every army formation will execute its assigned mission just as they would be called upon to do in case there were a war. This is the first time in the history of the Soviet Army that such maneuvers will be held. In addition, the People's Democracies will also take part in these maneuvers. These strategic maneuvers, lasting for a month, will take place throughout the entire U.S.S.R. and all of the countries of the People's Democracies, based on combating a hypothetical enemy in Germany.

The objective is to determine which units can best fulfill offensive missions, shock actions, and defensive operations while evaluating their state of training and combat readiness. Deficiencies in training can be corrected and experience in joint operations gained. But that is only one purpose; the second purpose is to have these huge forces in a state of combat readiness exactly at the time the peace treaty with East Germany will be signed, so that if any difficulties occur immediately after the treaty is signed, following the Party Congress, they will be in a position to strike a heavy blow. In other words what Khrushchev wants to do is to use the maneuvers as camouflage for actual large-scale military preparations at the time of the signing of the peace treaty with East Germany.[6]

Penkovsky then drew his conclusions for the team. "First of all, Khrushchev is preparing nine armies in and adjacent to the immediate German theater, and now he has ordered a tenth army to that area. In East Germany itself there are only two armies, but the others are nearby in a supporting role.

"His first purpose is to frighten us. However, if the Communist world expresses complete approval at the Party Congress in October, and he also feels that world opinion is with him, he may strike us. He wants to take advantage of any indecision on the part of the Free

World, and he may actually attack the leaders, which are the United States and England. He does not have all available means for carrying through such a strike to a final conclusion. The military people know this but they act meekly before Khrushchev. If he orders the beginning of hostilities they will comply."[7]

This was important news; it brought up to date the American and British evaluation of Khrushchev's intentions. His readiness to go to war over Berlin, if he could achieve the necessary support, was a shock, but it also served as an early warning of the importance of Allied unity.

Penkovsky had to pause so the tape could be changed on the recorder. "Before you continue we would like you to state who your sources were for all of the information you have given us, by individual item," said Kisevalter.

Penkovsky was annoyed. "I suggest you take notes on the items I report and ask me to clarify them later," he retorted. He did not like to be interrupted in the middle of a momentous report, especially when he was offering his own analysis and recommendations.[8] However, the team knew how crucial it was to have him specify the source of each bit of startling information for it to have credibility in Washington and London.[9] How to keep Penkovsky talking and yet fulfill the requirements of the Washington and London intelligence community was always a problem.

Penkovsky listed the names of the generals who supplied him the information. Marshal Malinovsky himself had told him that the new Soviet army to be sent to East Germany would be the Eighth Mechanized Army, composed of three tank divisions and two motor-rifle divisions.

Penkovsky said, "As a staff officer of our command all I can suggest is that we now begin a propaganda campaign pointing to the aggressive nature of Khrushchev and the coming Party Congress to show that we are not deluded. Many effective countermeasures can be taken. From what I read about the firmness expressed by the West, I know that this is causing Khrushchev anxiety. Your leaders should take full cognizance of what I have reported regarding these maneuvers; they should check from other sources what I have said and take appropriate countermeasures, the nature of which, of course, is their business."

The team was impressed with the content of Penkovsky's report and the high level from which he obtained the information. The full mobilization of Soviet troops and rear reserves could only mean that Khrushchev was seriously prepared to face the West in a war over Berlin if the Allies opposed his plan to sign a peace treaty and turn administrative control of Berlin over to East Germany. This informa-

231

tion was vital to the president, high-level planners, and the Joint Chiefs of Staff.

Penkovsky also had significant information on newly resumed Soviet nuclear testing in the atmosphere. Khrushchev, who had promised Kennedy in Vienna that he would not resume testing unless the United States did first, had broken his word. "Khrushchev felt it was impossible for him not to run these tests," said Penkovsky.

The first, earlier phase of the tests was to mount the individual nuclear warheads on towers and explode them or drop them from aircraft. The next step was for the missiles to be fired against a test target with a conventional charge of TNT in the warhead. When that was successful a nuclear warhead was placed on the missile and fired against the same target. In the current phase of the testing, Penkovsky explained, nuclear warheads would actually be detonated from missiles fired at targets.[10]

He revealed the existence of a "huge rocket launching base" at the Novaya Zemlya islands, north of the Arctic Circle, between the Barents and Kara seas, equipped to test warheads for R-12 and R-14 rockets, known as the SS-4 and SS-5 medium-range missiles in NATO terminology. The R-12 (SS-4), he reported, "is already adopted and is being serially produced. Its range is 2500 kilometers [1500 miles]. The R-14 [SS-5] is being prepared for serial production. It has a range of 4500 kilometers [2800 miles]. Both ranges I have given are for the rockets carrying atomic warheads."[11]

In Krasnovodsk, on the Caspian, and at Kirovabad in Azerbaijan, Penkovsky said, there were missile launching sites facing Iran and Pakistan.

Penkovsky revealed Khrushchev's plans to create a second front to increase pressure on the United States if the Berlin situation reached the point of open conflict. The proximity of the Soviet Union to Iran placed the U.S. at a decided military disadvantage. Khrushchev would make Iran a target of opportunity for Soviet expansion in an area it considered its historical sphere of interest. Since the days of Peter the Great (1672–1725) the tsars have sought warm-water ports to the south, and at the end of the nineteenth century Russia seized the northern part of the Persian province of Azerbaijan, including its oil fields at Baku. Penkovsky said: "Khrushchev is going to tie Iran to the German problem. He plans to send troops into Iran when complications develop in Germany in October. Khrushchev plans to deal with this matter in Iran because of the extensive American military bases there."[12]

Penkovsky said that he had been told the Soviet leadership was ready to use Iran as a pressure point against the West. "Our Intelligence reports that the entry of Soviet troops now would not be badly received by the local population. Khrushchev contemplated giving an ultimatum similar to the one he gave a short time ago to Turkey and to Pakistan: if any more U-2 flights were sent from their airfields these airfields would be attacked. The ultimatum to Iran would state that if American bases were not removed from Iran, Soviet troops would move in. Obviously no one would remove anything, and if he moved in his troops, war would begin. Then they began to think more deeply about this. Possibly a conflict would not work out well since there are U.S. bases in Turkey and Pakistan; therefore it would be better to delay this for a month until October and in the meantime build up preparations."[13]

Penkovsky also reported on the first detonation of a new sixteen-kiloton warhead that was exploded in the air from an R-12 (SS-4) missile. It was this test that had polluted the atmosphere with radiation traveling across Europe.[14] In connection with nuclear testing, Penkovsky said he found out that on August 17, 1961, there had been a decree issued by the Party and the government creating a civil defense command. The document was seventeen pages "and I held it in my hands about fifteen to twenty minutes," Penkovsky said. He promised to summarize the document and photograph it at the first opportunity. Immediately on his return to Moscow, he did so, providing the United States with full details of massive Soviet civil defense planning designed to make the country less vulnerable to nuclear attack. In the process of contributing information on the civil defense system, he also told the team where deep command-and-control shelters were located, thus enabling the United States to target them.[15] By destroying command-and-control centers, the U.S. would cripple the Soviet military's ability to function and coordinate an attack against the United States.

The civil defense plans provided by Penkovsky added to the impression that the Soviet Union was seriously preparing for nuclear war. His news prodded the United States government to formulate a more highly organized civil defense program. Initially Kennedy lent support to the program and the public responded, but the idea never took hold. Nuclear warheads proliferated faster than shelters. Pictures of schoolchildren huddled under their desks with their hands on their heads only served to underscore the futility of trying to survive a nuclear attack.[16]

At the Paris meetings Penkovsky literally gushed with information, recounting how Central Committee member Churayev, who boasted of his personal rose garden with 20,000 bushes, had gotten drunk quickly at Varentsov's birthday party. Churayev told everybody at the table about food riots outside Moscow in which 400 men attacked the militia. The crowd came to make a mass appeal for better food supplies. The militia fired warning shots in the air and at the ground, but the crowd would not leave. Only when troops were called did the demonstrators disperse. According to Penkovsky, both Malinovsky and Varentsov were astounded that so prominent an official as Churayev would reveal such grim details at the dinner table.[17] The team was fascinated with Penkovsky's table talk. It laid bare the Soviet Union's internal economic and political situation. The richness of the personalities and their foibles were a unique source of intelligence. Such stories were not known to diplomats or journalists.

Since his return from London to Moscow, Penkovsky said, Mrs. Serov had twice invited him to their apartment at number 3 Granovskovo Street, next to the Voyentorg [Central Military Department Store] and opposite the special Kremlin Hospital. He told the team that apartments in the building in which the Serovs lived were occupied by Marshal Zhukov, Presidium members Mikhail Suslov and Yekaterina Furtseva, army marshals, and the chief prosecutor of the Soviet Union. Penkovsky had brought Serov a shirt from London and gave his wife and daughter small presents. Smiling at the irony, Penkovsky told the team, "The caviar I have brought you is from the Serovs. They gave me caviar and sausage. I have not brought the sausage because it is available here in France."[18]

When he was at Serov's apartment, Penkovsky related, the GRU chief told him about the downfall of a colonel who had criticized Khrushchev at a Party conference. The colonel, chief of a department at the Frunze Military Academy, said that Khrushchev had correctly criticized the cult of Stalin, but now he himself was developing the cult of Khrushchev. The colonel was interrupted and immediately the Party head of the region proposed he be censured. His mandate as a delegate was revoked and he was thrown out of the conference for daring to criticize Khrushchev. (Penkovsky did not mention the name of the officer, but Serov was referring to the case of Major General Pyotr Grigorenko, a much-decorated officer who was disgraced as a result of his speech and later sent to insane asylums and psycho-prisons for five years before being permitted to leave the Soviet Union in 1977 for the United States, where he died in 1988.)[19]

"Let me go on to the next point," insisted Penkovsky. "You gave me the mission that I find out by all means possible what is being done in the U.S.S.R. about the development of an antimissile.

Khrushchev has established a special scientific research institute in Moscow and there is a special experimental rocket battalion that is developing electronic guidance assemblies to control rockets capable of intercepting a hostile missile in flight and destroying it. Right now there is just the institute and the experimental battalion. Everything else Khrushchev may say is foolishness, bluff, and propaganda. However, experimental work is being done."[20]

Khrushchev's emphasis on missiles was placing a strain on other armaments, Penkovsky said. "Varentsov cursed and told me, 'We are doing things in a one-sided way. We are placing emphasis on rockets, and it is proper that we should do this, but we are beginning to forget about conventional artillery. Conventional artillery is of course organic in all rifle divisions. We now have a shortage of conventional artillery.' "[21] Khrushchev's priorities were creating resentment within the military leadership.

Shergold suggested they take a break for wine and sandwiches. While they relaxed, Penkovsky said he wanted to tell the team the latest black humor from Moscow.

> Two Soviets meet. One asks the other, "How do you live? Do you go to the cinema?"
>
> "Yes, I live well. I go to the cinema."
>
> "Do you go to the theater?"
>
> "Yes, I go to the theater. I live well."
>
> "Do you read the newspapers?"
>
> "Yes, I read the newspapers. If not, how would I know that I live well?"[22]

Another joke involved a questionnaire Khrushchev distributed asking, "What will you do when we catch up with America?" Someone wrote, "When we catch up with America you can go on, but I will stop right there."

"This is the life of our people—humor through tears—bitter humor."[23]

Penkovsky gave the team a copy of his GRU assignments in France. He told them that the GRU mission in Paris was to obtain Western weapons, particularly a small-caliber U.S. mortar, a standard NATO rifle, and U.S. and British gas masks. They were also looking for the formula for an anticorrosive treatment of submarine hulls to reduce time in drydock. High on the acquisition list was electronic technology applicable to rocketry and a small U.S. rocket launched from aircraft capable of creating atmospheric disturbances to disrupt radar.[24] "Think up something interesting so that I can once again go home with results," Penkovsky urged. He reminded the team of the praise he had received for the good pictures he took of the British bombers and a new surface-to-air antiaircraft missile system at bases while on a trip to Sheffield and Leicester.

When he was in England, Penkovsky and Wynne had visited Karl Marx's grave in Highgate Cemetery. The grave was overrun with weeds and littered with trash. Penkovsky pretended he was outraged. Instead of just telling the Soviet ambassador, he wrote an indignant letter directly to the Central Committee. In short order the Soviet ambassador in London was directed to allocate money for payment of a caretaker at the cemetery to clean and maintain the grave. The embassy established a periodic check on the condition of Marx's tombstone. "They can see that as an intelligence officer I am alert from the military and political point of view," said Penkovsky.[25]

Again Penkovsky stressed the need for the team to supply him with French contacts for the GRU Station in Paris. "Give me a man who can fool them and do whatever is necessary for us. We can achieve something interesting through this link."

Shergold said to Kisevalter, "I think we ought to explain to him at this moment that France is not quite the same as England and we do not want to bring in the French in any way. We want to keep this entirely secret from them and therefore we cannot get the cooperation of the French. Although we will do the best to help him in every way we can, it is going to be very much more difficult for us while we are here."

"But surely there are steadfast people in French Intelligence who can be told and who are working wholeheartedly for the French and for us," Penkovsky said to Kisevalter, once Shergold's comments were conveyed to him.

"We do not want to share our knowledge about you," said Kisevalter.

"I understand that you are clever and experienced case officers, but surely France is our country," countered Penkovsky.

"Yes," replied Shergold, "but if we were to tell the French what we are doing here, this would complicate matters. They would want to be here too. We would not be able to maintain security and therefore we are not prepared to do anything which would involve bringing in the French."

Shergold and Bulik did not want to tell Penkovsky the British and American Services believed that the French Secret Service, the SDECE (*Service de Documentation Extérieure et de Contre Espionage*), had been penetrated by the Russians. In essence they did not want the French to know they were in Paris for fear of exposing Penkovsky.*

Penkovsky was not to be deterred, and returned to his favorite subject: "Well, I ask you to think about it. What you do should earn me thanks. This is your business as case officers. We must think up something good so that I get a decoration and am promoted to general."[26]

After he had delivered his reports and answered the team's questions, Penkovsky went down a list of his own requirements. He told the team that the battery-operated electric razors he gave as gifts had created a sensation, and his contacts, including General Serov and Gvishiani, each wanted one. He needed six more. Since the sixty-year-old bottle of cognac had been so successful for Varentsov's birthday, Penkovsky thought it would add the right touch to provide wine or cognac to his sources for the forty-fourth anniversary of the Bolshevik Revolution, on November 7, 1961. "I will get bottles of wine, vintage 1917, for Serov, Malinovsky, and Churayev. I'll ask Varentsov to take the bottle to Malinovsky. When he is told it is from the colonel he met who is walking around as a full colonel for twelve years now and it is time that he should be proposed for general, Malinovsky will probably say, 'Go and write the recommendation.' I am sure that Serov will not object. I am not losing by bringing them presents. It is prima facie evidence that they trust me by the fact that they accept my gifts. My story is very simple. I get along well abroad. I buy odds and ends out of the money I save. They even write letters and notes to me with their requests of what they want."

Penkovsky continued with his list of requests for gifts: a small gold lady's watch, either Omega or Longine, with easily read Arabic numerals on the dial, small bottles of Arpège, Chanel No. 5, and Mitsuoko perfume, but only small bottles. He needed phonograph records of the popular Russian cabaret singers Vertinsky and Leshchenko, who emigrated after the Revolution, but whose songs were still popular in Moscow. Also on the list were wallets, pocketbooks, watch straps, and twenty cheap ballpoint pens. Penkovsky had orders for a prescription medicine called Sustanon, which was

---

* In the fall of 1961 the CIA had reports from Soviet defectors that French Intelligence had been penetrated by the KGB. Peter Deriabin recalled that when he was serving in the KGB in Moscow in 1952, I. I. Agayants, deputy chief for disinformation of the KGB's First Chief Directorate, gave a lecture in which he disparagingly referred to French Intelligence as "that prostitute I put in my pocket."

In 1962 Kennedy wrote de Gaulle a personal letter informing him that information from a recent Soviet defector indicated the French Intelligence Service, and even de Gaulle's cabinet, had been penetrated by the KGB. See P. L. Thyraud de Vosjoli's *Lamia* (Boston: Little, Brown, 1970), pp. 298–318.

supposed to sustain sexual potency, and the laxative Ex-Lax. Then he read off a long list of requests from the Serov family.[27]

"I can see now why you need twenty-five days in Paris," said Joe Bulik with a smile.

Bulik suggested that Penkovsky have a free day. They should not meet again until September 22, in the early evening, after dark, so that no witness would be able to recognize Penkovsky when he was being picked up by the team. Penkovsky and the team also agreed not to meet too frequently; they set short intervals between meetings at the beginning of the twenty-five-day-long sojourn and stretched them further apart as time went on.[28]

The film Penkovsky had brought to Paris was being developed in London and would be ready for the next meeting. The meeting ended at 11:15 P.M., after nearly four hours, and a tired Penkovsky was dropped off near his hotel.

Penkovsky spent the following day touring Paris with Wynne. The Eiffel Tower, the Louvre, and a ride on a *bateau-mouche* along the Seine excited Penkovsky. He marveled at the elegance of the public buildings and the bridges across the Seine. According to Wynne, Paris was at its best for Penkovsky when he sat on the Champs-Élysées, below the Arc de Triomphe, sipping cold French beer and savoring the passing parade of well-dressed, attractive women. Parisians seemed free and high-spirited. The energy on the Champs-Élysées, the sense of purpose, and zest for life shown by the strollers elated Penkovsky. He flirted with stylish women, who smiled at his openness and sturdy good looks. Wynne had to restrain him from making dates.[29] He and Wynne ate a steak dinner with red wine followed by dessert and cognac at a small restaurant on the Rue Lincoln off the Champs-Élysées. After dinner Wynne suggested they visit some night spots, but Penkovsky was tired. He smiled and told Wynne, "I would not mind one night's rest."[30]

On Friday, September 22, at 7:30 P.M. Penkovsky crossed the Solférino footbridge on the Right Bank of the Seine and met Shergold and Roger King, who drove him to the safe house on Hameau Beranger, ten minutes away. Penkovsky had spent the day at the Soviet exhibit and meeting with the officers in the GRU *Rezidentura* in Paris. A key mission for the GRU Paris Station was to determine the composition of the new solid rocket fuel developed by France.[31]

Penkovsky's report on Khrushchev's intentions for Berlin at his last meeting in London had produced sparks in Washington. His comments had been encrypted and cabled to CIA headquarters, where they were written up in a report attributed to a "Senior Soviet officer with access to high ranking officials." The idea that Khrushchev was prepared to go to war over Berlin stirred deep concern, a flurry of speculation, and many questions. There was a requirements order for the team to follow up. Just what did Penkovsky mean when he reported that "If necessary Khrushchev will strike" at the time of the signing of the peace treaty with East Germany?

"Who told you this?" asked Kisevalter.

"This was not told to me by only one person," explained Penkovsky. "This concept was expressed to me by Varentsov and also by [his aides] Pozovny and Buzinov. In addition I have heard the same thing in the General Staff from those who are in a position to know and with whom I have friendly relations. This is all tied to the general theme I reported. If you retreat from Berlin, things will be quiet for a year or a year and a half. Then Khrushchev will start crowing again that we have achieved a victory, that Kennedy was afraid to face him.

> Let me tell you how it came about. Buzinov asked me if I had 500 rubles so he could get some supplies of butter and sugar because he felt that things would be very bad in October [1961]. I asked if he wasn't being panicky. He said, "No. I am an old soldier but I have a feeling from what I see, and you must see, through your channels, how difficult things can be in October. I have been running from one place to another and sending officers to all kinds of bases where preparations for combat readiness are being made. I know that if the West begins to fire after the peace treaty is signed, we must be ready to strike them a hard blow and we do not have sufficient reserves of rockets."[32]

"What specifically does Khrushchev lack to follow through with an attack on the West?" asked Kisevalter.

"He does not have a sufficient number of atomic warheads. They published in our press that we have 30,000 atomic weapons of various yields, and many fools believe this. They have weapons with various size yields, but few of them—they are still making them. Similarly, although the R-11 [SS-1] and R-12 [SS-4] [medium-range] rockets have been found to be satisfactory and are being mass produced, the R-14 [SS-5] [intermediate-range] is still not in serial production."

"What else does he lack?"

"Trained personnel cadres. Several more years are required. Is it not significant to have 2500 students at one time at one academy, the Dzerzhinsky Academy, in peacetime? They can be seen going to their studies every day."

"Any other fundamental items—how about submarines?" asked Kisevalter.

"There are insufficient submarines. However, they do have an announced plan for attacking the United States and England using ICBMs, submarines, and aircraft. This was announced at a diplomatic reception by Khrushchev himself, who also mentioned that they had a nuclear weapon of one megaton [equal to one million tons of TNT]. Varentsov told me many times about all these deficiencies I have mentioned. On this I swear," Penkovsky said solemnly.[33]

I also forgot to mention that there is a lack of perfected electronic guidance systems. There have been a small number of rockets developed, and with this small amount Khrushchev is attempting to scare us. However, this maniac, before the end of his life, may desire to make a tremendous attack, and that is what all the Russian people are afraid of. That is why I made the suggestion that it would be worthwhile to assassinate him. We could relax for a year or two before a new leader emerges, and there would be a big fight for control of power. The most outstanding candidate now, the smartest, is Mikoyan, who is still an old Leninist. Molotov is ill and will not compete; Kozlov and Brezhnev are complete fools and they don't like Mikoyan because they are stooges of Khrushchev.[34]

To convince the team of the seriousness of war preparations in the Soviet Union, Penkovsky offered a full review of maneuvers and rocket training exercises that would accompany the signing of the East German peace treaty. "In these general maneuvers there is not a single unit that will not have its wartime military mission to accomplish. All will participate. A mock war will be declared. Irrespective of where one sits, in which headquarters, all elements of troop deployment will take part to the point of establishing bakeries, laundries, and field hospitals."

Kisevalter asked if the Warsaw Pact forces would be used in the training exercises. Penkovsky replied:

Of course firing will be restricted or simulated, and atomic bursts will be simulated, but Varentsov and Buzinov told me that there will be rocket firing exercises. These may be done in the Kapustin Yar area or in some isolated place. This exercise is to train the rocket crews in target aiming. Although there will not be a general mobilization of the population, this mass deployment of the entire standing army as it passes through its maneuver phases will put it into combat readiness. The air force and all services will participate. Offensive as well as defensive phases will be scheduled. I forgot to mention another thing—all forms of signals communication will be used intensively to train those units properly.[35]

240

When he finished reporting, Penkovsky had some thoughts of his own which again startled the team:

I have been thinking for a long time that it would be a great advantage for us [the West] to provoke a small local conflict with the Soviets in some remote area, something like the Finnish War or the conflict in the Far East in the past [the Korean War]. Khrushchev does not want this.

It should be demonstrated that Khrushchev is the sole proponent of nuclear warfare and the only warmonger among all nations. He says that a local conflict will develop into a nuclear war. This is not true, and a conflict using conventional weapons in Korea or Vietnam could be created. If a local conflict were created on the borders of Iran or Pakistan or Turkey, and there were enough provocation for this, by the Americans and British, and a Soviet Army group of almost fifteen divisions were to be deployed in this direction, say 500,000 men, and both sides were employing conventional weapons, you would be surprised to see how many mass desertions by officers and men would take place from the Soviet Army to your side. Then this son of a bitch Khrushchev would see for himself how weak his position is, and he would have to cease all hostilities to patch up his army. The army today is seething; Khrushchev has abused it severely by his extensive discharges [of officers] in the past, which is something Stalin did not do. Khrushchev is called "the abuser of the army."

Referring to Kennedy and Macmillan, Penkovsky said:

Our leaders should recognize how much dissatisfaction there is among the officers of the Soviet Army. Of course it is not for us, particularly army men, to suggest political action. Wiser people will do this, and it is not even our concern. However, I mention these things because I feel you should report the extent of the dissatisfaction in the army. Khrushchev is today the new Hitler, an atomic Hitler, and with the help of his stooges who support him, he wants to start a world conflict so that prior to his death he can achieve his boast, "I will bury capitalism."[36]

The fact that Khrushchev said that there can be no exclusively local war is general conversation in the entire General Staff. Everyone speaks of this.[37]

Penkovsky liked to think of himself as a military strategist, and he enjoyed enumerating his theories to the team, much to their annoyance. Kisevalter had a long requirements list to go through.

241

When Penkovsky wandered off the list with his own ideas it took time to get him back on track.

Actually, Penkovsky's strategic musings reflected the debate going on among Khrushchev, the Presidium, and the military leaders over whether a nuclear war could actually be fought and won. Soviet nuclear strategy was still largely unformed, and internal debates were carefully guarded military secrets. Unlike the open debate in the U.S., there was no open discussion in the Soviet press of strategic doctrine by civilian strategists, nor were such issues critically reviewed. It was not until 1962 that the first edition of Marshal V. D. Sokolovsky's *Military Strategy* was published in Moscow, providing clues to Soviet military doctrine. In the summer of 1961 Penkovsky was leading the team through the highly classified Soviet debate on nuclear strategy that was still a controversial enigma to American policymakers and strategic planners.

The goal of American strategic doctrine, as it had developed through 1960, was deterrence first. Should that fail, it was vital to have the strength to inflict catastrophic damage on the enemy. If an enemy attacked first, the United States should still have enough nuclear weapons left to retaliate and destroy the attacker.

Soviet strategic doctrine stipulated that the Soviet Union survive as a nation with its ideology and strategic forces intact. The Soviet Union placed its emphasis on massive civilian defense and planning that enhanced the prospect that the U.S.S.R. could survive, and in some politically meaningful way defeat the main enemy. Its nuclear strategy stressed political ideology; American strategy was primarily psychological in orientation, based on uncoordinated SAC war plans.[38]

The difference in emphasis had important strategic implications. American strategy stressed massive destruction: disabling of the enemy's nuclear capabilities and crippling its society. Soviet nuclear strategy emphasized fighting a nuclear war; implying that a nuclear war could be fought and won. The strategy of massive retaliation, articulated first by the Eisenhower administration, was the declared American strategic nuclear deterrent from the mid-1950s. Massive retaliation was designed primarily as a deterrent; the policy assumed that no Soviet leadership would be foolhardy enough to challenge American nuclear superiority. However, massive retaliation was losing credibility as a deterrent following the launching of Sputnik in 1957 and Khrushchev's claims to nuclear superiority. The Soviet Union had demonstrated an ICBM potential that could demand an American response. There were calls to revise American scientific and mathematical education to increase the number of graduate engineers. The CIA established the Directorate of Science and Technology to meet the Soviet challenge of missile and space achievements. The U.S. had to face a new reality of a growing Soviet nuclear strength sufficient to destroy the American way of life.

Many members of the foreign policy establishment, led by the Council on Foreign Relations in New York City, argued that the threat to wage all-out nuclear war in response to aggression anywhere, of any size, lacked credibility.[39] A council study resulted in the 1957 publication of Henry Kissinger's controversial book *Nuclear Weapons and Foreign Policy*, which advocated the option of limited nuclear war and was the catalyst for a national debate. Kissinger, a member of the council, argued that with the ability to wage a limited nuclear war, the U.S. would be creating a "spectrum of capabilities with which to resist the Soviet challenges" and Soviet nuclear blackmail. In terms of deterrence, he wrote, "the ability to wage limited nuclear war seems more suitable than conventional war because it poses the maximum credible threat." Kissinger was not suggesting that a nuclear war could be won, only that a limited nuclear war strategy would broaden the range of options available to prevent a full-scale nuclear war. The refusal to run any risks, even of limited nuclear war, he warned "would amount to giving the Soviet rulers a blank check."[40]

Kennedy came to power with a heavy skepticism of the way the Defense Department was being run. Robert McNamara, who left the presidency of the Ford Motor Company to head the Pentagon, brought with him a team of industrial managers who became known as the Whiz Kids for their ruthless cost cutting and efforts to rationalize the procurement and management practices of the Pentagon. Much of their skepticism was turned to the public perception of the Soviet threat, which was the source of competition among the services for the funding of new weapons programs. Under McNamara there was an attempt to quantify and verify the Soviet nuclear threat as the basis for decision-making on funding for new weapons systems. The system that had proceeded unchallenged under Eisenhower was now called into sharp question. This led to a buildup of conventional forces in Europe.

The Kennedy administration shifted its strategic focus from massive retaliation to the concept of flexible nuclear response. The president and his senior aides, Secretary of State Dean Rusk, Defense Secretary McNamara, and National Security Advisor McGeorge Bundy, had only limited insight into Soviet strategic doctrine until Penkovsky arrived on the scene. They were anxious to learn and determined to take charge.

Penkovsky's reports, supplemented by his own interpretations of the men who shaped the political universe of the Soviet military, provided important insights into the internal Soviet military debate over the use of nuclear weapons and limited nuclear war.

Penkovsky, in presenting his personal view of Khrushchev, revealed the questions being asked within the command of the Soviet armed forces: could a nuclear war be won and, if so, how should it be fought? Until Stalin's death in 1953, the Soviet view was that war with the West was inevitable and that a nuclear war could be fought and won. This stemmed from Stalin's assertion, based on the "superiority" of Marxism-Leninism, that the U.S.S.R. would prevail in any future conflict.[41] Ideology would be the sustaining impetus for Soviet victory. To the West it appeared that the Soviet Union did not understand the true power of nuclear weapons. To the U.S.S.R., former deputy secretary of defense Roswell Gilpatric noted, "nuclear weapons were another form of artillery."[42]

During the power struggle after Stalin's death in 1953, Premier Georgi Malenkov and his supporters argued that war between the capitalist states and the Soviet Union was no longer inevitable. A nuclear war would bring "the destruction of world civilization," Malenkov warned. He was striving to shift resources from military to consumer spending and gain popularity with the Soviet masses. Khrushchev attacked Malenkov and won the support of the Soviet military when he insisted that a world war would bring victory to the Soviet Union and socialism. By 1957 Khrushchev had banished Malenkov; facing the reality of American nuclear might, he switched his position and now spoke of "peaceful coexistence." In Marxist-Leninist terminology, peaceful coexistence was "a specific form of international class struggle" that made it possible to avoid war at the nuclear level by making the issue ambiguous. The Chinese bitterly attacked Khrushchev for trying to bluff his way into a position of political superiority and backing away from the threat of inevitable nuclear war.

The Soviet military followed Khrushchev's lead; after the 1957 launching of Sputnik, Khrushchev's boasts seemed to have some merit, and more funds were available for Soviet missiles and the military. However, to enlarge Soviet strategic rocket forces Khrushchev soon cut back on conventional military forces and alienated the traditional military leadership. In his speeches he stressed Soviet nuclear superiority and continued to insist on the Soviet Union's right to support wars of national liberation, while paying lip service to peaceful coexistence.

Soviet military doctrine changed after Sputnik and became the subject of intense scrutiny and analysis by American strategists. Lieutenant General (U.S. Army, ret.) William E. Odom, a leading expert on the Soviet military, studied Soviet nuclear doctrine over the twenty-five year period after Sputnik and noted:

> The Soviet view of nuclear weapons has little in common with popular views in the West. While accepting the revolutionary character of nuclear weapons for modern warfare, the Soviet leadership has proceeded on the traditional assumption that war, even nuclear war, must be made subordinate to policy; that nuclear war might well break out; and that Soviet forces must be designed, organized, and trained to fight successfully under nuclear, chemical, and biological battlefield conditions.
>
> Most important, while nuclear weapons can be decisive in the initial phases of a war, they alone are not adequate for victory. All branches of service and weapons systems must be integrated doctrinally for a combined-arms approach to war. As the Soviet military theorists see it, nuclear weapons affect dramatically not only the strategic but also the operational and tactical levels of warfare. Far from being unthinkable, nuclear warfare requires enormous doctrinal attention, material preparation, special training, and psychological toughness. Finally the vast resources allocated for nuclear war preparations in line with Soviet doctrinal dictates suggest a seriousness about the matter only vaguely appreciated in the West.[43]

Under the policy of massive retaliation, the U.S. would mount an all-out response to an attack that would destroy the Soviet Union's and China's industrial and population centers. Nuclear bombs were to be delivered by the Strategic Air Command led by General Curtis LeMay. From 1951 to 1955 the SAC Emergency War Plan, approved by the Joint Chiefs of Staff, called for 114 nuclear bombs to be dropped on the Soviet Union six days after the start of hostilities. The estimate, however, was that even with such devastating bombing the Soviet Union's industrial capacity would be destroyed by only 30 to 40 percent. The U.S.S.R. would still have sufficient troop mobility to invade selected areas of Western Europe, the Middle East, and the Far East.[44]

After the explosion of the first Soviet hydrogen bomb in November 1955, the Joint Chiefs of Staff added Soviet airfields and "atomic energy industries" to the list of targets. SAC's guidance from Eisenhower was to hit its targets with a high level of "damage expectancy." LeMay was free to interpret this guidance any way he chose.[45] The U.S. Navy, with its carrier-based attack planes capable of carrying nuclear bombs, selected its own targets in the Soviet Union and China, independent of SAC.

In 1960, in an effort to coordinate targets among the services and limit nuclear overkill, Eisenhower ordered the establishment of a Joint Strategic Target Planning Staff to develop a coordinated plan for American nuclear attack. This became known as the Single Integrated Operating Plan, or the SIOP, which was so secret that it had its own security classification: *Extremely Sensitive Information*. In their study of the SIOP, the secret U.S. plan for nuclear war, Peter Pringle and William Arkin explain, "Competition for targets generated a demand for more weapons." By the summer of 1960, when the admirals and generals met to designate targets, the U.S. strategic stockpile had risen to 18,000 warheads, up from 1000 five years earlier. In the same period the number of Soviet targets had risen from 3000 to 20,000.[46]

President Kennedy was aware of the rigidity of the SIOP nuclear war plan. When he was shown the "net evaluation" of a strategic nuclear war between the U.S. and the Soviet Union, he commented to Dean Rusk: "And we call ourselves the human race."[47] The shift from massive retaliation to a graduated nuclear response was under way.

At the time of the Berlin crisis, in August 1961, with nuclear war threatening to erupt over the Berlin Wall, Defense Secretary Robert McNamara reviewed nuclear war plans with NATO Commander Lauris Norstad. McNamara found to his dismay that the approved response to the hypothetical defeat of American forces in Berlin was still massive nuclear retaliation against Soviet aggression, an all-out effort to destroy major targets including population centers. "This option did not give me any peace of mind," McNamara recalled.

McNamara's doubts about the validity of American nuclear strategy were compounded when he met with Lord Mountbatten, then the British equivalent of the American chairman of the Joint Chiefs of Staff, in London in the summer of 1961—not long after Penkovsky's visit there. When McNamara discussed the nuclear "option," Mountbatten asked: "Are you insane?"[48] The British, like the Americans, realized it was time to shift to a new approach. Graduated response was the first step.

Under Kennedy's direction, McNamara ordered a revision of the first SIOP, which contained five primary options and a variety of suboptions. Attack target priorities were:

1. Soviet strategic retaliatory forces such as missile sites, air bases, submarine pens, nuclear bomb factories, and storage facilities.

2. Soviet air defenses away from cities, especially those along the routes U.S. attack bombers would fly.

3. Soviet air defenses near cities.

4. Soviet command-and-control centers.

5. If necessary an all-out "spasm" attack—another term for massive retaliation.

The only detail of the new SIOP leaked to the press was the decision not to attack cities first—"the no-cities doctrine." McNamara's contribution to nuclear strategy was to become known as MAD, mutually assured destruction.[49]

Penkovsky's information in the summer and fall of 1961, especially copies of the articles debating nuclear strategy in the Top Secret *Voyennaya Mysl* (Military Thought), indicated that the Soviet Union was moving in the opposite direction from the new American thinking, toward a nuclear war–fighting strategy. Penkovsky's reports were influential in leading Kennedy to toughen his stand on Berlin rather than back away from Khrushchev's threats to sign a separate peace treaty with East Germany and invalidate the Allied role in West Berlin.[50]

In the heat of trying to meet the specific demands on the requirements list, Shergold was determined to stick to hard, provable facts that could be measured by professional standards. He was less interested in Penkovsky's theoretical ideas. Shergold pressed Penkovsky on the allocation of missiles between Varentsov and other commands: "I would like to get this absolutely right—who told him and when, that the atomic warheads were taken out of storage and delivered to the missile bases?"

Penkovsky replied, "When the situation over Berlin became more tense, Khrushchev, with the support of the Central Committee, ordered that these atomic warheads be placed on a ready status and be delivered to the launching site in order to support his political policy with force. Khrushchev realizes that we [the West] may strike him first."

"But who told you this?" insisted Kisevalter.

"First of all Buzinov [Varentsov's aide]. Then, when I was in artillery headquarters, I heard from various officers that they were being sent out to determine accurately in practice how long it takes to move up atomic weapons to their proposed launching positions. How long it takes to assemble and mount them into firing positions. What the reactions of the troops are to the concept of employing such weapons. In short, all previous paper calculations are now being checked out in practice. They are bringing themselves to the point that if it is necessary to use atomic weapons they will be ready to use them."[51]

Kisevalter asked Penkovsky to explain the contradiction between Khrushchev's current belligerent attitude and his support for the policy of peaceful coexistence with the West that he enunciated at the Twenty-first Party Congress in 1959.

Penkovsky replied, "I understand you perfectly." From the Soviet viewpoint, he explained,

> Everything is dialectically interwoven. At that time Khrushchev was saying something entirely different from what he is saying now. In fact, in 1958 he set specific dates when he would sign the German peace treaty and then renounced them. His threats are like swinging a club to see the reaction. If the reaction is not in his favor, he stops swinging it. At that time there were no military forces capable of supporting the policy he now advocates. Now he is sitting on a military horse, and although he is not fully equipped to exert maximum strength, he is beginning to talk in a different way. Why has he kept quiet for so many years and now is speaking loudly? He estimates that there are weaknesses in our Western countries; that we are not fully prepared. He also knows some of our potential strengths in detail, particularly through his Communist agents. He feels he has strength and can act this way so that Kennedy, Macmillan, and de Gaulle must take him into account. Now we are showing him firmness, so he is ill at ease, but he still hopes that we will swallow the second pill [meaning a separate peace treaty with East Germany].

> What you refer to as a contradiction is actually a dialectic deviation. He wishes to use increased military strength to gain a political victory in the German problem. If we falter he will win both a moral victory and additional time for himself. However, if Khrushchev is struck at with force, he may recoil and think about it for a year or a year and a half. Of course he will arm during this period, as will we. This will really be a war of nerves.

Penkovsky had set forth the essence of Khrushchev's strategy and forecast the arms race that was to continue between the Soviet Union and the United States for the next thirty years. Dialectical Materialism views history as a process of change brought about by perpetual conflict. Every idea, or thesis, generates its own antithesis; from the struggle between them emerges a new synthesis that retains elements of both and supersedes them. The Soviet theory of history argues that capitalism is a thesis that generates the seeds of its own destruction, the antithesis of socialism. In the ensuing struggle between capitalism and socialism, the new synthesis that emerges will be Communism, with the final withering away of all states in a perfect Communism. Marxism-Leninism and history, Khrushchev believed, were on his side.

"I repeat," said Penkovsky, "that any concession will be regarded by Khrushchev as a weakness on our part. Incidentally, all this stems from the problem that you yourselves invoked in 1956 in Egypt during the Suez crisis." (The British and French attacked Egyptian forces in the Suez, and Israel advanced into the Sinai after President Nasser nationalized the Suez Canal in the summer of 1956. Under United Nations pressure the French and British withdrew their forces from the Suez Canal and the Israelis withdrew from the Sinai.)

"In fact, now that you still tolerate Castro in Cuba, Khrushchev considers it an accomplishment on his part. You see, the contradiction is this: whereas you use complete reason and humanitarian thinking in your approach to him, he translates this into an indication of weakness."[52]

"Does Khrushchev actually plan to rely on the Satellite armies in case of war?" asked Kisevalter.

"He is sure of a certain percentage of the troops, but he does not trust them as a whole. That is why he relies so heavily on nuclear weapons. This is why he states that any local conflict will develop into an atomic war. It is absurd and indicates absolute aggressiveness. He is trying to frighten people by this, both ours and his own."[53]

"If the Allies succeed in forcing access to Berlin, could then Khrushchev start a general war?" Kisevalter asked gravely.

Penkovsky replied without hesitation that despite his talk, "Khrushchev does not want a world war and would attempt to defeat the Allies locally, but if he feels that he has sufficient strength to knock out the U.S.A. and England, who are the leaders of NATO, it is possible that he may strike first. Even though in the past our General Staff and our foreign policies condemned the concept of surprise attack, such as Hitler used, now they have come around to the viewpoint that there is a great advantage to the side that makes a sudden massive first strike, and they are preparing themselves to be in a position to do so.

"Khrushchev cannot muster enough strength to strike at all potential enemy countries simultaneously, so he is singling out the U.S. and Britain for his attack targets, estimating that the other Allies will disintegrate, due to differences among themselves, and be happy to survive. The conclusion: if he does not retreat from his wild proposals and impossible conditions, we should strike him first, otherwise he may strike us."[54]

Kisevalter asked Penkovsky what kind of support Khrushchev had for his views regarding Soviet policy toward Germany, particularly among high-ranking officers. Do they encourage Khrushchev?

"A minister such as Malinovsky agrees with Khrushchev completely, although to himself he may say it may be too early to embark on such a risk. No one can openly oppose Khrushchev. They would simply be removed. Each one is afraid of losing the benefits of his position. Do you think Churayev wants to lose his estates with his 20,000 rosebushes? They would rather see everything go up in flames and go up themselves with it than say anything in opposition now and be removed."[55]

"Since Khrushchev must be well aware of Western military superiority over Soviet armament, how can he be so arrogant?" asked Kisevalter.

"You see, he feels that the West is not fully prepared. He feels that if the West were better organized, then it would be stronger, but since there are contradictions within NATO it is possible that some of the nations would pull out of it and therefore it is weak."

"Does he not recognize the West's superiority in armaments?" repeated Kisevalter.

"He recognizes our [the West's] armament strength, but he feels that the contradictions within NATO are strong enough to justify his position. He anticipates winning because of this," Penkovsky said. Penkovsky was alluding to NATO's inability to agree on the ill-fated multilateral nuclear force and its fears of Western Europe becoming the first nuclear war zone.[56] Shergold's own veiled comments about France and the fear of Soviet infiltration of its Secret Service were evidence of serious concerns, but they did not have the grave implications for Western strength and unity. Khrushchev placed too much credence on the differences within NATO, not enough upon its unifying fear of him.

Shergold was anxious to talk about Wynne before they adjourned for the night. "We have got to bear in mind for the future of this operation that it is frightfully important Wynne do something for the firms which he represents. He has spent a long time hanging around in Paris. He has not carried out his tasks. He is due to go to Yugoslavia; he cannot stay here. Otherwise he is going to lose his job and his potentialities for the future," said Shergold.

Penkovsky said Wynne had told him the same thing. Wynne would stay for a day or so in Paris to show him the city and then go to Yugoslavia. When he had gone to lunch with Wynne, Penkovsky said, Wynne had changed clothes and forgotten his money. "I had to give Wynne money to pay for our lunch. He is a good fellow and we are fond of him. He is a little bit self-serving, of course, but he is an honorable man and has done a lot for us. He must be supported in the future; how, is your concern, not mine," said Penkovsky.[57]

The meeting ended at midnight. Penkovsky could look forward to a free weekend to discover the pleasures of Paris with Wynne.

Safety or Glory

PENKOVSKY WAS A NEOPHYTE IN PARIS, WILLING TO HAVE WYNNE guide him through a night on the town. They started Saturday evening, September 23, with dinner at the Royale Hotel. Wynne explained the menu and ordered for them. He pretended to be worldly about wine and food, but his personal tastes remained simple. He liked to show off for Penkovsky, whose daring he admired. Wynne wanted to share Penkovsky's glory. He hoped, if all went well, his role would be recognized and rewarded with honors.

Wynne was determined to help the Russian spy relax with small talk and the humorous stories at which he excelled. During the meal he gave Penkovsky instructions on a new rendezvous point for the next meeting on Monday, September 25, at 7:30 P.M. Penkovsky absorbed the information, but he seemed preoccupied despite the fine food and wine.

Finally he spoke out about what was gnawing at him: should he stay in the West? The team had told him that the CIA or SIS would set him up in Washington or London in a position commensurate with his colonel's rank. He could be a consultant, an adviser on Soviet military and intelligence developments. Of course they wanted more information from him in Moscow, but he had to judge whether to defect. His dilemma was something he could not discuss with his wife. What did Wynne think? Wynne, too, could only advise him that it was something he must decide for himself.

Penkovsky continued his deliberation aloud: "There's the question of work and there's the question of my wife. . . . If I stay here it will mean leaving Vera and Galina behind. I can't get them out with me, it's impossible. And if I stayed they would be used [by the KGB] to get me back. It would be very bad for them. And yet, you know

252

if I go back it won't really be for them, it will be for myself, for what I have to do. I've been taken over, that's what happened. I'm not just a husband and father anymore, I'm something else as well. I'm really two people, can you understand that?"

"Yes," Wynne replied, "I understand."[1]

After dinner they stopped at two cabarets in Montparnasse. Penkovsky was enthralled to find the women wanted to dance with him and drink his champagne. He did not realize that they were hostesses who were paid for pushing drinks. Wynne did not tell Penkovsky, not wanting to spoil his impression that they were attracted to him. Wynne paid the bills and later sent them on to MI6 for reimbursement.

The evening ended with the two men walking up the Avenue George V. Penkovsky was again fascinated to find well-dressed prostitutes, in their own cars, determined to pick him up. To maintain security, Wynne had been instructed to keep his guest from succumbing to prostitutes. The team would supply Penkovsky's women. So Penkovsky returned to his hotel room alone.

That Monday, at 7:55 P.M., Mike Stokes and George Kisevalter picked up Penkovsky and brought him to the safe apartment. Washington's urgent requirements continued to dominate the Paris meetings. The implications of Penkovsky's reporting on Berlin and Soviet missile developments were so startling that the analysts and policymakers wanted to know exactly how his information was acquired and under what circumstances. Was he reporting gossip from the officers' mess or were his marshals and generals carrying out policy decided upon and dictated by Khrushchev himself?

Penkovsky reviewed for the team the history of his close relationship with Marshal Varentsov. He spoke about Varentsov's trip to Kapustin Yar, seventy-five miles southeast of Volgograd, for testing of the new medium-range missile the Soviets were developing, the R-12, or SS-4, as NATO called it. Kisevalter spent a long time impressing upon Penkovsky how important it was for him to obtain the exact dates of the missile tests, along with any available technical data, so that his information could be collated with the data the U.S. derived from monitoring devices. Penkovsky told the team about an anti–ballistic missile training institute in the Pokrovsko-Streshnevo area, five miles northwest of Moscow. "There are large yellow buildings with a high wall around them. Military technicians work there, not only civilians. All the employees are under strict secrecy regulations not to speak about what they do. My friend Pozovny [Varentsov's aide] has been walking around that area and swimming in the river for days. He meets high-ranking generals and they speak about these things."[2]

Kisevalter pressed Penkovsky on the sources for Varentsov's information. Which of Varentsov's material came from the Supreme Military Council headed by Khrushchev, the ultimate source of Soviet military decision-making? "All I can say is that Varentsov is a very well informed man, and when he makes a statement regarding the current situation it may not be the result of decisions of yesterday's Supreme Military Council. What comes from Varentsov may come from a discussion with the chief of ground forces or between Varentsov and the minister of defense or the chief of staff."[3]

Kisevalter had finished his agenda. He lifted his head toward Penkovsky and said, "You see, questions of this type help to clarify and pinpoint your report."

Penkovsky understood perfectly the source of such questions. "Yes, and it helps me to clarify for you elements of doubt. I suggest you send a cable to your source of information who stated that there are five Soviet field armies in the GDR and ask him to check his data," he stated. He had told the team there were only three of them in East Germany, an assertion that had not been immediately accepted.[4]

"By the way," Kisevalter said, "I have a message here for you from our chiefs. It says that the evaluation of the material you have obtained in the artillery journals is rated very highly and you are to be commended for your initiative and judgment in selecting the articles that you did."[5]

Penkovsky was pleased, and sensed it was the right time to raise the question of whether he should have a dacha outside Moscow for weekends.

"Do you have a dacha now?" asked Joe Bulik.

"No, I didn't buy one or rent one. You rather discouraged me from doing this, but I do have money. Before I leave we will reconsider this matter and you can advise me if I should have one or not. I need a place to go should I have to leave Moscow suddenly," said Penkovsky, making an operational argument to convince the team. The team feared that the purchase of a dacha would attract attention to Penkovsky and raise questions about the source of his new funds.

The prospect of being arrested was also on Penkovsky's mind. "The only area I can think of from which one can get out of the country is the Baltic area, since things are shut tight in Germany now. That is better than dragging the family all the way to the Far East to make a border crossing there."

"How about the southern areas like those facing Turkey and Iran?" asked Kisevalter.

"The borders are very tightly controlled there."

254

"How about water exfiltration from the area of Batum on the Black Sea?" countered Kisevalter.

"That is a very good idea," Penkovsky replied, "and I know that area, particularly from the Turkish side, since I was involved in handling a plane that crashed there; the Turkish village is only seven kilometers away from Batum. I have a good friend in Batum whom I visit whenever I am there. I am as at home with him as with relatives. His brother was in Varentsov's command and was killed during the war. We often sat at the seashore, where he has his own dacha, and swam in the Black Sea. We could see the border illuminated by both Turkish and Soviet lights. Our border guards parade along the shoreline, accompanied by dogs.

"The only way to get out from there," Penkovsky continued, "would be by a small boat straight out to sea and then be picked up. The only other place that seems favorable to me is the Baltic area, where the people hate the Soviet régime and are waiting to be liberated. One could get out from there by boat. However, your suggestion about Batum is very good; it can be done from there."

"Do naval craft patrol the shoreline heavily?" asked Kisevalter.

"There are patrol boats there, but not many. Let me ask this question again," Penkovsky asked earnestly. "If I compromise myself, would I be accepted if I ran to a Western embassy?"

In an aside to Kisevalter, Shergold said, "The embassy can't do anything for him because they can't get him out of the country." Penkovsky understood the difficulty and said no more. He left shortly thereafter, at 11 p.m.

The following evening, Tuesday, September 26, a car picked up Penkovsky in the area of Les Invalides and drove him in the direction of Le Bourget Airport, a ride without a destination, for the purpose of a briefing. He had asked the team to arrange for him to introduce a member of the GRU Paris Station to an American or French businessman who would appear to be a source for industrial intelligence on the GRU requirements list. MI6 and Bulik came up with two possible sources. One contact was an American, George Hook, the head of the Paris office of ARMCO Steel Corporation, who agreed to meet Penkovsky and arrange a tour of his factory, where Penkovsky could gather the technical brochures he needed for his reports to the GRU. Penkovsky also hoped to take along on the factory tour a GRU officer from the Paris *Rezidentura* who would appear to be an embassy official. This would earn him a good fitness report since French restrictions made it difficult for GRU officers to make their own contacts in Paris. Penkovsky was desperate to get this material so he could fulfill his mission to Paris. He believed his future depended on his ability to show the GRU what a good operator he was. Even while he considered defecting to the West, another part of him aspired to be promoted by the Soviets to the rank of general.

When he had contacted Hook, Bulik used a pseudonym. He told the ARMCO official he was from the CIA and how helpful it would be to the U.S. government if Colonel Penkovsky could be permitted to visit the ARMCO factory with a colleague. Hook agreed to cooperate. Bulik told Hook that Greville Wynne would arrange to introduce Penkovsky over a drink at the George V Hotel.

In the car, Bulik told Penkovsky that Wynne would arrange the meeting before he left for Yugoslavia. During the hour-long drive Penkovsky reviewed the background information on Hook and the factory visit. He asked to be dropped off on the Champs-Élysées, near the Arc de Triomphe and Wynne's hotel. They had a date for supper together.

The supper did not go well and Penkovsky left the meal upset with Wynne. The following evening, in the car on the way to the safe house, Penkovsky told Kisevalter about "some unpleasantness." Wynne's disposition had been extremely bad during their meeting. Penkovsky said he would present his version of the facts. Wynne told him he did not want to work with Penkovsky or with the team any longer. Wynne felt insecure; when he pressed to know what returns he could expect for his services he was never given a direct answer. He did not know where he stood. Wynne felt he was doing important work, but his activities were a threat to his business. He was under pressure. His wife, Sheila, was twice contacted by telephone in London by his British business contacts, who inquired when Wynne would go to Belgrade. This concerned Mrs. Wynne and she had called her husband in Paris. Wynne confessed to Penkovsky that he had failed to make the necessary appointments for negotiations in Belgrade on behalf of the English firms he represented. Penkovsky had taken up so much of his time that he was gradually losing the confidence of his clients. He was unprepared to go to Belgrade; he first had to return to London to make the arrangements. Penkovsky told the team he thought it was Wynne's own fault because he did not take care of his business in his free time.

In general, Penkovsky said, Wynne deserved nothing but praise for his operational support work. He further added that one reason for Wynne's being upset was that his wife told him that all was not going smoothly with the reconstruction job on their home in London. This was a clear signal that Wynne needed money.

The report of the meeting notes: "When Penkovsky related the figures and conditions allegedly reported by Wynne, they were in complete error, according to Shergold. Either Wynne did not tell

Penkovsky the truth or he garbled the facts. Wynne himself was under a misapprehension, or possibly Wynne was cleverly laying the groundwork for additional future demands." For his initial work in Moscow Wynne had received 15,000 pounds, $42,000 at the prevailing exchange rate.[6]

Money was not the only source of Wynne's dissatisfaction. He complained to Penkovsky that he would not receive a decoration. Penkovsky confessed to the team that this idea had first come from him; he had told Wynne he would be rewarded when he first tried to get Wynne to carry documents to the West. Wynne further told Penkovsky that he found it awkward to spend so much time with him and not be able to discuss the substance of the materials and reports which closely bound them together.

Penkovsky told Kisevalter he believed money was at the core of Wynne's problems and that he no longer needed Wynne. Since Wynne had done everything for the team that was required of him in a commendable, patriotic way, and was well paid for it, he should be released if he felt ill-used. Then, in the same breath, Penkovsky said he would not need Wynne until January or February of 1962, when Wynne was due to come to Moscow with a British business delegation. In a parting shot, Penkovsky said that he did not need Wynne in Paris; however, it would be useful if Wynne would return to Paris just prior to his departure so that Wynne could deliver industrial brochures to him and see him off to his plane.

What was the meaning of these contradictions in Penkovsky's attitude toward Wynne? Was Wynne seriously disgruntled—hence a security risk—or simply positioning himself for more money and recognition? Roger King was immediately sent off to see Wynne. According to the team's report, the tensions turned out to be a tempest in a teapot. That evening Wynne denied to King that he wished to stop work. Wynne left for Belgrade the following day.

The misunderstandings were the result of accumulated pressure and Penkovsky's personality. Penkovsky wanted Wynne to be the recipient of his largesse and feel indebted to him, but he did not want to share his own funds, received from the team, with Wynne. Penkovsky wanted to be assured of Wynne's continued loyalty, and to that end he was trying to help Wynne receive more money, which he thought would tie Wynne to him and assure smooth functioning of the operation. It was not Penkovsky's role to make a plea for Wynne. Spies are supposed to follow the orders of their control officers and not become involved in placating their couriers, but Penkovsky was unique.

The team did not tell Penkovsky what Wynne was receiving in payment, nor that he was being reimbursed by MI6 for the expenses he paid on behalf of Penkovsky. The cash Penkovsky received in London was doled out by Shergold, who made Penkovsky ask for every pound he wanted for shopping. Good tradecraft requires that an agent not suddenly have spent so much money that he attracts attention to himself. Money is also a key means for controlling an agent, and Shergold made no concessions to Penkovsky's unique situation in Moscow. He kept him on a tight leash. Bulik found Shergold's caution excessive and thought he was being stingy. In London, when he thought Shergold was being too tight, he and Kisevalter provided Penkovsky shopping money from their own operational funds. This was always done with Shergold present; the Americans made it look like it was their turn to pay.[7] Penkovsky understood the rules of tradecraft. He had practiced them himself in Turkey, when he was a military attaché recruiting Turkish agents. In Paris Bulik handled the funds and there were no problems with the British over funds.

The team made light of Penkovsky's problems with Wynne. They spoke of "strained nerves" and assured Penkovsky that everything would be worked out. In fact, Wynne called Penkovsky that same evening at about 11 to invite him to go out on the town with him. Penkovsky could not leave the meeting, but just prior to Wynne's departure for Belgrade the following day, Penkovsky called Wynne and expressed gratitude to him for his many services and kindnesses. Penkovsky said he had spoken to his friends on Wynne's behalf and that they had agreed to take care of Wynne's problems and demands.

The 1961 report of that evening's meeting summed up the team's mood toward Penkovsky: "There is no question that subject both wittingly and unwittingly can be most trying in his often capricious demands and handling him on the part of all concerned requires great patience, even if understanding is not always possible."[8]

Wynne's own recollection of the strains between him and Penkovsky in Paris were quite different. In retirement, Wynne moved to Majorca, where he raised roses commercially. In September 1988 he insisted that the Americans on the team had tried to get Penkovsky to work exclusively for them without the British, which would have eliminated Wynne from the project. "Penkovsky was upset because he would not work without me," Wynne said. There is no documentation in the case files of an independent American approach to Penkovsky in Paris. None of the team members ever met Wynne. Bulik, who would have made the proposal, denies that any such move was contemplated or discussed with Penkovsky. Even a quarter century later, Wynne was underscoring his own importance to the project and its inability to function without him.

*   *   *

Wynne arranged the meeting for Penkovsky with George Hook of ARMCO Steel at the George V. When Wynne went off to order drinks, Penkovsky and Hook discussed points of interest at the Soviet Exposition. Then Penkovsky asked Hook's assistance to visit factories producing specialty steels and electronic parts. Hook carefully jotted down the data, said he was going on a short trip and would return on October 4 or 5. He promised to call Penkovsky on his return and arrange for brochures and visits to the plants. Penkovsky was gratified with Hook's cooperation and reported to the team that Wynne had done a first-rate job. He had no idea that Bulik had made the connection.

The other source for technical intelligence and contacts was a White Russian engineer working for a French company. He posed a problem for Penkovsky. Meeting with a White Russian was an entirely different matter from receiving help from George Hook, an American. When Bulik mentioned a White Russian an alarm bell rang in Penkovsky's head. Penkovsky requested additional checks be made prior to his contacting the man. He believed the KGB had contact with, and probably had recruited, the White Russian in Moscow, since he had visited trade fairs there. "As soon as my name is connected by the KGB with their own man, they will see that Penkovsky, the son of a White Army officer, had been drawn as if by a magnet to another White Russian. That would be the end for me."

All agreed that the KGB in Moscow would have an extensive dossier on the man, at the very least. Penkovsky had no idea, and the team did not tell him, that the White Russian contact was actually on the CIA payroll. The team decided the two men should not meet.[9]

Penkovsky brought along the September 26, 1961, issue of *Pravda*, and pointed out that the Soviet government had officially announced forthcoming large-scale military maneuvers for the months of October and November. The announcement supplemented Penkovsky's earlier report, gleaned from Varentsov and others, that the maneuvers would last a month, with a short possible extension. This was a bold public admission on Khrushchev's part that he would continue to have his armed forces in a state of readiness for combat during the tense period after the Party Congress when the East German peace treaty would be signed. Penkovsky explained that during and after the November holidays, the celebrations of the Bolshevik Revolution, Khrushchev would be in a position to back up his political moves in Germany with the maximum number of combat-ready forces. Of course the real purpose of having this force available—

war with the West—was not mentioned in *Pravda*, Penkovsky re-marked.[10]

There was a knock on the apartment door and everybody froze. Shergold got up, opened the door, and the group smiled and relaxed when Janet Chisholm walked in. Penkovsky embraced her warmly. She was the surprise of the evening. She had come to Paris to plan their future meetings in Moscow.

Janet described her normal pattern of movement on Mondays and Fridays in the Arbat area, not far from Penkovsky's offices at the State Committee on Gorky Street and at General Staff headquarters on Frunze Street. They established a schedule for the balance of October, November, and December. At 1 P.M. on Friday, October 20, they would see each other on the Arbat at the *komissionny*, a consignment store where antiques and other used goods were sold. They agreed to meet there every Friday at the same time through the end of November.

If one or the other did not show up for a Friday meeting, they would reconnoiter the following Monday. Should a Monday meeting be necessary, they would meet in the delicatessen on the second floor of the Praga Restaurant, also at 1 P.M. Only if no meeting took place on a Friday would Janet appear on the following Monday. However, even if they met on Monday, she would still appear the next Friday. The one exception would be Christmas Day, a Monday, which was omitted from the schedule.

They resolved to arrange an official meeting between Janet and Penkovsky, either at an embassy reception or at a party where it would be logical for both to be invited officially.[11]

When Penkovsky arrived for their next meeting at the apartment, he mentioned that Paris was a small town; he had spotted Joe Bulik and George Kisevalter drinking coffee on the Champs-Élysées and of course had walked by without signaling. This served as an example to Penkovsky how easily he, too, could be spotted by KGB surveillance.[12] Bulik recalled that the team had also noticed Penkovsky but did not acknowledge his presence. "I really felt bad that we could not even have a meal with him. We should have arranged a private room at a restaurant, but there was always the question of security," recalled Bulik in later years.[13]

George Kisevalter began the meeting by telling Penkovsky, "We have a little surprise for you. A first-rate technician of ours has arrived and he wants to show you equipment that can be available for two-way contact in the near future, even though you will not receive it now."

Kisevalter deliberately engaged Penkovsky in innocuous conversation while "John" was introduced. John was actually Quentin Johnson, chief of operations for the Soviet Division, who had brought the newly designed device to Paris. Kisevalter explained to Penkovsky that while the introductions were being made over a period of twenty-nine seconds, a message was being transmitted. Penkovsky said he heard no sound. He was impressed when "John" removed the transmitter from his clothing, showing Penkovsky exactly how it had been fastened and concealed.

Penkovsky then learned how the short-range (800 meters) transmitter operated. The sender manually entered a digital-coded message and turned a windup dial to load the transmitter. Then the press of a button transmitted a high-speed electronic burst. The transmission would be received and decoded by a special receiving device in the American Embassy. They discussed from what points in Moscow he could transmit within a radius of roughly 400 meters from the embassy. He should face the receiving station while sending to avoid his own body's insulation effect. To avoid possible structural obstructions between his sending position and the receiving station, they chose 400 meters instead of the maximum range of 800 meters to be sure his message would be received clearly. If he found a position that would afford a line-of-sight transmission, namely by simply being able to see directly the top of the U.S. Embassy, he could transmit at a distance between 400 meters and 800 meters away. He could resend his message at any time if he felt unsure that it was properly received. The device had a button to activate the receiving station's automatic recording mechanism. All he had to do was to press this button for a minimum of ten seconds prior to transmitting. With this system Penkovsky could communicate vital messages of up to 300 words without any personal contact or use of a telephone or dead drop.[14]

Penkovsky was enthusiastic. He eagerly agreed to utilize this communication link, but he did not want to risk keeping it in his apartment. Here was another argument in favor of permitting him to buy a dacha. At the dacha he would find a weatherproof hiding place for the small wireless transmitter. The dacha would be only one hour from Moscow, so the delay in transmitting vital information would not exceed a few hours, the time needed for preparing and coding the information, picking up the transmitter from its hiding place, and relaying the message to the embassy. Once the equipment had been custom made for Penkovsky and completely tested, it would be delivered to the British Embassy in Moscow by diplomatic pouch and passed to him by Wynne.[15]

Quentin Johnson had come to Paris not only to demonstrate the new transmitter to Penkovsky and train him in how to use it, but also to defuse a crisis between the British and American teams. After

261

one of the long sessions with Penkovsky, Kisevalter and Mike Stokes had gone out to unwind. According to Joe Bulik, "George drank too much, became too gabby, and actually repeated some of the details of that evening's meeting with HERO. They were in some bistro and before long George was buying everybody drinks." Shergold reported the incident to Leonard McCoy, who told Bulik about it. Bulik reviewed the incident with Shergold and Stokes and "satisfied myself that it was not part of the underlying professional jealousy which persisted throughout the operation." Then Bulik "asked Len [McCoy] to send a cable to headquarters on the crisis which included my own recommendation that another case officer be considered after the Paris sessions were over as a replacement for George."

Johnson, chief of operations in the Soviet Division, was in Paris to calm the situation and show confidence by headquarters in the team's and particularly Kisevalter's performance. Arrangements were made with Albert Ulmer, chief of the CIA Paris Station, to present Kisevalter with a Certificate of Merit with Distinction and a $1000 check. "This was done," Bulik recalled, "in a dignified, quiet ceremony and was well handled by the chief of station and Quent [Johnson] with Len and me present. We all congratulated George and had a fine lunch." Kisevalter continued to work as a valuable member of the team after the Paris meetings, translating and analyzing the tapes, but a new Russian-speaking case officer was assigned to join Bulik for future meetings with Penkovsky.[16]

At their next meeting in Paris, on October 2, 1961, Penkovsky and the team worked on a signaling system in case he had top-priority information to pass before the high-speed transmitter arrived. An elaborate system, code named DISTANT, was conceived by the British and worked out with the Americans so that Penkovsky could flash word of a planned Soviet attack. Penkovsky was given two phone numbers of American Embassy personnel, either of which he could ring. When a man answered the phone, Penkovsky was to blow into the mouthpiece three times, then wait one minute and repeat the procedure.

The Americans would then go to telephone pole number 35 on Kutuzovsky Prospekt and look for a freshly marked letter X on the pole. This signal meant that Penkovsky would leave a detailed message in the dead drop. If it was not possible for him to promptly service the dead drop, the phone signal would be sufficient for an immediate early warning. Additional instructions were to follow. Penkovsky had been told he must appreciate fully the significance of the early-warning communications system. His signal alone, whether or not the dead drop was serviced, would result in prompt action at a high level in the United States and Great Britain under three conditions: he must give such a signal only if he had learned for a fact that the Soviet Union had decided to attack, or that the Soviets had decided to attack should the West take specific action, or that the Soviet Union had decided to attack should the West fail to undertake specific actions.

The system was to be used only for a message so urgent that he could not wait for the next meeting with Janet, and was for information that had to be passed through a dead drop. Penkovsky was not told its code name.

Penkovsky would load the drop with his urgent message on his way to the office at approximately 8:45 A.M., knowing that the dead drop would be cleared within a half hour. Under no conditions would he say anything on the telephone; he was sure the KGB had a tape recording of all phone calls to foreigners. They could either match his voice or break it down phonetically if he were under suspicion. Silence was his defense against any possible accusation.

The next item on their agenda was the *Kremlevka*, the highly classified telephone directory for the Kremlin that Penkovsky managed to photograph and send to the team. The *Kremlevka*, installed at the end of World War II, had been the first push-button telephone system in the Soviet Union. It connected Khrushchev and the Presidium directly to top Party, press, and government leaders in their offices and homes.

"First of all, how did you obtain this *Kremlevka* directory?" asked Kisevalter.

"This directory belongs to Gvishiani [chairman of the State Committee]. I had been working in his office and I had the chance to photograph it. The cover was red; isn't Gvishiani's name written on it somewhere?"

"No, the name doesn't appear," said Shergold.

"Here is exactly how I did it. I was working in Gvishiani's office for him late on Saturday and there I photographed the Government Office telephone directory, but his *Kremlevka* I took home with me overnight and photographed it at home."

Kisevalter asked him to explain the peculiarities of the Kremlin telephone system.

"It is classified as a government telephone system. There are two such systems. One is called the V.Ch. [the abbreviation of *vysokaya chastota* or high frequency], which ties in Moscow offices to its central switchboard. The lines go throughout the land to all the cities and to all regional committees of the Party, wherever a responsible Party official may be stationed. It is a high-frequency system. One must request the central switchboard to be connected. One cannot dial a number on this system. The caller's number is asked for and given when a long-distance call is made.

"The *Kremlevka* is exclusively a Moscow circuit which interconnects all the main government offices. There is nothing like it in Leningrad. You have probably read in the instructions that the system is under KGB supervision. It is stated that Top Secret conversations are prohibited, but everything is discussed on this line despite the admonition," Penkovsky explained.

"Is it also called the *Vertushka*?" asked Kisevalter.

"Yes, it is."

Vertushka is the slang expression, while *Kremlevka* is the official designation. The *Vertushka*, literally a spinning top, is the nickname for the more limited phone system directly connecting senior officials to the Kremlin. These lines have only to be lifted to ring and establish contact.

Kisevalter asked if it were possible to be connected into the *Kremlevka* system from the municipal line or vice versa.

"No, absolutely not. The only thing that can be done is to tap into the cable if one knows where to do this, and the conversations can be overheard if technicians can analyze the frequencies."

"On what basis is it determined whose name appears in a directory and who gets a *Kremlevka* telephone and who does not?" asked Kisevalter.

"All those who have important positions in any committee have this telephone. Some people have two."

"Who makes the determination?" asked Kisevalter.

"This is set up by the executive officer of the Council of Ministers of the U.S.S.R.," Penkovsky said. "He also determines who should be included in the special and restricted dining room roster and who can enter closed stores. This also includes special hospital privileges. It is the same old system of who gets a more elegant dacha and who gets a shabbier one. This executive officer has a big office which services the Council of Ministers."

"Does the Central Committee propose who should be given this telephone?"

"Of course they do; the executive officer merely handles the mechanics, for which he is given instructions," Penkovsky answered.[17]

Command-and-control in the Soviet Union has always been of primary interest to Western intelligence organizations and Kremlinologists. From the Kremlin directory supplied by Penkovsky, an MI6 Soviet expert in 1962 produced the first chain-of-command and complete organization chart for the Kremlin. The British Kremlinologist analyzed the names and positions of those listed in the *Kremlevka* and compared it with what was known about the Soviet leadership organization. The telephone book's lowest numbers were for those with the highest ranks, thus making it clear who was who in ascending authority in the top leadership and what their responsibilities were. By sorting out the responsibilities of those surrounding Khrushchev, Western Soviet-watchers could better ascertain shifts in personnel and policies, thus piercing the secrecy surrounding the Kremlin.

The team's newest requirements list ranged over a broad spectrum. Penkovsky was able to tell them about the priorities for missile and aviation construction, noting that while the navy and civilian enterprises took budget cuts in favor of rockets, the air force budget was not reduced, especially for long-range bombers.[18]

The team was anxious to find out who actually controlled the nuclear warheads. Penkovsky provided the names of the Chief Rocket-Artillery Directorate (GRAU for *Glavnoye Raketno-Artilleriskoye Upravlenye*), which receives the missiles from the plants and serves as a customer for the defense industry. Penkovsky explained the structure of GRAU and its directorates.[19]

Kisevalter asked who in the Central Committee controlled the GRU. Penkovsky explained that a military department of the Central Committee of the CPSU was in charge, "but the Central Committee is squeamish about using that term. It is officially called the Administrative Department. It is the same thing. There is a group of officers there who are concerned with the General Staff of the Ministry of Defense and with the Ministry of Defense as a whole. They have the *Kremlevka* and they can simply call Serov at any time. This is the First Section, or the Military Section, of the Central Committee of the CPSU. The other section is the Main Political Administration of the Central Committee of the CPSU, which conveys the Party's directives to the army and navy. Thus the Central Committee, with these two powerful tentacles, controls all the armed forces of the U.S.S.R."[20]

The team's agenda shifted to Soviet nuclear testing. Penkovsky stressed that security was so tight that the presence of foreigners, even from socialist countries, was not permitted at the test sites. He told the team that Chinese development of nuclear weapons was progressing. "I think that in two or three years they will have their own nuclear weapons. They are working very intensely on them," Penkovsky said.*[21]

---

* The Chinese exploded their first atomic bomb in October 1964, the same week that Khrushchev was forced to resign from office.

265

At their thirty-ninth meeting, on Sunday, October 8, Penkovsky arrived at 8:15 P.M. First he described his date on Friday night, when he had taken a French interpreter, whom he had met at the French Exhibition in Moscow, to the Lido nightclub. Then Penkovsky listed the cultural centers in Paris he had visited so he could tell his colleagues in Moscow about the attractions of Paris without mentioning the nightclubs. He asked the team to arrange for Wynne to drive him to Versailles so that he could complete his tour of cultural high points.

The team's requirements list was still focused on Soviet military preparations over Berlin. There were long discussions about the differences between tactical and strategic Soviet missiles. Which missiles came under the control of Marshal Varentsov, the artillery ground forces commander, and which were under the command of Marshal Moskalenko, commander of the strategic rocket forces? Knowing the command-and-control system and how the Soviet rocket forces were organized would provide insights into the strength of the arsenal. Penkovsky told the team that rockets with a range of more than 600 miles were considered "strategic." Intercontinental ballistic missiles were still in the testing stage and none had been deployed yet. The only ICBMs were those on the test ranges. Moskalenko's only strategic weapons were a small number of medium-range ballistic missiles, and these required a lengthy fueling process.

Varentsov had mobile tactical missiles with nuclear warheads; even these were not directly controlled by him. The Soviet warheads were kept in special storage depots guarded by elite KGB troops and could be distributed only after a decision by the Military Council headed by Khrushchev.

Again and again Kisevalter pressed Penkovsky for specifics. Who had told him there was an aircraft factory in Dnepropetrovsk? What is produced at the Kiev metallurgical plant? Penkovsky studied photographs and identified KGB or GRU officers for the team.

At the end of three and a half hours, Penkovsky was shown the presents that the team had bought for him to take back to Moscow: a tennis outfit for Serov, battery-driven razors for those who had not received them after the last trip, and the bottles of 1917 wine that Penkovsky wanted for the forty-fourth anniversary of the October Revolution. Penkovsky was satisfied.

The time in Paris was drawing to a close. Penkovsky worked frantically to complete his assignments for Soviet Military Intelligence. On Tuesday, October 10, Penkovsky met for the fortieth time with Bulik, Kisevalter, Shergold, and Stokes. He had spent most of the day in meetings at the Soviet Embassy. He told the team how the embassy was in a state of turmoil because the ambassador was returning to Moscow for the Twenty-second Party Congress. Penkovsky had delivered to the embassy the pile of material he had collected on new steel-making processes and electronics. The brochures were divided up to be sent separately to the GRU and the State Committee. Penkovsky said he still needed one visit to a factory so he could introduce a member of the Paris GRU Station to a local contact. He pressed the team to produce one for him.

Bulik cautioned Penkovsky, "You should not be too successful here. If you are, they may send you back to Paris and this is the last place that we want to meet again. We want to meet in a place like London or America, under conditions that we can control and not in a place where we have no control."

"Remember," added Kisevalter, "there are French regulations here laid down by their Foreign Ministry with respect to visits to French factories by Soviets."

Penkovsky then repeated his request for an English-language book on rockets and missiles, with a brief summary description in Russian of its contents. "This book must be of a type that the Soviets would be interested in having fully translated and published," he explained. He would review the translation and write an introduction to the Soviet edition.* The team was ready for his request and offered *Man and Space* by Dr. Ralph Lapp, a history of space flight published in 1961 by Harper & Brothers.[22] Penkovsky was so excited that he insisted on taking the book back to Moscow with him and demanded a summary in Russian be prepared for him. Although the book was readily available in bookstores in the West, Penkovsky knew his discovery of it would demonstrate his alacrity and initiative. He said he would edit and retype the summary of the book at home and add the appropriate political slant before presenting it to be considered for full translation and publication. By broadening his expertise, Penkovsky hoped to win a promotion to general and increase his access to classified information.

Penkovsky had it all figured out. Varentsov would support his translation, and this would add to his credibility when constantly requesting Soviet documents as background material for the articles he was writing. This plan seemed "like blatant eyewash" to the team, according to notes made on the meeting, but the record adds, "It may be possible that Penkovsky knows what he is talking about and this can do him considerable good and no harm at all."[23] In fact,

* The Soviet Union did not join the International Copyright Convention until 1973. Until then the Russians felt no obligation to obtain permission to publish or to pay royalties for a book reprinted there.

Penkovsky was praised for bringing back the Lapp book. His superior at the GRU, Colonel Rogov, wrote a memorandum to General Serov urging it be translated into Russian because of its importance.[24]

During his last week in Paris Penkovsky spent his days at the Soviet Exhibition and embassy and his evenings with the team or Wynne. Back from Yugoslavia, Wynne was available for shopping and meals. One night Bulik arranged for Penkovsky to meet a prostitute at the Hotel California on Rue de Berri, opposite the office of the Paris *Herald Tribune*. Bulik rented the room, paid the woman, and told her she was for a friend, a Yugoslav businessman. Bulik went to the hotel bar and waited until Penkovsky was finished.

It was a busy time; the British arranged for Penkovsky to visit a diesel factory that made fuel-injector pumps, and ARMCO executive George Hook came through with a trip to a steel tubing factory. Hook remembers Penkovsky as "good looking and cultivated, not your run-of-the-mill Soviet official." Penkovsky was a guest for lunch at Hook's home in Neuilly-sur-Seine, on the outskirts of Paris. The conversation was informed and stimulating, recalled Hook. After dessert Hook provided Penkovsky with pamphlets on steel-making processes, "but not the latest dope."[25]

On Thursday, October 12, Penkovsky met again with the team at the safe apartment. He was given his operational instructions and final requirements briefing. (See Appendixes C and D.) Heading the list was the possibility of "information from responsible Soviet officials that the U.S.S.R. has decided to launch an attack against the West." Penkovsky was to supply "the plan, date, and time of attack, details of information acquisition." The other requirements dealt with strategic missiles, submarine ballistic missiles, antiballistic missiles, antiaircraft developments, and nuclear weapons. Penkovsky was also requested to provide "any indication that the RIS [Russian Intelligence Service] has a high-level penetration of a Western government."

Penkovsky visited the ARMCO factory on Friday morning with a GRU officer from the Soviet Embassy staff. Thanks to George Hook they were well received and invited to lunch. Penkovsky spent the rest of the day assessing the brochures and pamphlets he acquired from the factory and from the team. His package for the diplomatic pouch weighed nine pounds and was sent directly to the GRU.

French restrictions on travel by Soviet "diplomats" to curtail espionage made it difficult for GRU officers in the Soviet Embassy in Paris to operate on their own and make French contacts. Penkovsky, visiting Paris as part of the Soviet Exhibition, was not subject to such controls. He had made contact with an American and a British firm, something the Paris GRU Station was not able to do. Although

Penkovsky was not given a description of the latest technology for heat-resistant steel to be used for missile construction, the object of his assignment, the brochures and specifications were sufficient to make it appear he had acquired valuable industrial secrets.

On Saturday morning, October 14, when Penkovsky said his farewells at the Soviet Embassy, the GRU *rezident*, Cheredeyev, showed him "the very fine report" he was sending to Moscow on Penkovsky's performance in Paris. Penkovsky told the station chief that he would report most favorably on how he saw things being done at the *Rezidentura* in Paris. Penkovsky knew the rules of how to play the game: "scratch each other's back." Cheredeyev also asked Penkovsky to pass personal greetings to Ivan Aleksandorovich [Serov].

For the final meeting with the team, on Saturday night, Penkovsky was picked up at a new rendezvous point near the Pont de Grenelle. Although there was no indication he was being followed, it was good practice to vary the pickup site. At the safe apartment Penkovsky thanked the team for their help and said he was certain he had accomplished his GRU mission in Paris.[26]

Penkovsky was firmly told not to call and say goodbye to the French interpreter whom he met at the French Exhibition in Moscow and had taken to the Lido. Roger King would call her, say he was a French associate of Penkovsky's, and express regrets at his not having been able to say farewell personally. Penkovsky would contact her on his return to Paris in a few months. The purpose of this plan was to avoid a letter from the woman to Penkovsky arriving at the committee in Moscow. Penkovsky was not to do anything that would attract attention by Soviet Security. A letter from a foreigner was clear grounds for suspicion.

Most of the meeting was spent reviewing the operational instructions, which Penkovsky repeated from his notes. Then they reviewed requirements for Essential Elements of Information (EEIs), the CIA's equivalent of a journalist's Five W's: Who, What, Why, Where, When, and How. He also received requests to obtain manuals on the latest Soviet tanks, the T-10M and the T-55, and on the latest conventional artillery pieces.[27]

Penkovsky received instructions to provide precise data on nuclear yields and the accurate dates of explosions so his material could be correlated with test data from American atmosphere samples. He was also asked to pick up and record any information whatsoever on Soviet communications, cryptanalysis, cryptographic work, and personnel methods in this field.

In the final questioning, Penkovsky provided information about a classmate at the Military-Diplomatic Academy who was assigned to "illegal" work, so that he might be recognized abroad. Since illegals

269

are infiltrated into countries with false documents and live under-cover, Penkovsky's identification of the agent's picture from the class photograph at the Academy would be helpful in spotting him.

A sixteen-page translation summarizing Lapp's *Man and Space* was ready for Penkovsky. He was pleased, and the meeting broke for drinks, canapes, and photographs. Champagne toasts to continued health and success were followed by emotional farewells. In the Russian manner, Penkovsky hugged and kissed each case officer in turn. Then they all sat quietly for a minute, observing the old Russian tradition of silent prayer for a safe journey.

Unspoken was the question, would they ever meet again? Would they ever see each other in a world free of war? Penkovsky was the only agent reporting directly to the West on Nikita Khrushchev's plans for war soon after he revealed them to the Supreme Military Council. Could Penkovsky help save both his Motherland and his newly adopted countries from destroying themselves in a nuclear war?

At 5 A.M. Penkovsky was awakened in his room at the Hôtel Buffalo du Montana. He had moved there because the rooms were cheap enough to accommodate his thirty-six-francs-per-day allow-ance, about $7 dollars in 1961. Wynne called for him at 6 and drove him to Orly for an 8 A.M. Air France flight to Prague, where he would transfer to an Aeroflot flight to Moscow. It was a cold, gray morning and when they neared the airport fog closed in. The flight was delayed. Wynne and Penkovsky drank coffee and brandy and walked the airport corridors, awaiting a break in the weather and word of the flight. Wynne asked himself if the fog was a sign for Penkovsky. Did the gods caution him to stay?[28]

At 11 Penkovsky was still in the departure lounge when George Kisevalter and Mike Stokes arrived for a later flight. They saw him, but the rules of tradecraft prevailed. They did not greet him and tried to stay out of his line of sight.

Finally the departure was announced for 11:15 and Penkovsky walked to the gate. Wynne recalled, "At the door Alex stopped, and for a moment I thought he was going to turn around and come back to Paris and safety. He dropped the cases and stood there without speaking, and I waited and hoped. Suddenly he seized my hand, then picked up the case, and said, 'No, Greville, I have work to do,' and was gone."[29]

C H A P T E R   T H I R T E E N

Closing the Missile Gap

ON OCTOBER 21, 1961, WHILE THE TWENTY-SECOND COMMUNIST Party Congress was taking place in Moscow, Deputy Secretary of Defense Roswell Gilpatric decisively challenged Nikita Khrushchev's claims to nuclear superiority in a carefully prepared speech to the Business Council at White Sulphur Springs, West Virginia. The central theme of Gilpatric's speech—coordinated by McGeorge Bundy, assistant to the president for national security affairs, and approved by President Kennedy—was that the United States had more and better nuclear weapons than the Soviet Union. Gilpatric said the United States "has a nuclear retaliatory force of such lethal power that an enemy move which brought it into play would be an act of self-destruction on his [Khrushchev's] part. . . . The destructive power which the United States could bring to bear even after a Soviet surprise attack upon our forces would be as great as—perhaps greater than—the total undamaged force which the enemy can threaten to launch against the United States in a first strike. In short, we have a second-strike capability which is at least as extensive as what the Soviets can deliver by striking first. Therefore, we are confident that the Soviets will not provoke a major nuclear attack."[1]

Gilpatric's measured but powerful warning to Khrushchev made front-page headlines around the world. It was what McGeorge Bundy later called "a sober affirmation of America's nuclear strength, indeed superiority."[2] The conclusions stated by Gilpatric were based on the information Penkovsky had been supplying for the last six months, joined with new satellite photographs of Soviet missile sites over the summer. The CIA's Board of National Intelligence Estimates in September had utilized Penkovsky's material to revise

271

downward its estimate of the number of operational Soviet nuclear missiles.

So that there was no mistake about the intended meaning of Gilpatric's speech, Secretary of State Dean Rusk, in a television interview the following day, emphasized, "Mr. Khrushchev must know that we are strong and he does know that we are strong." For America's European allies the pronouncement of American nuclear superiority provided encouragement and political comfort.[3] With the Berlin crisis still unresolved, the Gilpatric speech, McGeorge Bundy would argue, "was part of the *political* defense of West Berlin, just as Khrushchev's threats were a part of a *political* assault on the Western presence there."[4]

Khrushchev was disturbed by the Gilpatric speech and trotted out Defense Minister Marshal Malinovsky to boast that Soviet warheads had greater yields than American weapons—twenty, thirty, up to 100 megatons—even if they had fewer warheads and delivery systems.

Gilpatric's speech had been preceded, four days earlier, by Nikita Khrushchev's six-and-a-half-hour diatribe at the opening session of the Twenty-second Congress of the Communist Party. Khrushchev, speaking as first secretary of the Party's Central Committee, was at his bombastic best when he addressed the "congress of builders of Communism," assembled before him in the Kremlin Palace of Congresses. The Soviet Union, Khrushchev said, stood for the "line of social progress, peace and constructive activity" against "the line of reaction, oppression and war." To prolonged applause, he assured the more than 5000 delegates that "today the Soviet Union is stronger and more powerful than ever!"

Speaking about Berlin, Khrushchev insisted a German peace treaty "must and will be signed with or without the Western powers," but he backed off from his June threat to Kennedy to sign unilaterally "one way or another before this year is out." Khrushchev said the time of an agreement "was no longer important. We have the impression that the Western powers are displaying a certain understanding of the situation and that they are inclined to seek a solution for the German problem and for the West Berlin issue on a mutually acceptable basis." He was referring to the talks in New York City between Dean Rusk and Foreign Minister Andrei Gromyko, which had been going nowhere for nearly a month, since September 21, 1961, but had created an impression in the press of momentum and reduced tensions. Gromyko was attending the United Nations General Assembly meetings.[5]

Penkovsky's role during this time was to provide background that enabled President Kennedy to know Khrushchev's intentions on

Berlin and the true state of Soviet nuclear strength. The new assessment was the result of a complex bureaucratic process. The final result, dramatized by Gilpatric's speech, represented the summation of Penkovsky's human intelligence reporting and estimates supported by technical data obtained from satellite photography. The state of the American overhead reconnaissance satellite programs was so highly classified that their existence was not supposed to be officially acknowledged.

Penkovsky's first report to the American intelligence community on the state of Soviet missile development had been distributed on May 16, 1961. It was titled, "The Soviet ICBM Program," and was disseminated through a Top Secret code-word channel to a select group of senior officials. The report listed the source: "a reliable senior Soviet Official who has close professional and personal contact with Soviet general officers concerned with the missile program."

The report said that

when the source was asked to comment on various statements by Khrushchev regarding Soviet ICBM tests, production, deployment and threats, he replied that Khrushchev was only bluffing. When asked to give the basis for this judgment, source made the following statement:

1. Khrushchev's basic idea in the entire matter is to be a jump ahead of and to impress the leaders of the Western powers—to represent that which he does not have or that which he has in insignificant quantities as something which he has already in hand. There are tests of one nature or another which in many cases are successful, but he is already ranting as though this were an accomplished thing. Thus the whole idea of Khrushchev and the Presidium is to demonstrate and to illustrate in one way or another such as by launching of an earth satellite, even of a man in space, in order to impress Western military leaders that the Soviet Union has everything. This is to force Western government leaders and military people to do their planning on the assumption that the Soviet Union already has a tremendous military potential when in reality it is only being developed.

2. Source then referred to Khrushchev's threats, and recalled that a senior general officer of artillery, responsible for one aspect of the Soviet missile program, with whom source has close professional and personal relations, had told source in early 1961 that "We are only thinking about these things, only planning, even though we have had some successes here and there. But in order to get anywhere one has to increase production tremendously and to train cadres." Source went on to say: "This officer has constantly said

there is an enormous amount of work to be done not only with cadres, but also with equipment, missile types, etc., while Khrushchev is shouting that we already have all this." The officer stated further that the Soviets have in their arsenal tactical missiles and missiles that can reach South America, the United States, or Canada, but not accurately.

3. These are test missiles which are still undergoing further tests and are not on bases. The U.S.S.R. does have the capability of firing one or two—there are not hundreds even in testing status. There may be only tens in that category. Even in sending up a satellite or a man in space all scientists are mobilized for the effort, and before a satellite is launched they have several failures. The main idea now of Khrushchev's statements is to create an effect for foreign ears, but the preparations are being carried out intensively. The objective is to obtain mass production.

4. Those missiles which have already been developed [medium-range missiles] are being produced in great quantities, and they can be launched at any time to the extent of their operational ranges. With respect to ICBMs, the Soviets have had one failure after another. They continue to throw millions into the effort, and if they have one success it is used to impress the West by pretending that there are hundreds. But there are no such hundreds. That is only idle talk. However, one day they will be there, since the entire economy and policy are geared for such development. The basic problem is to develop a missile with a large warhead yield, but with a high-caloric fuel which requires little space. On paper the Soviets have had some success there, but when one considers that millions of men's efforts are directed to this work and that the entire economy of a nation is directed by a one-party system to which all is subordinate, they can do this. Eventually they will perfect such missiles and they will ultimately be mass produced.

5. Even now it may be possible that somewhere in the Far East or at Kapustin Yar there may be some missiles which could reach other continents and detonate with an atomic, even hydrogen explosion, but such launching would be completely unplanned, uncontrolled and certainly not of a mass variety. Of this I am entirely sure but in two or three years there will be a different picture.

The distribution for this report included twelve people outside the CIA. Heading the list was McGeorge Bundy in the White House. At the Defense Department, Penkovsky's report was sent to the director of intelligence for the Joint Chiefs of Staff and the assistant chiefs of staff for intelligence of the army, navy, and air force. Copies went to the director of the National Security Agency and the director of intelligence and research at the State Department.

At the Agency there were about twenty people allowed access to Penkovsky's reports under the code-word system CHICKADEE, restricted to only those officials with a "need-to-know" the information. Code-word systems are used for such sensitive subjects as signals intelligence, satellite photos, and intelligence from high-level human sources—HUMINT. Those cleared included the director and his deputy, the chief of operations on the clandestine side, the assistant director for national estimates, the assistant director for current intelligence, the assistant director for scientific intelligence, and the assistant director for research and reports. IRONBARK was used to circulate the translations of the publications Penkovsky copied with the Minox cameras. These documents included operating manuals for missiles, classified Communist Party documents, and the highly classified Kremlin telephone directory.

Changing a National Intelligence Estimate is no small task. "Penkovsky's information ran up against the fact that it takes more proof to change an estimate than to create one because it involves an admission of error and there are vested interests in programs already under way," explained Edward Proctor, former deputy director for intelligence.

National Estimates were produced for the DCI by the Office of National Estimates (ONE) in CIA with representatives from the intelligence arms of the State and Defense departments, the CIA, the Atomic Energy Commission, and other agencies, as the estimate warranted. The estimate of Soviet strategic missile strength was revised annually, and more often if circumstances demanded. There were also estimates of other Soviet strategic programs. The first step was for the ONE to issue a paper stating the terms of reference for the estimate and ask the agencies for their contributions. The lead time for preparing a contribution was three to four months, sometimes longer. Coordination between the agencies and departments took from two weeks to two months, depending on the complexity of the estimate and the amount of disagreement.

"It is like writing a novel by assigning chapters to people with varying viewpoints and then trying to coordinate and revise the contributions into a consistent whole," explained a former member of the ONE. After the representatives report back to their principals, there is a meeting of the full United States Intelligence Board to coordinate the estimate. With the representatives seated behind the principals to whisper advice, the estimate was negotiated. In 1961 the USIB still met in an office of the South Building in the Navy Hospital compound overlooking the Potomac. In the end, if there is no agreement, the members agree to disagree and write footnotes to the estimate stating their objections. The arguments represent not only facts as known but bureaucratic interests. In the case of the Soviet missile estimate, the air force was deeply involved. The greater the Soviet missile threat, the bigger the air force budget and the larger the role of the Strategic Air Command and the air force missile program. By 1961 the responsibility for missiles with a range under 1000 miles was assigned to the army and those with a range over 1000 miles went to the air force. The navy had its Polaris program for submarine-launched missiles.

Inserting Penkovsky's information into the system was easier than getting it accepted. Although his first report on the Soviet ICBM program was rushed to completion so it could be included in the information presented to the Intelligence Board for its June 1961 update of the NIE, the information created little initial impact. Only a brief reference to Penkovsky's report was made in a footnote. None of the participants at the meeting referred to it, and it was not mentioned or even reflected in the body of the estimate. A member of the board told Jack Maury that "no matter how good the source was, since the subsource was unknown to the consumers and was given no evaluation in the dissemination, he would have to be considered F. The community was unwilling to accord an F source any consideration in changing a National Estimate." F in this case meant unsubstantiated.

Another factor was simply "that the CHICKADEE report did not exactly fit the views of anyone at the meeting." A member of the board recalled that "nobody wanted to accept it because it was so contrary to their established views and political positions, especially the air force. A revision would mean a change in their budget."

Although the members of the board did not argue with the clandestine-service evaluation of the source (Penkovsky), the subsource, Marshal Varentsov, from whom Penkovsky had received his information, was not named in the report for security reasons, which accounted for the skepticism with which Penkovsky's revelations was initially received. Yet the thrust of his material demanded attention and further analysis.[6]

Edward W. Proctor, then chief of the ad hoc guided missile task force in the Directorate of Intelligence, prepared a memorandum dated June 2, 1961, reassessing the NIE on the basis of Penkovsky's reporting. Proctor said "in the light of the extensive changes which would be necessary if the report is accepted as valid, it may be necessary to withdraw" the current estimate. The task force report was sent to Deputy Director for Intelligence (DDI) Robert Amory. It included a study on the implications of the clandestine report and urged a complete reversal of the NIE. The NIE stated:

The Soviet leaders, particularly Khrushchev, have been deeply impressed by what they regard as a major improvement of their strategic position resulting from their achievements in long-range ballistic missiles. . . .

We believe that the direct and indirect evidence supports the view that: (a) the USSR has been conducting a generally successful ICBM program, at a deliberate rather than an extremely urgent pace; (b) that USSR is building toward a force of several hundred operational ICBM launchers, to be acquired within the next few years.

On the basis of our sense of tempo of the program and our judgment as to the relationship between what we have detected and what we are likely to have missed, we estimate that probably the Soviet force level in mid-1961 is in the range of 50–100 operational ICBM launchers, together with the necessary operational missile inventories and trained crews. This estimate should be regarded as a general approximation. We estimate that the program will continue to be deliberately paced and result in force levels about as follows: 100–200 operational launchers in mid-1962, 150–300 in mid-1963 and 200–400 in mid-1964. Some of the launchers activated in the 1963–64 period will probably be for a new and improved ICBM system.

Proctor argued that

A full acceptance of [Penkovsky's] report would imply that the Soviets have *not* been conducting a generally successful ICBM program and that they do not have 50–100 operational ICBM launchers at present.

A reasonable interpretation of [Penkovsky's] report, together with other information would lead to the following description of the Soviet program.

1. The Soviets have developed a reliable booster which they have used and probably will continue to use in their space programs. From this they are deriving considerable psychological and political advantage in creating the impression that they possess a formidable ICBM force.

2. This booster has not developed into a satisfactory ICBM weapons system, perhaps because of poor accuracy and difficulties involved in deploying so large a vehicle.

3. They are developing a new ICBM with better weapon system characteristics which will be more easily deployed. This new system may now be undergoing tests in Area C at Tyuratam.

4. Because of the limitations of the present ICBM as a deployable weapon, there are only a few deployed at present. This situation will probably continue until the new system becomes available operationally.

5. If the new system is satisfactory and there are no major difficulties encountered, the USSR will probably have a high-priority program to deploy this weapon in the hundreds.

The USSR would probably have the following numbers of ICBMs on launcher. Comparable numbers from the current draft of NIE 11-8-61 are presented in parentheses.*

Date	Potential New Estimate	Draft of NIE 11-8-61
Mid-1961	25 or less	(50–100)
Mid-1962	25–50	(100–200)
Mid-1963	75–150	(150–300)
Mid-1964	175–250	(200–400)
Mid-1965	300–400	

Proctor stated the need for more information about the unknown source's credentials "because [the] acceptance [of his report] as an accurate reflection of the status of the Soviet ICBM program will modify substantially our estimate and could cause important changes in US policy. [I]t is necessary that we who are assessing this program have access to almost all the information available so that we can make an independent judgment of the validity of this report."

After serious consideration by Jack Maury and Dick Helms, the decision came down against further revelation of details that might point to the source of the report. There was deep concern that further discussion of who the source was, where he worked, and how he obtained his material would compromise him.

The result was that no revision of the estimated number of Soviet strategic missiles was made in June. However, the June 1961 national estimate said in an explanatory footnote that "we had information that the Soviet program was not as far along as Khrushchev and others would have us believe and we were examining it," recalled Howard Stoertz, the Board of Estimates officer in charge of estimating the Soviet strategic missile program. In a 1989 interview Stoertz said:

Penkovsky's information helped to bridge the gap between the other information we had and provided an understanding of what the

* The NIEs were assigned numbers, but not on the basis of date. The 11 series referred to Soviet strategic capabilities.

Soviet program was like. An estimator always wants to have an understanding of the Soviet program. We had a lot of technical information that had accumulated over a period of time. It was incomplete. It was in some respects contradictory and it was difficult to interpret. The Penkovsky information was the only piece of inside information that I can recall about Soviet thinking and planning about intercontinental missiles. His information said the Soviet Union did have a big program—like our other information indicated—but that it was proceeding much more slowly than we had forecast. That was the critical explanation.[7]

They had inquired as best they could into the authenticity of the source and they told me that he and the material were authentic. I had no basis for making a judgment. To that extent my ability to use the stuff was somewhat diminished. If I had a photo taken by a U-2, I knew what it was. There was an interpreter who could tell me what was being seen. I could never talk to this source and could never find out anything about who he was. That was protecting his life, but to that extent it somewhat diminished the utility of it to me. I accepted their word, but I was looking for other confirmation.[8]

Still, the analysts sensed that something was missing. The Soviet missile program should have been further along, and more sites should have appeared on satellite photos. Where were they? Were the missiles hidden, as the air force suggested? One insider's joke was that the air force counted a Soviet missile site under every cloud or flyspeck that appeared on the satellite photos.

The June estimate was a turning point because it signaled the breakup of the view that held to a higher production rate for Soviet missiles.[9] The analysts could now work with new photos from the Discoverer satellite program, which for the first time provided detailed pictures confirming the offensive capability of the Soviet missile launching site at Plesetsk, south of Arkhangelsk, near the Barents Sea.

The combination of the Discoverer project reconnaissance satellite photography and Penkovsky's reporting demanded a new estimate. The Discoverer satellite program had begun in 1958, and after a series of failures, began to produce pictures by August of 1960. Discoverer imagery established what the Soviet ICBM launching sites looked like and permitted analysts to eliminate suspected sites. They reduced the number of SS-6 ICBM sites to between ten and fourteen.[10]

Khrushchev's threats regarding Berlin were still a critical issue when the CIA issued its own report on September 6, 1961, on the "Current Status of Soviet and Satellite Military Forces and Indications of Military Intentions." Signed by Acting Director of Central Intelligence Charles P. Cabell, the report noted that neither the SS-6 nor the SS-7 would be operational ICBM weapon systems "during the coming autumn and winter." This led Cabell to conclude: "We now believe that our present estimate of 50–100 operational ICBM launchers as of mid-1961 is probably too high."[11]

This CIA view received the support of the army, navy, and State Department's Bureau of Intelligence and Research and became the consensus in a new National Intelligence Estimate, NIE 11-8/1-61, which reduced the projection of Soviet strength to fewer than thirty-five missiles. On September 21, 1961, this national estimate was approved by the U.S. Intelligence Board and passed to the president.

Kennedy, who was concerned that earlier air force estimates of Soviet missile strength sharply contradicted the intelligence community consensus, lost interest in the air force claims. The new evidence from Penkovsky and the Discoverer satellite photos overwhelmed unsubstantiated air force conjecture.[12] Shifting from the idea of American inferiority to American superiority would be a difficult public perception to change. A drawn-out bureaucratic struggle ensued before the shift was made public.[13]

The new lower estimate thus ended debate about the so-called missile gap between the United States and the Soviet Union that had been a key issue in the 1960 presidential race. During the 1960 campaign Kennedy had erroneously charged that the Soviet Union was ahead of the United States in ICBMs. He had relied on estimates from the air force and Senator Stuart Symington, former secretary of the air force (1947–1949), who himself had hoped to be the Democratic nominee. Despite the denials of many in the Eisenhower administration, including Vice-President Richard Nixon, the Republican candidate, Kennedy continued to press his vote-getting assertion that the Soviets had more missiles than the U.S. credited to them.

The combination of Khrushchev's continued bragging and President Eisenhower's unwillingness to discuss American nuclear weapons strength left an impression that Kennedy used in the 1960 campaign to reinforce the idea of Soviet nuclear missile superiority. Khrushchev had used the success of the Sputnik and other space shots—launched with the same rocket boosters as would be used on Soviet missiles—to create an image of Soviet invincibility. By February of 1961, a month after Kennedy entered the Oval Office, Defense Secretary Robert McNamara acknowledged at his first meeting with the Pentagon press corps that in fact there was no missile gap, "and if there is one it is in our favor." McNamara said he thought his remarks were off the record, but the reporters rushed from his office to announce the news. McNamara was so embarrassed by the headlines the following morning that he went to the White House and offered his resignation. McNamara had spent between 10 and 20 percent of his time during his first month in office examining air force intelligence estimates and photographs of Soviet missile strength. He concluded that the air force was not trying to deceive him but that they were wrong. Kennedy told him not to worry, but to let the issue rest.[14]

The issue persisted, however, while the Berlin crisis deepened over the summer. The revised NIE had finally produced a new bureaucratic consensus, and enough time had passed so that the missile gap controversy was replaced by the urgency of Soviet threats to Berlin.

There was no question that a major effort was under way to catch up with the United States in nuclear weapons, but for the moment the U.S. was ahead in the number of missiles, bombers, and submarines. The decision to let Khrushchev know that the U.S. knew the true state of the Soviet missile program was made deliberately, after careful consideration. Roger Hilsman, who headed the State Department Bureau of Intelligence and Research during this period, recalled in his memoirs, *To Move a Nation*, published in 1967, that telling the Russians would undoubtedly cause them to speed up their program. "On the other hand, Khrushchev's several ultimatums on Berlin indicated that, if he were allowed to continue to assume that we still believed in the missile gap, he would very probably bring the world dangerously close to war. Thus the decision was reached to go ahead with telling the Soviets that we now knew," Hilsman wrote. Gilpatric was chosen, Hilsman said, "because a speech by the Deputy Secretary of Defense was high enough to be convincing to the Soviets but not so high as to be threatening—whereas a speech by the President, the Secretary of State or the Secretary of Defense might have been."[15]

The Gilpatric speech was followed by a round of briefings of the Allies "deliberately including some whom we knew were penetrated, so as to reinforce and confirm through Soviet intelligence channels the message openly carried through the Gilpatric speech," wrote Hilsman.[16]

For the Soviets, the implications of the message were horrendous. It was not so much the fact that the Americans had military superiority—that was not new to the Soviets. What was bound to frighten them most was that the Americans *knew* that they had military superiority. For the Soviets quickly realized that to have reached this conclusion the Americans must have made an intelligence break-through and found a way to pin-point the location of the Soviet missiles that had been deployed as well as to calculate the total numbers. . . . The whole Soviet ICBM system was suddenly obsolescent.[17]

Hilsman overstated his argument. The Soviet ground-launched missile system was far from obsolescent, but it was vulnerable. At the critical moment between war and peace over Berlin, Penkovsky's reporting, the satellite pictures, and the Anglo-American team's careful probing for details all came together to expose that vulnerability. Khrushchev lost his taste for a showdown over Berlin.

Penkovsky returned to Moscow on Saturday, October 14, and by the following Friday, October 20, on a cold, cloudy day, threatening rain, he had again photographed secret documents on his requirements list. He was ready to meet with Janet Chisholm at the *komissionny*, the secondhand store, on the Arbat, at 1 P.M. She arrived first, coming directly from a diplomatic wives' ballet class in the ballroom of Spasso House, the American ambassador's residence, not far from the Arbat.

A bell tinkled when the door opened into the warm, musty shop. Crowded glass cases filled with used plates, crystal, tableware, silver cups, serving dishes, clocks, jewelry, and vases offered an excuse to browse. There were landscapes on the shop walls, portraits, and framed photographs—a collection of uprooted memories offered for sale. Most of the goods were of poor quality, but occasionally valuable prerevolutionary-era pieces came to market.

The *komissionny* was a better place to meet than the other rendezvous spot on the Arbat, the delicatessen shop of the Praga Restaurant. Chisholm had gone there first, found practically nothing worth buying, and realized there would be no excuse for loitering if Penkovsky happened to be late. The well-stocked commission store provided built-in cover.

Penkovsky arrived on time and made a quick tour of the shop to catch her eye. Following him when he left the store, she trailed behind him down the Arbat without speaking. The afternoon skies were leaden and the air was raw, damp, and nearly freezing, the kind of fall day Muscovites loathe. They prefer the crisp, dry, freezing cold of true winter to wet, indecisive autumn. Janet carried her shopping bag and wore a Soviet-made fur hat so she would not stand out as a foreigner. Penkovsky walked along Arbat Street toward Smolensk Square. He turned right at Arbat Lane, a small side street, and entered the last door on the right. It was an old apartment house near the end of the lane; number 7/4 was painted on it. There were two sets of doors and then a hallway. Mrs. Chisholm watched Penkovsky disappear behind the doors. No one was following them; she entered behind him. He beckoned to Janet. They were alone. He handed her a letter. They exchanged greetings and asked after each other's families. Penkovsky expressed disappointment that she had nothing for him in return. The meeting lasted less than a minute.

The following week, on October 27, they met again at the secondhand store at the same time and carried out the same routine. This time, however, when they lingered in the doorway of the apartment house an old woman came down the stairs. Penkovsky spotted her and quickly embraced Janet, hiding her face and making it appear that they were lovers. She did not resist. The old woman looked away from them and walked into the street. Penkovsky slipped a package of cigarettes with three Minox film cartridges into Janet's shopping bag. They parted in silence. On November 3 and 10 Penkovsky and Mrs. Chisholm again rendezvoused at the commission shop and repeated their routine. Penkovsky gave Janet five containers of film and two letters during the meetings.

Janet walked home or took the trolleybus after the meetings. When her husband returned for lunch to their apartment off the inner Moscow ring road, on Sadovo-Samotechnaya, she handed the material to him and he took it to the embassy. The handovers in the apartment took place in complete silence, and the Chisholms never discussed anything about the meetings with Penkovsky or the operation itself when they were in the apartment. Once safe in the embassy, the material was packed in the diplomatic pouch and shipped to London.

On the evening of November 16, Penkovsky was invited to the apartment of the British scientific attaché, Dr. Senior. Here he met Mrs. Chisholm and her husband socially. No materials were exchanged, but now that they had met under official auspices, Penkovsky would always have a reason for greeting Janet should they meet in public. The next day Penkovsky arrived at the commission store at 1 P.M. and made visual contact with Janet, then left. They did not speak. He again walked down the Arbat and turned right at Arbat Lane, entering the last door on the righthand side of the lane. In the hallway on the left were two metal boxes at waist height, one slightly higher than the other. Penkovsky showed Janet that the space between the boxes would be the location for a new dead drop. Then he gave her one film cartridge, a letter, thirty-eight pages of handwritten notes, and two pages of the latest jokes making the rounds in Moscow. It was to be their last meeting for a month. Penkovsky told Janet he was off for a vacation with his wife and daughter to Kislovodsk, the best mineral water spa in the North Caucasus mountains. He told Janet he would meet with her on December 9, when he returned.

Ever since Penkovsky's request in Paris at the end of September for a means of rapid communication, the CIA and MI6 worked on a way for him to reach them from Moscow in an emergency. When Penkovsky's first report on large-scale Soviet military preparations for Berlin came to headquarters from Paris, Jack Maury talked with Dick Helms about how to handle Penkovsky's material. Maury noted that Penkovsky "was now in a key position to give us information vitally affecting our own reaction to recent Soviet moves. For example, HERO could assure us that all the preparations we would be seeing over the next few weeks were, indeed, part of the maneuvers already described, in which case the Soviets would be able to take aggressive military action without alerting our indications mechanism." At some critical juncture, Maury suggested, HERO might provide information that the Soviets were bluffing and were not ready to strike despite their demands for significant concessions. Helms agreed that such questions would probably arise, but argued that the Agency should take the position that the consumers themselves would have to make up their minds about the answer. All the CIA could vouch for, said Helms, "was that, from strictly an operational standpoint, we had been unable to fault HERO and could see nothing in the operational and counterespionage aspects of the case which would cause us to question the validity of the information supplied."[18]

The DISTANT early warning system, conveyed to Penkovsky in Paris, was supposed to solve the problem of rapid access to him in case of an emergency. The CIA Station chief in Moscow was instructed to report immediately to headquarters the receipt of the early warning signal before servicing the dead drop. This would result in the dissemination of the warning several hours sooner than if the Moscow Station waited for the dead drop to be unloaded. Such a warning could result in a prompt change in the alert status of American forces.

The British were concerned that a DISTANT early warning signal, unless carefully controlled and evaluated, could lead to misinterpretation and an outbreak of hostilities. Maurice Oldfield, the MI6 representative in Washington, conveyed this disquiet in a letter to Jack Maury on the arrangements they proposed for dealing with any

"Flash" message from HERO "indicating a Soviet intention to attack the West." Flash is the highest priority for message traffic.

The DISTANT code-word message would be passed to the CIA Station in London and then to a meeting of the British Joint Intelligence Committee (JIC), which the CIA was invited to attend. "In this way it is hoped that an agreed Anglo-American assessment of the report will be secured before it is released from the intelligence community. A DISTANT report will not be treated by the U.K. as an indicator unless the JIC accept it as such," wrote Oldfield.[19]

This did not fit the American definition of how to deal with an early warning of an attack. Dick Helms insisted it was CIA's job to pass on the raw data once the source was confirmed. It was up to the consumers to decide its meaning themselves.

On October 28, 1961, a message drafted by Jack Maury in Allen Dulles' name and approved by Dulles went to the London CIA Station. It was an attempt to work out an agreement on how the early warning system would work. While acknowledging the British concern with the risks of passing critical early warning information to what the British considered "trigger-happy" customers, the Agency stood firm. The British never openly referred to the Strategic Air Command, but the primary responsibility for the American strategic nuclear response against a Soviet war initiative rested with SAC, and the air force, which had put forth high estimates of Soviet nuclear strength and was the first to argue for a pre-emptive strike strategy against the Soviet Union.

Dulles' message conceded that striking the proper balance between the hazard of misuse and the conceivably greater hazard of withholding such information would present extremely difficult problems. The Agency instructed the American London Station chief, Frank Wisner, to tell the British that the CIA could not tie its own hands and make a firm commitment to restrict dissemination of possibly critical early warning information. Even the few hours necessary to convene a special Joint Intelligence Committee meeting and the additional hours required for coordination between Washington and London could mean the difference between success or failure of an attack. Once the early warning information was passed to the CIA and the United States Intelligence Board (USIB), if the information was considered critical, it would have to be communicated immediately to top government officials outside the intelligence community.

The CIA said it would, of course, take into account the British views in considering future specific cases, but it was most likely that the final decision must depend on the situation at the moment

285

an early warning report was received from Penkovsky. The CIA insisted on leaving the way open for the report to be passed immediately to the president if circumstances warranted.

It was anticipated that Penkovsky would pass the material to a dead drop serviced by the CIA, but just in case he passed the message to the British the CIA spelled out that the message should be sent to the MI6 representative in London and Washington and passed to the designated officers of the Soviet Division "without awaiting interpretation or evaluation at any stage."

The matter was resolved on October 31, 1961, in London at a meeting attended by Sir Dick White, head of MI6; Allen Dulles, the outgoing director of CIA; and his successor, John McCone, who was visiting London to meet Sir Dick. The London CIA Station chief, Frank Wisner, and his deputy, Carleton B. Swift, Jr., also attended, as did Sir Hugh Stephenson of the Foreign Office and his colleagues Charles Ransom, John Taylor, and Norman Darbyshire.

Sir Dick took the high ground and in his inimitable style subtly conveyed to the Americans that the British Secret Intelligence Service was superior to, but tolerant of, its American cousins. Sir Dick explained the DISTANT procedure which had been drawn up in London by the JIC, commenting that it was designed to ensure that early warning reports received from HERO should be evaluated and assessed before reaching ministers; this was particularly so of political information passed by HERO. Under the DISTANT procedure Sir Norman Brook, secretary to the Cabinet, would be simultaneously informed of the receipt of an early warning report. This would enable him to summon the appropriate members of the Cabinet to consider the report immediately after evaluation by the Joint Intelligence Committee.

Allen Dulles said that whether the SIS or CIA channel was used from Moscow, or any other point outside the Soviet Union where HERO might report, would not seriously affect timing; either side should immediately communicate the report to the other. He went on to say that the CIA would handle such reports much on the same lines as proposed in the DISTANT procedure drawn up by London but that as director of Central Intelligence he could not undertake not to pass to the president, either directly or in his capacity as chairman of the National Security Council, even unevaluated material from this source. In that case the CIA would make sure to stress at all times the fact that the material had not yet been evaluated.

Dulles explained to the British that Kennedy was fully aware of the conditions of the source in Moscow and maintained a personal interest in his material. The president had been particularly interested in the Russian view of his talks with Khrushchev in Vienna earlier in the year, which Penkovsky had provided.

In an aside, Sir Dick, curious to know the state of KGB voice-monitoring capability, asked whether the CIA thought the Russian version was based on recorded material; could they have introduced a miniaturized recorder for this purpose? Dulles said that this was not CIA's impression; their feeling was that the report was based on translator's notes. However, he added, Sir Dick's speculation could not be ruled out.

Dulles said that in addition to informing the president of early warning reports from HERO, he would simultaneously inform the secretary of state and the secretary of defense. McCone, underscoring his agreement with Dulles on what should be reported to the president, commented that there appeared to be two slightly different systems in use for the treatment of intelligence at the highest government levels in London and Washington. The meeting resulted in agreement that neither Dulles nor McCone could be bound by an understanding to refrain from passing raw intelligence from HERO to appropriate members of the American administration.

Sir Dick stressed that the SIS is basically a collector of intelligence whose task it was to turn over such intelligence to the assessors on the Joint Intelligence Committee. The JIC, in turn, would evaluate the material before passing it on to the ministers and the Cabinet. The feeling of SIS and the British intelligence community in general about Penkovsky was that his political access was fairly sketchy: he was always at least one step removed from the policymakers on whose deliberations he was reporting. The possibility therefore existed that he could be unwittingly misled. Moreover, while at the time at which he obtained his information it might have been correct, in a fast-moving world his report might be superseded by the time it was being considered by the collators. In fact, the SIS pointed out, HERO had not hesitated to correct some of his reporting on Iran. What required careful watching were the datelines of his material—Berlin was a good example of this.

In conclusion, like an invocation over Penkovsky, Dulles warned, "We must all keep the possibility of provocation in mind in this operation." He added that it was not the CIA view that this was such an operation. Sir Dick concurred.[20]

Under heavy clouds threatening snow, Janet Chisholm waited in the park off Tsvetnoy Boulevard for Penkovsky to arrive on December 9, but he did not appear. Nor did he come that week to the alternate meeting places, the secondhand store and the Praga delicatessen.

Rauri Chisholm cabled London, which informed Washington. Concern for Penkovsky's safety mounted; the dirty fear that he had been arrested or turned into a double agent was in the air. But there was no way to check on Penkovsky without compromising him. The only thing to do was to wait.

One week passed. On the afternoon of December 16, Janet Chisholm walked the short distance from her apartment in Sadovaya-Samotechnaya to the park off Tsvetnoy Boulevard. She was delighted to see Penkovsky waiting for her in the freezing cold, and followed him into a doorway on a nearby side street. When they believed they were alone they exchanged letters, and Penkovsky gave Janet eight rolls of film and a Minox that needed to be repaired. He said he had been unable to come the previous week because bad weather had delayed his return from vacation.

The following week, December 23, they met again in the snow-sprinkled park and repeated their routine, but this time Mrs. Chisholm came with her two-and-a-half-year-old son. She had to persuade the youngster to leave the piles of snow in the park so she could follow Penkovsky.

It was always the same. Janet would dress plainly so that she would not feel conspicuous as a foreigner in the neighborhood. Penkovsky would enter one of the doorways along the side street, where there was not a great deal of vehicular traffic, but where pedestrian activity was always a threat. Inside, he stood behind the stairwell so that he could observe anyone coming down the stairs or through the front door. On one occasion he apparently changed the doorway he had originally chosen when he saw four people go in. No further incidents occurred.

This day, two days before Christmas, Janet Chisholm was with her son when she entered after Penkovsky. They were together for about twenty seconds. Penkovsky brought a three-page letter, five films, and New Year's cards for his American and British case officers. She passed the materials for him in a package of Russian cigarettes, and he passed the information to her in a package of British cigarettes. Janet placed the take in her bag and he pushed it down himself, being sure it was in place. They exchanged a comment or two about family or health. Penkovsky said they would meet again the next week as usual. They were not interrupted. Janet left with her son; it appeared she had taken him in from the cold for a respite. Then she returned home a few blocks away.[21]

At about 9 P.M. on December 25, 1961, the wife of an American military attaché assigned to monitor the phone number given to

HERO received two voiceless calls three minutes apart. When she lifted the receiver nobody answered, but there was no blowing into the phone, the signal to clear the dead drop. There were no further calls. A check of telephone pole number 35 showed that it had not been marked with an X. The CIA notified Shergold of the incident.

On December 27 Shergold reported a successful meeting with HERO was carried out on December 23. In view of this meeting on December 23, Shergold felt that the calls on the night of December 25 represented a false alarm. He drew the CIA's attention to the fact there were two things wrong: no marking on the post signaling clearance for the dead drop, and a gap of three minutes between calls. Shergold recommended no visit be paid to the dead drop. On December 30 Mrs. Chisholm went to the park with her youngest children and met with Penkovsky, who made no reference to any phone call by him on Christmas night. She gave him a letter and received a letter and two film cartridges from him.

On January 5, 1962, their first meeting of the new year, Penkovsky and Janet met at the commission store and, as usual, proceeded to an apartment house hallway. She gave him a laudatory letter from the team with New Year's greetings. Penkovsky dropped three rolls of film in a cigarette package into her shopping bag.

Their next meeting was on January 12, at the Praga. Janet followed him down the Arbat and off onto the side street through the doorway of the apartment house. She delivered a letter, a Minox, and eighteen rolls of blank film. Penkovsky gave her four rolls of film and a one-page letter and told her to come directly to the hallway of the apartment house the following week, January 19. When she arrived, Janet saw Penkovsky in a phone booth, using it as a vantage point to check for surveillance. She entered into the apartment house hallway and Penkovsky followed. He gave Janet four rolls of film and she delivered a letter to him. Penkovsky told her he would be leaving for Leningrad on January 20 and would meet her next on February 2. During this period Mrs. Chisholm returned to England for a medical checkup.

The frequency of Penkovsky's meetings with Mrs. Chisholm was of growing concern to the CIA Soviet Division officers handling him. On January 12 the case officer who replaced George Kisevalter after the Paris meetings wrote a memorandum on the dangers involved in too many meetings and the production of too much material. Penkovsky, in his letter passed on December 23, described how, when left alone for a few minutes in the office of General Buzinov,

Varentsov's aide, he spotted a Top Secret report of Varentsov's in the midst of a pile of secret papers.* He whipped out his Minox and photographed Varentsov's article on the spot. This incident, wrote the new junior case officer

> is but the latest and most dramatic illustration of a problem which has been troubling everyone connected with the case here for some time: the colossal and ever increasing risks we are permitting HERO to take in the pursuit and transmittal of documentary intelligence. Another good illustration is the 420-page manual on atomic weapons which we recently requested HERO to obtain, and which now looks as if it will be of no more than marginal interest. Our frequent admonitions to HERO to be careful, to think first and foremost of his own security, to meet ANNE less—in the context of our simultaneous requests for him to retake various pages of documents—are of a "stop it, I love it" nature, and have clearly been interpreted by HERO in this vein.

> It is clear that the great dangers to the operation in its present stage lie in the frequent meetings with ANNE, and HERO's photographic endeavors, the two being of course largely interdependent. It should be sufficient to note that HERO has had ten meetings with ANNE in the past 11 weeks (October 20 to January 5 inclusive) and that she has gone to the meeting site on several other occasions. In this same period HERO has passed 27 rolls of film. These risks are not a constant factor in our operational equation; they increase geometrically with the regularity and frequency of the meetings and the amount of material photographed and passed.

The case officer argued that "just because the risks were justified at one stage of the operation, does not mean that they are necessary now." He cited the backlog in translations and evaluation as potential problems: "Consumers have not had a chance to properly digest the documents already provided." And, he added, "it seems to me that it's entirely possible that we have reached a point of diminishing returns on some of the articles and manuals."

Penkovsky's information had become "increasingly timely, specific and well sourced," the memo continued. Therefore the risks of keeping him in place had also grown.

> In the light of these factors, it seems to me that we can well afford to call a halt on the photography for a few months. This will

---

* According to U.S. national security information classification, unauthorized disclosure of Top Secret information can be expected to cause "exceptionally grave damage" to the national security. Unauthorized disclosure of Secret information is expected to cause "serious damage" to the national security, while disclosure of Confidential information is expected to cause "damage" to the national security.

allow HERO to "cool off" and will enable us to get caught up on the backlog and to take better stock of what we have. Everything appears to be shipshape, and future prospects are brighter than ever, with HERO's rise in professional status and the avenues of access opening up before him. All the more reason to examine carefully at this time whether or not we are justified in jeopardizing this unique source in the interests of acquiring more military manuals (in this connection, the record shows clearly that HERO himself is *not* a good judge of what risks he can and should take).

The officer recommended that HERO be immediately instructed to suspend all documentary photography until further notice, and to concentrate on his own reporting. He also urged that scheduled meetings with ANNE be reduced to once every two weeks.[22]

On January 15, only three days after the memo urging that Penkovsky curtail his meetings with Mrs. Chisholm, Maurice Oldfield delivered a message from Harold Shergold to Jack Maury.

We have to report that ANNE believes herself to be pregnant. This development will have both a short term and a long term effect on the role she plays.

The short term effect is that she will soon have to stop going to the ballet classes. These provide cover for the Friday and Monday rendezvous [RVs] if they take place in town. We have considered the possibility of her attending these RVs on the same days on other excuses such as shopping. Normally this would be feasible but there is a snag. ANNE has a British nanny who would dearly love to attend the ballet classes; so far she has not been able to go as she had to stay at home to look after the youngest child. If ANNE does not go, it will be difficult if not impossible to find a valid excuse why she should not go.

ANNE could attend the town RVs on the shopping excuse, on other days of the week, i.e., Tuesday, Wednesday or Thursday. We have asked ANNE to continue with the present schedule up to the end of January. In February the problem is easier in that the basic RVs are in the park and she can attend them. For this month we propose asking HERO to agree to shift the alternative RV from Monday to Tuesday. . . .

In the long term we may have to consider withdrawing ANNE earlier than we had intended, i.e., by June or early July. We have a replacement standing by, but she gave birth to a child only some six weeks ago. We would like the baby to be six or seven months old before the mother has to go into action. She, like ANNE, is a former SIS secretary and the wife of our representative designate.[23]

291

Shergold asked for CIA's agreement to the new meeting arrangements. Maury responded by raising the question of reducing the number of meetings with Chisholm and curtailing Penkovsky's efforts in order not to compromise him. On January 23 Shergold replied:

> Throughout the course of our dealing with HERO, we have on several occasions tried to give him advice in the interests of his own security. Usually, . . . he has agreed with what we have said, thanked us for our concern about him, etc., but inevitably a few days later he has returned to the charge and endeavoured to persuade us that what he wants to do is the right course. On no occasion can we recall really having prevented him from doing what he wanted to do.
>
> The same applies to the carefully worded warning we gave him in December about the frequency of meetings with ANNE. He thanked us for our concern about his safety and continued as before to appear once a week. If we repeat the warning, he will probably pay lip-service to it, but still continue as before. All that we may succeed in doing by repeating the warning after such a short period of time, is to irritate him.
>
> We agree . . . that the course of action proposed by CIA is, according to all the rules, correct. It pre-supposes, however, that agents are ideal and logical persons. It is our view that such agents rarely, if ever, exist. HERO does not at any time consider that he is an agent. He pays lip-service to being our soldier and accepting our instructions and advice, but remains convinced that he knows best.
>
> All that we have heard from ANNE and Wynne about HERO's behavior on his own territory makes us feel that he really does know the form there and how to cope with it. To our mind the major risk lies in the act of photographing itself rather than in the transmission of the material to us. Even if we are wrong about this, we do not think that a further warning message from us will alter his ways.
>
> HERO revels in what he is doing, is determined to be the best of his kind ever (perhaps not appreciating that he has probably achieved this status already) and sees in his meetings with ANNE the symbolization of his relationships with the Americans and with us. This is important to him.
>
> We agree fully with C.I.A. that we should not add to the risks he is running by asking him to repeat missing or badly photographed pages. We should also in future be very selective in asking him to obtain any particular document or type of document.

292

To sum up the above we feel that it would be a tactical and psycho-logical mistake on our part to renew the warning at this juncture. If in the coming months we have an opportunity to see him, then let us do it as persuasively as we can.

On February 2 a letter was drafted to Penkovsky with new require-ments. He was asked to provide data on the current status of the Soviet antiballistic missile (ABM) programs and missile deploy-ments in East Germany, details on deployment for the Warsaw Pact exercises in October and November, and the Soviet evaluation of the exercises. Specifically, the letter asked him to point out what weaknesses and problems were noted and the measures planned to correct them. Penkovsky was also asked to report on several political questions, among them factional strife within the Central Commit-tee; the status of Molotov—who had been ousted from the Presidium by Khrushchev in 1957 and was now serving as the Soviet representa-tive to the International Atomic Energy Agency in Vienna—and the new investigation into the murder of Sergei Kirov, the Leningrad Party leader, who had been assassinated on Stalin's order in 1934. The search for Kirov's murderers and the "enemies of the people" who supported them served as Stalin's pretext for the Great Purge of the 1930s.* Penkovsky was given a full list of the materials that had been received from him since the last letter. This extraordinary step was taken since he maintained no records, and the volume of documents and manuals he had photographed was so great that it was necessary as a check for him to avoid duplications and become more selective. He was also given the phone number of U.S. Air Force Captain Alexis Davison, an air attaché in the U.S. Embassy, who would be listening for his early warning call at number 432-694.

The February 2 letter urged Penkovsky to be attentive to his per-sonal security and stressed the importance of his safety. Tension between the U.S. and the Soviet Union over the Berlin Wall had eased slightly when the twelve Soviet tanks stationed near the Wall were withdrawn on January 17, following the removal of a U.S. tank force forty-eight hours earlier. But Berlin remained a festering, unpredictable sore point, and the Soviet Union continued to impede Allied air traffic into West Berlin, thus prompting a joint British, French, and American protest against "aggressive and dangerous Soviet harassment" of their flights. The letter to Penkovsky also

---

* The 1962 report of the commission investigating Kirov's death had still not been made public in 1991. See *Khrushchev Remembers: The Glasnost Tapes*, pp. 20–25.

requested information on the Warsaw Pact maneuvers that would provide authoritative information on the combat readiness and effectiveness of Soviet forces in Europe.

Three days before this letter to Penkovsky was prepared on January 29, the nuclear test ban conference in Geneva was adjourned. The conference had convened 353 sessions over three years. Efforts to break the deadlock over a monitoring system for nuclear tests had failed. Penkovsky's reports on Soviet nuclear developments and intentions were therefore more vital than ever.

At the end of January 1962, Quentin Johnson, the chief of operations for CIA's Soviet Division, flew to London to meet with Harold Shergold. The reason for the trip was to discuss the case code named HERO; they agreed that Penkovsky's high volume of document photography was becoming too great a risk to the operation. Johnson and Shergold met with Mrs. Chisholm—in London briefly to consult a doctor on her pregnancy—and reviewed the Moscow operation with her before she returned to continue appearing at the rendezvous sites.

Johnson, an imaginative, skilled professional, had a very favorable impression of Mrs. Chisholm. He found her "fairly relaxed about her part in the operation." Johnson asked her about normal surveillance on her and her cover for action. She noted that her husband was heavily surveilled, but that she herself was seldom followed. Johnson observed that she was probably good at avoiding detection—her cover for being in a doorway would be to adjust her clothing or tend to her son out of the cold. "Janet has never made a record of the windows overlooking the contact sites, but feels that the normal traffic in these streets renders the whole action inconspicuous," Johnson noted in a report on the meeting.[24]

At the London meeting Shergold told Johnson he planned to withdraw Janet and her husband from Moscow by June 1962 because of her pregnancy. He had in mind another married couple to replace them, Gervase Cowell and his wife, Pamela, also a former SIS secretary. "They also have three children," Shergold explained. "Two are too old for cover use, but the third will be 'pram age' at her arrival in the area."

Shergold agreed on the need to supplement or if possible to switch from clandestine meetings on the street to meetings under the cover of diplomatic functions. At any rate, the personnel changes were likely to cause a slowdown on contacts.[25]

Johnson argued that it would be prudent for Penkovsky to curtail his activities for a few months or even a year. Shergold opposed this view, arguing that Penkovsky would take instructions to curtail or halt his activities as a sign the CIA and SIS had lost confidence in him. This could destroy him. He is in control, knows what to do in Moscow, and will not take orders, Shergold said. Johnson said the American view was that Penkovsky should be cooled off and saved for another day.

When he returned to Washington, Johnson met with his colleagues in the Soviet Division to review his talks with Shergold. Johnson told his colleagues that he was "somewhat reassured about the conduct of her [Mrs. Chisholm's] contacts with Penkovsky." A CIA memorandum recapping the meeting said:

> Shergold does not feel that Penkovsky would accept CIA's suggestion to reduce either this activity or the number of personal contacts with the Soviet Union for the following reasons:
>
> a. The personal contact with someone he knows is very important to HERO subjectively.
>
> b. HERO has not accepted previous suggestions to reduce the number of personal contacts.
>
> c. The case officer teams were not able to hold down HERO on the number of personal meetings during the Paris phase.
>
> d. HERO is loath to use the dead drop because of security considerations as well as because he derives satisfaction from personal contacts.

Joe Bulik, who had been in Paris with Penkovsky, listened to Johnson's report and took exception, noting that it was Shergold himself, not Penkovsky, who had pushed for more meetings when they worked out the schedule in Paris. Similarly, Bulik observed that it was true that Penkovsky did not prefer a dead drop but only so long as he had other means available to him. He was prepared to use one when there were no other ways to communicate. Bulik felt that the British were less sensitive to protecting Penkovsky than the Americans and were prepared to use him despite the risks that might develop from frequent meeting.[26]

Penkovsky had not shown up for his scheduled February 2 meeting with Chisholm in the park on Tsvetnoy Boulevard. She then went to the alternative meeting places on both February 5 and 6. Still there was no sign of Penkovsky. On February 9 and 16 Penkovsky did not appear for his scheduled meeting.

SIS in London was informed by Rauri Chisholm and asked him to "discreetly check" when the Anglo-American tobacco delegation, which Penkovsky was accompanying as the Soviet host during this time, had left the Soviet Union. Maurice Oldfield, the MI6 man in Washington, contacted Maury in Washington and suggested that the CIA also try to find out what happened to Penkovsky. Oldfield warned that the British "may have to consider trying to find out where HERO is in his office through our Scientific Attaché or Commercial Counsellor in Moscow." Shergold was anxious to hear from Maury on this problem.[27]

ANNE was instructed to continue to keep her rendezvous schedule. "To date," Oldfield reported, "she has noticed nothing unusual. Shergie points out that this may indicate that all is well and that, for reasons unknown, such as illness, HERO is unable to attend."

Again, on February 20, Oldfield wrote to Maury saying," I have just heard from Shergie that there was no sign of HERO at the reserve RV [rendezvous] scheduled for today [in the delicatessen shop above the Praga restaurant].[28]

A new coded radio message was drafted to Penkovsky telling him, "ANNE will attend reserve meetings in the park on Mondays at 1600 hours in accordance with the plan and basic meetings at 1300 hours on Fridays at RVs whenever she can, but this will not be possible every week. We are disturbed by your absence and hope all is well. Greetings."

It was not until March 9, 1962, that the CIA found out why Penkovsky was no longer coming to the meeting sites. After his meeting with ANNE on January 19, he had spotted a car making a U-turn on a one-way street. In the backseat of the car were two men in dark overcoats. ANNE was under hostile surveillance, he believed.

ANNE had also reported that on January 19 she noticed a car, which may have been following her, when she boarded the bus after her ballet lesson; but she had not seen it again. She had no idea that Penkovsky had informed the team that he spotted the same car tailing her later that day.

Penkovsky was concerned for ANNE's safety and tried to get word to her. From January 20 to 28 he was assigned to work with an American paper delegation in Leningrad and Moscow. During the trip and at social events Penkovsky singled out an American he thought would be receptive and spent a lot of time with him. He suggested the American delegation hold a cocktail party and invite the British scientific attaché, Dr. Senior. On January 27 the American economic attaché gave a cocktail party which Penkovsky attended. To his disappointment Dr. Senior did not attend and Penkovsky was not able to pass a message to Mrs. Chisholm.

Early on the morning of January 28, the day the delegation was scheduled to leave, Penkovsky called at the hotel room of the American businessman with whom he had struck up a working relationship. The American was packing when Penkovsky arrived and asked him to deliver a message in London. Penkovsky explained that the message should go to the person who responded to the telegram that the American would send when he arrived in London. The telegram was to be addressed to LABORICI, the name Penkovsky had been given by the team.

Penkovsky wrote out the telegram for the American: PLEASE MEET ME ON [time and place to be provided by the American sending the telegram in London] SIGNED ALEX.

The message from Penkovsky was then to be delivered to the person who responded to the telegram. Written in Russian, it said: BE CAREFUL, BECAUSE AUTOMOBILE WITH LICENSE NUMBER [the American could not recall the plate number] IS FOLLOWING YOU AND THEY ARE WATCHING YOU ALL THE TIME NOW.

The American businessman made notes as Penkovsky talked, then the hotel porter came for his bags and interrupted further conversation. At Sheremetievo Airport the American, convinced this was just the sort of provocation he had been warned to avoid, told Penkovsky he would not carry out his request to pass the message, and he destroyed the notes. Penkovsky was stunned and his previously ebullient spirits sank.

Penkovsky then asked the American to be sure to call him at the State Committee when he returned to the Soviet Union. The American, of course, made it a point not to contact Penkovsky, still thinking this might be a provocation. The American recalled that on the trip they had made earlier from Leningrad to Moscow Penkovsky had told him, "They [the Soviets] don't like you because you know too much."

Penkovsky had also informed the American that he would visit the thirty-second International Automobile Show, in Geneva, from March 15 to 25, and that he had applied for a visa to the Seattle World's Fair, opening on April 21.

Yet none of this was known until March 9, 1962, when, in London, MI6 contacted the American businessman who had been in the paper delegation in Moscow to ask him when he had last seen Penkovsky. The businessman, who had once worked for the CIA and wanted to avoid further dealing with the Agency now that he was in the private sector, finally told MI6 of his meeting with Penkovsky just before he left Moscow. He also passed on what he remembered of Penkovsky's message.

The CIA sent the new case officer, who had replaced George Kisevalter, to London to debrief the American businessman and to meet with Shergold.* It was Shergold's belief that HERO had deliberately broken contact because of surveillance on ANNE but otherwise was safe. The fact that HERO accompanied the American delegation to the airport on January 28, nine days after the surveillance was spotted, pointed to this, argued Shergold.

Shergold and CIA agreed that no further contacts between ANNE and HERO must take place. She should not go to meeting places on designated days or carry any compromising material at any time. In order not to break her behavior pattern sharply, she should go to the commission shop, the Praga, and the park at meeting times but on nonmeeting days. If she should see HERO by chance and he should indicate that he wished her to follow him, she should under no circumstances do so. MI6 was fearful that Penkovsky had been turned and that ANNE might be arrested by the KGB.

A radio message would be sent informing HERO that his message had been received from the American businessman.

Full preparations were undertaken for a possible Geneva meeting with Bulik and Shergold to arrive there on Sunday March 11.[29]

From March 16 to March 31, message Number 6 was broadcast to Penkovsky:

TEXT BEGIN NUMBER SIX. WE RECEIVED YOUR MESSAGE ABOUT THE SURVEILLANCE AND ABOUT THE POSSIBLE TRIPS. DO NOT RPT NOT ATTEMPT TO MEET IN MOSCOW AS IN THE PAST. UNTIL WE MEET SOON END.

While Shergold and Bulik waited for Penkovsky in Geneva, they discussed future communications with him. On his own initiative Shergold now urged abandoning street meetings as the primary means of contact and accepting reduced production as the price of increased security. A CIA memo summing up the Geneva talks between Bulik and Shergold noted that "whatever the past difficulties may have been, it appears that we will not have any trouble with Shergold on this score in the future." Shergold also agreed to an American proposal to send Penkovsky a set of prepared postcards which he could mail to accommodation addresses in England to signal key situations. Accommodation addresses appear to be normal residences, but are actually controlled by MI6 or CIA to receive mail from agents. The postcards would be provided to him with cover texts already written in English. Each card would signify one simple message, the key to which would be the signature, the picture on the postcard, and the accommodation address. It was agreed that the most important messages to be conveyed were: "I am under

---

* The CIA officer, now retired, refused to reveal his name publicly.

suspicion," "I am on an internal trip," "I am ready to do business again," and "I will be coming to the West soon." The cards for each eventuality were selected and Shergold agreed to have them all prepared with different British handwriting and innocuous tourist messages addressed to several different secure but seemingly innocent addresses in England.[30]

These elaborate preparations soon became moot. Penkovsky did not go to Geneva for the International Motor Show.

Suspicion and Surveillance

ON MARCH 28 PENKOVSKY WAS INVITED TO A COCKTAIL PARTY AT THE apartment of Dr. David Senior, scientific attaché at the British Embassy. The occasion was a visit by delegates of the British Baking Industries Research Association. Such parties were standard diplomatic treatment for a trade group, to introduce them to their Soviet counterparts and show the flag. The new intelligence-gathering strategy was to use such an occasion to receive materials from and pass materials to Penkovsky; only a spy of Penkovsky's value merited such audacious risk. Exposure would trigger severe diplomatic retaliation. Earlier, Khrushchev had warned American Ambassador Thompson that if the American Embassy was involved in spying "we will put you out of business."[1] Khrushchev refused to acknowledge Soviet espionage activities against Americans in Moscow and around the world.

There were forty-seven guests at the party, twenty-two British visitors, ten members of the embassy including the Chisholms, and fifteen Soviet officials, eight of whom were from Penkovsky's office. Consistent with normal Soviet practice, Penkovsky did very little circulating for about an hour. In the suspicious atmosphere of that time, the Russians stayed together in groups and Dr. Senior, the host, brought people to them for introductions.

After the party was in full swing and the Russians had relaxed, Penkovsky found himself near Janet Chisholm and her husband. When Rauri Chisholm saw Penkovsky approaching with a colleague, he engaged the Soviet official in conversation and steered him into the second reception room, leaving Penkovsky alone with Janet, whose pregnancy was now apparent.

After greeting her Penkovsky said, "You must be feeling rather

300

tired. Why don't you rest for a few minutes in the hostess's bed-room?" Janet smiled and excused herself. Two or three minutes after she had disappeared into the appropriate bedroom, Janet heard Penkovsky saying to the hostess, "What a lovely apartment, please show me around." When he was conducted into the bedroom, he apologized for disturbing Janet, winked at her, and turned to leave, casually exposing a packet of cigarettes in his hand behind his back. They were visible only to Janet. She lifted the packet from his grasp with "the pleasure of a dog receiving a bone from its master."[2]

Janet put the packet containing eleven rolls of exposed Minox film and a folded one-page letter into her handbag, completing the pass. She was deeply impressed by this superb and brazen stroke of trade-craft, perfectly executed and beautifully timed. Penkovsky rejoined the party with his hostess and Janet appeared a little later from another room.[3]

Two days after the party, Dr. Senior, in response to a standing request by Rauri Chisholm to provide details of foreign travel by members of the State Committee, handed Chisholm Penkovsky's visiting card. As part of his job Dr. Senior helped to arrange meetings and travel for members of the committee with British organizations and companies. Senior also gave him details of Penkovsky's planned visits to the U.S. in April and to the United Kingdom in the autumn. Then Senior commented that Penkovsky even asked Mrs. Senior if he could look around the flat. "When he did so your wife was resting in the bedroom," he told Chisholm, disapproving strongly of Penkov-sky's behavior.

Mrs. Chisholm had no way of knowing the contents of the letter she had accepted until the packet had been sent to London, the film developed, and the relevant parts sent back to her husband via coded message. The take from Penkovsky was never opened, processed, or read in Moscow; instead it was sealed and sent directly to London via courier.

In the letter passed at the party, Penkovsky wrote that on January 5, after his meeting with ANNE, "I turned my attention toward an auto entering the lane. Violating the traffic regulations, the car swung around, and one of the men in the car was looking out in-tently. ANNE had already left. Having waited a couple of minutes, the car moved off onto Arbatskaya Street and went toward Arbat Square. In any case I remembered the car."

On January 12, before and after their meeting, there was no surveil-lance, Penkovsky wrote.

On January 19, after the meeting, ANNE walked along Arbat Lane down to the side of the Arbat. Penkovsky, convinced that all was in order with her, said, "I turned from the lane onto Bolshoi Molchanovka Street and went toward the Arbat Square. As soon as I exited onto Bolshoi Molchanovka, I observed the same car in which there was one man in a black overcoat. I left without looking for surveillance on me. The car is brown colored with license No. м щ 61–45."

Penkovsky concluded: "Surveillance is being conducted on ANNE, perhaps periodically." He urged that meetings on the street be stopped for three or four months. However, ANNE should "continue to behave naturally and visit the meeting places, but she should not carry operational materials with her since 'hooligans' (KGB) might grab her purse."

Penkovsky recommended that he be invited once or twice a month to small receptions hosted by American, English, or Canadian representatives. "If something should be important and urgent, then I will transmit it via the dead drop." This was the same procedure the Anglo-American team agreed on in Geneva when Penkovsky failed to appear. There was no mention that he might be under surveillance too.

In his letter Penkovsky said he was scheduled to leave on April 19 for the U.S.A. to visit the Seattle World's Fair Exhibition Twenty-first Century. He also wrote that he was supposed to visit Italy with Gvishiani for two weeks in February and go to the Auto Show in Geneva on March 24. This letter closed, "With warm greetings until we meet soon my dear friends," and was dated January 26, 1962, but he had no opportunity to deliver it until March 28. Penkovsky also wrote letters dated March 5 and March 28 that he passed to Janet at Dr. Senior's party.

In his March 5 letter he noted that the trip to Italy was postponed and the Geneva trip was canceled. He was still hoping to visit America on April 19, but wrote, "at the present it's going badly because the KGB Counterintelligence are rummaging around concerning my father. They are continually searching for my father's burial place. They cannot find it and they are conjecturing that perhaps my father is alive and that in the future it would not be suitable to send me on assignment overseas. My command considers these fears meaningless and they are defending me from all these conjectures of the 'neighbors.' Everything must be decided soon.

"In March I must meet with ANNE at a reception. I will pass detailed information about myself and plans for the future, depending upon the situation which is in turmoil about me."

In his March 28 letter, written the same day he met Mrs. Chisholm at Dr. Senior's apartment, Penkovsky was still optimistic about being allowed to fly to the Seattle Fair on April 19. His visa applications had been submitted and approved by the State Committee and the

GRU. He wrote: "The KGB will have its say on the 15th of April. If I make the trip then, everything will be all right. If they do not give me permission to make the trip, then my situation will change sharply and become complicated. It will be necessary to leave the committee, and in the fall of this year, having fulfilled twenty-five years of service in the army, I will be discharged. We must plan our future work dependent on all of these contingencies of life. If I do not come to the U.S.A., then after the 20th of April it will be necessary to arrange a reception at which I will be able to pass my plans for the future."[4]

On April 3 Jack Maury and Joe Bulik went to the State Department to expedite HERO's visa application. They met Roger Hilsman, head of the Bureau of Intelligence and Research, and told him they thought their Soviet source was applying for a visa. They wanted to make sure that his application was not rejected. Bulik and Maury emphasized the sensitivity of the situation and asked how the matter could be handled without revealing the CIA's operational interest in their source. Hilsman suggested they ask Ambassador Charles E. Bohlen, President Kennedy's special advisor on Soviet affairs, to join them. Bulik pointed out that since Penkovsky had served as a military attaché in Turkey, he was no doubt listed in State Department records as an intelligence officer. Bohlen said the process by which visas were granted or turned down was quite mysterious and apparently arbitrary and that he would be reluctant to alert anyone in the office concerned with visa applications to the CIA's interest in any Soviet individual.

Bohlen suggested the "best bet" was to notify Dick Davis, then deputy assistant secretary of state for European affairs, since he had to sign off on all traffic to Moscow approving visas and could short-stop any correspondence. Bohlen then asked the name of the individual. When Bulik and Maury showed some hesitation in revealing it, Bohlen said it was "quite ridiculous to be cozy since the individual could be identified by looking at the airgram reporting the visa application." Maury then told Ambassador Bohlen and Hilsman "the true name of the individual, emphasizing the overriding importance of strictest security."[5]

Maury and Bulik talked to Bohlen about the difficulties of further communication with Penkovsky and about their hope of getting the embassy's agreement to use its officers for contact with him. Bohlen said this would create something of a problem and wondered if there was another way of keeping in touch with him. At that point Hilsman vigorously and eloquently spoke up, saying, according to a memorandum on the meeting, that "the information provided by

HERO was of unique and outstanding value and this was by far the most productive intelligence operation that he had ever known of and that, with the possible exception of technical sources, nothing else had ever produced material of such concern to the national interests. This seemed to reassure Bohlen, who asked to see some of the recent reports from Penkovsky."[6]

When Maury reported on the meeting to Dick Helms, Helms was disturbed that Penkovsky's identity had been revealed. "While perhaps we had no alternative, in the future I want to be consulted before we take such a step," he said. Helms asked Maury to call Dick Davis to impress upon him the importance of handling the matter with the utmost discretion.[7] Even the president did not know the name of the "reliable and well-placed Soviet official." It was standard practice for the CIA director not to know the names of the Agency's spies inside the Soviet Union.[8]

On April 5 a message from CIA headquarters to Moscow Station requested new dead-drop sites. The drops were listed as a top-priority requirement that could become an essential way to communicate with HERO. Considering the heavy surveillance on American Embassy staff members, finding new places for HERO to leave and receive materials was no small task. Only for a spy like HERO were such heavy demands and high risks warranted.

Also on April 5, Sir Dick White, in Washington on other business, visited CIA headquarters to meet with Helms and the Soviet Division officers involved in the Penkovsky case. The problem of how to interpret and handle an early warning message from Penkovsky of a Soviet attack remained unresolved. Helms opened the meeting by expressing the hope that "we can reach agreement on this matter which is vital to both services."

Maury emphasized that any such report would have to be put in the context of contemporary developments and that the U.S. would insist that in any circumstances the report should be treated with reserve. However, he added there was no alternative but to take the report and discuss it with the Office of Current Intelligence (OCI), which then would probably place it for priority consideration before the Watch Committee and perhaps the United States Intelligence Board (USIB).

Sir Dick White replied that the American procedure as outlined was nearly identical to that followed in the U.K., where a report is taken to the War Room of the Defence Ministry to be considered by the Chiefs of Staff; probably a meeting of the Joint Intelligence Committee (JIC) would also be convened. Sir Dick also noted that since the message would presumably be transmitted simultaneously from Moscow by both services, evaluation would be undertaken at the same time by both sides. He said the aspect that most concerned the British was their fear that if the information went straight to the White House, the president might call the prime minister before he had been apprised by the JIC.

Maury's explanation that such information would not go to the president without being fully evaluated and critically reviewed stilled Sir Dick's concern. Both sides agreed it was unlikely that a single raw report from HERO would get to such a level unless it were supported by reasonably firm collateral.

In the file on the margin of the memorandum for the record of the meeting with Sir Dick are undated handwritten annotations by an unidentified CIA officer that read: "Perhaps mislead. Note lesser reports have."[9] Somebody had read the file and felt compelled to add his warning footnote to history.

On the basis of Penkovsky's letter explaining that he was planning to come to the Seattle Fair on April 19, the CIA began feverish preparations for his visit. A safe house was rented in Seattle and false identities established for those who would work on the case. Detailed instructions were prepared for Penkovsky to make contact once he got to England or America.

Joe Bulik traveled to London to confer with Shergold on these preparations. In case Penkovsky transited London, Bulik asked MI6 to meet Penkovsky, and he gave Shergold instructions how Penkovsky could make contact in Seattle. Penkovsky was told: "Enter Seattle Public Library at Fourth Avenue entrance (between Spring and Madison streets). Take escalators up two flights and exit building at Fifth Avenue entrance, which has a fountain and benches. Sit on bench for a few minutes. You will see one of your friends there. Follow your friend when he leaves. If he is holding a newspaper in his hands, this indicates danger and we will not have a meeting that night. Should library be closed, walk around the building to the fountain area and sit down."

The CIA also prepared instructions it would retain should Penkovsky stop over in Washington, D.C. "Go to the Washington Monument approaching it on foot from Constitution Avenue and Fifteenth Street. Walk around the monument. You will see one of your friends. If he is holding a newspaper do not contact him. If he is not holding a newspaper follow him to a waiting car." In the event of Penkovsky's arrival in Washington, Bulik had arranged for him to meet secretly with Attorney General Robert Kennedy, who had agreed after being told of Penkovsky's desire to meet the queen of England and President Kennedy. There was no meeting planned with the president and none ever took place.[10]

An elaborate FBI-CIA watch was kept on all planes arriving from Europe but Penkovsky did not appear in April or May.

On May 31, 1962, the British legation in Moscow celebrated Queen Elizabeth's thirty-sixth birthday at their embassy.

The building was built in 1893 by Kharitonenko, a rich sugar merchant, and the street's original name was Sofiskaya Embankment, after the church of Saint Sofia, a few hundred yards to the east. After the death of the French Communist leader Maurice Thorez in 1964, the embankment was named after him.

The stucco exterior of the embassy, painted in yellow and white with inlaid faces of Greek gods, is a prime example of the Italian influence on the Russian architect Fedor Shekhtel. The first British ambassador to the Soviet Union took up residence in the house in 1919 and it has been the embassy ever since.[11]

In fair weather Ambassador Sir Frank Roberts and his wife would have greeted the guests on the lawn, but it rained all day. The guests entered the embassy and climbed the wide mahogany staircase to the reception rooms on the second floor. The embassy is decorated with rich rugs, dark woods, high-backed baronial chairs, and marble busts of former ambassadors, which give it a pre-Revolutionary air. The presence of 600 guests in the complex of reception rooms heightened the difficulties of Janet Chisholm's and Penkovsky's task. Briefing instructions for the meeting had been prepared for Penkovsky but there had been no opportunity to deliver them to him. Still, both Penkovsky and Chisholm knew as a matter of course to look for each other at the reception, even if they could not be sure in advance of the other's presence. They met briefly and Mrs. Chisholm told Penkovsky to follow her and meet in the cloakroom. An after-action report noted, "after a brief exchange of words HERO actually followed ANNE at a distance, with 10 to 15 people between them."

She led him through three reception rooms and allowed him to see her descend the main staircase. When they reached the main hall exit, Janet heard Penkovsky ask a junior British diplomat for directions to the cloakrooms. He was escorted to the east wing of the embassy complex, opposite the entrance, where Janet intercepted him. The actual exchange was conducted entirely unobserved in an alcove of the cloakroom. Penkovsky passed Janet a package from inside his jacket and she gave him a letter from the Anglo-American control officers, twelve rolls of unexposed Minox film, and a translation into Russian of *Man and Space* by Dr. Ralph Lapp.

Penkovsky returned to the reception. Janet remained in her husband's office in the wing of the embassy that included the cloakrooms. Within thirty minutes Rauri Chisholm arrived in his office and Janet delivered the material to him. Penkovsky had given her seven rolls of exposed film, a four-page report, a two-page coded message from his one-time pad, and a three-page letter.*

Penkovsky's letter, addressed to "My Dear Friends," had been written on May 15, 1962. In it he explained that he had hoped to see them in April but a series of developments forced a cancellation of his trip. His training to replace an officer assigned to the International Atomic Energy Commission based at the United Nations in New York or Vienna had been scheduled to begin in January. This was put off, and it was explained to him that it would first be necessary for him to travel to the U.S.A. for the State Committee to test the reaction of the FBI to his presence. Penkovsky was told by the GRU that they had intercepts of American traffic from Turkey in which he was twice listed by the Americans as a GRU officer. On the basis of this, Penkovsky wrote, "I was asked to wait until April to go to Seattle."

In April he wrote, "Serov personally proposed me to be the leader of the delegation to Seattle. We applied for visas. My group and I received visas. All of a sudden there was a telephone call and a letter from the Central Committee about the inexpediency of sending this delegation to the U.S.A. and that its trip to this fair is put off until September 1962."

Penkovsky elaborated. The reason for the postponement, he explained, was that the Central Committee learned "that the Americans were preparing some kind of tricks and provocations against the Soviet representatives at this fair. None of us went. The delegation was withdrawn. It was decided to boycott the Seattle Fair for now.

After this, in the middle of April, friends from the Committee and GRU offered to send me as the leader of the group from the committee to the Soviet Industrial Exhibit in Brazil. The leadership of the committee and the GRU agreed. Everything was submitted to the Central Committee and the visa was received. I even received the travel allowance. Two days before departure by air, someone from the KGB called Serov personally and stated the following: "For the time being it is inexpedient to send him to the American continent because supposedly the Americans are very interested in him. There were frequent telephone calls before issuing him a visa to Seattle; there can be various provocations against him at the exhibit." Serov had nothing left to do but to "take the advice" about

---

*A one-time pad system is considered unbreakable because once used, the pad is destroyed and the code is never repeated.

these warnings and refrain from sending me to Brazil. (Besides, consider Serov's own situation.) I was withdrawn from the trip. The group left for the exhibit. At present it has been decided not to propose that I go anywhere and to continue the work in the Committee.

Supposedly the "neighbors" (KGB) have information that my father did not die and is located abroad. This information appeared at the end of 1961. An immediate search of the place where my father was buried did not produce anything—the grave was not found. Also documents regarding the death of my father were not found. My command does not pay special attention to this and believes that my father is deceased.

The problem of his father's past still haunted his future. Time was running out. He wrote: "In September 1962 I will have twenty-five years of service in the army. If the 'neighbors' continue to delve into my biography I may be transferred to the reserve, or at best I will be transferred from the GRU to another position.

"I am sick and tired of all this. I feel that I already do not have sufficient strength and potentialities for my great friends and sponsors. I very much want to come to you. Even today I would leave everything and would depart together with my family from this parasitic world. What should be done for the future? I request your advice."

If he were discharged from the army, Penkovsky wanted to know, "Which city it is best for me to move to with my family, so that it would be easier to carry out my dream? Should I move to Batum, Sukhumi, Odessa, or Riga, or to somewhere in the East? If I am discharged I will move in the winter of 1962–63."

He also asked, "How much money do I have in my account for the work that I did? If suddenly the situation surrounding me should become worse, where should I hide by myself?

"I will definitely be in the committee until September. During this time it is necessary to work out questions of communication for the future. Whom should I maintain contact with for exchanges if ANNE won't be available? For the time being it is inexpedient to meet ANNE on the street."

In the event he were suddenly removed from the committee, Penkovsky said, he would be at the regular agreed-upon meeting place on the 21st of each month at 2100 hours. "I will expect your person according to the arrangements that you have from my first sheet handed over in August 1960. Dead drop No. 1. remains in effect. (The description of two dead drops and of two more new places for meeting on the 21st of each month will be given by me later.)"

He asked the team to "send film and a small pistol that can be conveniently carried. We will continue to work until the last opportunity."

Penkovsky said that Wynne could come to the committee and the Ministry of Foreign Trade once more in 1962, and he complained of the difficulty in understanding the coded radio transmissions.

He closed by telling the team, "My wife gave birth to a second daughter. Try to send a coat, dress, suit, a winter baby blanket, and baby shoes all for a girl one year old.

"I shake your hand very firmly." It was signed, "Always your friend, Oleg Penkovsky."

A post-action report on the meeting from Maurice Oldfield to Jack Maury pointed out that "The lesson to be drawn from this is that with prior briefing we think this exchange plan would have been foolproof, but that with the improvisation required many things could have gone wrong and ANNE feels that the improvised indoor hand-over should be avoided like the plague."

Shergold suggested that on the basis of ANNE's experience at the queen's birthday the upcoming American July 4th party should not be used operationally. Bulik agreed and Wynne, who was to be in Moscow in early July, was instructed to tell Penkovsky not to attempt to pass anything at Spasso House, the American ambassador's residence, where the party was to be held.[12]

Penkovsky was beginning to feel trapped. He sensed that the numerous phone calls allegedly about his American visa, and Central Committee fears of an American provocation involving him, could mean at least two things: the KGB had become suspicious of his movements and wanted to observe him to be sure the Americans had reached him, or they could really believe the Americans were planning to embarrass him because they knew he worked for the GRU. Yet things were going well at the committee. He still had Marshal Varentsov and General Serov as his protectors.

Penkovsky's May 15 letter generated a flurry of meetings and efforts to assuage his fears. Even if the Seattle Fair boycott were the result of the low ebb of Soviet-American relations and Soviet concern with American provocations, the other cancellations of his foreign travel were ominous. At the minimum they indicated the KGB believed Penkovsky was known to American Intelligence as a GRU officer or was considered unreliable because of his family background. At the worst he was under KGB surveillance for spying and would not be allowed to leave the Soviet Union. Shergold and Bulik agreed to reply to Penkovsky with an encouraging letter as soon as possible. They confirmed his invitation to the American ambassador's Fourth of

July party and made plans to send Greville Wynne to Moscow "under sound cover arrangements." Wynne would be briefed to pass and receive messages. He would warn Penkovsky not to try to exchange material at the July 4 reception.

In an effort to provide a new American contact for Penkovsky inside the diplomatic framework, the CIA sent case officer Rodney Carlson to Moscow on June 24 to serve under cover in the American Embassy. Carlson would try to develop a relationship with Penkovsky through the State Committee. That way Penkovsky and members of the committee would be invited to American functions and they could exchange messages and film. Getting a good "slot," an official State Department position, in the embassy for a CIA officer was difficult because the State Department traditionally opposed covert operations through the Moscow embassy. Ambassador Thompson stressed that embassy officers were to be used only for major items of importance and not for fishing expeditions.[13]

In June, with GRU backing, Penkovsky applied for a twenty-day visa to Cyprus in connection with the Soviet Exhibit at the Nicosia International Fair. He was scheduled to leave on July 10.

At noon on Monday, July 2, Greville Wynne returned to Moscow to meet with members of the State Committee and the Ministry of Foreign Trade to discuss bringing his traveling exhibition of British industrial products, displayed in a custom-fitted panel truck, to the Soviet Union. Penkovsky did not come out to the airplane at Sheremetievo Airport as he had done on previous occasions. Instead, he waited for Wynne in the airport lounge, where he greeted him formally and officially on behalf of the State Committee. Penkovsky showed his pass and whisked Wynne through immigration and customs as he always had. They got into an old black car and Penkovsky put on a show for the driver by pointing out old monasteries and new institutes and academies while they drove down the broad lanes of Leningradsky Prospekt toward the center of Moscow and then to the Ukraine Hotel. In the backseat Penkovsky passed Wynne nine rolls of exposed film before they reached the hotel. Wynne handed Penkovsky a letter, 3000 rubles in cash, and twenty rolls of unexposed Minox film. He also brought a brown paper parcel with baby clothes for Penkovsky's second daughter, Marina, born on February 6, 1962.

An ornate multitiered concrete wedding cake, the trademark of Stalin's architectural taste, the Ukraine Hotel is located on Kutuzovsky Prospekt, overlooking the Moscow River. The telephones in each room are connected directly to a central station, where they are monitored by the KGB. Penkovsky not only flashed his pass from the State Committee, to assure that Wynne received a good room assignment, but he accompanied Wynne to his suite.

As soon as they entered the sitting room, Penkovsky turned on the radio and broke down sobbing. Wynne motioned him toward the bathroom and they turned on the water taps in the sink and bathtub full force to make as much noise as possible. They hoped to prevent their conversation from being understood if it was being taped by the KGB, as was likely. Penkovsky looked sick, tired, and very nervous. He told Wynne that he was tired and frightened and that things had changed greatly. Yet again, Penkovsky said, his trip abroad had been canceled at the last moment. This time it was Cyprus. The KGB had called Serov directly and told him there was concern that Penkovsky would be the focus of a provocation. Serov had no alternative but to cancel the trip, Penkovsky explained. Penkovsky and Wynne agreed to meet again at 9 P.M. Wynne shut the water off in the bathroom and Penkovsky left.

Wynne washed, changed his clothes, and decided to go for a walk. When he reached the street he remembered that he had left something in his room and went back. The woman in charge of his floor who kept the room keys was upset on seeing him. She told Wynne his key was missing and went to look for it. He was forced to wait for ten minutes before his key was "found" and he was permitted to go to his room. When he entered, Wynne could see that his suitcase had been searched, but there had been nothing incriminating or suspicious in it.

Wynne's usual routine in Moscow was to have lunch with the three resident British correspondents at the restaurant in the National Hotel off Red Square. Ross Mark, the *Daily Express* correspondent in Moscow at the time, recalled that Wynne attached himself to the correspondents. "He was a dapper little figure in his dark suits, what a lower middle class Englishman thinks of wearing to put himself up a class," recalled Mark. "He was a hail-fellow-well-met with no harm in him. We never could pin him down on what he was selling to the Russians."[14]

At 8 P.M. Wynne visited the British Embassy Club, nicknamed the Pub, in a building adjacent to the embassy, in order to meet with Rauri Chisholm. After several drinks they adjourned to the men's room, where Chisholm gave him a small package to be delivered to Penkovsky. Included in it was an article written in Russian on air defense developments in the U.S. and the Soviet Union, which it was understood Penkovsky would publish in a military journal. The article was based on a classified U.S. Army field manual for Air Defense Artillery Missile Battalion Nike-Hercules, #FM 44–95, which the Russian Intelligence Service received from a spy and had

311

placed in the Special Collection of the artillery library. Now some of its contents were to be included in the article he would have published. This would explain why, if there were ever questions, Penkovsky had asked for access to the material in the Special Collection.

The article, written for Penkovsky, also included material on the Soviet SA-2 Guideline surface-to-air antiaircraft missile and articles from *Military Thought*. It made Penkovsky sound very knowledgeable. By publishing such an article in a military journal, Penkovsky still hoped to be promoted to general.

CIA Counterintelligence was anxious to know how the Nike-Hercules manual had found its way into the library. In a letter accompanying the article the team asked Penkovsky "to provide us with English language writing or ink stamped printing which would help us to identify the channel through which FM 44–95 reached the Special Collection."[15]

Wynne returned to his room at the Ukraine Hotel and at 9 P.M. Penkovsky came to receive the delivery. Penkovsky turned on the radio, and they went into the bathroom, where he turned on the taps. Penkovsky, Wynne would recall, again started crying. He said he would have to leave the Soviet Union. "My father's history is now counting heavily against me and I do not expect to get another job in the committee next September when I will have served for twenty-five years in the army." He would be considered to have been downgraded; he would be forced to retire on a pension of 200 rubles a month. No longer would he have access to his old friends. He would be unable to stay in Moscow.

Wynne showed Penkovsky pictures of the woman who would take Janet Chisholm's place in Moscow, Mrs. Pamela Cowell, the wife of Gervase Cowell, the new MI6 officer in Moscow. He also showed him a picture of the new American assistant attaché, Rodney Carlson, who would also be a contact. Penkovsky was told Carlson would be at the American Fourth of July party and to look for a man wearing the special tie clasp with the red stones he had been shown at the meeting so long ago in London. That way Penkovsky could be certain that he was talking to the right person.

The July 2nd letter to Penkovsky also contained information on how to operate with Pamela Cowell:

> Photographs of her and her husband will be shown to you. Please note that in no circumstances is her husband to be used as a contact. At social gatherings at which you and Mrs. Cowell are present in British private flats, we propose the following drill.

The lavatories of all British flats in Moscow have a tin of disinfec-

tant called HARPIC [a household cleansing powder]. We are arranging to have one such tin fitted as a device for concealing material
from you to us and from us to you. We hope that a sample tin will
be ready in time for Wynne to show you how to use it. Forty minutes
after you have arrived at the party, Mrs. Cowell will go to the
lavatory and will exchange the normal tin of HARPIC for one she
will carry in her handbag. The tin she leaves in the lavatory will
contain messages and material (e.g., film) for you. Shortly after you
have seen her return to the party you should go to the lavatory,
remove the material for you from the HARPIC tin, and put your
material in its place; the concealing part of the tin will hold up to
twelve Minox films and a typewritten message. When Mrs. Cowell
has seen you return, she will take a suitable opportunity to go to
the lavatory again to exchange the HARPIC tins, putting back the
original in its place and keeping the one containing your material.
This drill, which we would ask you to accept, will be applicable only
in British private flats. It will avoid any last-minute improvisation.

Chisholm had provided Wynne with a sample can of Harpic custo-
mized for storing messages and material. Wynne showed it to Penkovsky, demonstrating how the hollow part could be removed from
the bottom, making it possible to hide materials. Penkovsky then
took the can and practiced opening the bottom several times before
returning it to Wynne.

Penkovsky and Wynne agreed to meet again at 9 P.M. on July 3
near the statue of Karl Marx opposite the Bolshoi Theater. Wynne
arrived precisely at 9. At 9:10 Penkovsky pulled up in a taxi and
joined him. He had been driving around the area checking that it
was free of surveillance. It was an unseasonably cool but pleasant
evening for July and they walked away from the center of the city
to the Hermitage Gardens. Inside the park there are also two theaters
and a small restaurant. They ate dinner in the upstairs section,
lingering until the restaurant closed at 11. Then they walked together in the empty park for another twenty minutes and Penkovsky
spoke about his future. He asked Wynne "to inform my friends
that whatever happens I will carry on working until September."
Penkovsky repeated his request for a pistol and said that although
he would obviously like to have his family with him he was now
prepared to leave the Soviet Union on his own.[16] It was not something he could explain, it seems, but internally Penkovsky felt op-
pressed. He wanted out of the Soviet Union; even at the price of a
generalship, even at the price of being less useful to the West. He
still hoped to escape.

The next morning, July 4, was sunny and comfortably cool. Wynne
walked to the State Committee headquarters on Gorky Street for his

10 A.M. meeting to discuss bringing his Mobile Exhibition to Moscow. For nearly two hours, two committee members whom Wynne had never met before questioned him closely on the names of the companies that would take part in the exhibition. They expressed interest on behalf of the State Committee, but said that a final decision could be made only after Wynne gave them a definitive list of the firms joining the exhibition, along with the products they would display. Wynne raised the question of an exchange of technical delegations.

The meeting ended without reaching a decision. Wynne did not see Penkovsky again that day. Wynne spent the afternoon at the America House barbecue party; Penkovsky went off to the American Embassy party at Spasso House, the ambassador's residence.

Ambassador Llewelyn E. Thompson, a tall, genial man with an easy manner that masked his analytical toughness and insight into the Soviet system, had been ambassador to Moscow since June of 1957; usually a new administration appointed new ambassadors, but President Kennedy regarded Thompson highly and asked him to stay on when he took office in January 1961. The ambassador had an excellent relationship with Nikita Khrushchev; he knew of Penkovsky's secret role but maintained his best diplomatic poker face when he shook Penkovsky's hand and exchanged pleasantries when he passed through the receiving line.

Penkovsky appeared with Vassily Vassilevich Petrochenko, deputy director of the foreign relations department of the State Committee. Petrochenko was also a GRU officer. They circulated on the lawn in front of the white doric columns of the New Empire Style mansion built in 1914 by a wealthy merchant and manufacturer. Spasso House derives its name from the nearby Russian Orthodox Church of the Salvation on the Sands (*Tserkov Spasa-na-Peskakh*). The neighborhood, a mile west of the Kremlin, remains a cameo of the past. The splendid American Embassy residence sits on the small, quiet Spasopeskovskaya Square. In the seventeenth century the area was the home of the tsar's falconers and dog handlers.

Penkovsky scanned the faces of the guests, looking for Rod Carlson, the lean, intense man in the picture Wynne showed him, the man wearing the identifying tie clip with the red stones. Carlson, an experienced officer, had also been shown pictures of Penkovsky and watched for him.

Penkovsky moved carefully, staying with his group from the State Committee, and noticed Carlson. Later, the party thinned out, and they managed to be alone briefly. They introduced themselves and shook hands. Penkovsky said quickly that he had nothing for Carlson with him but would have something the next time they met.

Carlson said he had nothing to deliver that day either. The meeting was a success. They had established contact; it was a springboard for their next operational meeting. Penkovsky shifted the conversation back to a social plane "where it stayed from then on."[17]

The following day, July 5, was Moscow summer, warm with sudden rainsqualls that quickly cleared into bright sunshine. At 4 P.M. Penkovsky came to Wynne's room at the Ukraine Hotel and handed him six passport photos of himself, two rolls of exposed Minox film, a one-page letter, and two pages from his coded one-time pad. Wynne gave Penkovsky phonograph records by the Russian popular singer and poet Aleksandr Vertinsky, who had emigrated in 1919, two years after the Revolution, and whose albums were not for sale in Moscow because they were considered decadent. The CIA had purchased the records in New York for Penkovsky to give to Marshal Varentsov, General Serov, and other high-ranking sources. Penkovsky left within fifteen minutes after arranging to meet Wynne outside the Peking Restaurant, near the ring road just off Mayakovsky Square, at 9 P.M.

Wynne spent the rest of the afternoon and early evening wandering around Moscow, carrying the material Penkovsky had given him. At 8:30 he went to America House and sat down for a drink at the bar, where Rauri Chisholm was waiting. When he finished his drink Chisholm headed for the men's room. Wynne followed him there and handed over the material from Penkovsky.[18]

At about 8:45 Wynne hailed a taxi near the American Club and asked to be taken to the corner of Gorky Street and Mayakovsky Square. He walked across the square to the entrance of the Pekin Hotel, on Brestskaya Street off the Garden Ring Road. Wynne did not see Penkovsky in the lobby so he left, walked around the block, and returned to the restaurant entrance. Again he did not see Penkovsky. He continued to roam around the neighborhood side streets before circling back once again to the Pekin, where the restaurant was. When he approached the hotel he saw two men standing in a doorway. Wynne walked slowly toward the hotel, pausing to look in shop windows along the way. The two men seemed to be following him. This was the first time Wynne had noticed any surveillance.

When Wynne neared the Pekin again he saw Penkovsky walking toward him from the opposite direction, wearing sunglasses and a light raincoat. He was carrying an attaché case. Wynne paced himself so that he and Penkovsky arrived at the entranceway at the same time. When they made visual contact, Penkovsky signaled with a furtive gesture that they were not to make physical contact. Penkovsky entered the restaurant and quickly saw that all the tables were taken. People were standing in the back waiting to be seated. He walked out and turned the corner. Wynne, who had followed him into the restaurant, made a pretense of searching for a table. Then he left behind Penkovsky. The first thing Wynne saw was the two men who had followed him standing on the opposite side of the road near a policeman. Wynne got a good look at them and he decided they were following him. He kept his eye on Penkovsky and did not look back. Penkovsky, however, looked back two or three times. Wynne decided the best thing to do would be to return to his hotel and wait for Penkovsky to contact him there.

Wynne flagged down a taxi, but the driver did not want to take him to the Ukraine Hotel, which was only a short distance away. While he was trying to convince the driver, Wynne noticed Penkovsky head into a driveway leading to a group of apartment houses. He let the taxi drive off and walked toward Penkovsky, who stood against a wall at the entrance to the driveway and beckoned for Wynne to follow him. After they had walked into the courtyard and were alone, Penkovsky approached Wynne and said, "I see you are being followed. We must break contact immediately. I will see you tomorrow morning. You must leave on the first plane out."

While Wynne and Penkovsky talked, the two men shadowing Wynne appeared at the entrance of the driveway. On seeing them, Penkovsky turned and disappeared inside the apartment block. When the tails saw Wynne standing there, directly facing them, they were startled. One of the watchers jumped back in the direction whence he had come, the other walked away slowly. Wynne headed back to the ring road and walked along until he could hail a passing taxi. He asked the driver to take him to the Praga Restaurant on the Arbat. When Wynne looked out the rear window of the taxi he noticed the two men tailing him watch the taxi drive off. Wynne did not see them again, nor did he see any car that appeared to be following his taxi.

At Arbat Square the taxi stopped at a traffic light and Wynne noticed a taxi stand on the other side of the street. He paid his driver and crossed the street to hire another taxi. Wynne doubled back down Kalinina Prospekt, then asked the driver to take him to America House. He arrived there at 9:20 P.M. He checked for surveillance but saw nothing to arouse his suspicions.

Rauri Chisholm was still at America House. Wynne had a drink and waited until Chisholm, who was with a small group of American and British embassy officers, would have a chance to talk with him. After nearly an hour Chisholm went to the men's room. Wynne followed him there and briefly told Chisholm what had happened at the Pekin Hotel. On leaving America House, Wynne saw no signs of surveillance and nobody appeared to be following him when he took a taxi back to the Ukraine Hotel.

At six the following morning Penkovsky called to check that all was well. He said he could not call for Wynne at the hotel and asked Wynne to get to Sheremetievo on his own. Wynne checked out of the hotel and was at the airport, sitting on a bench near the main entrance, when Penkovsky arrived at 7:50. Seeing Wynne, Penkovsky slipped into his official State Committee role as the senior official escorting a foreign visitor. In a formal manner, he arranged Wynne's ticket and escorted him through customs and immigration. They had only a few minutes for a cup of coffee before Wynne's flight departed for Copenhagen.

In the coffee shop Penkovsky was very agitated. He told Wynne he was quite certain that it was Wynne who was under surveillance, not he. The previous day, he said, Yevgeny Levin, his boss at the committee, a KGB colonel, had called him in and asked a lot of questions about Wynne. Levin was especially curious why Wynne had come again on his own and not with a delegation. Wynne had now done this several times and the pattern was strange, Levin said. Penkovsky explained that Wynne was developing his new mobile exhibition project and was lining up companies to be represented. Levin appeared to be unconvinced and said the committee would wait and see what, if anything, Wynne produced.

"It is extremely important that you send the committee the fullest information about your mobile exhibition and the companies that have agreed to participate in the project, as soon as possible," Penkovsky warned Wynne. "It is now important for your own safety that something concrete should emerge." Penkovsky's mood had changed. Depression had turned to anger at the KGB's rough surveillance, clearly meant to intimidate them. After all, he was using Wynne for the benefit of the State Committee, and the KGB was out of line. Ever the optimist, Penkovsky told Wynne he would protest to Levin the way they were treated by the watchers the previous evening. Wynne should show the vehicles for the mobile exhibition to as many people as possible from the Soviet Embassy as soon as possible after his return to London. "Greville, we must not be seen together so much, but is it essential that you come back in September," said Penkovsky, escorting Wynne to the departure gate.[19]

End Game: The Cuban Missile Crisis

PENKOVSKY WAS IN LIMBO. WYNNE, UNDER HEAVY SUSPICION IN MOScow, returned to England. Janet Chisholm had left for home to give birth to her fourth child. Penkovsky waited for an invitation to meet again with his new American contact, Rodney Carlson. In case of an emergency he could turn to the DISTANT warning system; he could mark the telephone pole on Kutuzovsky Prospekt, call the prearranged number, and blow into the mouthpiece three times.

Wynne's report to MI6 on his Moscow visit and Penkovsky's state of mind were pessimistic in the extreme. Wynne's account of the rough surveillance at the Peking Hotel on July 5 and his hurried departure from Moscow the following morning sent shock tremors through the British and American teams.

On July 20 CIA director John McCone met with President Kennedy in the White House and, using the code name CHICKADEE for Penkovsky, told the president that "most recent reports were received July 4th and 5th, together with information leading us to believe CHICKADEE is in trouble. We conclude he is under suspicion, possible surveillance, and even might have been compromised to the point where he could be acting as a counteragent. We therefore are studying his most recent reports, which covered certain aspects of military doctrine most carefully, checking them against all sources available to us, and are not disseminating them pending a judgment as to their bona fides."[1]

After a six-day operational review, Penkovsky's material was judged to be reliable. The documents he had photographed most recently were, accordingly, translated and distributed inside the intelligence community. The British and Americans now agreed on a set of "Future Plans" for Penkovsky that stipulated:

318

1. Communications with HERO must be maintained in any event.

2. No pressure will be brought on HERO to produce intelligence, particularly in the event he should be retired.

3. If HERO goes abroad, we recognize that he may wish to defect and we will not induce him to return to the USSR.

4. If HERO should remain in the Committee, we will make every effort to restrict personal communications with him to a social-professional context.

5. We will examine the possibilities of clandestine exfiltrations from the USSR for the eventuality of his retirement.

6. WYNNE's role will in future be one of support for HERO's position in the Committee and his clandestine communications role will cease.[2]

The CIA and SIS were trying desperately to keep their man afloat.

On August 1 President Kennedy announced that the U.S. was willing to accept a system of national control posts, subject to international supervision, for monitoring a nuclear test ban; this was a significant concession. Four days later, on August 5, the Soviet Union unilaterally resumed its nuclear tests in the atmosphere with a forty-megaton explosion in the Arctic. On August 9 the Soviet Union officially and categorically rejected Kennedy's compromise proposals for a nuclear test ban treaty.

On August 10 CIA director John McCone dictated a memo to Kennedy expressing his belief that Soviet medium-range ballistic missiles (MRBMs) would be deployed in Cuba. On August 22 the president publicly confirmed reports that several thousand Soviet technicians and "large quantities" of supplies were pouring into Cuba. The following day he signed National Security Action Memorandum (NSAM) 181 calling for study and action "in light of evidence of new [Soviet] bloc activity in Cuba." The memorandum directed a study of the probable military, political, and psychological impact of the establishment in Cuba of missiles capable of reaching the U.S. It also called for an analysis of the military alternatives available should the U.S. decide to eliminate such missiles.

On August 27 Penkovsky was invited to a reception in the apartment of the American agricultural attaché in the yellow stucco embassy annex on Tchaikovsky Street. The embassy apartments were an oasis of American furniture, appliances, brand name foods, and soft drinks.

319

The three-bedroom apartment—two baths, living room, kitchen—was palatial by Moscow standards. The party, from 6 to 8 P.M., was being held in honor of an American tobacco delegation. Penkovsky arrived alone about 6:30 and worked his way through the guests, slowly moving toward Carlson, the clean-cut young attaché. They talked in Russian for a few minutes with Jane Danilova, an interpreter for the State Committee. Then Carlson went off to the bathroom and loaded the dead drop. Carefully, he taped the package, wrapped in waterproof oilskin, containing a false internal Soviet passport and a letter from the team, to the underside of the water tank cover of the toilet in the largest of the bathrooms. Carlson rejoined the party from another door and moved slowly toward the other side of the room, where Penkovsky was now talking to an embassy officer. The three men stood together for a moment; the embassy officer soon moved on. Penkovsky immediately addressed Carlson in English: "I have a small package for you. Do you have something for me?"

"Yes. Go to the bathroom, through this door and turn right. Under the lid of the toilet tank."

As soon as Carlson said "bathroom," Penkovsky said, "Yes, Yes." Two American officials approached and the conversation turned to innocuous subjects. After a few minutes Penkovsky, using his standard ploy, said, "This is a nice apartment. How many rooms? May I see it?"

Carlson and another embassy officer said "Yes," and the three moved off, Penkovsky leading. When they passed the bathroom, Carlson said, "This is the main bathroom." Penkovsky went in, looked around, came out, and the three went into the hall, where the host was showing interpreter Danilova the apartment. All went into the children's bedroom, then out into the hall again and past the bathroom. Penkovsky asked, "May I use it?" "Of course," replied Carlson. The host and Danilova by this time had moved back to the party. Carlson stood aside to let the embassy officer pass and said to him, "Go ahead, I guess he doesn't need any help in there." Carlson was now alone in the hall. He went into the bathroom with Penkovsky and locked the door.

Penkovsky gave Carlson a small package from his pocket and asked, "For me?" "You have for me?" Carlson said "Shh" and pointed to the toilet tank. Penkovsky did not move. Carlson took off the lid of the tank, turned it over, and placed it on a mat on the floor. He removed the envelope along with the extra tape that had been left so that Penkovsky could fasten his package in place. Penkovsky put the envelope in his pocket, said goodbye, and left when Carlson unlocked the door. There was no one in the hall. Carlson relocked the door, flushed the toilet, put the lid back on the toilet, and stayed for three minutes washing his hands. Then he slowly opened the door. Fortunately, there was still no one in the hall. He looked back and noticed that two hairbrushes that had been on the toilet lid had been left on the sink. He closed the door, replaced the brushes on top of the toilet lid, and left the bathroom. He walked back to the living room through the long hallway, entering the living room at the opposite end, from which Penkovsky had entered when he returned.

Moscow Station sent an operational immediate message to CIA headquarters advising: TWO WAY PASS ACCOMPLISHED AT RECEPTION WITHOUT INCIDENT. HERO PASSED SEVEN CASSETTES AND THREE OPERATIONAL MESSAGES. POUCHING 28 AUGUST.

In his after-actions report Carlson commented, "HERO was obviously somewhat nervous . . . and was in too much of a hurry." Penkovsky spoke only in English when referring to the operation. Carlson thought that Penkovsky had his mind set on a pass similar to that used in the past and did not listen to anything beyond where he was told to go for the exchange. However, this was not apparent to anyone else, Carlson thought.

After the exchange in the bathroom, Carlson said, he rejoined the party "without incident." He reported that while talking to Penkovsky and a Soviet colleague, Penkovsky said, "We will come to America."

"When? We will welcome you there," said Carlson.

"Sometime, sometime," Penkovsky replied cheerfully."[3]

One of the three written messages from Penkovsky was a long letter, written on August 25, 1962, noting, "It will soon be a year since our last meeting. I am very lonely for you and at the present time still do not know when we are fated to see each other. I and all the members of my family are in good health. I am in good spirits and capable of working."

More ominously, but seemingly unaware of the consequences of what he described for the first time, Penkovsky wrote, "I have already become used to the fact that periodically I note surveillance and control over me. The 'neighbors' continue to study me. For some reason they have latched on to me. There was some kind of stimulus for this. I confuse and lose myself in guesses and suppositions. I am very far from exaggerating the dangers and the causes. I am an optimist. Nevertheless, I am trying to objectively evaluate the situation. I value highly the fact that you are also doing this on my behalf. In drawing conclusions about my situation I want to

321

emphasize that I am not disappointed in my life or work. The most important thing is that I am full of strength and desire to continue our common and, as you write, important and necessary work. This is the goal of life. And if I succeed in contributing my little bricks to our great Cause, then there can be no greater satisfaction."

Penkovsky told the team, "It is not advisable to make a decision now to cease photography: it is necessary to continue this work until they take away my pass."

Aside from the surveillance, Penkovsky wrote, things were going well for him at the GRU and the State Committee. He had received a commendation and a cash award in rubles. He still hoped to be sent abroad on a temporary assignment in the near future. The possibilities were to go to Japan or Australia, to the U.S. with a book exhibition, or to France with Gvishiani. These trips should take place between September and December 1962. Penkovsky said he expected Gvishiani to propose one of the trips and to try to talk to the KGB and the Central Committee, where the KGB also controlled approvals for overseas trips. "Only God knows what the answer will be. If the KGB clears me of suspicion they will sanction my travel. If not, they will 'advise' what to do: either to leave me in the committee or to remove me from the committee but leave me in the army, or to dismiss me altogether.

"If they remove me from the committee and start to dismiss me, I will make a last attempt to remain in the army in any other job and will go with a last request to Malinovsky, to S.S. [Sergei Sergeyevich Varentsov], to Serov, and to other generals. If this doesn't help, I will not remain in Moscow. I ask you to understand this and to sanction these actions and decisions of mine."

Then Penkovsky devoted a special section of his letter to Wynne and his problems. He wrote that everything went normally until the day before Wynne's departure, when

> Levin [the KGB representative on the State Committee] told me that his people [KGB] were interested in the aims of Wynne's visit. I told him that besides the committee, Wynne must visit the Trade Council or the Ministry of Foreign Trade about the question of organizing the Mobile Exhibition. Levin said that he knew all this, but that for some reason they have become interested in W. I learned all this in the afternoon—after I had given W. the second batch of material. I had made a date with him for 2100 hours that same day for a farewell supper. I was working officially with W., and the organs [KGB] had been informed of this—in such cases the neighbors are not supposed to surveill us. On approaching the Peking I noticed surveillance of W. I decided to go away without approaching

him. Then I became afraid that he might have some return material for me before his departure from Moscow. I decided to enter the restaurant and to have dinner with W. in plain sight of everyone. Entering the vestibule I saw that W. was "surrounded" (and that surveillance was either a demonstrative or an inept one). Seeing that there were no free tables, I decided to leave, knowing that W. would follow me. I only wanted to find out if he had material for me and then to part with him until morning, having told him that I would see him off. Having gone 100–150 meters, I entered a large, through courtyard with a garden. W. followed me, and the two of us immediately saw the two surveillance agents following us. Exchanging a few words, we separated. I was very indignant about this insolence, and on the following day, after seeing W. off, I reported officially to my superiors that KGB workers had prevented me from dining with a foreigner whom we respect, have known for a long time, with whom we have relations of mutual trust, with whom I have been working for a long time, etc. I said that our guest felt uncomfortable when he saw that he was being tendered such "attention." My superiors agreed with me that this was a disgrace, and Levin was equally indignant about the surveillance. Levin said that the committee and I, as its representative, granted the necessary courtesies to Wynne and that we [the KGB] do not have any claims on him. But it seems that W. attracted the interest of control organs to himself by his rash actions; these I was unable to fully foresee, and although I tried to take preventive measures against some of them, it seems that W. did not carry them out.

Then Penkovsky complained about Wynne's inability to organize the traveling exhibition more expeditiously so that Wynne would be invited to Moscow in 1962. He also wrote that he had found out after Wynne left that Wynne had invited a Soviet girl and boy to his hotel room. "I do not know what conversations he held with them, or what the idea was to look for new acquaintances in such a manner. Was he lonely? These young people were questioned."[4]

Penkovsky also criticized Wynne for not exchanging a single British pound, "although I am sure that you gave him money for the trip. Every day he took 30–40 rubles [$27–36] from me, and I paid fully for his hotel room. When he asked for money it was embarrassing not to give it. Perhaps someone noticed that he did not exchange money although he lived, ate, entertained, and paid in rubles."

In conclusion Penkovsky urged the team to have Wynne quickly send committee all the materials requested and come up with a list of interesting firms so an exhibition could be set up in Moscow or Leningrad. "I request you to control and to assist W. in sending materials and prospectuses of good quality and appearance about the proposed exhibition. It is necessary to complete this in a solid way— then many of the suspicions about W. will vanish."

Penkovsky wrote that if he was not sent abroad on a temporary assignment he would "go on leave in the second half of September until the end of October. For the duration of my leave I will be listed in the committee regardless of what decisions may have been made about my future. After my leave I will return to the committee and will still be able to go to receptions. After my leave I will inform you about the future at one of the receptions."

Then Penkovsky, discussing the future, unburdened himself to the British and American team:

Dear Friends, I have a big personal favor to ask of you. I ask you to make an exception from the rules for me. I am extremely grateful for the system adopted for paying for my work at present and for the future, after I come to you. My present salary for life, plus a pension the size of the salary—this is very good and is sufficient for my future life in the world so dear to me, for the stability and eternity of which I fight with you. However, when I come over to you, I will have in my account 35–40 thousand [dollars]. I consider this sum insufficient to start from scratch, especially since I want to acquire right away my own active enterprise. When I arrive I would like to have more. I ask you to select from the total [number of] photographs which I have made, at least 100 of the best and most valuable ones: 5000 frames. Attach to them all the early handwritten materials (the genuineness and value of which I think have already been checked and determined), and deliver all this to my highest superiors for an over-all evaluation and to establish as a material encouragement to me of a one-time sum, taking into account the value of all the documents at once. In this connection I would like to remind you of the following. The existing system of payment during the period of my remaining in Russia was established by us during the first days of our mutual work when, modestly estimating my agent possibilities, we came to the mutual conclusion that I was basically limited by the framework of the GRU and that I would be able to provide genuine documents of value only on intelligence.

As a consequence of the subsequent evolution of our mutual work, and of proper foresight and guidance of my work, new capabilities were established and we went beyond the framework of the initial plans and supposition. We have obtained and are obtaining many other materials which have a definite value for our Command. I ask that this be taken into account in examining my request. I am very interested and concerned by the question of what I will leave my children and grandchildren. My well-being during my lifetime is not of disinterest to me, but what will remain after me for the people near and dear to me? I assure you at once, that if my request is turned down the quality of my work and all my enthusiasm will not diminish by a single grain and that I will continue to work just as I am working now. Believe this, in this is my strength.

Penkovsky, more mundanely, also asked for four mercury batteries for his transistor radio and said he had found what he considered to be "two very good dead drops," one near a church visited by foreigners and the other near the grave of the poet Sergei Yesenin, in the Vagankovskoye Cemetery. "I do not want to visit the dead-drop sites for detailed study while I still am being watched. I will send the descriptions later."

Penkovsky said he was working on an article from the translated material in Lapp's *Man and Space*, passed to him by Janet Chisholm on May 31 at the queen's birthday party. Penkovsky noted that the material "helped me open many doors and established me more firmly as a person who wants to do something new. . . . I embrace you warmly and shake your hands, Your Friend. 25.8.62."

In his package from Carlson Penkovsky found a long letter from the team and a Soviet internal passport made out to Vladimir Grigoryevich Butov, a worker at a design institute in Moscow. The passport, made especially by the CIA for Penkovsky, was to be used should he need to flee from Moscow. It contained his picture, which he had sent earlier via Wynne.[5]

On August 29, the day after Penkovsky's meeting with Carlson, the Soviet Union announced that the volume of its maritime shipments to Cuba in 1962 would be twice the 1961 total. On September 1 it announced an agreement to supply arms and military technicians to Cuba. Following the flurry of Soviet activity in Cuba, speculation burgeoned, and at a press conference reporters asked the president for a comment on the possible meaning of such steps. The United States, said Kennedy, will employ "whatever means may be necessary" to prevent aggression by Cuba against any part of the Western Hemisphere, but the president added, "The evidence of Cuba's military buildup showed no significant offensive capability."

On Wednesday, September 5, Penkovsky appeared at an American Embassy reception for a U.S. electric power delegation headed by Interior Secretary Stewart Udall. The reception was at Spasso House and there was no opportunity for Penkovsky to pass a message or films to Carlson, who was also invited to the party. The layout of the ambassador's residence prohibited a joint trip to the men's room by Penkovsky and Carlson. When Carlson went to the bathroom to load a letter for Penkovsky inside the cover of the toilet tank he was unable to make the tape stick. In any case, Penkovsky gave no indication that he had a delivery to make.

Penkovsky and Carlson did have a brief conversation about the anticipated American tobacco delegation; Carlson said he would contact Penkovsky. Carlson was developing a realistic cover for his relations with Penkovsky. Penkovsky told Carlson that he hoped to see him the following evening at a British movie showing and added in English, "There are many good places there." The British and Americans had periodic showings of the latest films, to which Russians were invited. However, Carlson was not invited because only Soviet citizens and British Embasssy officials were on the British guest list.

The following day Secretary of the Interior Stewart Udall met with Nikita Khrushchev, who told him, "Now, as to Cuba—there's a place that could really lead to some unexpected consequences."[6] That evening Penkovsky attended the British film showing of *A Taste of Honey*, starring Rita Tushingham, at the offices of the science and cultural attachés. Chisholm's replacement at the British Embassy, Gervase Cowell, who had just arrived in Moscow that week, and Penkovsky, acknowledged each other with eye contact at the reception before the film, but no words were exchanged between them. Penkovsky had been shown pictures of Cowell's wife, Pamela, but she was not there. No operational procedure had been established to transfer materials to Gervase Cowell, which is why Penkovsky looked for Mrs. Cowell, to whom he was supposed to pass material in a hollow Harpic can in the bathroom. In his report to London, Cowell wrote,

> The film show was given for Russian guests of the Scientific and Consular sections of the Embassy. The show began at 6.30 pm and the guests were invited for 6 pm. They came in a steady dribble over that period so social contact was sketchy; the punctual ones had a handshake all around, the later ones only managed a greeting to their official contacts before the film started.

> HERO materialised around the middle of this build-up. [He] did a very brief double take as he passed me, no more than any guest who had been to previous receptions might give to a new face, but being HERO I think it registered. I felt this was enough for one evening and I had no wish to give him the impression that I had something for him by contriving to make any further contact. As there was only one British wife for the greater part of the evening I was fairly sure he would have sized up the situation for what it was—an opportunity for us to both appear at a party.

Of the seventy Russians invited, only twenty-four turned up, but they included Levin, the top KGB official on the State Committee for Science and Technology, and his wife. Penkovsky had a good reason for behaving with caution. When the British sent Cowell's report to Washington they discussed the need to answer Penkovsky's September 5 letter and his acute concerns about how much money he would have when he came to the West. It was agreed that an answer should be prepared and agreed upon by September 10 in order to have it translated and in Moscow for a possible meeting with Penkovsky on September 13.

The British brought the Americans up to date on Wynne's activities. One of his mobile exhibition vehicles was on the road in Eastern Europe and had received reasonable publicity. Wynne had booked a site for it at the British Trade Fair in Bucharest in early October, but no plans were being made for a trip to the Soviet Union this year. "Wynne will write to Levin giving him full details of his Bucharest trip and of the firms participating," the report from London said.

To meet the deadline for agreement on a joint letter to Penkovsky by midday on Monday, September 10, 1962, Harold Shergold prepared a draft:

Dear Friend,

We thank you most warmly for your most informative letter and the valuable material you passed to us recently. The quality of your photography is as always excellent.

We were most interested to hear that there is a possibility that you may make a trip abroad to one of four countries later this year and most sincerely hope that this time you receive permission to go. We long to see you again as much as you long to see us and wherever you go, we will go, too, in order to meet you.

We have studied your comments on our financial proposals for your future very carefully. It appears that we did not phrase our letter containing these proposals to you properly since you have not drawn the conclusions we expected. There should not be any questions in your mind but that you will be treated very generously by our governments. It has been clearly stated in the highest circles that your efforts have been most successful and that the value of your material is of the highest order. Although we would have much preferred to postpone discussion of detailed financial arrangements until we could meet with you personally, in keeping with your request, our leadership has authorized an award of $250,000, which is being set aside for you until you come to the West. We have also given thought to the question of your children and grandchildren. When next we meet, we will discuss all these financial matters with you more fully.

We have taken note of all your comments with regard to [code name for Wynne] and will do everything we can to insure that he plays his part properly; you should know, however, that he has been in correspondence with the All Union Chamber of Commerce. He has received a letter from them to the effect that it is only possible to consider the organization of an exhibition in the Soviet Union in 1963. In view of this he clearly cannot make detailed plans with firms and exhibitions at this stage, although several firms, who will be of interest to you, have shown great interest in such an exhibition. In the meantime he is planning to send one of his mobile exhibition vehicles to the fair in Bucharest in October. In the very near future, he will be writing a letter to Levin giving details of the present situation; he will not, however, for the reason given, be able to provide a list of exhibitors and exhibits for the proposed exhibition in the USSR.

The letter continued with a review of Penkovsky's work.

We were naturally most pleased to receive the remaining pages of the Field Service Regulations, as this is of course a basic document. The other manuals and regulations are also of value. We are, however, already in general terms, familiar with the questions discussed in them, because of other materials which you yourself have provided us. In view of this and to the extent that you have a choice within the *Spetsfond* [classified library] you should know that the *Military Thought* articles, both top secret and secret, and the *Military News* collection are more valuable and we would welcome 1961 and 1962 issues in this range that we have not already received. We would also be interested in any similar collections of articles concerning for example the PVO [antiaircraft] Air Forces or the Navy if they are available in the *Spetsfond*. Incidently, we believe that we have not yet had a chance to comment on the GRU lectures by Serov, Rogov, etc. We were most interested in them and would welcome further papers, particularly any dealing with illegal operations. (We emphasize that the above guidance is not to be interpreted as a request that you intensify your efforts in this direction; our previous statements on this subject still apply and you should only do such photography as you consider safe and possible.)

Cuba and Berlin: In addition to the Berlin question, in which details of military-diplomatic preparation and timing continue to be of importance, we are very much interested at this time in receiving concrete information as to military measures being undertaken by the USSR to convert Cuba into an offensive military base. In particular we would like to know if Cuba is to be provided with surface to surface missiles.

All of your friends think of you all the time and sympathize with the difficulties you have. At the same time they are proud of the way you are facing up to these difficulties and continuing to fight for what you know to be right. Remember always that, although unseen, they are at your side. ANNE sends you warmest greetings and has asked us to let you know that she has given birth to a son. Both mother and son are well. We all send you our warmest greetings and once again express the hope of seeing you soon.

Bulik agreed fully with the text and the letter was translated into Russian for Penkovsky.

Pamela Cowell, known by the code name PANSY, arrived in Moscow on September 12. The following evening there was to be a farewell party for Dr. David Senior, the British scientific attaché, whose tour of duty was ending. The Cowells were invited as were Penkovsky and his wife, Vera.

There would also be a party on September 15, given by acting economic counselor Carroll Woods. Unaware of Penkovsky's espionage activities, Woods had routinely included him on the guest list of Soviet officials from the State Committee. When Rod Carlson learned of the party, he hastily arranged to have himself added to the guest list in his official capacity. Carlson made plans to receive material from Penkovsky and to pass the letter to him if Penkovsky failed to make contact with Pamela Cowell on September 13.

Indeed, on September 14 Mike Stokes called from London to tell Joe Bulik that Penkovsky did not attend the party given by the scientific attaché on September 13. "Very few of the Russians invited were present," explained Stokes. Shergold told the CIA London Station, "Either HERO thought he should not appear at both the 13 and 15 September parties, and therefore he may be opting for the 15 September party, or he may have been excluded or restricted for some reason from attending the September 13th party because out of a fairly large gaggle invited from his office only two persons appeared. Now we are awaiting results of the 15 September meeting."[7]

On September 16 a brief cabled message from Moscow arrived in Washington: HERO NO SHOW. Penkovsky had said he might be going on leave; his handlers, while concerned, could only hope for the best. They assumed that Penkovsky would appear according to plan after his leave at the end of October.

The increased shipments of Soviet equipment to Cuba were stirring suspicion and controversy in Washington. On August 31 Kenneth Keating, the Republican senator from New York, had told the Senate that there was evidence of Soviet missile installations in Cuba. Keating urged Kennedy to take action and proposed that the Organization of American States send an investigative team to Cuba. Keating soon mounted a campaign against the Kennedy administration charging a coverup of the fact that there were Soviet offensive missiles in Cuba. He never disclosed his sources and refused to document his charges, but they became a major issue in the congressional election campaign. Recalling the Keating charges years later, Dick Helms said he was convinced Keating "took a flyer based on Cuban refugee reports. I went into his charges in detail because my ass was being roasted every day on what Keating was using for his information. You know Senators can get away with that."[8]

On September 4 Soviet Ambassador Anatoly Dobrynin had called on Attorney General Robert Kennedy. The president used his younger brother Bobby to pass private messages and to handle diffi-cult and delicate situations. The president was thus able to make his views and concerns forcefully known while avoiding direct presi-dential involvement. Bobby Kennedy told Dobrynin "of President Kennedy's deep concern about what was happening" in Cuba. Do-brynin informed the attorney general that he should not be con-cerned because he, Dobrynin, had been instructed by Soviet Chairman Nikita S. Khrushchev to assure President Kennedy that there would be no ground-to-ground missiles or offensive weapons placed in Cuba. Dobrynin also told the president's brother that the Soviet military buildup was not of any significance and that Khru-shchev would do nothing to disrupt the relationship between the U.S. and the U.S.S.R. during the period prior to the election. Chair-man Khrushchev, explained Dobrynin, liked President Kennedy and did not wish to embarrass him.[9] Dobrynin passed along similar mes-sages to White House aide Theodore Sorenson and United Nations Ambassador Adlai Stevenson. That same day, after being briefed by his brother, President Kennedy issued a statement that there was no evidence of "offensive ground-to-ground missiles" or of "other significant offensive capability" in Cuba. "Were it to be otherwise," he warned, "the gravest issues would arise."[10]

Khrushchev continued the pattern of deception. On September 11 an official Soviet statement said there was "no need for the Soviet Union to shift its weapons for the repulsion of aggression, for a retaliatory blow, to any other country, for instance Cuba." The So-viet statement called on the United States "not to lose its self-control and soberly to assess where its actions could lead."[11] During this same period Robert Kennedy was told by Georgi N. Bolshakov, a KGB officer operating under cover in Washington as information counselor at the Soviet Embassy and editor of the magazine *Soviet Life*, that there were no offensive missiles in Cuba. Bolshakov met with Khrushchev and Mikoyan at Pitsunda on the Black Sea while they were on vacation in mid-September and was instructed by Khrushchev to assure the president that "no missile capable of reaching the United States will be placed in Cuba." Mikoyan added that only defensive surface-to-air missiles (SAMs) were being installed in Cuba.[12]

The only senior member of the Kennedy administration who suspected Khrushchev of placing offensive surface-to-surface missiles in Cuba was CIA director John McCone. On August 10, after examining U-2 photographs and secret intelligence reports that included Penkovsky's material and Cuban agents' sightings of what appeared to be missiles being unloaded and moved on trucks, McCone dictated a memorandum for President Kennedy "expressing the belief that installations for the launching of offensive missiles were being constructed on the island."[13] Despite the caveats of aides who recommended that he omit his statement of belief until it was completely documented, McCone persisted. At a National Security Council meeting attended by the president on August 17, McCone argued that the Soviets must be placing surface-to-surface missiles in Cuba. Secretary of State Dean Rusk and Defense Secretary Robert McNamara expressed the view that the buildup was purely defensive.[14]

McCone's argument was based on what he called "a judgment factor." He had no hard information that offensive missiles were in Cuba, but the U-2s flying over Cuba to study the Soviet buildup spotted the pattern of surface-to-air missile sites, for defensive anti-aircraft missiles. Penkovsky had told the Anglo-American team about the Soviet SAM plans in 1961 in London and provided a detailed manual on the SA-2 capabilities. McCone asked himself what the SAMs were protecting since they were not defending airfields. There had to be offensive strategic Soviet missiles in Cuba, he deduced.

"The obvious purpose of the SAMs was to blind us so we could not see what was going on there. There they were with 16,000 men with all their ordnance equipment and then came the ships. There was nothing else to ship to Cuba but missiles. That was my argument. We didn't see the missiles. They were on the ships and we had no agents on the ships. We really didn't know what was on the ships, but some things you can deduce. That was one of them," said McCone.[15]

McCone's position was not enviable. "I was taking a position that there were Soviet offensive missiles in Cuba and the whole Kennedy administration was opposing me, all Democrats. Here I was the sole Republican with a very different view. I had a devil of a time to persuade the President and his brother, Bobby Kennedy, that I was

331

not the source of information to a Republican Senator [Kenneth Keating]."*

"The excuse that was given by McNamara, Rusk and others," McCone continued, "was that they [the Soviet Union] had never put a missile outside of their own territory. That was true, but my argument was that Cuba was the only piece of real estate that the Soviets controlled where they could put a missile that could hit Washington or New York but couldn't hit Moscow. Of course they wouldn't put missiles in Albania or East Germany for fear the local people would put them away and fire them on Moscow."[16]

McCone was so upset that he went to see Michigan Republican congressman Gerald Ford, then a member of the House Appropriations Subcommittee, which passed on the CIA budget.

I was going on my wedding trip and I was beside myself because I couldn't get [support for] my view. I told Jerry Ford, "I can't get anybody to level in on this problem which I think is a serious problem." Ford said, "I'll tell you what I'll do, I'll arrange for the President to listen to you." I said, "You don't have to do that. I can see the President anytime." I went to see the President and I gave him my view, one-on-one. The President convened an NSC [National Security Council] meeting for the next morning [August 10, 1962]. Everybody there heard my shouts of danger—Rusk, McNamara, Bundy. I presented my side of the story. The President said, "John is leaving and I want a contingency plan of operations drafted so that if John is right we'll have a plan to operate." That was the quarantine, as it later turned out. I was quite disillusioned, because usually a contingency plan goes in the bottom drawer. So I didn't take a great deal of satisfaction from that meeting as I flew up to Seattle to be married.[17]

The question of Soviet offensive missiles in Cuba festered while McCone's wedding to Theiline Piggot took place on August 29. On September 1 McCone and his bride sailed from New York City on the *S.S. France* for a honeymoon in Saint-Jean–Cap-Ferrat, in the south of France. "I left orders to overfly Cuba every day and the ship had hardly left the dock when my order was canceled by Rusk and McNamara, especially Rusk who feared a U.S. plane with a civilian pilot would be shot down and create a hell of a mess."

McCone interrupted his honeymoon to meet in Paris on September 6 with Deputy Secretary of Defense Roswell Gilpatric and National Security Advisor McGeorge Bundy. He warned them that he

---

* McCone and Keating had dinner in Paris after the Cuban missile crisis. McCone asked Keating the source of his information but "he wouldn't tell me."

believed the Soviet Union was placing missiles in Cuba. McCone cabled from France recommending that a Special National Intelligence Estimate be made stating the opinion that the SAM sites discovered in Cuba were being developed to protect offensive surface-to-surface missiles. McCone's deputy, Lieutenant General Marshall S. Carter, ignored his boss. The report he sent forward by the United States Intelligence Board (USIB) to the National Security Council and the president did not include McCone's recommendation because the CIA estimator could find no new, hard evidence to support what Arthur Schlesinger, Jr., later called McCone's "presentiment." The Special National Intelligence Estimate (SNIE 85-3-62) noted:

> The establishment on Cuban soil of a significant strike capability with [medium- and intermediate-range] weapons would represent a sharp departure from Soviet practice, since such weapons have so far not been installed even in Satellite territory. Serious problems of command and control would arise. There would also have to be a conspicuously large number of Soviet personnel in Cuba, which at least initially, would be a political liability in Latin America. The Soviets might think that the political effect of defying the U.S. by stationing Soviet nuclear striking power in so menacing a position would be worth a good deal if they could get away with it. However, they would almost certainly estimate that this could not be done without provoking a dangerous U.S. reaction.[18]

When McCone returned home he found there had been no overflights over Cuba during his absence. "Everybody seemed to be rather relaxed about that. I was furious, so we immediately started a program of overflights. We ran into delays on the question of civilian pilots. That was solved by turning the U-2s over to the Air Force. Their pilots had to be checked out in what to look for in Cuba. After ten days or more of bureaucratic infighting aided by cloud cover over Cuba the question was resolved by the facts of the first flight on October 14."

That same day, a Sunday, Presidential Assistant for National Security Affairs McGeorge Bundy appeared on ABC's *Issues and Answers*. Still unaware of the information derived from the U-2 flights, he denied the existence of medium-range missile sites in Cuba. "I know there is no present evidence, and I think there is no present likelihood that the Cubans and the Cuban government and the Soviet government would in combination attempt to install a major offensive capability."[19]

A team at the National Photographic Intelligence Center reviewed the photos taken during the October 14 U-2 flight and identified a pattern that conformed to SS-4 medium-range missile sites in the Soviet Union. When checked against the manual for SS-4 missiles that had been supplied in 1961 by Penkovsky, the evidence was irrefutable. Penkovsky had copied it with the Minox camera and passed it to Janet Chisholm.

On the morning of October 16, Richard Helms went to see Attorney General Robert Kennedy in his office to discuss the entry into the United States of a defector. The attorney general was in his shirt-sleeves, his coat thrown over a chair. When Helms walked in, Bobby Kennedy asked, "Dick, is it true they've found Russian missiles in Cuba?"

"Yes," Helms replied.

"Shit," said Kennedy.[20]

Later that morning his advisers showed President Kennedy photographs of SS-4 medium-range missile launching installations under construction in San Cristóbal, Cuba. To the untrained, naked eye the photographs looked like a football field being excavated. To the analysts the pattern showed SS-4 missiles, with a range of 1100 miles, which could hit Washington, D.C. From the missile manual that Penkovsky had transmitted in 1961, the CIA knew all the operational details of the liquid-fueled SS-4 missiles.[21]

Three days later, on October 19, the CIA prepared a detailed memorandum on the SS-4 missile sites in Cuba that relied heavily on information provided by Penkovsky. What the photoreconnaissance team saw in the U-2 aerial photographs was a characteristic deployment pattern, or "footprint," of the SS-4s that was shown in the missile manual supplied by Penkovsky. This was confirmed by satellite pictures of SS-4 installations in the Soviet Union. While the identification of the sites was based on interpretation of aerial photos, changes in the status of sites could be analyzed with precision only by referring to the extensive details in the classified documents Penkovsky supplied. Thus, "triangulation," positive confirmation of the kind of missile being deployed in Cuba and its operational characteristics, was possible mainly because of the work of Oleg Penkovsky.

"Penkovsky's" manual assisted the CIA to estimate for President Kennedy how long it would take to complete the installation. "We looked at power and fuel lines, launching booms and all the other details which were in the manual. The assessment gave President Kennedy three extra days," Dick Helms would recall. "The big issue of the moment was whether to send in the Air Force to take out the missile bases and the whole Cuban Air Force. With the aid of the material Penkovsky delivered we were able to tell the President 'this

Minox camera film cassettes seized in Penkovsky's desk. (Russian matchbox illustrates scale.) *(KGB)*

This picture of Janet Chisholm and her children in Tsvetnoy Boulevard Park in 1961 was shown to Penkovsky to help him identify them. *(Courtesy of Janet Chisholm)*

KGB surveillance photographs of Penkovsky entering and leaving an apartment house on Arbat Pereulok for a meeting with Janet Chisholm in January 1962. *(KGB)*

Janet Chisholm caught on camera by the KGB entering and leaving her meeting with Penkovsky on Arbat Pereulok in January 1962. *(KGB)*

Telephone pole no. 35 on Kutuzovsky Prospekt, marked by Penkovsky as a signal to clear the dead drop on Pushkinskaya Street. *(CIA)*

Vera Dimitrieva Penkovsky in 1965, opening the secret drawer in Penkovsky's desk that contained incriminating evidence of his spying. *(Express Newspapers)*

Penkovsky at his trial before the Military Collegium of the Supreme Court in Moscow, April 1963. *(Vadim Biryukov)*

Greville Wynne after he was released from Soviet prison in 1964, with his son, Andrew, and wife, Sheila. *(Courtesy of Greville Wynne)*

Wynne at home in London after his release from Soviet prison. *(Courtesy of Greville Wynne)*

Richard Helms and President Lyndon Johnson at the LBJ ranch in Texas in April 1965 when Helms was named Deputy Director of Central Intelligence. *(CIA)*

President John F. Kennedy, Allen Dulles, and John A. McCone in November 1961 when McCone succeeded Dulles as Director of Central Intelligence. *(CIA)*

CIA officers at a farewell dinner for Allen Dulles held at the exclusive Alibi Club in 1961. *From left to right:* two unidentified men, James Critchfield, Brigadier General Jesse Balmer, Colonel Lawrence K. "Red" White, Allen Dulles, Richard Helms, Colonel Sheffield Edwards, Bronson Tweedy, Eric Timm, James J. Angleton, Lyman Kirkpatrick, and John M. Maury.

Форма № 51.

456

В ОТДЕЛ ЗАГС МОСГОРИСПОЛКОМА

оенная **Коллегия**
ерховного **Суда**
Союза ССР

: в : ь СПЕЦОТДЕЛ МВД СОЮЗА : ССР

к № ____делу____

ГЛАВНОМУ ВОЕННОМУ ПРОКУРОРУ
на № 4в-8131-62

0 . мая   195<u>63</u> г.

Прошу дать указание соответствующему отделу ЗАГС

№ СП-001/63

о регистрации смерти ___ПЕНЬКОВСКОГО Олега___

Москва, ул. Воровского, д. 13.

Владимировича ____1919____ года рождения, наступившей

__16 мая 1963 года_____ и выдаче свидетельства

о смерти его____жене - гр-ке ПЕНЬКОВСКОЙ Вере

Дмитриевне_____, проживающе<u>й</u> по адресу:_____
г,Москва, Набережная М.Горького, д.36,кв,59.

Заявитель об этом уведомлен.

Начальник секретариата
Зам. председателя Военной Коллегии
Верховного Суда Союза ССР

ПОЛКОВНИК ЮСТИЦИИ   И.Полюцкий

Photocopy of a court order to provide the certificate of Penkovsky's death on
May 16, 1963, to his wife, Vera Dimitrievna. *(KGB)*

is what we've got here and it will take them X days to be ready to fire.' It gave President Kennedy time to maneuver. I don't know of any single instance where intelligence was more immediately valuable than at this time. Penkovsky's material had a direct application because it came right into the middle of the decision-making process."[22]

The CIA's October 19 memorandum was able to provide the National Security Council Executive Committee (Ex Comm) with detailed information on the SS-4. The briefing paper showed the SS-4 to have a range of 1020 nautical miles, with an accuracy, or CEP (circular error of probability) of 1 to 1.5 miles. The 3000-pound warheads had a variety of yields from twenty-five kilotons to two megatons. The liquid-fueled missile launchers were capable of firing a second and even a third salvo. The refire time was five hours. There were usually two missiles per launching pad. "From command to firing time varies from eight to twenty hours. In an alert, missiles could be held indefinitely about 2 1/2 to five hours from firing." After that time, because of the instability of the fuel, it would have to be removed and replaced. The president was told that there were three SS-4 sites with four launchers on each site with two missiles per launcher. Two of the sites were already operational.[23] The U-2 photoreconnaissance also confirmed the beginning of SR-5 intermediate-range ballistic missile (IRBM) sites. These missiles, with a range of 2100 miles, could hit almost every city in the United States, and many in Canada and South America.

Penkovsky's detailed information on the SS-4s included their refire rate. This proved of key importance during an Ex Comm discussion of a proposal to bomb the missile sites. In the event the bombers did not destroy the sites fully on the first strike, the committee wanted to be able to tell President Kennedy how long it would take for the missiles to be ready for a second launch. Since each missile was potentially able to account for an American city, this was a vital question.[24]

In a discussion of the missiles in Cuba, the president remarked to McCone, "You were right all along."

"But for the wrong reasons," said Secretary of Defense McNamara.[25]

"There was a good deal of tension in high levels of the government and for that reason I didn't ask McNamara what he meant by that. I wish I had," said McCone.[26] Walter Elder, McCone's executive assistant, did ask McNamara what he meant. "McNamara said, 'I don't know. I had to say something.' "[27]

President Kennedy addressed the American people at 7 P.M. on October 22 and told them:

Within the past week, unmistakable evidence has established the fact that a series of offensive missile sites is now in preparation on that imprisoned island. The purposes of these bases can be none other than to provide a nuclear strike capability against the Western Hemisphere. . . .

This urgent transformation of Cuba into an important strategic base, by the presence of these large, long-range and clearly offensive weapons of sudden mass destruction, constitutes an explicit threat to the peace and security of all the Americas. . . .

But this secret, swift, and extraordinary buildup of Communist missiles, in an area well known to have a special relationship to the United States and the nations of the Western Hemisphere, in violation of Soviet assurances, and in defiance of American and hemispheric policy—this sudden, clandestine decision to station strategic weapons for the first time outside of Soviet soil, is a deliberately provocative and unjustified change in the status quo which cannot be accepted by this country, if our courage and our commitments are ever to be trusted again either by friend or foe.[28]

In the subsequent series of meetings by the Ex Comm to assess Soviet intentions and capabilities, from October 16 to November 2, when the Soviets dismantled the missiles and destroyed the sites, Penkovsky's information played a critical role in assessing the ability of the Soviet missiles in Cuba and overall Soviet nuclear strength. The analysts were able to read it authoritatively because he had provided the basic intelligence on which to determine their judgments.

Ray Cline, deputy director for intelligence (DDI) was in charge of preparing the CIA's briefings for President Kennedy. He believed that the initial photograph of the SS-4s at San Cristóbal—fully understandable only because of Penkovsky—was the key to successful resolution of the crisis. Afterward, Cline asked Bobby Kennedy and McGeorge Bundy how much they thought that single piece of evidence was worth. Both men said "it had fully justified all that the CIA had cost the country in its preceding years."[29]

Ambassador Charles E. Bohlen, who had become aware of Penkovsky's identity earlier in 1962, had been named ambassador to France. He walked into the president's office on October 17 in the beginning of the crisis, to pay his official farewell call. The president showed Bohlen the U-2 photos of the SS-4 sites being built at San Cristóbal and told him "though the data seemed scanty, our experts could determine the nature of the installations with precision."

In his memoirs Bohlen later commented, "Invaluable in analyzing the photos was material obtained from Oleg Penkovsky, probably the most successful Western espionage agent who worked in the Soviet Union."[30]

On October 22, 1962, Joe Bulik sent a message to the Moscow Station telling them to stress to HERO that information on Soviet nuclear intentions was of top priority. The time for the use of "early warning" had come. Referring to the letter that Carlson was to deliver to him, Bulik wrote: "P.S. You will appreciate that our letter was written before President Kennedy's historic announcement of 22 October. As the situation is changing rapidly from day to day it is not possible to give you specific questions. It will however be clear to you that all concrete information about military and diplomatic moves being planned by the Soviet Union either in Cuba itself or elsewhere in the world is of vital importance."

There was no way to contact Penkovsky since he was not at the State Committee and he had not been seen. The most optimistic way of looking at this was that he was on leave, taking his annual vacation. The worst case was that he had been arrested. Leaving nothing to chance Joe Bulik cabled the CIA Station in Moscow following Kennedy's speech: SUGGEST HERO EARLY WARNING PROCEDURE BE IN ALERT SITUATION WITH PERSONNEL IN PLACE.

At about 9 A.M. on November 2, two voiceless telephone calls were received on the primary number given to Penkovsky to indicate that he had loaded the Pushkinskaya Street dead drop. Unlike the voiceless calls at irregular intervals in December of 1961, this time the signal site, a gray telephone pole, number 35 on Kutuzovsky Prospekt, was marked with a chalked letter X. Penkovsky was signaling that he had left an urgent message in the dead drop at 5/6 Pushkinskaya Street. The decision was made to clear the drop, and Richard Jacob, a twenty-five-year-old CIA officer, under cover as an archivist in the American Embassy, was chosen to do so at 3 that afternoon. Jacob, responsible for preparing the diplomatic pouch and arranging for it to be sent and accepted at the airport, had been up until 4 A.M. waiting at Sheremetievo Airport for a pouch to arrive. The plane had been diverted because of foul weather and poor visibility. Jacob was sleeping when Hugh Montgomery, the CIA deputy station chief, came to his apartment and asked him to come to the embassy. Montgomery and Jacob met in the "bubble," the suspended plexiglass, soundproofed room designed for classified conversations and believed to be impregnable to Soviet electronic bugging. Montgomery appeared tense and "not happy" to Jacob. There was little discussion and Penkovsky's name was never mentioned. Jacob, however, sensed it must be Penkovsky who had loaded the drop. He had been advised of the case before going to Moscow and he had inadvertently met Penkovsky at Ambassador Thompson's 4th of July party at Spasso House.

Penkovsky had come to the party with his boss, Vitaly Petrochenko, chief of the Foreign Relations Department of the State Committee on Science and Technology. Jacob recalled that "Petrochenko seemed to be keeping his eye on Penkovsky. I talked with Petrochenko, then he took me over to Penkovsky, who was with Hugh Montgomery. I was concerned about meeting Penkovsky, but there was nothing I could do and I was introduced to him by Petrochenko. We exchanged greetings and then I left."

Moscow was Jacob's first overseas assignment for the CIA; he spoke Russian well—he had studied the language for five years at Dartmouth and continued to study it during his service in the army, where he did intelligence work. At Fort Meade, Maryland, he had been taught what to do during an interrogation: "Don't say anything that is untrue and don't give details which might be used against you."

Jacob had been psychologically prepared for Moscow by the conservative Russian teachers at Dartmouth, many of them emigrés from Saint Petersburg who glorified life under the old régime and reviled the abuses of the Bolsheviks. Yet he also had a Marxist professor who explained the goals of the Soviet state in glowing terms. Moscow was a challenge and Jacob was stimulated by the assignment. He knew there was intense physical and audio surveillance of the embassy, but Jacob did not let it bother him. He was determined not to repeat the performance of the hapless officer, code named COMPASS, whom Jacob described as "a poor guy."

"Russians are Pavlovians," said Jacob, "they instill psychoses and nervousness to render you inoperative or make you recruitable. I went to Moscow by train so I could get a feel of the country. I wanted to see the Great Russian plain and see a part of the national character. My train arrived in Moscow on a snowy January morning in 1962. There was nobody there to meet me. I gathered my bags and walked out into the heavy snowstorm. There was a line of nine or ten Russians waiting for a taxi. One of them looked at me and my clothes and asked me if I was a foreigner. When I said I was an American they pushed me to the head of the line. 'You are a foreigner—go to the head of the line.' I was impressed by this small act. Here were the Russians showing that they were generous to guests, but at the same time also showing a sense of inferiority while wanting to show that they could do something gracious. That would never happen in France or Germany."

Jacob recalled that he went out of his way to make it appear that he was not a CIA officer. He downplayed his Russian language ability and pretended that he wanted to improve it so he could later teach. He told the Russian secretaries in the embassy office that he was going to spend a year in the Soviet Union and then return to the United States to teach Russian.

When the young Belgian wife of one of the American political officers was mean to him and pulled rank on him he took it as an opportunity to demonstrate that he was not an intelligence officer. "I hated her, but I was also grateful to her. Whenever she abused me verbally I was careful to be very correct and apologetic. I figured if I was treated badly in public the Russians would not think I was working for the Agency," said Jacob. "They know that the KGB employs people as drivers and in jobs like pouch officers, but nobody in a Soviet Embassy treats them badly. Their rank is known and they are treated with respect."

On November 2 the skies were overcast and leaden, a dark slate color, the prelude to a light, first snow of the year. The air was blustery with gusts of wind but the temperature had not yet dropped to freezing. Jacob wore a sweater under a cheap American raincoat coated with plastic. It did not look expensive or foreign made. "Its great advantage was the pockets," recalled Jacob. "It had a regular pocket and then a slit that I could put my hand through, so if I wanted to discard what I had picked up I could put my hand through the slit and instead of putting the material into my pocket I could drop it."

The plan was for Jacob to drive to Kuznetsky Most with Robert K. German, the embassy publications procurement officer, who knew nothing of Penkovsky or that Jacob was going to clear a dead drop. While German went on his buying rounds at the bookstores on the street crowded with shoppers, Jacob walked to Pushkinskaya and into the bookstore on the corner of Pushkinskaya and Khudozhest-vennogo Teatra Lane (Art Theater Lane). The store has two entrances, one on the lane and another on the corner fronting on Pushkinskaya. Jacob used the entrance on the small lane, walked through the store, and exited on Pushkinskaya in hopes of losing any surveillance on him. He observed the four corners of the street. "My first reaction was to observe pedestrian traffic on both sides of Pushkinskaya Street, my own and the opposite side. In both cases it was heavy and quite fluid, no apparent loiterers or other conspicuous types on either side of the street. Proceeding past the meat store, I observed three Volgas parked at the curb, the first being some twenty feet from the lane. The first two were empty and the last had one passenger in the driver's seat."

In his after-action report Jacob wrote that he "noted no suspicious or abnormal factors" and entered the doorway of 5/6 Pushkinskaya, between the meat and vegetable stores.

My mandate was to clear the dead drop unless my own assessment was that I was clearly under surveillance. As I entered the dimly lit area at the foot of the stairs, I observed a middle-aged woman with a shopping bag. Her back [was] turned towards me waiting for a second woman who was coming down the staircase. Having visually located the radiator, I placed my right foot on top of it and tied my shoelace while the two women exited the building. I then turned my full attention to the radiator which was some three feet to the right of the door, with the end almost adjacent to the door itself. I swept my hand behind the radiator, but did not locate the drop at first, probably because I was going too low; I made immediate contact on the second try. I grasped the matchbox firmly in my right hand and lifted the wire hook from the brace with an upward motion of my arm. Clasping the matchbox firmly in my fist, I turned and took one step towards the door. At this moment, four men threw open the door. The first man immediately seized my arm, which I had already inserted into the slit of my raincoat and, ripping my coat down the side, attempted to grasp my fist. By this time I had already released the matchbox and moved back a step so that it could fall to the floor. Within fifteen seconds two men had pinned each of my arms behind me, while a third man, behind me, locked his forearm around my neck and under my chin. The fourth man stood in front, pressing me back against the wall. Each man behaved in a thoroughly professional manner, with no apparent confusion as to who should grasp what limb; nor was there any shouting or talking, excepting several unintelligible monosyllables.

I was immediately moved out of the building and pushed into a light green Volga sedan which was parked at the curb immediately opposite the doorway. It was not one of the cars I had noticed parked on the street. As I was being carried out, I noticed a fifth person who was wearing glasses and appeared to be directing the operation.

Inside the car I was locked between two men with my arms pinned behind me. The third man in the front seat was exerting considerable pressure with one of his hands against my chest, while the fourth man drove. The trip to the militia station was of relatively short duration, about ten to fifteen minutes. At the outset the man to my right said: "The bastard threw it away." Several minutes later the driver appeared to be unfamiliar with the route to the militia station and the other person in the front seat gave him verbal instructions.

When we arrived at the militia station the car drove up on the sidewalk, halting several feet from the main entrance. I was pushed out and the four men escorted me at close quarters to room 225, which we entered through a small office. No explanations were offered for our sudden appearance.

Two men were present and the four custodians delivered what appeared to Jacob to be a perfunctory oral report explaining the intrusion. For the first time Jacob had an opportunity to observe his four escorts carefully. Two were dressed in dark blue padded jackets, the type worn by manual laborers in Moscow. The third man wore a long dark blue overcoat, and the fourth had on a light brown sport coat with an open neck sport shirt. All wore sport caps except the man in the open neck shirt. During this brief ceremony each of Jacob's escorts was addressed as citizen (*grazhdanin*). The matchbox was produced by one of the escorts and they were dismissed.

At this point a third man entered the room. Jacob was ordered to sit in a straight-backed chair with his back to the door of the room. The office had a writing desk, a cabinet in the corner, a small writing table and a low table with a decanter of water and drinking glasses. There were portraits of Brezhnev, Lenin, and Khrushchev on the wall. They were in an office of the Moscow Militia Station.

When addressed, Jacob replied by saying he carried a diplomatic passport and demanded to be put in touch with "my embassy." Another official asked somewhat indifferently, "What embassy?" and Jacob added, "The American Embassy." The KGB surveillance that Penkovsky spotted had been on Janet Chisholm; apparently the KGB had expected a British agent and were surprised to find an American. Jacob, strong-willed and well-trained, refused to say anything other than that he was an American diplomat and that he wanted to contact his embassy.

The translator, a stocky man in his middle forties with regular features, spoke English with an American accent, and asked Jacob if he spoke Russian. "I replied that I spoke English, without specifically denying that I spoke Russian." The third man carried his medium height and soft Slavic features with command bearing. He opened the drop instrument at the small table. As per Penkovsky's original instructions, the drop consisted of a thin wire, hooked at the top. Some five inches below the hook, the wire was wrapped three or four times around a standard Russian matchbox, which in turn was wrapped in white paper with a string of Scotch tape fastened length-wise to the box. The Russian officer, wearing a gray suit and tie, unwrapped the wire from the matchbox and opened the box. He withdrew a tightly folded sheet of paper, about 7 × 10 inches, on which a typewritten text of some twenty to thirty lines was visible from Jacob's chair. With only a few seconds' hesitation, and with no visible indication of surprise, concern, or anxiety, the interrogator proceeded to read the text aloud, but indistinctly.

Jacob recalled that there were three main elements in the message that was read to him: "1, Our friend had not been able to contact us because he was undergoing preparation for a TDY [abbreviation for temporary duty, a trip], 2, He wished to receive a pistol to complement his passport and other documents, and 3, He expected to leave the USSR and wanted us to arrange a warm reception for him." Jacob wondered if a real text was being read to him or if he was being deliberately misled. He calculated that the time consumed in reading the text seemed to conform to his visual appraisal of the length of the message. Also the salutation read aloud was "my dear friends" and the conclusion "your friend" with no apparent evidence from beginning to end about the identity of the author, who sounded like Penkovsky.

Jacob had been briefed on the *in extremis* conditions of an imminent Soviet attack, the only situation that would require Penkovsky to use the dead drop to send his warning. While the letter was being read, Jacob strained "to note any indication that any element of this message might bear upon these conditions." Only the third point, that Penkovsky might leave the U.S.S.R., might have had some relation to the warning, but no mention was made of the specific destination of the trip he was to take.

After the letter had been read (although he was not sure it had been read aloud in its entirety), Jacob was asked in Russian who had written it. Replying through the interpreter, he said he wanted to be put in touch with the American Embassy.

"That will come later," replied the interpreter, expressing annoyance. "In the meantime you had better answer the questions." Jacob then produced his diplomatic identification card and demanded that the embassy be informed of his detention. The Russian asked the name of the American ambassador. Jacob replied that it would merely be necessary to call the embassy.

Jacob had been carefully instructed beforehand that in the event of apprehension he was to say only that he wished to phone the American Embassy. He followed those instructions and refused to speak Russian or acknowledge to his interrogators that he understood Russian. He responded to questions in Russian with a puzzled expression or a shrug of the shoulders. The Russians asked Jacob for his given name since the diplomatic card had only his initials "R. C."

The Russian sitting at the desk began to draw up a statement, which the Russians call an *akt*, describing Jacob's attempt to clear the drop. He worked on this for about an hour and during this period the interrogation was continued by two other men. Jacob refused to give his full name and again requested to phone the embassy. Thereupon, a ridiculous burlesque ensued, during which the interrogator tried to elicit his name, pointing out that the embassy would be contacted sooner if they had this information.

> I pointed out that I was the only "Jacob" in the Embassy and that this represented no obstacle to contact. This scene finally concluded with an observation by the interpreter that I was so ashamed of my dirty work that I didn't want to divulge this information. No reaction. The interpreter then asked me what my age was. When he received a neutral reaction, he responded with a somewhat rhetorical attack upon my vanity: "30, 40 years old?" No reaction. Both questions as to my given name and age were posed many time and in various forms. Occasionally my reaction was neutral, occasionally, I would repeat my demand to be placed in contact with the Embassy. At last the interrogator and the interpreter began to refer to me as an *avtomat* [automaton] and the interrogator delivered a curious peroration on the curious fact that I was behaving in a manner similar to that which we Americans associate with the Soviet system. No reaction.

At this point the interrogator, referring to Jacob's diplomatic card, asked if he were really a secretary-archivist in the embassy. To which the interpreter added, "Secretary-archivist or spy? Shall we put down the latter?" Then the interpreter asked who Jacob's chief was, who had given him the assignment, and how long he had been a spy. Jacob offered no reaction.

The interrogator tried again, asking Jacob how long he had been in Moscow. Jacob repeated his demand to be placed in contact with the embassy.

Several minutes later the interrogator appeared to have finished preparing the *akt*. Two other Soviet officials entered the room and conferred with the interrogator, editing and approving the final text. While they worked, the interpreter and the third member of the team sat in easy chairs at the end of the table and conducted a dialogue, replete with sneers and laughter, to the effect that Jacob's dirty career was now at an end and he would have to enter a "clean" profession, that his superiors would not be happy with the results of his work and that he would have to answer for his mistakes. In any case, American intelligence was very bad. Again, Jacob had no reaction.

At this point the interrogator indicated that the *akt* was finished and the four men who seized Jacob at the dead drop were ushered into the room. The *akt* was read, including the location of the drop behind the radiator, thus indicating that the KGB knew of the drop's location before Jacob cleared it.[31] The interpreter asked Jacob

343

whether he should translate the *akt* into English. The interrogator told him not to bother: "He [Jacob] understands the Russian version." Jacob interjected to say, "I have no intention of signing this *akt* whether you translate it into English or not." Then he added, "I also wish to say at this time that I have never in my life seen the materials that you have there on the desk," referring to the matchbox and the letter it contained. The interrogator shrugged and motioned to the four men who had seized Jacob to sign the paper. The interrogator wrote out what Jacob thought might have been an addendum noting that he refused to sign the *akt*. The four "escorts" then left the room.

The Russian who entered after the *akt* was completed and directed its editing now stood four feet from Jacob, staring at him. His full head of dark, wavy hair was well groomed and he wore a well-cut, dark blue suit. Solidly built, he had sharp but handsome features and appeared to be about fifty. Suddenly it struck Jacob that this was the same man—now without glasses—who had directed his seizure at the dead drop. He continued to stare and Jacob decided to meet his stare. "So I just looked up at him without smiling or any emotion on my face and stared him down. I guess it must have lasted about two minutes and I just decided that if he wanted to look at me I was going to look at him and I was going to make him lower his eyes first and he did after about two minutes. I don't know how I did it because I felt like laughing. I just decided at this point that in any way I could do it without talking that I would try to take a little bit of initiative. Then, he looked at me and said, 'Well your dirty career is finished.' "[32]

The interpreter again demanded Jacob's given name. "Why are you afraid?" he snarled. The wavy-haired official began to mutter in Russian, *trus, trus, trus* (coward) and *absyrdnost* (absurdity). Several exchanges took place between him and the interrogator to the effect that Jacob was young and inexperienced and would have a good deal of explaining to do in Washington. The interrogator told Jacob, "This, I hope, will be your last chance to speak Russian with good Russians." Just then, at about 5:15 P.M., a balding man in a light gray suit entered the room and was introduced as a representative of the Ministry of Foreign Affairs. Immediately, Jacob's guard went up. "I thought this might be just another technique and this might just be one of their boys and they would introduce me to him. They would naturally feel, and it was quite a correct assumption, that as soon as I thought that I was in contact with a Foreign Ministry representative my guard would go down, or at least that I would relax to the point that I might divulge more than I had. So I just assumed he wasn't [from the Foreign Ministry] right off the bat. I told him, 'My name is Jacob and I wish to be placed in contact with the American Embassy immediately.' He turned to the other men, and he seemed to be very uncertain of himself—a little bit frightened by the whole thing. They explained to him that I had engaged in espionage and had been detained. Then he said, 'I will contact your embassy.' "

When he returned to the room five minutes later, at about 5:30, the Foreign Ministry representative said he had called the embassy. For about ten minutes there was no questioning, then the Foreign Ministry man asked Jacob in English if he spoke Russian. Jacob again said he spoke English. The official asked, "Does Mr. Semler [a newly arrived Foreign Service officer at the American Embassy] speak Russian?"

Jacob assumed this would be of operational interest to the Russians and his guard went up. "I thought to myself: here it comes. They are going to try to get something about the people in the embassy out of me. So I simply said, 'I don't know.' " Another ten minutes passed without further questions and then Jacob was offered a cigarette and a glass of water. Jacob declined and asked the Foreign Ministry man to tell him the name of the person with whom he had spoken at the American Embassy. The official replied, "With some girls and the telephone operator." Jacob thought to himself, This guy hasn't called the embassy. He took the initiative and in English asked, "When did you call the embassy? Be specific and tell me, because if somebody from the embassy doesn't arrive here within fifteen minutes of the time you give me I am going to assume that you haven't called the embassy." The Foreign Ministry official was flustered and looked over at the other men. Then he left the room and was gone for two or three minutes. On his return he said, "I have spoken with Mr. Davies, the first secretary. They will be here to pick you up."

The interrogator was annoyed and frustrated with Jacob. He looked harshly at the American and said, "You have behaved very badly. This will be your last opportunity to speak with good Russians. I personally hope that you will not ever again have an opportunity like this. You would be just as well to speak with good Russians. I know you speak Russian." Jacob said nothing. Within fifteen minutes the phone rang and the interrogator answered. "They are coming," he announced. First Secretary Richard Davies and a consular officer arrived to claim Jacob. Davies refused to listen to the charges against Jacob. Firmly, and with anger in his voice, Davies protested to the Foreign Ministry representative the violation of Jacob's diplomatic immunity. Jacob noted that the interrogator "was looking at me with an expression of profound contempt. That was it. We all left."[33]

Jacob did not identify the man in charge of the operation to arrest him, Lieutenant General Oleg Gribanov, the head of the KGB Second Chief Directorate in charge of internal security and counterintelligence. Gribanov was an intense, hyperactive boss who had a reputation for heavy drinking, shrewd plotting, and abusive language to subordinates. He had been on the job for nearly twenty years when Penkovsky was arrested. It was Gribanov who had set up French ambassador Maurice Dejean through a classic entrapment ploy that began in 1955. For that operation Gribanov changed his name to Gorbunov and acquired a "trade wife," a KGB major who had served in Paris. Together they entertained the Dejeans and arranged for the ambassador to be seduced by Lora, a KGB professional. Her KGB officer husband surprised her and Dejean in a compromising position and threatened public court action against the ambassador. At that point Gribanov, as a friend, intervened and promised to keep the affair quiet, thus placing the French ambassador under his control.

Gribanov personally supervised the search and arrest of Penkovsky.* He coordinated the investigation of the case with Lieutenant General Nikolai F. Chistyakov, chief of the investigation department of the KGB.

The following morning, Saturday, November 3, after the Executive Committee met in the White House, DCI John McCone met privately with Kennedy and Rusk to explain the developments in Moscow. McCone reviewed the DISTANT warning procedure for clearing the dead drop "in the event of a sudden development of a dangerous situation." McCone told the president that "when a junior clerk in the embassy serviced the dead drop the clerk was apprehended and interrogated for three hours; interrogation was polite, he was subjected to neither recrimination nor physical violence, and then released." As a result of Jacob's seizure by the KGB, the CIA concluded "that HERO in all probability had been compromised and in an effort to save himself he had exposed this prearranged plan of the transmission of information," McCone told the president.

* In 1963 Gribanov was responsible for the arrest of Yale professor Frederick Barghoorn in Moscow when the Soviets needed an American to exchange for a KGB agent arrested in New York. When told that Barghoorn was the only possible candidate, even though he was not a spy, Gribanov ordered: "Make him a spy." Barghoorn was released on orders of Khrushchev after a public protest from President Kennedy.

Penkovsky had revealed to the KGB the dead-drop location and how to initiate contact, but whether he had told the KGB all the details of the DISTANT warning system was unclear and unknown.

Raymond Garthoff, the CIA and State Department analyst who wrote a study of the Cuban Missile Crisis, said that on October 22, the day the KGB says they arrested Penkovsky, "he had time to send a telephone signal to be used in the ultimate contingency: imminent war. . . . So when he was about to go down, he evidently decided to play Samson and bring the temple down on everyone else as well. Normally such an attempt would have been feckless. But October 22/23, 1962, was not a normal day. Fortunately, his Western Intelligence handlers, at the operational level, after weighing a dilemma of great responsibility, decided not to credit Penkovsky's final signal and suppressed it. Not even the higher reaches of the CIA were informed of Penkovsky's provocative farewell." Penkovsky did not call on October 22. Garthoff has the wrong date. The call was made on November 2, and was clearly a KGB-controlled effort to see who would service the dead drop. Once Jacob was detained it was clear that Penkovsky had been arrested and that the phone call was a provocation. The CIA evaluated it as such and Kennedy was informed by McCone.

In a footnote Garthoff says: "One of the key CIA clandestine service officers responsible for directly managing the Penkovsky case, whom I had come to know well as a reliable person, is my source for this information. He told me in strict confidence soon after the event. In the nature of such things, and given both continuing secrecy pledges and diminishing sources after a quarter of a century, I have not been able to confirm this report, but also not to disconfirm it. I believe it to be true."[34] Garthoff was wrong on all counts from the date (November 2, after the heat of the crisis, not October 22) to McCone's not telling the president.

On Sunday, Jacob was publicly charged with spying and ordered to leave the Soviet Union. McCone wrote in a memorandum for the record: "The situation suspected by the CIA did indeed materialize and we can only conclude that HERO in all probability is completely compromised and this source will be of no further value. And that now we must furthermore most carefully review recent reports (as we have been doing for several months) to be sure that information is not being 'planted' for the purpose of deception and misleading us."[35]

On November 4, Gervaise Cowell, the new MI6 officer, received a call at home from a Russian-speaking man asking him to meet him at the Moscow circus. "It is your friend," said the voice. "I must see you." Cowell did not reply. He knew that Jacob had been detained and that Penkovsky was virtually certain to be under arrest. Cowell informed MI6 in London, which passed the information on to CIA. It was further confirmation that Penkovsky had been compromised, since there was no operational plan to meet at the Moscow circus. The KGB was obviously fishing to find out who in the British Embassy was Penkovsky's contact.

Jacob was declared persona non grata by the Soviet Union. He left Moscow on November 6, 1962. From file photos, he identified the Soviet official who opened the matchbox seized at the dead drop as Vladimir Mikhaylovich Komarov, an alias for his true name, Vladimir Kovshuk, an official in the Second Chief Directorate of the KGB. Kovshuk was active in work against Americans in the Soviet Union since 1950, except for the period from March 1957 to January 1958 when he was first secretary in the Soviet Embassy in Washington. His cover position in Moscow was in the American Department of the Ministry of Foreign Affairs.

In Budapest on November 2, 1962, Greville Wynne hosted a cocktail party for Hungarian officials visiting his traveling exhibition of British industrial goods in Varosliget Park. Wynne was determined to run his custom-made trailer in Eastern Europe during the autumn so that he could prove to Soviet officials in Moscow that he was legitimate and be invited to Moscow again in 1963. Wynne had traveled through Budapest in early October and had arranged to return to Hungary for a self-sponsored showing of his industrial exhibitors after first showing at a British Trade Fair in Bucharest, from October 16 to 25. After Bucharest Wynne went to Vienna and spent three days with his wife before returning to Budapest on October 29.

Wynne's trailer arrived in Hungary without him while he was in Vienna for the weekend with his wife. In Vienna, he called London to ask if it was safe to return to Budapest, since there had been no word from Penkovsky since early September. Wynne claims nobody answered the telephone in London when he called the number given him by MI6.[36] Officials familiar with the case say that Wynne did speak with an officer and was advised not to return behind the Iron Curtain.[37] The reason he returned to Budapest, Wynne later insisted, was that he had expected Penkovsky to come to Hungary and rendezvous with his trailer at a gas station outside the city. Wynne said he planned to place Penkovsky in a secret compartment, under the front seats of the vehicle, and drive across the border into Austria. The compartment, Wynne said, was located under a false battery rack stretching across the front seats of the vehicle. Demonstration batteries camouflaged the hiding place, according to Wynne.[38] No CIA or MI6 case officers, including former Deputy Director for Plans Richard Helms, confirm the existence of a secret hiding place in the trailer. All maintain there were never any plans for one, and there is no mention of the trailer as an escape vehicle in the files or reference to a plan for Penkovsky to meet Wynne in Budapest.[39] There had been no contact with Penkovsky since September 6.

The CIA and MI6 had indeed studied several possibilities to get Penkovsky out of the Soviet Union. They considered documentation for him to pose as a Polish or Hungarian national, to disguise him as a merchant seaman, or to ship him out of Moscow in a wooden cargo box on a diplomatic flight, but none of the plans materialized. Why Wynne would have planned a rendezvous with Penkovsky when Penkovsky's ability to travel abroad had been so frequently withdrawn remains a mystery. Yet Wynne insisted that he had gone to Budapest in hopes of meeting Penkovsky.[40]

The evening light was pale, and Varosliget Park was still when Wynne walked down the steps of the exhibition pavilion with his translator, Ambrus. "I felt a stab of danger. The palms of my hands were wet. And I knew why. Because the Hungarian delegates whom I had been entertaining for the last two hours had suddenly, as if on order, left the party," Wynne would write in his memoirs.[41] At the bottom of the steps Wynne turned to speak to Ambrus, but he had gone.

> I saw him across the driveway. Between him and me four men appeared as if by magic. They were all short and thickset and wore their trilby hats at the same angle. One of them said quietly: "Mr. Veen?" and I said, "Yes, that is my name" and then, with the danger filling me I shouted to Ambrus and he called back, "It's all right, they speak good English," and walked away. If I had run they would have shot me. A sedan had drawn up beside us. It was a Russian-built Moskvich. There was another car by the entrance gates. I was tripped and my arms were seized. The back door of the front car was opened and I was hurled inside. As I fell head first I grabbed the far handle and opened the door and yelled to my driver, Charles. He was standing by the [trailers]. I had been trained that, if and when this thing happened, I must at any cost let someone know. I yelled at the top of my voice and in the second before the door was slammed against my head I saw Charles swing round and wave and start running toward the car. Then I was kicked in the kidneys by heavy feet and something metal hit my temple.[42]

Wynne was taken to a Hungarian prison where he was turned over to KGB officers and flown to Moscow on November 4, 1962, and held in Lubyanka. The Western press announced Wynne's arrest on November 6, 1962.

Wynne's arrest made it apparent to the CIA and MI6 that Penkovsky had been compromised and was most likely under arrest and interrogation, but exactly what had happened to him remained a mystery until December 11, 1962, when the Soviet press announced his arrest and the Soviet version of Penkovsky's spying. In an effort to save Penkovsky and Wynne, the CIA proposed a plan to trade them for Gordon Lonsdale, a.k.a. Konon Molody, the Soviet illegal who had been arrested on January 7, 1961, and was sitting in a British jail serving a twenty-five-year sentence. The British hoped to arrange an exchange of their own with the Russians, trading Wynne for Lonsdale.

Posing as a Canadian businessman, Lonsdale was an illegal who worked with two other illegals, "Peter and Helen Kroger," the alias for two American Soviet spies, Morris and Lorna Cohen; Harry Houghton, a former British Navy enlisted man; and his companion, Miss Ethel Gee. Houghton and Gee worked at the British Navy's underwater weapons establishment and stole classified plans and diagrams of advanced radar and underwater technology for Lonsdale and were tried for espionage and convicted.[43]

The negotiations were to be conducted through Vladimir Y. Semichastny, the chairman of the KGB, and General Ivan Serov, the head of the GRU, but the British were not prepared to alter their traditional policy of always denying involvement in intelligence operations. Sir Dick White approved the MI6 response rejecting the CIA proposal.

The British could not see any reason why the Soviet authorities should be expected to release to the West under any circumstances a Soviet national caught spying against his country and one, moreover, who had confessed his treason. The British warned that to suggest this to the Soviet Intelligence Services and government would invalidate any exchange proposal. The general rule is that spies must be tried first and convicted before they are considered for exchange.

Furthermore, the Foreign Office had denied in the House of Commons any involvement of Wynne in intelligence operations. The American proposal, which also included an option to publicize the sensitive information in the possession of Anglo-American Intelligence Services, would belie the Foreign Office statements. Even if the publicity were focused on Penkovsky, Wynne's role would inevitably become known because too many people knew of the association between the two men, the British argued.

The question of exchanging Gordon Lonsdale for Greville Wynne would involve lengthy negotiations that could not begin until Wynne had been charged and sentenced, said the British. The swap would be negotiated along similar lines to the exchange of U-2 pilot Gary Powers for Soviet spy Rudolph Abel on February 10, 1962. The British argued that a crash approach to the exchange would be fatal. Negotiations, according to them, had to be carried out in a manner allowing both sides to deny involvement. The Russians had not admitted Lonsdale was a spy, and the British would continue to deny that Wynne was one. In this way both sides could negotiate on equal terms, and in due course obtain the release of Wynne.

For the British the operation was no go. MI6 said it had given a lot of thought to operations that might help "our two friends" but they had been unable to decide on one which was feasible.[44]

On Friday, November 16, 1962, at 5:15 P.M. John McCone met alone with John F. Kennedy at the White House to review intelligence matters. Over a scotch and soda, while the president smoked a Cuban cigar, the DCI reported on Greville Wynne's arrest and the steps taken by the CIA to review and appraise Penkovsky's reports for authenticity. None of the material Penkovsky provided appeared to be planted, said McCone.

The Penkovsky operation was over. His career as a soldier of freedom for the West was finished. He was a traitor trapped in the homeland he had betrayed. Little mercy would likely be shown to him. In his biography Sir Maurice Oldfield is quoted as saying Penkovsky had been "the answer to a prayer. What he provided seemed like a miracle, too. That is why for so long he was mistrusted on both sides of the Atlantic. It seemed incredible that he could take such risks—not merely photographing Top Secret documents, but actually giving us the original documents in some instances."[45]

In all, the personal meetings with Penkovsky during his three temporary tours of duty in London and Paris totaled approximately 140 hours and produced some 1200 pages of transcripts. He supplied a total of 111 exposed rolls of film. An astounding 99 percent of these were legible. The film, together with other material he provided in written and oral form, resulted in an estimated 10,000 or more pages of intelligence reports. A CIA summary of Penkovsky's work noted: "He was extremely responsive to the requirements given to him and managed to acquire a considerable amount of information which was not strictly within his need to know. His positive intelligence was consistently highly evaluated, up to and including the last material received from him on August 27, 1962. His counterintelligence production though never formally evaluated in toto, was likewise highly regarded. As of August 1963, the Penkovsky operation was described as the most productive classic clandestine operation ever conducted by CIA or MI6 against the Soviet target."[46] Thirty years later, that judgment still holds.

The Trial

"COURT IS NOW IN SESSION. EVERYBODY RISE," ORDERED THE COURT commandant. Lieutenant General of Justice V. V. Borisoglebsky, the presiding judge in the trial of Oleg Vladimirovich Penkovsky and Greville Maynard Wynne, entered the Court Session Hall of the Military Collegium of the Supreme Court of the U.S.S.R. on Vorovsky Street and sat down. An audience of three hundred carefully selected Soviet citizens and a restricted number of diplomats and journalists then were seated and the trial opened at 10 A.M. on May 7, 1963.

Six months had passed since the KGB had kidnapped Wynne in Hungary and flown him to Moscow. There was no formal word of Penkovsky's arrest, which occurred on October 22, until December 12, when *Pravda* announced that Wynne had confessed and the two would be tried. The Soviets allowed Wynne's wife to see him at Christmastime, which the British regarded as an exceptional privilege.

The same presiding judge had officiated at the trial of Gary Powers in 1960. The Powers trial was held in the Hall of Columns of the Trade Union building and accommodated an audience of 2000, including specially invited guests from the Soviet Union and abroad. This would also be a show trial, but on a smaller scale. There was a greater need to maintain control over the defendants, Penkovsky and Wynne, and make certain they followed the script they had been forced to rehearse.[1]

It took an hour and fifteen minutes to read the full Bill of Indictment, which accused Oleg Vladimirovich Penkovsky of treason and Greville Maynard Wynne of aiding and abetting him.[2] The indictment said that "as a result of moral degradation" Penkovsky had

353

decided to become an agent "of the imperialist intelligence services." It said Penkovsky met with four British and American intelligence officers at the Mount Royal Hotel in London, England, on April 20, 1961. The British officers were named Grille (Harold Shergold) and Mail (Mike Stokes); the Americans, Oslaf (Joe Bulik) and Alexander (George Kisevalter). The names presented at the trial were phonetic approximations of what he thought they had told him. Bulik believes Penkovsky was trying to protect the team; but in any case Penkovsky was never told the real full names of the members of the British and American teams. The indictment said he had three meetings with the intelligence officers. Actually, he had seventeen meetings from April 20 to May 6, 1961, that consumed fifty-two hours and seven minutes. Ironically, despite the extensive surveillance of Penkovsky, the KGB still was in the dark on the full extent of his treason and relied heavily on his confession to create the case against him.

The indictment charged there were five meetings in the second phase, which occurred on Penkovsky's return to England from July 18 to August 7, 1961. Actually there were thirteen meetings, which lasted forty-seven hours and fifteen minutes. At the trial Penkovsky was referred to as a colonel in the reserves. In reality he was still on active duty as an intelligence officer of the General Staff, assigned to the State Committee for the Coordination of Scientific Research Work. To have admitted this would have publicly acknowledged that the State Committee is a cover organization for Soviet State Security and Military Intelligence.

The indictment charged that when Penkovsky was arrested on October 22, the KGB seized his instructions for servicing the dead drops. They had the telephone numbers to be called and the number of the lamp post to be marked. Thus, KGB Counterintelligence had been able to bait the dead drop with the matchbox containing an actual message written by Penkovsky.

The indictment listed Penkovsky's meetings with Janet Chisholm in the Arbat and in the area of Tsvetnoy Boulevard. It noted his meetings with her at diplomatic receptions and his encounters with Rodney Carlson of the American Embassy. The indictment said that on September 5, 1962, at a reception at the American Embassy, Penkovsky again met Carlson. "At that time Penkovsky had on himself four exposed rolls of film with Top Secret materials and one report to the intelligence center, but it was impossible for him to transmit them to Carlson." The indictment included excerpts from a letter Penkovsky had written to "My dear friends!" saying he had received the passport from Carlson. It quoted him: ". . . if I ever go on a trip to the United States or any other place, please arrange a reception at which I can transmit all the preparatory materials since I do not want to have our materials during the flight to you. Thank you very much for the concern shown me. I always feel your presence alongside of me." The film and letter to which the indictment alluded were the materials that Penkovsky had with him when he was arrested.

Penkovsky and Wynne were asked if they understood the charges and how they pleaded.

Penkovsky answered, "Yes. I plead guilty in all respects."

Wynne replied, "Yes. I plead guilty except for certain details about which I shall explain in detail."

The outline of Wynne's defense was clear. He would try to show that he had no knowledge of the spying operations of Penkovsky or the contents of the materials he passed back and forth.

The prosecutor led Penkovsky through a review of his missions and elicited that he had given to Wynne information on Soviet missiles copied from his course at the Dzerzhinsky Academy. Then the prosecutor showed the court the Minox and the code books Penkovsky used.[3]

"What type of information interested the intelligence men?" asked the prosecutor.

Penkovsky stressed in his reply that "Ninety percent of the materials I passed were of an economic nature."

The prosecutor showed the court a photograph of Penkovsky's desk and the articles taken from his hiding place in it.

"Accused Penkovsky, how did you use this hiding place? Did any members of your family know of the existence of this hiding place."

"No, they never saw them. I used this hiding place during the moments when no one was in the apartment. Mother was at work, my wife was walking with the child, and the older daughter was in school, and on Sundays—when they were busy with household matters."

"Was your desk open?"

"The desk's drawer was always locked and I always had the key with me, and no other key worked in that lock."[4]

To minimize his crimes Penkovsky never revealed the true number of meetings or the full extent of the materials he passed to the West. The trial was designed by the Soviet authorities to minimize the damage Penkovsky had done to Soviet military secrets. There was never any specific mention of manuals and operational orders he had copied at the Defense Ministry in the Special Library of Marshal Varentsov, nor of Top Secret and Secret journals of *Military Thought* he had photographed.

Penkovsky appeared confident and gave evidence almost eagerly, according to a British diplomat who observed the trial. He showed no sign of emotion or even awareness of the inevitable outcome for himself. He was self-assured, fluent, and seemed to derive satisfaction from the competence of his performance. He did not give the impression of having been brainwashed or drugged. There was nothing mechanical in his answers.

At the same time, the British diplomat noted that "his mental state was not entirely normal. He appeared to be acting under some kind of stimulus. Perhaps it was no more than the excitement and relief of performing in the limelight after months of intensive and lonely rehearsal. Penkovsky stubbornly resisted the procurator on the question of his motivation. While readily admitting everything else, he denied that he spied for material gain or that he planned to defect. He proclaimed himself a moral degenerate, but showed curious anxiety to deny apparently trivial aspersions on his character. He denied that he accepted presents from Wynne, that he did not sufficiently respect his wife, that he spent most of the night with a woman he met at a nightclub in London. During the opening sessions, at least, he showed no sign of the repentance his counsel ascribed to him."[5] Prosecutor Lieutenant General of Justice A. G. Gorny, in a tired, rasping monotone, asked Penkovsky why the agents did not trust the data he had copied by hand. Gorny was out to discredit Penkovsky personally and to show the court that it was only the documents that Penkovsky stole that were important.

"Later, when I began to supply intelligence abundantly, with materials which I had from the State Committee for the Coordination of Scientific Research, the agents said that I was performing great work and valued it highly," replied Penkovsky. "From this evaluation of theirs, one can say that I did not work in vain." The record indicates there was "a rumble of indignation" in the courtroom.[6]

The prosecutor asked Penkovsky to describe how he passed over films to Janet Chisholm in a box of Drazhe candies in the park off Tsvetnoy Boulevard. The trial record identified her incorrectly as Anna Chisholm, born on May 7, 1929, wife of the second secretary of the embassy, arrived in the U.S.S.R. on July 1, 1960.

Penkovsky recited from the script: "The lozenge-type candies were in a round box. I sat down on the bench where the children were sitting. I patted a child on the cheek, stroked him on the head, and said, 'Here is some candy for you, eat it.' Anna saw everything."

"Thus to camouflage espionage ties, even Anna's children were used?" asked the prosecutor.

"Yes, it appears so," replied Penkovsky.

The Soviet spectators in the courtroom interrupted with "noises of indignation" on hearing his answer.[7]

Then the prosecutor took Penkovsky through an account of his visit to Paris from September 20 to September 27, 1961, where Penkovsky and the team had five meetings that lasted for fourteen hours and fifty-five minutes. (Actually, Penkovsky was in Paris from September 20 through October 14, and had 12 meetings with the team.) Penkovsky was asked if he identified photos of Soviet officials and he said only that he was shown photos of trade representatives, economists, and technicians who were in France. There was no mention that he spent hours identifying GRU and KGB officials from photos provided by the British and Americans. It is unlikely that he confessed to this, and if he had, the Soviet authorities would not have wanted it revealed.

The trial adjourned for lunch at 2 P.M. and resumed again at 4. Asked if he had separate meetings with one of the two intelligence services, Penkovsky said there was one such meeting with the American intelligence officers. "Oslaf and Alexander [Joseph Bulik and George Kisevalter] invited me to their hotel room in the evening after the meeting. I accepted this invitation. A free and unconstrained atmosphere was created. I understood from the talk that the American side regretted having to work with me together with the British."

"Did you promise anything to the Americans or express any desires in regard to separate work with them?"

"No, I did not," replied Penkovsky.

The prosecutor next pressed Penkovsky on ten contacts with Janet Chisholm after his return from Paris. He admitted receiving letters, film, and enciphering notebooks from her.

"Until when did you meet with Anna on the street?"

"Until January 19, 1962."

"Why did you stop these meetings?"

"I considered it unsafe to continue the meetings."

"You mean you feared unmasking?"

"Yes."

The chairman of the court asked, "The accused, Penkovsky: did the idea not occur to you that it was time to give yourself up?"

"There was such an idea, but I did not bring it to its conclusion."

Under questioning Penkovsky told the court that he had transmitted 105 or 106 rolls of Minox film for a total of 5000 frames. Asked how many frames he transmitted through Wynne, Penkovsky explained it was more than half of the total.

The chairman asked, "Did Wynne know that he was receiving films from you?"

"Yes."

The chairman asked Wynne, "Did you know that Penkovsky was giving you exposed films from a Minox camera?"

357

"No, of course not," insisted Wynne.[8]

The prosecutor told the court that Penkovsky had been promised $2000 a month salary in the West.

"What sort of work did they offer you, or more precisely, promise to offer you?"

"Work of an intelligence nature. The specific work was not named."

"Was the department named?"

"Yes, it was. The Central Department [CIA] or in the Pentagon or in the Imperial [British] General Staff, depending on the choice which I could make in the future, of citizenship in England or U.S. citizenship."

"And did they even name a military rank?"

"They knew I am a colonel in the reserves and I was to maintain the rank of colonel in the British or American army."

Penkovsky was then questioned about whether or not he had dressed himself in uniforms of both a British and American colonel and if he was photographed wearing the uniforms. He admitted this was true.

"Which did you like better?" the chairman of the court asked.

"I did not think about which I liked better."[9]

"Did you conduct agreements on the possibility of your defection to the West?"

"It was not quite like that. American and British intelligence officers in Paris said that if my situation became very dangerous, there were many alternatives for moving to the West: a submarine, an airplane, and a land crossing of the border with the aid of various documents. In July, when Greville Wynne arrived in Moscow, he said that my friends were worried about me, that I should not worry, and that they would always help me when necessary."

Penkovsky, however, insisted he had not planned a defection to the West and "undertook nothing toward this. I never thought of abandoning my children and family and defecting alone. . . .

"I want to report to the court that during six months in 1962, I was abroad three times, twice in England and once in France. Three times I could have remained there. The British and American intelligence officers proposed that I remain. However, I rejected their proposal and said that I was returning to the Soviet Union."[10]

"How do you explain the fact that you took the way of crime? What personal qualities in you promoted this?" prompted the prosecutor.

"The meanest qualities," Penkovsky responded. "Moral decay, caused by almost constant daily use of alcoholic beverages, dissatisfaction with my position in the committee: I did not like the work in the foreign department. Plus marks against me about my birth undermined me. In difficult moments I was drawn to alcohol. I lost the road, stumbled at the edge of an abyss, and fell. Vanity, vainglory, dissatisfaction with my work, and love of an easy life led me to the criminal path. There are no grounds for this which would justify my crime to any degree. Morally base qualities and complete corruption—I admit this. Despite the fact that I do not belong to the group of people of a weak character, I could not take myself in hand and turn to my comrades for help. I deceived all my comrades and said that everything was well with me, that everything was excellent. In fact, everything was criminal: in my soul, in my head, and in my actions."

Prosecutor: "I have no [further] questions for Penkovsky."

Penkovsky's defense lawyer, A. K. Apraksin, an unimpressive figure with a weak voice, recounted Penkovsky's exemplary war record and told the court that he had four battle orders and eight medals. In response to his defense attorney's questioning, Penkovsky told the court that he became a regimental commander at twenty-five and a colonel at thirty.

"In answering the questions of the prosecutor, you spoke of marks against your birth. When did these marks appear against you? Have they really accompanied you your entire life or only recently?"

"I believe that they appeared on me in 1960," Penkovsky replied.*[11]

Penkovsky was asked if he had any dissatisfaction with the system or with the Party.

"No. I never had any differences of opinion with the policy of the Party and the government. I never grumbled. I was once an active fighter for the Party and the government, and struggled as a Soviet person. Sixty witnesses, including drinking buddies, have testified that they never heard me express dissatisfaction."

"And when did you acquire drinking buddies?" his defense attorney asked.

"When I decided to engage in criminal activity, that's when I began to drink."

Penkovsky and Wynne sat in formal wooden prisoner boxes on the side of the stuffy, crowded court. The judge sat in the center. The defendants rose when addressed and answered questions into a microphone

Wynne's defense attorney, N. K. Borovik, a heavily built man with thick white hair, presented a strong presence with his resonant,

---

* The "marks" Penkovsky was referring to was the apparent discovery of his father's records in the White Army.

fruity voice, when he cross-examined Penkovsky to help Wynne. The British diplomat who attended the trial found Borovik almost cloyingly affable but from the legal point of view the best performer of all the lawyers. Borovik worked hard to establish that Wynne was only a go-between for Penkovsky and knew none of the details of Penkovsky's meetings with foreign intelligence agents.

"Yes," agreed Penkovsky. "He was not told about all details. Later work showed that it was necessary to let him know about many details, and I told him, but altogether Wynne knows little about the character of the work in its full scope." Penkovsky was also trying to help Wynne. The first day of the trial ended early in the evening.

When the trial resumed at 10 A.M. on May 8, Wynne was questioned about delivering a package from Penkovsky to an Englishman at apartment 48 at house number 12/34 Sadovo-Samotechnaya in Moscow. Wynne made the delivery (to Ruari Chisholm's apartment) and was handed a package by Chisholm with written instructions: "Give this to your friend." The entire operation took two minutes.

"Everything happened silently?" the prosecutor asked.

"Yes, it was a silent scene. And why it was so I learned later," said Wynne.

"And why was it so?"

"I was told that there was a Russian girl living in this apartment in the next room, who was working for them as a nurse, and that this Russian girl had been seen in restaurants in the company of Soviet men in civilian clothes and that it was essential at this stage as few people as possible knew of the negotiations between Penkovsky and these persons, because otherwise the information on negotiations might be published in the press before the matter became official."

"I understand, at the time when you and the Englishman exchanged packages, there was no representative of the press in the apartment and it was unlikely that your conversations might get into the press," challenged the prosecutor.

"I must also say—I had been told that in the apartments occupied by diplomats in Moscow there are very often microphones for listening in," said Wynne boldly.[12]

The prosecutor was startled and angry with Wynne for departing from the prepared script. He paused, looking as if he had something unpleasant in mind, and Wynne, for an awful moment, wondered, he later recalled, whether he had gone too far and whether this would be the end of the hearing in open court. Then the presiding judge made a movement with his hand and shifted to a new line of questioning.[13]

Wynne pressed his defense that initially he did not know he was working for British Intelligence. It was when his contacts with Penkovsky increased that he began to have serious suspicions. "My statement now may sound naive to the professionals, but I am a businessman, a trader, and I did not know the methods of work of intelligence services. Now I understand them."

Wynne's remarks evoked laughter in the courtroom.[14]

"Tell me, defendant Wynne, how would you evaluate the behavior of an Englishman, working for the government, who, outside of his country's official channels, would be in secret communications with representatives of another state?"

"It all depends on what it is about. If it is a question of state secrets I would not touch this low, dirty affair for any price. But if it is a matter of business intrigues, commercial maneuvers, all kinds of business deals, I have been busy with them all my life."

"In short, we may understand you to say that your countrymen have deceived you?"

"Exactly so," replied Wynne. "It is exactly because of that that I am here now."

Again, the audience burst into laughter.

Wynne was asked to tell the court the places of entertainment he visited in London with Penkovsky.

"Two nightclubs and several restaurants."

"Were there meetings with women in London?"

"I have my own wife in London and I didn't have meetings with any other women."

"And did Penkovsky, with your help, have meetings with women?"

"No, no, I am not this kind of agent."

"I shall remind you that at the preliminary investigation you spoke of this more exactly. You testified that Penkovsky met at one of the clubs a woman and spent most of the night with her at her apartment?"

"This was not a decent woman," said Wynne.[15]

"How do you evaluate all your criminal action against the Soviet Union?" the prosecutor asked, changing the subject.

This was Wynne's cue. Both Wynne and Penkovsky were expected to follow a prepared script. The script called for Wynne to say: "I am sorry and bitterly repent my actions and the crimes I committed because I have always found in the Soviet Union only friendship and hospitality and peaceful coexistence."[16] He took a short breath and coughed into the microphone so he could tell if it was working properly. Then he said clearly: "I never had the intention of coming to the Soviet Union in order to abuse the welcome given me by the Ministry of Foreign Trade of the U.S.S.R."[17]

The prosecutor was furious and told Wynne: "Yes, but life showed otherwise. The trial process has shown that you committed great crimes against the Soviet Union. How do you feel about your actions?"

"I am fully in accord with the statement of the prosecutor. It is correct."

"What is correct?" insisted prosecutor A. G. Gorny. Even when annoyed, Gorny rarely raised his voice, showed no emotion, and did not attempt to arouse any.

"I agree that this is a dirty business, and if I had known from the very start that it was what it was, I would never have started in it. I do not believe that espionage is justifiable in peacetime, on either side."

"We are talking here about espionage on your part. How do you feel about your actions?" insisted the prosecutor.

"As concerns me personally, I did not want to become involved in it. I had no special preparation. It is true, I have learned a good deal about it in the past six months, and I don't like it."

Laughter from the audience greeted Wynne's reply.[18]

The court called on Wynne's defense lawyer, who led his client through a history of his wartime service against the Germans to gain sympathy for Wynne for fighting against the common enemy. Borovik said Wynne had taken part in paratrooper operations when the second front was opened in Normandy; that he was wounded in Belgium and awarded two medals. Borovik created this legend to gain leniency for Wynne, who claimed later in his biography that he served as an investigator for Internal British Military Security during World War II and did not see battle overseas.[19]

Borovik read Wynne's testimony from the preliminary investigation and asked him if it was correct: "I was very afraid that English Intelligence would pick up the phone and report about me to the proper places. I was afraid my business would collapse."

"Yes," replied Wynne, "that is correct, yet I would like to clarify one point here. At the time I had no solid proof of the nature of the affair. I did have definite suspicions, but I repeat, I had no concrete proof. That was my weakness in the battle with them."

At the end of the session Wynne was taken to what he called the "red cell," where he was visited by his "detested enemy," a KGB lieutenant colonel who stormed in with an interpreter and two guards. The KGB officer was furious. "How dare you disobey orders? Do you hope to escape punishment?" Wynne was raved at and screamed at and called every kind of criminal. He was reminded of all his stubbornness during interrogation and told that the only result of his folly would be to increase his sentence. He was threatened with dark unnamed punishments after the sentence. "Up to now we have been very patient," shouted the lieutenant colonel. "We have merely questioned you. But now you are going to be punished. You will see what happens to you, you will see!"[20] Then Wynne returned to the Lubyanka.

The third day of the trial, held in closed session, was for Wynne "not so much an anticlimax as an almost complete blank." Only the officials were present in the court. There were no press or representatives of the workers. Wynne could not follow the Russian testimony and was soon taken from the courtroom. In his cell Wynne wondered if his absence would damage his case. "I know that it will not, because I am sufficiently damaged as it is, but I cannot help wondering," he wrote in his account of the trial.[21]

In the official transcript the record says only that "at a closed session the Military Collegium considered problems relating to the nature and content of the information transmitted by the defendants to the British and American Intelligence." At no time in the open trial were any of Penkovsky's high-level contacts, such as Marshal Varentsov and GRU chief Serov, named.

There was still another day of testimony ahead; the character witnesses and expert witnesses had to be heard.

The first to be called was Igor Pavlovich Rudovsky, who drove Penkovsky to pick up Wynne at the airport on July 2, 1962.

Presiding Judge Borisoglebsky directed Rudovsky to tell the court where and when he met Penkovsky.

"Sometimes we just walked around the streets and ate in a restaurant or café after the working day. I and my friends had no conversations with him of an anti-Soviet nature. I introduced Penkovsky to Galina, a friend of my girlfriend. A great affection sprang up between them. Penkovsky was carried away with her. They met often; she did not know either his home or office telephone and my own telephone was the connecting link between them."

The judge: "Telephone switchboard?"

"Yes," explained Rudovsky. "Galya [Galina's nickname] called me and asked me to call Penkovsky and he called me and asked me to tell Galya when he would meet her. This happened three or four times. Galya worked near the Baku Restaurant and in the dining room Penkovsky asked me several times to meet Galya and bring her to the restaurant. It was not convenient for him to do so: he was married and I was divorced. At dinnertime I met Galya and entered with her into the dining room where Penkovsky was already at a table. Because this was the dinner hour we did not have any drinks. After dinner I drove Galya back to work.

"After a football [soccer] game we went to a restaurant and there was Penkovsky seated with a girl; I do not know her name. He said she was the secretary of the chief of the administration or department where he worked. He soon left with her. I know nothing about their relations. That is all I have to say on the matter of women."

There was laughter in the courtroom when Rudovsky finished.

"And Penkovsky never gave you anything personally?"

"A few things—a wallet, wristwatch strap, cigarette lighter, a key ring, and a bottle of toilet water."

"Can you tell the court about Penkovsky's range of interests?" the judge asked, seeking examples of the defendant's weak character.

"I observed nothing strange about his behavior. During our meetings he did not talk of anything except everyday matters and food. He showed no interest in literature, music, or art."

"What did you talk about at your gatherings?"

"Penkovsky liked most to talk about the flavor of roast meat, the importance of meat for health and things like that."

"May we conclude that he was interested only in eating and drinking and women?"

"I will say that he was respected by us for his important, responsible work, that he had relations with foreigners and so could speak to us about many things. We thought it was just willy-nilly that all his conversations got down to cooking and everyday matters."[22]

Penkovsky's defense attorney, Apraksin, was given a chance to cross-examine Rudovsky, but his questions only strengthened the case against Penkovsky.

Asked if he took money for driving Penkovsky, the witness Rudovsky replied: "Yes, I took money from him twice: the first time was one hundred rubles, the second time fifty rubles."

"Did you return this money to him?"

"Yes, through an investigator of the State Committee on Security."

"They understood your relations very well!" said Counsel Apraksin.[23]

Vladimir Yakovlevich Finkelshteyn was then summoned to the witness stand. Finkelshteyn told the court he had no quarrels of any kind with Penkovsky. Finkelshteyn, a fifty-year-old Jew from Penkovsky's hometown, said he had known Penkovsky for a little more than ten years. They had met through friends, and Finkelshteyn described how he joined Penkovsky after work and listened to Penkovsky's impression of life abroad. "Right up to the stunning moment when I read in the paper about Penkovsky, I considered him a man of authority carrying on necessary and useful work; however, I should tell the court that I noted in Penkovsky some traits of duplicity. On the one hand, he was an official who traveled abroad to various countries, on the other hand, he had many negative traits—vanity, arrogance, self-love, which he did not conceal; he was always agitated, always impatient, but also collected. In short, he seemed in an unnatural state and did not feel free as the rest of us did.

"We met Penkovsky at different times, often at football [soccer] games. We watched sporting events, went to the movie theater, dined in restaurants and sat in cafés. I am not a drinking man, or rather I drink very little, and I did not see that Penkovsky drank a lot. I would say that in our company he did not drink more than a hundred grams of strong drinks and then switched to dry wines. We still smile about him. His whole life was ruled by the clock; he was always hurrying off somewhere. Returning from abroad, Penkovsky brought souvenirs: lighters, watchfobs, and other small items which he generously distributed among his acquaintances."

Finkelshteyn insisted that his relationship with Penkovsky was not a friendship but rather that Penkovsky "was an interesting talker. Last year when he returned from England and France he gave his impressions of those countries. Since I worked in the art field, he talked about museums and architecture, that is, the sights of those countries.

"He reacted strongly to those who did not agree with him. He was punctilious in small things, very obstinate. He loved to pose, there was much of the histrionic about him. He seemed very demonstrative, but we felt and knew that he was not so actually."[24]

Penkovsky paid for dinners because he had more money than the others, explained Finkelshteyn, who painted a portrait of Penkovsky as a man not attracted to the theater or books. "He was a man whose interests were mainly concentrated on his work about which I, to speak honestly, know very little. I explained everything by the extreme pressures of his work. Yes, he always showed himself a gourmet. He loved to try new dishes, loved things that looked well. I got the impression he was training himself in some high-life style."[25]

"Was Penkovsky interested in politics?"

"Very little. At least at meetings with me he never talked about political matters. He even avoided them. If the conversation got onto public or political matters, he tried to change it to everyday matters."

The questioning was all directed toward showing the weakness of Penkovsky's character and that his motivation was not political. The prosecutor then instructed Finkelshteyn: "Tell me, witness, about the evening in the restaurant in which wine was drunk from a woman's slipper instead of glasses."

"This happened at the Poplavok Restaurant. A group of us, including two women, eight in all, met there. One of the women was

Galya, whom Penkovsky was attracted to, and the other was the wife of one of our acquaintances. We sat down, ate and drank. We drank a lot. Somebody said that out of respect for a woman we should drink from her slipper. We approved of this, laughing, and Penkovsky actually drank wine from Galya's slipper. Everyone present laughed."

"The slipper was taken from her foot?" asked the judge.

"It was."[26]

Penkovsky told the court, "Witness Finkelshteyn has described correctly and in detail the nature of our relations. With respect to presents . . . these little trinkets should not be considered presents. They were souvenirs which I myself received from foreigners and passed on to my acquaintances. I worked, for example, with a Japanese delegation of sixty persons and each of them considered himself obligated to give me a souvenir, with the result that I accumulated a stock of twenty pairs of handkerchiefs which I presented to my comrades."

The judge asked Penkovsky if he agreed with the witnesses that his "spiritual interests were limited."

"When I met with Finkelshteyn and the others we were just out for a good time," replied Penkovsky.

Wynne's defense attorney, Borovik, made a final effort on his client's behalf and asked him before the court if he had "received any money payments from British intelligence officers?"

"No, sir," replied Wynne. "Except for payments of expenses in Paris, I have never received anything and nothing has been promised to me."

Wynne explained that he had been reimbursed only for expenses. "I received no material reward; on the contrary, I paid all kinds of minor expenses out of my own pocket, or to be more accurate, my firm paid them."

Actually, Wynne had been paid bonuses of 10,000 pounds by the British and Americans after the first round of meetings with Penkovsky and 5000 pounds in 1962, but it was true that he was not on a regular salary. Wynne received a total of $213,700 in resettlement allowances shared jointly between SIS and the CIA after he was released from prison in the Soviet Union.[27]

The first part of prosecutor Gorny's summary was an indictment of American and British intelligence organizations. A summary of his speech appeared in the afternoon edition of *Izvestia*, while he was delivering it.

Gorny told the court: "The 'secret war' against our state was begun by imperialist intelligence services immediately after the victory of Great October [1917 Bolshevik Revolution] and has never ceased; on the contrary, it has become more active and has expanded and in a number of imperialist states has been raised to the level of state policy.

"A leading role in this belongs to the Central Intelligence Agency of the U.S.—with the support of the most adventurist circles in the U.S. Like a giant octopus it extends its tentacles into all corners of the earth, supports a tremendous number of spies and secret informants, continually organizes plots and murders, provocations, and diversions. Modern techniques are put to the service of espionage: from the miniature Minox cameras which you see before you up to space satellites, 'spies in the sky.'

"The British Intelligence Service, which has been in existence for about 300 years, is no less insidious and astute in its methods, but it attempts to remain in the background. The activities of these major espionage centers against the U.S.S.R. are connected and closely coordinated, as can be clearly seen in the present case, but this does not reduce the contradictions between them or their struggles against each other."

Gorny quoted from a January 26, 1960, speech of Allen Dulles to the Aeronautical Institute: "Our main task now," said Dulles, "is to determine the position of the Soviet Union in rocket technique and in other military fields, and what it will be in the immediate future."

Dulles, said Gorny, "complained bitterly about the monolithic nature of Soviet society and the high vigilance of our people, saying that 'in the military field the Russians are attempting today to maintain an impenetrable cloak of secrecy.' "

Penkovsky and Wynne, Gorny charged, were attempting "to penetrate the impenetrable curtain which Dulles complains of. It is not only professional intelligence officers with diplomatic passports who engage in espionage. Into this dirty business are drawn members of various delegations, scholars, commercial travelers, students, tourists, and this of course does not promote good faith among nations or the development of scientific and cultural cooperation and international trade.

"Imperialist propaganda attempts by every means to incite backward views and opinions among the Soviet people, survivals of the past—individualism, a fast-living attitude toward life, private property, psychology, raising hopes for ideological diversions in order to use the results for political diversions, one of the forms of which is espionage."[28]

Gorny tried to spread dissension between the CIA and the SIS by telling the court, "In Paris, the American intelligence officers evidently decided to 'cuckold' their British partners and to arrange

367

a meeting with Penkovsky unbeknownst to the latter." In summing up, Gorny told the court, "The question inevitably arises: how can it be that a man like Penkovsky, who was born, was brought up, and received his education during the years of Soviet power, within our society, could so completely lose the moral qualities of a Soviet man, lose his shame, conscience, and elementary feelings of duty and end up by committing such a serious crime?"

To a certain degree, Gorny continued, Penkovsky's depiction of himself in his testimony was true, "but it ought to be depicted in plainer colors in order to approximate the original. . . . The exceptional careerism, egoism, and ambition of Penkovsky manifested themselves long ago. He sought constantly to mingle with people of authority and influence, to please and to fawn upon them and to glory in his closeness to them.

"No matter how Penkovsky was able to camouflage his thoughts and real aims, he was never able to conceal them completely. In a character reference filled out on him back in 1955–1956, it was stated that he was 'a vindictive and a malicious person, an unparalled careerist capable of any trick for the sake of that career.' How precisely and how correctly that was put! But unfortunately his officiousness and toadying achieved what he wanted, and this damning statement was pigeonholed.

"Of course, such degenerates and renegades as Penkovsky, who evoke a feeling of indignation and loathing in all Soviet people, are a passing phenomenon in our society. But this example shows clearly what danger is hidden in the vestiges of the past, vestiges resurrected by an ideology which is inimical to us, and what they might develop into if we do not take notice of them in time and decisively uproot them.

"Nor must we be allowed to be distracted from the fact that imperialism, doomed to defeat, in its savage hatred of the new Communist society which is advancing to replace it, is placing a great deal of hope on inculcating its corrupt morality into the minds of certain unstable people. That is why we need to be constantly vigilant, need to concentrate, and need to be aggressive in the struggle to ingrain into our people the principles of the moral code of a builder of Communism!" The prosecutor was summing up the purpose of the show trial: to extol the virtues of Communism and condemn Penkovsky and the West. Penkovsky's "degeneracy" was the reason behind his crimes, committed in the ideal socialist state. There were no mitigating circumstances or compelling motivations such as fear of nuclear war or disillusionment with the corruption of Communism.

In recommending sentences to the court, the prosecutor asked that Wynne be sentenced to ten years' imprisonment and demanded that Penkovsky be sentenced to death. "There is no place on earth for this traitor and spy who sold out his Motherland."

Penkovsky's defense attorney repeatedly denied that his client was dissatisfied with the Soviet government and its authority, "which brought him up and raised him," and insisted that he was not politically motivated.

Rather, he argued, Penkovsky's head was turned by success and his providing of favors for friends and ingratiating himself with others "changed Penkovsky into a Philistine. But a Philistine with great possibilities, a man for whom personal career, gay times, and personal benefit were placed higher than the interests of society, higher than the well-being of his friends and relatives."

Penkovsky's decision to turn against the Soviet state because his father's past blocked his career was never acknowledged, but instead was characterized as a "petty, unprincipled grudge against his immediate superiors, who, in his opinion, were blocking his career—his career meant everything to him. Forgetting about the interests of his Motherland, interests which had guided his actions during the Great Patriotic War, he became a traitor."

The defense attorney quoted the testimony of Penkovsky's wife at the preliminary investigation: "Over the past year, in general, he became nervous and suspicious. By his very nature, Penkovsky was vain, touchy, and inclined toward adventures. The negative features in his character had been developing over the course of his entire life."[29]

"This all happened," insisted Apraksin, "because certain people think that a Philistine and Philistinism are inoffensive phenomena during a time in which our nation is moving forward toward Communism, that they are phenomena which concern only personal relationships. These people think that there is no harm in the fact that he is removed from the collective, that he is living in his own little world, that he is narrow-minded and conservative in his viewpoint, and that he is vulgar.

"A Philistine is a vestige which is very dangerous and very harmful . . . unfortunately, this truism was forgotten by many of the friends, comrades, relatives, and former superiors of Penkovsky.

"The Philistine betrays and marks for oblivion the basic principle of our Communist morality—devotion to our socialist Motherland. To live in our society and not be guided by this fundamental principle which determines all human actions means to vegetate, means to be a Philistine."

This idea of Penkovsky's fall from grace, straying from the model of the New Soviet Man, was typical of the thinking of the 1960s. It arose from Khrushchev's frequent assertions of belief in the moral superiority of Communism. The truths of Marxism-Leninism were supposed to motivate and sustain men. Independent thinking and ambition were traits to be avoided by the New Soviet Man, whose life was devoted to bettering the collective society. All strength and loyalty were derived from the collective. Any blood tie to the aristocratic elite of the tsarist past made a Soviet citizen suspect if he were being considered for a position of responsibility. In the intelligence services, an aristocratic or gentry family past of serving in the White Army was a mark for unequivocal rejection, no matter how honorably one had served in the war or on the job: there might be an inherited tendency toward luxurious living and individualism. If his father were still alive outside the Soviet Union, Penkovsky might try to contact him and join the White Russian cause against the Soviet régime. With a White Russian father from the gentry class, he was by his very nature not trustworthy, unfit to be a General Staff intelligence officer who could serve abroad.

As for his "moral degradation," Penkovsky's behavior pattern was more that of a good spy than a Philistine. He was covering his tracks by womanizing and hard drinking, making it appear that those were his primary interests in life, not spying.

Similarly, in cultivating Greville Wynne, Penkovsky stressed to his superiors that he was recruiting "a trusted person" who was under development as a Soviet source. This aspect of his deception of the Russian Intelligence Services was never revealed at the trial because it would have severely embarrassed both the KGB and GRU.[30] Penkovsky's strategy appeared to be that by confessing and cooperating with the KGB, he might avoid the death sentence. In the closed morning session of the court on May 11, 1963, Penkovsky was given the final opportunity to plead for his life and repent. This he did, with a firm voice and dignity, but without success.[31]

That afternoon at 4:05 the court announced the sentences. Penkovsky was judged "guilty of treason to the Motherland." He was sentenced to be shot to death. He was deprived of his rank of colonel and stripped of his orders and medals. All of his personal property was confiscated. Wynne was sentenced to eight years' deprivation of liberty, the first three years to be served in prison and the next five to be served in a harsh-regime correctional labor camp. The sentence could not be appealed to a higher court, but Penkovsky was granted the right to a final appeal to the Presidium of the Supreme Soviet with a petition of mercy. Wynne, convicted of a lesser crime, had the right to appeal for a mitigation of his sentence.

In a separate decision the court named the employees of the American and British embassies in Moscow who aided Penkovsky and asked that they be declared personae non gratae by the Ministry of Foreign Affairs.[32]

Joe Bulik and George Kisevalter were deeply distressed over Penkovsky's death sentence. On May 10, 1963, Bulik, chief of the Soviet Division branch dealing with operations inside the U.S.S.R., proposed a plan "to grasp whatever slim opportunity there may be to save Penkovsky's life."[33] Bulik had given a similar proposal to Howard Osborne, chief of the Soviet Division, and to James Angleton, chief of Counterintelligence, in November of 1962 after Penkovsky's arrest. It recommended that the KGB and GRU be contacted to open negotiations to save Penkovsky. Osborne never sent the suggestion forward within the Agency and it languished in Bulik's safe. Angleton, however, who had his own channel to the British, passed Bulik's idea to MI6 for consideration. The British quickly rejected it.

Angleton never told Bulik that the British had turned down his suggestion. "The reason given to me by James Angleton was that we do not communicate with an enemy intelligence service. That's a bunch of baloney. Of course you do. There are no rules of protocol in these matters," insisted Bulik, "but I was overruled."[34]

When Bulik raised the idea for a second time in May, he suggested the approach to save Penkovsky be made without the British. He went directly to Osborne, his superior, instead of to Angleton, who had his own separate counterintelligence channels to the British. Bulik argued that his plan would if nothing else counter the charge made publicly by *Pravda* commentator Yuri Zhukov that "CIA does not give a hoot about the fate of their agents. All the promises they made to Penkovsky . . . have been broken. The spy is caught and he is written off the books."

Since Zhukov's attack was directed against the CIA, Bulik urged the operation be undertaken without the British. "In no way," argued Bulik, "does the plan envisage the problem of Wynne and Lonsdale," referring to the possible exchange of the two men, which the British hoped to negotiate after Wynne's conviction.

Bulik and Kisevalter, who signed the memorandum, proposed the CIA contact the KGB and GRU station chiefs in West Germany, the Netherlands, Italy, and Denmark. The letter they proposed the CIA send said:

As regards Oleg Penkovsky, we are concerned that your government may take such action that would deprive him of his life or future freedom. This proposition may come as something of a surprise to you, and you may at first glance consider it outrageous and impossible. However, we feel it our duty to take whatever steps and actions may be necessary to protect the life and freedom of Oleg Penkovsky. We have a tremendous obligation to this brave man.

We fully understand why the death sentence must be passed on Oleg Penkovsky by your court. We do urge that you give the fullest possible consideration to keeping Oleg Penkovsky alive until a *mutually* satisfactory arrangement is worked out between us. All of this can be done quietly, without public knowledge.

Should you not concur to this proposal, you must be aware that certain courses of action are open to us which could cause the deepest embarrassment to your Government, to the KGB. Even Penkovsky himself did not understand the full import of certain contacts and documents which are of the greatest value to us. They include matters not unrelated to considerations deeply affecting the leadership of the Soviet Government and the leadership of the KGB. As you and we both know, it is impossible to fully assess damage, whether on Penkovsky's case or other cases.

We frankly desire to pay the price for this unfortunate incident involving this brave man and are willing to consider those situations in which you may be willing to pay a price.

We should like to maintain communication with you or other authorized representatives and suggest you communicate your response by mailing it to P.O. Box [number] New York, N.Y. While recognizing that this matter is highly complicated, we would nonetheless appreciate at least an interim reply by June 1, 1963. If there is no reply, we will take it as your refusal and will proceed with our own plans.

A picture of Colonel Penkovsky with Marshal Sergei Sergeyevich Varentsov, Chief of Artillery, was to be included with the letter. Bulik argued that, if nothing else, the approach would serve as a counter to the Soviet charge that the CIA did nothing to save its agents. If the Soviet Union refused to respond, Bulik recommended, "We carry out our threat by appropriate publication in appropriate places of certain materials which Penkovsky gave us relating to Soviet espionage abroad and to Soviet subversive planning and warlike views of the Soviet government. There is much CA [covert action] grist which can and should be pulled out and exploited by the West."[35] Bulik envisioned a major campaign against the Soviet Union revealing Penkovsky's links with high senior officials, and selected leaking of materials he had provided.[36]

President Kennedy, unaware of Bulik's proposal buried inside the CIA, was curious about how Penkovsky, whose information had been so enlightening to him, had been caught. He sent a handwritten note to CIA director McCone, asking him what had happened. The Soviet Division prepared a response to the president's request. On May 15, 1963, McCone saw the president alone and left a copy of the memo, "The Compromise of Oleg V. Penkovsky," with him. President Kennedy was told: "The Agency does not at this time have any factual information which would reveal how or when Oleg V. Penkovsky was compromised to the Soviet Security Service (KGB) as an agent of the American and British Intelligence Services."

Having studied and evaluated the operation and the trial of Penkovsky and Wynne, the Agency said: ". . . our best speculation is that Penkovsky's compromise was due to a combination of circumstances, including the ever present possibility of a Soviet penetration of either the British or American official governmental circles."

Among the pertinent factors leading to this speculation, said the memo, was that "the Penkovsky operation was run on a fully joint basis with the British Secret Service (MI6). This alone from purely physical reasons multiplied the number of possible security leaks."

On May 17, 1963, *Pravda*, under the headline SENTENCE IS EXECUTED, wrote: "The Presidium of the Supreme Soviet of the USSR has rejected a petition for mercy submitted by O. V. Penkovsky, who was sentenced by the Military Board of the Supreme Court of the U.S.S.R. to be shot for treason to the Motherland. The sentence has been executed."

Bulik never received an answer or an explanation to his memorandum urging direct negotiations to save Penkovsky; it was returned to him on May 23 by Soviet Division chief Howard Osborne, without comment. Nobody had signed off on the memo. "There was no way to do that," said Richard Helms. In the intensity of the Cold War the CIA could not bring itself to negotiate for the life of a Soviet spy, no matter how valuable, and relations between the White House and the Kremlin were too strained to cut a deal to save Oleg Penkovsky.[37]

Aftermath

PENKOVSKY'S EXPOSURE, TRIAL, AND EXECUTION HAD NOT AFFECTED
the West's ability to further exploit the vast amount of information
he had supplied. No longer was there a fear of exposing him, but
there still remained the need to keep the KGB from knowing exactly
what materials, and in what quantities, the British and Americans
had received. It was the classic intelligence dilemma. The spy was
dead, but his take, some officials argued, should not be trumpeted;
it would be better utilized if kept secret. That way the opposition
team would not know what had been stolen and could not compensate for the advantage Penkovsky had gained for the West. If an
adversary knows he has been exposed, he may change his strategy
or devise countermeasures.

There is always a tendency inside government to hoard knowledge
in the belief that power lies in the hands of the holder of secrets.
The range of subjects and the depth of what Penkovsky delivered
were too important to let them molder in classified files. Following
the Berlin and Cuban crises, the Penkovsky archive offered continuing and valid proof of Soviet intelligence activities and internal military debates. It provided rich examples of privileged life within the
Soviet military elite, the military's dissatisfaction with Khrushchev,
GRU intelligence techniques and their objectives vis-à-vis the
United States.

Integrating Penkovsky's reporting and documents into the intelligence community bureaucracy was a difficult and delicate matter.
The operational demands of secrecy by the CIA's covert Soviet Division, and the anonymous grading system for intelligence sources,
often caused consumers to be suspicious of the Agency's materials.
Since there was no way to know who the source was, how could the

information be checked? What were the source's biases? Was his information real or planted? By the time information arrived it was often overtaken by events. Winning acceptance for Penkovsky and his materials had not been an easy task.

Penkovsky's documentary material, copied with the Minox, had proven to be unimpeachable. Here was the real stuff with no qualifications. The classified documents from the Ministry of Defense left no doubt of their authenticity and relevance. The CIA made a major effort to downgrade the security classification of materials Penkovsky had provided so that they would be more widely available within the U.S. government and to foreign allies. Many of the documents revealed Soviet intelligence efforts within NATO. Manuals on Soviet battle organization and tactics and the articles on nuclear strategy and chemical warfare in *Military Thought* were important for training of American military officers.

The Agency and SIS issued a flood of reports based on the photographed copies of *Military Thought*. Their security classification was downgraded from Top Secret to Secret, thus broadening the number of people who could read them. The production of new reports based on Penkovsky's materials continued well into 1965.

There was an internal debate within the Agency over which reports to release to the Allies; the concern was that the raw intelligence data should not be released because it might be misinterpreted. In an effort to prevent the KGB and GRU from knowing just how successfully Penkovsky had photographed documents, the CIA decided not to provide the original Russian-language documents. Instead they would declassify translations and reports based on Penkovsky's materials. The argument, first presented in April 1963, continued into 1965, when the Agency decided to make the Secret and Top Secret *Military Thought* available to NATO allies. The *Military Thought* series obtained by Penkovsky remain classified to this day, despite a lawsuit by the late Congressman John M. Ashbrook (R–Ill.) and J. F. and Phyllis Schafly in 1972 to have them declassified under the Freedom of Information Act. Ashbrook, a conservative Republican, challenged President Nixon for the Republican presidential nomination in 1972. In the suit against Defense Secretary Melvin R. Laird, Ashbrook and the Schaflys argued that the Special Collection of Articles "includes plans for a surprise attack against the United States" and that they "be revealed to the American Congress and to the American people so that efforts to provide the United States with proper defense expenditures and weapons will be fully supported."

The Defense Department argued that the Special Collection contained material of the highest classification, much of which was still extremely relevant to current Soviet strategic doctrine and war plans. In a letter to Ashbrook on February 1, 1972, then Deputy Assistant Secretary of Defense Lawrence S. Eagleburger wrote: "When arrested by the Soviets Colonel Penkovsky himself could not remember which documents he had passed to the West. Therefore, in all likelihood, the Soviets still are studying intensively the question of which of their secrets Penkovsky has compromised. We believe it would not be in the national interest to assist them in this undertaking by declassifying the papers, since the knowledge of which secrets had been compromised would enable the Soviets to take countermeasures to the disadvantage of U.S. security interests." The United States District Court for the Southern District of Illinois upheld the Defense Department on July 17, 1972, and the appeal against the decision was denied by the United States Court of Appeals for the Seventh Circuit on June 7, 1973. Nearly twenty years have passed and the Special Collection is now an important body of historical documents that should be declassified and studied because it is a vital part of the history of the Cold War.

Much of Penkovsky's information remained highly classified because it dealt with specific Soviet operational secrets that were deemed vital to national security. The Soviet Division prepared a Top Secret summary of "Penkovsky's Positive Production." It included information on Soviet air defense capabilities, performance data and technical characteristics of the V-75 surface-to-air missile, which had the NATO designation SA-2, GUIDELINE. Penkovsky's information had disclosed the altitude, 4000 feet, at which the SA-2 became operational. With this information the Strategic Air Command devised new attack tactics to fly below the altitude at which the SAMs became effective. Other contributions included:

- *The Soviet Armed Forces Field Service Regulations and the 1962 draft revisions.* These were the most recent Soviet manuals on general nuclear combat operations. Their data on the projected effects of nuclear weapons in the battlefield and full operational procedures for the protection of troops was unique.

- An article from the Top Secret *Information Collection of the Artillery*—"the first available Soviet policy document on the intended use of chemical weapons and on the identification of these weapons."

- Full technical characteristics of all Soviet tactical surface-to-surface ballistic missiles and free rockets, together with details on their ground-support equipment, also unique information.

- An article by minister of defense Malinovsky in the first 1962 issue of the Top Secret version of *Military Thought* regarded by the CIA to be "the best single document on Soviet armored fighting vehicles ever received by the Department of the Army." This article on the Soviet T-62 had a major impact on the design of the new American battle tank, M-60.

A former senior CIA official involved in the case said, "Penkovsky made lasting contributions that enabled us to understand Soviet capabilities, evaluate them and meet them. Penkovsky provided the essential information on where the Soviets were in strategic weapons and where they wanted to go."[1]

The information Penkovsky supplied was so voluminous that it provided insights into the Soviet military's internal debates over nuclear strategy, and about air force and naval force strengths.

Following his exposure, any questions about Penkovsky's bona fides were eliminated by the Soviet Union's wholesale recall and reprimand of senior military officers and officials associated with him. Marshal Varentsov was demoted to major general, expelled from the Central Committee, and ousted from his seat as a deputy to the Supreme Soviet "for having relaxed political vigilance and committed unworthy acts." General Ivan Serov was demoted to major general and fired as head of the GRU in March 1963. He was supposed to become assistant chief of staff of the Volga Military District, but never assumed his new post. Serov began drinking heavily and is reported to have committed suicide by shooting himself in an alley in the Arbat after he was expelled from the Communist Party in 1965, following Khrushchev's ouster.[2] Major General A. Pozovny and Colonel V. Buzinov, aides to Varentsov, were branded as "close acquaintances of Penkovsky" and subjected to "severe disciplinary measures," their careers wrecked. Central Committee member and close Khrushchev aide Viktor Mikhaylovich Churayev was heavily disciplined. An estimated 300 GRU and KGB officers and military personnel whom Penkovsky had identified to the British and Americans were recalled. Some 170 ballistic missile and artillery officers with whom Penkovsky had been in contact were reprimanded, downgraded, or transferred from Moscow to provincial posts. There was a shakeup and purge of State Committee officials who worked with Penkovsky. V. V. Petrochenko, deputy head of the Foreign Relations Department of the State Committee for the Coordination of Scientific Research, was dismissed and severely reprimanded.[3]

At the same time the British set the stage for the exchange of Wynne and Gordon Lonsdale. The *Times* of London on May 13, 1963, in what appeared to be a government-inspired editorial, noted that although the trial might have been "a straightforward process of law . . . it is, however, hard to reject the suspicion that the affair has been blown beyond its real size. The apparent clumsiness of Penkovsky's attempts to make contact with American Intelligence and the careless nature of his subsequent relationship with Wynne could strengthen the theory that he may have been under Russian control throughout. If this is truth, the evidence of Wynne needs explanation. It may be found in the six months' preparation for his trial. Both he and Penkovsky must have been under every kind of psychological persuasion. There is no need for the cruder forms of pressure that leave unmistakable signs. Neither man had been reduced to an automaton."

The *Times* of London suggested that aside from the propaganda effects of the trial a more specific objective of "the whole carefully staged affair" was that "after a decent interval the Soviet Union might offer to exchange Wynne for Lonsdale." The *Times* cited the exchange of Francis Gary Powers for Rudolf Abel in February 1962 as a precedent.[4]

The CIA believed it was essential to find out how Penkovsky had been compromised, and mounted a major counterintelligence effort to determine the cause. No smoking gun emerged and the postmortems continued for years, speculation that continues to this day. A broad range of theories emerged, but although many questions are resolved by the available records, others continue to gnaw and remain unanswered. The British, for whom MI6 does not officially exist, have long declined on-the-record interviews or access to documents. A source close to British Intelligence and the case suggested that Shergold harbored a sense of guilt about Penkovsky's demise. Shergold, he said, felt that the team had overused Penkovsky; but it was hard not to, given his demoniac drive. In hindsight the team should have tried harder to slow him down and put him on ice until suspicion had passed. The requirements that the CIA and MI6 gave Penkovsky to fulfill were so extensive they had to lead to his being discovered. But how was he trapped? In death, more than in life, Penkovsky was a symbol of the ultimate Cold War spy. Rumors and speculation swirled around him.

The Soviets launched a campaign soon after his death, suggesting Penkovsky was a double agent—that he had disseminated only what the KGB and GRU fed him. The earliest rumors were that he was not executed but was still alive, saved from death because, in truth, he had been a double agent. One of the first attempts to plant this hypothesis came from Nikolai Trofimovich Fedorenko, Soviet ambassador to the United Nations, at a dinner on May 27, 1963. Fedorenko discussed the Penkovsky case with a Western diplomat who had contact with the CIA. The diplomat suggested to Fedorenko that the Penkovsky revelations had been a severe blow to the Soviet Union. Fedorenko smiled and replied, "Do not believe everything you read in the newspapers. Penkovsky is very much alive and was a double agent against the Americans."[5]

A July 1963 report from one of CIA's reliable Soviet sources said, "Khrushchev mentioned in December, 1962, at a gathering in Kiev attended by Tito and others, that Penkovsky had done a lot of harm, but also that he had done some good simply on the grounds that now the United States knows the strength and technological advancement of the Soviet Union."[6]

At the same time the KGB and the Soviet military worked hard to minimize the broad public impact of Penkovsky's spying. In a controlled press the task was not difficult. The editors of *Izvestia*, led by Editor in Chief Aleksei Ivanovich Adzhubei, Khrushchev's son-in-law, called upon prosecutor Gorny for an interview on May 29, 1963. Gorny responded to letters from readers who wanted to know the extent of the damage caused to Soviet defense capabilities by Penkovsky's spying.

Gorny disparaged Penkovsky's role, insisting he had not given secrets connected with military equipment and the defense capacity of the Soviet state. "Such claims are without foundation. Penkovsky in his position was far removed from information connected with the armament of our troops and their deployment and with the employment of new types of weapons. He passed on to foreign intelligence services information only some technical reports of Soviet specialists who had gone abroad and some scattered data of a military nature that he had pumped out of loose-tongued friends and had taken from classified publications. . . . However, it can be asserted with full responsibility that the materials he passed could not cause any serious harm to the defense capability of the Soviet Union," said Gorny.[7]

In fact, the Soviet military authorities did not know the full extent of Penkovsky's work because he had kept no inventory of what he had photographed and had destroyed the summary he had been sent by the British and American team. When he confessed, Penkovsky tried to minimize what he had stolen and photographed. The initial insight the KGB had into the kind of highly classified materials he photographed on a regular basis would have come from whatever was on the undeveloped film found in his desk when they arrested him. Even before Penkovsky's and Wynne's trial, the CIA and MI6 were considering plans for long-term exploitation of his material against the KGB. A CIA memorandum, written before the trial in May, outlined a serious counterpropaganda effort to minimize the effects of the trial, but it stipulated: "Certain documents pertinent to the general subject of Soviet espionage in the West will be released for surfacing provided it can be done without risk or direct attribution to Penkovsky."

Thus the seed was planted for *The Penkovsky Papers*, a bestselling book compiled from "a series of hastily written notes, sketches and comments."[8] The May 1963 CIA memorandum noted,

> Preliminary discussions between the British and ourselves concerning long term exploitation have taken place already. Conversations were scheduled in London during the time of the trial. As presently foreseen, the major effort will be the preparation of the "memoirs" of Penkovsky, based upon the voluminous information from contacts with him, to present as thoroughly and carefully as possible Penkovsky's own views on the nature of the Soviet regime, its history and its prospects. To accompany those memoirs, appropriate documents will be selected from those available to us for release to the public. These two items, the memoirs and the documents, would then be made public with the explanation that they had been left in the West in the personal possession of a confidant who was charged by Penkovsky with making them public in the event his efforts to struggle against the party dictatorship in the Soviet union led to his arrest. This explanation will stress the idea that Penkovsky's arrest stemmed not from service as a Western intelligence agent, but rather from his burning desire to fight the Soviet regime as currently established. In addition to other considerations, putting this plan into effect will have to await a final resolution of the fate of Wynne. In the meantime, however, preparatory work on the memoirs has begun in London.[9]

The British, at an early point in the gestation, suggested that the memoirs—to be prepared by MI6—portray Penkovsky as a KGB agent working inside the GRU. Turning Penkovsky into a KGB traitor would discredit the KGB and demonstrate that one of its own officers was spying for the West. This would tarnish the image of the KGB as the elite organization it claimed to be.

MI6 produced the first sample chapter to discuss with the CIA in Washington. The British writing style and voice created for Penkovsky were unconvincing. On June 24, 1963, the CIA passed a memo to the British arguing firmly against their approach.

> We believe that to base the story of Penkovsky's life on the fiction that he was a KGB agent throughout most of his career is wrong. . . . in the opinion of those most familiar with the case here, the allega-

tion would not be accepted as true by those whom we most want to impress with the documents—the officers of the Soviet intelligence services and other Soviet officials. The introduction of this element in the story might make it more complicated and difficult to understand in the West. Western journalists seemed to have had considerable difficulties understanding Penkovsky the man and in analyzing the case based on the facts now overtly available. To throw in this further twist might confuse them totally.

We think that not only would the story be more valid, but also more dramatic if it sticks closer to the main facts and to Penkovsky's own words. The contact report in which he gives the history of his life in some detail, for example, could be used almost verbatim to cover a considerable part of his life.[10]

After the American critique it was agreed the CIA would take over, subject to British agreement on the final product. The British now wanted to distance themselves from the project because it was an unprecedented undertaking that would publicly link the theoretically nonexistent SIS to real intelligence documents. The British were also concerned about jeopardizing the release of Greville Wynne; they did not wish to disturb the ongoing negotiations to trade him for Lonsdale.

In July 1963 the British urged Washington to delay publication of the Penkovsky project pending the possibility of an early release of Wynne. However, a senior British diplomat, Sir Humphrey Trevelyan, Her Majesty's Ambassador in Moscow, said he would much prefer that the Americans publish the materials first in order to avoid allegations of Her Majesty's Government's connivance, but he took note of "the likely disadvantage as regarded control of the operation."[11]

Trevelyan warned that an attempt to paint Penkovsky in the colors of a knight in shining armor would ruin any chance of a positive impact on public opinion and could only result in the memoirs being called a clumsy forgery. The ambassador said he "was happy to be quoted in this view."[12]

In mid-July SIS's Maurice Oldfield wrote to Howard Osborne, who succeeded Maury as head of the Soviet Division, suggesting a variation of the theme that Penkovsky was under KGB influence and control: "Head Office are interested in your treatment of KGB pressure on HERO and like to consider the possibility that a KGB approach was made to HERO in the early 1950s before Stalin's death depicting HERO as hoping that the post-Stalin regime would bring this pressure to an early end only to find that the situation did not improve under Khrushchev. This would fit a deliberate Secret Police plan to spy on the army and the GRU worked out over a long period. They are prepared to skate over the question of the extent to which HERO actively collaborated with the KGB."[13]

This completely fabricated bit of British and American disinformation against the KGB never came to pass. Both the CIA and SIS decided to stick to the material in the debriefings and the documents that Penkovsky had copied with his American-supplied cameras. They decided not to fabricate any part of *The Penkovsky Papers*, but to edit the transcripts of the meetings into as coherent a narrative as possible. After joint consultations it was suggested that Peter Deriabin, a KGB Counterintelligence officer who had defected in Vienna in 1954, be asked to work on the Penkovsky "memoir." Deriabin at that time was a full-time CIA consultant specializing in Soviet intelligence organizations. He was given CIA-edited Russian-language transcripts of the tapes of Penkovsky's debriefings in London and Paris, and worked with a Russian-speaking CIA officer to translate them into English.

In August 1963 John McCone discussed the CIA's plans to publish Penkovsky's "memoirs" at the White House with McGeorge Bundy, National Security Advisor to President Kennedy. McCone returned to CIA headquarters in Langley with approval to continue the project without further clearance. The expectation was that the British would concur once Wynne was released.[14] Later in 1963 Kennedy had decided against releasing the documents after consultation with Ambassador Thompson because negotiations for the Test Ban Treaty were then under way and "it was considered inappropriate for the government to release a document of this sort."[15]

At 5:35 A.M. on April 22, 1964, Wynne was exchanged for Lonsdale at checkpoint Heerstrasse on the border between West Berlin and East Germany. The Russians initiated the exchange, anxious to retrieve from jail Lonsdale, whom they valued highly. The initial Soviet approach came in a letter dated July 10, 1963, mailed from Warsaw to Mrs. Sheila Wynne signed by Halina Lonsdale, a woman who said she was the wife of Lonsdale. The letter suggested the two women approach their respective governments to expedite the return of their husbands.[16]

The British press speculated that the Cabinet approved the deal after lengthy debate "despite the obvious inequality of the bargain" because Wynne's health was deteriorating after nearly eighteen months of harsh Soviet imprisonment and interrogation.[17] Given Wynne's contribution to delivering Penkovsky's information to the West, the trade was more than fair and redounded to the credit of the British.

With Wynne free, work accelerated on the Penkovsky materials. David E. Murphy, the new chief of the Soviet Division, who succeeded Osborne in September 1963, approved use of the Penkovsky debriefing transcripts so that a full elaboration of Penkovsky's views on the critical issues of East-West tensions and Soviet internal conflicts could be prepared.

Over drinks at the Century Club in New York City, retired CIA director Allen Dulles met with Frank Gibney, then the publisher of *Show* magazine and a former *Life* magazine writer and *Newsweek* editor. Dulles knew Gibney from his stories on the Soviet spy Rudolf Abel and his articles on Deriabin. He asked Gibney to cooperate with him on a television series based on his own life. Dulles said he would put him in touch with a couple of people at the Agency who could provide the material. Gibney recalled that there was little commercial interest in the Dulles project. Then his CIA contact, Donald Jameson, raised the possibility of developing a book from the Penkovsky material. The TV series on Allen Dulles became *The Penkovsky Papers*.

Gibney was responsible for the format and decided to structure the book as a biography of Penkovsky. He edited and annotated Deriabin's translations and included some of the intelligence material Penkovsky had provided on GRU agent handling and communications in the U.S.

The details of Penkovsky's life came from the autobiography that Penkovsky provided at his first meeting with the team in London. The trial transcript, which had been published in Moscow, filled in the operational details to which Penkovsky and Wynne confessed.

In the trial KGB Counterintelligence, perhaps deliberately, perhaps because of inadequate information, misrepresented the total number of meetings and the full extent of what Penkovsky provided, but most of the spying tradecraft disclosed in Moscow was accurate.

Gibney and Deriabin had collaborated on *The Secret World*, an account of Deriabin's life as a Kremlin Guards and KGB officer, which was published successfully by Doubleday & Company. Gibney planned to take the Penkovsky book to Doubleday and other publishers.

By the summer of 1964 Gibney was working on the Penkovsky material and writing speeches for Lyndon Johnson from an office in the Old Executive Office Building next to the White House. Because of the delay and President Kennedy's hold on the material in 1963, the CIA again cleared the publication plan with McGeorge Bundy in October 1964 at the White House.[18] Bundy held the view that *The Penkovsky Papers* should not appear to be U.S. government sponsored or directly linked to the government. The controversial nature

383

of the materials, he felt, should not intrude on diplomatic negotiations between the Soviet Union and the United States. This time around there were no sensitive negotiations in process, and the documents were to be incorporated in a book which was to "appear under private auspices rather than have it released by an official agency of the U.S. Government."[19] Bundy refused to meet with Gibney. Gibney said that Bundy had developed his own imperious style that Gibney found "so pompous he made Henry Kissinger seem self-effacing."[20]

In preparing the material for clearance, a CIA memorandum listed the statements "which might be considered politically or diplomatically sensitive." Finally, the list fell into two categories—information that was retained and information that was removed:

a. In virtually every chapter, there is some sort of attack on Nikita Khrushchev. He is described as a stupid braggart who alarms the West unnecessarily with his sabre rattling, as a war monger, an adventurer who plans to "bury capitalism under a rain of rockets." [These references were retained because the book was published after Khrushchev's ouster in November 1964.]

b. Cyrus Eaton offered his services to Khrushchev as a Soviet agent. [This was removed from the text because the charge was not substantiated and Eaton had no access to classified materials. The Agency did not want to be accused of character assassination.]

c. The Soviet Union should have been sharply confronted in 1956 over Hungary. [This was not removed from the text, because Penkovsky had said it and many in the clandestine service believed he was right.]

d. President Kennedy's actions vis-à-vis Cuba were exactly right. [This was removed from the text as too self-serving.]

e. Soviet intelligence knew that Syria was planning to break away from the UAR [United Arab Republic] in 1961, but said nothing, since Khrushchev wanted Nasser weakened. [This was removed from the text because of political sensitivities regarding President Nasser, then ruling Egypt.]

f. He [Penkovsky] makes the assertion in discussing Yerzin, former KGB resident in Turkey and presently Rector (and KGB resident) of Patrice Lumumba Friendship University: "These negroes sell themselves without any hesitation." [The quote was removed from the text because of its racist overtones, but the item on Patrice Lumumba Friendship University being KGB controlled was retained.]

g. All Jews have been weeded out of the RIS [Russian Intelligence

Service] as a matter of policy. [This was removed from the text since there were a limited number of Jewish linguistic specialists employed by the KGB and the decision was made not to raise the issue of anti-Semitism in the context of Penkovsky's other revelations.]

h. The Soviet Ministry of Defense did not admit to Khrushchev that it shot down our RB-47 over neutral water [on July 1, 1960]. [This was removed from the text since it was uncertain what the Ministry had told Khrushchev.]

i. The GRU considers Canada a happy hunting ground for intelligence collection. [This was removed from the text in deference to Canadian sensitivities.]

j. The Soviets continued to test nuclear weapons secretly during the moratorium. [This was removed from the text because of pending talks on a test ban treaty.]

k. Soviet intelligence operations in India are presently "on ice." [This was retained in the text because the Indian government had been privately informed of GRU activities reported in Penkovsky's information.][21]

The initial Deriabin translations of the "Penkovsky Memoirs," which he gave to Gibney, came with a cover sheet that said they "were compiled from tape recordings made during personal meetings with Oleg Penkovsky and Soviet Division officers. They are Penkovsky's own words. Although little editing has been done, his comments are not necessarily presented here in the same order or the same context in which they originally were expressed. His comments on 'Soviet Dissatisfaction,' for instance, appear together under one chapter heading, though they have come from the tapes of several different meetings. These 'Memoirs' gave considerable insight into the character and motivation of Penkovsky and a wealth of information on Soviet attitudes and 'Soviet Realities.' "[22]

Within the Agency there was a strong faction that opposed opening intelligence files to the public. Actually saying where intelligence information had come from was anathema to many old-school covert operators. A senior official directly involved in *The Penkovsky Papers* recalled:

Doing it at all was a tremendous innovation, the idea being, first of all, that it isn't proper for an intelligence organization to open its files and talk about a case in that detail so soon after the fact. Maybe you are supposed to wait twenty years or something. It was basically the main idea that this is not something that one does. I think also that there is something to the argument that the CIA

385

should not deliberately go ahead and do something like this. After-wards, we had another source and this guy said, "Don't do to me what you did to Penkovsky." That is, if he got caught he didn't want to end up being a famous hero, and what it might mean to his family. It might be seen by people in the Soviet Union as just not the proper way the people who ran him as an agent should have acted. Although I must say I don't see what difference it makes. What we tried to do was to imply that the man had done all this on his own initiative—this was outside the agency, he had done this on his own.

We never had any twinge of conscience that we were not acting as he would have wanted us to act. We did not want to make anybody, including the Soviet Union, feel we had done the wrong thing by Penkovsky.[23]

The decision was made to prepare the book in Penkovsky's own words, as if he had written them, rather than say the material was taken from the CIA-MI6 transcripts. In the Cold War climate of 1965 the Agency did not want to acknowledge its role and thus associate the U.S. government directly with the book. Part of the reasoning, according to those involved in the case, was not to let the KGB know how Penkovsky was run as an agent. A former senior CIA official close to the case explained, "If it came out under the CIA imprimatur people would say it was made up. We thought it would be more acceptable and have a greater impact if it came out in the man's own words."[24]

Taking the transcriptions and turning them into a book that was based on Penkovsky's own words was no small task. To avoid open-ing classified operational reports and letting the KGB know the full extent of the Penkovsky operation, the CIA limited the parameters of the book to the excerpts from the debriefing translations, the trial record, and Penkovsky's basic biography.

Dick Helms later called *The Penkovsky Papers* "black propa-ganda."* Although the contents were not fabricated, their presenta-tion was flawed by not acknowledging that the real source was the transcripts of Penkovsky's debriefings in London and Paris.

In an introduction to a reprint of the book in 1982, Frank Gibney

---

* Black propaganda is an intelligence term of art for material designed to inform or convince people of a particular matter without direct attribution to its actual source. In the case of *The Penkovsky Papers* the CIA did not want to directly attribute the material to the debriefings of Penkovsky. Similarly, the CIA distributed copies of Khrushchev's speech revealing Stalin's crimes at the Twentieth Party Congress with-out attribution to the CIA as the source of the speech. If black propaganda material contains erroneous information to mislead an adversary, it becomes disinformation.

explained how the *Papers* were compiled from the transcripts and the CIA's insistence that they not be cited as the source. "The only constraint on me," wrote Gibney, "was that I not reveal how the *Papers* got to this country and not *publicly* mention that they had been held by the CIA. I thought this a reasonable restriction, which did not interfere in any way with the authenticity of the *Papers*. If Penkovsky were to be the subject of a book it had to be on the material's intrinsic merits."[25]

After clearing the manuscript with the CIA, Gibney offered it to several New York publishers. Doubleday offered a $50,000 advance. The actual contract for the book was made between the Penkovsky Trust in New York City and Doubleday. The Trust was administered by Herbert P. Jacoby, of the New York City law firm Schwartz & Frohlich. The Penkovsky Fund, a charitable fund registered with the Internal Revenue Service, was administered by a group of prominent businessmen that included Herman Dunlop Smith, a respected Chicago investor and philanthropist; Charles Francis Adams, the chairman of the board of Raytheon Corporation; and Carl Gilbert, chairman of the board of the Gillette Corporation. They were chosen for their discretion, loyalty, and experience.

Doubleday editor Le Baron Barker suggested "The Penkovsky Papers" for the title. The view of Bromley Smith, secretary of the National Security Council, was that there should be no official government sponsorship of the publication of the papers. However, he reassured Barker that the *Papers* were genuine. "It is absolutely in the national interest for you publish them. For a variety of reasons we do not say they came from here, but I can assure you they are authentic."[26] Doubleday was unaware of the real nature of the Penkovsky material.

Gibney and Deriabin received 40 percent of the royalties from the book. The rest was placed in the Penkovsky Fund, which distributed $78,000 to graduate students of Soviet studies and to defectors. In a review of *The Penkovsky Papers*, John Le Carré said he was looking forward to seeing the first Penkovsky scholar enrolled at Moscow University. The book became a bestseller in its hardcover edition. Doubleday sold 110,000 copies in the United States, there was a British edition (published by Collins, with a foreword by Edward Crankshaw), and the book was published in France, Germany, Sweden, Korea, and Japan.

Following the initial publication in November 1965, the provenance of the material attributed to Penkovsky raised a firestorm of controversy. Leading the attack on the authenticity of the material was Victor Zorza in the *Manchester Guardian*. Zorza argued that Penkovsky would never speak the way he did in the book and questioned if it was really based on his words. He said the Agency should have done a better job in presenting the *Papers*, but he wrote: "The release by the Central Intelligence Agency of the reports it received during 1961–1962 from one of its most successful Russian spies, Oleg Penkovsky . . . is an event unprecedented in the history of espionage."[27]

The Soviet government was outraged at the publication of the book and its syndication in October 1965 in some thirty American newspapers. The Soviet Embassy in Washington publicly protested the publication of *The Penkovsky Papers* in the *Washington Post*.

The statement said: "In fact, the so-called 'Penkovsky Papers' is nothing but a crude forgery cooked up two years after Penkovsky's conviction by those whom the exposed spy had served. This is not the first case of publishing slanderous stuff about the USSR and it has the only purpose—to smear the Soviet Union, to poison the international atmosphere, to hinder the search for ways of improving relations between nations." The Soviet statement called the *Papers* "nothing but a premeditated act in the worst traditions of the Cold War." In reprisal for publishing the excerpts, the Soviet government closed the *Washington Post*'s Moscow Bureau and expelled its correspondent in Moscow, Stephen S. Rosenfeld.

The Penkovsky Papers were a revelation in their day. They were the first authoritative look inside the Soviet intelligence system and military structure to appear in the West. Even such critics of the book as Victor Zorza, who said it could not have been written by Penkovsky and that it was made up of debriefings and intelligence reports from Penkovsky, were awed by its content.[28] For the first time in the Cold War, Western Intelligence was on the offensive and not merely reacting to KGB successes such as Kim Philby and George Blake. From Gibney's evaluation in the *Papers*, Oleg Penkovsky emerges as "a flawed hero" who was "a hero nonetheless."[29] In the light of glasnost and perestroika, Penkovsky's revelations of the Soviet Union's weaknesses were prophetic.

A venture like *The Penkovsky Papers* is not likely to be repeated. Following the Church Committee investigation of the CIA in 1976, the line on CIA "special activities" influencing domestic opinion was clearly drawn. The current Executive Order 12333, December 4, 1981, permits special activities "in support of national foreign policy objectives abroad which are planned and executed so that the role of the United States Government is not apparent or acknowledged publicly and functions in support of such activities, but which are not intended to influence United States political processes, public opinion, policies or media." In short, no special activities for domestic American consumption, even at arm's length.

* * *

A British historian archly noted that a man is never so dangerous as when he can identify a private grievance with a matter of principle.[30] Penkovsky rationalized betraying his country because of the personal wrongs he suffered under the Communist system. Alan Studner, a CIA psychiatrist who has studied defectors, notes that "nobody ever defected because he was happy." Most defectors are from broken homes and split families with incomplete or split bonding. "I've never seen a man who had a good relationship with his father become a defector and be disloyal to the régime," said Dr. Studner.

Among the types of defectors Studner identified there is a wronged person who elevates his private dissatisfaction into a political principle. Such defectors often feel abandoned by a parent they have lost through separation or death. Added to this is the motivation of an oppositional personality who all of his life has been a fighter and counterattacker. More often than not these defectors did not succeed and so they become sideswipers and backstabbers. These are the ones who readily become volunteers, who are motivated by vengeance and justification. This kind of person feels no loyalty toward a régime that he believes has reneged on its part in an implicit compact of reciprocal obligation. These are all characteristics that describe Penkovsky. He was a grievance accumulator who throughout his life perceived himself as the unjust victim of jealous or incompetent but powerful rivals.

The defector also exhibits the trait of narcissism that is more than just self-love. Defined by Dr. Studner, it is a pathologic self-absorption, a preoccupation with the self at the expense of others. Penkovsky clearly had a grandiose sense of his own self-importance and saw himself to be a mover of history—all characteristics seen in the pattern of defection. From an early age he felt that special things were expected of him because of his family heritage as members of the gentry class. To be a general was the equivalent of being in the gentry class of his forefathers. Because he was a child of the Civil War, bereft of a father (his mother never married again) who could have helped to advance his career, others adopted him and helped him, most notably Marshal Varentsov. To have been promoted to general and become a member of the Communist Party military leadership class, a member of the small inner circle that was the equivalent of the prerevolutionary gentry, would have fulfilled his patrimony. This kind of fulfillment was barred to him and his grievances multiplied, providing him with the energy and rage for vengeance.

"When he did not make general, it created a murderous rage in him. He expected that Varentsov would be his father," explained Dr. Alan Cameron, who did a psychological study of Penkovsky. When Marshal Varentsov was not strong enough to win for Penkovsky the respect and recognition he believed he deserved, Penkovsky betrayed Varentsov.

Dr. Cameron theorized that Penkovsky sought a parent with whom to identify but never found his father and lost the development of personality that grows from early contact with parents. "If you miss that, you have no firm grip on who you really are. You pick up outside signals. Penkovsky's desire to become a colonel in the British or American army is an example. There was a need for great reassurances."

Penkovsky lived on the edge of the inner circle of Soviet military leadership and preyed upon it, using whatever he could take away to help him fulfill his ambition to be the greatest spy in history. His personal problems and ambition came together with the needs of the Western allies to know the strength and motivations of the Soviet Union, creating a fortuitous juncture in history. He volunteered his services to the West at a time of tension and distrust. While he spied, the precarious Cold War balance between the United States and the Soviet Union tipped toward nuclear war, first over Berlin and then over Cuba.

To the psychiatrists looking clinically at Penkovsky, he was supremely overconfident. "He could not imagine he would get caught. Normal mortals get caught, not a child of destiny with a vision," explained Dr. Studner. Another Agency psychiatrist who studied Penkovsky said, "He was like a teen-ager driving down the road at 140 miles per hour thinking he was in control."

Debate over the Penkovsky case and the bona fides of Penkovsky was influenced by the controversial defector Anatoli Golitsyn, who cast doubt on Penkovsky. Golitsyn, a KGB major in the First Chief Directorate, working against NATO targets, defected in Helsinki on December 15, 1961, and arrived in the United States on December 19. For two years he was debriefed by the CIA and provided valuable material which was used to trap the British Admiralty spy John Vassall in 1962.[31]

When Golitsyn's well of current information ran dry, he proposed that the CIA sponsor a multimillion-dollar study by him of how the Soviet intelligence system was involved in a massive deception campaign against the West. Golitsyn insisted that the KGB already had implanted an agent in the highest ranks of U.S. Intelligence and that Soviet-controlled agents, masked as defectors or double agents, would supply disinformation to build up the mole's credibility.

Dissatisfied with a negative response to his proposal from the CIA, Golitsyn went to England. From March to July 1963 he spent long hours with Stephen de Mowbray of MI6 and Arthur Martin and Peter Wright of MI5, who supported his views and encouraged him. When he returned to Washington, Golitsyn pawned off his massive deception theory on Counterintelligence chief James Angleton. So deep was the deception described by Golitsyn that the Sino-Soviet split was part of it. The plot, which began in 1959, included the writings of Andrei Sakharov, Golitsyn said.*[32]

Golitsyn found few supporters for his theories inside the Agency, except among Angleton and his Counterintelligence staff. Angleton embraced Golitsyn's long-term, massive-deception theory. For Golitsyn every Soviet agent who had come to the West since 1959 was part of the plot—including Penkovsky. "There is serious, unresolved evidence that Colonel Penkovsky was planted on Western Intelligence by the KGB," wrote Golitsyn.[33]

Golitsyn turned every CIA success into a failure. He was a major source for Edward Jay Epstein's *Deception*, a study of the invisible war between the KGB and the CIA. Epstein says Golitsyn supplied information that undermined *The Penkovsky Papers*. "He [Golitsyn] demonstrated, by diagramming hidden Soviet microphones in the U.S. Embassy in Moscow, that Penkovsky's early debriefings had to have been monitored by the KGB. Even if he had been a legitimate traitor then, Golitsyn argued, he would have been forced, in a deal that he could not refuse, to deliver the documents the Soviets wanted delivered to the CIA. He was, in other words, a Soviet postman at the time of the missile crisis."[34] On the contrary, Penkovsky was never debriefed in the American Embassy in Moscow. There is no evidence that he came under Soviet control until he was arrested. Nonetheless, Angleton agreed with Golitsyn's assessment; for Angleton the only new question was when had Penkovsky come under Soviet control.[35]

Golitsyn insisted that Penkovsky was a provocation and that his messages were used to control the reaction of the Kennedy administration to Soviet moves. The missiles were put in Cuba, insisted Golitsyn, to be bargained away. They were there to manipulate Kennedy into accepting a hostile Castro régime in Cuba and thus in effect giving up the Monroe Doctrine.

Golitsyn and Epstein fail to deal with the facts of Penkovsky's

---

*Andrei Sakharov was instrumental in the creation of the Soviet Union's hydrogen weapons before becoming a human rights advocate and the moral compass for his country. Awarded the Nobel Peace Prize in 1975, Sakharov, despite harassment and persecution, lead the struggle for glasnost until his death in December 1989.

contributions and arrest. Penkovsky never directly advised the Anglo-American team that Khrushchev was placing medium- and intermediate-range missiles in Cuba, although he correctly sensed long in advance that Cuba would become a point of Soviet-American conflict. Penkovsky's contribution to resolving the crisis was different. He provided the manuals and missile characteristics enabling the government analysts to interpret what they had seen in Cuba, and the president to act from knowledge and American strength when dealing with Khrushchev.[36]

Golitsyn's grand theory of a massive Soviet disinformation plot against the CIA was based on his doubtful premise—advanced at a moment when his own usefulness to the CIA was declining—that the KGB had infiltrated the Agency and had a high-ranking American official working as mole, a Soviet agent in place. After Penkovsky's demise, Angleton called Bulik to his office to tell him that all Bulik's Soviet agents recruited since 1960 were compromised and, Angleton believed, part of a Soviet disinformation plot. "I was so angry I just turned and left and we never spoke again," said Bulik.[37]

Yet the records demonstrate that Angleton initially supported Penkovsky's bona fides and urged that his information be brought directly to President Kennedy. While Penkovsky was alive and sending information, Angleton never questioned the validity of the material. The record does show that Angleton argued in one discussion that Penkovsky was an anarchist who would like to see a war between the United States and the Soviet Union.[38]

After Golitsyn sowed his theory, Angleton's suspicions grew and he argued that Penkovsky was a provocateur. "It is hard to convey just how perverse this seemed to the Soviet Russian Division under Jack Maury," Thomas Powers wrote in his study of Richard Helms' career, *The Man Who Kept the Secrets*.[39] "Penkovsky is credited as the single most important spy ever recruited by the Americans against the Russians. CIA people who saw the 5000 frames of microfilmed documents provided by Penkovsky, two pages to the frame, were dazzled by the quality of his information. The rule of thumb is that a provocateur must provide 95 percent true information if he is to be trusted and believed. The idea that Penkovsky was a plant, and that the Russians deliberately surrendered so much true information, strikes CIA officers as insane. One man in the DDP, arguing the point with Angleton, was finally fobbed off with an appeal to secret knowledge. 'You aren't cleared for certain sources,' Angleton said enigmatically, and would add not another word."

The chief of Counterintelligence argued against the bona fides of the CIA's best spy, but only after his death. Angleton's conversion against Penkovsky was only one element in the internally divisive search for a mole in the Agency. Angleton's belief in Golitsyn went to the extraordinary length of letting him review the personnel files of CIA officers who spoke Russian or had been posted to Moscow to see if he could spot the mole. Such a breach of security is without precedent. The mole was presumed to be in the Soviet Division; eventually officers from the division upon whom suspicion had been cast were transferred out of Soviet and East European affairs to less sensitive posts.[40]

For a long time Tennent Bagley, former deputy chief of the Soviet Division, argued that Penkovsky had not been apprehended earlier because the KGB was protecting a mole inside the CIA and feared exposing him by arresting Penkovsky. His argument was that the CIA's investigation to discover how Penkovsky was exposed would have led to the mole.

Former CIA director Richard Helms recalls that "the idea of Penkovsky as a double agent first came from Jim Angleton, who was too close to Golitsyn. It was a conception of Angleton's that we couldn't run a case without Soviet infiltration. We disagreed about this. If it was left to him none of our defectors would have been bona fide. As long as I was in the Agency I handled Angleton. When I left, the Agency lost control of him.

"It is great fun—if I may use such a vulgar phrase—to poke holes in the other guy's operation. Watching Jim perform was like watching a magician," said Helms, pantomiming a magician pulling a rabbit out of a hat. "The business of Penkovsky becoming a double agent did not become lively until Penkovsky was lost."[41]

A series of reviews was conducted by the CIA on what happened to Penkovsky and how he was caught. On June 26, 1963, John McCone discussed the case with the president's Intelligence Advisory Board. When a board member asked what motivated Penkovsky, McCone replied, "It was primarily emotional—that the man resented his failure to advance higher in the regime and was motivated to work against the present leaders." McCone told the distinguished group of presidential advisers, which included Dr. Edward Land, chairman and chief executive officer of Polaroid, that "the British had taken the principal rap on the case because of Wynne, who was a courier working for MI6. We think that the case was blown because of a penetration in the British government who saw Wynne and Penkovsky together. We also think that Penkovsky got careless and when they searched his apartment they found all of the espionage equipment."

Another board member asked if there was a danger that Penkovsky had been planted. McCone replied, "This was something that we always feared. We had checked his bona fides extremely carefully,

393

and held up dissemination of reports in order to insure their validity. After most careful checks with all other types of intelligence, we came to the conclusion that this was authentic."[42]

Continued efforts to find the source of Penkovsky's downfall produced a series of dry holes and raised tensions between the American and British Services over who was to blame. The American and British team leaders, Joe Bulik and Harold Shergold, neither of whom had ever met Greville Wynne, felt that he might have been a leak. The obvious answer was the one that both the British and American sides seemed to reject because it suggested poor tradecraft. Penkovsky had met Mrs. Chisholm twelve times between October 20, 1961, and January 19, 1962, and eleven of these meetings were in public places where they could be watched.

The idea of a mole or a security leak was more appealing and less incriminating than plain old sloppy tradecraft: meeting too often with the same person. Penkovsky was a driven man after he returned from Paris. He worked with a demoniac fervor to film documents in the secret library of Varentsov's artillery command. He refused to slow down, and he showed up at the meeting places in the Arbat and in the park off Tsvetnoy Boulevard with a total of thirty-five rolls of Minox film during the October to January period. Penkovsky also gave Janet Chisholm eight letters to the team that continued his reporting on strategic intelligence and a meeting plan for 1962. It was an intense and concentrated period of valuable work.

Penkovsky was a sideshow in the CIA's internal struggle that Golitsyn had unleashed, but the charge that he was under KGB control was perpetuated even more strongly in Great Britain by Chapman Pincher, the controversial British journalist specializing in intelligence matters. Pincher initially accepted Golitsyn's assessment that the Penkovsky affair was a major successful disinformation operation. "So do some senior officers of the British Security (MI5) and Intelligence Services (MI6)," he wrote.[43] Pincher remains in doubt about Penkovsky, noting that "there are many who cannot bring themselves to believe that Penkovsky was a fake, if only because, having accepted him as the greatest Soviet defector ever, their professional reputations are bound up with his integrity. Some of these, however, do not deny that he was 'blown' soon after contact with the West was made. One of these, James Angleton, suspects that the KGB source of this act of treachery was British and could well have been a high-level officer of MI5." Pincher noted that MI5 head Sir Roger Hollis, who was in charge of security and surveillance for Penkovsky, "had taken the unusual step of asking for the defector's name and had been given it" when Penkovsky arrived in London for the first time in April 1961. Pincher charged that Hollis was a longtime Soviet agent.[44] Pincher, however, failed to close the alleged link between Penkovsky and Hollis. Why was Penkovsky allowed to return to London for a second visit and then go to Paris if the KGB knew he was spying for the British and the Americans?

Peter Wright, former assistant director of MI5, in his autobiography, *Spycatcher*, wrote: "As I read the files, a number of reasons made me believe that Penkovsky had to be the deception operation of which Golitsyn had learned in 1959." Wright, despite his former official status, is incorrect on many facts, and says that initially Penkovsky "was interviewed by the CIA in their secure compound. . . . The Americans decided Penkovsky was a provocation and refused his offer." Penkovsky was never interviewed by the CIA in Moscow either inside or outside the embassy and his offer was never refused. Wright was also suspicious of Penkovsky because he had "apparently picked up not one trace of intelligence about Soviet intelligence assets in the West." In fact, Penkovsky identified all the members of his class at the Military-Diplomatic Academy, the GRU Station members in Ceylon, India, Egypt, Paris, and London, plus hundreds of other GRU and KGB officers.

Instead, Wright swallowed the Golitysn disinformation line and helped to influence Angleton. Wright argues that Penkovsky was deliberately sent to the West to reveal the inferiority of the Soviet missiles. "He [Penkovsky] helped to lull suspicions in the West for more than a decade, and misled us as to the true state of Soviet missile development." Wright never read Penkovsky's warning: the Soviet Union was behind, but not for long. Penkovsky's material explained the shifting Soviet missile strategy, based on internal documents that have never been refuted.[45]

Phillip Knightley, in *The Second Oldest Profession*, a history of spies and spying in the twentieth century, has troubles with Penkovsky and his bona fides. He can't make up his mind and presents both sides of the argument. Knightley's favorite, but unsubstantiated, theory is that Penkovsky was a controlled agent from the start who provided only the materials he was told to feed into a massive disinformation exercise.

In contradiction, Knightley also argues that "Penkovsky was used by a faction in the Kremlin to pass a vital message to the West." The message was that whatever Khrushchev might threaten, he did not have the capability to carry out that threat. According to this theory, Penkovsky's message was not only his own but also the message of an anti-Khrushchev group. Knightley speculates that Penkovsky's arrest in the midst of the Cuban missile crisis was a signal to the Americans that Khrushchev was conceding defeat: he knew that Kennedy knew of the inferior state of Soviet missile strength because Penkovsky must have told the Americans.[46]

In death Penkovsky became the focus for those who would spin conspiracy theories or sow dissension between the American and British. Within the White House and the State Department, McGeorge Bundy and Raymond Garthoff tried to minimize Penkovsky's contributions and dismiss him as a crank and misfit. In *The Crisis Years*, Michael Beschloss reports Bundy's inordinate pride in writing his history of nuclear weapons, *Danger and Survival*, so that "he had managed to avoid even a single reference to the spy."[47] Penkovsky's analysis of the Soviet system did not fit their own views on arms control and Soviet intentions. He was a spy. How could he be trusted or believed? Accepting stolen goods is distasteful, especially when they are used to influence policy decisions. In hindsight it is easier to credit one's own insight and omniscience.

Penkovsky and the record of his labors are a historical reality. In addition, he has been immortalized in fiction. He is a prototype for espionage novelists John Le Carré and Tom Clancy. In *The Cardinal of the Kremlin*, Clancy's hero, Colonel Filitov, an aide to the defense minister, was designated by Penkovsky as his handpicked successor. Le Carré's Soviet traitor Goethe, who betrays his country to save it in *The Russia House*, has the zeal of Penkovsky, who betrayed his country to prevent nuclear war.

Christopher Creighton and Noel Hynd, in their novel *The Khrushchev Objective*, insist "the broad base" of their story is true.[48] Their novel explains the death of British frogman Commander Lionel Crabb during Khrushchev's visit to England in April 1956. According to the authors, Section M of British Naval Intelligence foiled a plot by then KGB chief Ivan Serov to assassinate Khrushchev. Crabb was killed in the effort to defuse mines planted under Serov's direction on the Soviet cruiser *Ordzhonikidze*, at anchor in Portsmouth Harbor. Serov, according to the novel, was confronted with the evidence by the British and agreed to become a spy for them rather than face exposure to Khrushchev. According to the novel, Serov "kept the bargain made in London in April, 1956. Over the years that followed, top-rated secret information flowed from Moscow. . . . At no time was it more valuable than in 1962, when Kremlin estimates of their own naval strength were leaked through the British Admiralty to the United States Navy, which then confidently blockaded Cuba during the missile crisis of that October. Shortly thereafter, the leak in Soviet intelligence was traced to Serov."[49]

Serov became the head of the GRU at the end of 1958. The tale of his role as a British spy would make Penkovsky's close relationship to Serov and his family explicable only if truth is stranger than fiction.

In *Cuban Bluff*, a novel on the Cuban missile crisis, Nigel West, a.k.a. Rupert Allason, MP, and the author of several controversial histories of British intelligence organizations, credits Penkovsky with betraying the weakness of Soviet missiles to the West. In the novel, West re-creates a real meeting that took place between Washington-based KGB officer Aleksandr S. Fomin and John Scali, ABC State Department correspondent, at the height of the Cuban missile crisis. In the fiction Fomin tells Scali, "There was a single motive for deploying our missiles in Cuba . . . parity. The only way we can achieve equality in strategic weapons with the US is to place our shorter-range rockets closer to North America."

"And they were spotted just in time?" asked Scali.

"No. The Politburo was only informed on Tuesday that the CIA had planted a spy in Moscow. He betrayed the relative weakness of our missiles. The KGB says that the CIA has known for the past eighteen months of the technical problems that have wrecked the Soviet strategic missile program."

"Who was this spy?" asked Scali.

"His name was Penkovsky. He told the Americans everything. He has been arrested, and he has confessed."

"I've never heard of this guy," replied Scali evenly, making a mental note of the name. "But how can one man have precipitated all of this? It's not possible."

"Oh yes, my friend. It has happened. Believe me. Ask your State Department about the incident in Moscow on Monday, when a CIA agent was caught red-handed. They will tell you."

Nigel West was apparently referring to CIA officer Dick Jacob, who was detained at the Pushkinskaya dead drop on November 2, after the crisis was resolved, not on October 22. This fiction stems from Raymond Garthoff's incorrect assumption that Penkovsky tried to activate the DISTANT warning system on October 22, when the KGB said he was arrested. (See page 347 for details.) In all probability Penkovsky was arrested before October 22 and never had a chance to signal himself. Since he did not speak when the signal for clearing the dead drop was given on November 2, there was no way of knowing if it was Penkovsky himself or a KGB stand-in making the phone call. The signal itself was to clear the dead drop, and while indicating the message to come might signal an attack, it was the actual message to be delivered that would be the key, not merely the phone call.

When queried about West's novel, Scali said he had never heard of Penkovsky during the missile crisis and that he and Fomin never

397

discussed Penkovsky. Fomin, however, did offer Scali the formula for removing Soviet missiles in Cuba in exchange for removing American missiles in Turkey and Italy, which was to lead to the resolution of the crisis.

How Penkovsky was caught and whom he worked for remain an area of intense interest. Controversies over arcane points of fact and motivation are the substance of the ever present shadow war between the KGB and Western intelligence agencies, of which most of the world is unaware. Even after the end of the Cold War, both sides of the intelligence world compete for a foothold in the continuing struggle to penetrate the other side's secrets. The ideological edge of the battle has been blunted, but the intelligence agencies still seek to prove their superiority and control over each other.

In May 1991 Tom Bower, in cooperation with Novosti Press Agency, a Soviet propaganda organization with close links to the KGB, produced an hour-long documentary on the Penkovsky case called *Fatal Encounter* for the British Broadcasting Corporation. The show combined KGB footage, a fictionalized account of Wynne's life, and interviews with Soviet and American officials connected with the case.

The documentary, directed by Bower, alleges without foundation that MI6 was cheating on its American teammates. His information supports the old KGB effort to suggest duplicity between the American and British Intelligence Services.

In Bower's report the former KGB chairman, Vladimir Semichastny, reveals that the KGB saw a brush contact between a British diplomat, believed to be an MI6 officer, and a Soviet citizen, in the GUM department store in Moscow during the winter of 1962. Bower said this meeting was unknown to the Americans and unauthorized. Semichastny did not say who the diplomat was, nor did he give an exact date, but it was in January 1962, according to Bower. Semichastny says the KGB did not know who the Soviet citizen was. Bower jumps to the conclusion that the meeting in GUM was between Penkovsky and Roderick Chisholm, the MI6 station chief in Moscow. It was at this meeting, Bower asserts, that Penkovsky came under suspicion by the KGB, but he does not offer any other evidence to support his theory. "This was confirmed by British sources," said Bower, who never named the sources.

Sir Dick White, the head of SIS at the time of the Penkovsky case, insists that there never were any separate, unauthorized meetings between Penkovsky and MI6. "That is very implausible and most unlikely. We were in it together with the Americans and as a matter of good faith we would have told you everything. Penkovsky was an extremely difficult person to control. He took immense risks. He wanted to appear as the person who altered the balance of power between the two sides. His vanity was enormous. It is a common psychological position, people being attracted to do things by the importance it reflects on them. He couldn't have had a richer haul. To my mind, with such a rash man and such huge stakes this eventually had to come to an end. There is no need to place blame on any person. Everyone in that matter served well and it was a great satisfaction to me."[50]

Semichastny's revelation that Penkovsky was meeting with a British diplomat in GUM is not in the CIA files of Penkovsky's meetings. Mrs. Chisholm denies that her husband had any separate operational meetings with Penkovsky. A British official close to the case explained, "It was played absolutely straight. Obviously both sides thought they could do it better than the other, but it was played down the line. Rauri Chisholm never met clandestinely with Penkovsky."[51] (Chisholm died of cerebral malaria in September 1979.)

It is difficult to imagine separate British meetings with Penkovsky. There was every reason for Rauri Chisholm not to meet with Penkovsky at that time because Penkovsky had come to believe that Janet Chisholm was under surveillance; the U.S. and the British had called a temporary halt to the open meetings with Penkovsky.

Why would Bower accept the KGB story of a separate meeting by the British with Penkovsky? At Penkovsky's trial in 1963, the KGB worked hard to create a rift between the Americans and British. They tried unsuccessfully to put words into Penkovsky's mouth that the Americans tried to recruit him to spy only for them. It didn't work then and it doesn't work now. For everyone involved, the Penkovsky case was the high point of their careers, and their memories are clear that there were no separate meetings.

Bower told Joseph Bulik that British sources confirmed at least one separate meeting. After being told by Bower that there had been a separate British meeting, Bulik said he was shocked and concluded that "the Brits weren't honest with us." Bower told the same story to Mrs. Rene Peyton, a retired CIA officer, who reviewed the Penkovsky files to find out how he was compromised. Mrs. Peyton, however, stated, "There was no evidence in the files of Penkovsky meeting separately with the British."

Given the added risk of disclosure through unauthorized meetings, such practice would be highly unprofessional and unlikely. The material produced by Penkovsky was processed and shared jointly by the Americans and British. Both the British and Americans chafed under the agreement they made to run Penkovsky jointly, and there was keen rivalry between the two services, but in fact they worked honestly and closely together.

In a distortion of the case, Bower asserted in an article in the *Sunday Telegraph* (May 5, 1991) that Greville Wynne was responsible for Penkovsky's downfall. Bower alleged that Wynne was sent to Moscow in July 1962 without the knowledge of the Americans and that he was not supposed to be used for operational purposes with Penkovsky. Wynne, who in 1988 was living in Majorca (he died of cancer in 1990), described how he carried to Moscow a picture of Rodney Carlson, the CIA officer under embassy cover who was to be Penkovsky's American contact in Moscow. Wynne said he showed the picture of Carlson to Penkovsky when he arrived on July 2 so that Penkovsky could make contact with Carlson at the American Embassy Independence Day celebration. This assignment appears in detail in the files. With it are notes on the American and British coordination to show Penkovsky pictures of Carlson and Gervase and Pamela Cowell, the replacements for the Chisholms.

Wynne said he came under surveillance when he went to meet Penkovsky for dinner at the Pekin Hotel on the evening of July 5. He then went to America House, the American club in Moscow, to tell Chisholm what had happened. Wynne did not go to the British Embassy to meet Gervase Cowell, as Bower asserts. Cowell did not arrive in Moscow until September 1962, two months later.

Wynne came under suspicion of espionage when Penkovsky was spotted with Mrs. Chisholm in December 1961. Penkovsky had told his superiors in the GRU that Wynne was helping him fulfill his intelligence assignments in London; Penkovsky was then authorized to meet with Wynne after hours. By July, however, Penkovsky was under surveillance by the KGB.

Bower asserts that Wynne's trip to Moscow in July 1962 led to Penkovsky's downfall and that Wynne concealed "his personal responsibility for the KGB's abrupt arrest of Penkovsky." Then Bower goes on to claim that the KGB surveillance of Penkovsky produced nothing. In August, when General Oleg M. Gribanov, the head of the KGB Second Chief Directorate, asked General Nikolai F. Chistyakov, chief of the investigative department of the KGB, for permission to arrest Penkovsky, Chistyakov said Gribanov "needed something more conclusive." It was only when Penkovsky's apartment was searched on October 20, according to the KGB, that the evidence was found to arrest him. Bower then says that when Penkovsky disclosed Wynne's role after his arrest it came as "a revelation to the KGB." If it was a revelation, how could Wynne have betrayed Penkovsky? Thus Bower contradicts himself and discredits his own charge that Wynne was responsible for Penkovsky's arrest. Wynne was an accessory to the fact, but his role in the fall of Penkovsky was secondary. Wynne was arrested in Hungary after Penkovsky's confession implicated him.

Wynne, known for exaggeration and adornment of his own role, craved recognition and honor, but these were human frailties far short of the betrayal Bower alleges. Wynne performed bravely under extreme pressure in Moscow, even if he greatly overstated his role after he was freed from prison in the Soviet Union.

Wynne, whether as a spy or a writer, was, as John Le Carré has noted, one of those people who cannot leave a good thing alone. Yet in judging Wynne, Le Carré added: "The information which Penkovsky provided and Wynne purveyed led, there is little doubt, to the greatest moral defeat suffered by either side in the cold war: Khrushchev's decision to withdraw his rockets from Cuba."[52]

Traitor or Savior?

FEW SOVIET CITIZENS, EVEN IN THE TIME OF GLASNOST, HAVE PAUSED
to reevaluate Penkovsky's actions. No Soviet thanks Penkovsky for
saving them from Khrushchev's adventurism. Nobody lights a can-
dle to his memory for delivering them from a nuclear war with the
United States. They know only what appeared in *Pravda* and *Izvestia*
thirty years ago when it was reported that a decadent, alcoholic
military officer betrayed his Motherland. By becoming a spy for the
Americans and the British, Penkovsky crossed the line of no return
that made him an outcast in any society. He was a traitor.

In August 1990 we wrote a letter to then KGB chairman Vladimir
A. Kryuchkov requesting information on the Penkovsky case. We
were pleasantly surprised when the KGB agreed to discuss the case
with Schecter at their offices on Kuznetsky Most (known as "the
reception center"), where passes for visiting the main building on
Dzerzhinsky Square are issued and complaints of corruption or mis-
treatment are registered. (Schecter went alone to meet with the KGB;
it was unreasonable to expect them to receive Deriabin, a defector
who formerly served in Stalin's Kremlin Guard and the First Chief
Directorate of the KGB.)

A bald, energetic KGB official with a nervous smile waited in front
of the reception center and was the escort past the guards to a simply
furnished office. The official and his superior waiting there had both
taken part in the Penkovsky case, they stated. The senior KGB officer
looked like a rumpled professor in his early sixties, paunchy around
the middle, with graying, thin blond hair on an intelligent, high
forehead. The soft, self-indulgent silhouette gave him the look of an
intellectual who enjoyed the pleasures of academia. His face was
lively and alert with dancing eyes and a knowing, ironic smile. On

402

the surface his appearance was bright and charming, a Soviet version of George Smiley, with a deceptively gentle exterior and steel interior.* His rosy, unwrinkled skin conveyed a roundness in his demeanor that belied the stereotyped KGB image. Instead of the usual beefy, heavyhanded spy catcher, here was the Soviet prototype of cool-headed counterintelligence officers who devote their lives to tracking the enemy. He spoke about being a professional and gathering evidence. His quiet sense of humor and worldliness were impressive.

The KGB was uncharacteristically willing to discuss the questions that needed answers about the unresolved and disputed accounts of how Penkovsky was discovered and arrested. Had he been betrayed by a British or American mole within the American national security or British intelligence community? When was he actually arrested? When was he executed and how?

In *Contact on Gorky Street*, Greville Wynne stated that Penkovsky's death sentence was not carried out in 1963. It was in 1965 that Wynne said he learned how "Penkovsky, imprisoned for further interrogation in a small village, took his own life."[1] Another account said that Penkovsky, still alive, was thrown into a roaring furnace while an audience of GRU officers watched his execution, an object lesson on the fate of traitors. This was how Popov was said to have been executed. Michael Bruk, a translator at the Penkovsky-Wynne trial, explained that perhaps the story had grown from the fact that after his execution Penkovsky was cremated in an open coffin so his body could be seen and there would be proof of his death.[2]

The senior KGB officer said he thought he could help, but he would have to discuss how such information could be released. It would take several weeks.

Would there be a revision of the record on Penkovsky? Now that thirty years had passed, Khrushchev's memoirs confirmed what Penkovsky had surreptitiously photographed in classified libraries and overheard at the defense minister's birthday party. Would the remaining truths be revealed?

The KGB agreed to a meeting on Monday, October 8, 1990, at 3:30 P.M. at the Lubyanka. The shadow of the intimidating ten-story, heavy stone walls of the Lubyanka, KGB headquarters, looms large

---

* The character Smiley, a long-serving MI6 senior case officer, is said within the service to be modeled after the late Sir Maurice Oldfield, whose careless dress, tobacco-stained fingers, and skilled professionalism made him a legend. When Alec Guinness prepared to play the role of Smiley in the television series based on Le Carré's novel *Tinker, Tailor, Soldier, Spy*, he invited Oldfield to lunch to study his mannerisms. Afterward, Oldfield was asked what he thought of Guinness. "I still don't recognize myself," replied Sir Maurice.

in Soviet life. This is the building that Russians look upon with dread. In years past it was easy to spot people crossing the street to avoid walking on the sidewalk in front of the main entrance. Was it fear of being forced inside or meeting ghosts of tortured prisoners? Taxi drivers pointed to the pale yellow and rose colored stone walls and said *strashno*, terrifying, when passing through Dzerzhinsky Square.

The Lubyanka was known to be a building of no return because of the prison located in the interior. In the past men and women did not return, or if they did, only with broken bodies and lives. Within this lair occurred the acts of brutality and deception by which absolute power is maintained. The Lubyanka is no longer a prison. It has become a storehouse and cafeteria. Some cells are preserved, now a museum. The change came quietly in the late 1960s, but the image of dread prevails. Those in the KGB's employ considered themselves to be professionals preserving the Soviet state and its security. Until the abortive coup of August 1991, the KGB was the keeper of the Russian Empire, a political, military, and law-enforcement conglomerate charged with intelligence gathering and maintaining internal security. Equipped with the latest technology, it has the largest information network in the Soviet Union, and was said to be the only efficient organization for controlling the republics. The KGB and the Communist Party were the coercive forces in Soviet society until the coup failed and their powers were sharply curbed.

Since the introduction of glasnost, the Committee for State Security has a public relations department and pays lip service to the rule of law. However, it has still failed to come to terms with its past and faces an identity crisis from within. In the fall of 1990, for example, its public relations department sponsored an opening exhibition of the new KGB Museum located in the KGB Club next to the headquarters. The club has a bar, two restaurants, several auditoriums, and reception rooms. The historical exhibit opened with pictures of Felix Dzerzhinsky, the founder of the Cheka. The title is derived from the Cyrillic initial letters of the first two words of its full name: *Chrezvychaynaya Kommissiya po Borbe s Kontrrevolyutsiey, Spekulaytsiey i Sabotazhem*: Extraordinary Commission for Combating Counterrevolution, Speculation, and Sabotage.[3] From Dzerzhinsky the display jumped to Yuri Andropov, who headed the Committee for State Security from 1967 to 1982, and then on to Vladimir Kryuchkov, the chairman of the KGB, who was jailed for his role in the August 1991 coup. There were no pictures or mention of the men who ruled between Dzerzhinsky and Andropov, the forty-six years that included Yagoda, Yezhov, Merkulov, Kruglov, Abakumov, and Beria, all remembered today because they were Stalin's executioners. Stalin's Great Terror devoured an estimated 20 million people.[4] The Soviet holocaust began with the collectivization of agriculture, continued through the Party struggles and purges of the 1930s, followed by the forced deportation of nationalities through the beginning of World War II. The KGB and its predecessor organs, the VChK, OGPU, NKVD, and MVD, were Stalin's enforcers for these mass denunciations, phony trials, and executions.

The search for "enemies of the people" was the rallying cry and rationale for the purges. Any hint of a pro-tsarist past in a family tree was grounds for suspicion and denunciation. For Oleg Penkovsky, the family connection with the father he never met was to be his undoing. Was it because his father was a White Russian officer whose grave could not be found that Penkovsky's chances to advance were destroyed? Or was it his own self-doubt and driven need to establish an identity? Would the KGB reveal anything new about him? How had Wynne and Penkovsky felt when they had been brought to the Lubyanka? Had they abandoned hope the way "enemies of the people" did when entering these walls?

On the outside of the KGB headquarters on Dzerzhinsky Square was a marble portrait of Yuri Andropov with fresh red carnations resting on the ledge below; the heavy stone plaque commemorated the years when he was chairman of the KGB.* Entrance 1-A is a pair of tall, heavily varnished, blond wooden doors. In the past the front doors facing on the square were rarely used; all business was conducted through the entrances in the rear.

Inside the dimly lit entrance stood two young lieutenants in blue and gray woolen uniforms with calf-length black leather boots, checking identification of all who entered or exited. The KGB escort's red leather passbook notes that "the bearer is authorized to carry arms." When the guard demanded identification, I showed him my Washington, D.C., driver's license. The guard checked the picture and the escort nodded, indicating all was correct.

---

* The plaque for Andropov was removed after the August 19, 1991, coup failed. The statue of the KGB founder, which long towered over Dzerzhinsky Square, named for him, was torn down, and the square and metro station in front of the KGB headquarters were renamed Lubyanka Square.

The KGB is being drastically reorganized. The First Chief Directorate, in charge of foreign intelligence, was made an independent agency by Mikhail Gorbachev and renamed the Central Intelligence Service. The Second Chief Directorate, concerned with counterintelligence, has been renamed the Inter-republican Security Service. It will absorb the Fourth Directorate, dealing with transportation security, and the Sixth Directorate, dealing with economic crimes, fraud, and corruption. The Border Guards Directorate had been made an independent agency under the direction of the State Council. Other directorates are being reorganized, eliminated, or reduced in size and budget.

405

On the third floor, off a corridor newly paneled with composition board, a display room commemorates KGB exploits defending Soviet borders and fighting crime. The next room along the hallway is the "Press Bar." Indeed, the room seemed to be designed for informal meetings. It was decorated with crystal chandeliers, high-backed, nubby gray cloth lounge chairs, a bar with no bottles or glasses, and an espresso machine with no cups, saucers, or coffee. On a corner table stood a videotape player and a television set. The senior KGB officer from the Second Chief Directorate, for counterintelligence, would preside but refused to divulge his first name and insisted that neither he nor his colleague be identified. (Even the family names they gave could have been aliases.) Also present was a well-dressed young woman, an interpreter, who spoke poor English.

The KGB officer explained that he would offer a history of the case and provide new materials. His opening comment was, "We do not agree that Penkovsky was *le Sauveur du monde*." His use of French for the phrase "savior of the world" was a pleasant touch. "The case of Penkovsky," he read from a typewritten brief, "was not resolved by chance. The exposure of this dangerous spy was the result of hard work on the part of Soviet Intelligence."

The CIA and MI6 have never satisfactorily resolved the question of how Penkovsky was caught. In searching through the records, many possibilities emerge. One theory suggested that Soviet Communications Intelligence intercepted message traffic to the American Embassy singling out Penkovsky for a visa to the Seattle Fair in the spring of 1962. A Soviet spy in the National Security Agency, Sergeant Jack Dunlap, employed as a documents distribution clerk, may have compromised Penkovsky. When Dunlap's home was searched in July 1963, after he committed suicide, a number of Penkovsky's less sensitive documents, attributed to a "reliable Soviet source," were found. As a CIA study of the Penkovsky case noted: "While these documents would not likely have led to identification of Penkovsky as a source, they would certainly have indicated to the KGB that there was a penetration of the Soviet Government with access to internally controlled documents."[5] Another possibility was that Penkovsky had been betrayed by a Soviet spy, Lieutenant Colonel William Whalen, a code-word control officer in the Joint Chiefs of Staff in the Defense Department. The CIA study notes, "There is a strong possibility that he [Whalen] had access to Penkovsky's production and compromised it to the Soviets. This would greatly have reduced the time needed to isolate Penkovsky as a prime candidate for penetration of the Soviet defense establishment."[6]

Another possible source for compromising Penkovsky was U.S. Army sergeant Robert Lee Johnson, who late in 1961 was assigned as a guard in the Armed Forces Courier Center at Orly Airport, near Paris. With coaching from his KGB controller, Johnson obtained access to the triple-locked vault used to store classified material. Johnson was able to obtain a wax impression of the key to the vault, found the combination to the second lock in a wastepaper basket, and with the help of a portable X-ray device supplied by the KGB found the combination to the third lock. On December 15, 1961, Johnson entered the vault for the first time and delivered highly classified materials to the KGB, whose technicians copied it and returned it before Johnson's shift was over. According to the authors of *KGB: The Inside Story*, British historian Christopher Andrew and former KGB Colonel Oleg Gordievsky, on December 26, 1962, Johnson was given the congratulations of Nikita Khrushchev and the Soviet Council of Ministers, told he was awarded the Red Army rank of major, and presented with $2000 to spend on a holiday in Monte Carlo. By the end of April 1963, Johnson had provided seventeen flight bags full of documents that included cipher systems, the location of U.S. nuclear warheads stored in Europe, and NATO and U.S. defense plans.[7]

Since Penkovsky's information on Soviet planning in Berlin was passed to senior American commanders in Europe, it is possible that Johnson compromised them. Again, Penkovsky was never named directly but referred to as a reliable Soviet source or a senior Soviet officer, which would have given the KGB the spoor to track down. And Johnson's penetration of the vault coincides with the timing of the surveillance on Mrs. Chisholm and Penkovsky in Moscow.

If Whalen, Dunlap, or Johnson compromised Penkovsky's production, even if KGB Counterintelligence did not know Penkovsky's name, a check would have provided enough information for the KGB to track him down through a security search of all those Soviet officers with access to the tightly controlled documents in the possession of the American authorities. By reviewing who had signed the Soviet Defense Ministry registry logs for access to these classified documents, the KGB could begin a process of elimination of suspects.

A Soviet source familiar with the workings of the KGB and the handling of the Penkovsky case explained in an interview in 1990 that when it became known in 1961 that classified military materials were leaking to the United States, an investigation was initiated by the KGB to see who had access to these materials. From 1000 officers and staff personnel, the list was reduced to the point where Penkovsky came under suspicion.[8] In his memoirs Khrushchev raised his fears of a Soviet spy. "When the Americans made public the number and location of our missiles in Cuba I asked [Defense Minister Rodion Y.] Malinovsky: 'How do they know about the number of our missiles and their location? Can it not be that we have an agent in our armed forces? I do not exclude that.'

"Malinovsky replied: 'Neither do I. This is possible. It's difficult to give you a guarantee against that. However, aerial reconnaissance at present gives the Americans the possibility to observe our work. They fly systematically and take pictures regularly, then drop them in containers. Therefore, the Americans literally can follow us step by step. We also have the capability to do that, so this issue should not be sharpened into a confrontation.' " Khrushchev apparently knew that documents were missing and suspected the worst.[9]

Some of the translated Penkovsky documents might have been seen by Soviet spies in England. Two convicted British spies were functioning during the Penkovsky operation: John Vassall, a clerk in the secretariat of the Naval Staff, was arrested on spying charges in September 1962, and Frank Brossard, a senior intelligence officer of the Joint Intelligence Bureau, worked undetected from 1961 to 1965 until he was arrested and convicted.[10]

There was also the George Blake connection. On Friday, April 9, 1961, Blake was interrogated in the SIS offices at 3 Carlton Gardens, overlooking Pall Mall and St. James's Park, by a team of MI6 officers headed by Harold Shergold. Blake had been brought back to London from Lebanon, where he was studying Arabic. It was the fourth day of questioning. Still Blake refused to admit that he had been working for the Soviet Intelligence Service since he returned from a Korean prisoner-of-war camp in 1953. The evidence indicated Blake had betrayed British intelligence operations in Berlin in 1955, but Blake stolidly resisted confessing.

The group broke for lunch and when they returned Shergold had only one question left for Blake: "We know that you worked for the Soviets, but we don't understand why. While you were their prisoner in Korea, you were tortured and made to confess that you were a British intelligence officer. From then on you were blackmailed and had no choice but to collaborate with them."[11]

Blake snapped. "All I can say is that it was a gut reaction. Suddenly I felt an upsurge of indignation and I wanted my interrogators and everyone else to know that I had acted out of conviction, out of my belief in Communism, and not under duress or for financial gain. This feeling was so strong that without thinking what I was doing I burst out, 'No, nobody tortured me! Nobody blackmailed me! I myself approached the Soviets and offered my services to them of my own accord.'

"A gut reaction this outburst may have been but it amounted well and truly to a confession. Having now admitted to my interrogators—as unexpectedly to them, I am sure, as to myself—that I was a Soviet agent, I went on to explain exactly the reasons that impelled me to become one," Blake wrote in his autobiography.[12]

After breaking Blake, Shergold turned to preparing for the arrival of Penkovsky in London on April 20, 1961. Blake's arrest was announced discreetly in the British press on April 22, 1961, the day Penkovsky set off for a trip to Leeds with Greville Wynne. How were Penkovsky and Blake linked?

The story began in June 1960, the KGB officer explained, when Charles Roderick Chisholm, age forty-five, arrived in Moscow to be second secretary of the British Embassy. "We knew he was a British spy by the time he arrived in Moscow. We knew that," insisted the Soviet Counterintelligence officer.

In 1954–1955 Chisholm worked in the Russian section of the SIS Intelligence Station in West Berlin. At that time he actively tried to recruit Soviet military personnel. He used forged documents acting as a British businessman, B. Coster or Kastor, and H. Erickson, a British student. The wife of Chisholm played an important role. Usually we don't speak about wives. She was four years younger than her husband.* We knew he was an SIS spy who used forged documents. In June of 1955 the British government recalled Chisholm from Berlin. He made too many mistakes and was revealed as a spy. He was too active. After he was recalled he worked in the central apparatus in London against the socialist countries. In 1960 he appeared in Moscow. You can understand the feeling of Soviet Counterintelligence. It is only natural that we could not let him out of our sight.

In 1961 Soviet Counterintelligence began following Mrs. Chisholm. Twice, at the end of 1961 and in 1962, Counterintelligence saw Mrs. Chisholm, while walking, stop to enter the entrances of apartment houses. Soon they saw a stranger nearby who appeared to be very nervous and trying to discover if there was surveillance of him. The houses were not of historical or architectural value. That stranger was Penkovsky.

At this point the Russian interrupted himself to screen a videotaped copy of a twenty-minute KGB film on Penkovsky, which included KGB surveillance footage of Penkovsky meeting Chisholm in the park off Tsvetnoy Boulevard and in the Arbat beginning in December 30, 1961. There were HERO and ANNE. The videotape showed Penkovsky in a phone booth, looking for surveillance, then

---

* Mrs. Chisholm told the authors that she was an SIS secretary and was not involved in any operational activities in Germany.

entering and leaving an apartment house entryway. "In December 1961 we noted for the first time that Penkovsky or someone had a meeting with Anne Chisholm. (He used her code name ANNE instead of Janet.) By January, when we saw this man again, we recognized him as Penkovsky. It could have been an accidental meeting. We needed proof that it was not an accidental encounter," said the Russian Smiley. "There were no other meetings in the open in which we saw Penkovsky with foreign diplomats," he added, contradicting assertions that Penkovsky had unscheduled meetings with a British intelligence officer unknown and unreported to the CIA.

Why was Penkovsky allowed to continue to operate in Moscow from December 1961 until his arrest ten months later on October 22, 1962? Was the KGB protecting a mole in the American or British services who had fingered him? If Penkovsky had been arrested would the mole have been discovered?

The Soviet counterintelligence officer smiled and shook his head. "No, no. This is sheer imagination. Americans are good enough to make up such things. You people are very rich in such imagination, as well as everything else, but it was clear to us that it was Mrs. Chisholm that led us to the Penkovsky case. We did not need to have a mole," he said.

The junior colleague added, "Penkovsky was found with the help of Chisholm only."

Exactly why the surveillance was started on Mrs. Chisholm, the KGB officials declined to elaborate, other than to repeat that they knew she had tried to help her husband recruit Soviet citizens in Germany; because of this, both were marked for surveillance in Moscow from the first. The senior KGB officer said (erroneously) that Mrs. Chisholm met with Penkovsky four or five times, and he recounted the circumstances of the first meeting in the park at Tsvetnoy Boulevard.

George Blake had served in Berlin with the Chisholms; had this been the key?

"You can imagine what you want," replied the senior official, refusing to answer the question.

Suddenly it was clear. Blake served in Berlin at the same time as the Chisholms and had revealed their intelligence roles to the KGB.

How could a shrewd, experienced operative like Shergold, who had the intuitive power to break Blake, go from one case to the other without realizing that the Chisholms were tainted by the very fact of having served in Berlin with George Blake?

For Shergold the use of the Chisholms in Moscow was an operational necessity. "Everybody in the British Embassy was under surveillance. The name of the game was to avoid surveillance," he later recalled. Operating under known surveillance is one of the most controversial aspects of intelligence fieldcraft, and experts are divided on whether activity should be attempted under such conditions. In Moscow there was no alternative except to cease operations, but Penkovsky's insistence on continuing to operate negated that option. There was no simple alternative to the Chisholms. The CIA's officer in Moscow, COMPASS, had been a failure and his replacement did not arrive until July 1962.

The senior KGB official continued his analysis. "Soon after analyzing the results of our surveillance we came to the conclusion that Penkovsky and Anne Chisholm were involved in dead-drop operations." The senior officer and his colleague reviewed the Penkovsky case much the way it was presented at the trial. "Penkovsky was not motivated by any political ideas toward peace or any other humanitarian ideals, but by maliciousness, distorted self-pride, ambition, and personal immorality. He confessed all this during the investigation and at the trial," said Smiley. "Penkovsky wanted to achieve two aims. The first was to take revenge on his superiors. They knew him very well and did not want to advance his career. The second was to gain material profit. The Americans and British promised Penkovsky the rank and salary of a colonel [$13,955 in 1962 with allowances] when he defected, plus $1000 for each month he had spied for them."

We have seen in chapter 15 that when Penkovsky grew agitated about his future and the possibility of defecting to the West, the CIA and MI6 agreed to set up a $250,000 trust fund to settle him and his family in the West. Penkovsky would have been paid this $250,000 plus his salary of $1,000 per month, which retroactively came to $29,000.[13]

In discussing Penkovsky's motives, the senior official quoted from a fitness report that Penkovsky received from his superior, the military attaché, during the time he served in Turkey from March 1955 to December 1956: "Penkovsky is not a hard worker and did not perform his work scrupulously. At work he is not enthusiastic and has a tendency to be toadying. He spent long hours collecting and spreading gossip about the life and work of officers at the embassy. His surface discipline is more show than substance. By nature and conduct Penkovsky is a spiteful, vengeful person capable of stooping to any means to further his career." The officer who wrote the report was General Rubenko, the man whom Penkovsky had reported to Moscow for violating orders. For a lazy man, how feverishly Penkovsky worked for revenge when he became a spy!

The KGB did not arrest Penkovsky immediately upon discovering his espionage because it wanted to learn the full extent of his activities and with whom he was working. "We started to suspect Wynne when we suspected Penkovsky." Then he described the July meeting between Wynne and Penkovsky in the Ukraine Hotel and "their amateurish efforts to hide their conversation [by turning on the water taps and the radio]. Penkovsky was not arrested until October 22."

Gaps remained in the story. Where was Penkovsky from the time he was last seen until his arrest?

"Penkovsky was hospitalized on the 7th of September, 1962, at his request," explained the KGB officer. "He really was suffering from a skin disease for a long time and because of this illness he repeatedly turned to doctors for help." He was discharged from the hospital on September 28, 1962, according to the KGB account.

However, the CIA had been told by the controversial defector Yuri Nosenko that Penkovsky had been deliberately incapacitated by the KGB. A poisonous wax was supposedly smeared on the chair in his office. When Penkovsky sat on the wax his body heat melted it and the corrosive effects of the poison in the wax were released, irritating his buttocks so badly that he required hospitalization. Nosenko's version was based on an internal KGB memorandum he claimed to have seen in Moscow before defecting in Geneva in 1964.[14]

The KGB official denied that any "dirty tricks" were used against Penkovsky. "The idea that the KGB was involved in the operation, in the infection of Penkovsky, is purely an invention," insisted the officer.

The KGB official would not budge from this explanation that Penkovsky's hospitalization had been for a chronic skin ailment. "It was dermatological, but the hospital would know the exact name and there were records. This is possible to find out in the hospital. All the records are kept there, but it will take a long time. Maybe Penkovsky's wife knows, she visited him in the hospital," said the official.

This explanation of a chronic skin disease was hardly credible in view of an earlier internal KGB report that the CIA had obtained clandestinely saying that Penkovsky had been deliberately hospitalized by the KGB in order to get him out of his apartment so it could be searched without his knowledge.[15] The account of Penkovsky's being poisoned was also presented by Andrew and Gordievsky in their book, *KGB: The Inside Story*.[16] Gordievsky, a KGB colonel who escaped from the Soviet Union in the summer of 1985, had been appointed KGB *rezident* in London. Since 1974 he had been working for MI6 as a penetration agent inside the KGB. "What Gordievsky said is on his conscience," said the Russian Smiley with a shrug.

Patiently but firmly the KGB official interjected: "I want to repeat some details on the last period of Penkovsky's life, the existence of Penkovsky as a spy. The thing is that Gordievsky had nothing to do with the case and the case file on Penkovsky was kept a tightly held secret. Counterintelligence even now cannot disclose how Penkovsky was uncovered. In my opinion such secrecy may explain the appearance of numerous versions, especially in the West. I repeat once more that Gordievsky had no relation of any kind to the Penkovsky case, and he could not know anything about this case except rumors. Let's go further if we can."

The question of Penkovsky's arrest on October 22, 1962, was again raised. What had he done, and where had he been, between the time he was discharged from the hospital and his arrest? The evidence indicated that Penkovsky had been arrested before October 22. He was last seen on September 6 at the British Embassy film show. According to KGB practice, it would be standard to detain him for at least two weeks to obtain a confession before his formal arrest. Penkovsky was most likely detained after his discharge from the hospital, once his apartment had been searched and the incriminating materials discovered in his desk.

"He returned to work," explained the KGB senior briefer, as if that were the most natural and expected thing.

The two-or-three-week leave Penkovsky had expected to take in the fall had not come to pass. Penkovsky, the KGB now explained, "was arrested right when he was at work . . . when he was coming out of the office he was arrested. He was arrested with one of our minor officers of the State Committee." According to Tom Bower's BBC program, Penkovsky was told his passport for a trip abroad was ready and a friend from the KGB came to pick him up to take him to receive his passport. When he arrived at KGB headquarters Penkovsky was arrested.[17]

Again the KGB official referred to his typed briefing notes and told me, "It happened during the daytime in front of the building of the State Committee on Scientific Research. After his arrest he was brought to a solitary confinement cell in the KGB prison and he was kept there until his execution. Penkovsky's interrogation was conducted in the same building. The building to which he was brought was the internal jail of the KGB, address: Dzerzhinsky Square, Building Number 2.

When the sentence was announced for the Penkovsky case it was the death sentence. The duty to carry out the sentence was entrusted to the organs of the Ministry of Internal Affairs (MVD). You know that Penkovsky had all the rights of a convicted person. His appeal, to the Presidium of the Supreme Soviet of the U.S.S.R., the highest court, was rejected. The sentence was carried out and Penkovsky was shot on May 16, 1963, during the daytime. This did not happen here because the KGB organs do not carry out sentences. Sentences, jailing or executions, are carried out by the organs of the Ministry for Internal Affairs. As far as it is known, Penkovsky was shot in Butyrki Jail, located at Novoslobodskaya Street. In 1963 it was a special criminal jail. Butyrki Jail now is a transfer prison.

Penkovsky's body, after he was shot, was cremated. According to the laws at that time the urn with the ashes was not passed to the relatives. Our laws are different from those of other countries. The urn with Penkovsky's ashes was buried, where I do not know. Penkovsky's wife was given a death certificate, you can ask her. We do not have a copy of this certificate because Penkovsky's widow has it.

But the KGB officer produced a copy of a document which authorized the Registry Office to give Mrs. Penkovsky her death certificate.

The KGB officers denied that Penkovsky was burned alive in a crematorium as a gruesome example of the fate of traitors. However, the story persists. The Nobel Prize-winning poet Joseph Brodsky (in an article prepared for *The New Republic*) wrote that he was told that Penkovsky's execution was filmed. "Strapped to a stretcher, Penkovsky was wheeled into the Moscow city crematorium's chamber. An attendant opens the furnace door and two others start to push the stretcher and its contents into the roaring furnace; the flame is already licking the screaming man's soles. At this point, a voice comes over the loudspeaker interrupting the procedure because another body is scheduled for this time slot. Screaming but unable to kick, Penkovsky is pulled back; another body arrives and after a small ceremony is pushed into the furnace. The voice over the loudspeaker comes again: now it is Penkovsky's turn, and in he goes. A small but effective skit. Beats Beckett hands down, boosts morale, and can't be forgotten: brands your wits. A kind of stamp, if you will, for intramural correspondence."*

Then the KGB officers attempted to make the case that Penkovsky and the materials he passed to the West had no influence on decision-

---

*Brodsky heard this account of Penkovsky's death from the sculptor Ernest Neizvestny, who had a commission to create a bas relief for the Donskoi Cemetery crematorium in Moscow. After work one day, while drinking vodka with the director of the crematorium, Neizvestny was told by him how Penkovsky was executed by fire. "I believe it is a real story," Neizvestny said in an interview with the authors. "Maybe it is getting like a folk story, but the basis is real. Gossip is always true. The director of the crematorium told me while we drank vodka together and I spoke with people around me who worked with me. They told me a lot of stories of how they took gold from dead people, and good dresses."

making for peace or war. "Having analyzed all the materials at our disposal during the trial, as well as the Penkovsky file during the secret investigations, there is nothing to support the idea that he helped to eliminate a nuclear conflict between the United States and the Soviet Union. First of all, Penkovsky did not have access to information of the nuclear potential of the Soviet Union. Neither, I think, did he have any access to information of the nuclear potential of other countries."

It was ironic that for nearly thirty years the insignificance of Penkovsky's role was loudly trumpeted by the KGB when it was mentioned at all. Now full disclosure of his arrest and execution had not led to honesty about his importance, only further denials.

Smiley insisted that Penkovsky's information was of no importance during the Cuban missile crisis, but he did acknowledge that Penkovsky was given the task from British Intelligence to get information about the conclusion of a peace treaty with the German Democratic Republic and the location of Soviet troops in the GDR.

"I think that there is no use to review, to reestimate, the contribution of Penkovsky to the prevention of nuclear conflict at that time. And the analysis of materials before and during the investigation proves that.

"In short, we can't manage to find anything in the material of the investigation, anything to prove your version. To call Penkovsky a savior of the world is interesting to us, but it is not proved by the documents of the case."

He read off a list of items that Penkovsky gave to the CIA and MI6.

Penkovsky gave the names of the GRU officers, including the names of the staff of three intelligence stations and the names and operations of military and naval attachés. He told of the general organizational structure of the GRU staff and provided information on the methods of operation of Military Strategic Intelligence. He explained the rules of work and the ciphers [for cryptographic systems] used by the GRU in 1955–1956, when Penkovsky worked as a military attaché in Turkey. He provided the text of lectures of the Intelligence Department of the GRU and gave to foreign intelligence copies of the secret journals and magazines of the Soviet Army including *Voyennaya Mysl* (Military thought) from 1961 and 1962. He also provided secret copies of *The Artillery and Missile Journal* from 1962.

Penkovsky also provided the names of the staff of the Military-Diplomatic Academy and provided a list of students at the academy when he attended classes there. He also gave them information on the personalities of foreigners who cooperated with Soviet Military

Intelligence. This is the most important information that Penkovsky gave to the foreign special services.

The KGB official repeated the effort made during the trial to drive a wedge between the British and American Intelligence Services. He produced three pages of Penkovsky's handwritten testimony during the pretrial investigation. In it Penkovsky speaks of being invited by the Americans "for a cup of coffee" shortly before he left Paris in October 1961, but it contains no separate offer by the Americans to Penkovsky to work for them.

It is correct that both the British and the Americans would have preferred to run Penkovsky separately. Although MI6 and the CIA share the information they receive from most Soviet agents and defectors, historically they spurn joint operations because of the compounded risk of exposure in coordinating these. In the Penkovsky case, however, the difficulties of working in Moscow necessitated a team effort, especially since he approached both the CIA and MI6 before either could sign him up.

Penkovsky noted in his written pretrial confession, made available by the KGB, that

At the time of my meetings with the British and American intelligence officers in London and Paris, as well as in the letters of instruction I received from them, I could not feel any different approach toward me or any uncoordinated actions between them. Outwardly, in my presence, they made an effort to demonstrate full harmony, the same view, and a united plan of their joint work. In my presence there were never any arguments or reproaches to each other. They tried to demonstrate the presence of a well thought-out, well-coordinated joint operation.

This is the outward side. By intuition I felt that even if I was not a witness to any kind of open contradictions between them I did not really know the nature of their relations. Without me, but to themselves, the British and Americans thought: it would be good if there were only one of them because either of them separately could manage the work independently. Here it is necessary for one intelligence service to open its questions and tasks and give an evaluation in front of the other. I myself felt to a small degree the general antagonistic differences between these countries when their intelligence officers sat down together around one table and began to meddle with each other. To give up the idea of jointly working with me, and to lose what is already in their hands, that means to give a gift of everything to one side with nothing being received by the other.

I felt that they were annoyed with themselves about me because I had come to both intelligence services. The Americans were more disappointed with themselves than the British. They lost patience and told me frankly about it in their hotel, without the British being present. The Americans were sorry that they had delayed their answer to me for five months from the time I approached them [in July 1960]. The British, being more cautious, told me nothing like that.[18]

The KGB official's interpretation of Penkovsky's statement was similar to the organization's other efforts to spread dissension between the Americans and the British. Joe Bulik recalled that, in a postmortem of the Penkovsky case for new recruits and junior officers, he told them, "Never enter into a joint operation with any intelligence service. Despite that I always leveled with Shergie and the Brits. The only time I met alone with Penkovsky was when I met with him and females in Paris. The Brits did the same thing in London. The whole thing is just a bunch of garbage by the KGB trying to split the CIA and MI6."[19]

In his confession Penkovsky wrote, "Foreign intelligence officers never told me about the methods and means of their verification of my information. Nor did they tell me if the authenticity of some of my information was doubtful. Foreign intelligence officers often controlled and checked my conduct abroad. From conversations with intelligence officers I felt that they knew everything in detail from Wynne about the time I spent with him. Sometimes I noticed surveillance in the areas of hotels and exhibitions in London and Paris. I paid no attention to this surveillance and did not try to shake it."

In fact, there was not supposed to be surveillance on Penkovsky in Paris or London. This restraint was an effort not to attract attention to him. If the Soviets had noticed surveillance on him in London, it would have been reported back to Moscow and questions would have been raised. If there had been a surveillance team on him in Paris, either the KGB Paris Station or the French might have been alerted. Either event would have led to complications and possible compromise.

The KGB official offered a copy, in Russian, of the Military Court's evaluation of Penkovsky's crimes and his sentence. Then he talked of Penkovsky's personal qualities "to show how unscrupulous he was. During the investigation Penkovsky expressed his readiness to cooperate with the KGB and to help us to expose and denounce the activity of British and American Intelligence."

When pressed to offer evidence of this surprising assertion, the KGB official harshly added: "Of course, it was on the condition that

417

he be set free, but still he very easily betrayed his ideals. He had no ideals and no principles at all.

"We knew a number of people, unlike Penkovsky, who would not so easily betray their ideals and would be steady in their convictions. At the very first interrogation he immediately proposed his plan for exposing British and American Intelligence. He gave the Soviet Counterintelligence all the information, enough, for example, to catch American and British intelligence officers in Moscow. We did not mind that at all; but that shows how steadfast he was."

Perhaps he was trying to save his life?

"Indeed, indeed. He was trying to save his life. In one attempt he was trying to prolong, to save his life, and maybe he even hoped for something. God knows. We knew a number of people who were held under very difficult conditions and would not deal with Counterintelligence even to save their lives. Even to save their lives," said the official.

To further underscore his point about Penkovsky's character, he insisted that Penkovsky "was not forced, he was not physically forced or compelled to do something. We said to him if you want to give your evidence please do and he did so. He asked for some paper and pen. All day long he wrote his confession and his plan of exposure."

"It was his goodwill," said the junior KGB officer, mocking Penkovsky's efforts to save himself.

In 1990 the KGB pressed the same propaganda points they had pressed at the trial, but now the KGB footage of Janet Chisholm and Penkovsky together was part of the historical record. The KGB's reticence about George Blake clarified the sequence of events that led to Penkovsky's arrest.[20]

There was another stop to make before leaving Moscow. Vera Dimitrievna Penkovsky, Penkovsky's widow, was still living in Moscow in 1990, where she had been an editor at a publishing house before her retirement in 1989. She declined to be interviewed; her memories of her husband were too painful. She said in a phone call that her two daughters had changed their names and "are living a good life. The elder is married. We were not purged and we are not afraid, but we do not want to return to the past. Of course, I see things of those years in a new light." She did not explain what she meant by that.

A final journey through Penkovsky's Moscow was in order. On the front door of the house with the dead drop at Pushkinskaya Street 5/6 there is now a number-coded combination lock on the front door, a type of lock increasingly prevalent in Moscow. No one without the code is able to enter and see whether the radiator where the matchbox was placed is still there. When I pressed against the door, however, the lock was broken and it opened. The hallway was dark. On a whim I reached behind the radiator and felt for a message. Instead, I sensed a piece of cloth and pulled out a child's torn, lost glove left behind to dry. The concrete electric poles on Kutuzovsky Prospekt, including the one Penkovsky would have marked in case of the outbreak of war, are still standing. The heavy, polished wood and Persian-carpeted elegance of the British Embassy remains unchanged; it is easy to retrace the route Penkovsky followed to his rendezvous with Janet Chisholm in the cloakroom. It is possible to enter the shabby apartment house on Arbat Lane where Penkovsky and Janet Chisholm exchanged messages and materials. Tsvetnoy Park, where Penkovsky brought his films in a box of candy, is still a favored spot for young foreign wives walking their children from the nearby journalists' and diplomats' apartment house complex on Sadovaya-Samotechnaya. Soviet Army officers, on their way to the Defense Ministry and GRU headquarters, still cross Red Square near the bridge where Penkovsky first met the American students.

Imagine Penkovsky, not the way he would look now, aged by thirty years, but the way he was then, fired by injustice to himself and the Russian people. He sensed that the way to unseat Nikita Khrushchev, the "reckless adventurer" who led his country, was not through violence or a coup d'état. The way would be cleared by letting Khrushchev's adversaries know his weaknesses. Little did Penkovsky imagine under the yellow streetlights of the Moskvoretsky Bridge to what extent he would succeed in tipping the balance of terror away from nuclear war.

The volume of his reports, their insights, and their timeliness were critical in forming President Kennedy's views of Nikita Khrushchev and how to deal with him. Kennedy delighted in seeing the Soviet version of his talks with Khrushchev in Vienna because it revealed what Khrushchev considered important and how the Soviet leader played the talks in the Communist world and to Communist parties in the West. Such material, which emphasized Khrushchev's determination to proceed with a separate peace treaty with East Germany, gave Kennedy a better feel for the Soviet leader, whom he had found so difficult to reach in Vienna. He learned the Soviet leader's true measure long before the Cuban missile crisis. Penkovsky, KGB claims to the contrary, had provided Kennedy with the hard information to manage the Berlin crisis of 1961 and the Cuban missile crisis of 1962.

419

Oleg Penkovsky was the greatest Soviet spy to serve the West after the end of World War II. No Soviet spy has provided more material or had a greater impact on history.[21] He was a fearless prophet who warned the West of Khrushchev's plans to overtake the United States in nuclear weapons production. He provided the hard specifics of Soviet military strength and weakness. He identified for the West the vast Soviet intelligence apparatus: how it worked, who were its agents, their assignments and priorities.

The scope of information that Penkovsky supplied to the West was unrivaled. He changed the West's perception of Soviet nuclear weapons; he helped the Free World to understand the inadequacy of the Communist system. The military tactics and strategy he described and documented remain relevant to understanding contemporary Soviet doctrine, whose essentials have not changed. Penkovsky's Minox photos offered an insight into Soviet military thinking at a time of critical policy realignment. The U.S. could see the factories being built, sample the air, and photograph the missile-silo construction, but we could not read the debates over strategy or fathom Soviet intentions until Penkovsky made them available. His reports are still the measure by which intelligence analysts judge their sense of reality of the Soviet system.[22]

Penkovsky was motivated to defect by the police state's discovery of the White Russian past of his father. He had only his mother's word for it that the man who sired him and disappeared forever was married to her and that his name was Penkovsky. Yet by her assertion his fate was tied ineluctably to a noble name that could only bring him trouble. It was not an identity that would do him any good in the Soviet state.

Times have changed since Penkovsky was executed in 1963. The site of the murder of Tsar Nicholas II and his family in Sverdlovsk, again named Ekaterinburg in August 1991, is now a shrine. Photo exhibitions of life among the nobility before the Revolution draw crowds of nostalgic onlookers seeking a return to the family values of the old régime. To be attached to a family of illustrious gentry now indicates the possibility of a distinguished gene pool rather than pro forma confirmation of being an "enemy of the people."

Yet despite glasnost, Penkovsky's image, where it is remembered, remains as it was engineered at his trial in 1963. If anything it has tarnished over the years. The primary focus in 1963 was on his weak character, his greed, and his excessive love of women. Throughout the trial there was an effort to denigrate his importance as a spy in order to minimize and deemphasize the secrets he had stolen and transmitted to the West. At the trial Khrushchev was trying to protect himself and state secrets, at the same time that he struggled to re-instill vigilance. Yet, whatever strength Khrushchev tried to recoup at Penkovsky's expense, Penkovsky had made Khrushchev vulnerable. His ouster followed in October 1964.

The events of the past two years in Eastern Europe and the Soviet Union confirm Penkovsky's 1961 assertion that the building of the Berlin Wall was an act of desperation. Khrushchev says in his memoirs: "Paradise is a place where people want to end up, not a place they run from!"[23] Thirty years ago Penkovsky had the courage to state that Communism was not a paradise but a failure. When he said that to the Anglo-American team in the smoke-filled room of the Mount Royal Hotel, he was utterly alone and his life was at risk.

His surrogate fathers in the CIA and MI6 gave him the recognition he had failed to receive from his Motherland. He did please his surrogate fathers. The drama of his show trial confirmed for him that he had succeeded in foiling Khrushchev. He had seen Khrushchev back down in the Cuban missile crisis; he had accomplished what he had set out to do.

Penkovsky was a child of a peculiar moment in history. During the years 1947 through 1962 the world saw the development of nuclear weapons. Penkovsky was a product of this time. During his most productive years he found himself involved in defusing the world crises that surrounded their possible use. He helped the world pass through a period in which the use of these weapons seemed imminently possible, to a more enlightened time in which a greater understanding of the impossibility of their use has become the new reality.

At his trial Oleg Penkovsky appeared calm and resolute. The impression he left upon the world was that he was not really sorry for what he had done. He had used every intelligence trick he knew to save his wife and children and then to save himself. Even when he knew there was no hope for himself, he accepted his fate with dignity, according to those who saw him in the final closed session of the court.[24] The Soviet public, of course, had not seen his last emotional letter to the team, and it was not read at the trial. His stoic acceptance of his fate reflected his final words to his friends: "I am not disappointed in my life or work . . . important and necessary work. This is the goal of life and if I succeed in contributing my little bricks to our great cause, then there can be no greater satisfaction."

Appendix A
Penkovsky's 1961 Letter
to Allen Dulles

My Dear Director:

My dear friend Joseph will report to you everything about me. I only wish at the present moment once more to confirm that, despite my great desire to be with you even now, I feel that for another year or two I must continue in the General Staff of the USSR, in order to reveal all the villainous plans and plottings of our common enemy, i.e., I consider, as your soldier, that my place during these troubled times is on the *front line*. I must remain on this front line in order to be your eyes and cars, and my opportunities for this are great. God grant only that my modest efforts be useful in the fight for our high ideals for mankind.

Please believe, that your soldier shall take a worthy position among his comrades who fight for justice. I wish you, my dear Director, the best of health and great success in your difficult work. As your subordinate, I shall lay my "bricks" in our work and hope that thereby I shall be able to lighten for you the resolution of the great problems facing you, and shall thereby help you in this. If I am able to fulfill this in a small way, I shall consider my own problem fulfilled.

I grasp your hand,
Your O.
6. X. 61
2400 hours

[handwritten letter in Russian]

Original (in Russian) of Penkovsky's 1961 letter to Allen Dulles.

A history of Communism. Left to right: Marx, Lenin, Stalin, Khrushchev.

Appendix B
Dead Drop Number 1

Description of Dead Drop Number 1

Address and Location:

> Moscow, corner of Proezd Khudozhestvennogo Teatra and Pushkinskaya ulitsa. The dead drop is located in the main entrance (foyer) of Number 2, located on Pushkinskaya ulitsa—between the store Number 19 "Myaso" and the store "Zhenskaya obuv'."
>
> The main entrance is open 24 hours a day. The entrance is not guarded, there is no elevator.
>
> In the entrance (foyer)—to the left /upon entering therein/ a dial telephone, No. 28, is located. Opposite the dial telephone /to the right as one goes into the entrance hall/ is a steam heat radiator, painted in oil paint in a dark green color. This radiator is supported by a single metal hook, fastened into the wall. /If one stands facing the radiator, then the metal hook will be to the right, at the level of one's hand hanging from the arm./
>
> Between the wall, to which the hook is attached, and the radiator there is a space of two-three centimeters.
>
> For the dead drop, it is proposed to use the hook and the space /open space/ between the wall and the radiator.

Method of Using
the Dead Drop:

> It is necessary to place and camouflage any written material, for example, in a match box, then, the box should be

wrapped with soft wire /of a green color/, and the end of the wire bent hook-shaped, which will permit the small box to hang from the hook (or bracket) of the radiator between the wall and the radiator.

The location of the dead drop is on the unlighted right-hand corner of the entrance hall. In the entrance hall it is convenient to make a call on the dial telephone and it is very simple and easy to hang some type of small object on the indicated hook.

The site for placing the signal indicating that material has been placed in the drop, is located at a five minutes' ride from the dead drop /or a fifteen minutes' walk/. Thus the time that the material is in the dead drop can be held to a minimum.

I will await the signal indicating placing of the material in the dead drop after 12.00 and after 21.00 each day, beginning with 15.8.60.

PLAN (DIAGRAM) OF DEAD DROP SITE AND ITS LOCATION

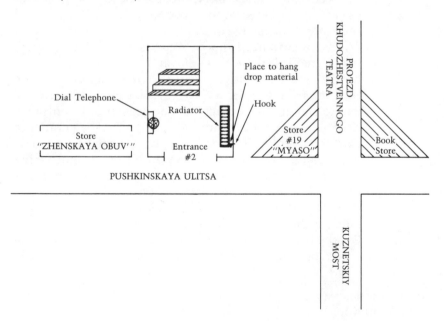

Description of the Site for Marking the Signal

Address: Moscow, Kozitskiy Pereulok Number 2, Korpus (unit) No. 8. In the entry Number 7 /between the store "Ovoshchifrukty" and the entrance to the Polyclinic Number 18/ there is a dial telephone, number 746. This telephone is mounted on a wooden board to the wall—on the left going in.
This entry into hallway number 7 from Kozitskiy Pereulok, is located between the streets: Ulitsa Gor'kogo and Pushkinskaya Ulitsa /not far from the Yeliseyevskiy gastronom./

Spot for
Marking the
Signal: The dial telephone is fastened to a wooden board (back board). Below—under the telephone /under its right corner/ on the wooden board, a piece of veneer has been broken off. This makes a light spot on the back board, on which the signal should be placed.

Meaning of
the Signals:
/Use Red
Pencil/   Signal for material having been placed in dead drop.

Signal that the drop has been unloaded.

427

Appendix C
Operational Notes for Penkovsky, October 1961

OPERATIONAL

1. <u>ON ARRIVAL</u>

RING NUMBER G3-13-58 AT 2130 HOURS SUNDAY 15th OC-
TOBER. THREE RINGS INDICATES THAT ALL IS WELL :
SEVEN RINGS INDICATES THAT ALL IS NOT WELL.

2. <u>MEETINGS WITH JANET</u>
   a) FRIDAY 20th OCTOBER AT 1300 HOURS AT THE COMMIS-
      SION SHOP ON THE ARBAT
   b) ALTERNATIVE : MONDAY 23rd OCTOBER AT 1300 HOURS
      IN THE PRAGA DELICATESSEN SHOP.
   c) SAME PATTERN TO CONTINUE THROUGHOUT REST OF
      OCTOBER AND NOVEMBER – BASIC MEETING ON FRI-
      DAYS WITH ALTERNATIVE ON FOLLOWING MONDAY :
      JANET WILL ONLY GO TO ALTERNATIVE MEETING IF HE
      FAILS TO APPEAR ON THE FRIDAY. EXCEPTION DURING
      THIS PERIOD WILL BE TIME HE IS OUT OF MOSCOW ON
      LEAVE : HE WILL NOTIFY JANET OF THIS PERIOD AND
      TELL HER DATE OF THE FRIDAY ON WHICH HE WILL
      EXPECT TO SEE HER AGAIN.
   d) IN MONTHS OF DECEMBER PATTERN WILL CHANGE
      AND BASIC MEETING WILL TAKE PLACE ON FRIDAYS AT
      1600 HOURS IN THE PARK : THE ALTERNATIVE MEETING
      WILL BE ON THE FOLLOWING MONDAY AT 1300 HOURS
      IN THE PRAGA DELICATESSEN SHOP ; THE ONE EXCEP-

TION TO THIS WILL BE ON MONDAY 25th DECEMBER (CHRISTMAS); DURING THIS WEEK THERE WILL BE NO ALTERNATIVE.

e) NOT LATER THAN THE FIRST FRIDAY IN DECEMBER HE WILL PROPOSE A PLAN OF MEETINGS FOR JANUARY AND IF POSSIBLE FOR FEBRUARY : THIS WILL GIVE US TIME TO AGREE OR SUGGEST ALTERNATIVES : HE MUST BEAR IN MIND THAT JANET MUST ADHERE TO A NOR- MAL MOVEMENT AND BEHAVIOUR PATTERN.

f) HE WILL PASS TO JANET AT MEETINGS MINOX FILM, TYPEWRITTEN NOTES AND POSSIBLY OTHER SMALL PACKAGES. JANET's HUSBAND WILL READ ANY TYPE- WRITTEN MESSAGES IN CASE THEY CONTAIN OPERA- TIONAL SUGGESTIONS OR INFORMATION OF VITAL IMPORTANCE.

g) AS SOON AS POSSIBLE AFTER HIS RETURN FROM LEAVE WE WILL TRY TO ARRANGE A PARTY UNDER AUSPICES OF DR. SENIOR SO THAT HE AND JANET CAN MEET OFFI- CIALLY : IN MEANTIME HE SHOULD USE COVER STORY THAT THEY HAVE ALREADY MET AT HOUSE OF MR KING IN DECEMBER 1960. MATERIAL MAY BE PASSED TO JANET AT A PARTY BUT NOT UNDER ANY CIRCUM- STANCES TO HER HUSBAND.

3. <u>USE OF DEAD DROP</u>

<u>NOTES</u> : i) DEAD DROP WILL <u>ONLY</u> BE USED TO PASS IN- FORMATION ON MATTERS LISTED IN POINTS ONE AND TWO OF FINAL BRIEF : IT WILL NOT BE USED TO PASS ANY OTHER INFORMATION MATERIAL.

ii) DEAD DROP MAY ALSO BE USED AS EMER- GENCY MEANS TO INFORM US THAT HE HAS BEEN POSTED AWAY FROM MOSCOW AND CAN NO LONGER ATTEND MEETINGS WITH US IN MOSCOW : THIS MEANS ONLY TO BE USED IF TIMING DOES NOT PERMIT HIM TO INFORM US THRU JANET.

iii) DEAD DROP SHOULD NEVER BE USED TO PASS INFORMATION WHICH CAN WAIT UNTIL NEXT MEETING WITH JANET : NORMALLY WE WOULD NOT EXPECT IT TO BE USED ON DAYS WHEN HE HAS MEETING WITH JANET.

iv) HE MUST REMEMBER THAT WE CAN ONLY CLEAR DEAD DROP ONCE IN SAFETY : THIS EMPHASIZES EMERGENCY NATURE OF ITS USE.

a) TO INDICATE THAT HE INTENDS TO FILL DEAD DROP HE WILL MAKE MARK IN FORM OF ROUGH CIRCLE WITH DARK COLOR ON POST 35 FACING ROAD SOME THREE FEET FROM GROUND : THIS MARK CAN BE MADE AT ANY TIME.

b) AT ANY TIME OF ANY DAY, AFTER MAKING SIGNAL ON POST 35, HE WILL TELEPHONE NUMBER 43-26-94 OR 43-26-87. IF NO ANSWER OR OBVIOUSLY SOVIET MAID ANSWERS HE WILL RING THE SECOND NUMBER. IF PROPER PERSON RESPONDS HE WILL PUT DOWN RECEIVER AND AFTER ONE MINUTE HE WILL DIAL SAME NUMBER AGAIN AND HANG UP AGAIN. THERE WILL ALWAYS BE SOMEONE AT EITHER OF THESE NUMBERS TO ANSWER HIS CALL. IF PROPER FEMALE VOICE RESPONDS SHE WILL SAY "HELLO, MRS. DAVISON (or MRS. JONES) SPEAKING". ON RECEIPT OF THIS SIGNAL THE POST WILL BE EXAMINED TO SEE IF THERE IS A MARK ON IT : IF THERE IS, EFFORTS WILL BE MADE TO CLEAR DEAD DROP AS QUICKLY AS POSSIBLE.

c) DEAD DROP MUST BE FILLED EITHER BEFORE SIGNAL OR WITHIN 10 MINUTES OF TELEPHONE CALL.

d) AFTER FILLING DEAD DROP HE MUST UNDER NO CIRCUMSTANCES RETURN TO IT TO SEE IF IT HAS BEEN CLEARED.

e) SIGNAL TO INDICATE TO HIM THAT DEAD DROP HAS BEEN SUCCESSFULLY CLEARED WILL BE PLACED WITHIN 12 HOURS OF RECEIPT OF TELEPHONE CALL ON WALL WITH POSTER AT ENTRANCE TO GASTRONOM. SIGNAL WHICH WILL TAKE FORM OF DARK SMUDGE WILL BE TWO INCHES DIAGONALLY FROM BOTTOM RIGHT HAND CORNER OF POSTER. ONE SMUDGE WILL INDICATE SAFE RECEIPT OF MATERIAL: TWO SMUDGES WILL INDICATE THAT DEAD DROP HAS BEEN VISITED BUT NO MATERIAL FOUND.

4. <u>EMERGENCY SIGNAL WITHOUT USE OF DEAD DROP</u>

IN THE EVENT THAT HE KNOWS SOVIET GOVERNMENT INTENDS TO GO TO WAR AND ONLY UNDER THESE CIRCUMSTANCES, BUT IS UNABLE TO PASS MESSAGE TO THIS

431

EFFECT EITHER THROUGH JANET OR THROUGH DEAD DROP, HE SHOULD USE FOLLOWING METHOD:—

a) TELEPHONE NUMBER 43-26-94 OR 43-26-87 AT ANY TIME ON ANY DAY. IF MALE VOICE ANSWERS AND ONLY IF MALE VOICE ANSWERS, BLOW THREE TIMES INTO MOUTH PIECE AND HANG UP. THIS TIME THE CALL SHOULD NOT BE REPEATED.

b) IN ADDITION TO THIS TELEPHONE CALL HE SHOULD IF POSSIBLE PLACE MARK ON POST 35. THIS MARK SHOULD BE MADE BEFORE THE TELEPHONE CALL.

5. <u>CANCELLATION OF PREVIOUS INSTRUCTIONS</u>

IN VIEW OF ABOVE NEW ARRANGEMENTS FOR SIGNAL-LING LOADING OF DEAD DROP ON ANY DAY, PREVIOUS ARRANGEMENTS WHEREBY HE COULD NOTIFY US OF THIS BY A TELEPHONE CALL ON MONDAY EVENINGS ARE CAN-CELLED. THE TELEPHONE NUMBER GIVEN HIM FOR THE MONDAY EVENING CALL SHOULD NOT BE USED AGAIN.

6. <u>MESSAGES FROM US</u>

MESSAGES FROM US TO HIM WILL FOR TIME BEING BE PASSED BY FOLLOWING MEANS:—

a) WIRELESS MESSAGES EVERY MONTH WITH 2 MESSAGES PER MONTH BEGINNING IN NOVEMBER. FIRST MES-SAGE WILL BE SENT ON SCHEDULED TIME 1-15TH OF MONTH AND SECOND MESSAGE FROM 16TH TO END OF MONTH.

b) TYPEWRITTEN MESSAGES IN RUSSIAN HANDED TO HIM BY JANET. HE MUST NOT EXPECT TO RECEIVE SUCH MESSAGES EVERY TIME HE MEETS JANET. IF SHE HAS A MESSAGE TO PASS IT WILL PROBABLY BE CONCEALED IN A CIGARETTE OR SIMILAR CONTAINER. IF SHE OF-FERS HIM A CIGARETTE OR A CIGARETTE PACKET HE SHOULD TAKE IT APART UNTIL HE FINDS THE MES-SAGE.

7. <u>PHOTOGRAPHIC EQUIPMENT</u>

a) NEW MINOX CAMERA TO BE TAKEN TO MOSCOW BY HIM. CAMERA WHICH NEEDS OVERHAUL TO BE HANDED TO JANET.

b) MINOX CASSETTES WILL BE SUPPLIED THROUGH JANET AS AND WHEN THEY ARE REQUIRED. AT PRESENT HE

HAS FORTY. WHEN WE KNOW THAT HE HAS ONLY TEN LEFT WE WILL PASS HIM AUTOMATICALLY RESUPPLY. IF HOWEVER HE REALISES THAT HE WILL NEED RESUPPLY EARLIER HE MUST ASK FOR IT IN A MESSAGE TO BE HANDED TO JANET. SHE WILL THEN HAND THEM OVER AT NEXT MEETING IN SUITABLY DISGUISED FORM— PROBABLY SWEET BOX.

Appendix D
Final Brief for Oleg Penkovsky, 1962

<u>FINAL BRIEF</u>

I. <u>INDICATIONS</u>

1. INFORMATION FROM RESPONSIBLE SOVIET OFFICIALS THAT THE USSR HAD DECIDED TO LAUNCH AN ATTACK THE WEST--THE PLAN, DATE AND TIME OF ATTACK. DETAILS OF INFORMATION ACQUISITION.
2. INFORMATION THAT THE USSR WILL ATTACK THE WEST IF CERTAIN SPECIFIC CONDITIONS ARE NOT MET BY THE WEST, OR IF THE WEST COMMITS CERTAIN ACTIONS OR ADOPTS CERTAIN POLICY.
3. INFORMATION THAT THE USSR WILL NOT ATTACK THE WEST.
4. INFORMATION THAT THE USSR WILL ATTACK HER ON A CERTAIN DATE OR IF CERTAIN CONDITIONS PREVAIL.

   ALWAYS GIVE DETAILS OF WHEN, WHERE, FROM WHOM YOU GET INFORMATION. THIS IS PARTICULARLY IMPORTANT FOR THE ABOVE QUESTIONS, BUT SHOULD BE APPLIED AS WELL TO ALL YOUR OTHER INFORMATION. KEEP AN AIDE MEMOIRE FOR EACH ITEM OF INFORMATION. AND GIVE YOUR OWN EVALUATION OF EACH ITEM IN A SUBPARAGRAPH.

II. STRATEGIC MISSILES

    1. NUMBERS DEPLOYED OR PLANNED TO BE DEPLOYED IN EACH RANGE.
    2. WHAT IS THEIR WARHEAD YIELD

III. SUBMARINE BALLISTIC MISSILES

    1. WHEN WILL ATOMIC OR CONVENTIONAL SUBMARINES HAVE BALLISTIC MISSILES ON THEM

IV. ANTI-BALLISTIC MISSILES

    1. WHEN WILL THE ABM BE READY FOR DEPLOYMENT
    2. WHAT METHOD IS CONSIDERED BEST FOR DESTROYING A BALLISTIC MISSILE (ILLEGIBLE)

V. VURS

    1. HAVE ANY NEW ZURS BEEN DEVELOPED SINCE THE V-750
    2. FOR LOW FLYING AIRCRAFT
    3. FOR HIGH FLYING AIRCRAFT

VI. NUCLEAR WEAPONS

    1. WHAT SUCCESSES WERE ACHIEVED IN THE RECENT TEST SERIES, AND WHAT WEAKNESSES WERE DISCOVERED
    2. WHAT CHANGES IN PRODUCTION, STORAGE, OR DELIVERY VEHICLE POLICIES RESULTED FROM THE TESTS.
    3. WHAT WERE THE SMALLEST AND LARGEST WEAPONS TESTED, AND WHAT ARE THEIR USES.
    4. HAVE ANY "FANTASTIC WEAPONS" DEVELOPMENTS TAKEN PLACE

VII. SECURITY

ANY INDICATION THAT THE R.I.S. HAS A HIGH-LEVEL PENETRATION OF A WESTERN GOVERNMENT

VIII. TACTICAL MISSILES

    1. IDENTIFY BY DESIGNATION OR RANGE THE WEAPONS APPEARING ON THE 7 NOVEMBER PARADE.
    2. DETERMINE THE DEPLOYMENT STATUS OF THE

VARIOUS MISSILES, INCLUDE NUMBERS, GEOGRAPH-
ICAL LOCATION, AND UNIT DESIGNATIONS.

DOCUMENTS

1. 18 AUGUST CC <u>POLOYZHENIYE</u> ON THE <u>KOMANDOVAN-
   IYE</u> <u>GRAZDANSKOY</u> <u>OBORONY</u> AND ANY OTHER PARTY
   OR DEFENSE MINISTRY DOCUMENTS ON THE GERMAN
   CRISIS AND THE <u>OSOBYY</u> <u>PERIOD.</u>
2. SECRET CC DECREES AND CONCLUSIONS REGARDING
   THE PARTY CONGRESS AND FUTURE POLICIES OF SOVIET
   AND INTERNATIONAL COMMUNISM
3. REMAINDER OF <u>VOYENNAYA</u> <u>MYSL</u> <u>SPETSBORNIK</u>
4. 1960 ISSUES OF THE <u>ARTILLERY</u> <u>SBORNIK</u>
5. 1961 AND 1960 <u>VOYENNY</u> <u>VESTNIK</u>
6. THE PTURS MANUAL

Author's Note
by Jerrold L. Schecter

OLEG PENKOVSKY HAS LONG BEEN A SOURCE OF FASCINATION AND speculation to the authors. My interest in the Penkovsky case began in 1965 in Tokyo, when I was *Time-Life* Tokyo bureau chief, and Frank Gibney, fresh from his success with *The Penkovsky Papers*, moved to Tokyo. Gibney had been *Time* bureau chief in 1949 and 1950 and was wounded covering the Korean War. After the publication of *The Penkovsky Papers*, he became president of TBS-Britannica in Tokyo, a joint venture that published the Encyclopaedia Britannica in Japanese. We played tennis regularly at the Tokyo Lawn Tennis Club and one afternoon over a lemon squash after a match he told me the story, as he knew it, of how *The Penkovsky Papers* was written from the transcriptions of Penkovsky's debriefings in London and Paris. Gibney spoke highly of Peter Deriabin, the Soviet defector with whom he had written two books and who translated the *Papers*.

We remained friends over the years, and my life became intertwined with the Soviet Union when I was posted there from 1968 to 1970 as *Time-Life* bureau chief. Penkovsky was somebody I knew about, but I never ran into traces of him in those years. The only spies one heard about in Moscow then were connected with Soviet spying successes: Kim Philby, who lived within a few blocks of my office and who was quoted as saying he had "become bored with caviar"; Richard Sorge, whose statue was unveiled commemorating his service in Japan before and during World War II; and Colonel Rudolf Abel, who spied in New York. One day our children said they had heard the British spy George Blake lived in the next building, but we never saw him.

In 1986 Gibney introduced me to Deriabin, who had retired from the CIA in 1982. Deriabin had written a book on the KGB for which he asked my wife to be his literary agent. I was impressed with Deriabin's encyclopedic knowledge of the Soviet Intelligence Services and his intellectual curiosity, not only about past but present Soviet leaders, their personalities, and their motivations. Deriabin told me how much he wished he could have met Penkovsky. He felt he knew Penkovsky from reading the edited debriefing transcripts, but many questions remained unanswered. He had never been shown the files or the full transcripts while working for the CIA.

How was Penkovsky discovered and arrested? What did he really bring to the West? What was his true motivation? Was he a double agent? Deriabin knew that the CIA files, which he had never seen, held the answers.

In 1987, twenty-five years after the Cuban missile crisis and the arrest of Penkovsky, Deriabin suggested it might be time for the Central Intelligence Agency to open the files of the Penkovsky case.

We wrote a letter to the CIA information and privacy coordinator requesting permission to be afforded access to historical documents in search of relevant materials for a biography of former GRU Colonel Oleg Penkovsky. Our request was based on the policies and procedures of the CIA for handling of their records under the Freedom of Information Act. According to the revision of 32 CFR 1900.61—Access to Historical Records, published in the Federal Register on December 8, 1987—the CIA information coordinator can make the records available subject to a review of the manuscript by the Agency "for the sole purpose of determining that no classified information is contained therein."

On June 7, 1988, Deriabin and I requested access to the Penkovsky archive under the provisions of the revised regulations. On September 26 permission was granted subject to security clearance by a CIA publications review board. Such clearance, the letter of permission said, "is concerned solely with a determination that no classified information is contained in the manuscript. It does not constitute an Agency endorsement of the author's point of view or the factual accuracy of the manuscript."

The material available for review came in seventeen cardboard boxes and filled ten file-cabinet drawers in four steel safes. The only security caveats the Agency attached to using the materials were protection of sources and methods insofar as these were not general public knowledge. Other CIA operations that might relate to the Penkovsky case were not open for review or discussion and the Agency declined to cooperate in regard to them.

The CIA also withheld research and studies it had conducted concerning the cause of the compromise of the Penkovsky operation, saying that these studies were heavily dependent on a wide variety of sensitive foreign sources. We were free to draw our own conclusions on how the case was handled and how Penkovsky was compromised.

Even now, thirty years later, there is still great sensitivity about the Penkovsky case. We interviewed former CIA officers involved, who agreed to cooperate voluntarily. Most of those interviewed permitted their names to be used. Some spoke only if they would not be personally named. A few refused to cooperate and did not want their names mentioned in the book. George Kisevalter declined to cooperate on the book, as did the former CIA officer COMPASS. The few currently serving CIA officers involved in the case were not made available by the Agency and declined to be interviewed. Charles Beling, a former senior CIA operations officer, who had been peripherally involved in the Penkovsky operation, agreed to come out of retirement to serve as a consultant and liaison with the CIA.

The authors collaborated closely to interview principals in the Penkovsky case. Alone or together we visited London, Paris, Colorado, Majorca and Moscow to find those who had been involved with Penkovsky. Schecter did the writing. Deriabin provided the institutional memory and translated the transcripts of Penkovsky's meetings with the team. Together we checked the CIA files for consistency and accuracy.

Although Penkovsky's code name changed periodically, we have used the code name HERO, which the Americans used informally, rather than his British code name, YOGA. British code words have not been used, but there was a parallel British system to IRONBARK and CHICKADEE called RUPPEE and ARNICA.

The material from the transcripts and the operational record of the case referred to in the notes is being declassified and will be available under the Freedom of Information Act. The authors' request for declassification of Annexes A and B of the document "Positive Intelligence Contribution of the Penkovsky Operation" has been denied and is being appealed.

441

Notes

PROLOGUE

1. Penkovsky letter dated July 19, 1960. The names in the postscript were American military attachés serving in Turkey while Penkovsky was in Ankara.

CHAPTER ONE **Approaching the Americans**

1. Memo from John Abidian to Edward Freers, August 13, 1960.

2. Interview with Eldon Ray Cox, October 10, 1989.

3. Joseph J. Bulik interview with Cox, October 6, 1960, pp. 33–34.

4. Ibid., pp. 33, 35, 36.

5. The RB-47 fliers were released by Khrushchev the day after John F. Kennedy's inauguration in January 1961. Khrushchev's decision not to release Gary Powers and the RB-47 fliers before the election was part of his effort to defeat Richard Nixon. The Soviet leader believed their release would benefit the Republicans, and he later boasted that he cast the "deciding ballot" in Kennedy's election "over that son of a bitch Richard Nixon."

6. Interview with Cox, November 10, 1989, and February 1, 1990. Powers was traded for convicted spy Colonel Rudolf Ivanovich Abel, a.k.a. William Fischer, on February 10, 1962, on the Glienicke Bridge spanning East Germany and West Berlin.

7. Interview with Cox, November 10, 1989.

8. Interview with Cox, October 10, 1989, and February 1, 1990.

9. Ibid. and "Memo on Debriefing of Henry Lee Cobb From 1100 to 1500 hours on Sunday, September 11, 1960."

10. Interview with Cox, October 10, 1989.

11. Joseph J. Bulik, October 5, 1960, memo for the record on debriefing Vlad Toumanoff.

12. Abidian, in an interview in 1989, recalled receiving a message telling him that the letters sounded like they had come from a Soviet spy who had gone underground and was now trying to recontact the Agency. There is no copy of such a message in the file and no evidence that Penkovsky ever worked for the CIA or was in contact with the CIA before August 1960.

13. Interview with Charles Beling, December 11, 1989.

14. Interview with Bulik, March 1991.

15. Interview with Cox, February 24, 1989.

16. Memo for the record of meeting August 31, 1960, with Richard Helms attended by John H. (Jack) Maury, Bulik, and the Moscow Station chief to discuss new case. Interview with Bulik, July 28, 1988.

Contrary to later accounts by Greville Wynne and others, Penkovsky did not approach the British or the Americans for recruitment in Ankara.

17. Interview with Colonel Charles Maclean Peeke, November 10, 1989, and Bulik, July 27, 1988.

18. Peter Deriabin, who was the chief of the KGB Counterintelligence Group in Vienna in 1953, knew Popov.

19. C. I. Tsybov and N. F. Chistyakov, *Front Taynoy Voyny* (The Front of Invisible War). Moscow: Voyenizdat, 1964. Tsybov and Chistyakov say that Popov worked for the CIA as their agent from 1952 to 1956 "and maybe even earlier." Ronald Payne and Christopher Dobson, *Who Is Who in Espionage*. New York: St. Martin's Press, 1984, p. 138.

20. Interview with Mrs. John M. Maury, September 22, 1989.

21. Interview with CIA officer, March 16, 1991.

22. When Senator McCarthy tried to get William Bundy, then assistant to Robert Amory, deputy director of intelligence, to testify, he failed. Amory told Bundy to go on leave outside of Washington so that he was not available. Then Allen Dulles reached Vice President Nixon, who arranged for McCarthy to back away from attacking the CIA. See John Ranelagh, *The Agency: The Rise and Decline of the CIA*. New York: Simon & Schuster, 1986, pp. 238–246.

23. Authors' interview with retired Soviet Division officer.

24. Interview with Quentin Johnson, November 28, 1989.

25. COMPASS letter to Bulik, December 6, 1960.

26. Ibid., paragraph 7.

27. COMPASS letter to Bulik, December 10, 1960, paragraphs 8, 9, and 10.

28. COMPASS letter to Bulik, December 6, 1960, paragraph 5.

29. Ibid., paragraph 10.

CHAPTER TWO **The British Connection**

1. Greville Wynne, *The Man From Odessa*. London: Robert Hale, 1981, p. 175.

2. Ibid., pp. 60–87.

3. Ibid., pp. 60–87.

4. Gordon Brook-Shepherd, *The Storm Birds: Soviet Postwar Defectors*. London: Weidenfeld & Nicolson, 1988, p. 145.

5. Wynne, pp. 25–73.

6. Greville Wynne, *Contact on Gorky Street*. New York: Atheneum, 1968, p. 31.

7. Ibid., p. 33.

8. Press release on "Trade & Technical Delegation to Russia" in authors' possession.

9. Transcript of meeting #1, paragraph 126.

10. John Barron, *KGB, The Secret Work of Soviet Secret Agents*. New York: Bantam Books, 1974, pp. 170–192.

11. Authors' information.

12. Debriefing of Merriman from London in classified file.

13. Transcript of meeting #1, paragraph 126.

14. Harrison diary and letter to authors, October 24, 1989.

15. Ibid. and Penkovsky meeting #1.

16. William Van Vliet letter to Canadian ambassador.

17. Ibid.

18. Phillip Knightley, *Philby, K.G.B. Masterspy*. London: André Deutsch, 1988, pp. 182–183, 194–199, provides a skillful account of Philby's purgatory when he returned to England in 1951.

19. Interview with Richard Helms, March 6, 1991.

20. Interview with Joseph J. Bulik, July 27 and 28, 1988.

21. Interview with Raymond Rocca, October 18, 1989.

22. For examples see Anthony Cave Brown, *"C": The Secret Life of Sir Stewart Menzies, Spymaster to Winston Churchill.* New York: Macmillan Publishing Company, 1987, pp. 416–417.

23. Authors' information. Also see Nigel West, *The Friends.* London: Weidenfeld & Nicolson, 1988, pp. 17, 21, 124. Shergold was never a member of MI5's Security Intelligence Middle East (SIME) as West asserts.

24. Interview with Bulik, July 27, 1988.

25. Letter of February 2, 1961, paragraph 4.

26. Meeting #1, paragraph 127.

27. Wynne, *Gorky Street*, p. 42.

28. Interview with Bulik, July 27, 28, 1988.

29. Interview with Bulik, January 2, 1990.

30. Interview with Bulik, July 27, 1988.

CHAPTER THREE **London at Last**

1. Wynne, *Gorky Street*, p. 76.

2. In *Contact on Gorky Street*, page 77, Wynne describes an entire floor of the hotel taken over by British Intelligence. "Most of the rooms were filled with unsuspecting civil servants who never knew what went on behind the few remaining doors. There were two or three offices, a conference room, and (the heart of the matter) an operations center. Here in place of the prim bedroom furniture, were installed typewriters, tape recorders, coding machines, radio equipment, a private line to Washington, and a projector for slides and films. Stenographers, typists, and interpreters in case of technical language difficulties. A doctor with stethoscope, syringe, and pep pills to keep Alex awake and alert; during his stay in London he never had more than three hours' sleep a night. And relays of British and American Intelligence officers to question, question, question." This was not the case at all; there were only the two rooms and the Anglo-American team of four men. On occasion the team would bring in an instructor for the Minox camera Penkovsky was using or a doctor to examine him. The whole operation was geared to a minimum of activity so as not to attract attention.

Wynne also imagined that there was a party of defectors gathered to greet Penkovsky. When the authors interviewed Wynne in Majorca in September 1988, he acknowledged that he never saw the party taking place and that he only heard voices in the room. There was no such welcoming party with invited defectors for obvious security reasons.

3. Interview with Joseph J. Bulik, July 27, 28, 1988.

4. Meeting #5, paragraph 74.

5. Meeting #5, paragraph 75.

6. Meeting #2, paragraph 85.

7. Meeting #1, paragraph 87.

8. Meeting #1, paragraph 86.

9. Meeting #1, page 8, of transcript.

10. Oleg Penkovsky, *The Penkovsky Papers*, trans. P. Deriabin. New York: Doubleday, 1965, p. 60.

11. Confidential source.

12. Meeting #1, paragraph 35.

CHAPTER FOUR **Life and Times**

1. Meeting #2, paragraphs 100, 101, 102.

2. Meeting #2, paragraph 144.

3. Meeting #1, paragraph 48.

4. Meeting #1, paragraph 59. Shortly before the end of World War II, under orders of Stalin and Beria, special groups consisting of KGB and military counterintelligence officers were organized to capture the laboratories and documents connected with atomic and rocket research in Germany. In Germany, General Ivan Serov, then a deputy to Marshal Zhukov, was in charge of this task. The equipment and papers captured in the laboratories were moved to the Soviet Union at the same time German scientists were captured and taken to the Soviet Union as prisoners of war. One of the key facilities was Peenemünde, the German rocket testing site on the Baltic.

Two settlements of German scientists were organized, one near Moscow in the village of Bogorodskoye, the other near Kuybyshev on the Volga, where the Soviet government was temporarily situated during the war. They came under the direction of Beria, who in 1945 became the First Deputy Chairman of the Council of Ministers and chief for development of nuclear weapons.

The Soviet Union also developed a policy of recruiting German scientists in 1945 at a time when the United States and its allies still had not made up their minds whether to treat scientists as war criminals or sign them up to continue their research work. See Tom Bower, *The Paperclip Conspiracy*. Boston: Little, Brown, 1987, pp. 131–156, and Linda Hunt, *Secret Agenda*, New York: St. Martin's, 1991, pp. 1–39.

5. Meeting #1, paragraph 60.

6. Meeting #1, paragraph 95.

7. William J. Broad, "Rocket Run by Nuclear Power Being Developed for 'Star Wars,' " *New York Times*, April 3, 1991, p. 1.

8. Meeting #1, paragraph 61.

9. Meeting #1, paragraph 64.

10. Meeting #1, paragraph 67.

11. Richard Rhodes, *The Making of the Atomic Bomb*. New York: Simon & Schuster, 1986, pp. 343, 711.

12. Meeting #1, paragraphs 74, 75, 76.

13. Authors' information.

14. Paul R. Josephson, "Atomic Culture in the USSR Before and After Chernobyl," in *Soviet Social Problems*, edited by Anthony Jones et al. Boulder: Westview Press, 1991, pp. 61–67.

15. Meeting #1, paragraph 83.

16. Meeting #1, paragraph 88.

17. Meeting #1, paragraph 89.

18. Meeting #1, paragraph 92.

19. Meeting #1, paragraph 97.

20. Meeting #1, paragraph 101.

21. Meeting #1, paragraph 102.

22. Meeting #1, paragraph 106.

23. Meeting #1, paragraphs 108, 109, 110.

24. Meeting #1, paragraph 84.

25. Interview with Richard Helms, March 6, 1991.

26. Meeting #1, paragraph 77.

27. Meeting #1, paragraph 78.

28. Meeting #1, paragraph 79.

29. Meeting #1, paragraph 80.

30. Meeting #1, paragraph 81.

CHAPTER FIVE **Hitting the Jackpot**

1. Meeting #2, paragraph 69.

2. Meeting #2, paragraph 71.

3. Meeting #2, paragraph 72.

4. Meeting #2, paragraph 73.

5. Meeting #2, paragraphs 89, 90, 91: discussion of dead drops and how to use them.

6. Meeting #2, paragraph 9: Wynne's role described.

7. Meeting #2, paragraph 113: General Staff Planning, Khrushchev's intentions, and Cyrus Eaton.

8. Meeting #2, paragraph 114.

9. Michael R. Beschloss, *Mayday*. New York: Harper and Row, 1986, p. 340.

10. National Security Archive copy of Top Secret Memo by Lawrence McQuade, forwarded by Paul Nitze to McGeorge Bundy, from John F. Kennedy Library NSF. Box 296–298. Missile Gap 2/63–5/63.

11. John Prados, *The Soviet Estimate: U.S. Intelligence Analysis and Soviet Strategic Forces*. Princeton: Princeton University Press, 1982, p. xi.

12. Meeting #2, paragraph 115.

13. Meeting #2, paragraph 116.

14. Meeting #2, paragraph 117.

15. Interview with Quentin Johnson, November 28, 1989.

16. Meeting #2, paragraph 121. See *Penkovsky Papers* (1965), p. 364, for an abbreviated version of this story.

17. New jokes transmitted by Penkovsky to Janet Chisholm on November 17, 1961.

18. Meeting #2, paragraph 119.

19. Meeting #2, paragraph 123. "Placing rockets in the satellites and nuclear warheads in East Germany."

20. Meeting #2, paragraph 130.

21. Meeting #2, paragraph 135.

22. Meeting #2, paragraph 137. Colonel Peeke retired from the U.S. Army in January 1965.

23. Meeting #2, paragraph 139.

24. Meeting #2, paragraphs 143–149.

25. Meeting #2, paragraph 144.

26. Meeting #2, paragraph 145.

27. Meeting #2, paragraph 148.

28. Meeting #1, paragraph 146.

CHAPTER SIX **Penkovsky's Travels in England**

1. Meeting #4, paragraph 1. In Greville Wynne's *Contact on Gorky Street*, pp. 80–82, he writes that the stomach ache was used as an excuse for Penkovsky to meet with the debriefing team. Bulik, in an interview, said this never happened. All the meetings outside London were scheduled at the end of the day in a different hotel from the one Penkovsky was staying in with his delegation.

2. Meeting #4, paragraphs 3, 4.

3. Lavrenti Beria was arrested on June 26, 1953, and executed on December 21 or 22, 1953. Lieutenant General P. Batitisky is said to have actually shot Beria. See *Krasnaya Zvezda* (Red Star), Second Edition, March 18, 1988, p. 4.

4. Meeting #4, paragraph 16.

5. Meeting #4, paragraph 25.

6. Meeting #4, paragraph 29.

7. Meeting #4, paragraphs 30, 31.

8. Meeting #4, paragraph 34.

9. Meeting #4, paragraphs 36, 37.

10. Meeting #4, paragraph 42.

11. Meeting #4, paragraph 44.

12. Meeting #5, paragraph 2.

13. Meeting #5, paragraph 8.

14. Meeting #5, paragraph 9.

15. Meeting #5, paragraph 41.

16. Meeting #5, paragraph 42.

17. Meeting #5, paragraph 43.

18. Meeting #5, paragraph 43.

19. Meeting #5, paragraph 43.

20. Meeting #5, paragraph 64.

21. Meeting #5, paragraph 65.

22. Strobe Talbott, trans., *Khrushchev Remembers*. Boston: Little, Brown, 1970, p. 293.

23. See *Penkovsky Papers*, (1965), p. 313, for an account of how Varentsov helped Kupin after his mistress in Germany committed suicide.

24. Meeting #5, paragraph 77.

25. Meeting #5, paragraph 78.

26. Meeting #5, paragraph 76.

27. Meeting #5, paragraph 80.

28. Meeting #5, paragraph 81.

29. Meeting #5, paragraph 82.

30. Meeting #5, paragraph 83.

31. Meeting #5, paragraph 84.

32. Report on U-2, April 20, 1962, with copies of reports.

33. Meeting #5, paragraph 85.

34. Meeting #5, paragraph 86.

35. Meeting #5, paragraph 87.

36. Meeting #5, paragraph 89.

37. Meeting #5, paragraph 90.

38. Meeting #5, paragraph 91.

39. Meeting #5, paragraph 92.

40. Meeting #5, paragraph 93.

41. Meeting #5, paragraph 94.

42. Meeting #5, paragraph 95.

43. Meeting #5, paragraph 96.

44. Meeting #5, paragraph 98.

45. Meeting #5, paragraph 101.

46. Meeting #5, paragraph 103.

47. Meeting #5, paragraph 104.

48. Meeting #5, paragraph 105.

49. Meeting #5, paragraph 106.

50. Interview with Joseph J. Bulik, July 27–28, 1988.

51. Meeting #5, paragraph 112.

52. Meeting #5, paragraphs 113, 114.

53. Meeting #5, paragraph 115.

54. Meeting #6, paragraph 1.

55. Meeting #6, paragraph 3.

56. Meeting #6, paragraph 7.

57. Meeting #6, paragraph 9.

58. Meeting #6, paragraph 14.

59. Meeting #6, paragraph 29.

60. Meeting #6, paragraph 30.

61. Meeting #6, paragraph 31.

62. Meeting #6, paragraphs 40, 42–45.

63. Meeting #6, paragraph 46.

64. Meeting #6, paragraph 47.

65. Meeting #6, paragraph 57.

66. Meeting #6, paragraph 58.

67. Meeting #6, paragraph 59. Penkovsky is referring to Marshal Varentsov and other marshals and general officers when he refers to "powerful people in the leadership."

68. Meeting #6, paragraph 61.

69. Meeting #6, paragraph 64.

CHAPTER SEVEN **Trading Secrets**

1. Meeting #7, paragraph 1.

2. Meeting #7, paragraph 2.

3. Meeting #7, paragraph 4.

4. Meeting #7, paragraph 5.

5. Meeting #7, paragraph 6.

6. Meeting #7, paragraph 8.

7. Meeting #7, paragraph 9.

8. Meeting #7, paragraph 10.

9. Meeting #7, paragraph 11. Penkovsky's words are reminiscent of the traditional peasant saying: "God is too high and the tsar is too far away."

10. Meeting #7, paragraph 12.

11. Meeting #7, paragraph 13.

12. Meeting #7, paragraph 14.

13. Meeting #7, paragraph 17.

14. Meeting #7, paragraph 31.

15. Meeting #7, paragraph 32.

16. Meeting #7, paragraph 33.

17. Meeting #7, paragraph 34.

18. Meeting #7, paragraph 35.

19. Meeting #7, paragraph 36.

20. Meeting #7, paragraph 37.

21. Meeting #7, paragraphs, 71, 113.

22. Meeting #10, paragraph 1.

23. Meeting #10, paragraph 4.

24. Meeting #10, paragraph 6. See *Penkovsky Papers* (1965), p. 172.

25. Meeting #10, paragraph 22.

26. Meeting #10, paragraph 24.

27. Meeting #10, paragraphs 28, 29.

28. Meeting #11, paragraph 1.

29. Meeting #11, paragraph 4.

30. Meeting #11, paragraph 12.

31. Letter from Mrs. Sheila Wynne, March 29, 1991.

32. Based on the change in the American consumer price index between 1961 and 1990.

33. Meeting #11, paragraph 13.

34. Meeting #11, paragraph 14.

35. Meeting #11, paragraph 17.

36. Meeting #11, paragraph 18.

37. Meeting #11, paragraph 19.

38. Meeting #11, paragraph 20.

39. Meeting #11, paragraph 21.

40. Meeting #11, paragraph 23.

41. Meeting #11, paragraphs 24, 25.

42. Meeting #12, paragraph 1.

43. Meeting #12, paragraph 3.

44. Meeting #12, paragraph 19.

45. Meeting #12, paragraph 20. The KGB troops who provide security for nuclear storage facilities and the arming devices for nuclear weapons are known as OMSDON divisions, the abbreviation for their name in Russian, *Otdelnaya Motostrelkovaya Diviziya Osobogo Naznacheniya* (Independent Motorized Rifle Division for Special Purposes).

46. Meeting #12, paragraph 21.

47. Meeting #12, paragraph 3.

CHAPTER EIGHT **Meeting a Cabaret Girl and "C"**

1. Meeting #13, paragraph 6.

2. Meeting #13, paragraphs 1–4.

3. Meeting #14, paragraphs 1–6.

4. Meeting #14, paragraph 8.

5. Meeting #14, paragraph 8.

6. Meeting #14, paragraph 10.

7. Meeting #14, paragraphs 11, 12.

8. Meeting #14, paragraph 13.

9. Meeting #14, paragraph 15.

10. Meeting #14, paragraph 16.

11. Meeting #14, paragraph 19.

12. Meeting #14, paragraph 27.

13. Meeting #15, paragraph 28.

14. Meeting #15, paragraph 29.

15. Meeting #15, paragraph 48.

16. Meeting #15, paragraph 49.

17. Meeting #15, paragraph 50.

18. Prados, *Soviet Estimate*, p. 111.

19. William Randolph Hearst, Bob Considine, and Frank Conniff, *Khrushchev and the Russian Challenge*. New York: Avon Books, 1961, p. 249.

20. Meeting #15, paragraph 67.

21. Meeting #15, paragraph 73.

22. Meeting #15, paragraphs 76, 77, 78, 79.

23. Meeting #15, paragraph 81.

24. Meeting #15A.

25. Meeting #15, paragraph 7.

26. Meeting #15, paragraph 8.

27. Meeting #15, paragraph 9.

28. Meeting #15, paragraph 10.

29. Meeting #15, paragraph 15.

30. Meeting #15, paragraph 16.

31. Meeting #15, paragraph 26.

32. Meeting #15, paragraph 26.

33. Meeting #15, paragraph 42.

34. Transcript of meeting #2, paragraph 1, April 21, 1961.

35. Meeting #15, paragraph 85.

36. Meeting #15, paragraph 86.

37. Meeting #16, paragraph 11.

38. Meeting #16, paragraphs 12, 13.

39. Meeting #16, paragraph 14.

40. Meeting #16, paragraphs 20, 21.

41. Meeting #16, paragraph 22.

42. Meeting #16, paragraph 23.

43. Meeting #16, paragraph 24.

44. Meeting #16, paragraph 25.

45. Meeting #16, paragraph 26.

46. Meeting #16, paragraph 27.

47. See *Penkovsky Papers* (1965), p. 369.

48. Penkovsky Operation Seminar, Parts 3 and 4, taped October 22, 1966, p. 2, Penkovsky identified everyone in the GRU who was in Turkey before him, during his time there, and afterward. He also described who ran the Iranian and Egyptian desks, and provided full details on GRU operations in India, Pakistan, and Sri Lanka. GRU operations in London and later Paris were also described by Penkovsky.

CHAPTER NINE **Return to Moscow**

1. Meeting #18, paragraph 35.

2. Operating instructions, May 5, 1961, paragraphs 1 to 9 and note.

3. Maurice Oldfield memo to Jack Maury, June 17, 1961, paragraph 14.

4. Ibid., paragraph 15.

5. Ibid., paragraph 16.

6. Arthur M. Schlesinger, Jr., *A Thousand Days*. Boston: Houghton Mifflin, 1965, p. 367.

7. Talbott, *Khrushchev Remembers*, p. 188.

8. Thomas J. Schoenbaum, *Waging Peace and War*. New York: Simon & Schuster, 1988, p. 336.

9. Schlesinger, p. 373.

10. Schoenbaum, p. 331.

11. Ibid., p. 336.

12. Paul H. Nitze, *From Hiroshima to Glasnost*. New York: Grove Weidenfeld, 1989, p. 195.

13. David Halberstam, *The Best and the Brightest*. New York: Random House, 1972, pp. 75–77.

14. Maury memo on meeting with Ambassador Thompson.

15. Meeting #18, paragraphs 9, 10, 11.

16. Interview with Richard Helms, March 6, 1991. Helms said he did not want to know the name since this might put him under pressure with Congress if asked. He preferred to say he did not know rather than have to decline to answer on security grounds.

17. See *Global Corporate Intelligence*, edited by George S. Roukis et al. New York: Quorum Books, 1990, p. 288, note 1, for reference to IRONBARK. IRONBARK and CHICKADEE are also described in a BBC film on Penkovsky, May 8, 1991.

18. Interview with Robert Gates, March 15, 1988.

19. Interview with Raymond L. Garthoff, August 17, 1990, and Maury memo noting Hilsman speculating on the same source for IRONBARK and CHICKADEE material.

20. Interview with Walter Elder, October 6, 1988.

21. The defector referred to in the memo was Soviet Navy captain Nikolay Fedorovich Artamonov, who took the name Nicholas George Shadrin in America. The bona fides of Shadrin remain unresolved and his disappearance in Vienna in December 1975 when he went to meet KGB agents produced a mystery still unsolved. Was Shadrin killed by the KGB when chloroformed or was this the cover for his return to the Soviet Union? His bizarre end leaves unanswered the question of whether he was a genuine defector or a plant. If so, his being shown the copies of *Military Thought* in 1961 could have permitted a signal to Moscow of what was being leaked. However, Shadrin did not know the name of the Soviet source.

22. Memo for the record: briefing of foreign diplomat to load dead drop in Moscow.

23. Oldfield memo to Maury, May 18, 1961.

24. Memo for the record by John M. Maury, chief of the Soviet Division, July 13, 1961.

25. Memo for the record by Maury, July 22, 1961.

CHAPTER TEN **Return to London**

1. Meeting #18, July 18–19, 1961, paragraph 21.

2. Ranelagh, *The Agency*, p. 375.

3. Interview with Raymond L. Garthoff, August 16, 1990.

4. John M. Maury memo for the record on conversation with Mr. Angleton re CHICKADEE material, June 30, 1961.

5. Meeting #18, paragraphs 53, 57.

6. Schlesinger, *Thousand Days*, p. 376.

7. Meeting #18, paragraphs 86, 87, 92.

8. Meeting #18, paragraph 81, 82.

9. Meeting #18, paragraphs 88, 89.

10. Meeting #18, paragraph 60.

11. From July 17 to August 2, 1945, President Truman, Winston Churchill, and then Clement Atlee, who replaced Churchill when he lost the British elections, met with Stalin at Potsdam. The conference confirmed Soviet territorial gains in Poland and the redrawing of Polish-German boundaries, but disagreed over Stalin's demands for excessive German reparations from the zones controlled by the Allies.

12. Meeting #18, paragraph 62.

13. Meeting #18, paragraph 63.

14. See *Penkovsky Papers* (1965), p. 338.

15. Meeting #18, paragraphs 77, 78.

16. Meeting #19, paragraphs 3, 4.

17. Theodore C. Sorenson, *Kennedy*. New York: Harper & Row, 1965, p. 592.

18. Nitze, *From Hiroshima to Glasnost*, pp. 204–205.

19. Meeting #23, London, July 28, 1961, paragraphs 1, 23, 24.

20. Meeting #23, paragraphs 27 and 28.

21. Sorenson, p. 592.

22. Meeting #23, paragraph 30.

23. Meeting #23, paragraph 31.

24. Meeting #23, paragraphs 31–33.

25. Meeting #18, paragraph 36.

26. Meeting #18, paragraphs 37, 38.

27. Meeting #18, paragraph 40.

28. Meeting #18, paragraph 39.

29. Meeting #18, paragraph 44.

30. Meeting #18, paragraph 45.

31. Meeting #18, paragraph 46.

32. Meeting #18, paragraph 47.

33. Meeting #18, paragraph 48.

34. Interview with Joseph J. Bulik, July 27, 1988.

35. Meeting #30, paragraph 25, 26.

36. Meeting #30, paragraph 33.

37. Interview with Bulik, July 27, 1988.

38. Meeting #30, paragraphs 35, 36.

39. Meeting #30, paragraphs 35–38.

40. Memo for the record, July 25, 1961, development and plans file.

41. Memo for the record, August 3, 1961, Jack Maury, development and plans file.

42. Ibid.

CHAPTER ELEVEN **Paris**

1. Meeting #31, Paris, September 20, 1961, paragraph 21.

2. See *Khrushchev Remembers: The Glasnost Tapes*, Vol. III, trans. Jerrold L. Schecter and Vyacheslav V. Luchkov. Boston: Little, Brown, 1990, pp. 169–170.

3. Interview with Joseph J. Bulik, July 27–28, 1988.

4. Meeting #31, Paris, September 20, 1961, paragraphs 1, 2, 11, 12.

5. Meeting #31, paragraphs 17, 33, 35.

6. Meeting #31, paragraph 19.

7. Meeting #31, paragraph 29.

8. Meeting #31, paragraph 30.

9. Meeting #31, paragraphs 69, 70.

10. Meeting #31, paragraph 27.

11. Meeting #31, paragraph 28.

12. Meeting #31, paragraph 57.

13. Meeting #32, paragraph 71.

14. Meeting #31, paragraph 39.

15. Interview with CIA officer (name withheld on request), June 13, 1989.

16. See Schlesinger, *Thousand Days*, pp. 747–749, for a discussion of how Civil Defense attempts created a political backlash for Kennedy.

17. Meeting #31, paragraph 64.

18. Meeting #32, paragraph 90.

19. Meeting #31, paragraphs 67, 89, 90.

20. Meeting #31, paragraph 70.

21. Meeting #31, paragraph 78.

22. Meeting #31, paragraph 82.

23. Meeting #31, paragraph 85.

24. Meeting #32, paragraphs 7–11.

25. Meeting #31, paragraph 93.

26. Meeting #31, paragraphs 95, 96.

27. Meeting #31, paragraph 102.

28. Meeting #31, paragraph 107.

29. Wynne, *Contact on Gorky Street*, pp. 143–147.

30. Ibid., pp. 146–147.

31. Meeting #32, paragraph 11.

32. Meeting #32, paragraph 20.

33. Meeting #32, paragraph 21.

34. Meeting #32, paragraph 23.

35. Meeting #32, paragraph 24.

36. Meeting #32, paragraph 28.

37. Meeting #32, paragraph 48.

38. Fritz W. Ermarth, "Contrasts in American and Soviet Strategic Thought," in *Soviet Military Thinking*, Derek Leebaert, ed. London: George Allen & Unwin, 1981, p. 51.

39. Marvin Kalb, Bernard Kalb, *Kissinger*. Boston: Little, Brown, 1974, p. 52.

40. Ibid, pp. 53–55.

41. *Military Thinking*, p. 74.

42. Interview with Roswell Gilpatric, February 23, 1991.

43. Lieutenant General William E. Odom, "The Soviet Approach to Nuclear Weapons: A Historical Review," *The Annals*, AAPSS, Vol. 469, 1983, pp. 117–134.

44. Peter Pringle and William Arkin, *S.I.O.P., The Secret U.S. Plan for Nuclear War*. New York: W. W. Norton, 1983, pp. 59–61.

45. Ibid., p. 107.

46. Ibid.

47. McGeorge Bundy, *Danger and Survival*. New York: Random House, 1988, p. 351.

48. Interview with Robert McNamara, September 11, 1990.

49. Pringle and Arkin, p. 121.

50. Meeting #23, paragraph 28. Kisevalter handed Penkovsky President Kennedy's speech on Berlin and told him how his material had an impact on the president's thinking.

51. Meeting #32, paragraph 39.

52. Meeting #32, paragraph 61.

53. Meeting #32, paragraph 63.

54. Meeting #32, paragraph 67.

55. Meeting #32, paragraph 69.

56. Meeting #32, paragraph 75.

57. Meeting #31, paragraph 98.

CHAPTER TWELVE **Safety or Glory**

1. Wynne, *Gorky Street*, pp. 145–146.

2. Meeting #33, paragraph 34.

3. Meeting #33, paragraph 48.

4. Meeting #33, paragraph 50.

5. Meeting #33, paragraph 89.

6. Expenditures authorization, July 30, 1962.

7. Interview with Joseph J. Bulik, July 27, 1988.

8. Meeting #35, paragraphs 1–3.

9. Meeting #35, paragraphs 5, 6.

10. Meeting #35, paragraph 7.

11. Meeting #35, paragraphs 10, 11.

12. Meeting #36, paragraph 2.

13. Interview with Bulik, July 27, 1988.

14. Meeting #36, paragraph 21, and interview with Quentin Johnson, April 16, 1991.

15. Meeting #36, paragraph 22.

16. Letter from Bulik, September 10, 1988.

17. Meeting #37, paragraph 15.

18. Meeting #38, paragraph 20.

19. Meeting #38, paragraphs 22, 23.

20. Meeting #38, paragraph 25.

21. Meeting #38, paragraphs 30–32.

22. Dr. Ralph Lapp was a noted scientist and writer on space and nuclear fallout. He worked on the atomic bomb project and was deputy director of the Argonne National Laboratory.

23. Meeting #40, paragraph 11.

24. *Penkovsky Papers* (1965), illustration following p. 334 reprints the memo in Russian.

25. Interview with George Hook, September 8, 1990.

26. Meeting #42, Paris, October 14, 1961, paragraph 4.

27. Meeting #42, paragraphs 8, 11.

28. Wynne, *Gorky Street*, p. 164.

29. Ibid. and meeting #42, paragraphs 15, 16.

CHAPTER THIRTEEN **Closing the Missile Gap**

1. *Vital Speeches of the Day*, Vol. XXVIII, December 1, 1961, No. 4.

2. Bundy, *Danger and Survival*, p. 377.

3. Ibid., p. 378.

4. Ibid.

5. *Current Digest of the Soviet Press*, Vol. XIII, No. 40, p. 5.

6. Memo for the record. Conversations with Messrs. Ed Proctor and Jack Smith re use of CHICKADEE material in NIE 11-8-61. Also see Nitze-McQuade memo, "The Missile Gap Estimates," May 31, 1963, declassi-

fied July 25, 1979, DDRS (78)-263 (d) in John Prados, *The Soviet Estimate*. Princeton: Princeton University Press, 1982.

7. Interview with Howard Stoertz, September 28, 1989.

8. Ibid.

9. Prados, *Soviet Estimate*, p. 117.

10. William E. Burrows, *Deep Black*. New York: Berkley Books, 1986, pp. 100–107. Burrows has a complete history of the Discoverer program, also known as Corona, run by the CIA and the air force.

11. Prados, pp. 117–118.

12. Ibid., p. 119.

13. Ibid. Chapter 8, "The End of the Missile Gap," explains with rich detail the interservice rivalry and air force efforts to influence budgeting for missiles and bombers by maintaining a high estimate for Soviet missile strength.

14. Interview with Robert McNamara, September 11, 1990.

15. Roger Hilsman, *To Move a Nation*. New York: Doubleday, 1967, p. 163.

16. Ibid., pp. 163–164.

17. Ibid., p. 164.

18. Maury memo for the record, September 26, 1961.

19. Oldfield letter to Maury, October 27, 1961.

20. Memo for the record of October 31, 1961, London meeting.

21. Interview with Janet Chisholm, November 1990.

22. Case officer memo to Bulik on HERO dated January 11, 1962.

23. Oldfield letter to Maury, January 15, 1962.

24. February 6, 1962, memo for the record, Subject: Discussion between Soviet Division officers of Soviet Division's chief of operations European trip, February 1–5, 1962, and his conversations with Shergold.

25. Ibid.

26. Notes on the side of the memo of Johnson's meeting in London and Bulik interview with authors, July 27, 1988.

27. Oldfield MO/2503 30 Jan 1962.

28. Oldfield letter to Maury, February 28, 1962.

29. March 9, 1962, debriefing of American businessman by CIA case officer.

30. Memo for the record, April 2, 1962, by new case officer.

CHAPTER FOURTEEN **Suspicion and Surveillance**

1. Memo for the record, John M. Maury, April 5, 1962.

2. Oldfield letter to Maury, March 29, 1962.

3. Interview with Janet Chisholm, October 16, 1990.

4. Letter passed to Mrs. Chisholm with Minox films, translation dated April 10, 1962.

5. Memo for the record, Maury, April 13, 1962.

6. Memo for the record, Maury, April 3, 1962.

7. Ibid.

8. Walter Elder, executive assistant to Allen Dulles, and John McCone recall that both directors did not want to know the names of Agency agents or assets inside the Soviet Union. When he was director, Elder says William Colby told him he did not want to know the names of the CIA's Soviet agents "because I might talk in my sleep." Good tradecraft dictated that Penkovsky's name be known only by those who needed to know.

9. Memo of conversation of CIA officers on April 5, 1962, with Sir Dick White and Mr. Oldfield, including Mr. Helms, Maury, Osborne, Johnson, Roosevelt, and Cram (page 1 of three-page memo by Cram).

10. Interview with Joseph J. Bulik, July 27–28, 1988, and Richard Helms, December 8, 1990.

11. The Kharitonenko family was noted for its lavish entertainment, and the white and gold room of the house was used as a music room where Chaliapin, Caruso, and Bolshoi artists performed. Robert Bruce Lockhart, British vice-consul in Moscow in 1912, describes a party at the Kharitonenko mansion when a Russian naval officer, acting as aide-de-camp to the head of a British parliamentary delegation, shot himself after hearing by phone from his mistress in St. Petersburg that she no longer loved him. When the Soviet government moved from St. Petersburg to Moscow, the house was taken over as a Foreign Ministry guest house and entertainment center. Later it was occupied by Soviet diplomats and their families, including Maxim Litvinov, then assistant commissar for foreign affairs, and his English wife, Ivy.

12. Oldfield letter to Maury, June 1, 1962, and June 14, 1962.

13. Memo for the record, Maury meeting with Ambassadors Thompson and Bohlen, April 5, 1962.

14. Interview with Ross Mark, April 26, 1991.

15. Letter to Penkovsky, July 2, 1962.

16. Wynne's account of his activities in Moscow from July 2–6, 1962.

17. Carlson report of meeting dated July 6, 1962.

18. Wynne's account of his activities in Moscow from July 2–6, 1962.

19. Ibid.

CHAPTER FIFTEEN **End Game: The Cuban Missile Crisis**

1. Director's file, "Memorandum on Counterintelligence Activities," July 20, 1962.

2. Memo for the record, July 26, 1962.

3. Carlson after-action report, August 28, 1962.

4. Wynne follow-up report in 1972.

5. The CIA letter included with Penkovsky's counterfeit internal passport read:

> 1. The passport blank is of our manufacture. In appearance it cannot be distinguished from an original of the 1954 printing (RSFSR).

> 2. The first two pages are filled in according to the data in a passport actually issued to a certain Vladimir Grigoryevich BUTOV. The serial number, cachets, signatures, and all entries in points 1–8 are exactly the same as in the passport of the real BUTOV.

> 3. We did not fill in the "bearer's signature" since we believe it better for you to sign the passport yourself (in BUTOV's name of course): PLEASE DO NOT FORGET TO SIGN THE PASSPORT (p. 1, entry 4).

> 4. We never had any contact with BUTOV. We know about him only that he was a guide at the Brussels World Fair and on the "Gruziya" (Georgia a cruise ship??). We suppose that he is still living in Moscow, but we do not know his address or place of employment.

> 5. The main advantage of such a passport (as opposed to a completely notional identity) is that if there should be any inquiries, the 106th Militia Dept. in Moscow can confirm that such a passport was indeed issued to BUTOV, and that BUTOV was actually registered with them.

> 6. We had to take the place of work and the address from other sources, since we do not have this data for BUTOV himself. We registered you on Yakovlevskiy Pereulok 11, apt. 13, since this street is located in the 106th Otd Mil. We don't know who actually lives there, but believe this not to be an important point since you will use this passport only outside of Moscow.

> 7. Your place of employment is GSPI—the All-Union Design Insti-

tute No. 10 (formerly of the Ministry of Aviation Industry). It is located on Kutuzovskiy Prospekt 5-9, P.O. Box 1401.

8. BUTOV is liable to military service and we did not want to dream up his military history in order to fill out a *voyennyy bilet* [military record]. Therefore, with this passport you can travel around the country and register temporarily, but application for permanent residence could cause trouble on account of the military registration problem. We are preparing a second set of documents for you under a different name where you will not be liable to military service for medical reasons and will have a document to this effect. With this set you will receive cachets with which you can deregister and disemploy yourself, and will have the possibility of applying for permanent registration if that becomes necessary.

6. Raymond L. Garthoff, *Reflection on the Cuban Missile Crisis*, revised edition. Washington, D.C.: The Brookings Institution, 1989.

7. September 14, 1962, message to CIA Washington from London Station.

8. Interview with Richard Helms, December 8, 1988.

9. Robert F. Kennedy, *Thirteen Days*. New York: W. W. Norton, 1969, pp. 25–26.

10. Garthoff, p. 29–30. Dobrynin told Garthoff he had not been informed that the missiles were being deployed. At a conference on the Cuban missile crisis in Moscow in January 1989, ex–Foreign Minister Andrei Gromyko joked with Dobrynin about not telling him the missiles were being placed in Cuba and said, "Oh, I must have forgotten to tell you."

11. Roger Hilsman, *To Move a Nation*, p. 166, and Andrei Gromyko, *Memoirs*. New York: Doubleday, 1989, p. 175.

12. Garthoff, pp. 47–48. Bolshakov in his own version published in *New Times*, No. 5, January 27, 1989, said Khrushchev's message was: "Premier Khrushchev is concerned about the situation being built up by the United States around Cuba, and we repeat that the Soviet Union is supplying Cuba exclusively defensive weapons intended for protecting the interests of the Cuban revolution and not for perpetuating an aggression against any state on the American continent, the U.S. included. The Soviet leaders are perfectly well aware of President Kennedy's position, will not take any action with regard to the United States before the elections to Congress due in November 1962 and hope that after the elections we shall get down to a new round of active negotiations."

At the January 1989 Moscow meeting on the Cuban crisis, Pierre Salinger, White House press secretary under Kennedy and ABC News chief European correspondent, interviewed Bolshakov on camera, asking him if he knew about the Soviet missiles in Cuba when he conveyed Khrushchev's message to Robert Kennedy. "No, I didn't, Pierre," answered Bolshakov. *New Times*, No. 6, 1989.

13. Arthur Krock, *Memoirs: Sixty Years on the Firing Line*. New York: Funk & Wagnalls, pp. 379–380. Krock presents a detailed chronology of how McCone pressed his case that in outline, but not all details, is correct.

14. Interview with McCone, August 29, 1988. See Krock, *Memoirs*, pp. 379–380 for a detailed chronology of how McCone pressed his case.

15. Interview with McCone, August 29, 1988.

16. Penkovsky informed the Anglo-American team that the Soviet Union was basing medium-range missiles in Germany in 1961, but retained control of the nuclear warheads.

17. Interview with McCone, August 29, 1988. McCone was married at her home, The Highlands, in Norcliffe, on the outskirts of Seattle. Both were widowed and it was the second marriage for each of them.

18. Krock, p. 379, and Burrows, *Deep Black*, pp. 113–115.

19. Quoted in Garthoff, p. 34.

20. Interview with Helms, December 8, 1988.

21. James G. Blight and David A. Welch, *On the Brink: Americans and Soviets Reexamine the Cuban Missile Crisis*. New York: Hill & Wang, 1989, p. 213.

22. Interview with Helms, December 8, 1990.

23. CIA Top Secret briefing memo, October 19, 1962, declassified.

24. Thomas Powers, *The Man Who Kept the Secrets*. New York: Alfred A. Knopf, 1979, p. 329.

25. Quoted in Krock, p. 379.

26. Interview with McCone, August 29, 1988.

27. Interview with Elder, October 6, 1988.

28. Sorenson, *Kennedy*, p. 703. The literature on the Cuban missile crisis continues to proliferate. The essential accounts remain Sorenson: Schlesinger's *Thousand Days*, and Elie Abel, *The Missile Crisis*. More recent analyses include Graham T. Allison, *Essence of Decision: Explaining the Cuban Missile Crisis* (Boston: Little, Brown, 1971), James G. Blight and David A. Welch, *On the Brink: Americans and Soviets Reexamine the Cuban Missile Crisis*, and Garthoff's *Reflections on the Cuban Missile Crisis*.

29. Dr. Ray S. Cline, *The CIA Under Reagan, Bush and Casey*. Washington, D.C.: Acropolis Books, 1981, p. 221.

30. Charles E. Bohlen, *Witness to History 1929–1969.* New York: W. W. Norton, 1973, pp. 488–489.

31. Soviet defector Yuri Nosenko told the CIA in 1964 that embassy security officer John Abidian was under surveillance and was observed mailing letters and going to a dead drop, thus giving the KGB knowledge of where Penkovsky's dead drop was. When he confessed, Penkovsky must have told them where it was.

32. Tape #4, Friday afternoon, November 9, 1962, debriefing of Richard K. Jacob, p. 3.

33. Ibid., pp. 8–12.

34. McCone memo, November 5, 1962. Garthoff, in *Reflections on the Cuban Missile Crisis* (pp. 64–65).

35. McCone memo, November 5, 1990.

36. Interview with Greville Wynne, September 8, 1988.

37. Authors' information.

38. Interview with Wynne, September 17, 1988.

39. Interviews with Joseph J. Bulik, Richard Helms, and authors' confidential interviews. In *Contact on Gorky Street*, Wynne wrote: "London (I mean those I worked for) were very anxious to save Penkovsky. A concealed space had been built big enough for a man to lie down. This had been made overnight, on pretext of road tests, by workmen who had nothing to do with the engineers who had built the caravans [trailers] for exhibitions. The caravans cost over 35,000 pounds. London would have spent ten times that amount to save Penkovsky."

In *The Man From Odessa*, Wynne wrote: "The Hungarian government granted me permission to set up my caravans as from the last week in October. It all seemed business as usual, but I didn't like the way things were developing. A feeling that I was being watched. A new interpreter was assigned to me, and there was something about him I didn't care for at all. I was glad when I returned to Vienna and made contact with MI6. In Moscow, Alex was still passing information to us. The word from London was to go ahead. Proceed to Budapest and wait for our signal."

Wynne's imagination after the fact was very active. There was no plan in effect for Penkovsky to escape through Budapest.

40. Interview with Wynne, September 8, 1988.

41. Wynne, *Gorky Street*, p. 11.

42. Ibid., p. 13.

43. Roland Seth, *Encyclopedia of Espionage.* London: New English Library, 1975, pp. 449–465.

467

44. Appendix to Oldfield letter of November 28, 1966.

45. Richard Deacon, *"C", A Biography of Sir Maurice Oldfield*. London: Macdonald, 1985, p. 131. See also pages 130–138 for discussion on Penkovsky and doubts about him.

46. Evaluation of Penkovsky, 1963.

CHAPTER SIXTEEN **The Trial**

1. Interview with Greville Wynne, September 1988.

2. Crimes stipulated in Article 65 and Article 64, paragraph A, of the Criminal Code of the Russian Soviet Federated Socialist Republic. Each of the fifteen Soviet republics has its own criminal code modeled on that of the Russian Federation.

3. *Trial In the Criminal Case of the Agent of the British and American Intelligence Services, Citizen of the USSR, O. V. Penkovsky and the SPY Go-Between, British Subject, G. M. Wynne, 7–11 May 1963*. Moscow: Political Literature Publishing House, 1963, p. 39.

4. Ibid., p. 41.

5. Murrel, Third Secretary report, June 6, 1963.

6. *Trial*, p. 47.

7. Ibid., p. 54.

8. Ibid., p. 85.

9. Ibid., p. 87.

10. Ibid., p. 88.

11. Ibid., p. 94.

12. Ibid., p. 121.

13. Wynne, *Contact on Gorky Street*, p. 127.

14. *Trial*, pp. 122–123.

15. Ibid., p. 129.

16. Wynne, *Gorky Street*, p. 131.

17. Ibid., p. 134.

18. Trial transcript, p. 151.

19. Interview with Wynne, September 1988.

20. Wynne, *Gorky Street*. p. 134.

21. Ibid.

22. *Trial*, Ibid., p. 166.

23. Ibid., p. 169.

24. Ibid., p. 173.

25. Ibid., p. 175.

26. Ibid.

27. Memorandum on resettlement for Greville Wynne, February 17, 1966.

28. Wynne, *Gorky Street*, p. 190.

29. *Trial*, p. 227.

30. Lieutenant General Nikolai F. Chistyakov, *Po Zakonu i Sovesti* (On law and conscience). Moscow: Military Publishing House, 1979, p. 11.

31. Interview with Soviet source present at closed session.

32. *Trial*, p. 248. The British named were A. Rowsell, Gervase Cowell and his wife, Pamela Cowell, D. Varley, and F. Stuart. Americans named were Captain Alexis Davison, Hugh Montgomery, Rodney Carlson, Richard Jacob, and W. Jones.

33. Bulik memo to Howard Osborne May 10, 1963; Unsigned memo, November 28, 1962, concerning letter to KGB/GRU.

34. Interview with Joseph J. Bulik, December 14, 1990.

35. Memo from Bulik to Chief, SR Division, May 10 and May 14, 1963; Unsigned memo, November 28, 1962.

36. Interview with Bulik, July 27–28, 1988.

37. Interview with Richard Helms, December 8, 1988.

CHAPTER SEVENTEEN **Aftermath**

1. Interview with retired CIA officer, June 13, 1989.

2. Ilya Dzhirkvelov, *Secret Servant*. London: Collins, 1987, p. 147.

3. *Izvestia*, May 25, 1963.

4. *The Times*, May 13, 1963.

5. Quoted in message, May 31, 1963.

6. Memo to DCI from DDP Richard Helms July 8, 1963.

7. *Trial*, pp. 251–252.

8. *Penkovsky Papers* (1965), p. 4.

9. Memo May 3, 1963, "Possible Developments in the Trials of Oleg Penkovsky and Greville Wynne."

10. Excerpt from memo to British, unsigned, dated June 24, 1963.

11. Maurice Oldfield letter to Howard Osborne, July 1, 1963.

12. Ibid.

13. July 12, 1963, letter from Oldfield to Osborne.

14. John A. McCone's memo on White House meeting, August 1963.

15. Memo for the record, April 23, 1965.

16. Interview with Mrs. Sheila Wynne, January 19, 1991.

17. *Sunday Telegraph*, April 26, 1964, "Gentleman for a Player," by Gordon Brook-Shepherd.

18. Memo from David E. Murphy, October 20, 1964.

19. Memo for the record, April 23, 1965.

20. Interview with Frank Gibney, December 6, 1990.

21. Interview with Donald Jameson, May 10, 1991.

22. Introduction to translation of "Penkovsky Memoirs," undated.

23. Interview with CIA official, August 1989.

24. Interview with former senior CIA official, August 1989.

25. *The Penkovsky Papers*, New introduction and commentary by Frank Gibney, New York: Ballantine Books, 1982, p. xiv.

26. Interview with Gibney, December 6, 1990.

27. Victor Zorza article in *Manchester Guardian*, October 15, 1965.

28. Victor Zorza, "Soviet Expert Thinks 'Penkovsky Papers' Are a Forgery." *Washington Post*, November 15, 1965, and Zorza, "Soviet Expert Doubts Validity of Controversial 'Papers,' Usage in 'Penkovsky' Said to Prove Forgery." Ibid., November 16, 1965.

29. *Penkovsky Papers*, p. 396.

30. Alan Studner, M.D., "Psychology of Treason" (CIA study), quotes J. M. Thompson: "A private grievance is never so dangerous as when it can be identified with a matter of principle."

31. Vassall, a homosexual, was entrapped by the KGB while serving in the British Embassy in Moscow and spied for six years before his arrest, and trial in October 1962 when he was sentenced to eighteen years' imprisonment. See Pincher, *Too Secret Too Long*, chapter 31, for details on Vassall and the ramifications of his case. Golitsyn's information on Vassall was supplemented by Yuri Nosenko and clinched the case.

32. Anatoli Golitsyn, *New Lies From Old*. New York: Dodd, Mead, 1984, See chapter 16, pp. 153–182. "The feigned disunity of the communist world promotes real disunity in the non-communist world," insists Golitsyn. He says that if Sakharov's writing are "read as disinformation and decoded, his predictions of convergence are predictions of the victory of the long-range policy of the bloc and the surrender of the West with the minimum of resistance" (p. 237).

33. Ibid., p. 54.

34. Edward J. Epstein, *Deception*. New York: Simon & Schuster, 1989, p. 79.

35. Ibid., pp. 79–80.

36. Ibid., p. 80.

37. Interview with Joseph J. Bulik, July 27, 1988.

38. Maury memo for the record.

39. Thomas Powers, *The Man Who Kept the Secrets*. New York: Alfred A. Knopf, 1979, p. 283.

40. Robin Winks, *Cloak and Gown*. London: Collins Harvill, 1987, p. 416.

41. Interview with Helms, December 8, 1988.

42. Excerpt from Lyman Kirkpatrick's notes to President's Board, June 26, 1963.

43. Chapman Pincher, *Their Trade Is Treachery*. London: Sidgwick & Jackson, 1981, p. 156. Pincher repeats this in *Too Secret Too Long*. New York: St. Martin's Press, 1984, pp. 264–267.

44. Ibid., pp. 158 and 478.

45. Peter Wright, *Spycatcher*. New York: Viking Penguin, 1987, pp. 204–212.

46. Phillip Knightley, *The Second Oldest Profession*. New York: Norton, 1986, p. 325.

47. McGeorge Bundy denied remembering Penkovsky when queried by the authors and declined to discuss his role. Bundy told Michael Beschloss (*The Crisis Years*. New York: HarperCollins, 1991), that Penkovsky's importance had been exaggerated in the literature of the period (p. 768).

48. Christopher Creighton and Noel Hynd, *The Khrushchev Objective*. New York: Doubleday, 1987.

49. Ibid., p. 332.

50. Interview with Sir Dick White, June 15, 1991.

51. Interview with sources close to British Intelligence.

52. *Sunday Times*, October 15, 1965.

CHAPTER EIGHTEEN **Traitor or Savior?**

1. Greville Wynne, *Contact on Gorky Street*, p. 9. Wynne offered no substantiation for this statement and there is no evidence or rumor that such was the case.

2. Authors' interview with Soviet official in 1989.

3. Felix Edmundovich Dzerzhinsky (1877–1926), a Pole from Vilna, formed the Cheka on December 20, 1917, as an organ of the Bolshevik Party to suppress political and military opposition to the Bolshevik regime and take measures to reduce black market speculation during the Civil War, 1918–1921, the so-called period of War Communism. By a decree of September 5, 1918, concentration camps were set up under the control of the Cheka. Although the Soviet secret police is today called the *Komitet Gozudarstvennoy Bezopasnosti* (Committee for State Security), the term *chekist* is still used to refer to KGB officials.

4. See Robert Conquest, *The Great Terror*. New York: Macmillan, 1968; and R. J. Rummel, *Lethal Politics: Soviet Genocide and Mass Murder Since 1917*. New Brunswick, N.J.: Transaction, 1990.

5. McCoy, *The Penkovsky Case*, p. 12.

6. Ibid.

7. Christopher Andrew and Oleg Gordievsky, *KGB: The Inside Story*. New York: HarperCollins, 1991, pp. 460–462.

8. Confidential information.

9. Columbia University collection of Khrushchev Memoirs, tape 5, track 3.

10. Ronald Seth, *Encyclopedia of Espionage*. London: New English Library, 1972, pp. 85–88 and 646–649.

11. George Blake, *No Other Choice*. London: Jonathan Cape, 1990, p. 198.

12. Ibid.

13. Memos on creation of Penkovsky trust fund and final accounting.

14. Brook-Shepherd, *The Storm Birds*, pp. 158–159. Nosenko told the CIA he had seen an internal KGB memo on how Penkovsky was caught that included the details of making him so ill he had to be hospitalized.

15. Authors' information.

16. Andrew and Gordievsky, *KGB: The Inside Story*, p. 475.

17. The Penkovsky case as shown in *Fatal Encounter*, BBC 1, May 8, 1991.

18. Penkovsky pretrial testimony in authors' possession.

19. Interview with Joseph J. Bulik, December 19, 1990.

20. In October 1991 another effort was made to obtain further details on Penkovsky's arrest. The same officers from the Second Chief Directorate again declined to provide access to the actual documents on how Penkovsky was discovered, but the senior officer insisted that "the material we provided for you is from documents and is not based on people's reminiscences." He was referring to former KGB chief Semichastny's story that Penkovsky was spotted meeting a foreign diplomat in GUM department store. The counterespionage officials insisted that their directorate's files would not be made public, in order to protect sources and methods. They did, however, arrange contact with former Second Chief Directorate head Oleg Gribanov, who, at age seventy-three, is suffering from sclerosis. Gribanov, who works as an advisor to a state business concern, was polite but elusive. He refused to have his picture taken saying, "I avoided the camera during my entire career and I am not about to change now." He firmly refused to discuss any operational aspects of the case. The KGB's chief investigator of Penkovsky, Lieutenant General Nikolai F. Chistyakov, now retired, also declined to discuss operational details of the case.

21. 1963 memo to House Armed Services Committee, May 23, 1990.

Bona Fides of the Penkovsky Operation

1. We have no reason to believe that Penkovsky was a double agent or that any information he supplied us was wittingly provided to him as deception material by Soviet authorities.

2. Throughout this extraordinary operation, a recurring question for us, and one also in the minds of analysts trying to cope with the resultant flood of classified Soviet documents, has been the possibility of Soviet deception. This possibility was given serious consideration each time we received new material from Penkovsky. During the numerous long personal meetings we had with him we used subtle and varied tests of his loyalty to the intelligence community. He always passed all of the tests which could be levied . . . and his information has stood the tests of time and comparative intelligence.

3. On the basis of these checks and counterchecks together with our familiarity with the methods and purposes of Soviet deception operations, we have concluded that there is no possibility that this case represents planned deception, build-up for deception, fabrication or double agent activity. Rather it represents the most serious penetration of Soviet officialdom ever accomplished and one that will hurt them for years to come.

22. McCoy, *Penkovsky Case*, p. 14.

23. *Khrushchev Remembers: The Glasnost Tapes*, p. 203.

24. Authors' interview with Soviet source.

Index

Abakumov, 404
Abel, Col. Rudolf, 84, 351, 378, 383
Abidian, John, 8–10, 222, 444n12, 467n31
Acheson, Dean, 183–84
Adams, Charles Francis, 387
Adzhubei, Aleksei Ivanovich, 379
Aeroflot, 45, 197, 270
Aeronautical Institute, 367
Agayants, I. I., 237n
Agriculture, U.S. Department of, Foreign Agricultural Service, 11
Air Defense Artillery Battalion Nike-Hercules, 311
Air Force, U.S., 8–9, 77, 280, 333, 462n10
Air France, 270
Ajax, Operation, 18
Albania, 68, 116
Allason, Rupert, 397
All Union Chamber of Commerce, 328
Ambrus (translator), 349
American Broadcasting Company (ABC), 333, 397, 465n12
Amory, Robert, 276, 444n22
Andrew, Christopher, 407, 412
Andropov, Yuri, 404, 405
Angleton, James Jesus, 36, 65n, 189, 193–94, 204–5, 371, 391–95
Antiballistic missiles (ABMs), 293
Anti-Party Group, 82n
Apraksin, A. K., 359, 364, 369
Arbenz, Jacobo, 18
Argonne National Laboratory, 461n22
Arkin, William, 246

ARMCO Steel Corporation, 255–56, 259, 268
Army, U.S., 155, 191n, 311
Artamonov, Nikolay Fedorovich (aka Nicholas Shadrin), 456n21
Artillery and Missile Journal, The, 415
Ashbrook, John M., 375–76
Atlee, Clement, 457n11
Atomic Energy Commission, 275
Azerbaijan, 232

Bagley, Tennant, 393
Baltic States, 52, 59n, 82, 88, 127
Barghoorn, Frederick, 27n, 346n
Barker, Le Baron, 387
Batitisky, Lt. Gen. P., 450n3
Bay of Pigs invasion, 46, 182, 183, 191n, 203
Bekrenev, Vice Admiral L. K., 191
Beria, Lavrenti, 110–11, 120, 176, 177n, 209, 221, 404, 447n4, 450n3
Berlin crisis, 3, 181–92, 196, 199, 201, 204–13, 226, 229–32, 238–39, 246, 247, 253, 272–73, 279, 282, 284, 293, 374, 390
Beschloss, Michael, 471n47
Bessarabia, 52n
BIGOT list, 189
Biryuzov, Marshal, 171
Bissell, Richard, 203, 223
Blake, George, 44, 45, 161, 388, 408–11, 418
Board of Estimates, 278
Bohlen, Charles E. (Chip), 184, 222, 223, 303–4, 336–37

475

About the Authors

Jerrold L. Schecter, former Diplomatic Editor of *Time* magazine, was Time-Life Moscow Bureau Chief from 1968 to 1970. He served as Associate White House Press Secretary and Spokesman for the National Security Council (1977–1980), and later was foreign affairs columnist for *Esquire*. He has written four books including *An American Family in Moscow* and *Back in the USSR*, coauthored with his wife and five children. He was instrumental in the acquisition of Nikita Khrushchev's memoirs and translated and edited the third volume, *Khrushchev Remembers: The Glasnost Tapes* with V. Louchkov. He lives in Washington, D.C., and Moscow where he is a Founding Editor of *We\Mbl*, a joint Soviet-American weekly newspaper.

Peter S. Deriabin was born in 1921 in a small village in the Altai Krai of Siberia. He served in the Red Army from 1939 to 1944 where he was seriously wounded four times and awarded nine medals. His career in intelligence began in 1944 when he was sent to Military Counterintelligence School in Moscow. He became a KGB officer assigned to the Kremlin Guard in 1947. From 1951 to 1954 he worked in the First Chief Directorate of the KGB when he was assigned to the KGB *Rezidentura* in Vienna in charge of counterintelligence. He defected to the United States in 1954 and worked as a consultant to the U.S. Army and the CIA until his retirement in 1982. He is the author of four books on Soviet intelligence.